D1112110

INNOVATION
in EDUCATION

A publication of
The Horace Mann–Lincoln Institute of School Experimentation
Teachers College, Columbia University

INNOVATION

in EDUCATION

EDITED BY

Matthew B. Miles

Associate Professor of Psychology and Education
Teachers College, Columbia University

BUREAU OF PUBLICATIONS

TEACHERS COLLEGE, COLUMBIA UNIVERSITY

NEW YORK 1964

Foreword

IT HAS become platitudinous to speak of the winds of change in education, to remind those interested in the educational enterprise that a revolution is in progress. Trite or not, however, it is true to say that changes appear wherever one turns in education.

Under these circumstances, a book on innovation in education deals with one of the most fundamental of themes for these times. Professor Miles, through the work he has carried out in the Horace Mann–Lincoln Institute as well as through the assembly he has convened in this book, asks that we give serious and extended attention to the phenomenon of change itself.

You are invited in these pages to listen in on a many-voiced conversation among people who have been in the midst of educational change long enough to have thought about it. In some cases, these people have been involved in the educational revolution for more than a generation. What they say does not of itself amount to a comprehensive theory of innovation; much less does it suggest a recipe to be followed by those who undertake innovations in education. It does, however, tell of reality and thoughts about reality. It tells of solid success, apparent success that later proved abortive, and real failure. It is utterly human, utterly candid, for its authors take their subject and their readers too seriously to be anything less.

A generation ago, only three groups of people were actively involved in educational innovation: the curriculum-makers, the school administrators, and certain social theorists. What a contrast with the situation now! These people are still involved, but they have been joined by new, potent groups: scientists and other scholars, missing since early this century; foundation executives; journalists; government officials;

ad hoc groups of interested and concerned citizens. *Innovation in Education* is addressed to all of these groups, as well as to the scholarly community.

For all of these people, the book offers a wide range of experience to think about—and ideas to think about, too. It challenges some of the most dearly held dogmas: that novelty of itself breeds resistance; that involvement and consensus are the royal road to innovation. It seems that people are neither all that senseless—nor all that sensible. At least, not always. Not always.

The book will require some getting-used-to. It is neither comfortable nor easy, and it certainly is not bland. We do think it is important, however—so important to curriculum-makers, for example, that it may well be the source of some of the most illuminating controversy in years.

I should like to add to Professor Miles' statement of gratitude to the contributors my own, on behalf of the other members of the staff of the Horace Mann–Lincoln Institute of School Experimentation. The contributors, and the members of the faculty seminar that led to this publication, should all have a sense of satisfaction at this worthy result of their voluntary efforts.

ARTHUR W. FOSHAY
Executive Officer
The Horace Mann–Lincoln Institute
of School Experimentation

Editor's preface

THIS book had its genesis during the spring of 1960. It seemed to me then that the quickening of change in nearly all aspects of education since the mid-1950's not only was heartening but presented the opportunity—and indeed the need—for close study of innovative processes. Intuitive, vague, grandiose, and implicit formulations of just how educational change did (or "should") take place were not lacking, but serious thought was.

After some discussion with other members of the Horace Mann–Lincoln Institute staff, I proposed that we initiate a faculty seminar, which would take as its task the systematic conceptualization of innovation and change processes in American education. The seminar members were drawn from the Institute, from Teachers College, and from the Graduate Faculties. We met over a period of a year for what proved to be fifteen extremely interesting sessions, discussing case studies of innovation, generalizing, reviewing working papers, and in general enjoying ourselves. The members of this seminar taught each other a good deal; they included Lawrence A. Cremin, Amitai Etzioni, the late Hubert M. Evans, Arthur W. Foshay, Miriam L. Goldberg, Solon T. Kimball, Paul F. Lazarsfeld, Gordon N. Mackenzie, the late Paul R. Mort, A. Harry Passow, Goodwin Watson, Sloan R. Wayland, and myself. Mark S. Atwood of Rutgers University and Elizabeth Kelly of the Newark, N.J., public schools joined us for two case discussion sessions.

At the conclusion of the seminar, I proposed that a collection of papers from the seminar members and other interested persons might prove helpful. This idea received support, and further explorations, invitations, and harryings led in gradual stages to the present volume.

vii

I am indebted to many people beyond those in the seminar for their aid in the course of the book's development. Most of all to the thirty-four persons who contributed chapters; their vigorous interest in the area covered by the book, their willingness to think, and (not least) their patience with editorial demands led to some very satisfying collaborative relationships.

The initial support and continuing interest of my colleagues at the Horace Mann–Lincoln Institute, A. Harry Passow and Miriam L. Goldberg, and particularly Arthur W. Foshay, have been extremely helpful.

In a project of this sort, many secretaries go unsung; I can only acknowledge here the intelligent and unremitting assistance of Rhea Grubart, Jeanne Corr, and Grace Smith over the past three years.

F. Emerson Andrews, Stephen K. Bailey, Roald F. Campbell, Ernest V. Hollis, Hollis W. Peter, and other dedicated tipsters were helpful in alerting me to current work that deserved a place in the book. Richard I. Miller supplied data from the NEA Project on Instruction.

Stephen M. Corey, Norman Wilson, Arthur W. Foshay, and especially Betty Miles made insightful and helpful commentary on the initial and concluding chapters.

The lot of publishing personnel is, sadly, an anonymous one. I should, however, like to say that at the Bureau of Publications I found lively interest, sustained aid, and steady, discriminating scrutiny throughout the design and editing of the book. Every editor should be so fortunate.

M.B.M.

December 5, 1963

Contents

INNOVATION
in EDUCATION

CHAPTER 1

Educational innovation:
the nature of the problem

Matthew B. Miles

How does educational innovation proceed? For the classical view, there is C. P. Snow:

> In a society like ours, academic patterns change more slowly than any others. In my lifetime, in England, they have crystallised rather than loosened. I used to think that it would be about as hard to change, say, the Oxford and Cambridge scholarship examination as to conduct a major revolution. I now believe that I was over-optimistic. (Snow, 1961)

Who would deny that change in education is slow? But it *does* occur— Snow himself, or at least *The Two Cultures,* has already showed up on more than one American high school examination, and it may not be long until students will have to read F. R. Leavis' denunciation of Snow as culture hero to boot. And while rueful pessimism about educational change is hardly rare in America today, the present zest for educational innovation, and the remarkable rate and diversity of educational change do, in fact, frequently call out the label "revolution."

Whether we are actually moving into anything like an educational revolution will probably not be clear for a decade or so. But it *is* apparent that comprehensive changes in the structure and functioning of American educational institutions are now occurring, partly as a result of the steadily accelerating demands on these institutions. There

1

is a good deal of professed public concern about the adequacy of education, and an expressed interest in educational reform which is nothing short of striking. Innovations of all sorts—set theory, team teaching, trimester plans—are being advocated vigorously, installed, and (sometimes) evaluated. A very wide variety of strategies for creating and controlling educational change is being employed—polemical, manipulative, technological, prestige-based, experimental, moralistic—with varying degrees of success. The dominant focus in most contemporary change efforts, however, tends to be on the *content* of the desired change, rather than on the features and consequences of *change processes.* It is the thesis of this chapter, and of this book as a whole, that attention to change processes is crucial. We need to know, for example, why a particular innovation spreads rapidly or slowly, what the causes of resistance to change are in educational systems, and why particular strategies of change chosen by innovators succeed or fail. The current flurry of educational change in America offers an excellent opportunity to study problems of planned change in social systems—an area where our understanding is decidedly less than perfect. Given an increase in understanding, it seems likely that we may be able to manage educational innovation somewhat more skillfully than we have in the past.

This chapter first examines the current climate of educational change and speculates on the reasons for its existence; then underlines the need for inquiry into problems of educational innovation, provides definitions of terms used, and reviews the broad educational setting in which innovative efforts are taking place. It describes a range of current innovations, and reviews the strategies employed to install them; then concludes with a listing of interesting (that is, unsolved) problems in the study of educational innovation.

The Current Climate

It seems fair to say that something more than the usual American sense of meliorism is at work in the current educational scene. The first phase of rightist attacks on the public schools in the early 1950's, the following wave of charges of anti-intellectualism (both of which have been well reviewed by Raywid, 1962), and the enormous amount of journalistic disputation more or less appropriately tagged the "Great Debate" (Scott, Hill, & Burns, 1959) seem finally to have led to a climate in which there is not only a sense of impatience with the existing state of the educational establishment, but high willingness to alter it and—even—to get down to work. Residua from the "debate" are still in evidence (e.g., Koerner, 1963), but the time for exhortation, polemics, moralism, and defense seems to have passed. The present work output devoted to altering educational practices seems quite remarkable.

Current innovational activities

As a general indicator of the extent and nature of current innovation attempts, it may be useful to sample some activities presently under way.

The large-scale resurgence of academic concern with school subject matter signalized by the National Academy of Sciences' Woods Hole Conference (reported by Bruner, 1960) has generated a rapidly accelerating number of curriculum studies in academic subjects, largely developed along the lines of the Physical Science Study Committee (PSSC) project. A recent review (Fraser, 1962) lists ten projects in science, eleven in mathematics, one in English, two in foreign languages, and four in social studies, the newest focusing on anthropology. (This list includes only those projects actually preparing curriculum materials and testing them in the schools, and does not include pronouncements of commissions, "position papers," and the like.) Since Fraser's report, the Office of Education has announced the initiation of Project English and Project Social Studies, two similarly large-scale enterprises; Patterson (1962) has reported the imminence of a substantial humanities–social-science project; and a recent issue of the AAAS *Science Education News* lists four additional science projects, one math–science project, and a project with the ultimately appealing acronym ALL (Accelerated Learning of Logic). The National Education Association itself, far from confirming the image of "intrenched professionals," is sponsoring a large-scale Project on Instruction, with vigorous involvement of scholars from all disciplines.

The support of governmental agencies is no less striking. The Cooperative Research Branch of the Office of Education has disbursed approximately $10 million a year during 1956–61, covering a total of 407 research projects. This effort seems to have been largely responsible for the current burgeoning of interest in educational problems evinced by a wide range of behavioral scientists. The National Science Foundation disbursed approximately $159 million in 1960, $34 million of which went directly for teacher improvement institutes, attended by nearly 31,000 teachers.

Title III of the National Defense Education Act authorizes up to $75 million a year to state educational agencies. This has involved, among other things, the appearance of approximately 5,000 language laboratories, 53 language area centers, nearly $9 million worth of graduate fellowships, 161 research projects, and language institutes reaching more than 11,000 teachers of modern foreign languages. Title VII of the Act has also stimulated much research.

More than half of all moneys granted by the larger foundations currently go to educational enterprises; Andrews (1961) found that 54 per cent of the $389 million given by the 154 largest foundations in 1960 went to education. The Fund for the Advancement of Education has alone disbursed $50 million in the period 1951–61. Foundation giving accounts for over a quarter of all voluntary contributions to colleges and universities (Council for Financial Aid to Education, undated).

The outpouring of printed material on educational problems need hardly be detailed here (e.g., in the first quarter of 1961, the NEA *Magazine Report* reviewed 142 articles on education in national magazines and newspaper supplements). The *Saturday Review* seems to have had no difficulty in finding material for its regular Education Supplement, which has appeared monthly since its creation in the fall of 1960.

Meanwhile, the development of educational technology proceeds with avidity (for example, a recent issue of the *American Behavioral Scientist* was entirely devoted to discussion of educational television, films, programed instruction, language laboratories, information retrieval hardware, and related matters).

All this ferment seems to have focused most vigorously on the public elementary and secondary schools, but there are a good many signs of increasing concern about the adequacy of college and university education, evidenced in treatments as diverse as Sanford's (1962) encyclopedic collection *The American College* and Paul Goodman's (1962) proposal for a secessionist Utopia modeled along the lines of the medieval university.

The concern for change has spread into associated professions (see, for example, Carle, Kehas & Mosher's 1962 collection of articles on guidance and counseling); when one goes on to note the enormous growth in programs of management development and the current concern with improvement of training methods via research (Glaser, 1962), and remembers (with Clark & Sloan, 1958) that the nonformal educational enterprise represents a "third force" rivaling the schools and colleges in scope, only words like "explosion" will do.[1] But even given all this concern, it is fair to say that great needs for change still remain. Jencks (1963), after reviewing the progress of educational improvement since Sputnik, continues:

> Yet none of these improvements has appreciably diminished the fundamental parochialism of the majority of schools, the stultifying social standards imposed by the students on one another and tacitly supported by the teachers, the chauvinistic self-congratulatory view of the world conveyed by textbooks and staff alike, the subordination of education to community solidarity, symbolized by such practices as appointing football coaches to be school superintendents and building palatial assembly halls for community festivities while providing no money for hiring top teachers. All this and more persists.

Acceleration in change rates

Data gathered in the late 1930's by Mort & Cornell (1941) suggest a relatively leisurely diffusion rate for educational innovations. Once a "practical invention" (such as the kindergarten) had been devised to meet an underlying need—a process itself occupying fifty years on the average—approximately fifteen years elapsed before 3 per cent of school systems had installed the innovation. Though adoption rates increased rapidly after the 3 per cent "tipping point," complete diffusion of successful inventions appeared to take approximately fifty years after the first "authentic introduction." (See also Mort's findings in Chapter 13 below.)

---

[1] Although this discussion is focused by choice on developments in American education, it seems quite clear that similar concerns exist in all industrialized countries; for example, Fehr (1962) reports that reconsideration of the teaching of mathematics is under way in at least twenty countries. The amount of energy currently being poured into educational change in the developing countries, in proportion to gross national product, is of course even greater (see Dillon, 1960, and Lengyel, 1962, for sample analyses).

Informal sampling in a variety of available data suggests that this rate may have accelerated.

For example, data reported in Gotkin & Goldstein's chapter in the present book show that 11 per cent of school systems sampled were using some form of programed instruction. If we consider Skinner's machine, available in 1954, to be the "first authentic introduction of a successful invention," [2] seven years have elapsed; the prediction from Mort's average curve would have been for 2 per cent diffusion in this period of time.

According to a report in *Saturday Review* (Feb. 16, 1963), 46 language laboratories were known to have existed in secondary schools in 1957; this included approximately .2 of 1 per cent of the total number of secondary schools. Five years later, over 5,000 schools (approximately 17 per cent of the total) had such installations. Here again, the Mort prediction would have been for less than 2 per cent diffusion in the same period of time.

It may be argued that these innovations are primarily technological, and that organizational changes would diffuse at rates more nearly comparable to those found in the earlier studies. Data on the use of teacher aides and team teaching, two fairly drastic innovations in role definition at the local school level, are reported by the NEA Project on Instruction (1962). The first introduction of the teacher aide innovation (in which teachers are assisted by subprofessional personnel who perform routine duties such as record-keeping) was made in Bay City, Michigan, in 1952. Data from a national sample of elementary and secondary schools indicated that 9 per cent of elementary schools and 18 per cent of secondary schools were using teacher aides during 1960–61. The Mort prediction would have been for about 2 per cent diffusion for this period of time. Team teaching (in which a small group of teachers jointly plans and carries out learning experiences for a larger-than-usual group of students) can be seen as an extension of the teacher aide notion; although the first formal foundation support of a team teaching proposal did not occur until 1957, 5 per cent of secondary schools sampled were using team teaching in 1955–56;

---

[2] Pressey's invention of a programed testing device in 1926 appears to fall under the heading of a "false start," a frequent phenomenon in the period of early invention and trial before a diffusible device enters the educational system.

this had grown to 12 per cent by 1960–61; 31 per cent of the principals sampled expected to use team teaching by 1965–66.

An example from the area of curriculum materials suggests a similar acceleration. The Physical Science Study Committee was formed in 1956; the first text was available in 1957; according to Mayer (1961), the PSSC materials were in use in nearly 20 per cent of American secondary schools by 1961.

The NEA Project on Instruction study (1961) also contains some impressionistic data on acceleration in change rates. In a national sample of elementary school principals, nearly 30 per cent indicated that "much" change had taken place in the past 5 years, 53 per cent checked "some" change, 15 per cent "very little," and 2 per cent "no" change. When asked to anticipate changes during the period 1961–66, 39 per cent predicted "much" change, 43 per cent some change, 6 per cent little change, and 1 per cent no change (11 per cent made no usable predictions).

For a final example, note Mayer's (1961) comments on the need for drastic improvement in the English curriculum:

> Nobody is yet scared enough to do anything, but another decade of erosion in the relative importance of the English program should flush out large numbers of teachers willing to learn from college professors, and college professors willing to learn from teachers, and administrators and psychologists willing to recognize that there is still much to be learned. The revolution of method that must follow will extend far beyond the confines of the high school English department; it may even reach the students.

Only two years later, the Office of Education's Project English has established six curriculum study centers at universities with substantial financial support, and a recent survey article (Squire, 1962) lists a large number of groups, experiments, and projects under way.

These data are informal, but it seems fairly clear that the diffusion rates of the late 1930's and of the early 1960's, for a variety of reasons, are quite different.[3]

[3] It may be argued that these findings are artifactual, in that the Mort–Cornell data were biased in the direction of attention to larger-scale changes (e.g., kindergartens, reorganized high schools) or unpopular ones (e.g., homemaking courses for boys), and thus ignored more easily diffusible innovations. For example, though good data are hard to find, changes in the teaching of reading seem to have moved relatively quickly in the 1930's following the introduction

Causative Factors

It may be useful to speculate on underlying reasons for the climate of urgency and accelerated educational change which has been described above. The most obvious, and perhaps the most impressionistic, centers around the "struggle for national survival"; it seems undeniable that change rates showed a striking acceleration in 1958 following the launching of the first Soviet satellite (see data in Brickell's chapter in the present book).

But Sputnik aside, it is not difficult to deduce the idea that schools as a social institution will change more rapidly during periods of general social change. The dedication of American Education Week in 1962 to the theme "Education Meets the Challenge of Change" illustrates acknowledgement that new social orders do, in fact, dare to build new schools.[4]

The growing demands of an affluent society for manpower of a more intellectually sophisticated sort, accompanied by mounting technological unemployment at the semiskilled level, and the remarkable efflorescence of cultural and esthetic activities (cf. Jennings' chapter in the present book) are certainly relevant. Beyond this, the tremendous growth in the production of knowledge in contemporary America—along with the exponential increases in technological capacity for information handling and retrieval—cannot but have powerful back-effects on both the content and the rate of educational innovation. Expenditures by government, industry, and universities for research and development, for example, were approximately $15 billion

---

of new materials by publishers. And Allen (1956) did find that large differences in diffusion rate stemmed from the nature of the innovation and its support by nonschool groups (for example, driver education achieved 90 per cent diffusion in 18 years, while pupil study of the local community required 60 years for the same spread).

However, Ross's (1958) summary of Mort-type diffusion studies done through 1946 tends to support the fifty-year theory for that period. And added evidence for the recent acceleration of diffusion rates is suggested by Bushnell (1957). See also Finn, Perrin & Campion (1962) for data on diffusion rates in educational technology.

[4] See Kimball & McClellan (1962) for an excellent discussion of what the American transformation to a corporate society means for our notions about education. Clark's (1962) treatment is also relevant.

in 1961, a figure which more than halfway matches the expenditures for formal education; research and development expenditures are presently doubling every four years; the fraction devoted to basic research is accelerating almost as rapidly ($432 million in 1953, $1.3 billion in 1961); see Brozen (1962), also Machlup (1962).

Finally, and most crudely, the sheer size and growth of the educational establishment itself is exerting perhaps the most profoundly innovative effect of all. In his analysis of progressivism in American education, Cremin (1961, p. 128) points out that the first compulsory school attendance law was passed in Massachusetts in 1852; he suggests that this marked the begining of a new era in the history of American education, and goes on:

> Had there never been a progressive movement, had there been no social settlements, municipal reform associations, country life commissions, or immigrant aid societies, no William James, Stanley Hall, Edward Thorndike, or John Dewey, the mere fact of compulsory attendance would have changed the American school. What might have happened instead of what did is not, of course, the immediate concern of the historian. But that the situation was ripe for something to happen is. Compulsory schooling provided both the problem and the opportunity of the progressives; its very existence inexorably conditioned every attempt at educational innovation during the decades preceding World War I.

The formal educational system in America now includes approximately 29 million children in public elementary and 6 million in private elementary schools; 11 million in public secondary and an additional million in private secondary schools; and about 4.5 million college students. These bodies are housed in something over 95,000 elementary schools, nearly 30,000 secondary schools, and 2,139 institutions of higher learning. Elementary and secondary schools employ about 1,700,000 teachers; 313,000 people teach in colleges and universities. These enterprises are administered by about 100,000 superintendents, principals, and supervisors, and about 51,000 college administrators of various types. Approximately 184,000 lay persons are involved on the boards of local school districts, states, and institutions of higher education. A recent study (see DeCrow & Kolben, 1963) estimates that nearly 17 million adults were engaged in systematic educational experiences during 1961–62. When we include the nonformal educational establishments of industry, commerce, and the military, it is apparent that over one third of all Americans put their daily work time in on education. The portion of gross national product devoted to formal education is growing steadily (this is undoubtedly a basic factor in acceleration of change rates), and is now about 5 per cent; during the current year this amounts to approximately $27 billion. The expenditures of all nonformal agencies (including voluntary and youth-serving organizations as well as those above) are very hard to assess precisely, but a figure of perhaps $40 billion seems plausible as a total for all educational efforts.[5]

It is hardly necessary to review the assorted projections of the size of the American educational establishment over the next few decades; all of them are staggering, threatening, or exciting, depending on one's point of view. One of the most recent of these predictions is that the college population of the country is expected to reach twice its 1960 size within the next seven years; the current sharp increase in concern for innovation in higher education can hardly be unrelated to this expectancy.

The Need for Inquiry

Given these massive figures, and such heightened concern for educational change, it nevertheless seems apparent that almost all available funds, energy, and time are going into the development of innovations as such. The fraction available for examination of, planning for, and sophisticated execution of change *processes* seems to be minor. Ignorance about the conditions of change in social systems is not rare. A professor of education prominently associated with a large-scale change project says in a public meeting:

> I've been trying educational innovation for years, and the more I do it the less I know about it. The only thing I'm sure of is that everyone is human. So the key to innovation is, try something interesting. Experiment!

A distinguished "educational statesman" falls back on bromides:

[5] With operations costs of this size, it is not surprising that innovation attempts are expensive. For example, the PSSC diffusion rate described above was achieved at a cost of nearly $2 million annually for its first four years, if associated NSF institutes are included (see Marsh & Gortner, 1963).

The depressing thing about all this is that through recent advances in psychology, sociology, and education, we know better but are forever unwilling to do better. A fraction of the money spent for horse races, for tobacco, alcohol, or useless drugs, if added to our school budgets would at least give youth a better chance. In the end, nothing avails except the wisdom and fervor of parents, teachers, and citizens.

And, in one educational meeting after another, deliberate use of the "Hawthorne effect" is advocated—"So long as you do something new, the kids will learn more"—in blissful ignorance of the fact that the work of Roethlisberger and Dickson showed that sheer "newness" was not the issue. Rather, alterations in decision-making structure, the development of group norms, styles of formal and informal leadership, and the perceived reward structure of the organization were all factors at work in enhancing (and restricting!) output at the Hawthorne plant.[6]

And, as more than one observer has noted, the planners of some large-scale curriculum study projects seem to assume simultaneously (1) that any subject matter can be taught to children of any age, and (2) that the teachers who will do this teaching are an ineducable lot of dunderheads who are the main barrier to innovation.

A very wide variety of strategies for inducing educational change (see the section on *Strategy* below) are currently asserted to be efficacious, ordinarily without any intimation that the requirements of change in systems have been taken into account—and without any evidence whatever that the strategy employed does, in fact, account for the rate of change observed. Proposals for innovation are quite frequently made without accompanying attention to the processes by which the innovation is to be installed. See, for example, Koerner's (1963) call for drastic shifts in the present pattern of teacher preparation; it is as if an effort of the will were somehow sufficient to cause all remaining teachers colleges to be closed, to mention a typical reform he proposes.

Just how complex and difficult the pathways of thoroughgoing in-

---

[6] Even Cook (1962), conducting an extended study of the Hawthorne effect, defines it as "a phenomenon characterized by an awareness on the part of the subjects of special treatment created by artificial experimental conditions." This is the popular meaning of the Hawthorne effect, but such a formulation completely disregards the aspects of the social system which were, in fact, responsible for the changes noted. See Homans' (1941) account of the Hawthorne studies.

novation actually are is dramatized in the chapters of the present book (see, for example, Fox & Lippitt, and Clee & Reswick). Yet these processes are, over and over again, dismissed or treated simplistically.

Primitive constructions of the processes of educational innovation may perhaps be excused, given our current urgency and haste. Yet the relatively high rate of educational innovation we are now experiencing provides an excellent opportunity to understand the problems of innovation in educational systems with some clarity. It seems fair to say that, while a substantial body of empirical information on change in social systems of various sizes has accumulated, there is no really adequate theory of social change.[7] Thus the current situation presents a fertile ground for inquiry, and there is a very real possibility that our theoretical understanding of social change can be overhauled and refined.

It also seems fair to assume that increased clarity in our conceptualizations can lead to more intelligent control of change processes in education. Second-guessing from the armchair is easy; prediction is vastly more difficult (see Chapter 24 below); control in any meaningful sense of the word is hardest of all. Yet the social technology of planned change is already receiving thoroughgoing attention in fields outside education (see, for example: Bennis, Benne, & Chin, 1961; Bennis, 1963; Mann & Neff, 1961). Educational practitioners need not assume that change in the systems with which they are associated must be planless, automatic, or arbitrary; if we know more about educational innovation, the management of change as a planful process becomes more likely. Beyond this, the practical benefits of inquiry in this area are likely to show up in economy of energy. Given more understanding, it is less likely that educational innovators will (for example) ever again invest as much energy, with as little net effect, as was expended in the Eight-Year Study. We shall see.

[7] The reader who doubts this is referred to Loomis & Loomis (1961, esp. pp. 582–660) for a thoughtful review of the theoretical work of seven major American sociologists. However, interest in this field is growing rapidly. See Hirsch & Zollschan (in press) for a stimulating collection of empirical cases and theories concerning social change; Etzioni & Etzioni (in press) present material of similar scope. See also Rogers (1962) and Katz, Levin & Hamilton (1963) for thorough reviews of work on the diffusion of innovations. Moore (1963) has produced a thoughtful integration of existing work on social change.

Definitions

It may be useful to offer some rough definitions of terms which will be in recurrent use throughout the book. Usage from chapter to chapter varies and precision will not be attempted here.

Change

"Change" is very nearly an undefined, primitive term. It generally implies that between time 1 and time 2 some noticeable alteration has taken place in something. The emphasis in most chapters of this book is on alteration in the goals, structure, or processes of a *system*.

System

"System" has typically inspired a varied splendor of definitions, as Griffiths points out in the present book. A working definition for our purposes might be: a bounded collection of interdependent parts, devoted to the accomplishment of some goal or goals, with the parts maintained in a steady state in relation to each other and the environment by means of (1) standard modes of operation, and (2) feedback from the environment about the consequences of system actions. This is scarcely an elegant definition, but it can be seen to apply to systems as various as the classical candle flame, an air-conditioning system in a building, a man flying a jet fighter, a small group, and (even) the "American educational system." The systems of most concern in this book are social systems (thus the parts involved are persons, groups, or organizations) devoted to the achievement of educational goals. Educational systems come in a variety of sizes, from classroom to school building to school district to the state department and its relationship to local school districts, to far-flung systems like the College Entrance Examination Board's Advanced Placement program, to terribly diffused systems like "the mass media"—and, as suggested, the American educational system. Just how complicated, multifarious, and diffuse the latter is will be detailed in the next section.

Certain types of change in educational systems are excluded or barely treated in the present book. These include changes involving a general system *drift* over time (for example, accretion in the curriculum offerings of colleges); shifts in the *Zeitgeist* (e.g., the renewed concern with "excellence" and "achievement" characterizing the late 1950's), which serve as a backdrop for specific innovations, operating to support, reinforce, or block them; the *social movement* (e.g., "progressive education"); the *revolution* (if we follow the usual definition—a radical, violent change in the fundamental power structure of a social system—no educational examples come readily to mind); and lastly, *accidental* changes of an unplanned, entropy-increasing sort (e.g., the destruction of a school's records by fire).[8]

Innovation

Innovation is a species of the genus "change." Generally speaking, it seems useful to define an innovation as a deliberate, novel, specific change, which is thought to be more efficacious in accomplishing the goals of a system. From the point of view of this book, it seems helpful to consider innovations as being willed and planned for, rather than as occurring haphazardly. The element of novelty, implying recombination of parts or a qualitative difference from existing forms, seems quite essential (cf. Barnett, 1953). The element of specificity might more easily be labeled "thingy-ness"; innovations in education, as will be seen in the section below, ordinarily have a defined, particular, specified character, rather than being diffuse and vague. Finally, since the inhabitants of a system (or the persons, groups, and organizations in its environment) usually advocate or try to introduce innovations de-

[8] The term *reform* has been used only intermittently in the chapters of this book, mainly because it is a vague, diffuse term without very precise referents. Ordinarily, one thinks of reform as involving a large-scale change, often involving a structural shift, with a strong melioristic overtone. Norms and procedures operating in the system prior to the reform are generally seen as bad, undesirable, even morally wrong. Thus, reform ordinarily involves exposure ("muckraking") of the corrupt old and its radical excision, or at least modification, by "housecleaning" procedures. Examples of educational reform seen in these terms might be the drastic changes in American medical schools following Flexner's report on them in 1915, and perhaps the reduction in political corruption in the American schools following the reports of Joseph Mayer Rice in 1892–93 and Adele Marie Shaw in 1903.

If we stick to the definition offered here, the so-called curriculum reform groups (PSSC and others) operating at present can be seen more clearly as marketers of innovations—and as themselves innovations on a larger scale—than as purveyors of reform. Wholesale changes in teacher education, if they are ever achieved, might more legitimately be labeled a reform, since the elements of moralism, housecleaning, and broad structural change all have been or might be present.

liberately, as indicated above, the worthwhileness of an innovation is ordinarily justified on the basis of its anticipated consequences for the accomplishment of system goals.

Innovations in education

To give more concreteness to the universe called "educational innovations," some samples are described below. They are organized according to the aspects of a social system with which they appear to be most clearly associated.[9] In most cases, the social system involved should be taken to be that of a school or college, although some innovations take place within the context of much larger systems.

Boundary maintenance operations.   Social systems must induct and extrude personnel through their boundaries, which define who is "in" or "out" of the system. Innovations relevant to this aspect of systems include changes in teacher certification requirements, merit pay programs, perhaps, and pupil assignment laws.

Size and territoriality.   Social systems include specified numbers of persons or groups within their boundaries, and extend over geographical space. Innovations in this aspect of social systems include: school district consolidation; variations of class size, as in the Newton Plan and the college proposals by Ruml & Morrison (1959); and Goodman's (1962) experimental urban university of 10 teachers and 150 students.

Physical facilities.   Any social system operates in relation to an accompanying collection of technology, and thus can be fruitfully

[9] The aspects of social systems presented here draw on the treatment by Loomis (1960). Of course, it should be said that almost any given innovation is bound to have ramifying effects on many (or all) other aspects of the social system into which it is introduced. For example, team teaching, itself an innovation in the definition of roles within the local school system, also has effects on physical facilities, the use of time during the school day, class size, normative beliefs and sentiments (e.g., teacher attitudes toward autonomy and academic freedom), and the in-service training activities employed. Thus the classification used here is arbitrary, and is of primary use in indicating the wide range of educational innovations currently being advocated or installed.

Chapters of the present book which are particularly illustrative of a social-system approach to the study of innovation include those by Atwood, Wayland, Carlson, Barton & Wilder, and the editor.

thought of as a "sociotechnical system." Innovations in this aspect include methods used to insure flexible use of building space in schools (divider walls, flexible seating, and the like), language laboratories, closed-circuit and broadcast television, and programed instructional devices.

Time use. Any social system exists in and carries out operations over a period of time, which is punctuated, organized, and controlled in various ways. Examples here are the "year-round schools," the trimester plan for colleges and universities, the use of double shifts in schools, and flexible class scheduling.

Goals. Social systems exist in time and space *for* something, to accomplish a more-or-less specified purpose. One recent innovation which involves change in school system goals is the Higher Horizons Program in New York City, which implies that more system effort should be devoted to meeting the needs of underprivileged children. Another is the "structure" approach, implied by Bruner (1960) and advocated by most current curriculum "reform" groups; it implies that internalization of the basic concepts and methods of inquiry of a subject field should be a fundamental outcome of elementary and secondary education.

Procedures. An educational system, like any other social system, must employ a set of operations which serve as means for goal attainment. These are ordinarily arrangements of time, persons, and activities thought to accomplish work toward system goals. This is (supposedly) the area where most educational innovation is expected to take place—though innovations are also made in all other aspects of systems, and do affect goal attainment as well. Several subtypes of educational system procedure seem identifiable. These include: (1) the use of *curriculum materials* to support changed curriculum content— e.g., the text, film, instructional-device and experimental materials accompanying the curricula developed in physics, chemistry, and mathematics by national study groups; (2) *specific instructional procedures*—e.g., role-playing, independent study, use of programed textbooks, teacher "question boxes" for pupil feedback; (3) *general procedures*—e.g., the laboratory practices approach of the Citizenship Education Project, the Dalton Plan, the platoon school; (4) *curricu-*

lum organization—e.g., the Dual Progress Plan, involving a combination of departmentalized and "self-contained classroom" teaching for different clusters of subjects; (5) *classroom composition*—e.g., multiage grouping, the ungraded primary, the "teachable group" (Thelen, 1960).

Role definition. A social system must specify the behaviors expected, permitted, and prohibited for persons occupying its various parts. Innovations in role definition include the use of teacher aides, contract correction of English composition papers, and team teaching.

Normative beliefs and sentiments. As persons and groups interact in an on-going system, regulatory beliefs and sentiments tend to develop which insure the maintenance of standard behavior and system accomplishment. These are ordinarily less subject to direct innovation than most of the items mentioned previously, since they tend to be emergents of interaction. However, some innovations which have been advocated include a strong normative component. Among these are the idea that children should be made to work harder, the idea that ability grouping is not in itself "undemocratic," and the idea that centering the curriculum in the needs and wishes of the learner is less appropriate than drawing it from the basic disciplines underlying subject matter.

Structure (relationships among parts). The parts (persons, groups, departments, etc.) of a system ordinarily stand in a defined relationship to each other. One part is able to control the output of another, for example; one part sends messages only to (or receives them from) certain other parts. Within small systems, structural innovations include the use of curriculum councils, departmentalized organization in the elementary school, and the use of "houses" within large schools. Within much larger systems, such as that loosely labeled "the American educational system," a number of innovations in structure have been proposed, including a national council of advisors on education (as reviewed in the *New York Times,* November 25, 1962), national specialty boards for certification of teachers in subject matter areas (Lieberman, 1960), and state curriculum evaluation commissions (Alexander, 1962).

Socialization methods. As persons enter an on-going social system through its boundaries, they must learn the ropes, be taught to be effective and appropriate contributors to the system. They must accept its goals, use its procedures skillfully, and conform to existing normative sentiments. Innovations appropriate to this heading include fifth-year programs for the Master of Arts in Teaching, and the in-service training institutes held under National Science Foundation and other auspices.

Linkage with other systems. Any given social system must develop ways of making connection with other systems in its environment, with which it makes transactions of various sorts. Examples of innovations in this aspect of educational social systems are work experience programs (see Burchill, 1962), the use of Saturday seminars or "community resource pools" involving supplementary teaching by citizens, and the use of collective bargaining between representatives of teacher associations and local school district administrators.

This listing is sufficient to indicate the wide range of innovations now being advocated in American education. This method of organizing the range of current innovations has been used in order to stress the fact that innovations are *always* operant in relation to a given social system; they affect one or more parts of the system crucially, and are in a very real sense rejected, modified, accepted, and maintained by existing forces in the immediate system. Perhaps this is the place to point out that such a view of innovation is hardly novel: cf. Francis Bacon's *On Innovations,* written in 1597:

> It is true, that what is settled by custom, though it be not good, yet at least it is fit. And those things which have long gone together are as it were confederate within themselves; whereas new things piece not so well; but though they help by their utility, yet they trouble by their inconformity. Besides, they are like strangers, more admired and less favoured.

Strategy

"Strategy" is defined here as a means (usually involving a sequence of specified activities) for causing an advocated innovation to become successfully (i.e., durably) installed in an on-going educational system. The range of strategies now being proposed and carried out in America is very wide, and classification is difficult. However, a proposed typology of educational innovation strategies is outlined in Chart 1.

Dimensions of strategies. Any given strategy is thought of here as being ultimately aimed at getting an innovation installed in a "target" system (usually a local school system and its immediate community environment, or a college or university). Strategies may be initiated by the *target system* itself, or by *other systems* in the environment of the target system, such as state departments of education, mass media, foundations, and government agencies.

In either case, the strategy may involve the use of *existing* structures, or the creation of *new* structures. "Existing" and "new" must of course be defined with reference to the time at which the innovation is introduced.[10]

We thus have four ways in which a strategy may be initiated. Chronologically, we may then think of a series of stages which occur prior to the actual adoption of an innovation by a target system. These stages include: (1) *design*—the innovation is invented, discovered, made up out of whole cloth, produced by research and development operations, etc.; (2) *awareness-interest*—the potential consumers of the innovation, that is, members of the target system, come to be aware of the existence of the designed innovation, become interested in it, and seek information about its characteristics; (3) *evaluation*—the consumers perform a kind of mental trial of the innovation, and form pro/con opinions about its efficacy in accomplishing system goals, its feasibility, and its cost; (4) *trial*—the target system engages in a (usually) small-scale trial of the innovation, in order to assess its con-

[10] Two points need to be made about strategies involving the creation of new structures. First, these new structures (e.g., the Physical Science Study Committee) are *themselves* innovations in the larger system—innovations designed to further the installation of other, more specific innovations (e.g., the PSSC texts) in target systems. Second, new structures may be set up either on a permanent or temporary basis—but this distinction need not detain us here, partly because temporary structures tend to become permanent in social systems if they operate successfully in solving system problems. See the author's chapter on temporary systems in the present book.

sequences. If these are favorable, the innovation tends to be adopted, and the strategy is complete.[11] Note that, whether the *initiation* of a strategy comes from the target system itself or from the environment of the target system, this typology always assumes the strategy to be aimed at adoption of the innovation in the target system.

The four types of initiation, and the four stages prior to adoption by the target system, generate the 16 cells in Chart 1. They have been arbitrarily numbered for ease of reference; *no* sequence from row to row is implied.

A *comprehensive* strategy would involve all four cells across a given row, from design of the innovation through awareness-interest to evaluation and trial, although there is no reason why all stages of a comprehensive strategy should necessarily be accomplished by the same system, group, or person. As we shall see, many strategies are partial or truncated, and may even fall in only one cell.

Strategies initiated by the target system, using existing structures. Several types of comprehensive strategy may be placed in this row (cells 1–2–3–4). These include the curriculum councils and committees extensively used in school systems to prepare and install innovative curriculum guides; local in-service training programs and staff meetings, which appear to account for the design and installation of many specific innovations; and the model of "action research" commonly advocated in the early 1950's.

If we remember that the "target system" is defined here as including the relevant portions of the local community, the so-called "community-

---

[11] This formulation of stages, particularly the latter three, draws closely on the conceptualization of Rogers (1962), which was based on approximately five hundred studies of diffusion, drawn mainly, but not exclusively, from the field of agricultural innovation. Rogers' formulation omits the stage of *design*—since most of the studies he reports on began with the existence of an adequately designed innovation, such as hybrid corn. Rogers' stages of *awareness* and *interest* have been collapsed here for simplicity, and his final stage of *adoption* has been omitted, since this is a study of strategy, which presumably concludes at the point when adoption occurs. Of course, there may be more or less durable adoptions: discontinuances may take place, or the innovation may be adopted in a more or less drastically revised form. And there may be subsequent local evaluation after the adoption has been in force for some time. These sequelae do not concern us centrally, however, in the examination of strategies. (See also the chapter by Eichholz & Rogers in the present book.)

STAGES IN THE STRATEGY PRIOR TO ADOPTION BY TARGET SYSTEM

INITIATOR OF STRATEGY		Design of innovation	Local awareness–interest	· Local evaluation	Local trial
Target system (school, college, etc.)	Existing structure	1	2	3	4
	New structure	5	6	7	8
Systems in environment of target system	Existing structure	·9	10	11	12
	New structure	13	14	15	16

Chart 1. A typology of change strategies

by-community" approach derided by Lieberman (1960) would be a comprehensive strategy. An example is the procedure suggested in the "manual" prepared by Smith (1959) for the Council for Basic Education, which primarily advocates citizens' working with the local school board.

All of these comprehensive strategies involve attention to designing potential innovations (with or without research on the problems involved), developing awareness and interest, enabling evaluation of the proposals, and encouraging or requiring trials—which, hopefully, will lead to adoption. The usual arguments offered for using strategies of this type center around the importance of "local control" and of active involvement in decision-making of those who are affected by the decisions.

A partial strategy in this row of the matrix is the deliberate creation of conflict around particular innovations at the local school district level. This strategy, advocated by a number of super-patriotic organizations (see Raywid, 1962), covers only cells 2–3. That is, it seems to focus mainly on awareness-interest and evaluation, but does not usually lead to local tryout, especially where conflict is strong enough to be disabling to the participants.

Visits by local school system personnel to neighboring systems are also a partial strategy; they can be placed in cells 2–3–4. Brickell's chapter in the present book points out the crucial importance of such visits in the decision to try out and adopt a particular innovation.

Strategies initiated by the target system, using new structures. Some strategies, while initiated by the target system itself, do involve the creation of special structures to develop innovations and guide the progress of strategic attempts. Comprehensive strategies in this row (5–6–7–8) include specially appointed local curriculum committees, either at the school or college level; the creation of a council of administration and faculty for general college improvement, as advocated by Morrison (1959); and the use of a local group affiliated with the National Citizens Commission for the Public Schools (Dreiman, 1956) to aid the local school district in matters of reorganization, teacher recruitment, improvement of materials, and community financial support.

A partial strategy in this row of the matrix, covering only cells 6–7, is the community self-survey suggested by Raywid (1962). It seems designed to diagnose the state of community opinion in relation to the school program, thus aiding local awareness-interest in re particular innovations, and evaluation of them, but appears to stop short of encouraging the trial of innovations by school personnel.

The usual argument for creating new structures within the target system is that the norms and procedures of the local system have become overfirm and resistant to change, and that an additional stimulus for change is therefore needed. The value of attaching the new structure directly to the target system is said to be that understanding of the demands of the system is more likely to be complete. On the other hand, the major weakness of such strategies is that the new structure may become trapped in the assumptions of the existing structure and thus rendered impotent.

More importantly, as Lieberman (1960) has pointed out, *all* strategies involving the local system as initiator ignore *cross-system* problems, such as teacher certification, fiscal reform, and the position of professional organizations in the power structure of the larger system.

Strategies initiated by systems in the environment, using existing structures. Many strategies stem from systems outside the target system, and involve the use of structures in existence for a reasonable length of time prior to the introduction of the proposed innovation. One comprehensive strategy of this type (cells 9–10–11–12) is Lieberman's (1960) outline of possible steps for diffusing the innovation of collective bargaining between teacher organizations and school districts. It involves a coalition of the National Education Association and the American Federation of Teachers, and is designed to increase the power of existing structures (as is his advocacy of the strategy of teachers' withholding services from a local school district where practices such as salary administration are felt to be inadequate).

Another comprehensive (and thoroughly worked-out) strategy in this row, also proposed by Lieberman (1960), is aimed at installing the innovation of national teaching specialty boards. The steps envisioned include the use of foundation initiation and support to involve national professional subject-matter organization leaders (both teachers and professors), plan-making by these organizations, dissemination to local school districts, the use of professional conferences to assess the proposals, decision-making by a specified minimum number of school districts, and foundation support of these decisions.

Another comprehensive strategy in this row has been used by the Fund for the Advancement of Education; it involves the provision of funds on a matching basis for management surveys in institutions of higher education, operated either by consulting firms or by the institutions themselves. Such a strategy (itself an innovation) appears to have been useful in stimulating the local design of innovations, and in carrying them through to adoption.

Not surprisingly, there seems to be a concentration of single-cell strategies in cell 10 of this row. Many organizations appear to act as if their sole function were to increase local awareness-interest in particular innovations. One strategy of this sort is the production of a critical book or article, like those excerpted in Scott, Hill, & Burns (1959). Another is the production of a book designed to disseminate images of an as yet incompletely installed innovation. Examples are: the collection of journalistic descriptions of innovations such as team teaching by Morse (1960), entitled *Schools of Tomorrow—Today;* [12] and the Ruml–Morrison book (1959) nominally addressed to college trustees, showing novel images of class size utilization at the college level. The fellowships for educational reporting granted by the Fund for the Advancement of Education can also be called a cell 10 strategy. So can the so-called "promising practices" approach used by the Metropolitan School Study Council and similar groups; specific instructional practices are collected from teachers and circulated to a wider teacher group, often through magazines such as the MSSC *Exchange.*

Another partial (10–11) strategy in this row involves a book which discusses the pros and cons of a particular innovation very thoroughly, to aid the development of local awareness-interest and local evaluation. Examples of this strategy are the journal issue edited by Lipson (1962) on the advantages and disadvantages of the year-round school, and the discussion of the college trimester plan by Hungate & McGrath (1963).

Two other strategies initiated from the environment of the target system, using existing structures, are worth mentioning. Perhaps because they are restricted to single cells, each has attracted substantial amounts of criticism. First is the strategy followed by some foundations, notably the Fund for the Advancement of Education, in financing demonstrations of particular innovations in local schools. This amounts to restriction to cell 12, since the emphasis is primarily on local trial, rather than on the design of the innovation or the development of awareness-interest and evaluation. The reasoning behind this strategy has been described in a recent report (Fund for the Advancement of Education, 1961, p. 16):

> [The Fund] can, however, select areas of contingency and, with good timing, make its small efforts have large effects. It tries to study the power structure of the educational system, gauge the temper of the times, appraise the array of forces for and against any particular change, and then throw its weight at the right moment behind the most promising trends in the hope of converting them into dominant ones.

[12] Charmingly enough, this book gives no intimation as to the source of its title; an earlier book employing precisely the same strategy (*Schools of Tomorrow*) was written by John and Evelyn Dewey (1915) to describe the early experiments in progressive education.

This stance toward educational change has attracted a good deal of criticism, primarily assertions that the Fund was simply paying school systems to try out "untested" practices, such as teacher aides, team teaching, and educational television.

These criticisms have been strongest, not surprisingly, from persons favoring the other single-cell strategy in this row: classical educational research. This strategy has tended to be limited to cell 9: university and college professors have conducted research to answer fundamental questions underlying the design of innovations, and in some cases have developed innovations as a result. The responsibility for dissemination of research findings, so as to bring about local awareness-interest, evaluation, and trial, has, however, been ordinarily assumed to belong to some other group. For example, it has often been remarked that local school personnel do not read research journals with great voracity—but the classical educational researcher continues to assume that his responsibility ends with the act of publication.

Strategies initiated by systems in the environment, using new structures. There may be a growing tendency to build new structures to carry innovative enterprises. At least, this review found more currently-used strategies placeable in row 13–14–15–16 than in the other rows of the matrix. An example of a comprehensive strategy of this sort is the publication *Focus on Change: Guide to Better Schools* (Trump & Baynham, 1961), and associated materials. Produced by the Commission on the Experimental Study of the Utilization of the Staff in the Secondary School (a new group appointed by the National Association of Secondary School Principals of the NEA and supported by the Fund for the Advancement of Education), this publication makes an analysis of needed innovations, describes them thoroughly enough to develop local awareness-interest and evaluation, and outlines a series of strategic steps which can be used in the local school system to install particular innovations, such as flexible time scheduling.[13]

A by now familiar—and apparently effective—comprehensive strategy is that followed by national curriculum study groups (the Physical Science Study Committee, the Biological Sciences Curriculum Study,

[13] Note here that, as in the case of the CBE manual (Smith, 1959), a strategy may turn out to include the teaching of others (particularly persons in the target system) to use another, more specific, strategy.

the School Mathematics Study Group, and the like). Initially, it involves the convening of scholars from academic disciplines to agree on the basic concepts to be included in the new curriculum. This step is followed by the preparation of texts, materials, and supporting devices based on the concepts; careful field testing and feedback on the adequacy of the materials; training of selected teachers in the use of the revised materials; and follow-up supervision for these teachers as they begin to use the materials. (See Marsh's chapter in this book.)

Still another comprehensive strategy involving new structures in the environment is the coordinated research and development laboratory proposed by Gilbert (1962): exploratory research, fundamental and specific development work, design and testing of the specific innovations resulting, training of educational practitioners, and follow-through are all conceived as parts of the total enterprise.

The network of regional research organizations being proposed by the Oregon State Education Department under Office of Education financing can also be placed in cells 13–14–15–16; these organizations would conduct some basic research and would "emphasize field testing, development, evaluation, experimentation and implementation of all lines of educational research which hold promise for improving classroom and administrative practices in public elementary and secondary schools, and institutions of higher learning" (Nyquist, 1962, p. 14).

One more comprehensive strategy is that of collaboration between a university and the schools in the immediate area surrounding it, for purposes of innovation design, dissemination, evaluation, and trial. Such organizations now exist, for example, around the University of Pittsburgh (the Regional Commission on Educational Coordination and the Coordinated Education Center), the University of Wisconsin (Wisconsin Improvement Program), the University of Chicago (the School Improvement Program), and Harvard University (the School and University Program for Research and Development).

Many examples of partial strategies in this row of the matrix can be identified. One is the use of experimental or laboratory schools—actually educational Utopias, as Watson's chapter in the present book points out—such as those proposed or carried out by people as diverse as Maria Montessori, John Dewey, and Paul Goodman. This strategy actually covers only cells 13–14–15 at best, since no provision is made for supporting or encouraging actual trial in the target school system (namely, any other system than that of the experimental school itself). An adapted (and more nearly comprehensive) strategy, which might be called quasi-utopian, involves the creation of institutionally sponsored experimental colleges. The Fund for the Advancement of Education has supported the study of a "New College" plan, which would draw jointly on the resources of Amherst, Mount Holyoke, Smith, and the University of Massachusetts; it has also financed experimental subsystems within existing colleges, like Monteith College within Wayne State University. The linkage of such systems with their associated target systems presumably makes eventual trial of innovations more likely (though see Watson's analysis of the failure of an earlier New College to do just that).

Another partial strategy: the work of James B. Conant has included, among other projects, the creation of a new structure (The Study of the American High School) led by a man of high prestige and dedication. The strategy involved the study of existing school programs, the preparation of a number of innovative suggestions, the production of a report (which sold approximately 200,000 copies in the first six months), followed by numerous news conferences and television appearances to stimulate awareness-interest and to form a basis for local evaluation of the soundness of Dr. Conant's recommendations.[14] Note, however, that provision for actual local trial of the recommendations was absent from the strategy.

Other strategies are even more truncated, involving only two cells in the last row of the matrix. For example, Nyquist (1962) has described another regional research organization proposal (this one made by Pennsylvania State University under sponsorship of the Office of Education); it envisions centers for programmatic research in fundamental areas of learning, and associated development and dissemination activities, but contains no clear provisions for local evaluation and trial. A strategy suffering similar limitation (to cells 13–14) is the just-launched Project Social Studies of the U.S. Office of Education, which is to emphasize basic and applied research, the creation of curriculum study centers, and exploratory projects designed to stim-

[14] See Lieberman (1960, pp. 218–30) for a detailed and interesting analysis of the Conant strategy. It appears to have been followed again in Conant's more recent study of teacher education (1963).

ulate further research. Plans for local evaluation and trial of resultant innovations are not part of the strategy as presently conceived.

Other examples of 13–14 strategies are: the working conference which meets to develop or discuss particular innovations and disseminate knowledge about them, such as the Conference on New Schools for New Education sponsored by the Fund for the Advancement of Education; the series of Conferences on Teacher Education and Professional Standards in which academic scholars and professional educators met to discuss possible innovations in teacher certification (though the proceedings of these conferences were disseminated, evaluation and tryout of particular innovations at the local level were not part of the over-all strategy); and the use of an institute to plan further summer training institutes, as currently reported by Rosenblatt (1963) for the Commission on English of the College Entrance Examination Boards.

Several National Defense Education Act projects appear to involve primary attention to local awareness-interest and evaluation of innovations (cells 14–15): these include the in-service training institutes sponsored for teachers of foreign languages, and the program of graduate fellowships in this same field. (The program for construction of language laboratories does make explicit provision, of course, for actual local trial of the innovation, and thus can be located in cells 14–15–16.)

One other example of a 14–15 strategy involves the creation of a professional journal explicitly devoted to reporting new trends in education. Examples of these are the British journal *Forum*, and the journal of the Bureau of Educational Research at Ohio State University, *Theory into Practice*. Here too, explicit stimulation of the trial stage is lacking.

Finally, several strategies fall in single cells of the last row of the matrix. In cell 13, one could place the language area centers sponsored by NDEA (primarily designed to develop innovations, with little attention to dissemination and trial as such, since these are to be handled by other aspects of the NDEA program); the associated NDEA foreign language research program; the launching of Mortimer Adler's Institute for Philosophical Research to undertake "an analytic reexamination of Western humanistic thought, a project of considerable interest to those concerned with the goals of liberal education," according to the sponsor, the Fund for the Advancement of Education (1961, p. 20); and Jensen's (1962) proposal for the creation of separate departments of educational research, not affiliated with existing departments of education.

The support of the *Saturday Review* Education Supplement by the Fund for the Advancement of Education appears to be a strategy limited to cell 14. Finally, the "clearing house" function performed by many specially set up groups and organizations is another typical cell 14 strategy.

Generally speaking, the advantages of new structures (see also Miles' chapter on temporary systems in the present book) appear to be that they by-pass vested interests, provide protection for development and trial of innovations, and aid high focus on the work at hand. If careful provision is made in this type of strategy for a comprehensive approach, as is evident in several strategies reviewed here, decisions to adopt the innovation appear to be quite likely.[15]

This concludes the discussion of types of strategies in current use in the American educational scene. It may be helpful at this point to turn to a brief examination of that scene; without an ordered look at the context in which strategies are launched, and in which they live or die, our understanding of educational innovation can only be partial.

The American Educational System

A frequently encountered view of the American educational system is that it is not a system at all, but a vast, sprawling, complex semi-chaos. Another view sees it as a connected network of subsystems of various size, operating in a more or less coherent way. For the latter point of view, the reader is referred to the chapters by Wayland and Mackenzie in the present book (see also Campbell & Bunnell, 1963). No attempt will be made here to do much more than describe the various clusters of subsystems which make up the American educa-

---

[15] In passing, it should be noted that some strategies involve the linking of existing organizations, or the pairing of new and existing structures. This type of strategy appears to be a useful one; note, for example, the impact of the Trump Plan, which involves, in effect, a coalition between the NEA and the Fund for the Advancement of Education.

tional system. In effect, the reader is presented with a list of the main actors who may appear in the cast of any particular drama of educational innovation. Almost every chapter in this book selects a limited number of these subsystems, and examines their interrelationship during the development of a set of processes centering around a particular innovation or class of innovations.

Chart 2 is designed to aid the reader with the discussion that follows; it does not pretend to show, of course, how particular subsystems are connected with and affect each other.

Directly educative systems

A number of systems might be analogically termed the "production departments" of the educational system; in them, learners learn something.

Formal educational systems. A wide range of schools and colleges is included in this category. First, for children and adolescents, there are publicly financed elementary, junior high, and high schools (and, in some cases, community junior colleges), over which nominal control is exercised by local boards of education with jurisdiction covering a local school district (ordinarily a town or city, but not infrequently a region or a county).

In addition, there are private and parochial schools for learners of similar ages.

There are also institutions devoted to the learning needs of people who are about to become (or are) adults. McConnell (1962) has characterized them briefly:

> What in this country is called higher education . . . includes two-year technical institutes, two-year junior or community colleges, independent and denominational liberal arts colleges, teachers colleges, multipurpose state colleges, complex universities, land-grant colleges and universities, specialized colleges in music and arts, theological schools, and highly specialized, advanced scientific and technological institutions. And this list is by no means complete.

All these, of course, may be either publicly or privately controlled, as in the case of the lower schols.

The use of "higher" and "lower" is not coincidental. The institutions in which formal education is given are generally thought of as standing in a hierarchical relationship to each other. Downward influence is exerted not only on the curricula of the lower schools, via college entrance requirements, but on their teaching staffs and their social and intellectual climates as well.[16]

Institutions of higher education, as primary educational agencies, are, like the lower schools, target systems for innovative efforts. In addition, they perform two other functions important for educational innovation: the training of teachers and professional educators of all sorts, and the production of new knowledge underlying both educational subject matter and educational processes.

Many institutions of higher education also engage in an intensive adult education program through extension services, conferences, and other means.

Nonformal educational systems.   Directly educational programs of all sorts are carried out by industrial organizations, on the scale of $5–10 billion annually. The federal government sponsors an enormous military training establishment, operated by the Department of Defense, and a large number of educational enterprises conducted by other governmental agencies (notably the Departments of Agriculture, Labor, Interior, and State, and the Veterans Administration) for their employees and clients. In addition, a great many teaching and learning activities are operated by marketing and merchandising establishments, by voluntary organizations in the health and welfare field, by hospitals, and by other local service and governmental agencies.

The volume of educational efforts sponsored by the Agency for International Development (both here for outbound personnel, and in other countries), by the Peace Corps, and by the various programs of international exchange for study, teaching, and research (see Weidner, 1962) is already substantial, and can only continue to grow.

Finally, the nonformal educational efforts of youth-serving organ-

[16] Lieberman (1960) has pointed out, for example, that the relative emphasis on athleticism and anti-intellectualism in high schools, the ill-fated "life adjustment" curriculum about which so much scolding has occurred, and the restrictive effects of membership in high school fraternities, sororities, and clubs can be seen to stem from historical roots and current practice in the American liberal arts college. College recruiting of promising athletes, use of social acceptability criteria by admissions officers, the activities of fraternities and sororities, and the condoning of anti-intellectual norms are all examples.

izations of all kinds—Boy Scouts, 4H Clubs, denominational religious groups, settlement houses, welfare agencies, camps—exert a very considerable influence on their "students," and form another subsystem in the American educational establishment.

Regional associations of educational institutions. In recent years there has been an increasing development of voluntary regional associations of educational institutions. Such associations are formed to facilitate the pooling of facilities and personnel, exchange of students, fund-raising, cooperative program development, and research.

Some associations of this type are: the Southern Regional Education Board; the Western Interstate Commission for Higher Education; the Ohio Association of Colleges; the Committee on Institutional Cooperation, which includes the "Big Ten" universities and the University of Chicago; the recently formed consortium on political research which uses data-processing facilities at the Institute for Social Research at the University of Michigan, but involves the collaboration of political scientists from twenty-two universities; various "school study councils," where schools in an area around a university band together to support study and development activities (the Metropolitan School Study Council of Teachers College, Columbia University, being the first historical example); the Regional Education Coordination Center and its associated Commission centered around the University of Pittsburgh; and university-connected school improvement programs, such as the School and University Program for Research and Development, which involves Harvard University and several school systems in the immediate area.

Government agencies

Any educational subsystem (school, college, or non-formal) is of course influenced by governmental agencies at local, state, and national levels. Both general laws, and those relating specifically to educational enterprises, set bounds on, and enable, educational operations.

Local school systems receive a good deal of financing (usually 30 to 50 per cent) from revenues controlled by the state in which they exist. Accordingly, relevant state-level persons and systems exerting control over the local school district include the state department of education, the state board of education, the chief state school officer,

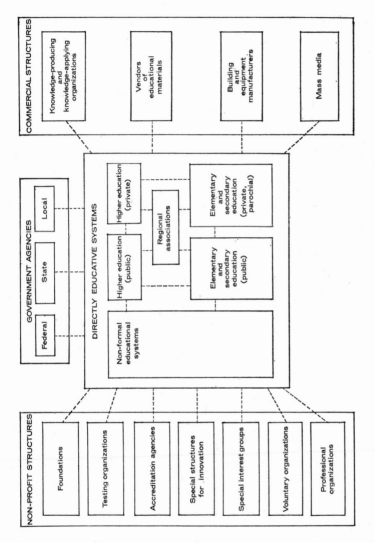

Chart 2. The American educational system

the state legislature, the governor, and various state courts. Public higher education is influenced at least as strongly by state agencies— and private institutions are regulated as well. The chapters by Colvard, by Johnson, and by Flesche, Masters, & Eliot in the present book illustrate well the importance of state agencies in affecting innovation.

At the national level, although public education is supposedly "locally controlled," there are nevertheless a number of groups and agencies which exert substantial *de facto* control. These include agencies which grant money for educational research and development, most prominently the Office of Education, the National Science Foundation, and the National Institute of Mental Health.

Though the Office of Education is supposedly prohibited from acting like a Ministry, it does in fact operate on a $750 million annual budget: it administers National Defense Act moneys for educational research, training, and facilities construction (see Johnson's chapter in the present book); collects and disseminates a wide variety of educational data; and through the Cooperative Research Branch in the past eight years has had a substantial effect on the amounts and kinds of research done in education.

A recently developed innovative force is apparent in the Labor-Department-supervised retraining programs for unemployed workers under the Area Redevelopment Act and the Manpower Development and Training Act; state agencies and the Office of Education are also involved in many of these.

Enabling all this activity, of course, are decisions made in the U.S. Congress; the intensity and variety of educational lobbying today testify to the importance of national legislation. In the executive branch, there are groups like the President's Science Advisory Committee, the White House Conferences on Children and Youth, and the President's Committee on Education Beyond the High School which stimulate innovative efforts. More directly, the President's education bills determine the outer limits of federal support for education. Finally, the drastic and sweeping effects, on education, of more than one Supreme Court decision demonstrate the ultimate influence of national judicial activity.

Commercial structures

Many profit-making systems affect directly educative systems. The distinction between profit-making and nonprofit structures is not minor; the quality, cost, and diffusion rate of educational innovations introduced for money-making purposes often turn out to be different from those associated with innovations proposed by systems with non-monetary goals. Commercial considerations are frequently of central importance when old investments and new products are at stake (see Forsdale's chapter in the present book).

Vendors of educational materials.   Although it is estimated that
school systems spend only 1.5 per cent of current outlay for textbooks,
(according to 1959–60 data presented by Bing, 1962), educational
materials (if we include films, film strips, tapes, workbooks, tests, and
teacher guides as well as textbooks) do exert an enormous influence on
operations in the classroom. The speed or slowness with which commercial firms are able to alter existing materials and distribute them
successfully has been frequently suggested as the major factor in educational change rates. Educational innovations which have a useful
(and profitable) supporting set of materials appear to diffuse relatively
rapidly; those without such a base tend to diffuse much more slowly,
or to disappear.

Building and equipment manufacturers.   The architects, construction firms, and suppliers who concentrate on school buildings exert
clear influence on educational innovation rates, as do the firms which
manufacture associated equipment of all sorts, from seating to audio-
visual hardware to floor wax. In some respects, the physical accoutre-
ments of the American school and college have changed much
more drastically than the operations taking place in and through
them.

Knowledge-producing and knowledge-applying organizations.   The
very rapid growth of systems devoted primarily to professionalized research and development activities is by now a familiar aspect of the
American scene. Although many of these are nonprofit organizations,
they are in effect run as business operations, often with as much attention to the marketing of knowledge to an interested purchaser as to its
development *per se.* The work of such organizations often has close
relevance to educational innovations and the strategies for installing
them. One thinks, for example, of the very large financial resources
administered by the American Institute of Research as it pursues
Project Talent, the fundamental studies of educational systems proceeding at System Development Corporation, and the training studies
being conducted by the Human Resources Research Office.[17]

The approximately 3,000 consulting firms in the U.S. are less am-

[17] Though the first two of these are nonprofit organizations and the last is a
government–university venture, they share a professionalized approach to knowledge production which did not exist even two decades ago.

biguously devoted to profit, and direct most of their energy toward work with profit-making organizations. However, the growing tendency to involve firms such as Arthur D. Little, McKinsey & Co., and Cresap, McCormick, & Paget in the innovation problems of educational organizations indicates a significant addition to the subsystems at work in the American educational scene.

Mass media.   Finally, we cannot ignore the brute fact that newspapers, magazines, radio, television, and books are themselves the primary informative and educative agents for nearly all adults and most children in our society. Beyond this, they serve to stimulate the need for educational change, to diffuse information about particular innovations, and to block the progress of others. For example, the importance of the mass media for the success of innovation strategies like those followed by J. B. Conant, the Fund for the Advancement of Education, and Admiral Rickover can hardly be overestimated. And, the FCC and *Publishers' Weekly* to the contrary, it is important to remember that the majority of mass media institutions exist for profit-making purposes. Educational television stations, for example, now number 75, or less than 15 per cent of television outlets.

Nonprofit structures

Many structures devoted primarily to educational improvement and change, without regard to financial profit, exist in the United States. These structures, too, exert influence on directly educative systems.

Foundations.   Financially most prominent, perhaps, are the more than 15,000 philanthropic foundations in present existence. This figure seems impressive, but it should be noted that approximately 1 per cent of the foundations control three quarters of total foundation assets. Thus the concentration of philanthropic power is relatively narrow. The assets of the Ford Foundation alone account for over one third of this concentration; adding the Carnegie and Rockefeller funds pushes the assets controlled by three foundations to approximately $4.2 billion. Assets do not necessarily imply expenditures, but of the $220 million given to education in 1957 by the top 1 per cent of foundations, the Ford Foundation supplied just under half (as part of a special teacher salary endowment project).

Testing organizations.   Many observers have remarked on the extent to which the curricula of formal educational institutions at all levels are now influenced by nationally standardized tests. The most vigorous effects probably stem from the work of the Educational Testing Service (through well-known instruments such as the Scholastic Aptitude Test and the Graduate Record Examination, as well as a large number of special-purpose instruments) and Science Research Associates (through the National Merit Scholarship examination). The diverse activities of the College Entrance Examination Board, including the Advanced Placement Program, also exert much influence.

Accreditation agencies.   Although a good deal of institutional accreditation takes place through governmental agencies such as state departments of education, voluntary regional accreditation associations like the North Central Association of Schools and Colleges considerably affect the quality of educational programs. The controversy currently raging around the National Council for Accreditation of Teacher Education (see Stiles, 1963) illustrates the crucial nature of such groups.[18]

Special interest groups.   Many organizations have particular interests which they attempt to have incorporated in school and college programs. These include a large number of business and industrial corporations; patriotic organizations such as the American Legion; business associations such as the National Association of Manufacturers; "nonprofit" groups like the National Advertising Council; various religious denominations; clearing house groups like the National Industrial Conference Board; and voluntary associations with a particular message, such as the 4H Clubs or the American Red Cross.

Voluntary organizations.   There is a very wide range of voluntary organizations, involving lay persons mainly, and devoted to educa-

[18] Accreditation agencies deal with institutional competence; the question of *individual* professional competence in education is now primarily dealt with by legal (state) certification requirements based on training and experience. Other professions, notably law and medicine, handle certification by direct examination of performance, conducted by voluntary boards drawn from the profession itself, and coordinated with the state legal structure. Whether this pattern will emerge in educaion is problematical (cf. Lieberman, 1960).

tional change in one form or another. Some of these are predominantly local, like associations of real estate firms or local taxpayers' associations. Others have both local chapters and a national organization devoted to advancing an over-all coherent program. Under this rubric would fall such organizations as the Parent–Teachers Association, the National Citizens Council for the Public Schools, and the White Citizens Council movement in the South.

Finally, there are voluntary nonmembership organizations which develop and advance a particular point of view on educational change, such as the Council for Basic Education.

Professional organizations.   A vast complex of associations devoted to the interests of one category or another of educational practitioner also exerts a good deal of influence on educational innovation. Such organizations help to set standards, hold conferences, issue journals, and engage in lobbying activities; they also produce knowledge which affects school and college subject matter, teaching methods, organization, and innovation processes.

Examples of such groups are the National School Boards Association; the National Education Association with all its subsystems for every variety of educational professional role; the National Association of Independent Schools; the American Association of University Professors; the American Federation of Teachers; an enormous range of learned societies (e.g., the American Sociological Association, the Modern Language Association of America); national councils (e.g., the American Council on Education, the Social Science Research Council); and a number of national institutes (e.g., the American Association for the Advancement of Science).[19]

Special structures

A number of structures appear to be devoted primarily to advancing educational innovation directly, having been created for that purpose.

Some of these structures have existed for some time, and are periodically reused, as it were. These include systems like the recurrent White House Conferences on Education; the conferences on teacher

[19] See Kiger's chapter in the present book for an illuminating account of these last three types of structure.

education sponsored by the National Commission on Teacher Education and Professional Standards, which brought together academic scholars and professional educators in a series of well-reported meetings; and the Educational Policies Commission of the National Education Association.

In addition, we are currently seeing the creation of many new structures explicitly designed to further educational innovation. A type of growing frequency is the special curriculum study group in an academic area, such as the Physical Science Study Committee (which itself has led to the creation of a supporting organization, Educational Services, Inc.). Other examples of newly created systems are the Educational Facilities Laboratories; the Learning Resources Institute; the Center for Programed Instruction; the Massachusetts Council for the Public Schools (just currently converting itself to a national organization, the National Committee for the Support of Public Schools); and the Southern Education Reporting Service.

In addition new knowledge-producing organizations are created steadily within universities. These include institutes or centers (such as the Center for Research on Human Learning just launched at Stanford), and extensive research projects focused around the operations of a principal investigator (such as the Yale-Hamden Hall Responsive Environment Study, now located at Rutgers University; it centers around the work of O. K. Moore on technologically aided methods of teaching very young children to read and write).

As we review this complex of subsystems, each exerting influence on educational innovation, it is hard to avoid the conclusion that it constitutes a listing of all the significant aspects of American culture. This is only half true, of course: the worlds of corporate life, the nuclear family, entertainment, crime (etc.) are largely lacking. What we must remember in examining the problems of educational innovation, however, is that nearly any innovation attempt will be conditioned by forces at work within or between subsystems of the general sort we have described here—educational agencies themselves, government systems influencing these, and a wide range of commercial and nonprofit organizations. The American educational system is not a simple structure, but neither is it, as we shall see in the present book, a chaos.

The Study of Educational Innovation: An Agenda

This book was begun in the belief that we know far less than is desirable about the nature of educational innovation. Basically, the problem is that we do not *understand*—do not know with any clarity or precision the answers to questions about almost every imaginable aspect of innovation in education. Perhaps it will serve as a prelude to the chapters which follow if an illustrative listing of classes of important questions is made here. Some of these are not dealt with closely in this book. Nor can it be claimed that the ideas in this book have succeeded in disposing of any of them as viable questions. Much, in short, remains to be done—as in almost any field of inquiry worth the name.

Special characteristics of educational systems. One basic class of questions focuses on the properties of *educational* systems—as opposed to other types of systems—which appear to exert pronounced effects on innovative attempts. For example, it appears to be difficult to measure the output of educational systems precisely; it has been suggested that this may slow down innovation rates and increase ritualization of behavior, since no clear criterion of appropriate behavior within the system is available. The fact that educational products are supposedly to be assessed over a very long span of time (such as a lifetime) may have similar effects. (See Kendall's chapter in the present book for useful evaluation procedures which help by-pass these problems.)

Another possibility is that the distance between lay and professional competence in educational systems is much narrower than in most other systems (partly because *everyone* has experienced an educational system and thus claims expertise); the existence of a considerable degree of lay control is both symptom and cause of this effect.

Still another possibility follows from the fact that educational systems are operated by persons who are themselves the instruments of change (compared, for example, with the situation in a steel mill, relatively little physical technology is employed). This may create resistance to evaluation and to innovation of any kind. Perhaps the fact that education is an enterprise directed toward the difficult (even threatening) task of altering persons also operates in this direction.

All these possibilities must remain speculations at this point, but they illustrate ways of thinking about the question: Do educational systems, as such, have special characteristics which affect the extent, rate, and fate of innovations?

Underlying characteristics of the innovation. Keeping in mind that innovation is defined here as a "deliberate, novel, specific change, which is thought to be more efficacious in accomplishing system goals," a number of legitimate questions arise about the crucial characteristics of the innovation itself.

For example: Does the fate of an innovation depend on the aspect of the target system with which it is primarily associated (i.e., is an innovation dealing with size and territoriality of a school system likely to fare any differently from one requiring new role definitions for members)? Furthermore: Are there formal characteristics of the in-novation—its complexity, the amount of extra energy its installation is likely to require from system members, its perceived "radicalness," the degree to which it is divisible into simpler parts—which exert critical effects on its progress into the system?

Prior states of the system. As the innovation begins its movement into the target system, questions must be asked about pre-existing conditions in the system which may facilitate or hinder change. For example: What is the role of the general *Zeitgeist* in serving as a sup-porter or blocker of specific changes, or as a creator of generalized openness or resistance to many changes in the system?

And: Are there conditions which might be characterized as making for "ripeness" of the system, a kind of latent disequilibrium which makes subsequent innovations actually welcome? What is the role of the external or internal crisis in making for openness toward innova-tion? What sorts of factors, whether personal (e.g., cognitive dis-sonance), interpersonal (e.g., status disequilibrium on the part of sig-nificant actors), or organizational (e.g., ambiguity in power structure) make for readiness for the innovation?

Processes during change. What, actually, seems to go on as an innovation encounters a system in which someone hopes it will be-come installed? Is the Lewinian notion of "unfreezing" of the system in the early stages of change an appropriate one? In what sense can "shifting" and "refreezing" be accurately said to take place? What is the true nature of the phenomena frequently—and too easily—lumped under the heading of "resistance"? In what way does "novelty excitement" play a part in acceptance of innovation? Can it be said to correspond to *"la joie de connaître"*? And can innovative processes be *managed* in any meaningful sense of that word?

Characteristics of the innovative person or group. What sorts of persons or groups characteristically serve as advocates of innovations? Where do their primary loyalties lie—inside or outside the target system? Do they operate most effectively in permanent or temporary subsystems of the larger system? Can there be said to be personality characteristics associated with the persistent advocacy of innovations? What sorts of assumptions do innovators appear to hold underlying the strategies which they employ?

The fate of innovations. Any particular innovation may or may not be incorporated, substantially as originally envisioned, into the subsequent operations of the target system. But what determines this? What kinds of revision are typically made in incorporated innovations, and what seems to cause these characteristic changes? Under what circumstances is an innovation likely to be rejected by members of the target system? What are the criteria for "success" commonly applied to an innovation by target system members, by innovators, and by dispassionate observers (if any such exist)? And, if these criteria are carefully applied, what proportion of adopted innovations is later judged, after all, to be undesirable? [20]

Reasons for changes in innovation rates. Finally: Under what circumstances does a system begin to innovate at a different rate than previously? Can there be said to be "learning" of a generalized stance toward innovation, such that the system is more open, experimental,

[20] Given diverse criteria, answers to this question are likely to be very difficult to obtain. For example, Keating's (in press) finding that—except for first-year spoken fluency measures—language laboratories were generally *inferior* to standard instruction provoked an immediate flurry of counter-assertions from teachers testifying to the efficacy of the laboratories. (*New York Times,* May 15, 1963.)

desirous of changing, more able to tolerate the ambiguity of the new— or perhaps more slavishly addicted to faddism and novelty? In what sense does the institutionalization of innovation (as, for example, via departments of research and development) in fact alter innovation rates in the surrounding system?

These are the classes of questions with which anyone seriously interested in the study of educational innovation must deal. If we come to understand them more clearly, we may be able to manage educational innovation in a more coherent, sophisticated way. But first we must understand.

References

Alexander, W. M. Assessing curriculum proposals. In A. H. Passow (Ed.), *Curriculum crossroads*. New York: Bureau of Publications, Teachers College, Columbia University, 1962. Pp. 11–21.

Allen, H. E. The diffusion of educational practices in the school systems of the Metropolitan School Study Council. Unpublished Ed. D. project, Teachers College, Columbia University, New York, 1956. Pp. 56–83.

Andrews, F. E. Report of the director. In *Annual report,* The Foundation Library Center. New York: The Center, 1961.

Bacon, F. *Essays.* London: Dent, 1906.

Barnett, H. G. *Innovation: the basis of cultural change.* New York: McGraw-Hill, 1953.

Bennis, W. G. A new role for the behavioral sciences: effecting organization change. *Admin. Sci. Quart.,* 1963, 8 (2), 125–165.

Bennis, W. G., Benne, K. D., & Chin, R. *The planning of change: readings in the applied behavioral sciences.* New York: Holt, Rinehart & Winston, 1961.

Bing, A. Educational publishing: problems and prospects. *Amer. Behav. Sci.,* 1962, 6 (3), 20–23.

Brozen, Y. The role of government in research and development. *Amer. Behav. Sci.,* 1962, 6 (4), 22–27.

Bruner, J. S. *The process of education.* New York: Harper, 1960.

Burchill, G. W. *Work-study programs for alienated youth: a casebook.* Chicago: Science Research Associates, 1962.

Bushnell, M. Now we're lagging only twenty years. *School Executive,* 1957, 77, 61–63.

Campbell, R. F., & Bunnell, R. A. (Eds.) *Nationalizing influences on secondary education.* Chicago: Midwest Administration Center, University of Chicago, 1963.

Carle, R. F., Kehas, C. D., & Mosher, R. L. (Eds.) Guidance—an examination. *Harvard Educ. Rev.*, 1962, 32 (4). Entire issue.

Clark, B. R. *Educating the expert society.* San Francisco: Chandler, 1962.

Clark, H. F., & Sloan, H. S. *Classrooms in the factories.* Rutherford, N.J.: Institute of Research, Fairleigh Dickinson University, 1958.

Conant, J. B. *The education of American teachers.* New York: McGraw-Hill, 1963.

Cook, D. L. The Hawthorne effect in educational research. *Phi Delta Kappan*, 1962, 44 (3), 116–122.

Council for Financial Aid to Education. *Guide lines to voluntary support of American higher education.* New York: The Council, undated.

Cremin, L. A. *The transformation of the school: progressivism in American education, 1876–1957.* New York: Knopf, 1961.

De Crow, R., & Kolben, K. (Eds.) *Continuing Education for Adults* (newsletter). Chicago: Center for the Study of Liberal Education for Adults. No. 32, March 31, 1963.

Dewey, J., & Dewey, E. *Schools of to-morrow.* New York: Dutton, 1915.

Dillon, W. S. Nation-building in Africa: Challenges to education. *Teach. Coll. Record*, 1960, 62 (2), 152–61.

Dreiman, D. B. *How to get better schools: a tested program.* New York: Harper, 1956.

Etzioni, A., & Etzioni, E. *Social change: sources, patterns and consequences.* New York: Basic Books (in press).

Fehr, H. F. Mathematics reform around the world. Paper read at Montclair State Teachers College, December 8, 1962.

Finn, J. D., Perrin, D. G., & Campion, L. E. Studies in the growth of instructional technology, I: Audio-visual instrumentation for instruction in the public schools, 1930–1960, a basis for take-off. Occasional Paper No. 6, Technological Development Project. Washington: Department of Audiovisual Instruction, National Education Association, 1962.

Fraser, D. M. *Current curriculum studies in academic subjects.* Washington: National Education Association, 1962.

Fund for the Advancement of Education. *Decade of experiment: the Fund for the Advancement of Education 1951–61.* New York: The Fund, 1961.

Gilbert, T. F. A structure for a coordinated research and development laboratory. In R. Glaser (Ed.), *Training research and education.* Pittsburgh: Univ. of Pittsburgh Press, 1962. Pp. 559–578.

Glaser, R. (Ed.) *Training research and education.* Pittsburgh: University of Pittsburgh Press, 1962.

Goodman, P. *The community of scholars.* New York: Random House, 1962.

Hirsch, W., & Zollschan, G. K. (Eds.) *Explorations in social change.* Boston: Houghton Mifflin (in press).

Homans, G. C. Group factors in worker productivity. From Ch. 4, The Western Electric researches. In *Fatigue of workers: its relation to industrial production* (Committee on Work in Industry of the National Research Council). New York: Reinhold, 1941. Reprinted in Maccoby, E. E., Newcomb, T. M., & Hartley, E. L. *Readings in social psychology.* New York: Holt, 1958. Pp. 583–595.

Hungate, T. L. & McGrath, E. J. *A new trimester three-year degree program.* New York: Bureau of Publications, Teachers College, Columbia University, 1963.

Jencks, C. Schoolmaster Rickover. *New Republic,* 1963, *148* (9), 14–16.

Jensen, A. R. The improvement of educational research. *Teach. Coll. Rec.,* 1962, *64* (1), 20–29.

Katz, E., Levin, M. L., & Hamilton, H. Traditions of research on the diffusion of innovation. *Amer. Sociol. Rev.,* 1963, *28* (2), 237–252.

Keating, R. F. Preliminary evaluation of the effectiveness of language laboratories as used in the Metropolitan School Study Council. New York: Institute of Administrative Research, Teachers College, Columbia University (in press).

Kimball, S. T., & McClellan, J. E., Jr. *Education and the new America.* New York: Random House, 1962.

Koerner, J. D. How not to teach teachers. *Atlantic,* 1963, *211* (2), 59–63.

Lengyel, E. Educational revolution in the Middle East. *Teach. Coll. Record,* 1962, *64* (2), 99–105.

Lieberman, M. *The future of public education.* Chicago: University of Chicago Press, 1960.

Lipson, S. (Ed.) The year-round school. *Theory into practice,* 1962, *1* (3). Entire issue.

Loomis, C. P. *Social systems: essays on their persistence and change.* Princeton: Van Nostrand, 1960.

Loomis, C. P., & Loomis, Z. K. *Modern social theories.* Princeton: Van Nostrand, 1961.

Machlup, F. *The production and distribution of knowledge in the United States.* Princeton: Princeton University Press, 1962.

Mann, F. C., & Neff, F. W. *Managing major change in organizations.* Ann Arbor, Michigan: Foundation for Research on Human Behavior, 1961.

Marsh, P. E., & Gortner, R. A. *Federal aid to science education: two programs.* Economics and Politics of Public Education Series, No. 6. Syracuse: Syracuse University Press, 1963.

Mayer, M. *The schools.* New York: Harper, 1961.

McConnell, T. R. Diversification in higher education. In H. Chauncey (Ed.), *Talks on American education.* New York: Bureau of Publications, Teachers College, Columbia University, 1962. Pp. 35–45.

Moore, W. E. *Social change.* Englewood Cliffs, N.J.: Prentice-Hall, 1963.

Morrison, D. H. Achievement of the possible. Part 4 in B. Ruml & D. H. Morrison. *Memo to a college trustee.* New York: McGraw-Hill, 1959.

Morse, A. D. *Schools of tomorrow—today.* New York: Doubleday, 1960.

Mort, P. R., & Cornell, F. G. *American schools in transition.* New York: Bureau of Publications, Teachers College, Columbia University, 1941.

NEA Project on Instruction, *The principals look at the schools: a status study of selected instructional practices.* Washington: National Education Association, 1962.

Nyquist, E. B. We must disenthrall ourselves. Paper read at 1962 Research Conference, Educational Research Association of New York State and New York State Education Department. Albany, New York, October 25, 1962.

Patterson, F. Social science and the new curriculum. *Amer. Behav. Sci.,* 1962, 6 (3), 28–32.

Raywid, M. A. *The ax-grinders.* New York: Macmillan, 1962.

Rogers, E. M. *Diffusion of innovations.* New York: Free Press of Glencoe, 1962.

Rosenblatt, L. M. Reappraisal of the English curriculum. Paper read at Educational Records Bureau Conference, Nov. 1, 1962.

Ross, D. (Ed.) *Administration for adaptability.* New York: Metropolitan School Study Council, Teachers College, Columbia University, 1958.

Ruml, B., & Morrison, D. H. *Memo to a college trustee.* New York: McGraw-Hill, 1959.

Sanford, N. (Ed.) *The American college.* New York: Wiley, 1962.

Scott, C. W., Hill, C. M., & Burns, H. W. *The Great Debate: our schools in crisis.* Englewood Cliffs, N.J.: Prentice-Hall, 1959.

Smith, M. B. *A citizens manual for public schools: a guide for school board members and other laymen.* Washington: Council for Basic Education, 1959.

Snow, C. P. Miasma, darkness and torpidity. *New Statesman,* 1961, 42 (1587).

Squire, J. R. English at the crossroads. *English Journal,* 1962, 51 (6).

Stiles, L. J. Wisconsin's challenge to NCATE: who is to control the education of American teachers? Paper read at Education Writers Association annual awards luncheon, in conjunction with American Association of School Administrators meetings, 1963.

Thelen, H. A. *Education and the human quest.* New York: Harper, 1960.

Trump, J. L., & Baynham, D. *Focus on change: guide to better schools.* Chicago: Rand McNally, 1961.

Weidner, E. W. *The world role of universities.* New York: McGraw-Hill, 1962.

Part I: Case studies
in educational innovation

In the development of theoretical understanding, there is no substitute for the close examination of concrete, particular situations. If we do not have a knowledge of acquaintance with the phenomena of interest, generalizations are bound to be naive and theory shallow. Each of the nine chapters of this section reviews the events of a particular innovative situation. The chapters are arranged in approximate order of increasing size of system.

Atwood's account of the vicissitudes of an organizational change in an urban high school follows the microprocesses of interaction between the people significantly involved. Clee and Reswick review the development of a shorter-range change—an innovative course in a technological institute. Watson's fascinating story of the rise and demise of an experimental college is used to illustrate the recurrent patterns appearing in most utopian enterprises.

The three following chapters examine educational change processes at the state level. Colvard provides a vivid, closely documented account of the intercollege struggles which occurred in the context of a state-wide innovation—a foundation-sponsored teacher education program in Arkansas. Johnson details the impact of federal funds on educational practice in California. And Flesche, Masters, and Eliot, viewing the political context of educational decision-making, describe an Illinois state-level commission as an innovation for the management of educational change.

The growth of educational technology is not, of course, limited by local or state boundaries, but occurs in a national setting. Forsdale provides a diagnostic view of the network of groups, roles, and persons which are likely to influence the diffusion of a new educational tool—in this case, 8mm sound film. Gotkin and Goldstein examine issues, illustrated in a number of case situations, which bear on the diffusion of programed instructional devices.

Finally, Marsh reviews the general strategy of what may prove a classic approach to innovation at the national level: the Physical Science Study Committee.

The authors of these chapters come from many disciplines and professions: anthropology, social psychology, engineering, sociology, education, political science, English, psychology. The assumptions they bring to bear vary accordingly; thus the degree of quantification, the methods of inquiry and sources of evidence used, and the theoretical schemes explicitly or implicitly underlying the presented generalizations differ too. Just how interdisciplinary the study of educational innovation properly "should" be is undoubtedly a fruitless question. At this point we need knowledge, regardless of its ancestry. Thus the importance of these case studies.

CHAPTER 2

Small-scale administrative change: resistance to the introduction of a high school guidance program

M. S. Atwood

THE major aim of this chapter is to describe in detail and analyze the steps by which the principal of a large city high school, in trying to improve the guidance services offered the students, changed the way his faculty performed guidance activities and by so doing aroused unexpected resistance.[1] This will provide an example of a small-scale educational innovation for comparison with the studies of large-scale or long-ranging innovations that appear elsewhere in this book. In generalizing from these case studies about the importance of differences in the size of a change, its duration, or its content for the processes and consequences of innovation, certain problems inherent in the process of comparison must be dealt with first.

If one is to compare large and small, long and short innovations, one needs a common language to describe the cases in terms that are

[1] The research on which this case is based was supported in part by the Cooperative Center for Educational Administration, a project of the Kellogg Foundation, and by the Advanced School of Education, both of Teachers College, Columbia University. The full study is reported in Atwood (1960).

THE AUTHOR is Assistant Professor of Education, Graduate School of Education, Rutgers, The State University.

49

reasonably free of the particular instances, but accurately reflect the specific cases. In addition, one needs to decide on a minimum set of common data to be described for each case. If a particular phenomenon is absent from the description, one must be assured that it is absent in reality. One must also decide how much of the context of an innovation is to be described. This context can be thought of as the conditions in which the innovation was introduced, and succeeded or failed. The immediately prior situation is often given as an adequate statement of these conditions. If it is adequate, one must still decide how much of the situation is "immediate." These are decisions that have usually been made from common sense. However important common sense may be to other aspects of research, it does not guarantee common data for precise comparison.

The second aim of the chapter is to explore the usefulness of one set of answers to these problems of comparison, that offered by anthropological interaction theory. This approach shares many elements with the other social sciences, as will be obvious from the other contributions to this book. But its combination of empirical, processual, contextual, and comparative features, and particularly its operational procedures, offer a way of describing and analyzing the nature of innovations that renders the data objective and comparable. The data of the case to be presented were collected and analyzed in line with the assumptions of this theory. A short statement of the theory will help in understanding the choices made in selecting the elements of the case and in judging the usefulness of the method.

Interaction Theory and Method

Anthropological interaction theory (Chapple & Arensberg, 1940; and its restatement and elaboration in Arensberg & McGregor, 1942; Arensberg, 1951, 1957; Arensberg & Tootell, 1957; Chapple & Coon, 1942; Chapple, 1953, 1962; Chapple & Sayles, 1961; Homans, 1950; Kimball & Pearsall, 1955; Kimball, 1958; Whyte, 1951) starts with the widely-held assumption that society and culture are products of social action. Social action consists of events in time and space in which people stimulate one another and respond to stimulation. Out of the recurrence of such interactional events emerge symbols, attitudes, values, beliefs, norms, and the like. These emergents have meaning primarily in the events of interaction in which they occur. They must therefore be referred back to the events as a first step in describing and interpreting them. This first step may be thought of as placing the phenomenon in its primary or *internal context*. Second, the connection between the phenomenon under study and the other elements of the events is made by observing the order of occurrence in time of each of the elements. Any new phenomenon or change is treated as an emergent from prior changes in the events in which it first appears. This procedure helps to reveal unsuspected causal relations. It represents observable reality more closely than static correlational approaches. This second step may be thought of as placing the phenomenon in a process in *time*. The internal contextualization is thus extended to include prior states of events.

Events take place and recur in a particular *environment* of physical possibilities and limitations. The connection between the events and their physical environment must be described. The environment consists also of other sequences of recurrent events. The connection of these other events to the events under observation must likewise be made. But not all the other events taking place in adjacent spaces and times need to be included in this examination. One distinguishes linked or tangent events occurring before and during the appearance of the events under observation. The linked events are those which share some of the same people interacting in the focal sequence of events. This physical and social environment forms the secondary or *external context*. This third step places the phenomenon under study in it.

So far, the features of the interactional approach which have been brought out are (1) its empirical bias—it deals mainly with observable happenings in space and time; (2) its processual nature—it regards reality as sequences of happenings which must be placed in the order of their occurrence; (3) its contextual emphasis—it makes the first task of the researcher that of looking for connections among the elements in space and time, placing a phenomenon in its primary context of events; and (4) its answers to the question of a sufficient secondary context—the physical context is described when the events are placed in space, the social context is adequately described by the linked events in which some of the same people interact, and the temporal context by the prior state of both of these.

The result of this approach is a number of cases of social action described in their natural setting. The next step imposed by interaction theory is to compare these cases. The classification of similarities and differences is based on the common properties exhibited by the events of interaction. These properties yield universal operations, the simplest of which are (1) enumerating the people taking part in an event, (2) identifying the actors, (3) specifying the order in which they act, (4) measuring the duration of each act in an event, and of events, (5) counting the frequency of occurrence of these orders of action or events, and (6) noting the regularity in time of their occurrence.

Whether or not the patterns of interaction are in fact prior to values and attitudes, and whether or not they are the significant feature of social life and changes in it, the operations that can be performed make interaction the empirical basis for comparative analysis and generalization. These operations give a description of events that is relatively free of the particular and yet more concrete than such nominal descriptions as "high morale" and "tight authority," or than definitions of an innovation as "new" or "representing a qualitative shift in an existing situation."

The way of applying interaction theory to the study of educational innovation is already clear. Educational innovations are to be treated as changes in patterns of social action, and as the emergence of new patterns of events. Educational innovations become processes described operationally as changes from prior states in the number and identity of the people involved, in the direction of action between them, in the frequencies of the specifiable kinds of events involving them, and in the duration and regularity of these events. They also become statements of changes in the spatial distribution of people and actions, and of changes in the preceding and concurrent sequences of linked events. Since the validity of this approach for education remains to be established, additional data on values, sentiments, behavior, and changes in these have to be included for examination against the operationally described patterns of interaction. Interaction thus defined offers a precise and objective framework within which to categorize and compare the observed facts of innovation.

The Case Study

The example of a small-scale educational change to be presented in this manner concerns the efforts of a new principal of a high school to introduce a centralized guidance program. Since the faculty of the high school were noted in the city for being "guidance-minded," he expected no resistance to his plans. And, since he had decided nevertheless to "go slow," the opposition that developed to the program was all the more difficult for him to understand.

The prior situation

The John Quincy Adams High School was started in a large Eastern city during the 1920's with two aims: to provide a high school education for difficult students and the apparently uneducable, or "motor-minded," and to give them an opportunity for technical training in a major industry of the area. The first principal and founder of the school, Mr. Doyle, persuaded the industry to donate expensive equipment. He also persuaded the Board of Education to hire technically trained men from the industry who were licensed to teach only at Adams. He asked the principals of the other city schools to send him their difficult students, those who would otherwise be recommended for discharge. His concern for these students continued within Adams. He went to see his teachers frequently to inquire about a student's progress, or to ask one of them to reconsider a grade or a demand for severe disciplinary action.

The school grew rapidly in the 1930's and then began to decline because of competition from another high school, decreasing high school enrollments throughout the city, and the start of World War II. In 1944 Mr. Doyle became ill and died. The assistant principal, Mr. Fall, became acting principal until 1946, when a second permanent principal, Mr. Lehrer, was appointed. Many of the faculty were sorry that Mr. Fall was not appointed permanently. They were disturbed by Mr. Lehrer's appointment because his major interest was audio-visual aids, not the industry around which the school had developed. They believed that this change in the goals of the school was but temporary until the Board could find a technically qualified man like Doyle.

The faculty under Doyle had thought of themselves as "special" and superior in training and experience to the faculties of the other high schools in the city. Even those of the faculty who disliked some of Mr. Doyle's methods shared this feeling. And even these people agreed that Doyle was wholeheartedly devoted to the welfare of his students, a goal that they accepted for themselves. Several talked with pride of the extra time spent after school hours to help students, and of the occasional teacher who had helped finance a college education for a promising student.

In addition to this change in principals and in the aims of the school, certain other changes took place at this time which disturbed the faculty considerably. First. Mr. Lehrer reversed Doyle's policy of acting directly on students' problems. He believed that the responsibility for handling students' problems delegated to the deans and others should carry with it the authority to make decisions. As a result, he saw teachers much less frequently about the students than had Doyle. Many teachers interpreted this decrease in interaction to mean that Lehrer was "not interested in students."

A second change affected not only Adams but the whole school system. In 1947 the salary scale for elementary school teachers in the city was made the same as that for high school teachers. The high school teachers objected to the Board of Education's setting the same maximum salary for both. High school teachers had to have more training, they said, and pass more difficult examinations than the elementary teachers. These differences should be recognized by different maximum salaries. Discontent with the single-salary scale reached its climax in 1950. The high school teachers in the city went on "strike": they refused to continue their extra-curricular school activities without additional pay.

The teachers at Adams also complained of a change in the students during the period "after the War." They said that the students decreased in intelligence, became more difficult to teach, and caused more and more disciplinary problems. They believed that the disciplinary problems began to become serious "before 1952." There are no records to support these beliefs, but there is some indirect evidence. In support of their statements about difficulties in teaching, one may note that the ethnic composition of the students had begun to change. In 1946, it had been mainly Irish, Italian, Jewish, and others, with about 5%

Negro. By 1952 it was about 20% Negro and about 1% Puerto Rican. The spatial segregation of the Negroes and Puerto Ricans in their earlier schooling may well have resulted in a different response to learning from that to which the Adams teachers were accustomed. This difference may also have contributed to the teachers' belief that the students were less intelligent.

As for the increasing disciplinary problems, the lenient policy in dealing with students under Doyle was reversed by Lehrer. Though there may not have been any more problems than before, after 1946 increasingly more students were being chastised by the school authorities and transferred (or, if of age, discharged). In addition, the proportion of substitute teachers increased sharply in the fall of 1950 and 1951 from about 4% of the faculty to 12% and then 16%. When a similar situation occurred in the academic year 1956–1957, the older teachers pointed out that the inability of the substitutes to control the students made more work for the experienced teachers, who had to re-establish discipline before their own classes could go on. If the increased number of substitutes had a similar effect in 1950 and 1951, this may have contributed to the belief, in recollection, that students were becoming more difficult at about that time.

In 1952 Mr. Lehrer was transferred to another school. The new principal of Adams, Mr. Daubner, was appointed to his first position. Daubner announced an "open door" policy: all teachers were encouraged to come to see him about any problems. Although this was a change from Lehrer's relations with many of the teachers, it was not a return to Doyle's pattern of seeking out the teachers. But many teachers described the difference between Daubner and Lehrer as the difference "between night and day." Daubner also reversed Lehrer's policy of dealing with disciplinary problems. In Doyle's tradition, he tried wherever possible to give students a "second chance." But now, many of the teachers regarded this as the "easy approach" to discipline. They saw it as his attempt to alleviate the worsening disciplinary situation. When the problems did not get better, but were aggravated by an influx of strangers wandering through the halls of the school (a problem affecting other schools at this time as well), and when complaints came in from people in the neighborhood that the students were blocking their doorways, some of the teachers asked Daubner to have a policeman stationed in the school. He refused, and recommended instead that the faculty be more vigilant themselves in patrolling the halls. He did arrange to have a policeman stationed outside the building to clear the students away from the houses in the vicinity.

During the following academic year, 1952–1953, when Daubner took the first steps in introducing a centralized guidance program, a number of teachers thought that the new program was his alternative both to the failure of his "easy approach" and to their proposed solution of a policeman to keep order. (They judged the program accordingly for its success in lessening disciplinary problems, a much narrower criterion than the aims and scope of the program.) Actually, the decision to introduce a guidance program was made before Daubner became principal. The Board of Education wanted such programs installed, but left the initiative to the individual principals. Daubner came from a school that had had one of the first pilot programs. From his own experiences, he was convinced of the need for a systematic and expanded handling of the various guidance activities provided by the high schools. He came to Adams prepared to start such a program without knowing of its immediate problems. Some teachers had surmised this, because of the pilot program in the school that Daubner had come from, and because of the comments of their acquaintances who had been Daubner's colleagues in that school.

Some teachers were apprehensive about the new program. They wondered if it would mean a change in their teaching. Still others, those who disliked the "easy approach" shown in the handling of discharges, worried that the new program meant the dominance of "the permissive philosophy of education." On the other side, some worried lest any guidance program be thought adequate to do what they believed only a psychiatrist could accomplish.

The administrative organization of the school.   In addition to this sketch of some of the major changes in personnel, aims, and behavior, and of some of the major values, beliefs, and sentiments of the faculty, it will be necessary to outline the organization of the school and the way in which guidance activities were carried out before the program began, so that changes in both can be seen.

In 1952 Adams High School had roughly 2300 students and about 115 teachers (See Chart 1.) Under Daubner, the principal, were two assistant principals, Mr. Fall and Miss Galway. Formally equal

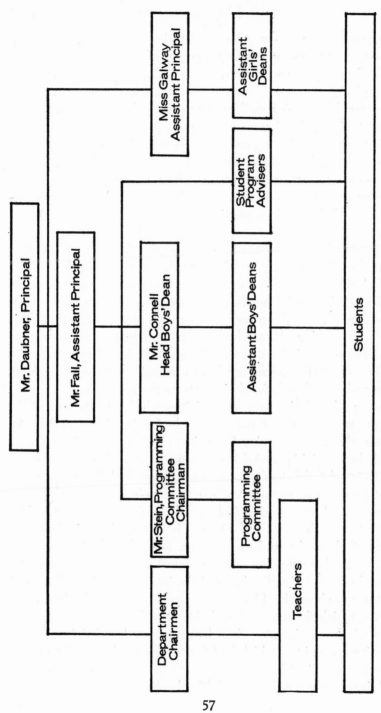

Chart 1. Organization of Adams High School in 1952, before the guidance program (position of boxes indicates relative power and prestige)

57

in pay and rank to them were the 14 chairmen of the subject departments. The regular monthly meeting of the principal with the people of this rank was called by the teachers "the principal's cabinet meeting."

The regular teaching staff were appointed from civil service lists, and were distinguished among themselves only by differences in pay based on academic training and on seniority in the city school system. Some "substitute" teachers were also appointed during each term. Each month, representatives of the teachers, the clerical staff, and the chairmen met to discuss grievances which were then taken up in the latter half of the "cabinet meeting" with the principal.

Teachers' duties. All teachers, except the department chairmen, taught five periods a day and had one home-room period in which the clerical records on the students were kept up, notices handed out, etc. The chairmen did not have a home-room class and, depending on the size of their departments, were exempted from one or more periods of teaching. All teachers except the chairmen were also assigned for one period a day, called the building assignment period, to police the four student lunchroom periods and the study halls, and to perform other duties decided on by the principal.

Among other duties were the activities which became part of the guidance program—the Deans' Offices, the Student Program Advisers' Office, and the Programming Committee. The number of teachers in any of these activities varied from term to term. About five teachers were assigned to be Boys' Deans, one as Dean and the others as Assistant Deans. Two to three teachers were assigned as assistant Girls' Deans to work under Miss Galway, the assistant principal, whose main role was that of Girls' Dean. These two offices took care of cutting of classes by students, absence, and other disciplinary problems. Some eleven teachers were assigned to the Student Program Advisers' Office. This office handled the intricate problem of counseling students about the 13 different courses of study leading to 13 diplomas which the school offered. The actual placement of students in a particular section of a class, however, was handled by the Programming Committee, which had four to five teachers assigned to it, with one named as Chairman.

All these teachers were excused, like the department chairmen, from a homeroom class and from one or more of their subject classes. The time released was spent on their duties in the offices. They were assigned for an indefinite number of terms to their jobs.

The other building assignments were rotated each term. The distinction between rotated and non-rotated building assignments had been a continual source of irritation to the rotated teachers. They complained periodically about the difference because, they said, the non-rotated jobs were easier. Since all teachers were formally equal, all should have access to the non-rotated "plums." The teachers in the non-rotated positions agreed with the other teachers that teaching five classes is the hardest job there is, and that time off from teaching is very desirable. But, they added that the other teachers did not recognize just how much work the non-rotated positions required. They often had to take work home at night, and to spend any free periods during the day on these duties.

Deans' Offices. The guidance activities in 1952 were carried out in the following way. When a student cut a subject class or was absent from a home-room class, the teacher had to send a card noting the offense to one of the Deans' Offices. When the student acted in ways that were unacceptable to the teacher (e.g., cheating, insubordination, refusing to work, etc.), the teacher attempted to restore the pattern of acceptable classroom behavior. If he was unsuccessful or believed that the offense required a more formal punishment, he sent a card to the Deans. They in turn sent a notice to the student through his home-room teacher, telling him to report to the Deans' Office at a particular time. The time at which the notice was sent varied from a few days to a week after the offense, depending on the seriousness of the case and on the amount of work the Dean who was handling the student's class had. Whatever action was taken, the Dean made a note of it on the original referral card and sent the card back to the initiating teacher. Instead of waiting for this notice, however, the teacher often stopped a Dean in the halls or in the cafeteria or came into the Deans' Offices to ask what had been done about a case.

The head Boys' Dean, Mr. Connell, had made contact with various city, religious, and welfare agencies and called on them as needed in dealing with a particular case. He took up any problems he could not handle with the assistant principal, Mr. Fall. Mr. Fall reported that he kept a daily eye on the working of the office, dropping in for a few minutes each day to sense the atmosphere and to look at the cards received from the teachers. Mr. Connell thought of himself as responsible directly to the principal.

The sentiments of the faculty about the Deans' Offices in 1952 cannot be reported. In retrospect from 1956, they all spoke well of Connell, often calling attention to his law degree as a mark of his qualities. He, however, in discussing (in 1956) the complaints of the faculty about the office under his successor, said that he saw little difference in the way the two offices were run, and that the teachers had always complained about him also.

Program Advisers' Office. The students talked to their Program Advisers each term in making up their program for the following term. The Advisers sent notices to the home-room teachers, who passed them on to the students whom the Advisers wanted to see. When the Advisers had a problem they went next door to Mr. Fall, the assistant principal, who "always knew the answers." They also advised the students about colleges, consulting Mr. Fall who kept the catalogues of various colleges in his office. The Advisers believed they were autonomous, and that they had no immediate superior: they went to Mr. Fall about problems because of his superior knowledge. Mr. Fall said they were directly under him but, because of his own many duties, he did not supervise them as closely as he would have liked to. He used their questions as a gauge of what they were doing, and interfered only when he thought that the direction of their activities was "getting out of line."

Programming Committee. After the programs for each student had been made up, they were sent to Mr. Stein, the Chairman of the Programming Committee. Mr. Fall worked out with him a master plan of the class hours and the number of sections for each subject and grade. Then, Stein with his group of assistants worked out the specific assignment of students to sections. At the beginning of each term, the size of classes had to be "equalized," made as nearly equal again as possible, because mistakes and changes requested by the students often led to imbalances. If this were not done quickly the teachers complained that they could not begin their work. Stein thought he was directly responsible to the principal, but according to Fall was directly under the latter.

Many of the teachers, as well as the Advisers and Deans, felt free to take the initiative in discovering emotional, financial, or other difficulties of their students and attempting to do something about them. They usually called these to the attention of Mr. Connell, the Boys' Dean, for action. If they did not like his response or did not think it was sufficient, they took the matter up with Mr. Fall. Though they could no longer go to the principal as they had done with Mr. Doyle, they were proud of their "guidance" activities, and of their competence to continue them even without the support of Doyle's successor.

The start of the guidance program

Mr. Daubner became principal in February, 1952. Because of his belief in moving slowly in administrative changes, he "did nothing" about the program in his first term. In one matter alone—the treatment of disciplinary transfers or discharges—he acted immediately by reversing Mr. Lehrer's policy (in the direction of more leniency).

He took every opportunity, however, to discuss the value of guidance in particular instances with faculty members, and arranged to have some films on guidance shown at the faculty meetings. Meanwhile he looked about for someone to head the program. The obvious person was Miss Galway, the assistant principal, who was already acting as Girls' Dean. But she declined the job. There is some doubt as to her reasons. Daubner said that she was eligible for retirement and did not want to take the additional courses necessary to qualify herself as guidance head. Some teachers said that she did not approve of guidance. Whatever the reason, she agreed that he should prepare someone else for the position.

After observing the faculty in the spring term of 1952, he selected Mrs. Sheen, a Student Program Adviser, as a possible candidate, but did not tell her of his choice. She knew the complex courses of study of the school; she was interested in guidance; she always volunteered to do extra jobs; and she was willing to take the additional courses to qualify herself to work in guidance.

Mr. Daubner began to give her small jobs at first in 1952–1953, and had her attend some conferences on guidance. At the same time, he took the handling of girls' cutting offenses away from Miss Galway and added them to the work of the Boys' Deans. In their place, Miss Galway was given some of Mr. Fall's administrative duties in order to even the load of duties between them. One informant reported that Miss Galway began to complain about the amount of work. Some teachers who regarded themselves as especially friendly with Miss Galway were also upset. They said that "all the glamor [of her position] was being taken from Miss Galway and she was left with only the mechanics [the administrative work]."

The following term, the fall of 1953, Miss Galway resigned. To replace her, Mr. Daubner appointed Mrs. Sheen as acting assistant principal and relieved her of all teaching duties. The rest of the duties of the Girls' Deans' Office were transferred to the Boys' Deans' Office, the title of which was changed to the Deans' Office.

Development of the Guidance Office. During the rest of 1953–1954, Mrs. Sheen gave her full time to developing a new activity that was called the Guidance Office. The office took over the handling of all cases of emotional difficulties, welfare problems, college counseling; the honor and various achievement rolls; and the development of a testing program. It also became the official office for making contacts with agencies outside the school. Mrs. Sheen began to address the faculty at the monthly faculty meetings to tell them about her work, explaining which cases were to be sent to her office and which to the Deans, how to fill out the new referral forms, how to compute the various honor rolls, and so on. With succeeding terms, the number of periods of building assignment time for her use and the number of teachers working under her increased.

She was nominated in the fall of 1954 by Daubner to become the assistant principal in charge of guidance. She prepared to take the first part of a "closed" examination in February, 1955, for the position. (The "closed" examination is administered by the city civil service, but is not competitive. This kind of examination was resented by some of the teachers because it prevented them from competing for the position.) She received her formal appointment in the spring of 1956.

Mrs. Sheen was then officially in charge of her Guidance Office, and the Deans' Office and Student Program Advisers' Office were

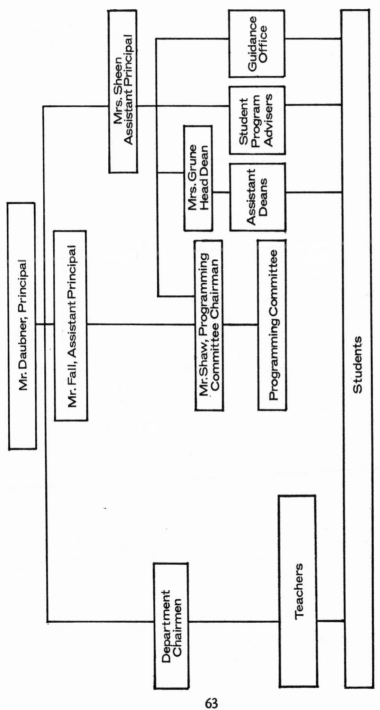

Chart 2. Organization of Adams High School in 1956, with the guidance program (position of boxes indicates relative power and prestige)

Mr. Daubner, Principal

Mr. Fall, Assistant Principal

Mrs. Sheen, Assistant Principal

Mrs. Grune Head Dean

Department Chairmen

Mr. Shaw, Programming Committee Chairman

Programming Committee

Assistant Deans

Student Program Advisers

Guidance Office

Teachers

Students

under her direct supervision, the three divisions together forming the Guidance Program. (See Chart 2.)

In addition, she now began to take part in the development of new classes, and to work with department chairmen in the modification of existing classes and curriculum. In the fall of 1956, for example, as the result of a poor showing in mathematics on a school-wide testing program for scholastic achievement which she had instituted, she arranged for more remedial sections to be given the following year in that subject.

Changes in the Program Advisers' Office.   Next after the development of the Guidance Office section of the program, the Students' Program Advisers' Office received Mrs. Sheen's major attention. Beginning with the fall of 1955, they were placed under her direct supervision. The attention she gave to them may in part be attributed to the immediate problem at this time of cutting down the number of classes that had to be "equalized." Two sources of the uneven class enrollments were the errors in the Program Advisers' work, and the changes they made at the students' request. In addition, with the Advisers there was no problem as there would have been with the Deans of placing her, a former subordinate, over a head Adviser. Putting the Deans under Mrs. Sheen's supervision was delayed until she became formally an assistant principal.

Mrs. Sheen began to codify the procedures of the Advisers and put them into writing. The Advisers received a continuing stream of directives telling them what to do and informing them of changes required by the Superintendent's Office. They complained to Mr. Fall. He pointed out that these directives merely stated in large part what they were already doing. But some of the directives contained errors, and new directives followed with corrections and further instructions. Further, they were forbidden to make decisions on problems that occurred without consulting Mrs. Sheen for a ruling. Because she often did not know what to answer at the beginning and had to consult Mr. Fall or Mr. Daubner, and because her other duties occupied her full time, she frequently delayed a few days before making decisions. In addition, she called a number of meetings with the Program Advisers, which they described as "lectures."

The Advisers disliked the delays and the meetings as well as the directives, and during 1955–1956 they continued to go to Mr. Fall for advice. At the beginning he accepted this, for he believed it would take time for the Advisers to become accustomed to the change. Toward the end of the year, he saw that they had no intention of making the change. He began with increasing frequency to refuse to answer their questions until by June, 1956, he was insisting that all problems be taken to Mrs. Sheen. By the spring of 1957 the number of circulars and meetings decreased considerably (which some of the Advisers had not recognized, until the interviews of the present study brought this out).

Changes in the Programming Committee.   In the period after 1952, the efforts of the Programming Committee in making classes nearly equal in size appear to have been less successful than before. Complaints appeared in the minutes of the Teachers' Council, the formal grievance body, about the disruption of classes at the beginning of the term because of this. In the fall of 1955, the term in which Mrs. Sheen completed her examination for assistant principal and the term before she expected to receive her formal appointment, the Chairman of the Committee, Mr. Stein, asked to be relieved of his duties and returned to full classroom teaching. Mr. Daubner agreed, but persuaded him to continue on as a Program Adviser. One of the assistant Deans, Mr. Shaw, agreed to take over the job of Committee Chairman. In the last half of the fall of 1955, he left his work in the Deans' Office to be trained in the new job. He became the new Chairman in the spring of 1956.

Although the Committee's work was still formally under Mr. Fall, the consequences of the work brought it to Mrs. Sheen's attention. In an effort to cut down the inequalities in class size, she insisted that all requests from Program Advisers and department chairmen for special placement of students, or for changes in their placement, be sent to her first for approval before going on to the Programming Committee Chairman. By the spring of 1957, the following year, teachers reported that there were fewer changes in programs and fewer disruptions of their classes than before. They attributed the decrease to Mrs. Sheen's work and were pleased about it.

Changes in the Deans' Office.   The first consequences of the start of the program for the Deans' Office have already been described. In the spring of 1953, the Boys' Deans' Office was assigned all cases of girls' cutting, so that Miss Galway in turn could be given some of Mr. Fall's administrative duties. The Boys' Deans did not receive additional time for taking over girls' cutting offenses. The administrators said that adding duties to an already operating office did not require adding an amount of time comparable to that originally assigned to perform them. Further, the steadily decreasing enrollment in the school, a trend throughout the city which continued until the end of the next year, decreased the number of teachers in the school and thus the number of building assignment periods available. In the following term, the fall of 1953, during which Mrs. Sheen became acting assistant principal, the number of periods was cut from 17 to 10. Some teachers believed this time was taken from the Boys' Deans for Mrs. Sheen's use.

In the next term—spring, 1954—all the girls' cases were assigned to the Boys' Deans, who then became the Deans. Mr. Connell, the Head Dean, was unhappy about the amount of time allowed him for his work and repeatedly asked for more time, only some of which he got. In the fall of 1955, the term before Mrs. Sheen's appointment was formally made, the Deans' Office lost one man through sickness for most of the term. For the last two months of the term, Connell also lost the man who was to become the new Programming Committee Chairman to replace Mr. Stein, who had announced his resignation effective in the spring of 1956. After Stein announced his resignation, Mr. Connell asked to be relieved of his job.

In the next term, the spring of 1956, one of the assistant Deans, Mrs. Grune, was named to be Head Dean, and the Deans' Office was formally placed under Mrs. Sheen's supervision. All cases that required contact with outside agencies were now turned over to Mrs. Sheen. Otherwise the office functioned as it had before. However, by 1956–1957 the results of Mrs. Sheen's efforts to cut down the amount of change in class size at the beginning of the term began to affect the Deans' Office. Her interposing herself among the department chairmen, the Program Advisers, and the Programming Committee forced the students to get her approval for a requested change of class section. She rarely gave this. The students responded in two ways. They began to ask the Deans to intercede for them with Mrs. Sheen. And an increased number of them stopped registering for any classes, and thus became additional disciplinary problems for the Deans.

Summary of changes.   In short, the introduction of a guidance program led to the consolidation of punitive activities in one Deans' Office, and to the coordination of the Deans' Office, some of the Programming Committee's work, and the Program Advisers' Office under one person, the new assistant principal (Mrs. Sheen). It led further to the development of another division, the Guidance Office, which took over college advising and approval of program changes from the Advisers, and the out-of-school contacts formerly made by the Dean. In addition, the Guidance Office took over the treatment of emotional and financial problems which formerly had been handled by the faculty and by the Deans' and Advisers' Offices. The Guidance Office also began a testing program and began to participate in curriculum planning. As a result of the consolidation and coordination of these activities, the teachers lost much of their former control over them.

Associated with the over-all program were the resignation of one of the assistant principals (Miss Galway), the appointment of a former teacher and Program Adviser in the school (Mrs. Sheen) to the position, and the resignations of both the Dean (Mr. Connell) and the Chairman of the Programming Committee (Mr. Stein) in the term before the new assistant principal was formally appointed.

Response to the changes

Actions.   After the program began in 1952–1953, five major types of action characterized the response of many faculty members to the program. In the "first year" of the operation of the Guidance Office, the teachers "flooded" the office with cases, including "many things that any teacher could handle." Then this stopped, and the teachers had as little to do with the office as they could. Third, they began to make nasty comments about Mrs. Sheen to others, and directly to her. Fourth, they were slow in sending back forms, etc., which she had requested. (This refusal to respond on time to her orders continued until the spring of 1956, when she became the formal assistant principal. Then, they said, she had "the right" to make such requests.) Somewhat after these initial responses, about 1954–1955, Mr. Fall reported that the teachers began increasingly to ridicule the program to him. This action continued to the time of the study (1956–1957). The responses of the teachers upset Mrs. Sheen. Mr. Daubner had foreseen this and arranged for her to "let off steam," not by responding to the teachers' actions but by complaining periodically to him.

Sentiments.   At the time of the study in 1956–1957, the sentiments expressed by the faculty about the programs revealed a divided faculty, the division following the length of experience in the school. About 55% of the faculty had been in the school before 1952, and about 45% had been hired after 1952. Of the teachers in Adams before 1952, almost 90% had been there from 1944 or before. They made up the "experienced" teachers. Of the teachers hired after 1952, 86% came to the school in 1954 or after. Thus, between most of these "newcomers" and most of the experienced teachers there was at least a ten-year gap. Although most of the newcomers were young and inexperienced, some were not. They had transferred to the school from others in the system. The term *experienced* thus refers primarily to the length of service in Adams.

The sentiments expressed (in interviews) during 1956–1957 by a sample of 45 of the 111 teachers and department chairmen were treated for the *tone* of the comments. Tone refers to the liking or disliking, the approval or disapproval, expressed or implied by a comment. For example, those who criticized the Dean for being too lenient with the offenders and those who criticized her for being too harsh were both considered unfavorable in the tone of their sentiments. This treatment by tone revealed the following differences in sentiments about the guidance program:

	For	Against	Totals
Experienced teachers	8	22	30
Newcomers	12	3	15
	20	25	45

The *content* of the sentiments expressed will be summarized for the two major groups of teachers. The favorable newcomers knew little of the details of the program, but thought that "guidance was a good idea." The sentiments of the unfavorable experienced teachers covered several areas of content. They complained, first of all, about the "philosophy of guidance." By this some referred to the questionable need for a program, since they were already doing the job. For some, the program signified a "permissive" approach which would be interpreted by the students as a sign of "weakness." Second, for many the time spent on the guidance program was time "taken" by the principal from them. Without this program, there would have been more people to handle the clerical tasks, etc., and thus lessen each person's load. Third, for some the interest of "the Board" in guidance was "reason enough to be against it." It was, they said, "a fad."

Fourth, if there was to be a program, they disagreed about who should get the time to do guidance. Some believed the time ought to be given to the classroom teachers, as the ones best able to deal with guidance. Others thought that more time should be given to the Deans. Both Deans and Program Advisers thought that more time should be allocated to themselves. Fifth, the teachers complained about who received the attention of the program. Some resented the time spent on "the 5% [the troublemakers] at the expense of the 95%." Others resented the attention given to "the 20%" [the academically-minded], since the school had originally been for the "motor-minded," the apparently uneducables. Sixth, they complained about the lack of results obtained from the program. They saw no improvement in class cutting, absence, or disciplinary problems. Further, they did not know what was going on "down there" (in the Deans' and Guidance Offices): the cards they received reporting on the action taken had inadequate notes on them, and were returned at irregular intervals. Seventh, the teachers complained about their relations with the people in the program, particularly the Head Dean and Mrs. Sheen. The people in the program were accused of being abrupt, and of "acting as if guidance were the answer to everything and as if the teachers knew nothing." People in the program, the teachers said, did not consult them.

Eighth, the teachers criticized the choice of personnel for the program. This sentiment was intimately bound up with their long-standing criticism of non-rotated assignments. These jobs were easier than others, they believed, because they carried "time off," and it was unfair not to rotate the jobs. Since the jobs were not rotated, this implied a special merit among the people selected for the guidance program. But young, inexperienced people had been given some of these jobs. Further, the head of the program was a woman "who had not been such a hot teacher in the classroom that she could now tell everyone else what to do." The new Dean, Mrs. Grune, would have been "all right" as an assistant Dean but not as Dean. Some men said she was "too harsh"; others, "too lenient." The men who made these criticisms believed that the heads of the program and of the Deans' Office should have been men. None of the experienced teachers could understand the appointment of the new people. The lack of special merit demonstrated by the appointment of people they saw as new, inexperienced and not particularly qualified was support, the teachers believed, for their contention that the jobs could be and should be rotated. And it supported their belief that the principal had shown "favoritism"; some of his choices would be incomprehensible otherwise.

Conclusion.   Despite considerable differences in the content of the responses by various segments of the faculty to the guidance program, the major distinctions followed the length of experience of faculty members at Adams. The majority of newcomers to the school were favorable to guidance, and said that they used the program whenever necessary. The majority of the experienced faculty were unfavorable to the program, and said that they used it as little as they could.

Analysis

The course of events by which a guidance program was introduced in a high school, and the actions and opinions of the faculty relevant to the program have been outlined. The favorable sentiments of the newcomers were in accord with the sentiments which the experienced faculty had expressed toward guidance earlier. But the unfavorable sentiments expressed by the latter in 1956–1957 represented a marked shift from their earlier sentiments. In this section an explanation of the differences in the tone of the sentiments of the faculty will be presented.[2]

The explanation of the differences between the sentiments of the experienced teachers and the newcomers, and between the later and earlier sentiments of the experienced teachers was based on the assumptions of interaction theory. The significant feature of the innovation process was assumed to be the changes in operationally-described in-

[2] For the complete analysis, including data on the major types of action as well as sentiments, see Atwood (1960, Chs. 5ff.).

teraction patterns. These changes were assumed to precede changes in sentiments and individual behavior.

Effects on the interaction of experienced teachers

Examining the introduction of the guidance program as to its consequences for the interaction of the pre-1952 teachers revealed the following changes. Each interaction change is summarized first, and then followed by illustrations of the happenings from which it is derived.

Decreased initiation. The pre-1952 teachers experienced a decrease in the frequency with which they initiated action for others, and initiated action successfully (that is, got the response they wanted). By centralizing the program, the principal inadvertently took away the initiative in some of the guidance events from them. Because the program was set up under a formal superior, they lost control of a case once it had been turned over to the program. Further, they did not know what happened in a case until they received a report from the office. If they did not approve of the action taken, or of the time interval between their action and the response to it, they could now do little about either.

Increased response required. The teachers experienced an increase in the frequency of events in which they had to respond to someone else. Mrs. Sheen issued instructions which they had to follow; she sent around notices which they had to fill in and return; she addressed them at the faculty meetings for longer periods of time than had Miss Galway.

Irregular response from others. The teachers experienced more irregularity in the time between their initiating action on a case and the report to them of what had been done.

Value violation. The teachers experienced violations of valued characteristics of their interaction which had become part of their identity. They had been used to going to a man, and to a colleague or older person. Now they had to go to women, which bothered the men particularly, and to younger people in the program, which distressed the older people. The values the men brought into the school from their society—about men rather than women taking the initiative— may account for part of their resentment. Their view had been reinforced by Miss Galway's position in the school. Although formally their superior, she did little to make that position felt, initiating relatively little action for them. In addition, though, the jobs of Dean and Programming Chairman had always been held by men in Adams and were stepping stones in the system to assistant principalships. The appointment to the assistant principalship of a woman, a person who had held neither position, violated both expectations (held particularly by the older men teachers) about the jobs. The appointment of the young violated the expectations of all the older teachers about jobs with "time off." These jobs had come to be looked on both as the perquisite of seniority and as the symbol of competence to deal with children. The older teachers saw the jobs go to those who had not earned the right to the "plums" by their years of service, or by their ability to deal with children, which came only with the years.

Of more importance, the characteristic pattern of the teachers' daily interaction in the classroom had itself become valued. They valued taking the initiative and being responsible for everything that happened in the classroom. They said, "A good teacher handles his own problems." The Deans supported this view in different language: "Only the weak sisters come down here [to the Deans' Office] all the time." The consequences of setting up the program, especially the first two described above, violated the values of independent and self-dependent action, values which had become part of their notion of themselves as teachers.

The operation of the program continued these violations, by requiring the teachers to go outside the classroom more frequently than before, to turn over all cases and potential cases not only to the Deans but now also to Mrs. Sheen, and to give up control over the disposition of a case. The continuing complaints against the Deans' Office before the program began, reported by the former head Dean, may have partly expressed the inherent contradiction between its operation—requiring the teachers to go outside the classroom for help—and the values of independent and self-dependent action of the faculty.

Effects on newcomers

The change in the sentiments toward guidance shown by the majority of the experienced faculty can be correlated, as we have seen, with preceding changes in properties of their interaction patterns. This approach also accounts for the favorable sentiments of the majority of the new faculty. The latter had not been in Adams long enough to develop a pattern of interaction sufficiently stable to suffer change. (It must be assumed that they brought in their generally favorable attitude toward guidance from the outside.) Although they said they used the services of the program as often as necessary—the unfavorable people said they used it as little as possible—the newcomers to Adams did not actually use it significantly more than the other group. It is unlikely that they developed their favorable sentiments from interaction with the personnel of the program. But this explanation, based on change or its absence in interaction patterns, still leaves unaccounted for the eight experienced faculty members who were favorable and the three new people who were *un*favorable to the program.

The exceptions to the explanation

Six of the eight favorable experienced teachers were found to be working in the guidance program. But two of the three unfavorable new people were also in it. Neither a position in the program, nor the relative change in status from getting such a position, was able to account for the sentiments of these people. It was found, however, that the six experienced people were in the Deans' or the Guidance Offices, and the two new people were in the Program Advisers' Office. Examining the interaction patterns of the positions in the Deans' and Guidance Offices revealed that these appointments *reversed* the changes in interaction which the experienced faculty had undergone. Such positions (1) increased the frequency of events in which teachers took the initiative and took it successfully, (2) decreased the frequency with which they had to respond to others, and (3) reinforced their identifying characteristics as people who took the initiative and were competent to deal with students' problems. Because of the very rough quantitative measures used, it was not possible to tell whether the difference in their sentiments was connected to the reversal, to the degree of reversal, or mainly to the stabilization of their interaction patterns in these positions.

The Program Advisers, on the other hand, went through still another set of changes which, nonetheless, had the same interaction consequences as those undergone by the experienced faculty. Mrs. Sheen's action in tightening her supervision of the office resulted in a rapid decrease in the frequency of events in which the Advisers could and did take the initiative (making of decisions about problems). Her supervision increased the frequency of events in which they had to respond to her (continually revised instructions to them, and meetings). It resulted in longer and more irregular time intervals between their initiations to her and her responses. It changed the identity of their superior from a man to a woman, from one who had only been nominally a superior to one who was formally and actually their superior. The Advisers were denied access to the confidential files of the Guidance Office; they believed their competence to counsel the students was impugned, and their own identity was consequently affected. Thus, although the content of the changes affecting the Advisers was different from that experienced by the faculty, the changes had similar consequences in interaction, and the Program Advisers expressed sentiments whose tone was unfavorable, like the rest of the experienced faculty. Since there is no reason to believe that the two new Advisers differed at the start from the other new teachers in their generally favorable sentiments about guidance, their agreement with the unfavorable older group can be attributed to the similarity of their preceding social experiences, just described as changes in interaction.

The difference between these two segments of the guidance program suggests that change alone is not sufficient to account for the resistance and unfavorable sentiments of the experienced faculty. Only when the innovation resulted in the changes in interaction specified above (decreased initiative, increased response to others, etc.) did their sentiments change. The difference in the *content* of the changes affecting the general faculty and the Program Advisers was shown to be misleading. The resultant *interaction* changes experienced by both were similar, and were followed by similar changes to unfavorable sentiments. Where other changes nullified the changes in interaction, as in the Deans' and Guidance Offices, the sentiments of these people remained favorable or became so.

Linked Changes

The limits on the size of this chapter do not permit a detailed examination of the changes in the preceding or concurrent linked events. Most of the changes have already been described in the section on the prior situation. The changes preceding the program were: (1) the death in 1944 of the first principal and founder of Adams; (2) the decision of the Board after his death to change the goals of the school and thus the special status of the school and its faculty; (3) the equalization in the school system of high school and elementary school salaries; (4) changes in the ethnic composition of the student body beginning about 1946; (5) a general "strike" in 1950, the refusal of the high school teachers in the city to carry out extra-curricular activities without pay; and (6) the increasing discipline problems. Concurrent with the development of the program were: (7) a continuation of the change in the composition of the student body; (8) a continuation of the discipline problems, and (9) a steady increase in the number of clerical demands on the teachers. All these changes have been shown (Atwood, 1960, Ch. 6) to have had consequences in interaction for the faculty similar to those described above as the results of the introduction of the guidance program.

Since most of these linked changes having similar interaction consequences for the faculty occurred before the program began, the guidance program may be seen as an intensification and a reinforcement of the changes already occurring in the school and continuing during its development. In judging the strength of the correlation in this case between the changes in sentiments and behavior about guidance and the interaction changes resulting from the program, this state of the external context must be considered. How important such conditions are for the course of events in an innovation remains to be discovered from comparative study. In this instance, the development of the program appears to have exacerbated the feelings of the faculty. Their complaints about guidance served in part as a channel for expressing the feelings of "pressure" resulting from the other changes in the system.

Summary

The unexpected resistance that a high-school principal met from his faculty when he introduced a centralized guidance program was examined with the help of anthropological interaction theory. The theory offered a set of answers to some of the problems of describing this small-scale administrative change for comparison with other instances of educational innovation. The theory prescribed the significant elements in the process of innovation as operationally defined interaction and changes in it. The theory also specified the amount of context in space and time to be included. It provided further a scheme for analyzing and interpreting what happened. Interaction analysis revealed the similarities in the structure as well as the results of overt differences in changes. It enabled the diverse changes in the course of events in the case to be compared and added or subtracted from one another.

Resistance to the innovation was shown to be preceded by changes in the properties of interaction. The experienced teachers and the newcomers who became unfavorable to the innovation underwent a decrease in the frequency with which they took the initiative in guidance activities, an increase in the frequency with which they had to respond to others in the school, and an increase in the irregularity of the time lapse between their initiations and responses to them from others. They also suffered a series of changes diminishing valued characteristics of their identity as teachers. On the other hand, where other changes stabilized the interaction of some faculty members and partly restored their earlier pattern, the innovation was accepted by them.

It must, of course, be kept in mind that the connections noted here among the elements in the course of events occurred in an innovation still in progress. Further, the innovation took place in a social context already undergoing interaction changes. Whether or not the sentiments of the experienced faculty will change after the program as a whole stabilizes cannot be determined. Last, the usefulness of the approach for a comparison of innovations has not been attempted, and remains to be examined.

References

Arensberg, C. M. Behavior and organization: industrial studies. In J. Rohrer & M. Sherif (Eds.), *Social psychology at the crossroads.* New York: Harper, 1951. Pp. 324–352.

Arensberg, C. M. Anthropology as history. In K. Polanyi, C. M. Arensberg, & H. W. Pearson, *Trade and market in the early empires.* Glencoe: Free Press, 1957. Pp. vii-ix and 97–113.

Arensberg, C. M., & McGregor, D. Determination of morale in an industrial company. *Appl. Anthrop.,* 1942, *1* (2), 12–32.

Arensberg, C. M., & Tootell, G. Plant sociology: real discoveries and new problems. In M. Komarovsky (Ed.), *Common frontiers of the social sciences*. Glencoe: Free Press, 1957. Pp. 320–337.

Atwood, M. S. An anthropological approach to administrative change. Unpublished doctoral dissertation, Columbia University, 1960.

Chapple, E. D. Applied anthropology in industry. In A. Kroeber (Ed.), *Anthropology today*. Chicago: University of Chicago Press, 1953, Pp. 819–830.

Chapple, E. D. Quantitative analysis of complex organizational systems. *Human Organization*, 1962, 21 (2), 67–87.

Chapple, E. D. (with the collaboration of C. M. Arensberg) Measuring human relations. *Genet. Psychol. Monogr.*, 1940, 22, No. 1.

Chapple, E. D., & Coon, C. *Principles of anthropology*. New York: Holt, 1942.

Chapple, E. D., & Sayles, L. R. *The measure of management*. New York: Macmillan, 1961.

Homans, G. C. *The human group*. New York: Harcourt, Brace, 1950.

Kimball, S. T. Problems of studying American culture. *Amer. Anthrop.*, 1958, 57, 1131–1143.

Kimball, S. T., & Pearsall, M. Event analysis as an approach to community study. *Soc. Forces*, 1955, 34, 58–63.

Whyte, W. F. *Pattern for industrial peace*. New York: Harper, 1951.

CHAPTER 3

Collaboration in teaching and learning: an experimental course for engineering students

JAN E. CLEE
JAMES B. RESWICK

A SMALL group of engineering faculty and students, meeting at a 1962 summer conference in Bethel, Maine, conceived a plan to improve the effectiveness of learning through increased cooperation between faculty and students. In this chapter, the origin and background of the plan is examined, and an account is given of the implementation of the idea in a specific engineering course at Case Institute of Technology.[1]

[1] What is reported here represents the efforts of students, instructors, and consultants involved in the course. Although the authors are indebted to all the students, they would like to name the co-initiators of the plan explicitly: Robert C. Corell, James Emshoff, William Schultz, and Richard Weber. They would also like to mention the names of the council members. They were:

Instructors:		Students:	
J. Wilson	C. Kramer	R. T. Bond	R. A. Ginsburg
R. Dutton	R. Fox	A. M. Foster	J. E. Kindling
G. Kraft	R. Corell	J. A. Artherholt	R. H. Rubin
B. Lehtinen	L. Goodman	D. Japikse	

Dr. L. Goodman was lecturer for a part of the course material. The advice and support of Dr. R. E. Bolz, Head of the Engineering Division at Case Institute of Technology, and of Dr. H. A. Shepard, head of the Organizational Behavior Group, were of significant value to the success of the experiment.

THE AUTHORS are both affiliated with Case Institute of Technology, and are respectively: Instructor, Organizational Behavior Group, Division of Organizational Sciences; and Professor of Engineering and Director, Engineering Design Center.

Through all phases of development and application, cooperation was the explicit and central theme of the described experiment.

An educational experiment does not ordinarily represent the sheer implementation of an idea. Rather, it is the product of a process of building and development, and is molded by the social forces of the system in which it is applied. This process of modeling can be seen as a necessary adaptive process through which every innovation must go before it is accepted by a social system. Although they were not always successful, the experimenters approached every step in this process of adaptation on the basis on which the course plan was built, namely, that of optimal cooperation.

The Plan

The origin of the idea

Since 1960, the National Training Laboratories of the National Education Association has promoted conferences in College Leadership Training at Bethel, Maine. Faculty and students holding responsible positions in their colleges and universities are invited to attend, with teams of at least four members encouraged. The goal of "laboratory" training is described in a brochure (NTL, 1963) as: "Growth in individual perspective and performance and—through such growth—change in groups, in organizations and in institutional patterns." This means for the classroom situation, an important learning environment, "more significant involvement of students in the teaching–learning process."

The major part of the two-week program of these conferences has been built around "training groups," each including about twelve persons, college instructors and students, and a staff member. These groups are designed to enable the individual participant to learn more about the way in which his own behavior influences others. Cooperation, leadership, and barriers to working and learning are some of the phenomena on which attention is focused. These subjects are, however, always related to specific events, occurring in the training group itself, which are discussed and analyzed (thus the name "laboratory" for this type of conference).[2]

[2] For a summary of the current status of this type of training see Miles (1962). Underlying value premises have been discussed by Bennis (1962).

In addition, lecturers usually cover such topics as methods of decision-making, leadership roles and skills, and the barriers to effective group problem-solving raised by status and lack of trust.

Finally, opportunity is given for college teams to study specific problems on their campuses, and to make plans for innovations in classroom and campus life.

It was in this type of conference that the initiators of the experimental course plan recognized that cooperation and understanding are not automatic or self-evident. In designing and implementing educational innovations, hard work, patience, and courage are required to overcome fantasies and stereotypes, so that trust can be built and help given and accepted as common objectives are faced.

During June, 1962, a group of three students, a graduate assistant, and a faculty member from Case Institute of Technology [3] participated in the conference. This group joined approximately 100 other students and faculty, mainly from liberal arts colleges and universities. The Case team had the opportunity to apply their learning by working on a specific problem, the design of a new core engineering course in Dynamic Systems, for which Reswick (the faculty member of the team) had been given responsibility.

Description of the engineering course

The course, Dynamic Systems E-3, was to be the first of ten core subjects to be given to all engineering students under the revised curriculum program of the newly formed Engineering Division (a consolidation of the Mechanical, Electrical, Civil, and Chemical Engineering Departments) at Case Institute. It was to be given in the first term of the sophomore year to all engineering students, totaling 200. These students would be confronted for the first time with the

[3] Case, located in Cleveland, Ohio, is devoted to education in engineering and science. It has approximately 1600 undergraduate and 500 graduate students, with a faculty of about 200. It is situated in University Circle, an area of Cleveland in which cultural and educational institutions are concentrated, adjoining Western Reserve University.

Case, like many other engineering schools, is deeply concerned with improving engineering education. Grants from the Carnegie and Ford foundations have permitted searching self-study, and have resulted in major changes in philosophy, attitudes, organization, and curricula within the engineering departments (now formed as a single division). These activities have attracted national attention, and Case is becoming known as a place where the climate is conducive to innovation.

engineering approach to modeling and solving for the behavior of dynamic (time-varying) engineering systems.

The students would not have had a prior course in differential equations. Many topics, heretofore only considered at more advanced levels, would be presented and the required mathematics would be developed within the course. The dynamics of mechanical, electrical, and other systems would be studied from a unified point of view.

Newly developed portable analogue computers [4] would be loaned to the students for the duration of the course. Six students were to share two computer sets. (As it turned out, the computers were "owned" by the learning groups of six students which evolved during the course, as described below.) The computers would permit the student to obtain solutions to some homework problems much more quickly, and allow him to experience the nature of dynamic equations.

Assumptions underlying the course

The Case team originated the idea of organizing the E-3 course along presuppositions adopted during the conference. The presuppositions were:

1. Cooperation between instructors and students is not necessarily inherent within a university culture. Relationships are, frequently, not supportive of learning.
2. This situation can be changed if the opportunity is given for cooperation, and if instructors and students are willing to communicate about basic problems related to the teaching–learning process.
3. Learning and teaching are interdependent processes which are occurring continuously and simultaneously within the classroom situation.
4. While the instructor has the task of teaching, and can therefore be regarded as having knowledge and experience relevant to this task, it is the student who has knowledge and experience about the ways in which he learns.
5. Student and instructor have a common goal within the classroom situation: to create a situation in which optimal learning can occur. The objective of both is: learning for the student.

---

[4] A total of 75 analogue computers were developed by Case and Pastoriza Electronics of Boston, Massachusetts, under a grant to Case from the National Science Foundation. The computers are portable and battery-operated, and can thus be used anywhere at any time. With each set, it is possible to solve differential equations up to second order.

6. Students and instructors share responsibility for the amount of learning occurring in the classroom situation. Cooperation between the two groups is therefore necessary.
7. In a permissive, cooperative atmosphere, feedback can be given by the students to the instructors about teaching methods. The instructor can give feedback about the quality and amount of measured learning of the students.

The Case team, assisted by fellow participants and NTL conference staff members (mainly university faculty from the behavioral sciences), became deeply involved in the task of creating a concept for the E-3 course based on the presuppositions mentioned above. This occurred during a part of the conference designed to encourage teams to deal with "back home" problems.

The evolution of the course council idea

Some of the questions which this team asked themselves were:

1. How would it be possible to enhance communication among instructors and 200 students?
2. In which way and in what areas would it be possible to share real responsibility with the students?
3. How could a cooperative atmosphere be developed, to allow feedback among students and instructors?
4. How would it be possible to overcome the natural suspicions of students educated in a competitive culture?

The answer was found in the idea of forming a course council, which would make all possible decisions affecting the course. It would be composed of student representatives of the seven sections in which the group was to be administratively divided, their instructors (seven graduate assistants), and the two faculty members responsible for the course content material.

The course council would provide the opportunity for the students to give the faculty feedback about the way in which the course was taught, while instructors and faculty could express their thoughts about the expressed attitudes of the students. It was assumed that the council would function as a communication channel between students and instructors, and that more personal relationships in the council would enhance the relationships among students, instructors, and faculty outside the council.

It was the conviction of the originators of the plan that the council could only be of value if it had real responsibility; areas had to be identified in which the decision-making power of the council could be felt. It was also recognized, however, that limitations of the power of the council should be made explicit.

The distribution of responsibility among students, instructors, and faculty was delineated by the Case team as follows:

1. The Council of students and faculty to have responsibility for all aspects of the learning environment.
2. Final responsibility for course content to rest with the senior faculty member.
3. Instructors are resource persons in the subject matter of the course.

The meaning of "learning environment" as defined by the team included:

1. Formality of classroom: class discipline, class participation during lecture periods, attendance (required vs. unrequired).
2. Material presentation: suggestions to promote better understanding of course material.
3. Grading: absolute or curve; letter grade or number grade.
4. Types and nature of examination: proctored, unproctored, or take-home; open or closed book; unannounced or announced.
5. Homework: required or optional; graded or ungraded; method of review.

The basic idea of a council seems simple. It is an idea regularly applied in industry, but its implementation in a university culture has various aspects which became obvious only in the later stages of the course. The council concept implied a drastic shift in the authority structure—especially drastic in a situation where authority is used to enforce learning, and also provides the necessary security for students in the world of science with its many unknowns.

Another implicit consequence of the council is a change in roles. Instructors were to become resource persons listening to the needs of the students and responding to them. Students were to become specialists in the area of learning, an area normally recognized consciously only by the most mature among them. The council was to widen the world for all of its members. Fantasies of instructors and students about each other could be corrected: students were discovered to be interested in more than grades alone; faculty professors and instructors emerged as interested in more than research; both groups became more interested in each other, in the course content material, and in the possibility of creating real innovations in learning.

Implementation of the Plan

The first steps

Although the Case team at the Bethel conference went back to Cleveland with enthusiasm about the new course plan, it also had its doubts. There was concern among the members about the feasibility of the plan, in the face of organizational limitations, attitudes of tradition-oriented faculty members, and the willingness and ability of the students to take the kind of responsibility expressed in the plan.

Social reality forced the group to recognize that only one member of the team, namely the course leader (Reswick), could take the necessary steps towards implementation. Students became students again. However, the group did not cease to exist. It had an important function as a supportive audience to whom the course leader felt committed. This group continued to meet irregularly, functioning as a sounding board for the activities of its members whenever they were engaged in activities concerning the improvement of education and campus life.

The actual work, the formal implementation, had to be done by the course leader. His activities had various aspects. Information had to be given to the people who would be involved in any stage of the course (Head of the Engineering Division, Vice-President for Academic Affairs, Deans, and others). Insecurities and doubts on their part had to be changed into a supportive attitude. The enthusiasm of the initiators had to be transmitted.

All this, however, was not easy. It was difficult to transmit the concept that explicit cooperation between instructors and students would bring about marked improvement in learning. Long discussions on a personal level seemed necessary. It was not as much rational conceptual clarification as authenticity and enthusiasm which turned resistance into friendly skepticism.

The initial development of the course and its introduction to students and instructing staff was seen as an area where social scientists on the staff at Case could give much support. Accordingly, the course leader formed a new group around him. Members of the group were a Professor of Behavioral Sciences, the Director of Academic Affairs, a graduate assistant in engineering (one of the originators of the plan), and a graduate assistant in the Behavioral Science program of the Department of Management. The task of this group was mainly to plan the introduction of the course to instructors and students. It was also helpful to the course leader in considering the ways in which the course could be implemented with a minimum of resistance. The idea of small learning teams was first suggested in this group, to be picked up later by the course council and implemented.

The life of this planning group was short. It stopped meeting after the council was installed. It was suggested that the graduate assistant in the Management Department (Clee) should become a consultant to the council and its members. His role in the council was mainly seen as supportive to the instructors and the course leader, and as a source of help in the area of group processes. He also helped the council to be more sensitive to issues of teaching–learning processes in the course, and helped protect the objectives of the experiment when members sought security in more traditional behavior.[5]

Two things seem necessary to realize an idea: a person who can carry the idea, and continuing support. Different groups have supported the course leader as the carrier of the idea. In the beginning it was the team which had created the idea at Bethel. Later, on the campus, a group more knowledgeable about the Case system and more organizationally rooted replaced the team. When the course started, support was given by an individual serving as a consultant to the council.

---

[5] This occurred, for example, before the mid-term examinations. The council recognized that not enough effort was being given by students to the E-3 course, because of pressure of examinations in other courses. The council asked the course leader to warn the students that this behavior could lead to unsatisfactory performance.

The consultant then asked the council to evaluate what this would mean in terms of the objectives of the course. Council members did so, and realized that this action would deny the presupposition of students' knowledge of their own best learning modes. The decision was then made to slow down the introduction of new material, and to make an effort to review more carefully concepts which were not well understood. The council also agreed to change the date of the test. It was realized that a test would only be a good measure of student performance after adequate opportunity for development of knowledge and skills had been given.

Introduction of the plan to the instructors

The introduction of the plan to the instructors can be regarded as unsuccessful. This was mainly caused by the fact that most of the instructors were recruited just a few days before the course started. The ideas and the "philosophy" of the course could not be transmitted to them in such a short time. In addition, the course was, for many of them, a first teaching experience. Anxieties about this were increased by the experimental character of the course. Their image of the course was incomplete, and insecurity inhibited them from seeing the problems related to participation in such a course. It was difficult for them to resist using their authority to build tightly organized sections, in which the students would be taught and evaluated in traditional patterns.

On top of this, the council had to overcome inherent difficulties in becoming an effective working group; a sort of authority-vacuum existed during the first weeks. The desire of the instructors to do a good systematic job, and the pressures from the students to decide on a clear set of rules with respect to homework, tests, etc., led to extreme frustration for all. The support of the Behavioral Science consultant was critical at this time. His efforts, along with the insights of the course leader gained at Bethel the summer before, were probably responsible for the ability of the council to survive this period and become an effective decision-making group.

It is now recognized that much more attention should have been given to the introduction and training of the instructors. An effective job here will take considerable effort, because it involves more than information-giving, and the transfer of rules and guide lines; it means changing the traditional image which the instructor has of the teacher's role. It means the creation of resource persons who are able to help the student in the process of learning.

The introduction to the students and the election of representatives

The introduction to the students was very carefully planned in every detail, and probably therefore more successful. It was clear that a failure to introduce the course in the proper way could make the difference between ultimate failure and success. The following action steps were planned:

1. To invite all the students for a meeting on registration day (the day before classes officially started) in the Auditorium.
2. To explain the approach to be taken in the course, and introduce the assumptions on which the course is built.
3. To adjourn into seven 30-man sections, and to form five discussion groups of six men within each section.
4. To exchange ideas within the discussion groups about the ideas and thoughts mentioned in the introduction.
5. To select a spokesman for each discussion group to report to the section about the discussion in the small group.
6. To select a representative for the section out of the five spokesmen.
7. To meet again with all the sections in the Auditorium.
8. To hear the reports from the seven newly chosen representatives about the discussions in the sections.

The meeting was very successful. More than 75 per cent of the students attended the meeting. There was a surprising lack of cynical reactions. The representatives' reports were realistically enthusiastic; the emphasis in their reports was more on the responsibilities of the students than on the opportunities given to them by the new structure. Typical of the whole meeting was the closing remark of one of the representatives: "Now that we have the opportunity to influence a course in a meaningful way, it will be the students' responsibility to make this course a success." Expectations were high at the end of this general session. Probably too high, because for some students it was disappointing to find that the new approach did not mean a reduction in the work load, or the abolishment of tests.

The start of the course

On the same evening, after the introduction to the students, a dinner meeting was arranged for the council at the home of the course leader. The objectives of this meeting were to get acquainted with each other, and to make a decision with respect to the distribution of the available class time. The behavior of the students was quite conservative; they did not seem to know how to use the freedom presented to them. Exciting new ideas were not created during this meeting, despite the efforts of the faculty members to encourage the students to explore the opportunities presented to them. The seven instructors (graduate assistants) were observant and careful. One faculty member made an effort to break the ice by telling something about his background; this resulted in a series of formal autobiographical speeches by each of the instructors.

The minutes taken by a student are illustrative of the first meeting:

COURSE PLANNING COUNCIL

E-3 Dynamic Systems

Minutes of Sept. 18, 1962

1. Faculty and Graduate students give their backgrounds.

2. It was announced that Resnick and Halliday's *Physics Part I* would be the textbook for the first part of the semester.

3. It was decided that there will be three lectures and one recitation of one hour each per week. However, if the council feels that the course material warrants two recitations a week, then the amount of lectures will be reduced to two.

4. A *tentative* decision was made concerning the delicate problem of quizzes. The decision goes as follows: Quizzes will be given every recitation period. They will be taken directly from the previous week's homework. They will be able to shift a student's grade, in the final analysis, by a small percentage.

5. The next meeting will be held on Thursday, September 27, 1962, at 12:00 o'clock in the Vose conference room. Meetings will then be held every Thursday at 12:00 o'clock.

Respectfully submitted,

Roy Ginsburg

Secretary

The process of decision-making in the first meeting was difficult. The students and instructors expected the leader of the course to initiate action, and turned to him to make the decisions. He refused because of his reluctance to help in developing a situation in which he, instead of the council, would become the initiator and decision-maker. This created a deadlock, since other procedures for decision-making had not yet been created by the group. Besides, carefulness with each other prevented the issues from becoming clear. But the spirit was good, and the members were eager to go ahead.

Class meetings started the day after the introduction to the students. The structure of the course was not different at this time from the other courses for sophomores; it included three one-hour classes by a faculty member and one recitation hour under the guidance of a graduate student. The only difference in the E-3 course which an outsider could have observed during the first four weeks was the greater amount of confusion.

Students and instructors discussed with each other and among themselves the pros and cons of homework, various questions on grades and tests, attendance problems, etc. Most of these discussions were held during the section recitation hours. They resulted in a drawing together of the section and its student representative and instructor. The sections were therefore represented in the council by an instructor and a student who together felt obligated to press for the desires of their section, as they understood them.

Developments in the council

The problems of decision-making became more serious after the course had started. Some of the reasons have been discussed above. In the first meetings, positions were taken by the students on the one hand and the instructors on the other, while the faculty took an observant role. This changed gradually: the instructors identified themselves more and more with their sections, and, with their student partners, represented more and more the opinions expressed in their sections. In the council, these section pairs became reluctant to deviate from the opinions expressed by "their" students.

The tensions in the council increased because of the students' pressures on their representatives and instructors to make decisions according to the advice of their sections. Trust among the council members was threatened by these developments. And the one-hour luncheon meetings once a week were too short and pressured to develop better relationships.

The course leader decided, therefore, to hold an extra evening meeting on October 18. This meeting became a milestone in the development of the course, because the working approach of the council changed drastically.

The main concerns of the students, and therefore of the council members, centered around the criteria and means of grading. During this meeting, it soon became clear that the positions on these issues were too far apart to be bridged. The discussion was bitter, and occurred in an atmosphere of defeat about the inability of the council to do productive work. The consultant suggested, with support of the course leader, that the council evaluate the last four weeks and attempt to find the roots of the situation in which they found themselves. The council members then recognized that the council was not able to act because the representatives were committed to their section members, and not to the council. Thus they felt obliged to represent the opinions of their sections only, without taking responsibility for council decisions. It was seen that improvement of learning would be endangered if the students' and instructors' freedom of thinking were limited by the opinions formed in the sections. The council members became aware that they did not represent the sections only, but were moreover responsible for the development of the course.

This recognition changed their loyalty from their sections to the council itself, with its responsibilities. The following tentative decisions about grades were then made:

1. The final grade will be determined from:
    a. Departmental exams (to be "1 hour" exams, but not time-limited)
    b. Final exams (a "2 hour exam" to be given in 4 hours)
    c. The instructor's subjective opinion about the performance of the student.
2. Each of these parts to represent approximately ⅓ of the final grade.

Relationships in the council improved tremendously after this meeting. Students and instructors became much freer in relating to each other across section lines. Instructors talked freely with each other, and with the students, about problems they had in helping the students. The number of discussions which the consultant had with individual instructors dropped significantly. Students became more open in expressing their own opinions, or those of the student body in general.

There was a negative part of this development, however: the increased identification of the student representatives with the council caused them to become alienated from their sections. They were therefore less able to act as a communication channel between students of their sections and the instructors, an objective explicitly expressed in the plan originated by the Bethel group.

The formation of the small work groups

The developments in the council (described above), and particularly the development within the group of instructors, led to a major change in the course organization. The discussions in the council meeting, the enthusiasm of the course leader, and the eagerness of the students to participate in solving problems related to the improvement of learning, changed the insecurity of the instructors to concern for the development of the course.

The feedback which the instructors got in the course council about the recitation hours, and about the methods they used to test amounts of learning, made them aware of the impact of their approach on the learning process. The students felt that the behavior of the instructors during the presentation of the course content material was inconsistent with their behavior during the discussion of course procedures in the same section meeting. The recitation hours were, in the opinion of the students, too formal. Discussions among the instructors helped them see the many ways in which they could be of help to the students. They saw that they could not only transmit new knowledge, but also aid the thought processes of the individual student, by helping him when he was faced with a concept which he could not grasp.

They recognized, therefore, that they could not be of much help to the students in the recitation sessions of thirty people. Most of the instructors felt the need to have a closer relationship to the students. All kinds of suggestions were topics of discussion among the instructors. The suggestions ranged from special group meetings for the weaker students (voluntary) to meetings of the instructors with each of the students individually, on an involuntary basis.

These suggestions were brought to the council. It was then decided that, as an experiment, each instructor would meet an additional hour with a group of six students. The students were asked to form their own six-man groups by choosing their own partners. Most of the groups were easily formed, but others had extra difficulty in finding a time to meet and in their cooperation with each other. There are some indications that the members of the groups that were less cohesive and that had difficulties in being formed were handicapped. The test performance of these students averaged 0.3 grade points lower, though this difference is not statistically significant.

The creation of the plan meant, in fact, that each instructor had responsibility for at least five groups, and that his contact teaching load was therefore increased five times. The meetings with the small groups were so satisfactory, however, that it was decided at a council meeting to advise the sections to cancel their recitation hours, and to replace them with the small work groups, each of them with its own life and development. It was thus possible for the instructors to give individual attention to the students who needed this help. Efforts were also made to improve the teamwork in the small groups. Since homework was not required, the extra time load on the instructors was somewhat offset by their not having to correct papers.

The remainder of the course

No major structural changes occurred after the first four weeks of the course. The 32 small work groups continued to meet for a minimum of an hour once a week; the three one-hour lecture classes for all two hundred students also continued. Homework was assigned, but students were not required to hand it in. Some instructors gave occasional quizzes to aid them in their evaluation of student performance. The council met every week during the term of the course and made decisions as required. They decided on a specific percentage distribution for the final grade as follows:

10% for each of three departmental exams
35% for the final exam
35% for a performance grade to be given by the instructor

The intense involvement of the council is exemplified by their concern for two students who claimed at the end of the course that their unsatisfactory performance was caused by confusion at the beginning of the course and by its experimental character. The council considered the cases of these two students, and while much concerned about being fair to all members of the course, decided to give each of them an extra examination. This opportunity was gladly accepted. The spirit of the course at this time was best expressed by one of the students, who said, "Never before at Case were so many instructors and students concerned about two individuals."

Course outcomes

In an attempt to evaluate the outcomes of the course quantitatively, a questionnaire was prepared; it was filled in by 150 of the 200 students, one month after they received their grades. The consultant handled the data, which were reported back to staff and students only in general terms. Although the questions could be answered anonymously, all but six of the students gave their names. Most of the questions used a 7-point scale in which 7 and 1 represented the "positive" and the "negative" extremes, while 4 represented a neutral answer.[6] Averages were calculated. The character of the data, however, makes it questionable to draw definite conclusions: a weak statistical significance was only found in a few cases. The averages, therefore, can only be seen as expressing trends in the data.

It is difficult to judge the outcomes of a course carried out under experimental conditions, with measures designed by the experimenters. However, the staff involved believed that the students did, indeed, learn more subject matter than they would have had the course been organized along conventional lines. Students also made favorable estimates; a question concerning the amount students learned was included in the questionnaire, and the mean of the answers was 5.1 on the 7-point scale ("We learned more than average").

The final grades were, of course, under the control of the instructors, and therefore open to some question as a measure of learning. However, they do give an indication of the large number of students who successfully completed the course. They were as follows:

A—42 students (21%)
B—58 students (29%)
C—78 students (38%)
D—15 students (7%)
F—10 students (failing) (5%)

This distribution indicated far more A's and far fewer F's than is typical in engineering courses at Case. And, in the opinion of the students, the course was certainly not an easy one. Only 7 students found the course easy, and of the 147 who answered the question regarding the difficulty of the course, 108 found it difficult or very difficult, and 32 felt it had an average degree of difficulty.

More important to the instructors was the clear feedback from

[6] Sample questions were:

Q. 2) I consider this course as:

7) .... Too difficult
6) .... Very difficult
5) .... Difficult
4) .... Average
3) .... Easy
2) .... Very easy
1) .... Too easy

Q. 5) The influence of this course on my other course work was:

7) .... Very positive
6) .... Positive
5) .... More positive than negative
4) .... No influence
3) .... More negative than positive
2) .... Negative
1) .... Very negative

students that they felt the course had given them real insight into the nature of engineering—and that they liked what they saw. The importance of the interaction in the small groups between students and instructors, who represented engineering through their own deep involvement, cannot be overemphasized. Students at Case are generally critical of the fact that graduate assistants are recruited as instructors. The criticisms usually heard are that the graduate assistants are too young and too inexperienced in teaching, that they do not know the material, and that they are too "tough" with respect to grading. The general experience is therefore that the relationship between students and graduate assistant instructors is not conducive to learning.

However, student opinions about the graduate assistant instructors in the E-3 course were very favorable. Of the 148 students who answered the question on the effectiveness of the instructors, 120 answered that the instructors were very effective, 19 were doubtful, and only 9 expressed the opinion that their instructor was ineffective. (Mean, 5.6 on the 7-point scale.) Also, the relationships between the instructors and the students were seen as very good (Mean, 5.7).

The differences across instructors were interesting. The instructors receiving the highest scores regarding relationships with the students averaged 6.6, while the lowest averaged 4.7. The perceived relationships with the instructor were not reflected in the final grades. They were, however, reflected in the activity of the students. The small groups led by well-liked instructors met considerably more outside the official work-group hours than did the small groups of less-liked instructors. Our estimate is that the success of the participation of graduate assistants as instructors may be related to the "training in cooperation" which the instructors experienced while working in the council, as well as to the opportunity given them in the small groups to develop a personal work relationship with the individual students. Nearly all students (92%) were positive about the small groups; 85% reported that their groups met beyond the one weekly required hour, and for 36% this was for periods of four hours or more. The commitment of the instructors to the course, expressed in the many hours and the amount of energy spent by them, was beyond any expectation of the course leadership. In some instances this investment led to role conflict; some of the instructors gave so much of their time and energy that their own course work and research duties suffered.

As reported earlier, the relationships between student representatives and students deteriorated. In general, the representatives failed to function as a bridge between the council and the students; 89 of the 150 students did not realize they had any influence upon the council. The original objective of the council's function was therefore not reached. But the council accomplished its task in a far better way, namely by promoting the small work groups and by functioning as a platform for all of its members to understand the problems and opportunities in the teaching–learning process. It was here that the course leadership and the instructors were able to come to grips with some of the real issues in teaching and learning, and to deal with these issues without personal threat or fear. In an issue [7] of *Case Tech*, a newspaper published by the students of Case Institute, there appeared this paragraph summarizing an article written about the E-3 course:

"Students and instructors realize the importance of open relationships and close cooperation for the effectiveness of the teaching–learning process. Students and instructors are working to improve the course on the basis of a recognized common goal and a shared responsibility. Students are beginning to realize that they can influence the way in which they learn."

[7] January 11, 1963.

References

Bennis, W. G. Goals and meta-goals of laboratory training. *NTL Hum. Relat. Training News*, 1962, 6 (3), 1–4.

Miles, M. B. Human relations training: current status. In E. H. Schein & I. R. Weschler (Eds.), *Issues in human relations training*. Washington: National Training Laboratories, 1962. Pp. 3–13.

National Training Laboratories. Towards the improvement of campus life. Washington: National Training Laboratories, 1963

CHAPTER 4

Utopia and rebellion:
the New College experiment

Goodwin Watson

INNOVATION in education has often taken the form of an experimental school. Pestalozzi, Montessori, and Dewey, among others, founded schools in which to demonstrate their new educational theories.

A model school may usefully be distinguished from a limited educational reform. In the larger society, reforms attempt to alter one specific feature of the social complex. Attempts to found communities which are designed to incorporate an ideal state of affairs are commonly called utopian.

Any new experimental school is a kind of utopian project. Its organizers seldom wish to advance a limited reform—they plan to introduce a new integrated whole. Each sets out to design the best possible combination of the many good features of schools known to the founders. The new institution constitutes a dream come true.

Part I. The Utopian Project

New College, an experimental demonstration undergraduate school for the preparation of teachers, will be described to bring out hy-

THE AUTHOR is Professor of Social Psychology and Education, Teachers College, Columbia University (on leave), and Distinguished Professor, Newark State College.

potheses which may fit other innovations following the utopian model. Many of the principles which operated in the birth, life, and death of New College can also be seen to apply to creative experiments in lower schools, social agencies, idealistic factories, and utopian colonies. Each of thirteen such principles will be stated and discussed here first in its general form and then as illustrated in the New College history.

The facts in brief

New College was established at Teachers College, Columbia University, under the strong leadership of Professor Thomas Alexander in the fall of 1932, and existed for seven years.

The College used the facilities of Teachers College, had a faculty of thirty-five to forty members (some of whom were also on the Teachers College staff), and enrolled about three hundred students in a program which took five twelve-month years and led to a Master of Arts degree from Teachers College. About one hundred prospective college teachers had some practice teaching in New College while doing doctoral work at Teachers College.

The New College program was characterized by:

1. Individual guidance, differentiated programs, and no uniform credit ladder—accompanied by extensive testing and all-round individual evaluation.

2. Relatively few lectures; more individual reading programs, projects, conferences, and seminars.

3. Effort to achieve closer contact with "life"; requirement of a period of work (on a farm, in industry, in a welfare agency), and some months of study in a foreign country.

4. More contact with children: observation, case studies, twenty-four-hour child-care experiences, practice teaching, a required year of internship in a classroom with special supervision.

5. Close relations among students and with faculty. The initial "Announcement" (1932–33)[1] said: "Great emphasis will be laid upon the association of students among themselves and with members of the staff. Many of the greatest values of college life accrue from intimate intellectual and social contacts among members of the college body." This was accentuated during residence at the North Caro-

---

[1] Published by Teachers College, Columbia University, but now out of print.

lina farm (New College Community) and in the period abroad. Nicknames and first names were commonly used by students in addressing faculty.

Student enrollment never reached the set maximum (360); the budget showed an annual deficit of $35,000 to $40,000; the depression hit Teachers College about 1935; student withdrawals from New College ran over 50 per cent; and the radical political orientation of a minority of faculty and students disturbed the Teachers College administration. On November 10, 1938, Dean William F. Russell suddenly and bluntly announced to students and faculty that New College would end the following June.

This was followed by several months of strenuous but unsuccessful rebellion by devoted students and faculty members determined to "Save New College."

Beginnings

An ideology first. Most of the ideas worked into the design of a utopian experiment have been around for a long time. People have become aware of a discrepancy between ideals and practice. The project usually takes the form: "At long last we shall practice what we have been preaching!"

New College was an attempt to apply principles on which most educators would agree: the importance of individual differences; evaluation of actual learning rather than time-serving as a basis for a degree; students active rather than passive; breadth of experience as a foundation for relating to children from many walks of life; the value to students of close, friendly association with competent, talented faculty members.

Appropriate social matrix. Utopias spring up in clusters during certain historic periods. The social milieu which gives rise to one such experiment usually stimulates others also.

New College belongs in the series of experiments in higher education which included Rollins College, Bennington, Antioch, the Meiklejohn College at Wisconsin, Black Mountain, and Sarah Lawrence College. It was founded in the years when the Progressive Education Association was strongest, and when the Eight-Year Study was launched.

New College must also be viewed against the background of the

Depression and such movements of educational and/or social protest as the Social Frontier, the John Dewey Society, and the Society for the Psychological Study of Social Issues. Some of the same people participated actively in the leadership of all of these and in that of New College. The times of economic and social unrest stimulated designs for a better economic order, better government, and, of course, better schools. These were the days of the New Deal, the Blue Eagle, the Wagner Act, and the birth of the C.I.O. and Social Security—as well as innumerable proposals (Technocracy, New America, the Townsend Plan) for more radical changes.

Paternalism.   Most utopias center about a strong, benevolent father figure. (The Shakers' Mother Ann was an exceptional woman.) One thinks of George Rapp, Robert Owen, John Humphrey Noyes, Joseph Smith, and other patriarchs of the communal settlements in North America.

For New College, the central person was its founder and Director, Professor Thomas Alexander. He had cherished for years the dream of a teachers college which would improve on the traditional "normal school" pattern. He was responsible for the programs in Teachers College which prepared graduate students to go out into the profession of teacher education. He needed something like New College as a demonstration and practice school that would do for his students what the Horace Mann and Lincoln schools had done for the departments of elementary and secondary education.

He sold the idea to some of his colleagues and to his long-time friend, Dean William F. Russell. He personally selected the faculty and many of the first students. He secured the budget and the quarters in Teachers College dormitories (Emerson and Whittier Halls) which were not fully occupied.

He held innumerable meetings of planning committees but kept most vital decisions in his own hands. He was a creative maverick who wore no educational or political brand. He was an individualist with little confidence in collective decisions. He was basically kind and fair-minded, but he rather enjoyed shocking people with unexpected or extreme pronouncements. His bark was much worse than his bite. New College was indeed the "lengthened shadow of a man."

Escape to freedom.   Founders of Utopias have usually sought some place where they would be free from expectations and pressures to conform to the norms of an established culture. Lewin has noted that when the value system of a group "conflicts with the values of the larger cultural setting . . . it is necessary to separate the group from the larger setting. . . . The effectiveness of camps or workshops in changing ideology or conduct depends in part on the possibility of creating such 'cultural islands' during change." (Lewin, 1951, pp. 231–232)

The opening of the North American continent stimulated the fantasy of escape from the crowded ugly cities and the restrictive laws and customs of the Old World. It seemed an ideal setting for new kinds of communities.

New College did not have the freedom of Bennington or Black Mountain. It was closely tied to and dependent upon its parent— Teachers College. Yet there were many devices of separation. Most of the faculty and students of the parent institution had no contact with New College and knew little about what was going on in those isolated quarters. New College teachers and students spent a fair amount of time away from the campus. At New College Community, a North Carolina mountain farm, they lived in a world which had little connection with New York. In small cities of Germany and France, little colonies of New College students lived and studied for many months under conditions very different from those back home.

Participants

Appeal to intellectuals.   The mental capacity to grasp an ideology, and to imagine a life quite different from that of everyday practical experience, is most likely to be found in those with high verbal abilities. It has been characteristic of Utopias that, like the ill-fated Brook Farm, they attract people who want to read, to meditate, and to discuss ideas—but who are not much good at farming or the construction trades.

In the experimental colleges, the selection of persons interested in ideas has been an asset rather than a problem. Entrants to New College averaged 76th percentile on college entrance ability tests, and even higher (82nd percentile) on general culture. They were unusually bright, and shared the strong interest in the arts and world affairs which distinguished the graduates of the more outstanding progressive schools in the Eight-Year Study (Aiken, 1941; Redefer, 1950).

The faculty who came to New College were likewise among the most intelligent and creative. New College offered no appeal to those who sought security or who wanted to practice the customary routines of instruction or scholarship. It drew those who wanted freedom to experiment and who were willing to work long hours at low pay for the sake of their ideals.

Appeal to rebels.   People who leave the beaten tracks and customary comforts to go off into the wilderness and found a new type of community have often been motivated by rebellion against restrictions of the old order. They have been alienated from accepted creeds and established authorities. They are deviates, "odd-balls," iconoclasts, "way out." They make community life very difficult.

Every new educational venture appeals to many persons who for diverse reasons are disaffected with the traditional schools. Some of them have emotional problems which will make them sooner or later as dissatisfied with the new school as they were with those they knew in the past. At first, they are enthusiastic. They enter the project with unrealistic hopes. Before long they become disillusioned and resentful. They repeat their pattern of rebellion.

At New College, more than half of the students who seemed so interested and suitable that they were awarded scholarships the year the college opened, withdrew before graduation. Many of the others made exceptional demands for guidance and personal counseling. The faculty as well as the students—perhaps more than the students— were drawn from among protesters against traditional education. It is likely that, if the terminal crisis had not arisen, several disillusioned teachers would have been in search of more freedom elsewhere.

Communal cohesion.   The little band of dedicated souls who leave their homeland to start a settlement in a new world are bound together by special ties. Their new companions must make up to them for the loss of all their old ties to family and friends. Often, a hostile external environment increases their dependence on one another.

Students and faculty who leave the accepted educational path through the recognized colleges are not taking so drastic a step, but they do feel some isolation and need for social reinforcement. Their friends and families would have understood their going to Vassar or Yale or the University of Chicago, but what was this strange "New College"? All colleges foster lifetime friendships, but New College built even stronger ties. The informal intimacy of life in the New College dormitory, at the Community in North Carolina, and in the little colonies of expatriates living abroad strengthened the cohesion. Students and alumni from New College greeted one another, wherever in the world they might meet, like members of a very special fraternity.

Problems

Insecurity. No Utopia can afford its members the solid security provided by the established order. Arrangements are necessarily improvised, untried, and tentative. Sooner or later, the initial impetus wanes, and participants begin to wonder whether they have been wise to give up the savory fleshpots of Egypt to wander in a wilderness. Nostalgia for the old comforts and certainties increases. If the Atlantic could have been crossed as easily as it can be today, most of the Pilgrim Fathers would probably have returned.

At New College, there were many kinds of insecurity. No one knew when he would graduate. If he inquired, he was told that he still had a lot to learn, and the faculty would decide when he had met their high but still fluctuating standards. Some of the requirements—like the farm work—were unusual, demanding, and not seen by all as clearly educational. Others, like the sojourn abroad, seemed impractical for students with limited resources.

Most Utopias move far enough away from the old civilization to break off contact. But New College students were often in touch with friends attending other colleges. The tales of fraternity life, campus social affairs, summer vacations (New College ran a twelve-month year), and courses which provided easy and certain credits had their inevitable appeal. Many students sought transfers, while the number of new applicants did not increase.

The faculty likewise suffered from insecurity. No one had tenure or a dependable line of career promotion. Duties changed as the program was frequently revised.

Continuing revolt. Idealists seldom find that any Utopia is perfect. Since they are deeply committed to seeking perfection, there is constant ferment. Splinter groups arise, each claiming to represent the only Truth. Unrealistic expectations mean inevitable disillusionment. Participants who are beginning to feel how much they have given up for the sake of the Perfect Life are particularly resentful when the Utopia falls short of their dreams.

New College had to meet impossible demands. It had to provide perfect freedom for individuals, but at the same time to operate as a going institution and meet expectations for high standards of scholarship. The faculty were expected to devise new and better curricula, to use new and better methods of instruction, to develop new and better measures of achievement—meanwhile meeting burdensome hours in committees, weeding vegetables under the hot summer sun at the Community, shepherding students around Europe in winter fog (sharing the European student's low standard of creature comforts), and offering continuous individual guidance on all kinds of educational and life problems.

Resentment at unexpected demands and unfulfilled hopes was unavoidable. Since both faculty and students had strong rebellious and creative impulses—that is why they chose New College—there were endless proposals to change every feature of the program. Resistance to change and experiment was unbecoming for a New College student, teacher, or administrator. The ferment was exciting but wearing. Innovations hardly had a chance to make a contribution before they were altered. Stability was hard to achieve.

Insolvency. Most Utopias are bedeviled with financial worries. Few can begin with a Robert Owen. Most have arisen among the outcasts and underprivileged who have little money to invest. The prosperous seldom seek a new social order. Lack of capital means lack of equipment and of funds for hard times and emergencies.

The idealists who found and direct Utopias hate to be bothered with sordid financial details. They are concerned with higher matters. Auditing tends to be casual. Attention is on the great objectives, and those ends seem to dwarf considerations of bookkeeping.

The relative success of Bennington and Sarah Lawrence is probably due in considerable measure to substantial endowment, providing campuses which attract students who can afford high tuition. New College had no endowment. It operated on a financial shoestring, and that was borrowed from Teachers College. It had no grounds or building of its own, except for the farm structures in North Carolina, and those were lent by Dr. Alexander.

The years from 1932 to 1938 brought a decline in Teachers College enrollment and in available money. Teachers College depended very largely on student fees. At first, the Depression sent unemployed college graduates back to graduate school for certification and special training, but after several years of lag Teachers College felt its full impact. Neither the faculty nor the administration felt certain that they would ever see an economic upturn. The drain of even $35,000 a year had to be viewed as a serious threat to the survival of the parent institution.

The students at New College came largely from homes of modest income, in or around New York City. (The teaching profession has been recruited largely from the lower middle class.) The students could not afford increased fees. They objected strenuously to any items of extra cost.

In consequence, faculty salaries remained low. Some able professors, after a year or two of idealistic sacrifice, accepted offers elsewhere at salaries far above what New College was ever likely to pay. Even very dedicated teachers find it difficult to take their compensation in purely spiritual satisfactions for long. The heavy year-round burden of work, combined with the insecurity and lack of pay, made it remarkable that so many of the original faculty did continue to serve. Some had part-time positions in Teachers College and so found a little reassurance about their future.

Insularity.   Most Utopias are isolated, independent ventures. They are not part of a larger movement which can give them guidance, support, and status. Catholic monasteries and Jewish *kibbutzim* are exceptions; they are projects within larger organizations and can count on some backing. The early consumers' cooperatives were independent, and most of them failed. The formation of the Cooperative Wholesale Society in England (and parallel organizations in other countries) gave the necessary direction and assistance to enable local projects to avoid errors and weather storms.

As indicated above, the "cultural island" is useful in freeing the brave new project from traditional conformity restraints. It operates, however, to deprive the enterprise of some potential sources of support. In the case of New College, the involvement and warm support of leading educators outside the project itself could readily have been developed. In particular, it accorded with many of the principles and ideals of teachers of education in all leading universities; but these educators were not made to feel they were allied with or wanted by the experiment as advisers or supporters.

New College, although it was under the wing of Teachers College and of Columbia University, was largely on its own. It was an appendage, not integral to the welfare of Teachers College or the University. Alexander valued independence of action and sought to be free from the controls which might have been exerted if the affiliation had been closer. Most of the faculty and students in Teachers College had no first-hand contact with the plans for New College or with its operation.

Similarly, New College was not a real part of the Progressive Education Association. Although there were many similarities in educational goals, there was no organizational tie. The Board of the P.E.A. was never consulted during the organization of New College, and none of the New College faculty or administrators held any office in the Progressive Education Association. There was even less tie to the American Association of Teachers Colleges, the National Education Association, and other national bodies.

While this independence made for freedom of action, it hampered recruitment, publicity, and effective support. When help was sought after New College had been officially condemned to death, it was already too late.

The peculiar dependent-independent relationship to Teachers College turned out to be a decisive liability. Actions of militant New College students, faculty members, and the nonconformist Director brought a series of headaches to the Dean of Teachers College. He was in the awkward position of having to stand as sponsor for activities over which he did not have direct control. This would have been resisted by any administrator, and Dean Russell was particularly disturbed. His friendship with Tom Alexander had led him at first to accept a kind of organization which he later found unworkable and intolerable. He carefully removed Alexander a year before he publicly announced his decision to close New College.

Out-group hostility. Set any strange cohesive group within a different larger community—Mormons in Illinois, Dukhobors in Canada, or a socialist camp in a capitalist region—and mutual hostility is likely. Utopian colonies are looked at askance, called names, ridiculed, and sometimes forcibly attacked.

This is a hard lesson for experimental schools to learn. The founders are so convinced of the purity of their motives, and of the valuable service they are rendering, that it seems incredible to them that others should distort what is going on and even seek to destroy it. A common technique of out-group attack is to accuse the experimentalists of subversion or immorality. Like Socrates, they are charged with misleading youth. There may be rumors of "Red networks" or even of "free love." The trials of Highlander Folk School in Tennessee afford a grim example. A school for labor organizers, it practiced racial equality, which was not approved by the surrounding culture. The school was attacked as "subversive" but ably defended by Mrs. Eleanor Roosevelt and others. Eventually it was closed by court orders obtained on a charge of selling beer without a license.

New College also attracted hostile attention. It could hardly have been welcome for some older faculty members at Teachers College to see accustomed content and methods of instruction repudiated. If New College were right, the requirements and teaching practices of almost every college of teacher education in the country must have been wrong.

The students aggravated the problem. Some of them were extreme in their ideas, their talk, and their behavior. Even had they been no more outlandish than their contemporaries at Harvard, New College was more vulnerable. Everyone knew Harvard must be basically sound, and so some deviate individuals could be forgiven. But when many people suspected that New College might be unsound, the deviates became convincing evidence.

Threat minimized. It is difficult for members of a utopian experiment to take seriously the dangers due to external hostility. The leaders of the experiment are engrossed in its internal operation. They trust to relative isolation to save them from the need to worry about foreign diplomacy or public relations. They have gone apart from the world to strive for perfection within their own creed; they do not attack the outsiders; why should they not be allowed to live their new life in peace?

The psychological principle here is that a common way of dealing with threat is to dismiss it from mind. People who live on the sides of a volcano become accustomed to ignoring it. Experiments with films threatening men about the danger of venereal disease or children about the sad consequences of failure to brush their teeth properly (Hovland, 1953, ch. 5) have revealed that such warnings are easily ignored. The current world reaction to deadly radioactive fall-out, and to the imminent holocaust of nuclear explosions, is to assume that some way out will surely be found.

New College did not take its peril seriously. If the faculty and students were aware that they might be an embarrassment to the Teachers College administration, they doubtless felt that a little discomfort in the traditional power centers could be healthy. Alexander was spending his time and energy inside the complex college; public relations were largely ignored. Effort to get public opinion informed and aroused did not begin until after the announcement of intent to terminate the experiment had been made. That announcement fell upon unbelieving minds: "It can't happen here!"

Part II. The Rebellion

When Dean Russell bluntly announced the closing of New College, the faculty and student body received the announcement in stunned silence. This was followed by a series of militant acts designed to force reversal of the decree. The pattern of events resembled, on a small scale, what commonly takes place in ship mutinies, political revolts, and other rebellions. As the founding of New College has been compared above with the establishment of utopian communities, the effort to compel the authorities of Teachers College to back down on their decision will be described as similar in half a dozen ways to the general course of greater movements of revolt. As in Part I, the characteristics (designated by subheads below) will be presented first in terms of the general social pattern, and then as illustrated by what happened at New College.

Save self first. The first reaction to common danger is to try to find an individual escape hatch. Panic runs on banks, and hoarding during shortages, betray this tendency. Refugees stream from every center of destruction. Family bomb-shelters are a natural first response to the possibility of world-wide devastation.

Interviews with a sample of faculty and students present in the chapel on that November day when Dean Russell pronounced the death sentence on New College have indicated that the *immediate* response was to take care of oneself. "I'd better follow up that job at Brooklyn." "How much credit will I get for my three years at New College if I transfer now to Rutgers?"

Collective action galvanized. History tells many tales of the exciting moment when a bewildered crowd is transformed by an orator into readiness for unified, purposeful action. This occurred in Milbank Chapel after the first few moments of silent incredulity and thoughts of personal escape.

Some New College students with experience in leadership of striking unions and left-wing youth movements jumped to their feet. They articulated what everyone felt. "New College must be saved! The united efforts of faculty, students, parents, and an aroused public can force Dean Russell to reverse his decision!" The rebellion was on.

The sense of solidarity was profound. A mass movement was sweeping all—including even the hesitant and doubtful. One lone faculty member rose to ask whether there might not be some reason for the Dean's decision which they did not fully understand. She was hissed into silence and ostracized thereafter. For days, students cut her classes and faculty cold-shouldered this "traitor."

Everyone went to work on the campaign. Most classes were suspended. Some said that saving the college was more urgent than any course project. Others emphasized the valuable learning that comes from active participation in a worthy cause. The curriculum became experimental political science. There were petitions and delegations to the Dean, the trustees, the President of the University, the Mayor, and the Governor. There were press releases and new pep rallies each day to report progress and keep up morale.

Participants during those first days of dedication and solidarity experienced an extraordinary *élan*. It was one of those occasions of high uplift which one remembers throughout life. Students lived on their emotions for days, neglecting meals and sleep. Individuals who had been drifting, confused, or in conflict about their role in the world suddenly experienced integration and release. Now all became clear sailing! They had a purpose in life. It was challenging and important; it was shared by their fellow students and teachers. Internal and external demands were unified. The sense of identity, life meaning, and social support resembled that which dedicated participation in an important war effort sometimes brings.

Radicals vs. conservatives.   The apparent unity was not real. The spearhead of action was the band of students and teachers who had radical political inclinations. A few had been in the Young Communist League; more had been in the Young People's Socialist League. They saw the rebellion as a small prototype of the Coming Revolution. The fight meant more to them than just saving New College. It was a training and testing ground for militant action. They were exercising the leadership that would one day emancipate the workers of the world.

These radical leaders were high in intelligence and verbal skills. Ninety per cent scored above the American college average in tests of reading ability. They spoke and wrote fluently. They were also in the top 10 per cent in their knowledge of history, economics, and other branches of social science.

The initial wave of protest swept everyone into the movement, but soon the more conservative students felt uncomfortable; gradually, one by one, they quietly withdrew. They still regretted the closing of New College, but they conceded that the authorities might have had good reasons. They did not feel that they could set up their preferences against what the wise, high, and mighty had decided. So, not in protest groups, but singly and inconspicuously, they turned their attention to their studies and began trying to improve their academic records so they could be accepted as transfer students in colleges with some prestige.

On the whole, the conservatives were less brilliant, but better socialized, than the radicals. Most of them came from slightly more prosperous homes (although there were few upper-class homes represented in New College, and some of the radicals did come from such homes). The conservatives were well-groomed; some of the radicals were very careless about appearance.

The conservatives' attitude toward the termination of New College was one of disappointment rather than defiance. They were slow to find themselves as a group, because they had not had much experience in differentiating themselves from the prevailing norms. Radicals are all set to separate and to protest. It is not until a rebellion has made substantial progress that the counter-rebellion becomes effective. The counter-rebellion, however, has the strongest allies in the world around, and usually prevails.

The division of New College students into rebels and conservatives split some formerly strong friendships. It was interesting to see that the bonds built up by associates who had gone to high school together, had worked and played at the Community in North Carolina, and had lived in tight cohesion abroad, could not hold together persons who, in the crisis, joined separate camps. In a similar way, politics made new bed-fellows. Students who had never been drawn to one another or to certain faculty members before, now formed close alliances as they worked to save the college. Since the conservative response was more individualistic, it did not build so cohesive a group.

Splintering. The division between radicals and conservatives was only the beginning of schism. Utopian and left-wing protest movements are notorious for angry cleavages. When groups fail to achieve their ends, they tend to put the blame on errors of leaders or factions. Studies of dying churches have shown great bitterness and hostility among members and officials as frustration and resentment increase.

The principal division at New College occurred as the "liberals" began to differentiate themselves from the radicals. The liberals were offended by the harsh, defiant language of demands sent to the Dean. The tone was an echo of strikers' demands on the bad boss, and was out of harmony with the way these students spoke to parents, teachers, and other authority figures. They didn't see why one wouldn't get further by being polite. Many of the faculty felt the same way.

All groups in the rebellion wanted to be effective, but they placed different values on the means. Liberals expected that if one were considerate and friendly, the authorities would be more responsive. Radicals were convinced that the rulers could not be persuaded and must be overthrown and defeated. Power struggles, they maintained, are not won by fair phrases.

The power of the liberals was enhanced by a decision which a liberal faculty member pushed through the central planning committee in the early days of solidarity. She persuaded them that all action policies must be unanimous. This gave a veto to the minority of liberals on that central committee. The radicals were incensed, of course, at such frustration.

Splintering was further accentuated by loyalties to factions in the divided political left; these were transferred into the New College rebellion. Socialists, Lovestone followers, Communists, and Trotskyites were fighting one another as betrayers of the Revolution.

Some of the division among factions was internalized within individuals who had friends in antagonistic camps. Many New College students had been politically naïve; they were confused by, and later torn among, the competing ideologies.

The Galahad syndrome.   In vital contest, each side magnifies its own virtue and attributes satanic qualities to the enemy. Each sees itself as a knight pure in heart, out to slay a vicious dragon.

The rebels of New College saw themselves as campaigning for ideals of freedom, democracy, and personal integrity. They saw Dean Russell, Provost Del Manzo, and the Trustees as the incarnation of tyranny and duplicity and as forerunners of American Fascism.

The Dean saw himself as acting responsibly and carrying out with statesmanship his duties as chief executive of Teachers College. He felt that the rebels did not share his devotion to the welfare of the institution, and that their attacks on him were besmirching its reputation. He suspected that the students were being misled by Communist agitators not really interested in New College but bent on the overthrow of our democracy.

Recognition of defeat. When it became apparent that protests, pressures, and publicity would not sway Dean Russell or the Trustees, the rebels had to face defeat. The conservatives gave up the struggle after the first week or two. The liberals persisted for several months. The radicals fought hardest and longest.

The possibility of moving New College to some other place was explored. Some favored a parallel to Black Mountain College, to be located at the New College Community in North Carolina, but Black Mountain's struggle for survival raised serious questions. Moreover, most of the students of New College lived in or around New York, and could ill afford board away from home.

A partial transfer was made to Adelphi College, where Agnes Snyder, one of the staunchest faculty leaders, found her next job. The teacher education program at Adelphi adopted those aspects of the New College program which could most readily be incorporated in a traditional institution, but the vitality was gone.

Each faction found some rationalization for giving up the fight. Conservatives said, "The duly constituted authorities know best; it is presumptuous to question them." The liberals said, "We did our best. It is too bad that Teachers College has become reactionary and lost its leadership." The radicals said, "This was only a preliminary bout; we have learned important lessons for the real fights ahead!"

Part III. Aftermath

Founders of Utopias anticipate that their demonstration will be imitated. Founders of experimental schools see their project as the first of many. These hopes are almost never fulfilled. The experiment usually stands alone.

New Harmony was located where Father Rapp had founded Harmony; but Robert Owen did not incorporate many of the ideas of the earlier community in his new designs. Albert Brisbane propagandized Fourier's ideas so successfully that some forty Phalanxes were founded; but their beginnings were simultaneous, and only three lasted more than two years. They achieved no enduring influence.

In education, John Dewey's experimental school at the University of Chicago was followed by numerous "progressive" schools—most of which differed considerably from the Dewey school and from one another. Lincoln School is only faintly preserved in the New Lincoln school, to which several staff members transferred when Lincoln School, like New College, was suddenly closed by order of Dean Russell. Few progressive schools now survive. At the moment, attempts are being made to found two new schools in the United States modeled on A. S. Neill's experience at Summerhill (Neill, 1960).

On the college level, the original experiment of Morgan at Antioch continues, but without well-known imitators. The Experimental College organized by Alexander Meiklejohn at Wisconsin died without an heir. Leigh's experimental Bennington regressed to become just another good college for women. The innovations once introduced at Rollins College have not spread. Sarah Lawrence is admired but not copied.

Three kinds of influence from New College live on. One is the lives and memories of those who were part of the experiment. The little book, *We Asked the Mole,* designed to recall in pictures and unusual captions the exciting days spent at New College, may strike a critical reader now as "sentimental mush," but it has powerful emotional value for those who lived in the experience. A second influence comes from articles and pamphlets written by New College faculty members during the experiment; something like a hundred of these have been reported. The third type of influence is most difficult to measure—it is the adoption here and there, in bits and pieces, of some of the features of the model. These residues are hard to locate and are seldom clearly connected with New College. There are colleges today with individualized methods, guidance programs, travel opportunities, work experience, close tutorial association between faculty and students—but might they not have grown up in these patterns even if New College had never existed?

In retrospect, it seems to the writer that New College, like other projections of the creative human spirit, should be evaluated not so much by its persistence over time as by the vitality of the enterprise when it was under way. New College was a great educational experiment, not because of its duration or its residues, but because in it, if only for a brief time, students and teachers became truly inspired and dedicated. They experienced life together at a spiritual elevation rarely achieved in ordinary college studies. The losing battle to save New College was probably, for many of those engaged in it, the high point of their educational curriculum—and quite possibly the most memorable event of their lives.

Hence, the appropriate sequel to New College will not be any imitation of what was tried there in the 1930's; it will be the launching of another and quite different innovation, born of the spirit of a new age, but able again to challenge the participants to heights of adventurous experience far transcending the ordinary curriculum and the cautious little reforms.

References

Aiken, W. *The story of the Eight-Year Study*. New York: Harper, 1941.

Hovland, C. I., Janis, I. L., & Kelley, H. H. *Communication and persuasion*. New Haven: Yale University Press, 1953.

Lewin, K. *Field theory in social science*. (D. Cartwright, Ed.) New York: Harper, 1951.

Neill, A. S. *Summerhill: a radical approach to child-rearing*. New York: Hart, 1960.

New College, Teachers College. *We asked the mole*. No publisher given: 1939.

Redefer, F. L. The Eight-Year Study . . . after eight years. *Progressive Educ.*, 1950, 28, 33–36.

CHAPTER 5

The colleges and the "Arkansas Purchase" controversy

RICHARD COLVARD

The significance of a novelty [an innovation] must be understood to be the meaning it has for the acceptor. That is not necessarily the meaning it has for its introducer (Barnett, 1953, p. 338).

IT HAS now been over ten years since the "Arkansas Purchase" controversy first flared into prominence on the American teacher education scene: time enough, surely, to allow some of its highlights to be sketched and interpreted without danger of drawing the combatants back into open conflict. The following account reviews the complex course of organizational interaction involved in this important but insufficiently understood controversy. The emergent analysis stresses the necessity of considering the professional, political, and economic contexts of college operation, when innovations in American higher education are analyzed or attempted.

Overview

The original proposal

As dramatically announced to a large gathering of Arkansas educators assembled in a Little Rock hotel in October, 1951, the Arkansas

---

THE AUTHOR is Associate Professor, Department of Sociology, State University of New York at Buffalo.

117

plan was to be a bold new program in teacher education. The hopes of its major advocates, an official of a newly established philanthropic foundation and the president of the University of Arkansas, were made clear by the latter in his opening address:

> [The Foundation] selected Arkansas as the pilot state. . . . If we can make it work here—and I'm confident we can—there is no reason why it should not work in any state. That, of course, is what the Foundation is interested in. If our bold experiment succeeds, the Arkansas plan of teacher education will become standard throughout the United States.[1]

Those in the audience were not aware that the announcement had been preceded by preliminary negotiations between foundation and University officials, the governor, some officials of the state education department, and the state's leading newspaper editor. They *were* aware that the announcement was an open bid for all fourteen of the four-year colleges then training teachers in the state—seven private colleges as well as five state multi-purpose colleges and two state teachers colleges—to cooperate with the University in planning and establishing a state-wide conversion to a new teacher education curriculum, an $85,000 grant having already been made to the University for this purpose.

In the proposed curriculum, the prospective teacher, instead of having four years of combined general education and professional education, would have four years of the former, then go on to a fifth "professional" year. This year would combine formal study of education with extensive supervised "internship" in cooperating public schools.

If state-wide agreement could be reached on such a change, the assembled educators were told,[2] the foundation would pay all the costs of strengthening the general education offerings and staffs at all the institutions, plus all costs of staffing and operating the fifth-year centers on various unspecified campuses. Such financial support, likely to run into the millions, would last for the considerable (though as yet undetermined) time it would probably take to get the new system established. Eventually, possibly in ten years, said the University president, financing would have to come through regular channels.

Both the parent foundation's annual report for 1951 and a *Time* magazine article a few weeks after the original announcement made it pretty clear that, if the proposal were adopted, undergraduate schools

[1] *The Arkansas Gazette,* Little Rock, Arkansas, October 27, 1951.
[2] *Ibid.*

of education in all the institutions would give way to fifth-year training centers in various places throughout the state, and that the two teachers colleges would, at the undergraduate level, be converted primarily to liberal arts colleges:

> The preparation of teachers for the public schools seems to demand, contrary to the present requirements of many states, liberal education and practical experience rather than technical training that concentrates on method at the expense of content. The Fund for the Advancement of Education has entered into discussions with educational leaders in Arkansas looking toward the transformation of the teachers colleges of the State into colleges of liberal arts, with appropriate modifications in the program of education for teachers. The University of Arkansas has received a grant [$85,000] to assist it to develop a state-wide plan of liberal education for teachers, to be followed by a period of internship. The understanding is that, if a satisfactory scheme can be produced, the Fund will cooperate in the initial financing of it.[3]

Reactions of the surprised educators summoned by telegram to hear the announcement were varied, to say the least. But in general, both in this first meeting and in three rounds of formal negotiating sessions during the following seven months, the seven private colleges were enthusiastic, the two state teachers colleges were resistant, and the five state multi-purpose colleges were ambivalent. Representatives from all the colleges were much more interested in the prospect of enriching general education work than in the prospect of putting all professional training into a fifth year.

The actual project

The project finally agreed upon by the various Arkansas educational representatives eventually assembled as a "Committee of 36" was a compromise between what the foundation and the University administration wanted, and what the administrators of the other Arkansas institutions were willing to try. What happened, in essence, was that a state-wide agreement was reached to establish a fifth-year curriculum as an "experimental" alternative route into teaching, not as the sole teacher education program in the state.

The agreement was reached in May, 1952; after extensive planning, the new program formally got under way in 1953. What came to be called the "regular" fifth-year program, with training centers on two

[3] Ford Foundation (1951, pp. 17–18). Cf. *Time,* Nov. 12, 1951, pp. 82–83.

campuses, was set up and overseen by a state-wide Executive Committee for three years, on a scale much smaller than the proponents had hoped for: 29 students graduated in 1954, 64 in 1955, and 33 in 1956. Grants were tapered down after 1955, when conflict persisted among the college presidents and other representatives on the Executive Committee, and it became apparent that the program was attracting fewer students.

In 1955–56, the University, with the foundation's support, set up an "alternate" fifth-year program under its own direction. This program, which put the trainee in the public schools on a regular salary, was deemed to have a better chance of independent survival. Thirty students graduated from the program in 1956, 16 in 1957, 15 in 1958, and 7 in 1959—its last year.

Total foundation support (for the two programs—"regular" and "alternate") from 1951 through 1959 came to a little over three million dollars. About $540,000 of this sum went to the fifth-year work directly; approximately $277,000 went to administrative expenses for the coordinating state office; and the remainder—most of the money—went to the improvement of the general education programs on the various campuses.

Graduates from the new fifth-year programs seemed, in the subsequent over-all evaluation of the Experiment made by non-participants in 1956–57, to be able to teach as well as the graduates of the conventional four-year programs—as the proponents of the fifth-year idea had maintained all along. But the evaluation of this and several other aspects of the Experiment, although very systematic, could not be scientifically precise, because few testable procedures were used consistently in any of the new programs, and because the "regular" fifth-year program was discontinued before it was able to draw students exposed to the strengthened general education program for four years. The directors of the evaluation concluded that the enrichment of the general education programs would probably be "the most lasting tangible effect of AETE." (Spalding & Krathwohl, 1959, p. 183)

It was obvious to all that both the original proposal and the actual project, which was then the largest-scale but by no means the only program of this sort sponsored by the foundation around the country, unquestionably called widespread attention to the problem of how to give prospective teachers an effective balance of general and professional education. But opinions varied then—and still vary—as to whether the results in Arkansas were worth the struggle and the money. This is an important question but one which would be impossible to answer satisfactorily, partly because the Arkansas efforts were unprecedented in scope and partly because there are few criteria of effectiveness in higher education anyway.[4]

Scope and task of this study

The question of interest in this study is not whether, or in what respects, the actual project finally attempted was successful, but why the compromise proposal—and we mean the term "compromise" in a neutral sense—was adopted instead of the original one. In the larger study from which this work is drawn (Colvard, 1959),[5] a great many forces affecting the actions of the foundation and the University were examined in considerable detail. Here, because of space limitations, attention will be concentrated primarily on interorganizational aspects of forces affecting the colleges'—and especially the state colleges'—reactions to the original proposal, as the latter were revealed before and during the stormy sessions of the Committee of 36. This is only a part of the AETE story, but one which should be of general interest to

[4] Brim (1958, p. 22), in an interesting study, has suggested that "general, unappraisable ends serve the function of protecting educators (and, in other contexts, other professional groups) from public control, since the public has no way of determining if a good job is being done."

For added comment on the status and usefulness of fifth-year programs, see Herzog (1960) and Radcliffe (1959).

[5] For details of methodology, see Colvard (1959, pp. 428–454). See also Spalding & Krathwohl (1959), and the shortened version of that report (Arkansas Experiment in Teacher Education, 1960). See also Lindsey (1956), and especially Wolfe (1960); the latter includes a more detailed and systematic analysis of how Arkansas faculty members and administrators responded to AETE than is attempted here.

In the present account, wherever the dictates of documentation have allowed, identities of individuals and organizations have been withheld. Quotations not explicitly footnoted are from interviews made by the author and many other members of the group conducting field studies for the evaluation of AETE in 1956–57. The evaluation study involved research teams from Michigan State University, the University of Oregon, and Portland State College. W. B. Spalding served as director, D. R. Krathwohl as associate director. The interviews, other basic evaluation data, and summary materials have been deposited in the main library of the University of Illinois. See also Spalding (1958) and Krathwohl (1958) for brief accounts of the study and its findings.

those interested in the nature—or nurture—of educational innovation. Some sociological "morals" are offered at the end of the analytical section, but the reader looking for heroes, villains, or fools must find them for himself. The only value premise we are conscious of here is the one we share with Tawney: "The disputes which matter are not caused by a misunderstanding of interests but by a better understanding of diversity of interests." (1920, p. 40)

Central Issues

Three issues stood out in the seven months of negotiations following the announcement of the original proposal. Though they shaded into each other, and the shadings will show up in the eventual more detailed analysis, these issues can be preliminarily identified as follows: (1) the *educational legitimacy* of the proposed new curriculum, i.e., the "soundness" and professional acceptability of a teacher education program capping four years of general education with a fifth year involving internship in cooperating public schools; (2) the *organizational autonomy* of the academic organizations involved, especially the state colleges' concern not just to survive but to maintain substantial self-control over their own evolution; and (3) the *economic security* of the colleges contemplating participation in the new program, particularly those which felt they were likely to lose students if they did agree to the proposal and likely to lose legislative appropriations if they didn't.

Educational legitimacy

The original proposal set off a major battle which soon spread beyond the Arkansas borders. The president of the University was no longer to take an active part in it, because (to the considerable disappointment of the proposal's proponents in Arkansas and elsewhere) he had been offered the presidency of another university, and left to accept it shortly after making the announcement. But he vigorously threw down the gauntlet in his original statement:

> A great many educators have felt for a long time that emphasis on techniques has gotten out of hand in this country. Undergraduates who plan to enter the teaching profession have been spending an increasing amount of their time on subjects that are facetiously referred to as "blackboard engineering." The result has been that their general education has

suffered. In some cases they spent more time studying teaching methods than they did studying the subject they would be called upon to teach. . . . Specialized training in teaching techniques is necessary, but we believe it can be given best in concentrated doses under actual classroom conditions. This is exactly what . . . [the fifth-year] internship centers would do.[6]

In a memorandum which one of the early opponents of the proposal sent to the National Citizens Committee for Public Schools a few months after the original announcement, the president's challenge was answered as follows:

One of the basic tenets of this philosophy [we in teacher education in Arkansas and many other states have been holding] is that professional selection, guidance, and training should be carried on over as long a period of time as possible under the supervision of professionally competent persons, and integrated closely with the student's total college program. This had been considered a psychologically sound idea, although teacher education programs in practice fall short of its full implementation. One of the most emphatic efforts of the American Association of Colleges for Teacher Education during the past four years has been in the encouragement of a higher level of integration in the programs of its member institutions. The . . . [fifth-year] idea is directly opposed to this prospect, since it proposes to postpone any significant emphasis on professional preparation during the student's four years of college work.[7]

The question of whether the fifth-year idea—for a "dichotomized" curriculum—was educationally sound was never really settled, even in the actual Experiment. But it was the major professional issue in the struggle which was eventually to involve not only the colleges and the foundation, but regional and national accrediting orgnizations as well.

Organizational autonomy

The second issue was sometimes labeled by participants as the issue of the "advance commitment," although there was more to it than that phrase implies. The foundation consistently regarded the proposed program as a demonstration more than an experiment and stressed (in Arkansas and elsewhere—e.g., before a later Congressional committee investigating foundations) the political and professional support it had found for the program before the original announce-

[6] *The Arkansas Gazette, op. cit.*

[7] Teacher education in Arkansas and the Ford Foundation proposal. Memorandum in AETE files, January 6, 1952, p. 6.

ment. (U.S. Congress, 1953) But the foundation clearly insisted that the colleges must definitely decide whether or not they were willing to substitute the new type of curriculum for the old, as the University had already preliminarily agreed to do.

At the end of the first round of committee sessions, for example, a foundation official came down to Little Rock. In a long-discussed meeting, he reviewed the foundation's interest in the fifth-year idea, stressed that a plan was "of no value unless the people who carry it out have belief in it," [8] and summarized the question before them this way:

> This is the problem for you:
> 1. Are you interested in a teacher education program that concentrates general education in four years?
> 2. Are you interested in developing professional education in a fifth year —this to be connected rather closely with the public schools?
> This is the idea concerning teacher education we want to see Arkansas develop. . . .[9]

The minutes of the meeting record, among others, the following questions and the official's replies:

> Q: Does the plan envisage the abolishment of teacher training colleges?
> A: The idea was not intended to abolish professional teacher education. It is a question of what year in the education of teachers it will be given. . . .
> Q: Is state-wide participation necessary before the Fund will be interested?
> A: The Fund is interested in this as a state program. We assumed a state-wide program.
> Q: Will the Fund approve the plan without participation of all colleges?
> A: What is a state-wide program for Arkansas? The plan would need to be in terms of such a program. . . .
> Q: If we submitted a program on which the Fund had some questions, would it give us recommendations or suggestions?
> A: If your plan and our ideas are far apart, we would reject the proposal. If reasonably close, we would give interpretations and suggestions. . . .
> Q: Would your Fund approve a parallel plan, where the State Board would continue issuing certificates on our present [four-year] plan as well as that recognized by the proposed plan?

[8] Minutes of the Planning Committee Sessions, January 30, 1952. Cited in Colvard (1959, p. 463). (In AETE files. Also reproduced in Colvard, 1959, pp. 456–471. These minutes were transcribed from detailed notes at the meeting but were not completely verbatim.)

[9] *Ibid.*, p. 464. Cf. Woodring (1957).

A: Wouldn't that be saying that Arkansas could not make up its mind about what it wanted to do in teacher education? [10]

Shortly after this meeting, a leading official of the American Association of Colleges for Teacher Education introduced a resolution condemning the original proposal, in what quickly became known as the "Arkansas Purchase" speech:

> . . . It is not bold; it is brazen—the brazen attempt to impose a philosophy upon a whole state school system. It is not an experiment; it is a conclusion. . . . Apparently the Arkansas plan constitutes the purchase of a philosophy, its acceptance by a whole state being bought and paid for, cash on the barrel head. . . .[11]

The resolution itself was adopted "without audible dissent" (Colvard, 1959, p. 368) by the several hundred professional educators attending the AACTE session. It read in part:

> The people of Arkansas have every right to determine for themselves what kind of education they want for their teachers. . . . The proposed curriculum reorganization presented to us is replete with dangers to teacher supply in the state. . . . A more serious matter . . . [is that the] record indicates that a tax-exempt foundation . . . is offering highly attractive financial support if a particular pattern of education is . . . not tried out . . . but *put into operation.* . . . Centralized control by the proffer of money with strings attached can be just as effective and consequently just as dangerous as control by regulation and dictation. We condemn attempts to control by either means.[12]

One Fund official indicated to an interviewer [13] later on that he thought the "Arkansas Purchase" charge was "stupid." The AACTE "didn't check the facts . . . just went off half-cocked . . . before

[10] *Ibid.,* pp. 468–470.
[11] Statement concerning the Ford Foundation plan for teacher education in Arkansas. Reproduced in Colvard (1959, pp. 479–482).
[12] *The Ford Foundation teacher education proposal in Arkansas.* A statement by the American Association of Colleges for Teacher Education, February, 1952. Cited in Colvard (1959, p. 368). Also included as: The Ford Foundation teacher education proposal to Arkansas. *Progressive Education,* 1952, 29, 174–175.
[13] This material was paraphrased from skeletal notes after the interview by the research team member involved, and is marked LP, for "later paraphrase." In other cases, the researcher attempted to keep verbatim notes during the interview, or worked from a transcribed tape recording; these materials are marked AV, for "attempted verbatim." This notation will be used throughout. As indicated earlier, material not explicitly footnoted should be understood to have been drawn from research interviews.

anyone knew what it was going to be all about." Just a few hours before the meeting, the Executive Committee of the AACTE had talked with him very cordially about a project they were initiating. And "as far as he was concerned, the AACTE represented [a] professional reactionary point of view at its lowest ebb." [LP] Another Fund official less immediately involved in these events indicated—a little differently —that the AACTE's reaction had been anticipated, and that:

> The Fund was never concerned about it. . . . The decision not to consult with [the AACTE] or the NEA was a deliberate one because their primary *raison d'être* is not to experiment. The Fund has had the same reaction from them in the teacher aide program and they didn't get the information straight there either. The NEA exists to improve teacher welfare and to improve education, but the latter function is often in conflict with the former. The NEA tends to want to protect [the] status quo and it really is not set up to promote experimentation in education. [LP]

Whether the foundation was more free to reject the colleges' plans than the colleges were free to reject the foundation's stipulations— once the original proposal had been publicly made—was another subject that was never settled.[14] But mutual concern with the protection of autonomy, in the sense of trying to achieve and maintain "a condition of independence sufficient to permit a group to work out and maintain a distinctive identity" (Selznick, 1957, p. 121) was the second major issue affecting the whole course of negotiations. As later sections will show, the colleges' relations with each other—and with the University and the state legislature—were involved here even more than their relations with the foundation, whose own position on this autonomy issue was eventually summed up by one official this way in a research interview:

> The Fund was interested only in the local development of a program in accordance with the basic concept upon which it wanted to make the grants. . . . The Fund was not interested in squandering its money, but it did not seek to dominate a program either. It wanted to stimulate a creative approach on the local level within the state. [LP]

Economic security

Maintenance of the economic security (or, more accurately, reduction of the economic *insecurity*) of the colleges was the third issue—

---

[14] Broader contextual analyses (Colvard: 1961; in press) suggest that foundations in America are very much dependent on the educational and scientific organizations to which they make grants.

important in its own right and very fundamentally affecting the consideration of the other two issues: educational legitimacy and organizational autonomy. All the colleges, state and private alike, were in dire need of funds; the chance to get money with which to bolster general education programs was an exhilarating prospect, even to the administrators most ambivalent about or opposed to scrapping the undergraduate professional work in favor of a fifth-year internship program. But, they asked, where would the money come from when the new program would eventually have to be freed from foundation support? Because student fees were a major source of income at all the colleges, the potential effect of the new program on enrollments—and (for the state colleges) on legislative appropriations—was a crucial consideration to be taken into account.

Views of different educational institutions

The different kinds of institutions, it should be noted, had different definitions of the economic situation posed by the proposal.

The *University* was widely regarded as likely to gain students and income at the other state institutions' expense if the proposal were adopted (even though by no means all of its teacher education people favored the fifth-year idea). Said a state college dean, of this prospect:

> One other problem—the most important thing—distrust of many of the colleges of the University . . . the feeling that . . . the University would dominate the program and use it for its own purposes, competitively.[AV]

The *private colleges*, realizing (1) that their percentage of enrollments in the state had been declining for decades (from 68.4 per cent in 1900 to 25.1 per cent in 1950),[15] (2) that many of their students were in fact if not in theory prospective teachers, and (3) that their operations were very dependent on such students' tuition, felt they probably stood to gain—economically as well as professionally—from backing even the ultimate compromise proposal for a fifth-year program. Whether correctly nor not, one private college president recalled having sized up the situation as follows:

> We [had] to look at it this way: we had nothing to lose if this plan proved to be the best way of training teachers, and we had everything to win. You see if the best teachers [came] out of general education, we

[15] Governor's Advisory Commission on Education (1950, p. 27).

would get many students . . . who now go to the teachers colleges. We had everything to gain and the teachers colleges were the ones who were going to lose. So we went into it wholeheartedly while they dragged their feet and didn't want the program in any respects to become too successful.[AV]

The *state colleges* (both multi-purpose and teachers colleges) were not sure whether they stood to gain or to lose students, or income from tax sources. One key figure put part of the dilemma this way:

The members of the state legislature were interested. They said, "What the hell is the matter with [X teachers college] up there? They don't want to take fifty or one hundred thousand dollars that someone wants to give them and yet they're up here at the legislature crying for money all the time." [AV]

Heads of the *multi-purpose* state colleges generally kept out of the public wrangling, but one said to an interviewer later:

[The state colleges] . . . have all been very pleased with general education, but each of them had some skepticism for the fifth-year program. . . . You must remember that . . . I could not dare to get the school out on a limb to sustain the experiment, knowing at the same time that the college could not carry it out after it no longer had . . . [foundation] funds. Therefore, anything we went into, I asked the college to approach cautiously and conservatively. I didn't want to be made an ass of by having to drop an experimental program because we couldn't pay for it ourselves.[AV]

But, in part of a long letter, actually published as a full-page advertisement, the president of one of the *teachers colleges* who led much of the opposition wrote as follows to the editor who had been vigorously supporting the proposal:

Your editorial is misleading . . . because it states that the . . . plan offers Arkansas an opportunity "to acquire substantial financial aid for its colleges." This is not the case. What it offers is merely enough money to finance the junking of what we have in the way of teacher training and the setting up of a new system. . . . Then when the new system is set up the flow of money from [the foundation] . . . will cease and Arkansas through additional taxation will have to find the money to carry on. . . .

We of the teachers colleges . . . are participating in a study of the proposal. We are in favor of any improvement that can be made. We hope we can reach a working agreement . . . that will be realistic, workable, and endurable. . . .[16]

[16] Letter to *The Arkansas Gazette,* February 4, 1952.

Whether the various kinds of colleges' economic hopes and fears were warranted or not was, again, a matter which was not conclusively settled by the establishment and operation of the compromise project. But concern with enrollments and general economic insecurity ran like a ragged stream of red ink through the voluminous records of the negotiations, as more detailed analysis of these sessions—and of these three issues just sketched—will make clear.

Elaboration and Analysis

Implicit here is the notion that one group responds to the pressure of the other because, in anticipation, it can visualize the response that a particular activity will stimulate and then, in terms of its own estimate of the effects of this response on its own interests, it acts accordingly.[17]

Right after the original announcement in Little Rock, the editor whose support had been gained in the pre-announcement negotiations waxed optimistic:

In the next few months, the affected educational agencies and colleges will have to decide whether or not they will go along with the program. The indications so far are that the great majority will and it is difficult to see how any could hold out of a program that promises to give education in Arkansas—and in the nation at large—the greatest single boost it ever had.[18]

This editor, nationally prominent and on the board of one of the state teachers colleges—and also on the board of another large foundation—explained part of his interest and optimism to an interviewer this way:

There is something that you have to consider here—speaking practically. There is a natural law in education . . . that ignorance militates against public education. . . . You have to raise the level . . . to get people . . . to accept increased taxes for the schools. . . . Our important advancement this year [1957; sales tax raised to 3 per cent to aid schools] in the legislature [is] a result of trying to put this natural law into effect. . . . We were well adapted for such an experiment [as AETE] because of our extra need for very strong improvement of education from the University down to our kindergarten. Also our means for doing this are as limited as any in the country. We needed something to goose the system up in Arkansas as quickly as possible.[AV]

[17] Easton (1953, p. 178), here interpreting Bentley (1908).
[18] *The Arkansas Gazette*, October 28, 1951.

But the University School of Education official who somewhat re-luctantly took the torch handed him by the departing president was far less sanguine—especially after he made a post-announcement tour of the various colleges to sound out the prospects. In his own metaphors:

> . . . I went up to New York and had a visit with [the foundation official], and told him just how the land lay. They knew what the deal was. It wasn't all beer and skittles by any means. . . . After I made my rounds of the colleges here and saw how the wind was blowing . . . I told [the foundation] just how the land lay. I wasn't trying to kid them. . . . I told them it wasn't going to come off.[AV]

Educational legitimacy

Those identified with the professional education tradition (which stressed the importance of integrating general and professional work in a developmental sequence at the undergraduate level) felt strongly that the original proposal threatened the educational legitimacy of that whole academic tradition. And inextricably bound up with their pro-fessional convictions about the merit of the ideas undergirding their existent programs were fears that participation in the new program would jeopardize (1) their relations with the public (including poten-tial students) and the public schools, as prospective employers of stu-dents; (2) their standing with national teacher education accrediting associations—a prospect which might reduce both prestige and enroll-ments; and (3) their relations with schools and colleges in other states, particularly the other North Central Association states in which their graduates might want to teach or take further training.

Would they lose students and employers?   Bolstering the first fear was the fact that there was an extreme teacher shortage in the state. When students could teach with only a year or two of undergraduate work, why—many in the Committee of 36 asked—would they bother with a program which would take five years and, even then, probably not give them much more salary? (Even in 1954, graduation year for the first fifth-year graduates, Arkansas teachers' salaries were to average only $2300, the national average being $3740; the per-capita personal income in the state in 1954 was $979, against a national average of

$1770.) [19] Again, if, as in fact was common in the state, students could drop out and teach in Arkansas after their freshman or sophomore years, did it make either educational or economic sense to set up a single program offering no professional work in those undergraduate years?

In the earlier-cited letter to the National Citizens Committee for Public Schools, the history of teacher education in Arkansas was reviewed and "The Current Situation in Arkansas" summed up this way:

> . . . Arkansas is at the present time in very difficult circumstances with regard to the training, tenure, and professional competence of its teaching force. Arkansas teaching salaries are the lowest in the nation. The quantitative level of college training among Arkansas teachers is among the lowest in the nation. The State's certification regulations permit the issuance of the certificates on a basis of from one to five or more years of college training. Only a handful of states continue to issue certificates to persons with only one year of college training.[20]

The situation was improving, but not even a majority of certificates were given to people with Bachelor's degrees:

> . . . The certificates issued in Arkansas on this [one-year] level of training have declined . . . from 50 per cent of the total number of certificates issued in 1943–44 to only 13 per cent issued in 1950–51. The proportion of certificates based on the Bachelor's degree has risen from 11 per cent to over 38 per cent during the same period of time.[21]

No polls of prospective student opinion were taken, but public school representatives were present when the negotiations were formalized into the "Committee of 36," and these representatives, although generally favoring longer periods of training for teachers, were well aware of the "current situation's" shortages, and were strongly identified with the traditional professional education position. Other educational groups and prominent laymen concerned with the teacher shortage and the certification situation were not mobilized in support

[19] Spalding & Krathwohl (1959, pp. 134, 136). Citing Beaseley (1955, p. 13), the authors note that in 1954 the beginning salaries for teachers with bachelor's degrees ranged from $1,063 to $2,825, *and* that teachers earned about twice the average income in Arkansas—a fact doubtless complicating efforts to raise teachers' salaries.

[20] Teacher education in Arkansas . . . , *op. cit.,* p. 2.

[21] *Ibid.*

of the proposal, as had originally been intended by the departed University president.[22]

Would they lose accreditation?   The second fear, that of weakening college standing with national teacher education accreditation associations, was not equally shared. Not all of the colleges belonged, for example, to the American Association of Colleges for Teacher Education. The University deliberately did not belong, and several of the private colleges were not overly concerned with what AACTE might think of the dichotomized curriculum. But colleges which either belonged already (including especially the teachers colleges) or which aspired to belong (as was the case with a few of the private colleges) were dubious about going completely into a program they felt AACTE might consider unsound.

The concern about "what AACTE might think" came out in many ways in the meetings, but the most succinct statement was again made in the previously cited letter to the NCCPS. The writer, a State Department of Education official responsible for certification matters, pointed out that the proposal had been developed "without the support of the American Association of Colleges for Teacher Education, the National Commission on Teacher Education and Professional Standards, or the Association for Student Teaching . . . ," and that for this and other reasons:

> There has . . . been raised among faculty members of teacher educating institutions in the state a serious question as to the desirability of the plan. Four institutions in the state are involved as members of the [AACTE] in comprehensive programs of curriculum development. These institutions would necessarily be called upon to abandon their present plans for improving their programs in teacher education in the event that they attempt to participate in the proposed . . . plan. To a less dramatic extent, the same difficulty would face the faculties of all other institutions in the state which have undertaken seriously to keep abreast of improved practices in teacher education.[23]

Committee spokesmen—primarily administrators—from all the colleges conceded that their teacher education programs could be im-

---

[22] See text in Colvard (1959, pp. 164–166). (Request for funds to initiate a proposed project in teacher education . . .)

[23] Teacher education in Arkansas . . . , *op. cit.*, p. 6.

proved. But the heads of the state teachers colleges, in particular, argued that their programs were being improved constantly as it was, already gave considerable stress to general education, and involved close links with the public schools (e.g., in practice teaching). And they considered accreditation by AACTE a symbol of achievement and quality: it was a definite attraction to students who might be interested in teaching, not only in Arkansas but in other states, where graduation from a nationally accredited college might be a condition of employment.

Would they alienate colleges in other states, and the North Central Association? The latter point leads in to the third fear that continually crept into the debate about the educational legitimacy of the fifth-year idea: the fear of jeopardizing relations with schools and colleges—and accrediting agencies—in other states where Arkansas students might teach, or to which they might transfer. When Committee members wrestled with the question of the kind and amount of credit that might be given in the fifth year, and when they pondered the possibility of fellowships or other forms of financial support for the prospective "interns," a frequent subject of discussion was how various decisions might be regarded by colleges in other states, and by the North Central Association (which helped set standards for many schools and colleges in a wide adjacent region serving as a major market for Arkansas graduates).

There was actually more widespread concern among the college representatives with NCA's standards than with those of AACTE, but there were great differences in the degree to which the different kinds of institutions worried about whether credits granted in the new program would be accepted in other states. The University and the teachers colleges were at the extremes here, as on most other questions.

The University could grant credit, and was not too worried. As the School of Education official handling most of the University's AETE negotiations described the contrasting positions:

> We had people tell us when we were planning this thing that it was absolutely impossible. That it was illegal and immoral and everything else to let a person take a graduate course in a field in which he hadn't 12 junior or senior hours. Hell, graduate courses are courses taken by graduate students. . . . They were constantly worried about the North Central Association, some of these people.[AV]

And as the dean of a private college noted:

> [The president of one of the teachers colleges] was so afraid that this whole thing was going to undermine the standing of [his college] in AACTE and NCA, etc., he even conducted his own private research on what credits would be accepted in a major university. He wasn't going to be too quick to go into this thing.[AV]

The concern which the teachers colleges—and the other state colleges —felt in this matter was intensified because the NCA had recently been very critical of the extension work in teacher education which several colleges of both types had undertaken, partly in response to demand from school teachers who wanted additional training closer (than the University) to their home communities. An administrative official of one of the teachers colleges filled in this part of the picture:

> [A big question was] how in the world that thing would ever be accredited. The fact that it [i.e., the fifth-year program] was under the aegis of the University . . . would naturally mean that . . . any work earned under it bears the University accrediting. . . .
>
> The state universities can more or less thumb their noses at the accrediting agency. [But] at one time the NCA clobbered us for off-campus work which we were offering. They left the University alone, but every man on that board in Chicago [who] voted on this [earlier] thing was from a large school which was doing the same thing.[AV]

The private colleges, finally, were also concerned with out-of-state (and particularly NCA) reactions, but in a different way. Their administrators were most interested in the undergraduate phase of the proposed program, and they hoped that by strengthening their general education work they could actually improve their standing with NCA. For, during the period that included the announcement and the subsequent negotiations being highlighted here, four of the six private colleges were not accredited by that organization. As one University administrator long familiar with accreditation matters in the state described the situation:

> [As far as these colleges go] . . . you have a little bit of everything. Matthew College [24] has always rated highly academically [and is accredited]. Daniel College has been in and out; has been accredited three or four different times. . . . Of course Levi College has never been

[24] This and the following Biblical names are pseudonyms for the private colleges; the state teachers colleges will be referred to as "X" and "Y".

accredited. Yes, in 19— it was accredited to a certain extent by the University. Luke College . . . was accredited in 19—. Goliath College . . . is not accredited. And Joseph College . . . is not accredited.[AV]

The case of Daniel College was extreme, but is instructive here. Said Daniel's new president of this period:

> Our general education program came in coordinate with this [AETE] program. This was necessary for us to regain accreditation with NCA. I don't know which influence was greater on our general education program . . . the NCA or the AETE. . . .
> We lost our accreditation as a result of the fact that the college put a great deal more emphasis into football athletics than it did on the educational program. . . . Things were pretty bad when I came here, but we've made a lot of progress and have achieved our accreditation back. I think it was a good thing for the campus to get rid of the football tramps that we had hanging around here.[AV]

His dean put the matter even more bluntly:

> We got thrown out of the NCA in 19—. We were desperately trying to get back in at the time that AETE started. One of the weaknesses was the general education program. In fact, the examiner said we didn't have a general education program. So there was a double impetus; the support was all the more welcome.[AV]

One college president said this of NCA's apparently ambivalent attitude and its effects:

> The NCA has had very little influence [on AETE]. However, Dr. ——— [an NCA official] discussed at one time [the fact that] experimentation is helpful to education. . . . If the institutions [were] not permanently changed by AETE, they [NCA] would not object to their [the colleges'] participating in the experiment, so long as the basic pattern, organization, etc., were not changed beyond [that] which the school was approved for. They [NCA] would not attempt to dictate the participation of the colleges in the . . . experiment.[AV]

The college representatives in the Committee of 36 of course spent a great deal of time on many other matters of much importance and relevance to the question of the educational legitimacy of the fifth-year idea: Was it accurate to lump all professional education under the heading of "methods"? What about students who couldn't go even four years? Could a student who had taken, e.g., Human Growth and Development 322, enter the program, or would this be ruled out as a professional course? Just what was general education anyway?

How was it different from liberal education? Would general education include a course in child psychology, or (asked the private colleges) a course on the Bible?

The point we have stressed here is that each kind of college had external professional-economic relations to organizations in its environment which had to be taken seriously into account. In wrestling with a collective response to the original proposal, none of the Arkansas colleges could afford to ignore the complex web of relations it had with the public and professional groups which had historically supplied its raw materials and either certified or purchased its undergraduate products. The question of the "soundness" of the proposed new curriculum could be meaningfully considered only in the context of both the internal and external consequences of adopting it as the sole means of training teachers in the state.

Organizational autonomy

"Latent opposition from the first announcement," read a front page *Arkansas Gazette* story on the early Committee meetings in January, 1952, "has centered around fears that the state colleges would lose a degree of their autonomy." [25] State college fears of (1) domination by the University and (2) increased regulation by the state legislature were the major unwritten items on the agenda early in this round of meetings, and state college resentment of (3) what some termed "dictation" by the foundation was to be a central one at its close.

From now on, the hopes and concerns of the University and the private colleges may seem to fade from the picture. Their representatives were far from inactive, but they were definitely outnumbered. The problems confronting the state colleges began to take priority in part because the following distribution of Committee membership had been agreed to:

Colleges and Universities	
University of Arkansas	1
State Teachers Colleges	2
State Multi-Purpose Colleges (1 Negro)	5
Private Colleges (1 Negro)	7
	—
	15

[25] Neill, J., State educators hesitate about adopting Ford plan. *The Arkansas Gazette,* January 15, 1952.

State Education Organizations

Future Teachers Association	1
Parent Teachers Association	1
Arkansas Teacher Association (Negro)	1
State Department of Education	3
Arkansas Advisory Council on Teacher Education	6
Arkansas Education Association [26]	9
	—
	21
	—
Total	36

Inclusion of the state education organizations which would be affected by any major change in teacher education programs had been suggested by one of the state college presidents; and this man, together with several other college presidents and in consultation with the University's representative, proposed specific representatives. One teachers college president said later of the resultant composition of the Committee, "The teachers college people plus the public [school] people really took it over." [LP] That statement was too strong, but it was not all wrong. While the bulk of the public-school-oriented state education organization representatives tended to defer to *all* the college people, regarding the whole matter as mostly a college "show," they *were* there partly as a counterweight to the University. And, to cite this more militant of the two teachers college presidents again, "The AEA and its affiliates stood by the teachers colleges and voted with us every time." [AV]

Would the University dominate the program?   There were several bases for the state colleges' suspicion of the University's motives in pressing for the fifth-year program. At this particular time, the University carried on all the graduate work in the state—at its own campus, and at extension centers on other state campuses. It was able to accredit this latter work, and also pass on the competence of state college people who might teach in the extension centers. Even if the proposed fifth-year centers were located on various state college campuses and staffed by state college personnel, the University might still be in considerable control of such work. Some feared the University might become able to put state colleges out of the teacher education business at the undergraduate level, whether they wanted to be out or not. And, under-

[26] Representation here was from each of the major AEA divisions, e.g., Association of Classroom Teachers.

graduate work aside, as some of the state college people looked to the future they could see that the fifth-year programs might put a crimp in their own plans for setting up graduate programs. Both in the short and in the long run, then, the colleges' freedom to change curricula at both levels, to assign faculty, and to advise students might all be seriously diminished if the University had too much to say about the whole matter.

The School of Education official (a liberal arts college graduate) who represented the University in the meetings said, later on, that although he and his president had "frequently considered closing down the [University's] training school as a means of decreasing emphasis on professional education," [LP] he had personally felt the internships would probably be more effective in the fourth rather than the fifth year. Although he had been willing to try to reach an agreement on the fifth-year idea, he had never shared the view that the proposed new curriculum was going to replace the old ones completely. Such a view, he said, was "not realistic in a state which is short of teachers, where only 60 per cent had four years of training." [LP]

The University official's frank and cooperative performance in the meetings had reduced some of the concern about University domination, but there were still a lot of people present who remained fearful that, in any event, the University would (1) get the most money from the foundation, (2) get the bulk of tuition payments for the fifth-year work, and (3) get the major credit, in legislative appropriations, for the fifth-year enrollments—even if the work was done outside its own campus. For although the state colleges were historically bitter rivals among themselves for appropriations—so much so that the legislature was then giving each type the same amount of money regardless of size—the University was their ancient mutual antagonist, whose every action was suspect when money was involved. The University president who made the original announcement of the Experiment recalled that in general:

> There was an uneasy truce between us. They looked to the University for leadership but then they didn't follow it. They were always fearful of one another, not only the University, but each other as well. There was an atmosphere of complete suspicion between them. And I guess the one thing they had most in common was the fear that the University would dominate the scene.[LP]

The governor, whose defeat in a bid for re-election in 1953 was regarded by some foundation officials as another serious blow to the
chances for success of the actual AETE project, pointed up the financial aspect of this tradition of rivalry as follows:

> There is always a certain amount of jealousy . . . a fear that the
> University would have too much influence. . . . The basis [of the fear]
> is appropriations. They [the state college people] feel that the University
> gets more than its share of appropriations. They are always revenue-
> starved. It's economic.[AV]

The colleges' jealousy of the University's appropriations was easily
come by: in 1945–49, for example, the latter had got $1,746,800 in
appropriations, slightly more than the total appropriated for all the
other institutions combined (Arkansas Commission on Higher Education, 1951, Part II, p. 176). But autonomy was involved here as well
as economics, as was borne out in an early memo to the Committee
of 36 from the president of one of the state multi-purpose colleges:

> . . . It is recognized that this program must be a state program built
> through the united efforts and most careful thinking of all components
> of our state educational system. A wholesome condition can exist in this
> program only if the program is not subject to the domination of a single
> educational institution or outside agency.
> In whatever program may be developed, adequate safeguards must be
> established to protect the autonomy of the individual colleges and sec-
> ondary schools against the type of regimentation that leads to the stifling
> of institutional initiative. [From document in AETE files.]

Would a plan for centralized state control be revived?   The specter
of a future state legislature rustling its red tape and changing the
clasps on its coffers was summoned up in another way by the state
college presidents in these same spirited sessions. The fear here was
that even if the University did not prove to dominate things, the
proposed program might revive a plan for a centrally controlled system
of higher education which they had just helped lay to rest a few
months before the original announcement of the fifth-year proposal.
The governor sketched the background of this fear as follows:

> At that particular time we were also trying to establish a state board
> which would be the board for all the colleges and [the] University and
> have an integrated and planned educational program for the whole
> state. There was opposition because it was felt that this would be a step

toward your over-all planning commission. That would be more advantageous but I don't know when you'll see it come, because each college is politically autonomous. They are kind of like a state in a way. They don't want to lose any of their sovereignty. . . .

The senators and representatives from those areas: one of their primary jobs is to protect that institution against encroachment. They each did this but they also combined against the University or whatever group [was] getting the upper hand. It is a kind of check and balance. It's got nothing to do with education. It is a logrolling proposition. A pork barrel. That was the big argument for your central board. You assign a special course of instruction and they could teach this exclusively, etc. . . .[AV]

And the prominent editor who supported the fifth-year proposal said of this earlier effort, which he had also strongly favored:

The . . . [Commission recommending the central board] was set up by the Legislature, which was damn sick and tired of the squabbling and jockeying for positions and appropriations. They had [had] a bellyful of that sort of thing.[AV]

The Commission itself, finally, had reported on the history of the whole matter:

Historically, the General Assembly has exercised the principal control over these [state] institutions through its appropriations. Each institution is at present autonomous, operating under a board of trustees fully empowered to conduct its internal and external affairs. There are virtues in this independence. . . . But there are also hazards. There has been a natural tendency for the General Assembly to consider the problems of each institution—and they are usually financial—separately. The institutions, therefore, have had no option but to compete for legislative favors. The result has been a piecemeal approach to appropriations for higher education in Arkansas which has sometimes favored one institution at the expense of the other. (Arkansas Commission on Higher Education, 1951, Part I, pp. 8–9)

Subsequent chapters . . . concern themselves with various elements in the Arkansas higher education scene. They are replete with evidence of intense and sometimes bitter institutional rivalry, of duplication of effort, of program extension motivated by the desire to maintain a strong position in the keen competition for students and funds rather than the needs of the State, of efforts to stake out and protect claims with a view to the enhancement of institutional prestige. (Ibid., Part II, p. 24)

The Commission's formal recommendation had been that the institutions should maintain considerable autonomy in internal matters, but be brought under a single board. Among other things, the board would be empowered to (1) coordinate budgets and budget requests, (2) allot functions among the University and the various colleges, and (3) maintain a continuing study of higher education in the state, with an eye to advising the legislature.

The state college presidents involved in the Commission's study were put in the ambiguous position of recommending a diminution of the powers of the very boards which had employed them. They formally signed the report, but not all actually favored it. And those who were strongly opposed to it ultimately banded together long enough to muster sufficient support in the Assembly to kill it. "The Commission's recommendation," said the *Gazette* editor in a 1956 editorial urging a reconsideration of the Commission's recommendations, "died in the 1951 session, a victory of the very competition among the state institutions which had led the Commission to make it." [27]

Whatever the precise history of the earlier struggle against establishing a central control board, the major point here is that many of these same state college administrators were fearful that, *whatever* they decided about the fifth-year program, the just-buried bones of contention might rise again: if these administrators went along with the University and private college people advocating a state-wide fifth-year program, the coordinating machinery necessary for the new program might naturally serve as an eventual nucleus for a comprehensive state control system; if they didn't go along, the legislature might become alienated enough to force such a system on them anyway.

The latter prospect loomed large at the end of these first sessions, when, after failing to reach agreement on an advance commitment to the fifth-year idea, the Committee of 36 made its first counterproposal to the foundation. This "Proposal A" was essentially a holding action. Its main tenets were described in an interview with one of its principal architects (the state department of education official who had written the previously cited letter to the NCCPS, and had otherwise rallied much of the early opposition):

> That suggestion [Proposal A] started out with the concession that what we would hope to ultimately come out with was a Fifth-Year Pro-

[27] *The Arkansas Gazette*, December 12, 1956. It is interesting to note in this connection that a commission on coordination of educational financing *was* eventually set up by the legislature—in 1961.

gram. It did say, however, that we weren't in a position at the outset to
say [how] professional education ought to be distributed in terms of
quantity of time within the structure of the five-year program, and that
we hoped through an analysis of two or three years—through an exploration of several plans—to find the best balance of general education,
specialized preparation and professional education, and to find the
best time sequence for those. . . .

And so, on January 30, when [the foundation man] was due down
here . . . we had ready for him a plan which had no substance to it as
far as the nature of the program was concerned, but it was a plan of
action. . . .ᴬⱽ

The proposal "had been voted by a majority of the Committee of
36," he went on:

It had been voted by all of the state college people [and] the teachers
college people. It had the support of the public school people. And it
even had some support of the liberal arts people because they saw that by
then they were not going to be able to get any complete overhauling of our
whole programs. . . . Some of them went along with this idea, figuring
that was the only thing they could hope to get out of it. . . .ᴬⱽ

However, Proposal A did not prove to resolve the autonomy issue—
or the others, either—for according to the same somewhat embittered
respondent:

[The foundation man] didn't like the plan. In fact he was very trite.
He was standing at the rostrum . . . there was a table over at the side,
and he tossed it [the Proposal A report] over the table and said, "Of
course the Fund wouldn't be interested in any such thing as this." ᴬⱽ

The University representative coordinating the contacts with the foundation official, with whom he had worked in the experimental general
education program of a northern university many years before, described the situation in these somewhat different terms:

In connection with . . . turning down the request, [the University
man] indicated that he had . . . gone over the report with [the foundation man] ahead of time. [The latter] had had the same reaction which
he displayed at the meeting. . . . They agreed that this was not definite
enough . . . it was just a blank check.ᴸᴾ

The impasse reached on this first counterproposal, in any event, not
only set off the "Arkansas Purchase" charge already discussed but also
accelerated the fear that public display of an inability to get together

would antagonize the state legislature. And, not at all incidentally, it was soon to set off another round of meetings.

Would the foundation "dictate" the program? The still-open prospect of getting money from the foundation was itself a big incentive for the Committee to keep going, and not simply because all the colleges were chronically and competitively short of funds. More particularly, "outside" money would presumably be relatively free from the control of the state legislature, or—in the case of the private colleges, who were still very much interested in getting an agreement and improving their general education work—the control of church or other donor boards. Money from the foundation, in other words, might help bolster the colleges' autonomy, as well as be a means of strengthening their general education work. At least this would be so during the uncertain but presumably lengthy period during which funds would be available—*if* the University didn't control the program too much, *if* the legislature didn't start trying again to set up an over-all state board, and *if* the foundation didn't put too many strings on the money.

The first "big if," fear of University domination, was diminishing at this point, because the University representative was cooperatively yielding leadership in the sessions to the most active representative from the State Department of Education. One college president said of this latter development:

> [One,] we didn't want to have anybody from the University. . . . Two, the SDE was a convenient neutral agency . . . [and this SDE official] was in a strategic position for influencing the state. Three, and probably best of all, [he] had the respect of the people of Arkansas and had a basic integrity which certainly influenced every person involved.[AV]

The second fear, that of the legislature's reviving the plan for centralized control, was intensified by the rejection of Proposal A; this prospect was to be circumspectly lived with and, if possible, stalled off.

It was the third fear, the state colleges' fear that the foundation was not going to prove receptive to anything but a state-wide program very definitely along the lines of the original proposal, that was most prominent now. And mixed with this fear was the strong feeling that the legislature would retaliate on appropriations if an agreement of some kind was not reached.

When the Committee members returned to Little Rock a few months after the abortive effort with Proposal A, a reporter sized up their sentiments this way:

> Efforts would be made to work out the plan with the cooperation of the Fund officials. "It would be embarrassing if we hatched up a plan and dropped it in their laps and they said no. . . . We want a plan we know beforehand they will approve." [28]

All was not to be sweetness and light in the next sessions, however. Attacks and counter-attacks were to be made, not only in the Committee and in the Arkansas press, but in wider orbits of publicity, in and out of professional education. The AACTE, for example, was to distribute to its members twelve thousand copies of the "Arkansas Purchase" resolution for local press release. Said one state college president of the latter action and of the whole final phase of negotiations:

> When we heard [the foundation man's] proposal in January we simply said [the foundation] be damned. So pressure was put on [them] by us from the very beginning. Over and beyond us, the professional journals and other national professional associations got into the picture by putting screws on to them too. [AV]

We cannot deal sufficiently here with the foundation's concern with its own organizational autonomy, but have argued elsewhere that grant-making philanthropic organizations are not as all-powerful as they are often believed to be. [29] The final resolution of the struggle over the original proposal, which is outlined in the next section, would seem to be a case in point.

To summarize the *college* concerns that we have been able to deal with up to now: analysis of the contextual aspects of the educational legitimacy issue revealed the early caution-engendering consequences of the state colleges' relations (1) with the public, from which their students came, (2) with the public schools, public and private colleges, and universities, to which their students went, and (3) with the national and regional accrediting associations which might affect student supply and demand in both directions. On the organizational autonomy issue, similar consequences of the state colleges' historically competitive relations with the University and the state legislature, and their emergent relations with the foundation, have been identified.

But it has also been shown that these colleges, which felt the great-

[28] *The Arkansas Gazette,* March 29, 1952.
[29] Colvard (1961). Cf. Andrews (1956, p. 186) and U. S. Congress (1953).

est threat to their autonomy, were the ones most able to press their concerns in the Committee of 36 and in the larger political environment as well. For the tactics of (1) giving the sympathetic state educational people voting membership, (2) shifting the Committee leadership to the State Department of Education and away from the University, and (3) bringing national professional pressure to bear on the foundation, were imperfect but by no means inconsequential methods for protecting autonomy—methods employed by those who saw themselves as either on the fence or with their backs to the wall on the "advance commitment" issue. And not at all paradoxically, the professional relationships which had engendered educational caution at the times of the first announcement and the University representative's subsequent follow-up tour of the campuses were an important support for political boldness in the subsequent Committee sessions just reviewed.

Economic security

To sketch the major events in the next round of Committee sessions before analyzing them in more detail: this final round—some six months after the original announcement—began in a mixed mood of calm and belligerent resolution, slowly proceeded a long way in the direction of agreement on the original proposal, then nearly broke up altogether. The crisis came when the teachers college president in the vanguard of the fight against an "advance commitment" came in with a "farewell letter," as the detailed document came to be labeled, and strongly threatened to submit it and to withdraw his college from the deliberations.

It quickly developed, however, not only that the other state college leaders wanted participation to be on an "all or none" basis, but also that the dissident president was receptive to their argument, partly because of the prospect of retaliation by the state legislature. After the application of pressure on both scores, and a strong plea by another state college president that "they should not be like children and pick up their marbles and go home," [LP] the pace of negotiations quickened and the final counterproposal was made to the foundation.

Enrollments and the pressure for "all or none." An important basis of the effort to prevent the threatened withdrawal was that colleges considering committing themselves to what was really a "four years plus one" program were likely to lose students to the only college with a four-year program. And, questions of size and prestige aside, student fees were a crucial source of income at all the institutions.

The depth of the state colleges' dependence on student fees, in fact, had been a matter of great concern to the previously cited Commission which recommended a state board:

> All the institutions, from their inception, have operated under severe financial handicaps. While the state has made regular appropriations for each institution, the appropriations have rarely kept pace with their steady expansion. One result has been that the college students of Arkansas have had to bear a large share of the financial burden of operating these institutions. (Arkansas Commission on Higher Education, 1951, Part I, p. 8)

In 1949–50 the percentages of the state colleges' current income received from student fees had ranged from 19.2 to 54.0, with a median of 39.2, very close to the University's percentage: 38.2 (*Ibid.*, Part II, p. 176). Noting that the "original limitations of transportation which had dictated the geographical location of some institutions have long since vanished," and that "all the colleges now gladly accept, if they do not actively recruit, students from any section of the state," (*Ibid.*, Part I, p. 9) the Commission pointed out in particular that students had long since become the major source of funds for college buildings:

> The book value of all existing buildings, exclusive of the medical center . . . amounts to over $28,700,000 while appraised value is approximately $35,900,000. Over the years the contribution of State appropriations to the cost of these buildings has amounted to a total of only $5,582,000—about 19 per cent of book value and 16 per cent of appraised value. Both student housing and educational structures have been financed in the main through student fees pledged against the debt incurred. . . . In some of the institutions all or almost all of the student fees are pledged to bond issues. . . . (Governor's Advisory Committee on Education, 1950, pp. 30–31)

The financial situation contributing so greatly to the pressure for "all or none" was not, however, restricted to the already incurred debts for buildings. At the very time of these negotiations, a state audit had shown that the colleges were actually getting more of their revenue from student fees and other nonlegislative sources (e.g., dining halls and dairies) than from state appropriations:

> Every state institution of higher education except one [one audit incomplete] received more funds last year from outside sources than it did from state tax money. . . . The audits . . . brought into sharp focus the dependence the institutions place on their so-called cash funds.
>
> The cash funds are money received by the schools in fees, for services, from grants and from similar sources. They are spent at the discretion of each school's administration and autonomous boards. Several abortive attempts have been made in past legislatures to bring cash funds under the control of the legislature.[30]

The "cash funds" were not only economically vital; in the absence of an over-all control system they were also an important internal bolster to organizational autonomy. But all the colleges were dependent on them, and when his hand was called, even the president of X College deemed the stakes too high to run the risk of getting out of the game. Actually, as counterpressure was applied, it began to be clear that X's president hoped he would not have to make good his threat. For when the University representative returned to the stalled meeting (as an interviewer reported his feelings later):

> He was . . . much surprised to find that [X's president] and others did not want the possibility abolished, and particularly they seemed not to want to bear the onus of killing it. They wanted the money.[LP]

Said the University representative himself:

> I just invited [the president of X] to take off one day and he refused to go. We finally said, "If that's the way you feel about it, goodbye, and we're glad to have known you." Well, they didn't want to go, and he was made to stay and said, "We can't afford not to go in on this thing, because some of the people are going to ask too many questions."[AV]

Appropriations and the pressure to reach agreement. The State Department of Education official who was now leading much of the effort to bridge the differences and develop another proposal for the foundation pointed up the role of threatened legislative retaliation in the Committee's decision to go ahead and try to reach agreement:

[30] Harris, S. G. Outside income tops state support at all but one college in Arkansas. *The Arkansas Gazette,* January 23, 1952.

Q: Why did you [i.e., the Committee] continue?
A: I think that the potential money value of the thing was the primary reason. This was the year before the '53 Legislature [would meet], and I think none of the state college presidents or deans could afford to pass up this by action on their own. One or two . . . got almost to the point of saying: "Well, let's throw the whole thing out." But no college president relying upon the state's money could afford to be on record as saying, "We're going to pass up this money. . . ." AV

This interpretation of these events was borne out by the governor:

Q: Could you identify some central features of higher education in Arkansas which it's imperative for us to understand?
A: I think it is essential you understand the political origins of these colleges and how they have to fight for their appropriations. . . .
Q: Some people have felt that one of the reasons why some of the educators who were in many ways opposed to the [AETE] program actually went along with it was because they were afraid that if they didn't it would look bad in the legislature. What do you think of that?
A: As a matter of fact we were able to keep people from opposing it openly because of a fear of retaliation on appropriations. Some went along that wouldn't otherwise.
Q: Which ones would fall in that category?
A: Well, your teachers colleges. Both of them. As a matter of fact I had a long conversation with most of them [state college presidents]. I told them that they would be in a poor light to come before the legislature with a big chance for money which they turned down just because of contrariness. AV

Of course what the governor deemed "contrariness," the dissident president of X College tended to see as the defense of professional integrity and organizational autonomy. He had helped lay the groundwork for the "Arkansas Purchase" resolution (see Colvard, 1959, p. 366), which the *Gazette* editor had disparaged as being not only "overheated" and premature but also economically misguided:

. . . If our professional educators are going to stand rumps together and horns out against any critical examination of their internal affairs, how can they expect to obtain public backing for the increased financial support which they usually point to as the only salvation for public education? [31]

And in the previously mentioned letter printed as a full-page advertisement in that same paper, X's president had argued in this vein:

[31] *The Arkansas Gazette*, February 26, 1952.

We welcome this interest in improving teacher education. But let's proceed on the basis of facts, not myths. X and Y are top-ranking colleges, fully accredited by leading associations. They meet standards set for liberal arts colleges and do *not* overstress methods. They *already* tie their teacher education in closely with the public schools. [The foundation man's] analogy with medical education is fallacious. Doctors get professional training *before* their internship.[32]

Still, however he felt professionally, as an administrator X's president was realistic about the problem with the legislature. When interviewed, he said at one point that the major purpose of the Committee of 36 was "not to be too hasty," [LP] and at another:

> They were afraid they couldn't turn down the money when people were talking about millions of dollars and still make a good showing before the legislature. So what they were seeking was to find a way to postpone action while still keeping the offer open until the legislature had adjourned, when if they had to turn it down, they could do it with less disastrous effects so far as the legislative support went.[LP]

With the prospect of legislative retaliation as a club and the foundation money as a carrot, then, the stalled negotiations began rolling again. A state education official said of the decision to keep moving:

> The state college people and the public school people—none of them could afford to stand up and get on record of saying positively, "Let's throw this thing back." Then there was [a] certain amount of human nature operating in the thought that maybe we can work out something [so] that we wouldn't have to lose this [foundation] money.[AV]

And as an interviewer summarized the statements of one of the state college presidents on this general issue:

> A point to which the president returned several times during the interviews was that . . . the opportunity of having several million dollars in a state which needed money as much as Arkansas needed it led people to make compromises which they would not otherwise have made. He did not see these as compromises in principle because he felt that the presidents had not been willing to give up educational programs and the practices in which they were certain they were correct. He did say, however, that they were willing to try out procedures which they might not otherwise have been willing to try out in order to get the money. He pointed out that the major activity among the college presidents, including himself, was trying to find out how to get as much money as possible to improve his school within the framework of the grant.[LP]

[32] *Ibid.,* February 4, 1952.

The compromise proposal.   After a great deal more discussion, and one last unsuccessful effort by X's president to get the Committee to agree on a proposal under which the "fifth year for each participating college" would be "organized and directed by [its] department of education" and guided by "the regulations for the certification of teachers of the State Board of Education" (Colvard, 1959, p. 390), a motion was made and carried which included the following provisions:

1. *That* the 5-year plan . . . be developed as an experimental project . . . as a part of Arkansas' total program of teacher education . . . ;
2. *That* the project be understood to be subject to continuous review with the ultimate object either of establishing [it] . . . as the required program for all prospective teachers, of abandoning it altogether, or of continuing it as a part of the state's program of teacher education;
3. *That* the institutions of the state within the regulations of the State Board of Education reserve the right at any time in the future to make whatever adjustments both in the present program of teacher education and in the experimental program as shall appear to be beneficial to the education of teachers in the state. . . . (Colvard, 1959, p. 391)

As the State Department of Education man, chief architect of this turning–point motion, summed it up less formally:

We came up with a compromise—or what ultimately turned out to be a compromise. . . . I made this proposal: that we send to the Fund an idea, or plan, to put this thing into effect, but we [will] preface this plan by saying that we will not make any commitments about ultimately tearing up our present programs. . . . If the Fund believed strongly enough in the idea, then we would put everything we've got into trying it out and ask the Fund to commit itself to the support of the Experiment.[AV]

The final document ultimately submitted to the Fund six weeks later, as one president present recalled:

. . . was prepared by a large group consideration of small group recommendations and the recommendations were really torn apart and amendments made. . . . They would spend all afternoon discussing a phrase at a time. . . .[LP]

It included verbatim the three provisions cited above, but also the following rationale, reviewing the facts of Arkansas educational life:

At the present time, only slightly over half of Arkansas' teachers hold college degrees. Fewer than half of the state's elementary school teachers have degrees. Although this situation has improved greatly during the past few years, the state will have to continue to supply beginning teachers with less than five years of preparation for as long as they are required, as determined by the State Board of Education. It is not possible, of course, to anticipate how long this will need to be. A conservative estimate would be ten years, unless the General Assembly appropriates enough money to place teachers' salaries in the state at least on a par with those in neighboring states. . . . (Colvard, 1959, pp. 393–394)

After seven months of debate, the original proposal had again been rejected. The big question now was: would the Fund accept the compromise proposal? As far as the Committee was concerned, this last effort was "it." As a state college faculty member described the prevailing mood, "The Committee of 36 had no intention of discussing the matter further. . . ." [LP]

Some were fearful that the foundation wouldn't go along, but those most active in working out the proposal felt it would. Said the University's representative:

Now, let's be realistic about this. They weren't in any shape to turn it down. . . . They'd strung along with this thing and there had been a lot of talk about it. [The University president] had kind of put them over the barrel with his big talk, and they had said, "We're interested in this program," and I just don't think they were in very good shape to run out on us at that stage of the game.[AV]

And said the State Department of Education official:

The Fund actually, I think, was in a position where it had to back our final proposal. By that time it had been soundly chewed by AACTE . . . and a number of professional associations around the country. . . . At the time, we said we were very interested, that we hoped that the Fund is sufficiently interested to finance a trial, but we also held reservations on what we wanted because we needed to have freedom to move in the direction good for the Arkansas colleges. Because of these pressures, I actually don't think that the Fund people were in a position to deny our basic proposal.[AV]
. . . The Committee of 36 and the . . . [initial] proposal . . . [were] practically impossible to get together because Arkansas was just not set up for experimentation, and the Fund was just not set up for social reform. . . .[AV]

The Committee's final proposal *was* accepted. Interviews with various Fund officials, like those with Arkansas educators on all the issues reviewed in this study, showed considerable diversity of opinion about why this decision was made—and, indeed, about the initial impressions and intentions of the earliest (Arkansas and foundation) advocates of the original proposal leading to the Little Rock announcement.

One Fund official who had been actively involved in several stages of the negotiations indicated, for example, that as he saw some of the issues leading up to the eventual decision: (1) a demonstration had been sought because educational research was inherently inconclusive—it was important to try things and evaluate them; (2) controversy was desirable because it stirred people to action (and was inevitable anyway where vested interests were involved), but the AACTE "Arkansas Purchase" resolution had been an irresponsible condemnation of a program which was only in the discussion stages, and had been initiated by Arkansas people; (3) the Fund had been definitely interested in a state-wide program, but would have accepted a proposal which was in keeping with the Fund's educational convictions, even though it did not include all the colleges. But the Fund official most directly involved in the final negotiations on the compromise proposal made it clear that—whatever others might have felt about what had been intended, or about what had been or should have been done—he felt that both Arkansas and the Fund had taken a beating, in the press and in the professional journals as well. In his judgment, something had to be done and a grant should be made.

"No group," said Cooley many years ago, "is a trustworthy critic of its own premises." (1937, p. 728) "Each group," said Easton more recently (in the rest of the theme with which this analysis began), "responds to the actual and anticipated activity from outside itself, and is limited in its actions by the presence, actual or imputed, of these activities." (1953, p. 178)

If the application of national-level criticism and professional pressure increased the probability that the foundation would supply funds for a compromise project, the application of local-level economic pressure increased the likelihood that at least a congruent compromise project would be proposed by the Committee. Actual intercollege pressure for participation to be on an "all or none" basis, together with imputed legislative pressure "to reach agreement," weighed enough against the uneven balance of opinion in the Committee to keep it from permanently swinging the scales toward complete rejection—or complete acceptance—of the original proposal.

Implications

"You cannot completely understand a specific act . . . ," wrote Barnard a few years before the complex course of events traced here was completed, "without knowing all the organizations in which the *act* functioned as a part." (1948, p. 115) Our analysis of the action in Arkansas has fallen short of that sociological ideal, but has come close enough to it to point up the importance of taking into account, in efforts to understand changes in college curricula, the complicated context of professional, political, and economic relationships which officials of academic and philanthropic organizations must ultimately take into account in their own efforts to undertake such changes.

In Capen's vivid imagery:

The internal history of higher education in America is a history of discarded curricula. The abandoned wrecks of curricula once thought to be the perfect vehicle for conveying youth to intellectual maturity and professional competence line the long road that runs back to 1636. (1953, p. 265)

But the Arkansas colleges' decision to try out a new model "demonstrator" without trading in their old vehicles clearly suggests that a strictly internal history of such matters would miss some of the main forces at work. For educational innovation may be stimulated from without as well as from within: by the promise of foundation funds, the threat of legislative fiat, or the prospect of student fees, as well as through the internal hope of educational improvement. It may also be resisted from without as well as from within: by the rallying of colleagues, the manipulation of committees, and the mustering of constituents, as well as through the internal calculation of the merits of competing claims.

The economic situation in Arkansas was extreme, but the colleges coping with it were not unique in being political and economic as well as educational institutions. The scope of the original proposal was unprecedented, but educational legitimacy, organizational autonomy, and economic security are common—and competitive—college concerns. The organizational bonds of cooperation and bones of contention uncovered in this analysis are not absent, just better hidden, where the grass is greener and the ivy thicker. For in our pluralistic society, at least, colleges and grant-making philanthropic foundations alike are "outward bound" organizations. They are affected not only by each other's actions, but by actions undertaken by—or imputed to—a whole host of other organizations in the structure of the larger society.

References

Andrews, F. E. *Philanthropic foundations.* New York: Russell Sage Foundation, 1956.

Arkansas Commission on Higher Education. *State-controlled higher education in Arkansas.* Report of the Commission to the Governor and the General Assembly. Little Rock, Arkansas: The Commission, January, 1951.

Arkansas Experiment in Teacher Education (L. B. Kinney, Ed.). *A report on the Arkansas Experiment in Teacher Education, September, 1960.* Pamphlet (no publisher cited) available from Fund for the Advancement of Education, 1960.

Barnard, C. I. *Organization and management.* Cambridge: Harvard University Press, 1948.

Barnett, H. G. *Innovation: the basis of cultural change.* New York: McGraw-Hill, 1953.

Beaseley, L. R., *et al. Public school information.* Little Rock, Arkansas: Department of Education, 1955.

Bentley, A. F. *The process of government.* Bloomington, Indiana: Principia Press, 1949. (First published 1908.)

Brim, O. G., Jr. *Sociology and the field of education.* New York: Russell Sage Foundation, 1958.

Capen, S. P. *The management of universities.* (O. A. Silverman, Ed.) Buffalo: Foster & Stewart, 1953.

Colvard, R. The foundation and the colleges: a study of organizations, professions and power in the Arkansas Experiment in Teacher Education. Unpublished doctoral dissertation, University of California, Berkeley, 1959.

Colvard, R. Foundations and professions: the organizational defense of autonomy. *Admin. Sci. Quart.* 1961, 6 (2), 167–184.

Colvard, R. Risk capital philanthropy: the ideological defense of innovation. In W. Hirsch & G. Zollschan (Eds.), *Explorations in social change.* Boston: Houghton Mifflin (in press).

Cooley, C. H. The fallibility of scientific groups. In F. V. Calverton (Ed.), *The making of society.* New York: Modern Library, 1937.

Easton, D. A. *The political system.* New York: Knopf, 1953.

Ford Foundation. *Annual report for 1951.* Detroit: The Foundation, 1951.

Governor's Advisory Committee on Education. *Educational program for Arkansas.* New York: Englehardt, Englehardt, Leggett & Cornell, Educational Consultants, 1950.

Herzog, J. D. (Ed.) *Preparing college graduates to teach in schools.* Washington: American Council on Education, 1960.

Krathwohl, D. R. Study of the Arkansas Experiment in Teacher Education. In *The future challenges teacher education,* 11th Yearbook, American Association of Colleges for Teacher Education. Oneonta, New York: The Association, 1958. Pp. 115–122.

Lindsey, T. The Arkansas Experiment in Teacher Education: its assumptions, its purposes and its outcomes. Unpublished Field Study No. 1, Colorado State College of Education, August 1956.

Radcliffe, S. A. Teacher education, fifth-year programs: a selected bibliography. Bulletin No. 9. Washington: U.S. Department of Health, Education and Welfare, Office of Education, 1959.

Selznick, P. *Leadership in administration.* Evanston: Row, Peterson, 1957.

Spalding, W. B. Results of the Arkansas Experiment in Teacher Education. In *The future challenges teacher education,* 11th Yearbook, American Association of Colleges for Teacher Education. Oneonta, New York: The Association, 1958. Pp. 123–131.

Spalding, W. B., & Krathwohl, D. R. A report of the evaluation of the Arkansas Experiment in Teacher Education, 1959. (Mimeographed.) (Copies distributed by Executive Committee of AETE to participating institutions in Arkansas, the libraries of the Universities of Illinois and Oregon, and elsewhere.)

Tawney, R. H. *The acquisitive society.* New York: Harcourt, Brace, 1920.

U.S. Congress, Hearings before the Select (Cox) Committee to Investigate Tax-Exempt Foundations and Comparable Organizations, 82d Congress, 2d Session. Washington: U.S. Government Printing Office, 1953.

Wolfe, D. L. Conflicts in academic commitments to organizational change: a study in the sociology of education. Unpublished doctoral dissertation, University of Oregon, 1960.

Woodring, P. *New directions in teacher education.* New York: Fund for the Advancement of Education, 1957.

CHAPTER 6

Title III and the dynamics of educational change in California schools

DONALD W. JOHNSON

WHETHER or not the National Defense Education Act was inspired by the orbiting of the first Russian Sputnik, there can be little question that the intent of the legislation was to accelerate the development of educational programs suitable for students living in a space age. The selection of science, mathematics, and foreign languages for special emphasis showed that Congress considered education to be an instrument of national policy, and wished to use it to ensure a continuation of America's leadership in science and technology. The foreign language emphasis marked the death knell of isolationism; it was a clear statement that the United States' obligations in the world could be met more effectively by men and women who spoke the language of the people with whom they were to work.

These were the intents behind the provisions of the NDEA. The crucial question remains: what are the actual effects of this legislation, as seen at the local school level? This chapter reports data gathered to answer that question.

THE AUTHOR is Administrative Consultant, Research and Communication, in the Bureau of National Defense Education Act Administration, Department of Education, State of California. The material in this chapter is drawn from Johnson (1963), a study of the effects of Title III of the National Defense Education Act on the schools of California.

California: the Context

The history of our country during the past five years is too well known to need repetition here. What is not so well known, however, is the recent history of California, a state which is now the most populous in the nation. The first great fact of life of the post-World War II era in California has been growth—and more growth. California's population was estimated to be 17,391,000 (Holman, 1963) on January 1, 1963, an increase of 2,932,000 over the 1958 figure. Each day, one thousand automobiles enter the state, to leave it only for vacations or to "visit the folks back home." Subdivisions of a thousand homes are constructed and occupied in a matter of weeks, financed under traditional "G. I." and F. H. A. arrangements, and by California's unique Cal-Vet program.

The concept that California's new population consists of retired Midwesterners seeking sunshine is dispelled by school enrollment data. The 1958–1963 population growth of 2,932,000 represents an increase of 20.3 per cent. The five-year growth in graded student enrollments was 938,614, an increase of 32.4 per cent over the enrollment of 2,898,927 on October 31, 1957 (California State Department of Education, 1963).

California has invested over $1.5 billion from the State School Building Fund to provide classrooms for the added students in the state's approximately 1,600 school districts. These districts range in size from small one-room schools in the Sierra Mountains, which must each have at least five students, according to the state Education Code, to the sprawling Los Angeles Unified School District, which had a graded enrollment of 569,611 on October 31, 1962.

California's school districts not only vary in size, but differ in the grades for which education is furnished. Some districts enroll students for grades one through eight, others for grades one through six, still others provide for kindergarten through grade fourteen, and there are combinations of K–6, K–12, 9–12, 9–14, 7–12, 7–14, and 13–14. There are elementary school districts, union elementary districts, joint union elementary districts, high school districts, unified school districts, and junior college districts. Some of these are city school districts, defined not by geographical location, but by certain powers unique to this type of school district. All are fiscally independent in terms of taxing powers, but the money is disbursed by the office of the local county treasurer.

Superintendents and personnel directors of California's larger school districts spend the spring months traveling from Maine to Missouri recruiting the teachers needed for the classrooms that the state is building. Each year approximately 19,300 teachers (Hurd, 1961) are needed to fill vacancies created by death, retirement, and the construction of additional classrooms. Of these, six to seven thousand must be recruited from other states.

The second great fact of life in California is movement. Each year, 3.5 million persons, one fifth of the population of the state, move from one block to another, one city to another, and one county to another. And each year, one out of every five teachers is new to his teaching assignment for that year.

Thus the growth and mobility of California's population have imposed a burden on its complex and diversified public school system; they have also forced the state to examine its system of higher education as well.

The sixteen state colleges have become an independent system with a separate Board of Trustees, and have adopted a more restrictive entrance policy. The University of California, already the largest in the nation, concurrently planned to establish three more campuses, and has stiffened its entrance requirements too. The competition for available spaces in the state colleges and the five campuses of the University of California has forced the high schools to place more emphasis upon their college preparatory programs. A conservative movement, referred to as "The Challenge from the Right," resulted in the appointment of a Citizens Advisory Commission by the Joint Interim Committee of the California Legislature on August 22, 1958. The report of this Commission (Joint Interim Committee, 1961) made sweeping recommendations for the restructuring of school programs.

California and Title III

In this context, the Superintendent of Public Instruction moved to develop plans to implement the National Defense Education Act. The

California State Plan[1] for the administration of Title III was submitted to the United States Office of Education only two months after President Eisenhower signed the bill in late 1958. Each applicant for matching funds to purchase equipment and materials was requested to answer each of the following questions:

1. What is your present program?
2. What changes do you propose to make?
3. What equipment and materials do you need to implement your plans?
4. How will you provide teachers with necessary in-service education?
5. How will you determine if your program was improved?

During the first four years of the operation of the Act (1958–1962), California school districts requested $14,427,022 in federal funds, and received approvals totaling $10,861,657. In the first three years of the program (1958–1961), 887 school districts in California, enrolling 81.1 per cent of the total average daily attendance of the state, received approvals. Districts operating elementary schools submitted approximately 50 per cent of the approved projects; districts operating high schools submitted approximately 40 per cent, and districts operating junior colleges submitted approximately 10 per cent of the approved projects.

More than one half (56.9 per cent) of the approved projects have been in science, 24.3 per cent in foreign languages, and 14 per cent in mathematics; 4.8 per cent of the projects included more than one subject area.

Section 302(b) of Title III allocated federal money for the expansion or improvement of supervisory and related services, and the administration of the Act. The funds thus made available have been used in California to finance the administration of the program, to add consultants in the Division of Instruction in the Department of Education, and to employ consultants to work with school districts on a per diem basis. There were 137 projects for consultant service approved during the fiscal years 1960 and 1961, making 1,697 man-days of service available to school districts and offices of county superintend-

[1] The common term used to identify the *State Plan for Financial Assistance for Strengthening Instruction in Science, Mathematics, and Modern Foreign Language under Sections 301–304 Inclusive of Title III of P.L. 85–864—Amended.* It was approved by the U.S. Office of Education on February 9, 1959.

ents. During fiscal 1962, an additional 1,163 man-days of such service were provided.

The Study of Title III

In April, 1961, the California State Department of Education initiated an evaluation of Title III of the National Defense Education Act to determine its effect on the schools in California, and to obtain information needed to improve its administration of Title III.

Responsibility for the direction of the study was given to the writer. Wilbur Schramm, Director of the Institute for Communication Research, Stanford University, was employed as technical consultant. An advisory committee representing school districts and offices of county superintendents of schools assisted in developing the procedures and questionnaires used.

As a result of the advisory committee's recommendations, all school districts which participated under Title III were asked to complete a questionnaire. It was designed to obtain information regarding changes in their school districts, the extent and nature of the influence of Title III on these changes, and recommendations for improvement in state administration.

The offices of the 58 county superintendents of schools assisted in the distribution of the questionnaires during the fall of 1961. By April 1, 1962, 1,507 usable questionnaires had been received by the Department, describing the effects of 98.8 per cent of approved Title III projects. The 877 school districts responding had 80.2 per cent of the average daily attendance of California schools.

The questionnaires were coded and the responses tabulated with data processing equipment. Analysis of the responses showed internal consistency: administrators reporting (by rating) the greatest extent of change in their instructional programs and organization also reported the largest number of specific changes in their reports.

An analysis of the characteristics of school districts which participated under Title III of the National Defense Education Act in California revealed that participation varied directly with the size of the district, directly with the level of the school (using grade levels taught as an index), and inversely with its wealth. Geographical closeness to major population centers also resulted in increased participation.

Sixty-five per cent (approximately $10 million) of the expenditures approved under Title III was for specialized equipment and materials suitable for instruction in science, mathematics, and modern foreign languages. Twenty-five per cent ($3,850,000) was invested in basic audio-visual equipment and room darkening. Only two per cent of the total of slightly more than $15 million was used for remodeling of existing classrooms.

Changes in instructional programs

Five out of six administrators responding felt that significant changes had taken place in their instructional programs, and two out of three felt that these changes in program had brought about equally significant changes in the organization for instruction within their schools.

The extent of change in the instructional programs of California's schools is shown in Table 1.

Table 1. Reported Changes in Instructional Programs, by Educational Level and Subject Area *

GRADE LEVEL AND SUBJECT AREA	N	PER CENT OF RESPONSES FOR EACH DEGREE OF CHANGE				No Answer (N)
		Great	Considerable	Some	Very little or not at all	
Elementary						
Science	470	3.0	23.6	59.0	14.4	4
Mathematics	141	2.9	8.5	67.9	20.7	1
Foreign Lang.	139	35.4	23.1	30.0	11.5	9
Secondary						
Science	281	4.7	17.2	56.5	21.6	8
Mathematics	113	2.8	11.3	53.8	32.1	0
Foreign Lang.	199	9.4	35.2	41.8	13.6	0
Junior College						
Science	84	4.8	16.9	63.9	14.4	1
Foreign Lang.	36	7.9	28.9	52.7	10.5	0

* 44 responses were not suitable for use in this summary, 12 in junior college mathematics and 32 covering more than one subject area.

Although the extent of change in organization was not as great as that in the instructional program, Table 2 indicates substantial amounts of reported change here as well.

Table 2. Reported Changes in Organization for Instruction, by Educational Level and Subject Area *

| GRADE LEVEL AND SUBJECT AREA | N | PER CENT OF RESPONSES FOR EACH DEGREE OF CHANGE | | | | |
		Great	Considerable	Some	Very little or not at all	NO ANSWER (N)
Elementary						
Science	470	5.0	13.8	40.8	40.4	7
Mathematics	141	1.4	11.3	51.4	35.9	0
Foreign Lang.	139	34.9	19.4	24.8	20.9	10
Secondary						
Science	281	3.3	15.3	44.0	37.4	6
Mathematics	113	1.9	16.5	46.6	35.0	10
Foreign Lang.	199	5.3	14.9	43.3	36.5	12
Junior College						
Science	84	1.2	20.0	45.9	32.9	0
Foreign Lang.	36	2.8	13.9	69.4	13.9	0

* 44 responses were not suitable for use in this summary, 12 in junior college mathematics and 32 covering more than one subject area.

The changes reported by California school districts indicate that a revolution is taking place, characterized by increased specialization of assignment of teachers, the development of specific instructional programs for groups of students with identifiable special characteristics, and applications of new technology. The specific changes reported in each subject area at each level of education are summarized here.

Elementary science.   Much greater emphasis is now being placed on science in the elementary schools of California. This emphasis, in general, has taken the form of scheduling science as a separate class with additional time, and an emphasis on problem solving and concept formation. Content has been added, primarily in the physical sciences, including space science. Many school districts reported the development of courses of study with specific allocation of content to specific grade levels.

To provide more skilled science teachers, districts departmentalized programs in the 7th and 8th grades, organized for cooperative teaching in the lower grades, and employed supervisors and consultants.

Ability grouping of various kinds, science clubs, and accelerated programs provided for the more able students.

Elementary mathematics. California administrators reported that they were waiting to see the direction which new mathematics programs would take. Districts used experimental mathematics programs on a pilot basis, conducted in-service programs in newer mathematics, and increased their emphasis upon mathematical relationships. Manipulative materials were used more in the primary grades, and a few mathematics laboratories were equipped for 7th and 8th grade classes. Some districts solved the problem of providing more expert instruction through departmentalization. Ability grouping to provide for more able students had also increased.

Elementary foreign language. Enrollment in foreign language classes had increased tremendously during the period 1958–1961, but administrators reported that this instruction had been only moderately effective in many cases. Most districts selected Spanish, with emphasis upon conversational skill, but there was little agreement as to the grade in which instruction was to start, the role of the classroom teacher in this instruction, or the time to be devoted to it.

One school district reported the initiation of foreign language instruction through televised programs, and found enthusiastic responses during the first few months of the program. During the second year, however, the enthusiasm of teachers had waned, the students found it impossible to keep up with the televised instruction, and the entire program was dropped.

Districts employing special teachers who spoke the language well reported significant success. If the school district depended solely upon television instruction, the program was considered to be ineffective. The consensus of the reports received by the Department suggests that television, programed instruction, and tapes and records are only supplements to a competent teacher, and cannot provide students conversational fluency and accuracy in a particular language.

High school science. The reported changes in science instruction in California's high schools included tremendous expansion of laboratory facilities and programs, adoption of problem solving and discovery techniques of instruction, addition of content to existing courses, establishment of advanced courses, and adoption or adaptation of national science programs such as PSSC physics, CHEM chemistry, and BSCS biology. Districts have provided additional preparation time for teachers, and established departmental organization to provide administrative service to teachers. Combined with accelerated programs for college preparatory students was the development of science courses for terminal students.

High school mathematics. The most unusual change in high school mathematics combined two or more courses. An example is "Algeo," a combination of algebra and geometry. The change in emphasis from computational drill to understanding the structure of mathematical systems dictated this reorganization. Much experimentation with newer mathematical programs has taken place, the SMSG program being used more than any other.

There has been an increase in the number and variety of mathematics classes, and a similar increase in students enrolled. Increased variety of program, and specialization of course offerings, has resulted in further specialization by teachers; students thus have opportunities to pursue accelerated programs or to spend greater time in mastering basic mathematical skills.

High school foreign language. The reports indicated that foreign language programs in California high schools now emphasize conversational fluency as one of the major objectives. One result has been the adoption of the language laboratory as an essential tool of instruction. This shift in emphasis is also considered to be partly responsible for the rapid increase in enrollments in foreign language classes, such enrollment increasing at a rate almost double that of the student population increase. Part of the growth in enrollments has occurred as a result of the addition of other languages to the course of study, and the provision of additional years of instruction.

Increased use of technology has required the employment of laboratory assistants in the language laboratory, and the provision of increased time for the preparation of instructional materials (tapes) by the teacher. Some districts have provided this time by reducing the number of periods of instruction, while others employ language teachers during the summer months. Articulation with elementary schools and with the colleges continues to be a pressing problem.

Junior college science. Junior college science programs are even more highly specialized than those in high schools, resembling in many ways those in four-year colleges. The major trends in junior college science have been in the development of more modern classes, the addition of higher-level programs to accommodate the accelerated students being received from the high schools, an increase in the amount of laboratory time required of students, and increased specialization and complexity of departmental organization.

Junior college foreign language. Junior colleges in California have adopted audio-lingual teaching of foreign languages, and have installed language laboratories to facilitate this instruction. The result has been a significant change in emphasis and methods of instruction, and the employment of additional staff in language departments to supervise the laboratories, prepare necessary material, and provide for individual student practice. The emphasis on audio-lingual skills has also resulted in increased attention to listening ability in admitting students to foreign language classes.

Title III and teacher competency

Powers of generalization, the development of analytical tools, and a demand for higher levels of performance on the part of students are consistently emphasized as objectives of the newer programs. These programs require teachers of great knowledge and skill. There has therefore been considerable expenditure of time and money under Title III for in-service programs for teachers.

To determine whether teachers were more capable and more effective, administrators were asked to indicate the extent to which they judged that teachers were more effective. Five out of six administrators in the state felt that the teachers in their schools were significantly more effective as directors of classroom instruction. One out of fourteen felt that the effectiveness was shown in "almost all" techniques of instruction; one out of three saw it in "many" techniques, and two out of five in "some" techniques of instruction.

The questionnaire also asked administrators to judge the relative importance of eight factors generally considered to be of significance in affecting the quality of the classroom teachers in a district. These factors were: (1) quality of teacher preparation before employment; (2) recruitment and selection practices; (3) local in-service programs; (4) National Defense Education Act college and university programs; (5) workshops and conferences; (6) locally produced curriculum guides; (7) the availability of new media (television, audio-visual equipment and materials, etc.); and (8) improved teacher attitudes. Each respondent was asked to rate each of the eight factors as of "very great importance," "considerable importance," "moderate importance," "slight importance," or "little or no importance." For analysis, these responses were weighted from 5 through 1 respectively; Table 3 shows the results.

Table 3. Factors Relating to Teacher Effectiveness, as Rated by 1,507 Administrators of California School Districts

Factor	Mean weighted score
Quality of teacher preparation	4.20
NSF and NDEA college and university programs	4.18
Improved teacher attitudes	4.13
Recruitment and selection practices	3.90
New media of instruction	3.85
Local in-service programs	3.45
Locally produced curriculum guides	3.15
Workshops and conferences	2.98

Although this question provided only an approximation of the opinions of administrators responding, analysis of the weighted score is of some value. The factor considered by the respondents to be the most important in achieving improved effectiveness of the teaching staff was the pre-service preparation of their teachers. Following this factor closely were the college and university programs financed by the National Science Foundation and the National Defense Education Act. Many secondary school administrators in California reported that the National Science Foundation institutes had been "the greatest impetus for change in the history of education."

The third most important factor was the changed attitudes of teachers in science, mathematics, and foreign languages. The selection of these content areas by Congress for special attention appears to have given teachers in these fields a sense of importance. Institute programs for teacher training and the development of national curriculums have also contributed to this change in attitudes. In addition, many of the teachers were, for the first time, able to obtain an adequate amount and quality of classroom equipment. It is difficult to tell which of these factors was most important in changing teacher self-concepts, but the evidence suggests that the role of national programs in these content fields was a leading one.

The relatively lower importance (averaging "moderate") which administrators attach to local in-service programs, curriculum guides and courses of study, and workshops and conferences deserves greater attention than this study could give. The fact that the short-term consultant program under Section 303(a)(5) which provided outstanding experts to work with districts and teachers has been successful does not contradict this evaluation of local programs.

Rather, it supports the observation that the success of any in-service program is dependent upon the competence of the leadership in the substantive content of the subject. The great changes which have taken place in the content of science and mathematics have made it extremely difficult for school districts to provide leadership in these areas from within their own staffs.

Title III and student achievement

The judgments of administrators regarding their teachers were just that—judgments. The reports concerning the extent of pupil achievement in science, mathematics, and modern foreign languages were similarly based upon subjective judgment.

The questionnaire asked respondents to indicate the extent to which they felt student achievement had improved during the time in which their Title III projects had been in operation. Nine out of ten felt that significant improvement had been made in student achievement in the three subject fields financed under Title III. These judgments were considered to be significant, for the instructional changes reported had attempted to provide students with greater understanding of function and relationship in science and mathematics, and with an increased ability to perform independently of direct teacher supervision. Although pupil achievement in elementary foreign language programs was reported to be poor, the high schools and junior colleges submitted judgments of significant achievement by their students in conversational skills. They reported that the ability to converse in a foreign language had not adversely affected the students' mastery of grammar, vocabulary, and reading of a foreign language.

Yet very few districts had developed an adequate objective evaluation of the programs in science, mathematics, and modern foreign language. Two out of three reports from school districts contained no objective data regarding pupil achievement. Of the one in three that did include objective information, less than 30 per cent included test data. The balance of the objective information was limited to enrollment figures, library circulation figures, or data regarding participation in science fairs, science projects, and after-school science clubs.

Of the 1,507 usable responses in the study, only 68 gave an affirmative response to the question, "Have you evaluated any of the changes you have instituted by means of scientifically designed and controlled research?" When these 68 responses were analyzed in terms of meeting the usual requirements of "scientifically designed and controlled research," less than 10 of the 68 qualified. Thus less than half of 1 per cent of the responses described a clinical attempt to evaluate the effectiveness of a changed program.

Many administrators reported that adequate evaluation of their program changes had been very difficult. Adequate evaluation was inhibited, they felt, by the lack of adequate supervisory and administrative staff capable of conceiving, administering, and interpreting an evaluation program. A second factor was the lack of suitable tests designed to measure the changed objectives of changed instructional programs. The lack of standardized tests forced the use of teacher-made tests to assess the extent to which students had achieved the new goals. Thus it was impossible to compare the results from one classroom to another, or from one district to another. Thirdly, many districts reported that insufficient time had elapsed since the introduction of the changed program to determine the effect of the changes. Thus they desired to postpone evaluation until they felt teachers had become effective in the use of the materials and techniques.

The results of this study of Title III corroborate in many ways

Brickell's findings on evaluation (as reported in the present book) in his analysis of educational innovation in New York State. In California, as in New York, evaluation of educational change has been made largely on the basis of student reactions as observed by teachers.

Thus we have at least two apparent contradictions in the data received by the Department: considerable improvement in instructional programs, teacher competency, and student achievement was reported, in spite of the facts that (1) in-service programs often could not be carried out, or were considered to be of little relative value, and (2) program evaluations were not completed.

The dynamics of change

Traditional curriculum change processes involve the following steps: (1) the evaluation of an existing program with the use of standardized achievement tests identifies specific content or skills which students are not mastering; (2) research literature is reviewed to determine if more effective methods should be used to teach students the needed content or skills; (3) a revised course of study and teacher guides are developed, incorporating the modifications suggested by the research; (4) additional equipment and materials needed for these modified instructional techniques are acquired; (5) in-service training meetings are conducted by administrative and supervisory staff in the use of the new equipment; (6) the new program is introduced to the classrooms.

We have noted that school districts reported they were unable to complete their in-service plans, or to conduct adequate evaluation of either existing or changed programs. Thus the changes and improvements reported did not occur within the traditional boundaries of curriculum change. Then by what process was the improvement achieved?

The answer to this question seems to depend on the number of teachers involved in program change. For example, in high schools where only a small number of teachers were involved in a physics program, the process of change was effected by (1) sending one or two teachers to a summer institute or workshop; (2) providing consultant help to insure that the resulting experimental course was being taught as specified by the institute; (3) having the experimental and other physics teachers meet frequently during the year; (4) gaining approval from the board of education to continue experimentation for a second year; (5) submitting an NDEA project for equipment and consultant help; (6) holding a workshop of three to seven weeks for physics teachers; and (7) having all physics teachers institute the new program with constant consultant help.

On the elementary level, almost 50 per cent of schools in California reported that they were having extreme difficulty with their in-service programs. The large number of teachers to be trained, and the inability of administrative and supervisory staff to provide effective leadership in the substantive content of new programs made formal in-service work relatively ineffective, according to the administrators. In these cases, an informal approach, which used equipment and materials as devices to motivate teachers to obtain necessary in-service training (at their own expense and on their own time), appeared to be more effective. Administrators reported that they could not institute program change uniformly among all the teachers in a district because teachers, like students, were motivated by different forces and would develop their knowledges and skills at varying tempos and in varying ways.

The process in many of these districts, centering around the provision of equipment and materials, appeared to be cyclical. Regardless of the care exercised in any one selection, the equipment purchased was subject to criticism. This criticism was expressed by rejection of new equipment and materials, or by stated preference for items other than those furnished. These critical attitudes were communicated to principals and district administrators. After a certain amount of intercommunication, additional purchases of equipment and materials were made, based upon the recommendations of the dissident teachers. These teachers then accepted the responsibility for obtaining skills needed to use the additional equipment and materials, often through self-financed extension and summer school courses. The equipment and materials were introduced to the classroom, further informal evaluation of equipment needs and instructional techniques took place, and another cycle of change was instituted.

The three main aspects of this informal change process appeared to be (1) increased depth of involvement by the individual teacher, (2) increased numbers of teachers included, and (3) enrichment in the quantity and quality of instructional equipment and materials made available to teachers and students.

It is impossible to tell how many years it would take to involve all teachers in a school district with such a process. It appears that the time required would be in proportion to the number of teachers affected and the amount of change desired. The approach described as appropriate at the high school level involved only a few teachers, but took a three-year period to complete.

District plans for further change

Administrators in California school districts had extensive plans for further improvement of their instructional programs. More than half of the responses mentioned plans for the purchase of additional equipment and materials and the construction of laboratory facilities for science and modern foreign languages. Continuation and expansion of in-service education programs were to occupy the attention of one administrator in three. Almost all of the respondents anticipated continued or additional program and organizational changes; one in seven hoped to evaluate their changed programs.

Many problems faced districts as they moved forward in improving and strengthening their programs. The most common problem (mentioned by 24 per cent of respondents) [2] was the shortage of money. Next in order of frequency (16 per cent) was the lack of consultants and administrative staff to conduct in-service programs. Closely related to the second problem, and ranking third in order of frequency (14 per cent) was difficulty in obtaining teachers capable of effective instruction in the changed science, mathematics, and modern foreign language programs.

For this reason, the service most frequently requested from the state Bureau of NDEA Administration was increased consultant services, under Section 303(a)(5) of Title III, for the conduct of in-service training programs. Two out of every three questionnaires requested consultant service, for in-service programs, assistance in developing courses of study, and help in evaluation.

Effects on the school as a whole

The most frequent criticism of categorical aid programs is that they create an imbalance in the local school, and thus detrimentally affect the program as a whole. The Department of Education was concerned about the validity of this criticism, and sought information from re-

[2] The percentages show the proportion of the 1,507 respondents mentioning each particular problem; most respondents, of course, mentioned several problems. This also holds true for the percentages presented below in the section on effects (of NDEA) on the school as a whole.

spondents as to the effects of Title III on programs in nonsupported subject areas.

The responses indicated that, on the whole, other subject areas were benefited by a district's participation under Title III of the National Defense Education Act. The benefit most frequently referred to (by 360 respondents, or 24 per cent of the returns) was the spare time use of audio-visual equipment in other subjects. The emphasis upon improvement brought about by NDEA stimulated a "climate for quality" in the schools (19 per cent), strengthened curriculum development processes in the district through the appraisal of existing programs (14 per cent), and improved organization for curriculum development within the school unit (12 per cent). Twelve per cent made reference to the development of instructional techniques through NDEA-supported programs which were utilized by teachers in other content areas. Increased and more effective cooperation—between school districts, offices of county superintendents of schools, colleges and universities, and the State Department of Education—was reported by 8 per cent of the respondents. In addition, there were 322 references to other results that strengthened all the instructional activities of the district.

Estimates of unfavorable effects of NDEA on other subject areas were also invited. Those most referred to were overloading of administrators and supervisory staffs (5 per cent) and creation of the feeling that money had been taken from other areas of the curriculum (6 per cent). There were a few references to the creation of staff jealousies as a result of selecting certain subject areas (3 per cent) and to the feeling that supervisory time had been reduced in other areas (3 per cent).

No specific details were submitted in support of these reported favorable or unfavorable effects—but there is no reason to believe that the feelings do not have sound bases.

In general, then, most school districts in California felt that the National Defense Education Act had been a stimulus for program improvement in all areas of the curriculum, and that its favorable effects far outweighed any unfavorable effects.

Title III—resource or stimulus?

One of the questions which must be asked about the basic impact of a program like NDEA is: Has it primarily assisted in the completion and implementation of plans already in existence, or mainly stimulated new plans among the districts? An area of concomitant questions, only partially answered above, deals with peripheral effects on evaluation, in-service education, and other subject-matter areas.

Districts were asked to respond to questions asking in which of these three broad areas Title III had been most effective. Their responses indicated that in approximately 85 per cent of the cases Title III had assisted them in the completion of plans which existed prior to the passage of the Act; in 90 per cent of the cases it had stimulated the development of new plans. Thus most school systems were encouraged *both* to complete old plans, and to develop new ones. Comparatively speaking, Title III appears to have had only a marginal effect on district evaluation of programs, local in-service education activities, and spillover into other content areas.

Successes and failures: a summary

This study of the effects of Title III of the National Defense Education Act on school districts in California attempted to determine in what ways Title III had effected program change in the school districts. In general, Title III seems to have been successful in the following respects: (1) It has made it possible for more students to be educated in science, mathematics, and modern foreign languages. (2) It has improved the quality of teacher training in science, mathematics, and modern foreign languages. (3) It has directly aided the implementation of prior plans for curriculum improvement, and it has initiated new thinking and planning. (4) It has been part of a general pattern of change in science, mathematics, and modern foreign languages which touches program, organization, instructional facilities, pupil achievement, and teacher effectiveness. (5) It has assisted in financing the purchase of additional equipment and materials. (6) It has provided expert consultant assistance to school districts. (7) It has helped create a climate for increased emphasis on science, mathematics, and modern foreign languages. (8) It has assisted offices of county superintendents of schools to provide more effective coordination services. (9) It has provided resources at the state level for program development. (10) It has achieved its results without adversely affecting other subject areas (on the contrary, it has contributed to the improvement of instruction in other subjects).

On the other hand, Title III of the National Defense Education Act was unsuccessful in providing for the development of improved evaluation procedures and techniques, or in the stimulation of research and experimentation.

It also appears that Title III has encouraged many school districts to start curriculum improvement activities which they could not complete. For example, one large school district reported:

> This program has failed because of several factors: (1) Our assumption that teachers untrained in foreign language could teach by tapes was shown to be false. (2) Trying to make the program effective without a core of trained consultants is not being realistic. (3) Finding the needed time to make progress in the language is a difficult problem.

The problems reported by school districts indicated that they did not possess sufficient staff to develop new programs, provide necessary in-service training, or evaluate changes produced. This leads to the conclusion that present staffing patterns in the state are related to the maintenance of an existing program, and are inadequate for the development and implementation of new programs.

Title III and constructive change

If one uses the steps of program design, evaluation, and dissemination as defined and used by Brickell (1961), it becomes apparent that Title III of the National Defense Education Act in California has basically served the purposes of program dissemination. It has been effective in motivating district administrators to change. The provision of matching funds for the acquisition of equipment and materials needed for new programs has reached administrators of school districts enrolling over 80 per cent of the students of California. The consultants employed under Section 303(a)(5) of the Act, however, have been only partially successful in their attempts to provide teachers in the state with the additional knowledge in content areas and the instructional skills necessary for new programs.

These program dissemination activities were considered to be successful in the case of science programs developed by national curriculum groups and supported by extensive institute programs for training teachers. In those cases where adequate program development did not exist, and where institute programs for teachers were not available, Title III has initiated change with little evidence that such change was either constructive or orderly.

Title III was an experiment in educational legislation. As in any other experiment, failure of the program was possible, and identification of its partial successes and failures was a necessary step towards improvement.

The evidence obtained indicates that, on the whole, the experiment was a success. Title III has had a dramatic impact on educational programs in California. It has increased the emphasis upon science, mathematics, and modern foreign languages, and increased the time devoted to these subject areas in the public schools of the state; it has added greatly to the amount of content which students now master; it has provided for greater attention to individual needs of students, permitting the able and the slower student each to move at his own pace; it has improved the abilities of the teachers in these subjects; and it has changed the purposes of instruction to reflect modern needs more faithfully.

Guides for the Future

Some legislative principles

From the information obtained by the Department of Education in this study, it is possible to draw some generalizations and to develop some principles regarding incentive legislation.

The first and most important finding of the study can be worded as follows:

> Relatively rapid and dramatic improvement of educational programs can be achieved by legislation which provides matching funds for the purchase of equipment and materials at the local level, and for expanded activity in program development and in-service training of teachers.

Until the National Defense Education Act, there had been no attempt to improve a broad segment of public education through an incentive program. Previous federal legislation in the field had been limited to areas involving relatively few teachers in highly specialized areas, such as agriculture and vocational education. NDEA had the potential of affecting the educational progress of every student in the public schools of the United States. Its success suggests that similar programs can be developed in any content area that needs significant improvement and modernization.

State legislatures may, with equal certainty, move forward to initiate program improvement without waiting for federal action. The essential nature of incentive legislation lies in rewarding, with assistance in the acquisition of equipment and materials necessary for strengthened programs, the school districts whose administration and school board devote their energies and resources to improved educational practices.

Should the state government or the federal government desire to provide such incentive legislation, the five principles set out on the following pages, derived from California's experience with the National Defense Education Act, should guide the writers of the law.

1. Participation in an incentive program should require commitment to the program through financial participation of the applicant agency (whether state or local school district) to the extent of its realistic abilities.

Although additional financial resources may assist a school district in educational improvement, such resources cannot take the place of the will of its staff to improve. In the absence of such desire, the provision of additional money may even prove to be a deterrent. For this reason, the granting of money to a district to improve its educational program must be contingent upon tangible evidence of its desire for change. The most appropriate index of such desire is the commitment of financial resources to the program.

2. The legislation should be broadly written, specifying the intent as clearly as possible, but leaving to each participating unit the right to structure its administration of programs to meet the unique organizational pattern of its area.

The fifty states in the United States have many patterns for administration of public education. In some, the county is the basic administrative unit; in others, local school districts vary greatly in size and resources; in others, the state department of education is the sole service agency to the local units; and in still others, the state agency is supplemented with intermediate units which provide some of the services generally delegated to state departments of education.

The present National Defense Education Act is successful in eliminating criticism of federal domination through its provision for the submission and approval of state plans for the administration of the Act. However, certain technical requirements, such as the provision that all personnel providing service under the supervisory and related services section of the Act shall be employees of the state, violate the intent of the Act, which was to improve the educational leadership of the state agency. In states such as California, where the office of the county superintendent of schools has a long history of effective service to local school districts, restricting the expenditure of supervisory funds to the state agency is an arbitrary and unwise provision of law. The California Department of Education has shown, in its administration of Title III, that it is possible to provide for the unique needs of almost nine hundred school districts which have submitted over four thousand individual requests for financial assistance since the passage of the Act. It is certainly possible that the U. S. Office of Education, with only fifty state plans to review, could insure compliance with the intent of the Act.

> 3. A portion (up to 10 per cent) of the incentive funds should be reserved for reallocation to participating states and districts for program development and program evaluation in the content field.

Program development and program evaluation are necessary adjuncts to incentive legislation. Education has not yet reached the point where all questions are answered and there is a predetermined "best" program. Few school districts possess the resources necessary to conduct depth research programs to test the effectiveness of changed programs of instruction. Since it would be uneconomic, as well as unnecessary, to provide all school districts with these resources, selected districts should be assisted in this evaluation. Thus each state should be provided moneys for the purpose of field testing new instructional programs in a scientific manner.

In addition, any incentive program, if it is successful, institutes a cumulative process of change. Science programs in California, for example, have just begun to reflect the total change which is the potential of the National Defense Education Act. As the elementary students in the state master the additional content now provided in the grades, it will be necessary to devise new and strengthened secondary science programs. These again will be reflected by continual change at the junior college and college levels. During the time that a student proceeds from kindergarten to college, continual program development and experimentation will be necessary if he is not to be doomed to repeat studies he has already mastered.

4. Both summer and academic year institutes should be provided for teachers in content areas, operated by institutions of higher education, at which attendance is limited to those teachers who have the endorsement of their employing district. The endorsement should provide for specific plans to use the teacher in a leadership role in the employing district upon his completion of the institute.

The summer and academic year institutes financed by the National Science Foundation and the National Defense Education Act have been considered to be the greatest single force for curriculum change by some administrators in California. The significance seen in this program by administrators and teachers in the state is indicated by the frequent use of the word "awarded" in identifying teachers attending such institutes. One of the values of the institute program is the status it gives to its participants. Secondly, participants are paid for attending, a recognition of the importance of the task to which the teacher has been called and a reminder of society's stake in its successful completion. A third value is that the quality of instruction at these institutes has been high, and the content unique; participants have an educational opportunity otherwise unavailable. The only currently observed weakness in the program is that participation by a teacher is not based on his contractual relationship with an operating unit of public education. Effective use of the returning participant by the local school district is therefore not structured into the administration of the program. If the institute approach is to match its success in all districts with its success in some, this planned use of the trained teacher is a necessity.

The many reports received by the Department which contrasted the effectiveness of National Science Foundation institute programs with local in-service programs leads one to believe that most local programs do not provide sufficient time for the achievement of the desired result, are generally scheduled at a time least conducive for effective learning (i.e., at the close of the school day), and are conducted by individuals with less than desired competency in the substantive content to be learned.

5. Incentive programs should be continuing in nature, since they do not reach their full potential until an entire school generation has completed its formal education.

Since change is cumulative and continuous, the incentive for change should also be cumulative and continuous. Reference has been made to the fact that content is being taught at earlier grades than previously, and thus each succeeding higher grade is continually forced to revise its offerings to challenge the student and avoid repetition. Inasmuch as program change requires different items of equipment and materials, improved competency on the part of the teacher, and the development of different instructional skills, the incentive and reward for making such change should be provided for an indefinite period of time.

Some administrative principles

In the administration of incentive programs at the state level, certain general guides for action were similarly derived from California's experience with the law and from the evaluations and recommendations submitted by respondents of the study. Among the principles thus identified three have sufficient importance to be reported here.

1. Incentive money for the purchase of equipment and materials must be administered as a *curriculum* program, with equipment and materials related to specific instructional use.

In a period when the actual content and techniques of teaching in a subject area are undergoing continuous change, there is no one list of equipment and materials which is suitable for any one grade level for any period of time. If this statement is true, then considerations of economy dictate that a specific planned use be described for any proposed purchase. Consideration of flexibility demands that each school district be provided freedom to proceed on this process of change at its own rate.

Considerable evidence has been accumulated suggesting that the effectiveness of instruction is directly related to the tools provided the teachers. These tools are the equipment and materials used in the classroom, determining not only what is studied but, in many cases, the manner in which it is taught. For this reason, the selection of equipment and materials is a curricular decision which must be made at the operational level—namely, that of the school district.

2. A significant portion of the moneys made available for state supervisory and related services should be reserved for the employment of part-time consultants whose special competencies are appropriate for the unique needs and problems of the school districts and offices of county superintendents of schools which the Department serves.

It is impossible at this time to state as a percentage what "a significant portion" should be. Many of the consultants provided under Section 303(a)(5) were considered to be very effective in their work with teachers, most particularly when a specific instructional problem was the focus of the consultant's work. Where the consultants were requested to assist in the development of a course of study, their work was of only marginal utility in affecting the classroom behavior of the teachers actually carrying on the program thus developed. Nonetheless, the consultant program must be considered to be an effective use of some of the resources provided for supervisory and related services. The use of consultants for direct training in the conduct of instructional programs such as BSCS biology and American Language Material has been particularly effective.

The Department has been able to provide more consultant services through the use of per diem consultants than it could have with full-time employees. It has been able to employ truly capable people on a part-time basis who could not be employed full-time. Many of the outstanding people in science, mathematics, and modern foreign languages are currently employed in positions outside the field of education, and their services are available to school districts and the State Department of Education only on a temporary basis.

The Department has been able to insure that the consultants selected are appropriate for the specific assignments by involving the applicant school district in the identification of the consultant desired. In addition, such a program seeks out those individuals whose ability and personality permit them to exercise effective leadership in their chosen fields. Last, the use of part-time consultants, many of them employed in colleges and universities within the state, provides these institutions a better understanding of the problems of the school districts in which their graduates will serve.

3. Administration of incentive programs should be separated from the on-going supervisory aspects of a department of education.

The dilemma posed to a state department of education in the administration of incentive programs designed to change curriculum is not an easy one to resolve. An incentive program is by its very nature designed to institute a continuing process of change. The supervisory program of a department of education, on the contrary, is designed to promote and promulgate "best known practices," and by its very nature cannot "approve" programs for which adequate research is unavailable. For this reason, a department of education must establish an administrative organization which may finance program change without implying program approval. With this tool, a state department of education can establish the cutting edge to test new theories, new practices, and new concepts so that those which are successful can be incorporated in the activities of the supervisory bureau.

Where the supervisory and administrative powers are lodged in the same unit, the program change aspects are restricted, the cutting edge is dulled, and an inherent tendency to use financial incentive as a weapon to coerce conformity cannot be withstood.

References

Brickell, H. M. *Organizing New York State for educational change.* Albany, New York: State Education Department, 1961.

California State Department of Education. *California's teachers: their professional qualifications, experience, and the size of their classes, 1956–1957.* Vol. 27, Bulletin No. 10. Sacramento: the Department, 1958.

California State Department of Education. *California's need for teachers, 1960–1971.* Vol. 30, Bulletin No. 9. Sacramento: the Department, 1961.

California State Department of Education. *October enrollment reports.* On file in Bureau of Educational Research, Sacramento, 1963.

Holman, H. California's population. Sacramento: California State Department of Finance. Unpublished analyses, 1963.

Hurd, B. E. *Teaching in California schools.* Vol. 30, Bulletin No. 5. Sacramento: State Department of Education, 1961.

Johnson, D. W. *The dynamics of educational change.* Vol. 32, Bulletin No. 3. Sacramento: State Department of Education, 1963.

Joint Interim Committee of the Public Education System. *Final report of the Citizens Advisory Committee.* Sacramento: Senate of the State of California, 1961.

CHAPTER 7

The Illinois School Problems Commission: an innovation in decision-making at the state level

DONALD C. FLESCHE
NICHOLAS A. MASTERS
THOMAS H. ELIOT

MANY informed citizens have a very strong tendency to forget that "politics" plays an important and crucial role in educational decision-making, and that there is a constant need for durable and workable political structures for such decisions at the state (or any other) level of government. A strong commitment to the position that education is essentially a public responsibility, coupled with the fact that a public school system is a costly and complicated operation, has placed considerable burdens upon those who must decide how scarce resources are to be allocated. Thus, those concerned with changing the pattern of education or with introducing major innovations (which normally involve increased expenditures) are compelled to negotiate with political officials who are under pressure from interests which desire other goals, such as increased expenditures for mental health or reductions in taxation. The question that arises, then, is this: at what point in time and place do the educational innovators—those who

---

THE AUTHORS are, respectively: Assistant Professor of Political Science, Kalamazoo College; Associate Professor of Political Science, Pennsylvania State University; and Chancellor, Washington University. The chapter grew from their work in the Carnegie Project, State Politics and the Public Schools, Washington University. Donald C. Flesche was Research Associate; Nicholas A. Masters, Associate Director; and Thomas H. Eliot, Director.

desire change—confront the political decision-makers? The discussion that follows is about such confrontation in one state, Illinois.[1]

Illinois has arrived at a formula in educational policy formation that provides for "progress without significant controversy." The Illinois School Problems Commission (SPC) is an agency that for a variety of reasons has been able to combine stated ideals and goals in education with a recognition of the realities of the political system to achieve results. For the past decade, the SPC has served as the key agency for the major decisions made at the state level affecting public schools. Although it possesses no *formal* power other than advisory, virtually all of its recommendations have been incorporated into law.

The significance of the role of this agency in decision-making is not commonly appreciated. In Illinois, as in most other states, the authority of the state government has expanded considerably in the last few years. Today, a substantial share (about 25 to 30 per cent) of the public schools' operating and capital funds is provided from state money. Decisions on school reorganization, teacher welfare, the manner and time of election of school boards, and the auditing and accounting of part of the local districts' fiscal arrangements are not matters of exclusively local concern; the state plays a significant role. The pervasive myth of local autonomy cannot withstand close scrutiny.

The purpose of this chapter is to describe and analyze the role of the SPC in state decision-making. Data have been derived from unstructured interviews with members of the SPC, members of the General Assembly, representatives of organized educational interests, and personal observations. The survey covered largely the post-war period, with special attention to developments in 1960 and 1961.

The Illinois School Problems Commission: A Continuing Agency

In 1957, the SPC, a quasi-legislative and quasi-executive agency, was put on a permanent or "continuing" basis. This arrangement is

[1] This study represents part of a forthcoming larger study which deals with educational decision-making in three states: Illinois, Missouri, and Michigan. This study was made possible by a grant from the Carnegie Corporation to the Department of Political Science, Washington University, St. Louis. We alone, however, are responsible for any errors of fact or interpretation.

evidently an outgrowth of the earlier practice in Illinois of using temporary commissions to deal with problems in education. Although the SPC was not made a permanent part of the state decision-making machinery until 1957, in actual practice it had achieved this status almost from its inception in 1949, when the first SPC was established to meet the challenging problems in education that emerged following World War II. The need for such an agency resulted from at least three factors.

First, the post-war problems in education had reached crisis proportions. Over 12,000 separate school districts existed in the state; there was a desperate shortage of teachers (over 4,000 emergency certificates had to be issued to temporary instructors in an attempt to alleviate the situation); and many local districts had insufficient funds to meet heavy enrollment. Moreover, each proposal to solve these problems created additional complications. A representative of the Illinois Education Association (IEA) summarized the problems in "mathematical" terms:

Inflation + many more students + more unsolved school problems = too complicated a situation for the existing machinery to handle.

The diffuse decision-making arrangements which had existed for decades were uniformly regarded by all those interviewed as no longer adequate to meet the complex problems that the public schools faced.[2]

Second, despite numerous recommendations from various sources, the Illinois General Assembly, apparently jealous of its own prerogatives, had repeatedly refused to establish a state board of education—and, indeed, continues to refuse to do so. Thus, the state legislature had come to be regarded as the "state board" for educational purposes.[3] Yet the leaders of the legislature were fully aware that they lacked the necessary expertise to recommend positive legislation.

[2] From 1907 to 1949, the Illinois General Assembly created fifteen special legislative commissions to deal exclusively with public schools. Virtually all were concerned primarily with finance or reorganization.

[3] One Senator maintained: "The most important thing to remember is that in education matters the legislature is all-powerful." An IEA official remarked that since Illinois has no state board of education, "the state legislature has often boasted that *it is* the state board."

Third, neither the state superintendent nor the organized educational interests could offer, or were in a position to offer, a suitable program to fit the existing needs. The state superintendent, a partisan elected official, was too controversial to assume leadership or to be delegated broad authority by the legislature over educational matters. One IEA official pointed out: "The state office is an administrative department. You just don't get the layman's [as opposed to the professional politician's] point of view from it that you get from a state board." A Senate leader maintained: "The state superintendent is elected in a partisan state-wide election; his office is controlled by patronage appointments. His authority should not be extended beyond the administrative functions he is expected to fill." A leader of the State Association of School Boards was of a similar conviction: "The state superintendent just couldn't handle the job."

On the other hand, the various organized educational interests had only rarely been able to achieve unity among themselves; thus their demands for a state program varied widely and significantly. A leader of one of the key educational interests summarized the situation: "They apparently didn't know what they wanted." To get anything accepted, an IEA leader reported, it was necessary for each group to "find a friendly legislator, 'educate' him . . ., have him introduce your bill, and then see what happened." With all the diverse interests represented in the state, the result, according to a senatorial leader, was that "developing a program of school policy which was acceptable to everyone was almost impossible. Every group had its own plan for solving the problems, and if it wasn't accepted completely, that group was not satisfied."

The first SPC was created largely through the efforts of many people, but usually the efforts of the Research Director of the IEA, Lester Grimm, and the SPC's first Research Director, Dr. Richard Browne, are cited as being of special significance in the process of persuading the General Assembly to adopt this approach. It is doubtless true, however, that the creation of the first SPC did not break significantly with the pattern of handling educational decisions through temporary commissions. Only after the SPC began to function was it realized that this commission would serve as a major innovation in handling educational problems.

The Composition of the SPC

The salient feature of the composition and organization of the SPC is that all the major interests that have a direct and tangible stake in the outcomes of public school decisions are included. The SPC is structured to provide these interests with a formal and official voice in the decision-making process. The Illinois Constitution, though rigid with regard to the separation of powers principle, is flexible enough to allow for the creation of a special commission, to deal exclusively with one major policy area, that includes in its membership legislators, gubernatorial appointees, an elected state official, and organized interest group representatives.

By law, the size of the Commission is fixed at seventeen members. Each member serves a term of two years, but the normal practice has been for a member to remain on the Commission as long as he desires. Also by law, the legislative membership is fixed at ten, the governor appoints five, and two members (the State Superintendent of Public Instruction and the State Director of Finance) are *ex officio*. Beyond these ground rules, certain additional membership criteria have been developed.

Criteria for selection of legislative members. The main criterion in the selection of legislative membership is that representation on the Commission of all conflicting, or potentially conflicting, elements within the state legislature be insured. As is true with all other committees, both parties are represented. Since the practice is to select five members from each house, the majority party in each house is given three members, while the minority is accorded two. Each party, of course, is responsible for the selection of its own members.

Perhaps more important than party affiliation in the selection of legislative members is representation of the various geographical or area interests of the state. Geographical "interests" are not defined very precisely by members of the legislature, but they are acknowledged. Democratic legislators from Cook County, for example, elected with the support of Mayor Richard Daley's organization, insist that they have at least one member on the Commission from each house. In the

Senate, one Democratic assignee is from Cook County, and the other from "downstate," preferably central or southern Illinois. On the Republican side, representatives of the strong Republican areas in central Illinois demand, and usually receive, majority representation. For the past ten years, Representative Charles Clabaugh (Republican, Champaign) has served as the Commission's chairman; Senator David Davis (Republican, Bloomington) has been its vice-chairman for over five years.

Along with geographical factors, previous experience in educational matters weighs heavily in these assignments. Members who serve on this Commission have been typically drawn from the Senate and House Education Committees where they have established the reputation of being concerned and informed about public school legislation. Usually, although not invariably, appointments are made from the ranking or senior members of these committees.

Careful attention is also given to the personalities of applicants. Members of the Commission tend to recommend for membership only those who they feel will not upset the unity the SPC has been able to achieve. Legislators who are seen as seeking to manipulate the political process for their personal advantage, or who fail to gain the respect of their fellow-legislators, have little chance of being selected. Although it is somewhat difficult to document this point, those primarily responsible for making the selections indicated that to be eligible for SPC work, a member must be moderate and willing to compromise. Whether all assignments vindicate expectations is of course debatable, but as a ranking member of the Commission put it: "The leadership is usually *very* careful with whom they appoint to the SPC; this is not always true of . . . commissions of this type."

It should be mentioned that not all members of the General Assembly feel that the SPC is a desirable assignment. Several maintained that some of the work of the senior members of the Commission prevents them from becoming experts in this area; they have thus requested transfers on the grounds that there is little operative political warrant for remaining. One Senator resigned from this Commission when he became a candidate for a judgeship position in his home county, because he felt the Commission "involved too much work for what he gained from it politically." Conversely, members who for one reason or another have achieved the status of a public school "expert" have vigorously protested their right to retain membership. Seniority, however (unlike the situation in the United States Congress), does not guarantee tenure on the Commission.

Criteria for the selection of non-legislative members. The gubernatorial appointees, with few exceptions, have been representatives of the organized interests concerned directly or indirectly with education. Included in the membership of the SPC since its creation have been the Research Director of the IEA, the Secretary of Legislation of the Illinois Agricultural Association (who was an active leader in education in the years prior to the establishment of the SPC), a representative of the State Association of School Boards, and a member (often the president) of the Chicago Board of Education. The fifth gubernatorial appointee has varied from commission to commission, although this position on some occasions has gone to a representative of the Illinois Chamber of Commerce. Appointments made by the governor are not rewards for political work; that is, the power to appoint is too restricted to be used as a political weapon. Although the statute gives him broad discretion, the governor is limited by custom and "common sense" considerations requiring the aforementioned organizations to select their own representatives. Thus, the appointees to this Commission generally do not incur the same obligations to the governor that appointees to other state agencies do. In actual practice, the governor has only two appointees for which he alone is directly responsible: (1) the Director of Finance, an *ex officio* member; and (2) the one appointee not dictated by organized interests.

The remaining member of the Commission, the Superintendent of Public Instruction, serves in an *ex officio* capacity. It is his office, of course, that has the most direct and continuous contact with the local school districts, and it is only logical that he should be included, if for no other reason than that of the information at his disposal.

Once assigned, a member knows that he has joined a "going concern," an established group with its own set of norms.[4] From then on, a major factor in any decision he may reach in this Commission is the influence on him of this institutionalized group. The membership of the SPC is relatively stable, its chairman and vice-chairman are mem-

[4] For a study of group norms of committees, see Huitt (1954, pp. 340–65). See also Verba (1961).

bers of long commission tenure, and the majority of gubernatorial appointees have served on it since its inception. Change in membership is never complete, and seldom drastic at any one time, thus permitting a fairly continuous group life. This means that the group norms can be easily transmitted to new members. What are the characteristics of this group? What variables serve to integrate it? What must a member do—or avoid—to be accepted?

The basic norm of the SPC is that every member is expected to be interested in public education and to strive for its improvement, and to devote a considerable amount of his time and effort (either within the Commission or within the legislature) toward this end. The General Assembly provides practically no surveillance of the Commission's work, and is highly permissive in allowing the SPC to elaborate a definition of its tasks. The Commission operates under the assumption that in the field of educational policy formation, it has pre-eminence.

More precisely, the consensus of the Commission is based on the conception that it has one paramount task. That task is to solve the major problems of the schools in a business-like fashion, and at the same moment to guard against unreasonable drains on the state treasury. One Commission member described this pattern of consensus as follows:

> It is a working commission—we take a businesslike approach in attempting to solve the needs of schools which the state should solve. We are able to recognize the local needs and problems; we then try to recommend legislation within the framework of these needs. We are conservative in our recommendations; people by nature reject change and as a result we don't try to force undue change upon the General Assembly.

In terms of any action the Commission takes, the members maintain that they must display a high degree of agreement to the General Assembly. The realities of politics, they contend, demand this. Thus a major taboo in Commission work is to raise issues or to manipulate situations that will divide or bring about serious conflict among Commission members. Partisanship, for example, has no place in the Commission or any of its deliberations, regardless of the intensity of feelings or rivalries among the members in other policy areas. One Commission member, when asked about the relationships of political parties to the SPC, said: "The SPC is about as non-political as any commission in the state. Education just doesn't divide politically." Members of both parties on the Commission tend to condemn or censure any member who has the audacity to make education a partisan consideration. "Only one member of the Commission ever tried to make the Commission into a political agency and even members of his party [on the Commission] realized this and strongly disapproved."

Integration of the Commission is aided in several other ways. Commission members deal with the same subject matter year after year— and frequently more than once in a given year. "Substantive and procedural repetition," as Fenno (1961) has pointed out, "promotes familiarity with key problems and provides ample opportunity to test and confirm the most satisfactory methods of dealing with them." The absolute necessity that education be financed makes it urgent that the Commission find such methods. Moreover, the selection process serves as a deterrent against fragmentation. And, as we have seen, only those individuals who are predisposed to be cooperative and moderate in their approach, and who have a strong commitment to education (either by virtue of their past performance or their group membership), are selected.

How the SPC Operates

Responsibilities.   Established as an advisory agency to the General Assembly, the SPC is responsible for the following:

> The commission shall study: (1) The progress and problems of school district reorganization and the means of further promotion of an efficient school system. (2) Need of further codification and revision of the school laws. (3) State, county, and local school administration of the common schools and the interrelationship of such administration. (4) The adequacy and efficiency of present plans of granting state and common school aids of the various types, including the State aid formula and qualifying rates. (5) The methods of acquiring adequate revenue for schools and the definite sources of possible revenue for local school funds and for state school aids. (6) Any problems which may arise that may affect the general welfare of the schools.

> The commission shall also counsel and advise the Superintendent of Public Instruction on any school problem that he may bring to them for consideration. The commission may from time to time make recommendations for consideration of improvement in any public school area.

The commission shall also make recommendations to the Budgetary Commission prior to February 1, of each odd-numbered year, as to the amount of State school aid required for the succeeding biennium.

The commission shall consider and study all germane factors in an effort to determine the improvements necessary to raise the education standards of the public schools to a desirable level.

The commission shall make a detailed report of its findings and conclusions to the General Assembly not later than March, of each odd-numbered year, and shall submit recommendations for such legislation as it deems necessary. (Illinois School Problems Commission, 1961, pp. 3–4)

A broad statutory definition of functions, however, leaves significant questions unanswered. How, for example, does the SPC decide which problems it will consider in any given year? Does it consider *all* matters that require state action, even those of purely local application? Is any attempt made to avoid certain issues? The first step toward answering these questions is to look into the internal operations of the SPC.

Sources and types of problems dealt with.   The problems that the SPC considers and makes recommendations on arise in at least five ways. First, some problems come up more or less "automatically." Members of the Commission describe the following areas as "mandatory and routine": the state aid formula, qualifying rates for state aid, the amount to be provided under the state equalization formula, the amount of the flat grants, the sources of possible revenues for local and state school funds, and anticipation of the appropriation that will be needed to fill the equalization level authorized by the state.

Second, the General Assembly occasionally directs the SPC to take special cognizance of a particular matter. In recent sessions, for example, the SPC has been directed by the General Assembly, according to one SPC member, "to determine the best methods of obtaining additional revenue, to accomplish reorganization, and to improve the methods of transporting the pupils."

Third, the Commission retains its own research staff, which is constantly investigating and studying a variety of problems. Most of these studies are concerned with finance, although they cover the entire state education picture.

Fourth, many of the most significant problems handled by the

SPC are brought to its collective attention by the state's organized educational interests, by the state, county, and local superintendents of schools, and by individual Commission members, some of whom are regarded as oustanding educational leaders.

Finally, some problems are brought to the attention of the Commission through its open hearings or in informal communications. Conversations with individual members of the General Assembly, letters from constituents of the legislative members of the Commission, articles in professional journals, and newspaper accounts all have on one occasion or another brought educational problems before the SPC.

Problems excluded.   Almost as significant as what the SPC does and how its responsibilities are defined is what it carefully avoids. For example, the SPC by general agreement among its members refuses to consider matters that involve, or may involve, conflicts between parochial and public schools. Such proposals as the use of public funds to support transportation of students to parochial schools are left to the discretion of the regular education committees of the House and Senate or the General Assembly, with the SPC playing no overt or formal role. Issues involving racial problems in education, according to SPC members, also have no bearing on the Commission's responsibilities. Conflicts over segregation of schools or the treatment of Negro teachers and pupils are deemed by the Commission to be either primarily local matters, or within the jurisdiction of other agencies of state government. The line that can be drawn between issues which involve or do not involve religious or racial considerations is, of course, arbitrary. Some Commission members contend that the SPC has not entirely avoided raising these issues. It is a matter of opinion, therefore, how well founded the frequent claim is that the Commission does not deal at all with such problems.

Matters that are regarded as having application to a single school district or a few districts within a geographically-contiguous area, such as the validating of a school bond issue (which requires a state statute), are not matters of concern to the SPC. In addition, the SPC is generally of the opinion that recommendations to the General Assembly concerning teacher welfare (minimum salary law, tenure laws, retirement provisions) are handled effectively by the various organized interests, and that the SPC does not have to devote much time to their consideration.

Finally, the SPC makes no attempt to assume the General Assembly's constitutional responsibility for supervising the administration of public schools. If questions arise concerning the budget, methods, and policies of the State Office of Public Instruction, the SPC is not normally involved.

Procedure. The method of organizing the work of the Commission in 1959 is typical. The Commission first decides in its preliminary meetings where and when to hold its open hearings. Usually, the pattern is to hold them in every roughly-defined geographical area of the state; for example, several hearings are held in Cook County (the Chicago area) as well as in the "downstate areas." Following the hearings, the Commission divides into subcommittees, to which outside experts are often appointed. Each subcommittee is charged with the responsibility in a particular policy area. For example, in 1959 subcommittees were appointed to study such problems as the question of summer school, and a "number of technical matters pertaining to the length of the school day and year and with the financing of so-called 'Federally impacted' school districts." (Illinois School Problems Commission, 1961, p. 7) The final stage of the procedure comes after the subcommittees report (their views are usually incorporated by the research staff into a Commission report). At this point the SPC decides by majority vote what recommendations it will make to the legislature.

SPC's recommendations to the General Assembly in 1961 included the following:

> In the area of *finance*, it recommended keeping the equalization formula at the $252 per pupil figure established in 1959, appropriating $50,000 to the Superintendent of Public Instruction to continue a pilot study on a state program for gifted children, and appropriating $15,250,000 for reimbursements of school districts for transportation of pupils to and from school. In the area of *local district reorganization*, it recommended passing a county school district survey act, the creation of a State Reorganization Committee, and the setting by law of mandatory standards for reorganization. In the area of *state, county, and local school administration*, it recommended increasing the minimum academic training re-

quired for provisional certificates, permitting township school treasurers only in counties having at least 1,000,000 population, and recodifying the School Code. Certain recommendations concerning special education and the School Building Commission were also included. (Illinois School Problems Commission, 1961, pp. 11–27)

Much more than the manner of procedure is involved in the making of decisions, however. The open hearing plays a special and significant role in the total process. It has already been mentioned that some of the problems with which the Commission deals come first to its attention at these formal hearings. Most members, however, contend that the formal hearings are significant not so much for the information they yield but rather because they contribute to the structuring of consensus with respect to educational matters. Informed observers of the political process have long recognized that appearance before committee hearings has significant compensatory value. An educational interest group representative, an outraged citizen, or the spokesman for any interest may be mollified even if no concrete results are produced.[5]

The open hearings conducted by the SPC perform such functions. One interest group representative, a member of the SPC, suggested that the open hearings "are psychologically very important in that they make school administrators and interest group representatives feel that they are a significant part of the process by which decisions are made." A Commission leader maintained that the "real value" of the open hearings was "that they give the people interested in education a chance to get their problems off their chests and to make them feel a part of the whole process." A Senatorial member described their "real significance" as being "to give the school people a chance to feel close to the legislation eventually recommended."

Animating and guiding the formal procedure, then, is this practice of structuring the Commission's operations so that everyone has an opportunity to feel that he has played a part in the Commission's deliberations. This is a calculated effort to arrive at as wide a consensus as possible before the SPC makes any recommendations to the General Assembly for final decision.

[5] For a discussion of the significance of open hearings, see, for example, Truman (1951, pp. 372–77).

Relations of the SPC with the General Assembly

Members of the General Assembly have given virtually unanimous approval to almost all SPC recommendations, because it is an agency of the legislature's own creation and includes respected members of both parties. Moreover, the organized educational groups, the governor, and the representatives of other groups concerned with state policies feel that only this Commission is capable of presenting solutions to education problems which are acceptable to all concerned. Why do the members of the state legislature, in particular, feel this way? What accounts for the phenomenal success of the Commission?

First and foremost, it must be remembered that no one opposes public education, at least openly. There is no anti-school lobby. On the whole, public schools are not considered fit subjects for opposition by those who are ideologically against more spending or increasing the service functions of the state government. The great majority of the people—excepting some of the belligerents of the recent integration conflicts in the South—are firmly committed to the concept of education at public expense. Even those who vigorously oppose Federal aid to the public schools usually base their argument on the theory that public education is essentially a state or local responsibility.

The more or less special status the public schools enjoy is fully acknowledged by members of both parties. Legislators feel that it would be politically disastrous to be identified as a "public school enemy." And, on the other hand (except for a few members who have attained the status of experts), there is little political currency to be gained from being identified as an *advocate* of the public school cause.

Moreover, such generally useful political weapons as patronage and contractual arrangements for services authorized by legislative action are seldom aimed at the public schools. The public may come to accept or even expect the use of governmental power to gain obvious political or personal advantage. But this public tolerance is severely strained if schools are so used. Calculations of party and personal advantage have led virtually all legislators to the conclusion that their energies would be wasted in any political wars over education. In conflicts over public schools, it is doubtful that anyone could win and more likely that everyone would lose. Thus, the Illinois School Problems Commission serves the General Assembly in one important and fundamental way; namely, it reduces the chances of political fights over education.

Reasons for SPC effectiveness. There seem to be four reasons why the SPC has been able to perform this function so ably for the General Assembly. First, legislative membership on the Commission tends to maximize the chances that its recommendations will be consistent with, or made in consideration of, other budgetary and revenue estimates. In brief, legislative membership helps to insure legislative control. Second, the demands of the major organized interests concerned with decisions affecting the public schools are articulated through the Commission by virtue of their membership on it. Thus, on the whole, unity is achieved among the various organized educational interests prior to the legislative deliberations. Third, public education is removed entirely from the arena of partisan politics. This is of special importance to legislative members, since they know that organized educational interests and the public, as they perceive it, resent any manifestation of partisanship so far as public schools are concerned. Finally, and not mutually exclusively from the preceding points, experience with the work of the Commission in the past has justified the confidence and trust that virtually all legislators place in the Commission.

Examining each of these reasons separately, perhaps the most significant is that ten of the seventeen Commission members are legislators. Members of the General Assembly know that their legislative colleagues have had an integral part in the preparation of each proposal. Furthermore, five members in each house are ready to lead the effort to pass any SPC recommendation—members who have been actively involved in the months of study and who have precise information at their fingertips. One senator, a Commission member, said: "Our chief strength as a Commission lies in the fact that when we come in with recommendations, we have five members in each house who have fairly specific knowledge of . . . each recommendation . . . On our SPC the fact that the membership includes ten members who are actively engaged in the practice of politics gives us a more practical approach to solving the problems."

The legislative members of the Commission are professional, veteran politicians, familiar with the subtleties and nuances of legislative deliberations. They speak the language of legislators; they know which cues to respond to and which ones to reject. In many respects the General Assembly characteristics are similar to those of the Commission. It too is an institutionalized group with its own set of norms and customs. It should not be surprising then that special recognition would be given to recommendations made by its senior and respected members.

The respect accorded the legislative members of the SPC is not only for them as individuals but as symbols of a politically safe approach to a complex and potentially explosive problem. Thus, a Republican House member of the SPC and his Democratic counterpart in the Senate, both of whom may be deeply engaged in the tribal wars of General Assembly politics, are received, insofar as education is at issue, with unfeigned enthusiasm. If the basic question in politics is who controls, who is the man (or men) to see, then the answer is the legislative members of the SPC. They provide the bridge, the personal connections that are so vital in political negotiations. Representatives of the professional groups are delighted that they have found the men to do their bidding in Springfield.

Also of significance is the fact that the non-legislative members of the Commission, mainly the representatives of the key organized educational interests, are united in their support of what the state's problems of education are and how they can best be solved. In what ways does this serve the General Assembly? Unity among educational groups means that legislators know they are not going to be constantly pressured or harassed by a barrage of demands. It means that conflicts in the legislature are not likely to emerge, with one group of legislators advocating one interest and another group of legislators advocating some other interest.

Finally, past experience with the SPC has given the General Assembly confidence in its work. The General Assembly has found no reason on the basis of past performance to question SPC decisions which one member characterized as "representing the best thinking possible in the area of education." One House member put it more succinctly: "Its advice has always helped us out before; why wouldn't it work now?"

Other positive relations with the legislature. In addition to serving as the chief innovator of public school policy, the SPC has been able to assist the legislature in other ways. One function not previously alluded to is that the Commission, by virtue of its existence and importance, takes a lot of "the heat" off the other members which they receive from their constituents. Because of the widespread and active interest in the public schools, a phenomenon generally not characteristic of other state governmental functions, legislators are often subjected to an almost continuous barrage of requests to "do something about the school situation." Realizing that many of these demands are oversimplified or distorted, individual legislators look to the SPC and to its legislative members for aid in answering their constituents. This assistance may give the individual legislator the information he needs to relieve the existing pressure; it may be provided by the mere fact that the SPC exists. Constituency demands can be directed by the legislator to the SPC, thereby removing the immediate pressure from himself. One legislative member of the SPC explained: "The legislators look to us as a buffer between themselves and their constituents when they receive pressures from local interests to introduce controversial, unpopular, questionable, or unwise legislation. They can tell their constituents that they are ill-equipped to handle it and send it to us."

Moreover, the individual legislative members of the Commission provide services for the other members of the General Assembly. In essence, they serve as trusted confidants of the legislators on all educational matters, especially those that are introduced in the General Assembly without having been considered previously by the SPC. On such issues the *individual* legislative member of the SPC becomes, in the absence of official policy made by the entire SPC, the education expert whose advice is likely to influence a large portion of his party's representatives in his branch of the legislature. An interest group leader gave this description: "The members of the General Assembly look to the SPC for leadership in educational matters. An individual legislator wanting to introduce a bill without SPC approval would first take it to one of the legislative leaders on the SPC for his opinion. If one of these should disapprove, the bill would have little chance of being passed." One legislative member maintained: "There is *never* a bill concerning education that is called up that the members don't look to us for our opinion." Another said: "Any education bill has a difficult time getting passed unless it has the official support of the SPC or unofficial support of its members. The members of the legislature tend to go to the SPC members seeking guidance on how to vote."

Relations of the SPC with the Governor

Virtually the same considerations that govern the SPC's relations with the legislature affect its relation with the governor. The General Assembly, always aware of the tremendous formal powers [6] available to the governor—namely his veto and the patronage at his disposal—structured the SPC so as to include gubernatorial appointees. Moreover, the SPC fully appreciates the governor's strong position in the state and thus makes special efforts to accommodate its position to that of the governor. The SPC, basing its recommendations upon years of study and experience in the area of educational politics, advises the governor as to what the problems of education are, which of them can be solved, how they can best be solved, what is politically possible, and how the governor can use his influence to the best advantage to assure passage of these recommendations.

The governor, meanwhile, as the most powerful single individual in state government, relays his opinions, ideas, and recommendations to the SPC, where (particularly in the area of finance) they are given careful consideration. Leaders of the SPC have frequent contact with the governor, talking over each recommendation before it is officially announced. Mutual cooperation between the chief executive and the SPC, strengthened by mutual respect, has guaranteed general agreement between the two, and thus fits into the general pattern of achieving maximum consensus from all parties to the decision.

Concluding Comment

In sum, the SPC is a formal device that formulates policy separately from the General Assembly, where there are considerably more dimensions of conflict. Issues can be examined "on their merits" to some extent, with less anxiety about the final action to be taken. Moreover,

[6] See discussion of the role of the governor of Illinois in Steiner & Gove, (1960, p. 33).

the SPC has considerable informal power, is highly responsive to educational interests and appears to be highly effective. Many educators despair of anything resembling coherent educational decision-making at the state level, and resort to sporadic and frequently chaotic influence attempts. In Illinois, however, the SPC does not "buck," ignore or try to wish away the ordinary vicissitudes of politics—rather, it capitalizes upon them.

Two queries arise from this investigation of the work of the SPC. First, to what extent has the SPC encouraged or supported educational innovation? And secondly, can the lessons of the SPC be applied (*mutatis mutandis*) at the federal and local district levels? Addressing ourselves to the first question, we shall rely primarily on the participants' evaluations of their own success. All of the interviewees indicated that SPC was primarily a force for stability and moderation, not policy innovation as such. The members of the SPC attribute its success largely, if not entirely, to the fact that it is able to achieve consensus on educational matters. To achieve consensus, all agreed, the SPC must avoid recommending proposals that involve drastic and rapid changes in the direction of education policy.

The answer to the second query is much more difficult. All that can be said is that there is nothing inherent in the creation of a special commission that will insure that education will be insulated from conflict. The dimensions of conflict at each level vary, as do the stakes involved. However, the principles involved in the success of the SPC may well turn out to have wider application.

References

Fenno, R. F. House Appropriations Committee as a political system: the problem of integration. Paper read at Amer. Polit. Sci. Ass. annual meeting, September 1961.

Huitt, R. K. The Congressional committee: a case study. *Amer. Polit. Sci. Rev.*, 1954, 48, 340–365.

Illinois School Problems Commission, Report of the School Problems Commission, 6, March 1961.

Steiner, M. A., & Gove, F. S. *Legislative politics in Illinois*. Urbana: University of Illinois Press, 1960.

Truman, D. B. *The governmental process*. New York: Knopf, 1951.

Verba, S. *Small groups and political behavior: a study of leadership*. Princeton: Princeton University Press, 1961.

CHAPTER 8

8mm motion pictures
in education: incipient innovation

Louis Forsdale

THE MOTION PICTURE, like still photography and television, exists in technology. As Erwin Panofsky (1959) has observed of the rise of film art: ". . . it took place under conditions contrary to precedent. It was not an artistic urge that gave rise to the discovery and gradual perfection of a new technique; it was a technical invention that gave rise to the discovery and gradual perfection of a new art."

Because film rests in technology, technical advances affect it vitally. The addition of sound to theatrical film in 1927 revolutionized the industry; wide-screen processes helped save the teetering American film enterprise during the 1950's in the face of severe competition from television; beginning in 1932, 8mm fostered a thriving amateur film activity. Not all film inventions are this fruitful, of course: three-dimensional motion picture processes, after trial in the American market place, are now stored in laboratory corners, awaiting a more propitious moment for further trial.

THE AUTHOR is Professor of English, Teachers College, Columbia University, and Principal Investigator, Project in Educational Communication, Horace Mann–Lincoln Institute of School Experimentation.

8mm: An Incipient Innovation

A number of technical developments in the 8mm film field—both silent and sound—are now occurring, with the result that many observers feel that this hitherto amateur film size is ready to make an important contribution to educational film. As one enthusiast has put it, 8mm can be the "paperback of the film field."

The student of innovation has a striking opportunity for study in this prospective flowering of 8mm film in education. The development is still comparatively young, and it has a well-recorded history. The factors which must be considered to understand the 8mm scene are reasonably clear, yet there are enough "unknowns" to lend excitement to the study. Because the widespread acceptance of 8mm motion pictures in education will probably take many years, and because it may be a decade before the direction of the full impact is understood, the student of innovation has an opportunity to follow this particular development as it progresses. The purpose of this chapter is to present background information about the subject and sketch out the apparent present dynamics of the field, so that the reader can independently observe the course of this new small-gauge motion picture film in the years ahead.

What 8mm can mean in education

In the 1920's, educational film was distributed on 35mm film—the normal theatrical size. Reels and cans were bulky; projection machines were large and heavy. In the early 1930's, 16mm sound motion pictures were introduced in education, and this gauge soon dominated the field; it was through 16mm, with its greater ease of use and its lessened expense, that educational film came to its present state of development. Although smaller film size was obviously not the sole factor responsible for the advance of educational film in the last thirty years, it was a prerequisite.

Further miniaturization of educational film is now possible with 8mm film, both in sound and silent form. Technical problems have been solved in the main: the picture is good, if not perfect, and the sound track is good. A variety of sound and silent 8mm projectors is on the market, including striking new cartridge-loading machines which are simple enough for children to operate. Many laboratories are prepared to make prints in quantity. Educational film makers are studying marketing problems. Dozens of papers on 8mm subjects are being read in professional societies, both educational and technical. Enthusiasts speak of a breakthrough in educational film; even conservative observers see important new uses for 8mm film in the years ahead.

But why should anyone in education care about the growth of 8mm film? Don't we have a going system with 16mm—a system in which many millions of dollars have been invested by school systems throughout the nation and the world, by equipment manufacturers, and by makers and distributors of educational films? The answer to this question depends on the breadth of one's vision of the extent to which film *might* be used in an ideal setting.

Against this writer's vision of future possibilities, our present uses of motion pictures in education are peripheral and occasional. Moving visual information is simply not regularly provided for students, even in the best equipped school systems. This is not intended as criticism of the dedicated work of pioneer audio-visual people who gave birth to film libraries and distribution systems only yesterday, so to speak, and have carefully nurtured them to a state of happy adolescence (or is it childhood?) today. But surely the growth of educational film has not stopped. Is it not destined, in its maturity, to serve (like the book) as a ubiquitous medium of truly central importance in education?

8mm could help make films everywhere more accessible in education. Because of its more convenient size, its lowered cost, and—very significantly—its strikingly simplified new projectors, 8mm holds the promise of bringing film prints out of the centralized film libraries into the individual school or classroom. A cartridge-loading projector, such as the Technicolor 8mm "Instant Movie Projector," makes it possible for the average teacher to use films without fear. It also—for the first time in the history of the medium—enables a child, even a young one, to use the motion picture as an independent learning resource.

Such increased accessibility of films to teacher and learner, if realized, would be a most significant advance in educational materials. It is characteristic of all communication media—book, radio, motion picture, television—to be available at first only to the few, then gradually accessible to the many. For the motion picture to be widely and easily accessible in education, two problems must be solved.

First, costs of prints and projectors must be lowered. Cost is primarily a function of mass production and distribution; if we could achieve truly large numbers of sales, costs could be lowered dramatically. This is true of both 8mm and 16mm, of course, although given huge markets 8mm has a clear price advantage over 16mm.

The second problem which must be solved to make film readily accessible in education is convenience of use. Convenience depends on having film at hand—not in central libraries—and on ease of operating projection equipment. Even if a thousand film prints were stored on shelves in the average teacher's classroom in the United States, he would not feel easy in their use with today's 16mm projector. Both 16mm and 8mm projectors can be made simpler, but for a variety of technical reasons it has apparently been impossible so far to develop inexpensive cartridge-loading machines—probably the ultimate in simplicity—for 16mm film.[1] Meanwhile, sound and silent 8mm cartridge-loading projectors are available on the market today, as are other more traditional kinds of 8mm projectors.

Whether the 8mm development in education will succeed depends ultimately on the attitude of the teacher in the classroom. If he senses real innovation in the development, if he sees basic departure from current practice, a corner will have been turned. If he believes that 8mm is only "little 16mm," meaning more of the same in educational film, little gain will have occurred.

The network of agencies involved

But before the teacher can come to render that judgment, important decisions must be made within a network of supporting agencies. That network includes (1) *engineers,* who must design cameras, projectors,

---

[1] At least three cartridge-loading 16mm machines have been brought to prototype stage in the United States: one by Polan Industries in Huntington, West Virginia, on an Air Force contract; another by Astro Dynamics, Inc., in Burlington, Massachusetts; the third by The Motion Picture Research Council. Each projector is complex and expensive; of greater importance, each uses a cartridge which is filled with gears, rollers, and other devices, adding up to a cost for each cartridge which may exceed the cost of the film it contains. While it would be foolhardy to suggest that simpler cartridges cannot be made for 16mm film, it is a fact that no apparent progress has been made to date.

printers, and other essential pieces of hardware; (2) camera and projector *manufacturers*, who must make the economic decisions about whether and how to translate the engineers' blueprints into equipment purchasable in the market; (3) *processing laboratories*, which must be equipped to make quality 8mm prints of films in needed quantity; (4) educational film *producers and distributors*, who must make decisions, again primarily economic, about whether and how to introduce 8mm into the educational market place; (5) *educational officials*, who must be willing to purchase 8mm equipment and prints; (6) *leadership agencies and individuals*, who must be persuasive in pointing the way.

These various agencies are not tightly coordinated, although professional forums, such as the Society of Motion Picture and Television Engineers and the Department of Audiovisual Instruction of the National Education Association, offer periodic opportunities to exchange information about developments. Journals and newsletters provide useful channels for communication, too. But much information—particularly that which is related to the development of new products—is not shared, of course, until patents are granted or machines are in production. And because hardware plays such a critical role in the motion picture field, new developments (in the form of a new projector, for example) can appear with explosive suddenness.

Against this general picture of the present, in which the innovation must make its way, let us attempt to gain some perspective by examining the past 8mm scene.

The Development of 8mm Sound

8mm not new

The 8mm motion picture is not new, of course. Introduced in the United States in 1932, it has been used widely by amateurs since that time. As noted, the basic educational film medium in this country since the mid-1930's has been the wider 16mm form; however, Japan has for years made good educational use of 8mm along with 16mm. The occasional uses of 8mm film made in American education since 1932 were by teachers and students who wanted to make motion pictures locally in their schools. Frequently these films were explicitly instructional in purpose—a record of a science experiment, for example. Sometimes they were dramatic films, written, directed, and acted by students in cooperation with an interested teacher. In 1960, however, there was a sudden surge of attention to 8mm as a means of distributing professionally made educational films.

Sound on 8mm

The event which most captivated the attention of those who began to speak enthusiastically of important implications of 8mm in education was the addition of a sound track on this gauge of film. In 1960 and 1961, in Europe, the United States, and Japan, manufacturers introduced 8mm projectors which were capable of recording and reproducing sound via magnetic tracks on the film itself.

As with many technical advances, the magnetic sound track on 8mm film had existed in both experimental and practical form for many years. It was described as early as 1947 by Camras (1947); and in 1952 Lloyd Thompson of Calvin Productions in Kansas City had actually manufactured and marketed an 8mm sound projector using the magnetic stripe method (Thompson, 1961). It seems to have been released "before its time"; only one thousand of the projectors were sold (Calvin Productions, 1963), an insufficient number to warrant continued production.

The next two American firms in this field—Eastman Kodak and Fairchild—apparently introduced their projectors primarily for the amateur market, although representatives of both companies also spoke at the outset about the business and educational possibilities of the 8mm sound medium. A key spokesman in national forums was John Flory, advisor on Non-Theatrical Films of the Eastman Kodak Company, who suggested the attractive and serviceable analogy mentioned earlier, that of 8mm as "the paperback of the film field" (Flory, 1961).

Business and industry respond to 8mm sound

Industrial users of motion pictures for sales purposes were the first element of American society to respond clearly to the advantages of 8mm sound film. Soon such companies as the Do-All Manufacturing Company, the Ford Motor Company, and the Caterpillar Company had begun to make 8mm sound prints of films for use in their internal training and sales programs.

In 1961, the rear-screen 8mm sound projector was introduced by three equipment manufacturers in the United States. When folded for carrying, it is somewhat larger than a portable typewriter, and is therefore easily carried by a salesman. Its rear-screen is large enough for a small group of viewers. The film is threaded in conventional fashion, but in a loop (end spliced to beginning) so that the film goes around and around without rethreading. These machines found a ready market in the sales field for an obvious reason: products could now be displayed in motion, with accompanying sound track, in ways that revealed their capabilities to far better advantage than could a conventional film strip or book of still pictures. The Ford Motor Company is making widespread use of one of these machines in dealer showrooms.

The first important commitments to use of 8mm sound in the United States, then, were made by business and industry.

The Society of Motion Picture and Television Engineers

Through these early days of 8mm sound film, national and local meetings of the Society of Motion Picture and Television Engineers were frequently devoted to papers on the medium. Under the chairmanship of John Flory, a half-day of papers on 8mm sound film was organized for the 89th Semiannual Convention in Toronto in April, 1961. While most papers dealt with technical matters, Flory (1961) sketched with enthusiasm the future uses of 8mm sound in industry, education, church, and home. Education was represented at this convention in papers presented by Professor Steve Knudsen, of Iowa State University, and the present writer. Knudsen's paper (1961) presented the analysis of a massive vision—the setting up of a motion picture library in every classroom of the nation, using 8mm sound prints. The other paper (Forsdale, 1961) was optimistic about the changes in the uses of motion pictures in education which could flow from a successful development of the 8mm medium. It also called (as had statements of other educators through the years) for projectors which would be vastly simpler to thread than the present machines, suggesting that the ultimate solution would be a cartridge-loading machine. Of this more later.

Those who attended the Toronto convention seemed generally enthusiastic in their response to 8mm sound film; this has been typical in all recent SMPTE meetings.

8mm sound film was heavily represented in the programs of the

90th SMPTE meeting at Lake Placid in October, 1961, of the 91st meeting in Los Angeles in April, 1962, and of the 92nd meeting in Chicago in October, 1962. Indeed, the basic news release from the 92nd SMPTE convention dealt far more with developments in 8mm sound than with any other topic.

It is hardly surprising, of course, that a society such as the SMPTE would be ahead of most other agencies in disseminating information about the 8mm sound film development. Many of its members are the men who design the projectors, manufacture the film, and run the laboratories.

The laboratories prepare

Quantity runs of silent prints of 8mm films have been made in this country for some time, and particularly since World War II. The advent of 8mm *sound* film, however, called for a new look at the burgeoning 8mm medium, now moving from the status of amateur plaything to a position of who-knows-what significance. A processing laboratory which pioneered in 8mm sound film prints was the Geo. W. Colburn Laboratory of Chicago. Very early in the sound movement, they had designed and installed the equipment necessary to make reduction prints from 16mm to 8mm (Colburn, 1961); it was this laboratory with which Eastman Kodak contracted to print the small demonstration reels packaged with their new 8mm sound projector. Colburn's leadership has continued, and the attitude of management there, as in other respected laboratories, is a healthy one, that of maintaining high quality to preserve the integrity of the new field. In addition, General Laboratories of Kansas City and Hollywood, and Calvin Productions of Kansas City have also made important research, design, and equipment commitments to 8mm sound, and are now delivering prints. And, while there are undoubtedly other laboratories of importance in this field, special mention should be made of the Technicolor Corporation of Hollywood and London. It can play a large role through the years in the introduction of 8mm film, because its "dye transfer" film printing process is uniquely suited to mass runs of 8mm prints.

Educational motion picture producers and distributors hesitate

Educational motion picture producers and distributors have not responded quickly in this country to 8mm film, sound or silent. The three major houses—Encyclopaedia Britannica Films, McGraw-Hill Films, and Coronet Films—have taken somewhat different positions.

Encyclopaedia Britannica Films has not stated a policy in print, although its salesmen and officials frequently express a "wait-and-see" or an "it-will-never-happen-here" attitude toward 8mm *sound*. However, some eighteen months after the Technicolor *silent* 8mm cartridge-loading projector was marketed (see below), EBF announced that it would begin producing 8mm cartridge films in the science areas of the curriculum.

Vice President Ellsworth Dent of Coronet Films, in a statement at Teachers College in November of 1961, expressed doubt for a number of reasons—financial and other—about 8mm sound film, but also said: "We at Coronet Films will watch the progress of 8mm sound in education with great interest. . . ." (Dent, 1962). The clear implication of this is that Coronet prefers to wait until 8mm has achieved greater maturity before making significant investments.

Albert J. Rosenberg of McGraw-Hill Films has taken a stronger stand in his statement: "John Flory has characterized the development of 8mm as another milestone in the communication revolution. . . . We think he is right; it is not going to happen tomorrow or next year, but it probably will happen within the next five to ten years." (Rosenberg, 1962) McGraw-Hill Films also announced its decision to begin making cartridge films for the Technicolor projector at the same time as Encyclopaedia Britannica Films' announcement.

Most immediate action in supplying 8mm sound prints has been taken by a number of small educational film houses, who have undoubtedly had miniscule sales of 8mm prints. The Heath de Rochemont Corporation was atypical in its commitment; in late 1961 it offered a year's set of French language films—its "Parlons Francais" series—in a package together with an 8mm sound projector. This attempt to break the chicken-and-egg problem of owning projectors and having films available for purchase has not met with notable success, however.

The Methodist Film-of-the-Month

One agency which recognized the unique opportunities of 8mm sound film at an early date, and was willing to offer leadership in opening the field, was the Television, Radio and Film Commission (TRAFCO) of the Methodist Church. Early in 1962, they announced an experiment with an 8mm "Film-of-the-Month" plan for Methodist churches. Aware of the uncertainties of this innovation, TRAFCO set up a six-month experimental period in which to evaluate the market possibilities in the Methodist Church for the new film gauge. Selected churches were offered an introductory package of five 8mm sound color films (totalling 103 minutes in length), an 8mm sound projector, and a screen for a cost of $398; TRAFCO noted that the same package in 16mm would cost more than $1,300. The contracting church would also agree to purchase three additional films to be offered within a twelve-month period.

In its attractive color-illustrated brochure, TRAFCO offered a persuasive statement in favor of 8mm sound film, which is reprinted here to illustrate the kind of argument that has been used to persuade potential buyers to be attentive to the innovation.

> By starting your Film-of-the-Month library, films are available as you need them. No longer is it necessary to book rented films far in advance of their actual use.
>
> *   *   *
>
> This added flexibility brings new pleasure and efficiency into your audio-visual program. You now use a single film in part or in its entirety, or portions from several films, whichever will best fit your needs.
>
> Film-of-the-Month will save you money. By owning films, you eliminate most costs inherent in rental charges. Such items as film inspection, shipping charges and inventory control are reduced or eliminated.
>
> The average rental fee for a 15-minute color film in 16mm is $6. Now, large quantity purchases and low 8mm printing costs, make it possible to own this same film for less than $24, the cost of four rental showings.
>
> By owning your films, you show them as often as you wish to as many groups as you wish. No longer is it necessary to pull large groups together for every showing in order to justify rental costs. The cost-per-viewer on each film is so low that it is practical to use any film with even the smallest groups. (TRAFCO, undated)

The great potential of TRAFCO in opening up this new film field is its access to some 40,000 Methodist churches in this country, many of which are prospective purchasers. Since the Methodist educational curriculum for Sunday school work is recommended on a national basis, and is largely accepted by local churches, TRAFCO hoped that 8mm would enable each church school class to use the appropriate motion picture material at the same time—a goal which could never be achieved if the films were sent out on a rental basis from central libraries. This would, of course, make necessary large print orders at the laboratories—exactly the kind of situation tailor-made for an 8mm breakthrough.

Jeff Whatley, Associate Director of Audio-Visual Resources for TRAFCO, and an outspoken advocate of vigorous 8mm innovation, observes that their initial explorations into the probable success of the Film-of-the-Month plan were encouraging.[2] In the middle of the six-month experimental period, however, debates began within engineering circles: should the magnetic sound track of 8mm film be replaced in favor of a photographic sound track, or should some combination of the two be used? The problem which TRAFCO faced was whether it could in good conscience advocate purchase of a magnetic projector and begin sales of magnetic-striped films, if the chances of moving to the photographic track in the near future seemed high. The doubt cast by the sound-track indecision was compounded shortly when proposals in influential engineering quarters were made to change almost everything about 8mm sound film—size of the sprocket holes, placement of the sound track on the film, and size of the picture area on the film. (More of these important technical matters shortly.)

Disturbed by the presence of these questions of technical indecision, TRAFCO has now decided to wait them out. Their thinking about the long-range potential of 8mm sound film in Methodist educational plans remains optimistic, however. Whatley reports that in their initial demonstrations of 8mm sound film to Methodist church people in nine states, they found almost universal acceptance of the 8mm picture and sound. Indeed, they discovered that under proper conditions 8mm sound film could be used successfully with groups as large as 300, far more than the group of 50 or so normally recommended as maximum for 8mm. Further, TRAFCO feels that 8mm is the only solution currently available for the problem of placing copies of films on deposit in significant numbers of local Methodist churches.

The TRAFCO potential as a spearheading influence of great significance is dormant, then, awaiting resolution of technical problems which do not lie within its power to control.

[2] Mr. Whatley was good enough to read and approve this material on the Methodist Film-of-the-Month plan.

The Technicolor projector

While the addition of a sound track to 8mm film dominated interest in 1960 and early 1961, the attention of some observers turned to 8mm silent film when the Technicolor Corporation introduced a striking new 8mm silent projector in late 1961. It may play a most significant role in the future of 8mm in education.

The important feature of the machine is that *no threading whatsoever is required*. Four to five minutes of silent film is enclosed in a plastic cartridge which can be plugged into the projector instantly and without difficulty. Four- and five-year-old children can learn to operate it in a minute or so. The machine sells for from $60 to about $300, depending on the model purchased. It is the most striking advance in the design of projectors since Edison's day.

To anyone who has seen teachers struggle with the threading problems of the standard 16mm or 8mm projector, the Technicolor machine carries an obvious message: "Anybody can now use motion pictures." Teachers who have examined it respond positively and strongly. This type of machine will not only make the use of motion pictures easier for teachers, but, for the first time in the history of the medium, everyone—including very young children—will be able to use motion pictures in *independent* study. This latter fact offers educators the opportunity for development of striking new types of educational films which involve the viewer in more active learning than film has ever previously afforded.

These include illustration films conveying a single major concept, often from the sciences; drill films in mathematics and language arts, which capitalize on the unique pacing potential of motion pictures; reading films which invite the child to read as a necessary part of the film experience; skill films; films illustrating cyclical processes; and progamed material including motion.

Striking as the new Technicolor projector is, American educators have typically commented on its inability to play a sound track. British educators apparently often see a pedagogical advantage in the lack of sound—it permits the resourceful teacher to comment in his own way about a film during projection. Indeed, one British group, the Educational Film Centre, began—even before widespread release of the projector—to plan production of "single concept" silent science films for use in the Technicolor machine. Writing about the formation of the Centre, whose first object was to produce concept films for use in science classes, C. P. Snow, one of the founders, observed: *"I believe we are about to see an application of narrow-gauge film to education and industry which will be as revolutionary as the paper-back has become in publication and which will come far more speedily."* (1962, italics Snow's)

Late in 1962, the Educational Film Centre announced plans for publishing an occasional supplement, to be called *Concept Film,* in the English magazine, *The Science Teacher.* Writing about plans for the supplement, Roger Manvell, a director of the Educational Film Centre, observed: "We want *Concept Film* to act as a clearing-house for information about all concept films that either have been or are being produced, and to include articles about the concept film as a new factor in education and about the experience of teachers who are beginning to make use of the medium." [3]

Technicolor Ltd. also began in 1962 to make "single concept" films, working with a selected group of British teachers. They also started manufacture of a self-enclosed rear-projection screen machine (the 800-E) built around the mechanism of the Technicolor 800, the basic machine introduced a year earlier in the United States.

Meanwhile, there was also some early American response to the silent Technicolor projector on the part of film producers, although some educators were bemoaning its lack of sound. In 1962, Educational Services Inc., of Watertown, Massachusetts, began selling a package of nine black-and-white cartridges on wave-motion phenomena, adapted from existing 16mm footage. The set of cartridges could be purchased alone, or with a Technicolor projector at a discount price. Subsequently, Educational Services Inc. has packaged other cartridge sets in the sciences, and has announced plans for greatly enlarged production of cartridge films, drawing heavily on clips from existing 16mm films.

The Project in Educational Communication at Teachers College began exploring ideas for cartridge-loading films in 1961; in early 1963, this group was engaging in the professional production for research purposes of silent cartridge films in the areas of arithmetic, reading, the language arts, science, music, and the visual arts. Inter-

[3] Letter from Roger Manvell to Louis Forsdale, November 1, 1962.

estingly, the first cartridge film made by the Project was a *sound* film, completed in 1962, almost a year before the first cartridge-loading sound projector was placed on the market. This film, called *English Face-to-Face*, was the prototype of a method for use in teaching foreign languages through the aid of a cartridge-loading 8mm sound projector. Probably the first sound film ever designed explicitly to exploit the advantages of cartridge-loading,[4] this film was being appraised overseas in standard 16mm form when Fairchild announced its cartridge-loading sound projector.

Cartridge-loading 8mm sound projectors

Although the Technicolor cartridge-loading silent projector was the first such machine on the market, a cartridge-loading sound projector was not far behind. In February, 1963, the Fairchild Camera and Instrument Corporation announced development of a rear-screen cartridge-loading 8mm sound projector. Looking something like a small television set, it is intended to serve one viewer. It uses a cartridge, not compatible with the Technicolor cartridge, which carries up to thirty minutes of film. Meanwhile, Technicolor Ltd. of England has been working on a sound model of its pioneer silent machine. Other cartridge-loading 8mm sound projectors are reported in development by smaller organizations.

Unfortunately, one cannot report at this time how these machines are being received; it is too early, even for the Fairchild projector. This much is certain, however: bringing a machine to prototype stage or to marketing stage may assure its technical feasibility, but not necessarily its market success. It is probable that the latter will depend as much on availability of educationally sound materials which will exploit these machines' teaching potential, as upon the machines themselves.

---

[4] The film is designed for use in two cartridges. Cartridge A presents the lesson to be studied—two Americans talking with a foreign student in a natural street scene. When the learner is satisfied that he understands the language and cultural content of Cartridge A, he inserts Cartridge B, with which he practices. It is a replay of the first cartridge, except that the foreign student does not appear. The two Americans look out at the film viewer, speaking their lines to him and pausing for his speeches. The viewer is required to answer, filling in the gaps in the sound track, literally talking face-to-face with the characters on the screen.

Other types of simplified 8mm projectors

In addition to the cartridge-loading approach to simplification, other approaches are being made; these include an automatic threading 8mm machine, and a unique "channel-loading" 8mm machine (in which film is placed in a channel like that of a tape recorder, and is threaded automatically by the pushing of a button). The latter machine was designed by John Maurer of JM Developments in New York City, and, while only in prototype stage, is striking in its departure from traditional design. One has little doubt that other types of simple projectors are in various stages of research and development.

The Teachers College Project in Educational Communication

As technical advances were being made, thought was being given to the educational implications of 8mm. In the fall of 1960, the Project in Educational Communication of the Horace Mann–Lincoln Institute of School Experimentation at Teachers College, Columbia University, was set up; [5] it has played an important early role in bringing the attention of educators to 8mm film. Begun at the suggestion of Professor A. W. Foshay, Executive Officer of the Institute, the Project initially centered on 8mm *sound* film, although the attractiveness of the Technicolor silent projector as an educational tool shortly turned attention to the silent medium as well.

In the early spring of 1961, members of the Project decided that a major conference on the subject of 8mm sound film and education should be held to permit exchange of views and raising of critical questions. It would also serve as an occasion for the production of papers, which could be published for further dissemination of information. The conference, held November 8–10, 1961, was attended by some 150 leaders in the audio-visual field, with representation about equally drawn from the photographic industries and education.

The conference included the presentation of formal papers, informal presentations by individuals and panels, the showing of a number of 8mm sound films, and discussion from the floor. Part of an afternoon was devoted to the demonstration and inspection of 8mm sound equipment which had been provided by manufacturers. Sessions covered a

[5] Joan Rosengren, Stuart Selby, and John Swayze have served as Research Assistants in the Project.

range of topics: reports of industry readiness; speculation about educational uses; cost analyses; consideration of new film types suggested by highly accessible 8mm film. Emphasis was almost exclusively on 8mm *sound* film, although the Technicolor silent cartridge machine was shown during the equipment demonstrations.

The tone of the conference was in the main optimistic about 8mm sound film, although enough doubts about the medium, either from a technical or financial point of view, were expressed to temper unabated enthusiasm.

The conference aroused much interest. Although there is no reliable way of assessing its importance as a device for stimulating communication about the 8mm development, certain tangible results are apparent. Articles based upon it subsequently appeared in *Educational Screen, Audio-Visual Instruction, Film News, Popular Photography, Industrial Screen* (in England), *Teachers College Record, Art Education, Education U.S.A., Scholastic Teacher, Variety,* and various newspapers. Secondly, a paperback book, *8mm Sound Film and Education*, containing the conference proceedings was published (Forsdale, 1962). The circulation and influence of this document are not yet known, but would be interesting in assessing the effects of the conference as a facilitator of innovation.

The conference solidified for many people (both those who attended it and those who are still responding to material which came from it) the feeling that 8mm film has an important educational contribution to make. Members of the Project came away convinced that the technology was ready, or nearly ready, and that the primary weaknesses in the total system were in the availability of materials for use on the projectors, and in thinking about new techniques of distribution. Convinced that a breakthrough in 8mm depended, at the outset at least, on unique materials—not merely reductions of existing 16mm prints—they began to explore film ideas which were peculiarly appropriate for the cartridge-loading sound or silent machine. *English Face-to-Face*, the sound film made for a then nonexistent projector, has been described. In addition, a heavy concentration of effort went to exploration of silent cartridge film ideas. The primary goal of the Project since the conference has been to offer leadership by making and testing prototypes of the kinds of films which are suggested by the cartridge-loading development.

The Project in Educational Communication undoubtedly represents the greatest expenditure of time, talent, and money on the 8mm development within the educational enterprise. It has provided leadership in two key professional groups—The Society of Motion Picture and Television Engineers and the Department of Audiovisual Instruction of the NEA. It has provided the profession with a clearing house for ideas, and has been a way station for dozens of educators from around the world who are seeking information about the new development. It has supplied the press with a great deal of copy, both in the form of articles written by Project members and in the form of material for articles. (The press, alas, has reacted on occasion with astonishing inaccuracy, creating a totally or partially false impression of the current state of 8mm.) It has provided speeches and demonstrations for dozens of classes, meetings, and conventions. That the Project has been influential is apparent; how influential, and with whom, is not yet known.

Current Technical Issues

The magnetic vs. photographic sound track debate

In a field which rests upon technology, technical decisions—or *in*decisions—can *delay* development of the field. With respect to 8mm sound film, two technical debates which reflect such indecision should be noted. The first of these is on the question of magnetic vs. photographic sound track.

As noted earlier, the sound track on 8mm sound film is normally carried on a thin stripe of iron oxide, a magnetic material which is placed along the edge of the film. An alternative means of providing sound is the photographic (or "optical") track, in which sound is carried in the form of a visual image on the edge of the film; this system is normally employed in 16mm educational films.

Vigorous spokesmanship for the photographic track on 8mm film has been represented by John A. Maurer, a widely respected photographic engineer (Maurer, 1961). His advocacy has frequently been applauded, but has sometimes been met with expressions of dismay and bitterness by those who feel that customers are satisfied with the magnetic track, and that the success of 8mm sound film is being hampered by introduction of doubt. After all, they ask, what shall a customer do in the face of debate within the industry? He must ask himself: Which track will win in the long run, magnetic or photographic? Should he invest in 8mm sound equipment now, or wait until this problem is settled?

The magnetic track was probably adopted originally for two reasons. First, it is clearly the most useful technique for the amateur who wants to add a sound track to his silent film. He merely sends silent film to a laboratory for addition of a magnetic stripe; on getting the film back, he records his personal sound track on it while running the machine through the projector, as he would with a tape recorder. A second probable reason for the introduction of magnetic sound on 8mm is the assumption generally held among engineers that it offers a number of technical advantages. These include: (1) higher-quality sound reproduction than is generally possible with a photographic system; (2) a physical means of separating film on the spool (i.e., the magnetic stripe), which can serve to prolong the life of the picture; (3) assumed longer life of the sound track.

Proponents of the photographic track, on the other hand, argue that: (1) it will be cheaper to produce in the laboratory; and (2) it will be equal to or only slightly inferior in sound quality to the magnetic system.

Meanwhile, as this technical debate continues, those who are firmly committed to the magnetic system feel that nothing is served by the debate except the planting of doubt in the minds of potential users—who may choose to wait until the final decision is made before moving into the 8mm field. Advocates of photographic sound argue that inquiry cannot be halted merely to serve immediate commercial interest—and that, indeed, economic success of the 8mm sound film field may depend on their winning this debate.

The "new format" problem

The second technical debate was begun at the 91st meeting of the Society of Motion Picture and Television Engineers in Hollywood, in April, 1962, when a brief paper was read suggesting profound changes in 8mm sound film as we now know it. The paper (Staud and Hanson, 1962), written by two Eastman Kodak engineers (and widely taken to be an expression of Kodak policy) suggested, in rather vague terms, moving the sound track from one side of the film to the other and reducing the size of the sprocket holes. This would permit considerable enlargement of the picture area, providing a brighter and sharper image, a clear technical advance over current practice.

But if the theoretical advantages of the position presented by Staud and Hanson are clear, the practical results of moving in such a direction are not. A widely held assumption is that putting this new format into effect would require the purchase of new cameras, projectors, laboratory processing equipment, and other components which are needed in the system. All existing 8mm cameras and projectors would either have to be replaced or adapted in order to use the new format. Given the fact that we already have a useable 8mm sound film system, on which basic standards have been presented and approved by the American Standards Association, the introduction of a new format would probably mean the use of two systems (the old and the new), at least for a number of years. The situation could be parallel to the use of 45 rpm and 33⅓ rpm records: either separate projectors would be required, or dual-purpose projectors would be necessary.

Whatever the results of the Great Format Debate in the future, it has probably slowed the introduction of 8mm sound film in education, and in other fields. At least one audio-visual leader has concluded that in view of the Eastman Kodak "position," educators should not now make major investments in the 8mm sound film field, lest they be obsolete in the near future. Other observers, including the writer, have felt that a switch from the present format to a new one would take many years and that the old format would not be completely displaced even then. One cannot afford to wait upon stabilization of any technology, for in a society such as ours stabilization will never come. Progress in a technical society implies change; obsolescence is the price we pay.

What Does the Future Hold?

Given this picture—oversimplified as it is—of agencies and forces which constitute the major dynamics of the 8mm field in American education today, where do we stand?

We stand at a point where the photographic industry knows a good deal about the medium, and expects much from it. In the past three

years, "8" has probably occupied more time in SMPTE circles than
any other single subject: the engineers sense new technical triumphs;
the businessmen smell a hot commercial item. Educators are less well
informed about 8mm, although leaders in the audio-visual field are
rapidly learning of it through demonstrations, talks at national conferences, and articles in professional journals. A very few school systems have purchased new 8mm projectors and are experimenting.
School administrators who attend national conventions and keep up
with current literature have heard scraps here and there about the
development; some few have "made up their minds" pro or con, probably too early in either case. The average teacher has little idea that
anything of importance is stirring in the 8mm field.

What does the future hold? One can only seek opinions and speculate.

Opinion sampling about 8mm

At this writing, two questionnaire sampling studies are being made
by the SMPTE Ad Hoc Committee on the Utility of Small Format
Motion Picture Films. The purpose of these questionnaires—one of
which is directed at informed 8mm users in business and industry, the
other at educators who know the medium—is to seek guidance about
whether 8mm sound film in its present form is adequate in quality to
the task of presenting visual and auditory information in the kinds
of situations where it is being used, or where its use is contemplated.[6]
The Committee hopes that this information will be useful in illuminating the technical debate now occurring with respect to 8mm format.
Whether the data will help *solve* the format problem, one cannot say;
they will reveal much useful information about attitudes of 8mm
users, however. But these returns are not in.

Meanwhile, results of an earlier informal opinion-sampling study
about the future of 8mm are available. Conducted by Mark Slade,
Education Liaison Officer of the National Film Board of Canada,
the study was made shortly after the Teachers College 8mm conference, in late 1961 and early 1962. The questionnaire was sent to some
150 persons who attended the Teachers College conference, supple-

---

[6] This committee is chaired by the writer. The business–industry users'
survey is being conducted by William Hedden of Calvin Productions, Inc., of
Kansas City, Missouri, and the educational survey by Professor Robert Wagner,
Director of the Division of Motion Pictures of The Ohio State University.

mented by a number of state, provincial, and municipal audio-visual directors in Canada—180 people in all. In compiling the results, which are reprinted below in Table 1, the first 100 replies were used, simply as a matter of convenience.[7]

Certain observations about the responses may be useful. First, one should note the strong feeling (in response to Question 1) that 8mm sound film would be available for general classroom use before a decade was out, with the majority of respondents feeling that this would occur within four years. The 29 people who anticipated widespread availability in education within twelve months to two years were clearly wrong, however, and the three-year group is rapidly proving itself to have been overoptimistic, too.

Apropos of the feeling that greatest use and acceptance of 8mm sound film would be in the home (Question 2), it should be observed that home use to date is rumored to be quite small, although figures on projector sales are not a matter of public information. Business and industry have indeed responded. Education has not.

The division of opinion in response to Question 4, about the desirability and effectiveness of optical (photographic) vs. magnetic sound track, nicely reflects the near stand-off which prevails in engineering and business circles. The other technical issue—that of changing the format—had not been raised at the time of Slade's questionnaire.

Question 5, inquiring into 8mm sound film's probable effect on 16mm, treats an issue which is of utmost importance. Many school systems have large, hard-won, commitments to 16mm. The specter of 16mm projectors and print libraries becoming obsolete is frightening to some observers, but the respondents sampled here apparently felt the likelihood of this prospect was not great. (The writer feels that this doubt is graveyard whistling; *in the long run*, 8mm is quite likely to replace 16mm for most—although not all—educational purposes.) The fact that respondents accept the prevailing view (it's almost a cliché by now) that 8mm will not replace 16mm is a happy circum-

---

[7] Responses to each question do not always add up the numbers of people replying, because two answers were often checked, and "no opinion" or "don't know" answers were not tabulated. Slade observes, too, that while many answers were qualified, the table does not reveal this. He also notes that respondents vary considerably in the amount of thought they have given to the subject. "Armed with considerable hindsight," he regrets "the fuzzy wording of several . . . questions."

Table 1. Sampling of Opinion on the Educational Possibilities of 8mm Sound Film

SURVEY QUESTION		TOTAL SAMPLING (first 100 replies)			SELECTED GROUPS (from first 100 replies)	
		Total (100)	Educators, U.S. & Canada (69)	Company Executives, U.S. only (31)	University Faculty (15)	Educators, Canada only (33)
1. Do you expect that 8mm sound film will be available for general classroom use within the next:	12 months	6	1	5	1	0
	2 years	23	14	9	6	4
	3 years	19	12	7	4	1
	4 years	13	9	4	2	5
	5–10 years	33	26	7	2	16
2. Is the greatest use and acceptance of 8mm sound film likely to be in:	Classrooms	28	19	9	6	5
	Business & Industry	34	16	18	4	4
	Homes	40	31	9	6	20
3. Would you feel that 8mm sound film is unlikely to be widely accepted for classroom use unless the cost of film and equipment, compared with current 16mm prices, is:	25% less	15	9	6	3	3
	50% less	48	34	14	7	12
	60–75% less	38	27	11	6	13

Question	Response					
4. Which sound system is likely to be most desirable and effective in 8mm?	Optical	44	32	12	5	15
	Magnetic striping	41	24	17	7	10
	Not important	14	10	4	3	5
5. Relative to 16mm film, will the general acceptance of 8mm sound film in education tend to:	Make 16mm obsolete	22	16	6	1	12
	Supplement 16mm film	43	27	16	5	12
	Take a different form	45	30	15	11	4
6. Relative to the success of the medium, is cartridge loading of 8mm sound projectors likely to be:	Crucial	25	21	4	7	5
	Desirable	47	30	17	6	14
	Not decisive	30	18	12	2	11
7. Is 8mm sound film likely to make new demands on the producer to revise his outlook on the film as an art form?	Yes	60	42	18	11	15
	No	30	17	13	3	11
8. Is there a possibility, in your view, that publishers of text books will enter the educational film field as a result of 8mm sound film (i.e., "package deals")?	Yes	87	60	27	15	22
	No	8	6	2	0	6
9. Is the revival of silent film on 8mm for educational purposes a likely possibility in the relatively near future?	Yes	35	25	10	10	5
	No	58	37	21	5	25

stance, for such an outlook is nearly essential for successful introduction of 8mm into well-established audio-visual programs. And, in any case, the growth of 8mm will probably be so gradual that it will not truly threaten 16mm holdings—films and equipment—unless they are literally being *held* rather than *used*. For if they are being used, they will wear out and need to be replaced; that replacement can be with 8mm.

It is clear from Question 6 that respondents feel the cartridge-loading projector to be at least desirable. A group of respectable size doubts the need for such machines in making the innovation successful, however; they apparently see low 8mm print costs and projector prices—or perhaps simplified projectors of another style—as the great leverage point for change.

Although some ambiguity is apparent in the seventh question, it is probable that the 60 respondents who felt that 8mm film would cause the film producer to revise his outlook on "the film as an art form" were accepting, for example, the idea that 8mm calls for greater use of close-ups than does 16mm, to compensate for the lessened ability of the former to record small detail.

Question 8 shows an astonishingly large agreement that even more textbook publishers will enter the educational film field with 8mm. Probably embedded in this response is the view that new film distribution patterns will be established, an opinion in which the writer concurs.

Answers to Question 9 are undoubtedly colored by the fact that many members of the sample group had recently seen the Technicolor cartridge-loading silent projector at the Teachers College conference. One doubts if so large a number would have commented positively about the revival of silent film with the standard projector in mind. As events have subsequently worked out, the majority of respondents here were apparently too conservative; as this is being written, silent film using cartridge projectors is well on its way to becoming an educational reality, perhaps one of some importance.

Requirements for spread of 8mm

However optimistic about 8mm most of these respondents were, the innovation is still no more than incipient. What will be required to move 8mm into a central position in education?

It seems to the author that 8mm systems which are offered to the schools must be truly innovational, in three respects. First, because a taste of the possibilities has been given, projectors must be profoundly simpler to use than are present 16mm machines. They must be lighter and cheaper, too. Second, marketing techniques must be developed which will at first get projectors and films as packages into users' hands, and which will thereafter permit purchase of 8mm prints at prices well below the cost of the same subject on 16mm. The guess here is that 50 per cent reduction will do the job, but that is a big step. Third, to feed the new film market and viewing context created by the revolutionary cartridge projectors, fresh (often quite short) motion pictures film types must be developed.

The challenge of simple projectors is rapidly being met. Some thought has been given to the problem of marketing films; but in terms of the magnitude of the need, it is barely being touched. Unless we are able to depart from traditional numbers and procedures in educational film marketing, the essential low cost cannot be achieved. The development of new film types exploiting the new simpler projectors is being explored in few—too few—quarters. This may be the most vital problem of the lot; for high accessibility of motion pictures will call for re-examination of what films are for, for whom they are made, and when they are to be used. Negatives of existing 16mm educational films will provide many titles, and clips, for 8mm systems, but we dare not rely long on existing 16mm material. Providing *excellent* films for an 8mm film usage which is increasingly central to the curriculum will require a major effort, supported by large investments from business, government, and foundations.

The prediction, then, is that 8mm innovation in education will not occur quickly in breadth. It seems likely now that the cartridge-loading 8mm *silent* projector, with a growing stock of available short films for use with it, will lead the way. Silent though it is, the revolutionary nature of this machine, at its low price, will not be denied. Further, this machine, with its short film capacity and its small image, does not at the moment challenge existing 16mm systems—a matter of enormous importance.

8mm sound film will have its day in education, too, but there are increasing signs that the two big technical debates (magnetic *vs.* photographic sound tracks and present *vs.* new format) will have to be resolved in some fashion before large commitments are made in education. Given that accomplished fact, projectors of new design, and film prints of high quality distributed in quantity at low cost, will greatly increase the uses of film in education.

Meanwhile, in this study in the ecology of change, a last element should be noted: video tape. Ever since the introduction of video tape as a means of recording and storing moving images and sound, predictions have been made that briefcase-size, budget-priced recorders and playback units would soon be available. And video tape machines *have* come down in price—to "only" $15,000. The problem is to force the price much lower while building a machine which does not require an engineer to operate it. To observe that the electronics industry is aggressively innovative—far more so than the motion picture industry has been—is to state the obvious. Still, this writer believes that classroom or personal video tape has little chance yet of competing with 8mm film in cost, quality (including color), and ease of use. Other observers disagree. In any event, a race between the two systems could only increase the accessibility of moving images in education, a result worthy of the best efforts of many of us.

Panofsky reminded us that the film medium was a gift of technical invention: the process was given us, and then we learned how to use it. 8mm is another episode in the history of film innovation. All the components of the system—projectors, films, laboratory facilities, distributional channels—must be available at the same time, and at a price education can afford, if we are to learn how to use it properly for educational purposes. Unless the commercial interests risk funds generously and daringly now to supply these components, the innovation can remain indefinitely incipient. Only if industry works with education can the innovation be realized.

References

Calvin Productions, Inc. (Kansas City, Mo.) *The Aperture,* 1963, 70 (2), 2.

Camras, M. Magnetic sound for 8mm project. *Jour. Soc. Mot. Picture & Telev. Engrs.,* 1947, 49 (10), 348–356.

Colburn, R. A. 8mm color positive release prints with magnetic sound: a progress report. *Jour. Soc. Mot. Picture & Telev. Engrs.,* 1961, 70 (8), 603–606.

Dent, E. Coronet films looks at 8mm. In L. Forsdale (Ed.), *8mm sound film and education.* New York: Bureau of Publications, Teachers College, Columbia University, 1962. P. 83.

Flory, J. The challenge of 8mm sound film. *Jour. Soc. Mot. Picture & Telev. Engrs.,* 1961, 70 (8), 581.

Forsdale, L. An educator looks at 8mm sound film. *Jour. Soc. Mot. Picture & Telev. Engrs.,* 1961, 70 (8), 593–595.

Forsdale, L. (Ed.). *8mm sound film and education.* New York: Bureau of Publications, Teachers College, Columbia University, 1962.

Knudsen, S. 8mm and the classroom film library: potentials and requirements. *Jour. Soc. Mot. Picture & Telev. Engrs.,* 1961, 70 (8), 595–597.

Maurer, J. A. Photographic sound for 8mm film. *Jour. Soc. Mot. Picture & Telev. Engrs.,* 1961, 70 (8) 618–623.

Panofsky, E. Style and medium in the motion pictures. In D. Talbot (Ed.), *Film: an anthology.* New York: Simon & Schuster, 1959. P. 15. Originally published in *Bull. Dept. Art & Archaeol.,* Princeton University, 1934.

Rosenberg, A. J. McGraw-Hill studies the 8mm sound film field. In L. Forsdale (Ed.), *8mm sound film and education.* New York: Bureau of Publications, Teachers College, Columbia University, 1962. P. 87.

Snow, C. P. The new vision in the schoolroom. *Science Teacher,* 1962, 5 (5), 83.

Slade, M. Sampling of opinion on the educational possibilities of 8mm sound film. Paper distributed in February 1962. Multilithed, available from the author.

Staud, C. J., & Hanson, W. T. Some aspects of 8mm sound color print quality. Paper read at Soc. Mot. Picture & Telev. Engrs. meeting, 1962. Mimeographed, available from the authors.

Thompson, L. Problems in the design of an 8mm magnetic sound-on-film projector. *Jour. Soc. Mot. Picture & Telev. Engrs.,* 1961, 70 (8), 588–589. Reprinted from *Photographic Science and Technique,* 1954.

TRAFCO. *A new horizon in Christian communication: Film-of-the-Month.* Nashville: Television, Radio and Film Commission of the Methodist Church, undated.

CHAPTER 9

Programed instruction in the schools: innovation and innovator

LASSAR G. GOTKIN
LEO S. GOLDSTEIN

CURRENT interest in programed instruction, and the vitality of the field, are attested to by the large number of programs that have been written and are being offered for sale (Center for Programed Instruction, 1963a); the profusion of articles in both professional and lay journals pertaining to this new educational technology (Schramm, 1962; Silberman, 1962); and, to a lesser but rapidly growing extent, the increasing use of programed instruction in our nation's schools.

Any innovation, bringing with it solutions to some problems, is liable to create additional difficulties. This chapter [1] examines some of the ways in which programed instruction has been used in the schools, some effects the introduction of this technology has had on the curriculum and on classroom structure, and some problems of learner achievement and motivation which are beginning to emerge as the innovation spreads.

[1] This chapter was adapted from a speech delivered at the RCA Lecture Series, Radio Corporation of America, Camden, New Jersey (Gotkin, 1962).

THE AUTHORS, formerly affiliated with the Center for Programed Instruction, are Senior Research Associates, Institute for Developmental Studies, Department of Psychiatry, New York Medical College.

231

Programed Instruction in Schools

Present use

"Teachers" housed in programed textbooks and teaching machines have moved out of the laboratory into the classroom. A recently completed survey (Center for Programed Instruction, 1963*b*) found that 11 per cent (209 out of 1,886) of the responding school systems were using programed materials in some way.

While 57 per cent of the users indicated that they had been using programed instruction on a trial basis, only 1 per cent of the entire sample said that, on the basis of their experiences, they would not use similar materials in the future.

Asked about their plans for future use, those who had used programed instruction responded: for regular instruction, 68 per cent; for enrichment, 60 per cent; and for remedial instruction, 55 per cent.

Those who have had no experience with programed materials differ considerably from users in their plans for the future. Only 20 per cent of the neophytes said they planned to use programed materials for regular instruction; 34 per cent, for enrichment; and 29 per cent, for remedial instruction. It would seem that familiarity does *not* breed contempt, but instead broadens the purposes for which programed instruction will be used.

General reactions of teachers, administrators, boards of education, and parents were checked on a five-point scale ranging from "enthusiastic" to "strongly opposed." (In most cases, the local administrator's *estimates* of the reactions of teachers, parents, etc., are the data involved.) Approximately 75 per cent of administrators, teachers, and students were reported to be either "favorable" or "enthusiastic." Less than 5 per cent of each group were checked in the categories "opposed" or "strongly opposed."

The survey indicates that programed instruction is being used and that the users appear satisfied. The evidence from the survey suggests that fears engendered by the image of the "teaching machine" are readily dispelled by active involvement with programed instruction. The increasing availability of programed materials, as documented in the survey of publishers, *Programs '63* (Center for Programed Instruction, 1963*a*), leaves little doubt that programed instruction, as an innovation in education, has arrived.

Research

Educators considering adopting programed instruction are interested in evidence indicating that programed instruction will produce better results than those they now obtain. Such interest has given rise to a host of studies comparing "programed" with "conventional" instruction. The strategy of these studies has been to pit the classroom teacher against "the teacher in the program." Using the standard of the job being done in the schools, these studies (Silberman, 1962) show the teacher in the programed textbook, by and large, to be *as effective as, and more efficient than,* the classroom teacher: students learn as much in less time from programed instruction. These studies, however, though they have been necessary in the past and will be needed in the future, have three important limitations: (1) The results are not generalizable, since they depend on the particular program, the quality of classroom instruction, and the evaluative instruments used; (2) the results of such comparisons are *group* comparisons, and hide the failure of programs currently available for classroom use to really cope with *individual differences;* (3) in pitting "the teacher in the program" against the teacher in the classroom, to compare "programed" with "conventional" instruction, these studies have contributed to the practice of *limiting the teacher's role* in making use of programed materials to accomplish educational goals.

The role of the teacher has also been limited by the procedures employed in developing programed materials and in carrying out basic research. Gotkin and Goldstein (1962) have pointed out:

> The procedure of developing, testing, and doing basic research with programed materials is, unhappily, devoid of teacher involvement except in the instances where teacher and programer are one and the same. In the creation of a program, sequences of frames are tested by administering them to individual students and, on the basis of student feedback, the sequences are rewritten and refined. Ideally, this process is repeated until a polished, but not necessarily finished, product emerges. The program then undergoes field-testing in the classroom where teacher qua teacher participation is kept to a minimum, so that the program may be assessed on its own merits. Basic research investigating factors of programed instruction such as response mode, amount of reinforcement, pacing, repetition, etc., can be studied best in a 'teacher-less' environment.

Teacher Use of Programed Instruction

What ought to be the relationship between "the teacher in the program" and the teacher in the classroom? While theorists are preoccupied with speculation concerning the ultimate "ought," schools and teachers are beginning to provide evidence of flexible uses of programed materials, in and out of the classroom setting. The use of programed instruction, itself an innovation, may be incorporated into the educational system without disrupting existing classroom practices; or, the introduction of programed instruction in a school system may effect a change in either curriculum or classroom structure.

Nondisruptive use of programed instruction: homework

A study done in Huntington, Long Island, with a spelling program found that students working at home made gains equivalent to those who worked on the program in school.

In New Rochelle, New York, a 365-frame sequence on the gas laws was given to high school students with instructions to go through the program at home, writing their answers on an accompanying sheet which was to be turned in five days later. At that time a written test was administered. Mr. Daniel Wagner, the supervising teacher, felt that valuable class time was saved, and that students with a sound mathematics background did not need supplementary work on the program itself (though those without such a foundation required added instruction).

In Hillside, New Jersey, two classes used a grammar program in school, for forty-minute periods three days a week. Two other classes worked on the program at home three times a week, answering 50 to 100 frames per session, depending on the organization of the materials. The students who worked at home were given the entire program and told when each set was due. The paper on which the pupil had written his responses (his homework) was submitted to the teacher on the day it was due. The few children who had not finished the assignment were required to do it that day in order to keep up with the rest of the class. Some resistance from the homework group had been anticipated. Dr. Walter Krumbiegel, the principal who supervised the experiment, reported that none materialized. Some of the students who worked on the program in school and did not have the opportunity for classroom discussion intimated that they would have liked the chance to discuss the material in class. Matched groups from the in-school use and homework classes achieved statistically equivalent results on the standardized criterion test. Classes that worked on the programs at home were able to cover other topics in class.

In Skokie, Illinois, a vocabulary-building program served as the textbook for a summer course in vocabulary improvement for bright fifth and sixth graders. Students were required to work in class on the program only five minutes a day, but had over-all weekly assignments to complete. Merrel Flair, Coordinator of Special Services and Research, reported that the experiment with the children's working on their own was a success. The teacher has developed supplementary exercises for classroom use, based on the program. A summary report is being prepared.

In teaching statistics, one of the present writers has found that approximately half the students are unable to complete textbook reading assignments—and that about half of those who can are unable to hold intelligent discourse about what they have read. Classroom teaching then becomes a somewhat detailed presentation of the textual material at a rather low level. A most common report from students, indicating the ineffectiveness of this scheme, is, "I understood everything when it was presented in class, but when I looked it over at home, I couldn't understand it at all." With present use of programed instruction as homework material in a statistics course, students are coming to the classroom with intelligent questions and ability to discuss concepts at a high level.

Silverman (1963) has reported similar experiences, using the Holland and Skinner program in place of a textbook in an undergraduate course on the psychology of learning. Early in the course, the students (majors in psychology and education) went through the entire program as homework assignments. Posttests indicated that the majority of the students had mastered the content. Instead of spending time in class presenting the basic concepts, the instructor was able to begin with applications and then go into other learning theories. Silverman reported that spirited discussion made teaching a pleasure, and estimated that a 40 per cent saving in class time resulted from use of the program.

These uses of programed instructional materials as homework indicate that it is possible to incorporate programed materials into the curriculum without bringing about radical changes in the operating arrangements of the school. In using programs as homework instead of class materials, the teacher is freed of the problems created by radical differences in the rates of progress among students. Teachers can exert practical controls over the use of programs by collecting answer sheets and testing periodically.

A most intriguing advantage of using programed materials at home rather than in class was offered by a youngster who commented that when working at home he had time to *think*. In school he hurried, trying to maintain the pace of the faster students; he reported that he spent twice as much time on lessons when he worked at home.

Social psychologists have long been interested in social facilitation, the influence of the group on individual progress. The effect of group pressure on individual rates, attention span, and achievement seems worthy of exploration.

Programed instruction as a lever for innovation

Programed instruction provides educators with a lever for uprooting traditional classroom procedures. Speculations about the potential impact of programed instruction on the educational system have ranged from the removal of illiteracy in underdeveloped areas (Komoski, 1962) to the development of computer-based programs (Coulson, 1962). Instead of speculating, let us offer some illustrations of uses of programed instruction that show, here and now, some aspects of its potential educational impact.

An innovation in classroom structure. John McGowan, a teacher in Manhasset, Long Island, his principal, Henry Bruner, and the administration have used programed instruction to break the traditional classroom structure into a team approach that has resulted in more individualization. It is difficult to describe the Manhasset Plan, since each year the changes indicate further innovation.

This past year, one hundred eighth graders (four classes), working at the same time in one room, used *English 2600* (a grammar program) for three class periods a week. When a student completed a portion of the program, he took a test on that unit. While the test was being corrected by a participating teacher, the student began the next unit. Within a few minutes, the graded test was returned to the student. The teacher reviewed the student's errors with him. If the unit test achievement was below 80 per cent, the student was required to repeat the unit. An equivalent form of the unit test was administered upon completion of the reviewed unit. The mandatory achievement level had to be attained before the student was permitted to advance in the program.

The content of *English 2600* is equivalent to more than a year's work in English grammar at the eighth grade level in Manhasset. It was assumed that a student who completed the program with at least 80 per cent proficiency for each unit had mastered the material. Comparison with previous years' classes revealed a 10 per cent increase in standardized test achievement for those using the program. The increase is statistically significant, and was achieved in less time.

The problem of differing rates was handled by placing students in individualized composition classes upon completion of the program. The first 25 students constituted the first class, the next 25 the second class, and so on. The principles of grammar which the students had learned from the program were then applied to English composition.

Reports of previous trials with *English 2600* suggest that brighter students have been bored with the program. No such reaction has been reported for the Manhasset students. Perhaps elements that contribute to "boredom" were counteracted by: (1) permitting students to bypass units on the basis of pretest results; (2) using unit tests (for most students, seeing that their answers to individual frames are correct is of little consequence compared to obtaining scores that contribute to school grades); (3) providing the student with rapid feedback as to the results of unit tests, including individual explanation of the results; and (4) providing individualized instruction in composition upon completion of the program.

About 10 per cent of the students found the program too difficult; they were placed in a special class in which the program was augmented with classroom instruction and a variety of supplementary teaching materials.

This year, following upon the innovations of last year, programed materials in vocabulary-building and materials in spelling have also been adopted for use in the same over-all plan. Upon satisfactory completion of the spelling materials, students will be sent on to the grammar program, then to vocabulary-building, and finally to individualized composition.

The implications of the Manhasset Plan are many, but what is most unique are the changes in the logistics of classroom practice and teacher behavior. In the near future, we can expect large numbers of investigations of the use of programed materials in educational settings. For want of another and better term, we have been referring to these as *implementation studies*. Such investigations—unlike most current studies of programed materials—will include the *teacher* as a variable. In basic research investigating variables of programed instruction such as response mode, amount of reinforcement, pacing, and repetition, it is usually thought essential to keep the teacher's participation to an absolute minimum. But from the point of view of school usage, it is also important to investigate variables outside the program: not only the teacher's role, but the degree of administrative support, modifications of classroom structure, and procedures for coping with differences in individual rates.

The results of such studies will not finally define the parameters of programed instruction, but they will contribute to our scanty knowledge about the impact of programed instruction on the classroom.

Innovations in curriculum

Discipline-based subject matter.   In the summer of 1962, one of the authors supervised the field test of the first 27 units of a grammar program in English sentence structure (Rogovin, in press). The subject matter programed is based on Noam Chomsky's theory of linguistics, an approach to grammar rarely attempted until graduate school. In 20 to 25 hours, ten sixth, seventh, and eighth graders proceeded through these units. Supervising this field test was rather like being required to umpire a baseball game knowing only the rules of basketball. After a few days, the supervisor had the unnerving experience of being unable to answer questions posed by these junior high school students. Fortunately, their "managers" were not present to complain about the incompetence of the "umpire." The successful programing of such esoteric subject matter seems particularly relevant educationally in light of the currently increased concern with introducing children to modern curricula based on subject matter disciplines (Phenix, 1962) and the problems this raises for the role of the teacher (Lindsey, 1962; Wayland, 1962).

In-service education for teachers. Programed instruction offers a way of bringing new subject matter to teachers as well as to students. In the description below, the mathematics teachers in the Jefferson County, Kentucky, school system used programed instruction to study the modern mathematics they were to introduce into the curriculum.

> The group with whom these materials were used was not typical of those for whom the [programed] texts were intended, since all were members of a teachers' study group which was preparing for the following year's work in ninth and tenth grade algebra. In no way did we attempt to evaluate the outcomes in terms of learning for ourselves. . . . For us the books were available, the content was similar to that we desired to teach, and the possibility of homework assignments of a different kind was evident.

> The study group was composed of ten high school mathematics teachers who were charged with the responsibility of outlining a program in math for bright ninth and tenth grade pupils. All of us had obtained a bachelor's degree in mathematics, and all had attended institutes of various kinds during previous summers and academic years. . . . All of the teachers had taught the University of Maryland mathematics course for junior high school for 3 years and the SMSG geometry course for one year. Our next step was the preparation for our teaching SMSG algebra courses.

> Our in-service work consisted of sessions of 2½ hours on alternate weeks (excluding holidays) or 18 sessions in all, plus a three-week workshop held last June. During the June workshop, teachers were engaged for 6 hours each day, five days per week . . . the time spent on the Science Research Associates materials . . . was approximately half of the above time.

> The teachers followed the course exactly as their pupils would have been required [to], using the answer booklets provided. Our purposes were slightly different, however. We assigned ourselves three jobs to have been done before each session: (1) to make annotated references for each proposed lesson; (2) to suggest approximate length of all assignments to be made from the texts; (3) to note any errors in the content and to note content which would need to be taught prior to a pupil's use of the texts. The teachers did have in their rooms (thanks to National Defense Education Act) some fairly good references (from 50–70 volumes). Each "lesson" covered from 1–4 of the chapters in the ten books of the series.[2]

[2] Letter from Robert D. Neill to Lassar G. Gotkin, Feb. 6, 1963.

Advanced work for gifted children.   In Farmingdale, Long Island, an exploratory study (Gotkin & Massa, 1963) has demonstrated the potential of using programs to introduce advanced material for gifted elementary school children. The Farmingdale study also illustrates certain kinds of administrative problems that need to be faced in using programed instruction.

The auto-instructional program used was the first four books (10 chapters, 1,262 frames) of Dr. Susan M. Markle's *Words* (fifth experimental revision). The subject matter of the program might be labeled vocabulary-building, or word attack skills, but is more adequately characterized by the author:

> The verbal behavior that this program has attempted to produce as an end result might be called the ability to infer meaning. A student who has mastered such a skill can inspect an unfamiliar word, divide it into plausible units, search his own vocabulary for words containing these units, arrive at an approximate definition of each unit, construct therefrom an approximate definition of the new word, and test this definition for its reasonableness in the context in which the word occurs. (Markle, 1962*b*)

While the findings of this study substantiated the efficacy of using programed materials to present advanced subject matters to gifted children, the fourth and fifth graders failed to achieve the level of mastery obtained by eighth graders.

Possible explanations for the "failure" of these students to achieve a higher level of mastery fall into two categories, those of an administrative and pedagogical nature, and those intrinsic to the learner and the learning process.

These were administrative and pedagogical considerations:

1. Special classes were formed for the experiment, and more time was spent in moving from room to room than in the actual use of the materials.
2. The fourth and fifth graders were mixed in a single class; this seemed to influence the fifth graders negatively.
3. The time to complete the four books was compressed, especially at the end of the experimental period, when the work in the booklet was most difficult.
4. At the outset of the experiment, the teachers were not conversant with programed instruction.

5. The teachers were also not familiar with the content of the program; this was especially important for the teacher who was required to augment the program.

The main consideration related to the learner and the learning process was that the fourth and fifth graders lacked the "entry behavior" required for the program. This entry behavior might be generally described as the three to four extra years of experience with language that an eighth grader has over a fourth or fifth grader. The eighth grader has encountered informally, and perhaps formally, a considerable number of words and word parts taught in this program. Learning the meaning of words and word parts that are somewhat familiar is quite different from learning completely new material.

To raise the level of achievement of these fourth and fifth graders on this subject matter, two similar strategies seem possible. Both depend upon analysis of the test results and error rates. The first strategy involves rewriting the entire program to make it appropriate for gifted fourth and fifth graders; the second requires supplementary instruction by the teacher on those aspects of the program which are found through item and error analysis to be inadequate.

The first strategy would be revealing, since it depends upon empirical identification of the entry behavior required for learning from the program. However, in terms of time, money, and talent, it represents an enormous programing commitment. The effects of the second strategy are currently being explored in Farmingdale. Preliminary analysis of the results for this year (with the teacher interacting with the program) shows that every student in this year's fourth grade class has achieved above the mean performance of last year's fourth and fifth graders. Mean performance last year of fourth and fifth graders was 69 per cent; the lowest fourth grade score this year was 74 per cent.

The Farmingdale study is of practical significance for educators concerned with improving the education of the academically talented. Bruner (1960) has suggested, "Experience over the past decade points to the fact that our schools may be wasting precious years by postponing the teaching of many important subjects on the ground that they are too difficult." The content of the *Words* program represents innovation at the junior high school level, let alone at the elementary school level. The Commission on English of the College Entrance

Examination Board has recommended that the curriculum for college-preparatory high school students include systematic instruction in vocabulary-building and word derivation (Fraser, 1962). However, few teachers possess the subject matter training or competence to teach this recommended subject matter—which is the content of the program.

Ideally, the first step in introducing the new curriculum would be to enable the teachers to learn the content by going through the program. However, if time for such preparation is not available, as was the case in Farmingdale, programed instructional materials offer the teacher the opportunity to proceed through the program a few steps ahead of the students. Thus, the first time the program is used, the teacher functions as a learner, as a supervisor, and as an observer. In these capacities the teacher has the opportunity to assess the problems inherent in the program, and can formulate plans for remedying them.

The importance of the Farmingdale study extends beyond its relevance for introducing advanced subject matters early in the curriculum. The content of the *Words* program includes a *method of inquiry* for inferring and testing the meaning of unfamiliar words. What Dr. Markle is teaching is in harmony with Bruner's concern with the structure of knowledge:

> There is at least one major matter that is left unsettled even by a large scale revision of curricula in the direction indicated. Mastery of the fundamental ideas of a field involves not only the grasping of general principles, but also the development of an attitude toward learning and inquiry, toward guessing and hunches, toward the possibility of solving problems on one's own. (Bruner, 1960)

Three types of evidence were obtained that the students made gains in the ability to discover the formation and meaning of words:

1. The gains on the final test were proportionately greater for the section of the test requiring the construction of words.
2. Those students who achieved more on Books I and II scored higher on the pretest for Books III and IV, a result indicating transfer.
3. In a group meeting, subjects showed facility in deriving new words from unfamiliar roots.

Individual Differences and Programed Learning

Ability and achievement

The revolutionary promise of programed instruction has been that each student, proceeding at his own rate, would reach terminal behavior as long as he completed the program (Skinner, 1958). Upon completion of the program, a class's range of performance would be narrowed radically. The correlations between intelligence and posttest performance would be low. But despite the encouraging findings of time saved with equivalent and sometimes superior results, little evidence has been obtained of the *greater* promise of "assuring mastery at every stage," with subject matter approximating any meaningful segment of the curriculum, across a grade level of students with the usual range of abilities.

In Denver, where a grammar program was used with a single grade, no significant differences were found between gains made by the teacher-taught groups and the groups using the program (Reed & Hyman, 1962). When the results were analyzed by three ability levels, the highest ability group, starting with the highest pretest scores, learned the most; the lowest ability group, which had the most to learn, gained *least*. The posttest achievement of the lowest group did not even surpass the pretest achievement of the middle ability group. Results such as these seem to be the rule rather than the exception. (It should be mentioned that teachers were equally unsuccessful in coping with the lowest ability level.)

Boredom

One way to examine the failure of programed instruction to mitigate differences in achievement involves reference to the problem of *boredom* (Cf. Gotkin, 1962). Low motivation to work at a learning task is a typical feature of any learning situation. Practicing before a football game, listening to a lecture, or reading a text may all evoke boredom from a learner. Widespread boredom in any learning activity is presumably an index of a failure at genuine individualization of instruction.

Boredom is thus important for an educational innovation in at least two ways. First, it is evidence that the innovation may not be evoking vigorous, goal-directed activity from the learner; we may thus have legitimate reservations about his learning (though learners can and do learn a great deal without being excited about it). Secondly, regardless of the learning problems associated with low motivation, the existence of boredom seems to be very crucial in affecting the relative speed with which any innovation—programed instruction not excepted—is likely to diffuse through school systems. Brickell (1961) has pointed out how (in the absence of clearcut criteria for evaluation) teachers tend to judge the efficacy of an innovation by whether the "kids are interested."

The single most common comment students make about programed instruction, after using it for a period of time, is that it is a *boring* way to learn. (Anyone wishing proof that there is some basis for such reports should try the Holland–Skinner program. But remember: most students find textbooks boring too.) Programers have become increasingly sensitive about these reports. One of their favorite topics when they get together is, "How do you make programs interesting while insuring complete learning?"

To understand the meaning of reported boredom, we must recognize that the student is required to *work* when going through a program. In requiring the student to respond as he reads, the programer is coercing the student; he does not permit the student the luxury of "tuning out," as is the case in classroom situations. When a student becomes uninterested in a lecture or discussion, he merely lets his mind wander.

A sharp picture of another of the meanings of boredom was obtained in Manhasset this past spring with Markle's *Words* program, which was written for, tested with, and revised for average and above-average eighth graders.

On a very difficult posttest, half of the students scored 90 per cent or better, and over a quarter between 80 and 90 per cent. The test results are in harmony with the promise of "mastery at every stage." The test included items such as:

Your *composure* is
    a. your friend who writes music
    b. your way of dressing yourself
    c. your calmness
    d. your own writing for English class
    e. your nap time

Juxtaposed pictures are
  a. taken when a person doesn't expect to be photographed
  b. put next to each other
  c. painted in water colors only
  d. carefully arranged on the wall
  e. put away in a closet

These classes had also gone through *English 2600* earlier in the year. They were asked:

If the person who wrote *English 2600* and the person who wrote *Words* came to Manhasset to teach English this coming year, and you were given your choice of an English teacher, which one would you select?

Overwhelmingly, the students chose Dr. Markle. Their reasons were:

English 2600 was boring. All you ever answered was one word. The *Words* program was more interesting. There were stories about words, puzzle-like questions. It makes you think. There are chances to skip ahead. It's like someone is really talking to you. It's humorous.

Both programs were also used in Manhasset with classes of students constituting the bottom two-thirds of the ability range. Only a handful of students scored over 90 per cent on the posttest. While this group was definitely divided as to their feelings about the two programs, there was a large group that preferred the author of *English 2600* because:

It's not as boring. It's easier to know the words to fill in. It's easier to read. I didn't like those "your report" things in the *Words*. The instructions in *Words* were confusing. And I didn't like those wisecracks.

All of which suggests that one man's humor is another man's wisecrack, and indicates that different programs appeal to (and cause different amounts of learning in) different children.

Fitting the program to the learner

To make a program like *Words* appropriate for students in the lower ability range would require extensive revision. The revised program would eliminate all extraneous information. Longer frames would have to be broken down, and open-ended questions might have to be eliminated. The resulting program would have an entirely different style; it would read more slowly and be more repetitious. (Even with such revisions, there is no guarantee, of course, that the slower students could attain the terminal behavior.) The resulting program would no longer be the one that had appealed to brighter students.

It would seem that different students need quite different programs to cope with a given body of subject matter. The "headmaster" of a unique school being run in an Alabama prison has described (McKee, 1962) a system in which mathematics instruction is carried out through use of programs and supervised by inmates of the prison. The inmate-counselor may approach Dr. McKee with, "Jack is having trouble with the Temac algebra. I think his reading level is too low. Should he be shifted to the Grolier algebra?" Dr. McKee has discovered that his school does not need an algebra program; it needs algebra programs. His inmate-counselors have found that students who cannot learn from one program can cope with another.

What is being done here is far more radical than a Crowderian branch; learners are being branched onto an entirely different program. And examination of both programs suggests that neither would have much appeal for the above-average student. What is advocated here, then, is that the style of "the teacher in the program" must be matched with individual learning styles. It is time to give up the notion—often attributed to Skinner but not shared by him (Skinner, 1958)—that any single sequence is the optimal sequence for all learners. Otherwise, programed instruction will fall far short of its promise as an innovation.

Conclusion

Although evidence has already been provided in a limited number of areas that students using programed instruction learn as effectively and more efficiently, compared with conventionally taught students, there is little evidence that programs thus far written for classroom use *really* individualize classroom instruction. To pass through a single instructional path at one's own rate cannot be equated with the classical tutorial situation. To argue otherwise is to offer a naive notion of individualized instruction.

By enabling students to proceed independently, and at their own pace, programed instruction does break the traditional lockstep of classroom procedure. In breaking the lockstep it makes an enormous stride forward in individualizing instruction. But that is only one dimension of individualization. As Markle (1962*a*, 1963) has illustrated in recent papers, imaginative programers can do more to approximate the tutorial situation. And as McGowan and his associates at Manhasset have demonstrated, programed instruction can provide teachers with the opportunity to work with students individually. Imaginative programers and teachers will, hopefully, take advantage of the opportunity to bring the innovation of programed instruction to its full educational fruition.

References

Brickell, H. M. *Organizing New York State for educational change.* Albany, New York: State Education Department, 1961.

Bruner, J. *The process of education.* Cambridge: Harvard University Press, 1960.

Center for Programed Instruction, Information Division. *Programs '63: a guide to programed instruction materials.* Washington: U.S. Government Printing Office, 1963(*a*).

Center for Programed Instruction, Information Division. *The use of programed instruction in U.S. schools.* Washington: U.S. Government Printing Office, 1963(*b*).

Coulson, J. E. (Ed.) *Programed learning and computer-based instruction.* New York: Wiley, 1962.

Fraser, D. M. *Current curriculum studies in academic subjects.* Washington: National Education Association, 1962.

Gotkin, L. G. Programed instruction in the schools: individual differences, the teacher, and programing styles. Paper read at R.C.A. Lecture Series, Camden, New Jersey, September 26, 1962.

Gotkin, L. G., & Goldstein, L. S. School utilization of programed instruction: implementation studies. *Programed Instruction,* 1962, *1* (4), 3.

Gotkin, L. G., & Massa, N. Programed instruction and the academically gifted: the effects of creativity and teacher behavior on programed instruction with younger learners. Paper read at Amer. Educ. Res. Ass. meetings, 1963.

Komoski, K. An immodest proposal concerning the use of programed instruction in emerging nations. Paper read at Amer. Mgt. Ass. Conference, New York, August 7, 1962.

Lindsey, M. Decision-making and the teacher. In A. H. Passow (Ed.) *Curriculum crossroads.* New York: Bureau of Publications, Teachers College, Columbia University. Pp. 27–40.

Markle, S. M. Adjusting a program to individual differences. Paper read at R.C.A. Lecture Series, Camden, New Jersey, Sept. 26, 1962(*a*).

Markle, S. M. *Teachers manual for Words: a programed course in vocabulary development.* Chicago: Science Research Associates, 1962(*b*).

Markle, S. M. The lowest common denominator: a persistent problem in programing. *Programed Instruction,* 1963, 2 (3), 4–5.

McKee, J. The use of programed instruction in a correctional institution. Paper read at Amer. Psychol. Ass. meetings, 1962.

Phenix, P. H. The disciplines as curriculum content. In A. H. Passow (Ed.), *Curriculum crossroads.* New York: Bureau of Publications: Teachers College, Columbia University, 1962. Pp. 57–65.

Reed, J. E., & Hyman, J. L. An experiment involving the use of *English 2600,* an automated instruction text. *Jour. Educ. Res.,* 1962, 55 (9), 476–484.

Rogovin, S. *Modern English sentence structure: a programed textbook.* New York: Random House (in press).

Schramm, W. *Programed instruction today and tomorrow.* New York: Fund for the Advancement of Education, 1962.

Silberman, H. F. Self-teaching devices and programed materials. *Rev. Educ. Res.,* 1962, 32 (2), 179–193.

Silverman, R. E. Programed instruction in higher education. Paper read at Special Lecture Series, Teachers College, Columbia University, January 9, 1963.

Skinner, B. F. Teaching machines. *Science,* 1958, *128,* 1–9.

Wayland, S. R. The teacher as decision-maker. In A. H. Passow (Ed.), *Curriculum crossroads.* New York: Bureau of Publications, Teachers College, Columbia University, 1962. Pp. 41–52.

CHAPTER 10

Wellsprings of strategy: considerations affecting innovations by the PSSC

PAUL E. MARSH

EXCEPT for odds and ends—a handful of unmade films, some laboratory materials that weren't quite right—the Physical Science Study Committee had, by the fall of 1960, finished the job it had set for itself a little more than four years earlier. In 1956, the Committee had proposed to devise the teaching materials required for a high school course in modern physical science, and had agreed to demonstrate that what it created was scientifically, educationally, and commercially feasible. When established school supply houses took over production of the PSSC materials as a business proposition, that proof was in. The PSSC had satisfactorily completed a pioneering venture in modern American education.[1]

The PSSC: A Synopsis

A bare recital of the Committee's activities during those four years nearly makes a shambles of Mort's earlier schedule of curriculum innovation. In the spring of 1956, Professor J. R. Zacharias of the

[1] For more detailed discussion of the PSSC, see Marsh & Gortner (1963), and Marsh (1963).

THE AUTHOR is Research Associate, Massachusetts Education Study.

Massachusetts Institute of Technology wrote a letter to M.I.T.'s President J. R. Killian, Jr., suggesting the possibility that scientists could devise films to teach modern physical science to high school students. By the end of 1956, this notion had attracted powerful and widespread adherence among scientists, had won enough financial backing for a start, had become institutionalized into the PSSC, and had served to define the limits of the Committee's work. During the next two and a half years, over 250 scientists, teachers, and specialists joined the Committee, and spent over $4.5 million inventing, testing, and revising a textbook, a teacher's guide, laboratory guides and apparatus, films, and tests for a high school course in modern physical science. In the academic year 1959–60, over 800 school districts bought these new materials, the manufacture and sale of which passed into private hands for the beginning of the 1960–61 school year. The Committee had brought together massive resources to carry out a unique piece of work in short order.

That work, however, was only a fraction of the energy invested in the total program. Beginning in the summer of 1958, scientists at five institutions of higher learning in the North and along both coasts began to use the Committee's new materials to teach modern physical science to high school teachers at summer and in-service institutes. By the fall of 1961, over 2,000 teachers were introduced to PSSC physics in sixty-six such institutes; since then their colleagues have filled up about forty institutes a year. In 1957–58, 8 teachers tried out the materials with about 300 students; in 1958–59, some 250 teachers used them with roughly 6,000 students. Acceptance continued to double until, by 1962–63, knowledgeable estimates indicated that about a fifth of all secondary school physics students were using PSSC materials. Such an expansion is as great an innovation in the nation's school system as the Committee's work was in changing course content.

The PSSC Strategy: Unplanned and Planned

What made the whole program unprecedented was the organized and considered policy-making the Committee did. At this distance from the event, one cannot tell or even infer why the PSSC deliberated with such care about some parts of its program but not about the remainder. Much thought and effort went into determining the nature and competence of the Committee itself, and into insuring the quality of its products. On the other hand, Committee records actually have little—and nothing ultimately significant—to say about the process of getting PSSC materials into the hands they were designed for—the nation's students of high school physics. Perhaps the scientists and executives of scientific enterprises who worked together to create the Committee [2] simply planned in those areas where their experience told them policies were required. Perhaps the admitted novelty of their undertaking dissuaded them from putting time and thought to matters beyond their sure ken and control. Perhaps the absence of clear, straightforward information about the ways in which the nation's school system actually worked convinced them that systematic diffusion policies could not be made with any assurance of fitness. And perhaps the Committee felt its products could speak for themselves. Certainly it respected the independence of schools.

At any rate, even if its avoidance of explicit diffusion strategy was itself a deliberate policy, the PSSC's planning remained lopsidedly national, scientific, and technological. The subsequent evolution of the program seems to have vindicated the wisdom of this restraint.

A materials-centered approach

Whether or not alternatives to this concentration had been discussed and discarded at M.I.T. before Zacharias wrote his potent letter to Killian, or at the National Science Foundation before its original grant to the PSSC, the development of teaching materials was an elegant expression of the PSSC's thrust, and proved to be a successful approach to schools. Materials were more malleable than people: they could be changed and changed and changed again at small loss; once perfected, they could be reproduced and distributed anywhere

[2] These initially included, in addition to Zacharias and Killian, Professor I. I. Rabi of Columbia; Dr. Edwin Land of the Polaroid Corporation; and Professors N. H. Frank, M. Deutsch, and F. L. Friedman of M.I.T. Members added almost immediately to the Steering Committee included Professor E. Purcell of Harvard; Dr. Vannevar Bush, Chairman of the M.I.T. Corporation; Dr. Henry Chauncey of the Educational Testing Service; Dr. Morris Meister of City College of New York and the Bronx High School of Science; and Professor W. C. Michels of Bryn Mawr College, president of the American Association of Physics Teachers.

and anytime in whatever quantities were needed. The products of technology, they could be designed to illuminate scientific phenomena, and would keep this integrity in any school in the country. The scientists' concern was not what teachers might do with these materials, but what the use of such materials might do to students studying modern physical science.

This concern set the tone for Zacharias' original suggestion, and permeated the work the PSSC knew it was competent to do. Such a focus made sense in many ways. It was appropriate to the subject, for the physical world is ostensibly material, if not always tangible. It was appropriate to the discipline, for the lawfulness of physical science is revealed in phenomena which can be brought into a classroom or high school laboratory directly or vicariously by a great variety of media. It was appropriate to learning, for materials can appeal to a variety of senses. It was appropriate to schooling, for a range of materials lent itself to a probable diversity of classroom uses. The last consideration, however, was not a primary one for Zacharias. He was, after all, an experimental physicist, who knew how indispensable materials were to the study of physics.

Experimentalism

Furthermore, the Steering Committee knew as well as Zacharias did that experimentation depended on trial and approximation, and that advancement of knowledge in physical science came from testing ideas with full understanding that both the tests and the ideas were subject to refinement as a consequence. The way of physical science was not only to study the discipline, but to test it, with each experiment shedding a little more light, coming a little closer to the workings of the physical world. Mistakes were sure to be made, but analyzing and correcting them could teach as much as successes could. Great care went into designing experiments; this approach to physical science was neither irresponsible nor haphazard. Nevertheless, even the best designs were vulnerable, and—since humans drew them up—always would be. Trial and error were inseparable and inherent in experimentation, but the game was worth the candle because only through experimentation, with all its risks for error, did knowledge advance firmly.

Therefore, while the PSSC was not designed to encourage mistakes, its founders recognized, accepted, and allowed for the inevitability of error and the imperative of correction. This assumption of fallibility and the preoccupation with materials were both so ingrained among all scientists that the PSSC never thought to explain or justify this way of doing business. Yet this unspoken modesty was central to most of what the Committee proposed to do.

Concurrent work by others

Although the scientists who conceived the PSSC seemed relatively unselfconscious about their choice of entry and mode of access to high school physics education, others had done or were doing much of their spadework. A combined committee of physicists and high school science teachers supported by the Fund for the Advancement of Education had already surveyed laboratory apparatus for school use, and found it generally inappropriate—expensive, oversophisticated, elaborate. Only a handful of firms manufactured scientific equipment for mass sales, and they concentrated on their lucrative industrial and scientific markets. While these manufacturers were happy to have whatever school business they could get, none offered schools apparatus designed just to fit school needs. A companion study was aimed at high school physics textbooks, but its findings were not in when the PSSC began to take shape.

This is not to accuse Zacharias or the Steering Committee of opportunism. The professor first suggested a filmed course, a form of instructional materials outside the province of either study. The more reasonable inference seems to be that he and the other study committees reached their conclusions independently, that they were separate but congruent manifestations of a common concern about the content of high school physics courses.

A research and development approach

Be that as it may, the PSSC Steering Committee was able to devise an organization flexible and coherent enough to accommodate the making of films and the invention of laboratory paraphernalia, as well as the writing of textbooks and laboratory guides, when the second joint study committee on high school physics teaching supplies pointed out the need. After all, these supplies were all undeniably teaching materials, and coordinating their development both simplified administration and increased the possibility of their educational consistency. By claiming the development of course materials as its function, then, the PSSC was able to plan to create as many different kinds as seemed needed. The use and study of these supplies would teach physical science and the workways of physical scientists. And the PSSC's act of creation was itself to be conducted by the orderly scientific succession of investigation, design, approximation, experiment, and revision. Whatever resulted could be counted on to be tentative, but so could the whole edifice of modern physical science. What counted most was that the experiment be made.

Given this context, conditions for the essence of the PSSC program were logical and straightforward. It was, to begin with, a feasibility study, an experiment in research and development. What with the tentative nature of scientific findings, such openness was to be expected. It had, moreover, some obvious pragmatic advantages. The undertaking could be administered and financed like any other research project. This policy implied that the direction and management of the experiment ought to be consistent and highly coordinated, to protect its scientific integrity. Specialists and technicians might well come into the project, but only for its duration. Particular aspects could be stopped if their payoff looked uncertain; promising and unforeseen ideas could be tried out—all without redefinition of the essence of the program. The work could be evaluated in stages and steps, so that revisions could be made while they were inexpensive and easy to make.

Stages in the Production of Materials

Initial support

The National Science Foundation addressed itself primarily to this evaluative procedure. It was prepared to support the PSSC, but insisted that the experiment prove itself at each of three successive levels: scientific acceptability, educational feasibility, and commercial diffusion. Initially, both the idea of scientists' inventing teaching materials for schools, and the rough outline of what science those materials should teach had to demonstrate their acceptability among scientists. Neither the PSSC, nor M.I.T., nor NSF could act in this matter without reference to the nation's private scientific community-at-large, although each institution might act on that community's behalf. This requirement was *prudential* in that it relieved any of the three groups of exclusive responsibility for the program. But the requirement was more than that; it was *professional*, in that it concerned basic training of scientific manpower. Nor did NSF question PSSC claims that its work was *cultural*, in that it introduced students, whether potential scientists or not, to the scientific workings of the physical world in which all lived. Furthermore, science and government were growing increasingly intimate, the Committee maintained, so an informed citizenry needed increased knowledge of science.

Implicit in all these arguments was the assumption that scientists knew best what basic knowledge of science future scientists needed to start off with, how much science all adults needed to perceive the physical world with, and what kind of science citizens needed to maintain the government with. This assumption and its stated implications were in effect matters of basic national policy. They were never questioned.

The initial conference

Logically and procedurally, however, the PSSC and NSF needed demonstration of scientific feasibility first. Both insisted on involving the very best physicists the Committee could get—particularly to determine the outline of the new syllabus—and both recognized the prudence of widespread, hopefully national, approval and support from scientists. Massive backing from school people might perhaps meet the prudential requirements, but only physical scientists could define the structure of modern physical science. This point, generalized, was eloquently and persuasively argued by Bruner (1960) three years later.

A representative gathering of leading physicists could easily be convened, for they were not all that numerous. Such a meeting might require a considerable budget, but science, not money, was the prime consideration. In fact, the conference in December, 1956, at which the PSSC idea was approved and the content of the course hammered out, included almost fifty scientists, two from as far away as California and Kansas, and cost less than $100,000. The unanimity of the outcome showed that physicists could agree on matters of national educational policy, and—after three days of hot debate—on a viable introduction to modern physical science.

Organizational planning and recruitment

However basic, this step was only the first, essential one, allowing the institutional planning of the PSSC Steering Committee to proceed. Almost immediately, their policies brought the knowledge, experience, and ingenuity of a great many people to bear on a wide range of specific problems. From an operational or experimental point of view, the December conference had set the framework of the program, determining its scientific limits. Required next were research and development within that framework. In an appropriate balancing of material invention with logical coherence, the over-all management of the project now devolved on Zacharias, the experimental physicist, while responsibility for the course content was given to Friedman, the theoretical physicist. Under their direction, the work could be divided into segments and given to specialists for development. As many could be employed as budget and specific tasks called for, permitting —indeed encouraging—many people to address their talents to the practical problems at hand.

While Zacharias and Friedman at once hired as consultants many of the scientists who had contributed to the December conference, the program now required a different sort of competence as well. Whereas planning for the PSSC as a scientific experiment, and determining the syllabus, had called for (and got) executive and scientific talents of a high order, translating the syllabus into teaching materials called for competent technicians and teachers. Therefore, during the spring of 1957, the scientists consulting with the PSSC began roughing out in some detail the outline the Conference had agreed on, and the Committee began recruiting the wide range of scientists, science teachers, and technicians it knew were needed. This blend of specialists was what the program had to have in order to turn the science of the course outline into instructional supplies which might begin to teach that science to high school students.

Some nonacademic specialists—editors, photographers, scriptwriters —were hired by the Committee during the spring of 1957 on a full-time, short-term basis, and several science teachers near M.I.T. came in on weekends as consultants.

Producing first approximations of the materials

The major inventive effort of the program, however, was scheduled for that summer, when academic personnel were free from their classrooms. Although the PSSC had no real option in this decision, targets for the summer's work were the Committee's to set. It determined to try for a first approximation of enough of the materials of the course to permit classroom trial of its rudiments in a few schools during the 1957–58 school year.

To prepare for such a frontal assault, the Committee took advantage of its organizational flexibility. The devising of classroom and college entrance tests for students, a highly technical but wholly derivative segment of the program, was contracted out in its entirety to Educational Testing Service. Explorations were begun with Encyclopaedia Britannica Films, Inc., concerning its capacity to produce the teaching films the new syllabus called for. An Assistant to the Dean of the College of Education at the University of Illinois agreed to compile a comprehensive teacher's guide to accompany the materials. But the first order of business, and the one which could not be delegated, was the invention of the materials themselves.

For this purpose, the 150-odd scientists, teachers, and technicians at the PSSC for the summer were each given a major assignment to one of five heterogeneous task forces. One was charged with devising laboratory apparatus and experiments; each of the other four was asked to draft one of the major sections of the text. What counted, however, was creativity; and ideas and inspirations, regardless of their point of origin, were welcomed by the task force whose assignment they were. A casual but steady flow of people and suggestions went on between the laboratory group and all the other task forces. To foster such mobility, work space was as much centralized at M.I.T. as it could be. Since all tentative materials came back to Friedman, however, their coherence had a visible and congenial focus. Thoughtful and comprehensive planning, and careful placing of key personnel, had done what could be done to assure consistency among the essential items in the new course.

Obviously, the most pressing job for PSSC personnel that summer was invention. Both as individuals and as an organization, they were good at that job. Still, eight or ten weeks was certainly not time enough in which to do all the inventing that had to be done. By the middle of the summer, emphasis had to be shifted from the latter sections of the syllabus to the first ones, so that test schools might have teaching materials to start off the year with. Given task force organization, specific assignment, and a climate for movement, such a realignment caused little interruption. The organization of the PSSC had been so planned as to take such changes in stride. Indeed, when the Committee became convinced that its teaching films were integral with the text and the apparatus, it only needed to create a new task force with its own film studio, equipment, and technicians. And when the thrust of the program moved from invention to revision, these work groups were just as viable as ever, even though their tasks were different. The Committee's administrative structure was not such as to inhibit creativity.

Tryout and revision of the materials

Still, even the first approximations were neither easy nor quick to come by. When Labor Day, 1957, arrived, only Part I of the syllabus was ready for the eight test schools. But Part II was nearly done, and only Part IV was more unfinished than not. In fact, only once during the ensuing year were users of the course delayed for want of materials.

At this stage in the program, however, the crucial problem was not in the quantity of materials, but in their fitness for regular school use. The second major test set for the PSSC by the NSF was that its products be educationally feasible: that they demonstrate, in typical classrooms, in the hands of regular teachers and students, the capacity to teach the science the syllabus called for.

By all odds, this test was the longest, costliest and hardest for the PSSC to complete. While the creation of first approximations petered out about eighteen months after the outline had been produced by the conference in December, 1956, revisions to suit classroom demands began in the fall of 1957 and continued into 1960. While the expenses for creating new materials probably exceeded $1 million (perhaps $1.5 million), trial and revision cost the PSSC about three times that much. The Committee's tacit and deliberate policies, however, had fully anticipated this eventuality. Budgets had been openly prepared for the reworking of items, experimentation was the program's central theme, and all devices were considered to be approximations. The PSSC began by conceding its fallibility, and logically insisted on having the chance to correct its mistakes.

The trial–revision sequence. In order to learn what those mistakes were, the PSSC arranged to have its materials tested first in a very few schools, all handy to PSSC scientists; both they and the teachers (all of them Committee members) had to see and report on the supplies in action, so as to be able to propose revisions in accord with actual classroom experience. This scrutiny was close, careful, and ruthless. As a consequence, every segment of the course materials was revised, though Part II needed very little work. Parts I and III proved to require extensive overhaul, necessitating heavy revision in Part IV even before it got into the classroom.

Laboratory equipment, which at first was supposed to be constructed by teachers and students according to PSSC directions out of homey items purchased locally, was not only revised but procured and packaged into complete self-contained kits for student assembly. Some of the earlist PSSC teaching films were completely remade in the new studio. By the time the second year of classroom trial came around, most of the PSSC's teaching materials looked different from their prototypes.

There were also a very great many of them. Text and laboratory guides both came in four paperbacked quarto volumes. Seventy films were in print or planned. There were twenty-six apparatus kits and over two hundred other items of laboratory paraphernalia too commonplace to require PSSC distribution. There were already some seventy experiments for students to try out. The Committee's emphasis on disciplined inventiveness had paid off handsomely, and at the same time greatly increased possibilities for revisions.

Furthermore, classroom trial of the new supplies increased vastly for the 1958–59 school year. The number of test schools increased from 8 to 255, from schools close by the PSSC to those mostly quite outside its direct observation. While the collection of feedback—teachers' reports on the way materials worked in the classroom—and classroom visits from the Committee went on as a guide to further revision, the effects of both were much attenuated by the vastly increased amount of information they provided the Committee. It boggled at collating this massive written response, sent in chapter by chapter, and compromised by reading something like one out of five reports. Even so, revisions continued; everyone understood that the PSSC anticipated making further changes in its materials on its own initiative or on the basis of feedback, certainly until commercial houses took over production of the new supplies. Alterations, however, were generally less drastic and certainly less comprehensive than they had been earlier. Some parts of the text were expanded and clarified. Some films had explanatory sequences added to them. Some experiments and apparatus were simplified and refined. In general, this round of changes stressed clarity and coherence—factors bearing on the instructional effectiveness of details, and on the impact of the syllabus as a whole.

Timing.   At least as important as the nature and process of these revisions was their timing. Before PSSC materials were turned over to private manufacturers, the Committee had in hand statistical evidence that the new materials were getting across to their users a different body of knowledge from that of traditional physics courses (Ferris, 1960). A long, expensive, and difficult evaluation had been carried out precisely for that purpose. Changes had been made when they counted —prior to mass production—on the basis of agreement between scientists and teachers that the revisions were needed in order to fit all the new materials to teach the modern physical science of the syllabus. This massive, nation-wide, long-term collaboration between hundreds of teachers and scientists had produced a very large number of cunningly devised and carefully integrated instructional supplies of all kinds. And their classroom use, in almost any combination, under a wide variety of school circumstances, had demonstrated that the science they embodied was educationally feasible.

Diffusion of the PSSC Materials

The PSSC, however, was required to do more than show that the teaching materials it had devised enabled students to learn a different kind of physics. The Committee also had to demonstrate that large numbers of teachers were willing to investigate and use its supplies, and that large numbers of secondary schools were willing to pay for them. The proof of this commercial feasibility required a number of steps, occasionally unrecognized, but summed up in the willingness of traditional, profit-seeking school supply houses to mass-produce and sell PSSC materials in the forms devised by the Committee.

Informing the profession

Little of this phase of the undertaking was, or could have been, within the PSSC's control. Teachers as professionals, and school districts as autonomous governments, must be free to pick and choose the supplies they teach with and purchase. The Committee itself could only see to it that school people knew the PSSC existed, and could learn what its course materials were and how they worked. And this information had to be made available without promoting the purchase of PSSC supplies. The test of private, commercial feasibility could not be tainted with any suspicion of federal influence or control arising from the major financial backing of the PSSC by the National Science Foundation.

Informing and promoting are divided by a fine and tricky line, one along which the PSSC purposely did not travel very far. The success of Sputnik I, with its consequent surge of public interest in science education, gave the Committee's work virtually all the publicity it could have asked for, both in the press and in professional and scientific journals. Unsought by the PSSC, this dissemination of information was unquestionably fitting and proper. Policy was required, however, to determine just how far the Committee might go on its own initiative. Such policy was never really settled; this strategy remained a matter for debate until PSSC materials had passed into private hands. The absence of policy, however, did mean the absence of action; the PSSC went only as far as its policy makers could agree to go.

The institutes

The line of agreement was national, but also academic and scientific. The increasingly numerous teacher-training institutes, usually but by no means exclusively supported by the National Science Foundation at institutions of higher learning all over the country, were conceded to be appropriate vehicles for teaching teachers about PSSC materials. Every institute, however, was autonomous. Each director, commonly a scientist, was free to teach what and how he wished to whatever participants he chose to accept. The PSSC could do no more than ask institute directors to use PSSC supplies, and distribute them to those directors who agreed to do so. This procedure, in effect, constituted another test of the PSSC by academic scientists, only one or two of whom had been on the Committee. All of the forty-odd physicists who directed the sixty-six institutes with PSSC content for high school teachers between 1957 and 1961 had been free to judge the materials on their merits, and to use them or not, as they pleased. The scientists on the Committee, among them, did know most of the nation's physicists—a comparatively tightly knit group— and especially well those who shared the PSSC's concern for increasing and improving scientific manpower. Many of them had already demonstrated their interest by giving up their own research time in order to train teachers at previous institutes. The point, however, is that PSSC institutes were not at all the fruits of secret agreements among a handful of powerful men, but of a nation-wide concern for scientific manpower and education among a major segment of the nation's community of scientists.

Since both this community and its concern were widespread, the location of institutes in the early days showed a pattern consistent with the Committee's national thrust. The first five, held during the summer of 1958, were fairly evenly spaced across the northern half of the nation, from Bowdoin College in Brunswick, Maine, to Reed College in Portland, Oregon. In the next few years, PSSC institutes, with only one or two exceptions, were held in metropolitan areas— generally those of the East and West coasts, and of the North. Almost all these institutes were held where the majority of the country's students and teachers of high school physics were. The PSSC's program of disseminating knowledge of its new teaching materials by moving through the nation's scientific and academic community proved flexible and precise in reaching its potential users.

The local diffusion process

Even a partial analysis of the spread of the actual classroom use of PSSC materials, however, suggests that institutes, free as they were of PSSC control, primarily served to disseminate knowledge as such.

They were only one step in a larger, unplanned process by which PSSC supplies got into schools. That process was essentially local, educational, and pedagogical.

To begin with, while all the 2,100 teachers who participated in PSSC institutes up to 1961 conceded they had learned science, less than half of them had in fact adopted the new materials. Furthermore, about 150 teachers used the supplies without ever participating in an institute; some 10 more went to institutes only *after* using PSSC goods. In addition, the syllabus has been widely adopted both around Los Angeles and Chicago, major areas in which no PSSC institute has been held. New Orleans, the only other such metropolitan region, has had but one participant and one PSSC teacher. Nor are these institutional and geographical anomalies the only ones: 90 per cent of the 1,050 early PSSC users participated in their first PSSC institute during the same academic year (summer included) in which they adopted the PSSC syllabus. Such immediate adoption is a full year ahead of traditional administration of curriculum change, which, to permit orderly budgeting, commonly lags one year behind the decision to purchase new materials. Institute participation, then, does not seem to have been decisive as a reason for local budgeting for the use of PSSC materials.

Local clustering. A much more comprehensive explanation can be found in the geography of PSSC classroom use. Eight schools tested the first approximations of PSSC materials in academic 1957–58. From the areas these schools were in—usually metropolitan—came a quarter of all PSSC institute participants in the following summer, and about a third of all PSSC users during the subsequent school year. And most of these last taught in the immediate neighborhoods of the test schools. Such clustering together was a dominant characteristic of the early spread in acceptance of PSSC materials. Even in 1958, when institute directors were most highly selective in choosing participants, less than a quarter of the PSSC users were beyond easy reach of others. Over a three-year span, less than one out of five was geographically distant from others. Those who were thus cut off tended either to give up the new materials or to pick up colleagues nearby. PSSC supplies were most commonly used in tight groups and clusters of schools.

As often as not such groups were mixed, including without discrimination or distinction public, independent, and church schools. These heterogeneous groups have been commonplace in big cities, where the nonpublic schools have often had one or two specialized public high schools with them in a PSSC cluster. Sometimes, rural boarding schools have served as PSSC examples for neighboring public schools. While there is no evidence at hand suggesting leadership by any one type of school in beginning these groups, there is strong evidence of membership by all three types in the clusters. There seems to have been group response to the PSSC by physics teachers as such, regardless of the constituency their school served.

The importance of firsthand experience. Moreover, this reaction was by no means always favorable to the use of the new materials. Just as the PSSC evoked group acceptance, it also produced group rejection. This latter reaction was only easily visible, of course, among physics teachers who had participated in institutes but did not then use PSSC supplies. What made such teachers a majority (55 per cent of those attending) was, apparently, the lack of PSSC classrooms near enough to look in on. They had no visible proof that the new materials actually worked under regular school conditions. Until such proof was in their hands, these teachers may have felt they could not experiment with the PSSC, regardless of the quality of science it embodied or the eminence of its sponsorship. While there was no way in which this negative reaction could grow, it did not have to do so in order to prove influential. It gave "confirmation" to all those teachers whose firsthand experience was only with traditional high school physics. What negative response did was to brake the expansion of use of PSSC materials.

On the other hand, wherever neighboring teachers have been able to see for themselves—see PSSC supplies working in ordinary classrooms, in whatever kind of school—adoption of the new syllabus has spread year by year. Expansion of this sort took place as individual teachers or groups of teachers near PSSC schools adopted the new materials, often after going to a PSSC institute, but sometimes without going to an institute at all. Apparently the most typical pattern was that of first deciding to switch to the PSSC, ordering its supplies, and then attending an institute to learn how to use them. On this basis, adoption of the PSSC by teachers without institute preparation becomes understandable, as does spread of the course in areas like Chicago and Los Angeles, where no institutes had been held. This same reasoning may also begin to suggest the way in which most PSSC schools could begin using the new materials so soon after teachers' participation in institutes. For such teachers, institute participation appeared to be vocational education; what can be inferred to have tipped the balance toward the PSSC was the chance to see its goods working in classrooms.[3]

This process of diffusion has ignored the traditional boundaries of school administration. Clusters have crossed state lines as if they did not exist and, through negative groupings, have set up boundaries of their own. These boundaries appear to have developed systematically, but independently of the formal program of dissemination the Physical Science Study Committee itself had had a part in. Diffusion seems to have depended at least partially on a pedagogical judgment by teachers about the fitness of PSSC materials for ordinary classroom use. Such decisions, made on the basis of direct observation or of firsthand reports, and multiplied by all PSSC users and institute participants, determined the commercial feasibility of the program.

Flexibility of use. Local decisions were at once simplified and complicated when educational and commercial feasibilities came face to face. Though integrated and coherent, the materials devised by the PSSC in aid of its syllabus turned out to be numerous and, in sum, uncommonly expensive. To use them all took more than a year's time and more than a year's budget. This very abundance of coordinated supplies, however, allowed teachers to choose every year those particular materials which appeared most appropriate for the education of particular classes, while keeping within particular budget limitations. Its most economical cost-per-pupil came through varying class sizes, from large groups to individual instruction, depending on what materials were being used. The PSSC could maintain its scientific integrity and still be tailored to relatively precise local educational needs. By doing well at its scientific business, the Committee had enabled school systems to do well at the educational business of curriculum development.

[3] See also Brickell (1961), and his chapter in the present book, for a similar conclusion.

Retrospective Comments

In the final analysis, then, the limitation of PSSC policies to the invention and revision of teaching materials appears to have been sound strategy. The Committee's policy makers had great experience in the administration of scientific experiments, and could justify the policies they made. On the other hand, no one—neither these men, nor anyone else at the time—could have predicted the systematic reactions of the nation's schools to the materials. (Indeed, what is known about this response even now is far from complete.)

One thing, however, might have been suspected: the need for inventiveness in bringing modern physical science to high school students extended far beyond devising materials which embodied it. The goals of the program called for appropriate innovations by planners, foundation executives, administrators, scientists, technicians, teachers, businessmen, school administrators. Clearly, the PSSC could not have dictated or foretold what those innovations were to be. Yet it could have explained itself and its plans more fully than it did, in terms that its voluntary collaborators could understand and act on. Such an explanation is not a matter of promotion or of public relations, but one of open communication among a range of specialists at work on a common task.

The lack of such communication has ultimately had to be compensated for; its absence in the early days of the PSSC program made the work of innovation just that much harder. While, in the short run, the Committee's single-minded preoccupation with science teaching materials can be justified, in the long run this concentration cost the program support—especially among professional educators. Rather at fault themselves through their uncritical acceptance of an outmoded "professional" exclusiveness, some school people—often ones who could have contributed to the PSSC program—greeted it with suspicion and disapproval. Their opposition commonly had its roots in a want of knowledge about and understanding of the PSSC and its program. Since the PSSC did not of its own accord supply the information the profession needed, the upshot was a desultory and distracting power struggle, instead of limited but precise collaboration.

On matters of basic national policy, the two groups, the scientists and the schoolmen, stood four-square—but silent. They agreed in the belief that much larger amounts of money ought to be allocated to schooling. They similarly agreed that such financing could probably be anticipated mainly from governments of one level or another. They agreed that, even so, "politics" must not control the disbursement of those funds. They agreed that more of the nation's brainpower and manpower should be devoted to schooling, particularly to research and development in learning and teaching. They agreed that such an undertaking exceeded the resources and competence of any one set of specialists. They agreed that participation of any sort in such a program had to be voluntary. They agreed that they did not know beforehand just what the results and consequences of their efforts might be. They agreed that each needed the help and support of the other. Yet scientists and schoolmen did not communicate these common policies to each other.

This lack of communication put teachers on the spot. It forced them to evaluate PSSC materials on the basis of limited and partial information. In the absence of fuller, sounder advice, they looked to each other for rough and ready corroboration. Ultimately, then, it was classroom physics teachers, ignoring the tendencies toward exclusiveness of both scientists and educators, who reconciled scientific strategy and educational practice and made the Physical Science Study Committee program viable.

References

Brickell, H. M. *Organizing New York State for educational change.* Albany, New York: State Education Department, 1961.

Bruner, J. S. *The process of education.* New York: Harper, 1960.

Ferris, F. W., Jr. An achievement test report. In *Progress Report, Educational Services, Inc., 1959.* Watertown, Mass.: ESI, 1960. Pp. 26–28.

Marsh, P. E. The Physical Science Study Committee: a case history of nationwide curriculum development. Unpublished doctoral thesis, Graduate School of Education, Harvard University, 1963.

Marsh, P. E., & Gortner, R. A. *Federal aid to science education: two programs.* Economics and Politics of Public Education Series, No. 6. Syracuse: Syracuse University Press, 1963.

*Part II: Research and theory
in educational innovation*

As CRUCIAL as specific case studies are in the understanding of educational innovation, they are often not sufficient in themselves to extend our understanding to the point of prediction and control. The nine chapters of this section are devoted to efforts to gather data *across* a plurality of innovative situations, and to build theories capable of explaining the discovered regularities. In some respects, of course, placement of chapters in this section or the first is arbitrary—several of the case studies presented earlier included multisituation data, and many of them articulated supporting theory. But the basic intent of most of the present chapters is to systematize, to develop regularized means of studying innovative processes in educational systems, and to make generalizable sense of data collected.

The section begins with two classroom studies. Fox and Lippitt describe a systematic attempt to aid teachers in the improvement of classroom mental health practices; the fundamental innovation, indeed, was that teachers learned to use the methods of the behavioral sciences in planning and assessing the results of teaching innovations. Eichholz and Rogers develop and refine a generalized theory of *rejection* of innovations—in this case, audio-visual devices.

The next two chapters examine larger systems. The chapter by Mort reviews several decades of his work on diffusion lag and its correlates in school and community settings. Carlson demonstrates very clearly that the social position of the superintendent in the company of his peers (other superintendents) is closely associated with his innovativeness.

Research itself is usually asserted to be an important aspect of educational innovation—both in suggesting new practices, and in testing their efficacy. The next two studies deal with the techniques and sociology of research as such. Kendall's chapter deals with the formidable problems of evaluating educational programs; it presents some thoughtful ways out of typical evaluational dilemmas, using a study of an innovative medical school course as a vehicle. Barton and Wilder's devastating report examines the nature of research, educational practice, and the linkage between these in the special case of the teaching of reading.

The last three chapters in this section represent attempts at constructing general frameworks useful in the explanation of innovative processes. Mackenzie develops integrative generalizations on curricular change from a number of case studies. Griffiths proposes explanations of organizational change and stability, invoking the notion of "open system" as the primary mode of viewing organizations. Finally, Miles assembles a variety of empirical examples to illustrate the properties of temporary social systems, seen as a primary means for inducing individual and organizational change.

CHAPTER 11

The innovation of
classroom mental health practices

ROBERT S. FOX
RONALD LIPPITT

THE establishment of effective working relationships in the classroom has traditionally held high priority for teachers concerned with promoting educational achievement among their pupils. Although much of learning is ultimately an individual task, in the modern school it takes place in a social environment. Pupils learn through interaction with the teacher, by working in committees, by discussing with classmates, by checking homework assignments over the telephone. Their motivation to learn is influenced by their position in the classroom social structure, by the peer group standards toward classroom activities, and by the supporting or conflicting pressures from a great variety of forces which are a part of their life space.

Studying the process involved in the instigation and support of teacher innovations in improving the classroom learning climate became the focus for a research project [1] at the University of Michigan

---

[1] "The Introduction and Spread of Teaching Innovations to Promote Classroom Mental Health and Learning Efficiency," Grant OM-376 from the National Institute for Mental Health; and "Pupil-Teacher Adjustment and Mutual Adaptation in Creating Classroom Learning Environments," Cooperative Research Project No. 1167 of the United States Office of Education.

THE AUTHORS are, respectively: Director, The University School, School of Education, University of Michigan; and Program Director, Research Center for Group Dynamics, Institute for Social Research, University of Michigan.

beginning in 1959. Thirty teachers and their classrooms from school systems in southeastern Michigan have been involved over periods of from two to three years. As a result of examining the interpersonal situation within their classrooms, these teachers developed a variety of special techniques and procedures which proved useful in improving the learning climate. For example, one explored use of a "question box" to enable pupils to submit questions anonymously for class discussion. Another gave pupils opportunity to teach their own lesson plans, and still another developed a plan for involving older children in helping younger ones on academic tasks as well as human relations problems. Currently, data on the spread of such teaching innovations resulting from work in these classrooms are being gathered from the faculties of ten school buildings.

Questions Examined

It was hypothesized that teachers might be encouraged to make changes in their classrooms in at least two ways—(1) by collaboration with the research team in gathering and interpreting data about the state of affairs in the teacher's own classroom, leading to innovations designed to modify the situation; or (2) by examining the innovative efforts of other teachers in meeting situations similar to ones believed to exist in one's own class. In this second case, the challenge is one of adaptation—modifying the original innovation in ways that will fit the unique situation faced by the client teacher. The adoption of new ideas or innovative procedures developed by one's colleagues, or reported in the professional literature, becomes in itself an innovating activity for that teacher and that class.

These two approaches to improvement in the classroom may be restated in another way. On the one hand, teachers were involved in collaborative *action research* efforts, with a major emphasis on the gathering and analysis of data about their own classrooms as a basis for the introduction of new or modified procedures. On the other, special attention was given to the *communication linkage* between a teacher involved in change effort and his professional colleagues.

In addition to studying these general approaches, questions were raised regarding specific aspects of the helping relationships which stimulate or support innovation: What kinds of training activities would prove helpful? Would an intensive summer workshop produce results superior to consultation with the teachers in the field? In what ways can an outside consultant be most helpful? What kinds of support (or lack of support) do innovating teachers gain from their own colleagues?

Major Phases of the Project

Theory development and instrumentation

A first phase of the project focused on conceptualization of the professional growth process which stimulates the emergence of innovations in teaching practice relevant to improvement of mental health and learning conditions, and on conceptualization of the conditions within a school system necessary to facilitate the spreading of teaching practice innovations. (Some of the conceptual models which were developed are presented on pages 279–282.)

A battery of instruments was developed to explore aspects of the classroom group structure, peer standards toward learning and classroom behavior, and the valence for pupils and teachers of such other influences as family, other teachers, school administration, and scout troop (i.e., life space forces). Group interviews with pupils regarding classroom activities, and their desire for changes in the class or in the teacher, were planned. Instruments were designed to elicit information from teachers about their own self concepts, their concepts regarding mental health and learning, their teaching objectives and values, and their perceptions of classroom social structure and group standards.[2]

Recruitment

In its second phase, the project moved to recruiting a population of collaborating teachers to participate in a diagnostic measurement program. A sample of thirty teachers was obtained from schools in south-

[2] An inventory of these pupil and teacher instruments (Lippitt & Van Egmond, 1962) may be obtained from the Institute for Social Research, University of Michigan, Ann Arbor.

eastern Michigan serving rural, industrial, suburban, and university communities. Their grade level assignments ranged from fourth grade to twelfth grade, with sixty per cent at the elementary level, fifteen per cent at junior high school level, and twenty-five per cent at the high school level. Participating teachers ranged in age from 24 to 56 years, and had teaching experience varying from three to thirty years. An extensive measurement program was carried out with this sample of teachers in the spring of 1960, concluding the first year of the project.

Stimulation and support for innovation

Third was a phase of stimulating teachers to attempt the innovation of new practices to cope with problems identified by the diagnostic data, and to study the level of support needed to carry through the innovative efforts successfully. Stimulation and support were provided at three different levels of intensity:

1. *Maximum involvement.* During the summer of 1960, nine of the participating teachers attended a six-week, full-time workshop session. It was designed to aid them in using the data collected in their classrooms to make diagnoses, set goals, and make plans which they would implement in the fall.

The innovation attempts of these teachers were supported throughout the year by means of evening clinic sessions held each month involving the nine teachers and the project staff, and individual consultation with a project staff member as requested, usually on a monthly basis.

2. *Medium involvement.* Those teachers who had not participated in the summer workshop received a program of feedback conferences in the fall. This was done in two steps. First, the teachers were invited to attend one of four area meetings where the project goals were reviewed, general trends and diagnostic implications of the data were discussed, and support was given for trying out innovative ideas. Second, each teacher who had not attended the workshop met with a member of the project staff to review the data from his own classroom. Following this, teachers were offered an opportunity to request additional consultation. Those who did request additional consultation were identified as having medium involvement. Ten teachers were involved at this level.

3. *Minimal involvement.* The remaining eleven teachers, who did not attend the summer workshop, did receive feedback and interpretation of their classroom data, and did not request further consultation, were considered to be minimally involved.

This phase of the project was completed during the second year, along with a measurement program consisting of an abbreviated data collection in October and a more extensive remeasurement in the spring of 1961.

The spread of innovations

In its fourth phase, the project involved setting up a program for the planned spread to other classrooms of innovations which proved to have favorable impact on the learning atmosphere. Ten field sites (school buildings) where the systematic spread experiments are at present being conducted were identified in the fall of 1961. Change teams consisting of the school administrator, innovation teacher, and project staff consultant were established to plan the strategy and to facilitate the involvement of other teachers within the school. A wide range of activities and resources is being provided, the exact nature dependent upon the unique requirements of each school situation. These resources include conceptual tools for understanding classroom interaction phenomena, skill practice sessions (role-playing, administration of sociometrics), tape recordings of project teachers describing their innovations, written description of a number of the innovative practices, and a compilation of tools and instruments for gathering more precise information about the classroom learning environment. In addition, data regarding conditions which facilitate or hinder the involvement of the wider group of teachers in the building are being gathered by the project staff.

Teacher "A": Project Participant, Innovator, and Change Agent

A more detailed picture of how innovative practices were encouraged and supported by the project may be obtained through a case study of the activities of one of the maximally involved teacher participants. We introduce the reader to Teacher "A," one of the thirty teachers who became identified with the project in the early months of 1960.

Initial interests

In her application and in subsequent interviews, Teacher "A" expressed a desire to become involved in the project because she was concerned about how to achieve an appropriate balance between emphasis on furthering the academic skills of her pupils and emphasis on promoting improved interpersonal and group relationships. She saw these two major objectives as competing for time and energy. She was particularly concerned about the pressures some parents were putting on their children and on the teacher to bring about higher academic achievement. Teacher "A" perceived that many of these "pressured" youngsters were already experiencing difficulties in making social adjustments.

Other reasons given by Teacher "A" for becoming involved in the project were that she thought it dealt with learning atmospheres, which sounded interesting, and that through the summer workshop she might earn needed graduate credit.

Data collection activities

The first major involvement of Teacher "A" occurred in the spring of 1960. At the request of the project staff she completed instruments designed to obtain her perceptions and impressions of the following: her pupils, herself, classroom mental health practices and conditions, and interrelationships among these phenomena.

For example, she was asked to sort a set of cards, on which the names of the pupils in her class had been placed, into as many different piles as might occur to her. For each sorting, she was asked to record the main organizing idea around which the piles were sorted, the names of the students in each pile, and the descriptive titles that might be given to each of the piles. (She used such categories as "school achievement," "social maturity," "popularity," "sex," and "economic level.") This exercise was called "categorizing pupils." Furthermore, she was asked to describe the relevance of each of these pupil categories for teaching practice.

She was also asked to suppose that a visiting teacher from Russia had engaged her in conversation about school practices in this country. She was to assume that her visitor knew very little about American teaching practice. He was particularly interested in learning about mental health in classroom teaching, and what Teacher "A" considered to be good mental health practices and good mental health conditions in the classroom. She listed as many ideas as she could for the visitor, each on a blank 3 x 5 card. Cards were then grouped, and placed in rank order. A similar set of cards was produced around the practices and conditions conducive to effective learning. Teacher "A" was then asked to describe any connections or relationships she saw between the mental health variables and the learning conditions.

As a measure of her self concept, she responded to the statement, "As a teacher, I have the following characteristics: . . . ." She estimated which pupils were seen by the others as most influential, most expert, best liked. She indicated the types of resources possessed by each of her pupils by checking four-point scales regarding physical appearance, physical poise and coordination, friendliness or unfriendliness, social skill and poise, participation in classroom activities, degree of cooperation with the teacher, and helpfulness to other pupils.

A series of instruments was administered to the pupils by Teacher "A" at about the same time. These included "Impressions of Others," "Who Fit Together?," "Who Is Different and Who Is Average?," "Sociometric Questions," "Teachers," "How This Class Feels," "Parts of a Day," and "A Pupil's Life."

By having her attention directed to such aspects of the class environment, Teacher "A" was encouraged to attend more closely to these factors, and stimulated to seek further means of assessing her perceptions about the interpersonal situation in the classroom.

The summer workshop

During a six-week period beginning June 21, 1960, Teacher "A" became a participant in a summer workshop conducted by the project staff. Focus in the workshop was on the significance of classroom interaction phenomena for learning, and on the development of plans for improving the classroom learning atmosphere. Eight other project teachers were involved, representing four school systems and grade levels four through twelve. Teacher "A" enrolled for six units of credit ("Workshop in Elementary Education," 4 credits; and "Comparative Theory and Methods of Planned Change," 2 credits). Activities lasted from 9:00 until 4:00 each day.

Workshop activities were designed to have an impact on various aspects of the teacher's professional personality, on the assumption that change is most likely to occur when the balance of forces which affect the teacher's intentions and actions is altered. Attention was given to conceptualization, to diagnosis, to increasing sensitivity to the effects of an individual's behavior on the group, to skill development, to formulation of plans, and to support during innovative efforts.

Conceptualization or theory sessions. These provided Teacher "A" with the following opportunities: (1) to review relevant research; (2) to study theories that have been developed as tools to understand the classroom situation, the teacher's role, and the learning process; (3) to do reflective thinking about her own classroom situation; and (4) to clarify her ideas about what is involved in the process of change —the changing of classroom situations, and her own attitudes and performance.

Specific sessions were devoted to presentation of pupil and teacher life space theory, concepts for analysis of problems of classroom process and learning, concepts for understanding peer group formation and maintenance, theory of personal properties and resources, the relationship between social interaction and learning, and theory and process of change and changeability.

Once a week, in cooperation with another workshopper, she took notes on the presentation and discussion, typing them on ditto stencils and distributing them to all the participants on the following morning. As an example of a theory session, excerpts from her minutes of June 22, 1960, are presented below. (This particular session was the introductory one, and presented in very brief form the basic conceptual models which were developed in greater detail in subsequent sessions.)

Workshop Minutes

Recorder: Teacher "A" June 22, 1960

This session was a general overview of theory which seems especially relevant to teachers. Teachers are, in essence, applied social scientists. One of the great needs for the teacher is to reflect on his "day to day" job at times in order to gain greater awareness into what is going on in his teaching activity. Kurt Lewin once commented that "there is nothing so practical as a good theory." The purpose of these conceptualization sessions is to help us reflect on classroom dynamics using social scientific theory as our guide. There are a variety of frameworks dealing with what goes on in the classroom, involving both the description and explanation of classroom phenomena. Today's session will present these six orientations.

I. Life space of the child as a focus

This focus emphasizes the various socialization agencies which impinge upon and help to influence the child's behavior:

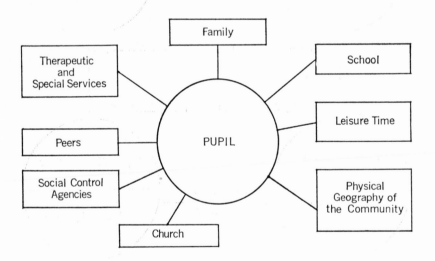

II. The world of peers (pupil-pupil interaction)

Research shows that there is a great deal of stability in the group culture with respect to the views of classroom members as to which pupils are high or low in likeability, influence, and expertness. In order to account for these facts we should focus on the so-called "circular process of social interaction." This circular process helps explain the great stability which occurs in the group social structure of the classroom.

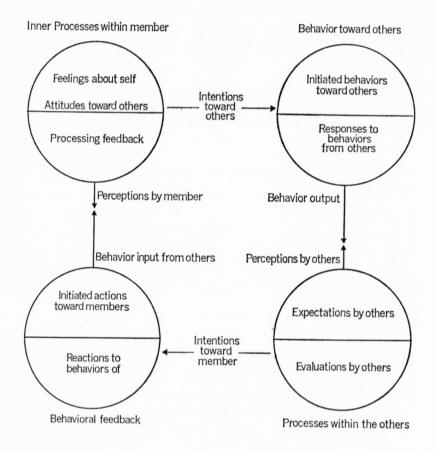

Inner Processes within member

Feelings about self

Attitudes toward others

Processing feedback

Intentions toward others

Behavior toward others

Initiated behaviors toward others

Responses to behaviors from others

Perceptions by member

Behavior output

Behavior input from others

Perceptions by others

Initiated actions toward members

Reactions to behaviors of

Intentions toward member

Expectations by others

Evaluations by others

Behavioral feedback

Processes within the others

III. Overlapping situations

The major problem posed here is that of conflicting goals and needs, of competing expectations for behavior. The analysis focuses on creative and non-creative resolutions of this multiple loyalty problem.

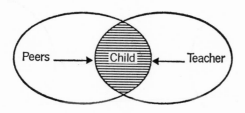

IV. Teacher life space

There are different influence areas in the teacher's life as well.

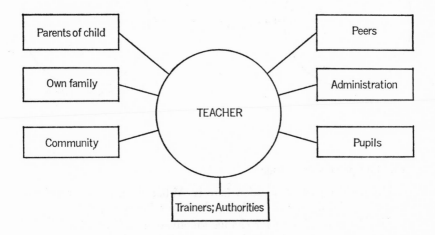

V. Interpersonal process in the classroom (between teacher and classroom group)

This is similar to the circular process situation diagrammed under II.

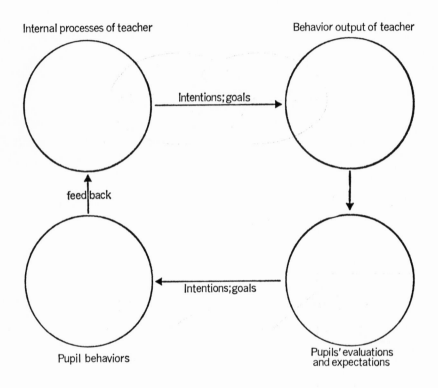

VI. The process of change

The most important question here is "What are necessary conditions
for change?" One model for change has the following steps:

1. Development of need for change (motivation and sensitivity)
2. Psychological acceptance of a source of help (help acceptance)
3. Formulating goals for change (conceptualization)
4. Skills; transforming intentions into action (intent–skill integration)
5. Consolidation of change (evaluation)

In addition, the circular process model may be helpful in thinking
about leverage points for change.

Human relations sensitivity sessions. These provided Teacher "A" with an opportunity to learn about herself and about groups. A two-hour period was devoted to this activity every Tuesday and Thursday. The experience constituted a "living case-study" in which the nine workshoppers came together as strangers and moved toward the development of a group. No agenda was provided and no leadership or rules for operation were imposed. A staff member designated as "trainer" assisted the participants to focus from time to time upon the processes that occurred while the group engaged in interaction. It was possible to examine such aspects of group behavior as the development of group norms, friendship and influence relationships, patterns of communication, relationships to authority, and leadership. Through involvement in such an experience-centered learning situation, Teacher "A" was provided opportunity to (1) gain personal skills and insights regarding her participation in group activity, (2) become more diagnostically sensitive to what happens in groups, (3) become more aware of the ways in which groups grow and mature, and (4) learn how certain group functions affect work level, motivation and problem-solving ability.

In addition to the trainer, a second staff member served as a nonparticipating observer, recording the important events of each session and duplicating the report for distribution prior to the next session. Excerpts from the record of the first session may give a "feel" for the way in which the sensitivity group moved into its task:

Report on Human Relations Sensitivity Group, Session 1

1. The trainer set the stage, explaining that one way of learning about a group is to let a collection of people start the process of establishing themselves as a group, while simultaneously examining their processes and procedures. The content of discussion is not important. Focus is on the present group. It is hoped that an atmosphere will be developed in which we can be frank; can try out new approaches.

As a point of departure we might consider, "What are things each of us does well or not so well in groups?" Or, "What information about other group members is it helpful to have in working with them? How can we obtain such information?"

2. The group was silent for a few minutes, broken by Teacher "B". Then, "The silence is like the reaction when confronting children with a misdeed." "The problem is too difficult." "We may need a chairman." "We need a topic." One teacher introduced "hobbies" as a topic. After brief reactions, discussion shifted to:

"What teacher does if she doesn't feel up to par?"

"Effect of student teacher on class."

"Reaction of class members to grouping practices."

3. After about 30 minutes of discussion by the group, the trainer called attention to the lack of involvement of part of the group in any of the topics discussed. He asked, "How did you feel during the silence?"

Near the conclusion of the session he asked, "What conclusions would you draw regarding this session?" Responses were:

"OK to object, but do so politely."

"Worthwhile."

"A waste of time."

"We need an educationally worthwhile topic."

"Team teaching. . . ."

"Let's set up a schedule of topics."

Teacher "A" observed, "Perhaps children have reactions to group activities similar to ours. If so, we would profit from analyzing our feelings."

In subsequent sessions of the sensitivity group, increasing attention was given to the roles each felt comfortable playing in the group process, and how helpful the group saw these to be. A particularly interesting problem with which the group grappled was the extent of dependence of the group, or members of the group, on authority. There was some speculation that many teachers find themselves in a role which continually demands and rewards compliance with authority. Members also explored through their behavior the relevance and contribution of emotionality in group relationships. These and other learnings, brought about through the opportunity to watch their own group behavior and then to interpret it with the help of a skilled trainer, caused the participants to value the sensitivity group highly among the various workshop activities.

Professional skills sessions.   A number of sessions were arranged to provide Teacher "A" with help in developing skills needed to implement some of the ideas growing from the theory. These dealt with the application of force field analysis to specific pupil or classroom problems; getting and using data about the effects of one's behavior on others, and giving others similar feedback data; utilizing pupil-teacher planning; role playing; developing instruments for assessing the interpersonal situation in the classroom; and testing techniques for presenting one's ideas and plans to teacher colleagues, school administrators, and parents. On several occasions groups of upper elementary children were brought in to assist in demonstration and practice of role playing.

One skill exercise, for example, was related to "feedback" skills. It was called, "Observing feedback in a role playing situation." Staff members took the parts in a cast comprised of a teacher, a passive resistant pupil, a frustrated pupil, an active resistant pupil, and an eager pupil. Workshoppers served as observers and were briefed as follows:

> You will be observing a classroom scene in which the teacher is attempting to explain a current event to the children, and to develop in them a more realistic evaluation of the nature of the problem. The children have been subjected to experiences in their everyday lives which have led to misconceptions. Your task as an observer is to listen and watch for the various types of feedback that the teacher gets and the uses he makes of this evidence. In addition, think of the skill requirements for developing ability to deal effectively with these kinds of situations. You are asked to act as a consultant to the teacher in regard to assisting him in developing better techniques for getting and using feedback from his pupils. As the scene opens the class has just finished reading from their *Junior Scholastics* about the Japanese reaction to President Eisenhower's Far Eastern tour.

The subsequent discussion by the observers as consultants to the teacher provided a variety of ideas and techniques for being sensitive to, and utilizing, feedback from pupils. For example, an observer pointed out that one pupil seemed very hostile toward the Japanese. The "teacher" berated the child for his attitude, and did not pick up several comments the child dropped about his father's war experience. Another observer suggested that the "teacher" arrange for a pupil to manage the discussion, thus freeing the "teacher" to serve as observer and be thoughtful about the contributions made by each child.

Data analysis and planning. Building upon these general experiences, Teacher "A" and the other workshop participants were encouraged to analyze their own classroom situations and develop a plan for improvement. Toward this end, some of the data that had been obtained the preceding spring from the pupils in Teacher "A"'s classroom were made available to her for study. In addition, a variety of activities and resources were provided which focused on the utilization of data in the improvement of classroom practices. The first of these was a case description of one of the project classrooms. Prepared by the staff using data from a classroom of a non-workshop teacher, the case of "Miss Hull" was used as a means of acquainting participants with the kinds of information available to them. In addition, there were several workshop sessions relating to general problems of measurement and analysis.

During the second week of the workshop some of the raw data from each teacher's own classroom, dealing with sociometric choices of the pupils, was brought in for coding and analysis. From these data Teacher "A" prepared sociometric matrices for her class dealing with attributed "influence" and attributed "expertness." She analyzed data from the instrument asking pupils for ways in which they would like the teacher to change, and from that calling for pupils to characterize their classmates and describe their standards for doing so. Differences in pupils' attitudes toward various aspects of their life space (home, school, clubs, playmates) were summarized. Data on classroom peer standards were examined. Teacher "A" found that her pupils placed high value on academic achievement. The leaders among the peer-group were all youngsters who were performing well academically and who thought school was a good place to be. Her pupils thought that their parents did not rate their academic performance as highly as did the teacher. Most did not think it was a good idea to help each other on school work.

These individual data analysis projects were followed by several discussions in which workshop participants split up into pairs or groups of three for the purpose of sharing data and interpreting them (making surprisingly clear the fact that extensive differences exist among classrooms). As an additional means of giving participants some appreciation of the differences across classrooms, a session was conducted in which a staff member presented several sets of data from a variety of classrooms, pointing up such significant sub-groupings for analysis as boys vs. girls, high achievers vs. low achievers, high ability vs. low ability, high utilizers vs. low utilizers.

Teacher "A" 's plan. A plan for improving the situation in her own classroom was developed by Teacher "A" at about the end of the fourth week of the workshop. Each teacher was given the opportunity, if he so desired, to present and discuss his plan with the staff and with the other workshop participants. Teacher "A" chose to do so. A tape recording of the discussion was made for her assistance in reviewing reactions and suggestions. Through subsequent study of the tape and conferences with her staff adviser, she refined her plan. In it she showed concern for the difficulties in interpersonal relationships among her pupils, as evidenced by expressions of intolerance toward others, unhealthy boy-girl competition, and ambivalence toward others in the class. She saw as possible sources of the problem the pupils' failure to accept individual differences in classmates, and their failure to recognize the importance of all members of the group. In view of this, her basic objective was to develop among her pupils more understanding of the individual differences existing in the classroom. She also wanted to explore ways of involving them more in the planning of learning activities.

Her plan included considerable detail which cannot be presented here, although it may be of interest to examine the outline she followed. The outline seemed to stimulate more attention to diagnosis and strategy planning than is often given in plans for classroom change.

Outline of Teacher "A"'s Plan of Action
1. Difficulties that need correcting.
2. Sources of the problem.
3. Criteria for judging appropriateness of changing the situation.
4. The change goal.
5. Resources for this change effort.
6. Resistances to this change effort.
7. Possible ways of working toward this change goal.
8. Decisions about starting points.
9. Plan for evaluation of success.
10. Complementary goals.

Her ideas regarding ways of working toward her change goal show considerable ingenuity. Some of these were:

—Increase knowledge of children in other lands. Observe differences in standards of behavior (what "everyone" does).
—Use role playing to develop appreciation of the "new" or "different" pupil.
—Use school newspaper to increase recognition of importance and contribution of pupils of all age levels in the school.
—Use small, heterogeneous groups regularly to work on specific skill areas or to consider problems of individual adjustment.

—Develop simple diagrams of concepts of "force fields" and "life space" to increase children's ability to perceive and appreciate the problems of the troublemaker.

—Demonstrate normal curves of learning. Use charts showing range of individual differences within the classroom. Use material from Terman Study of Gifted Children to point out variability among those having similar ability.

—Stress different kinds of usefulness in the plant and animal worlds. Tie this in with variety of ways to be useful in the school and community.

—Use questionnaire on room jobs once a month to encourage recognition and appreciation of various abilities and encourage additional breadth of experience for all members.

Among Teacher "A" 's plans for getting the project started in the fall was having the class prepare an inventory or directory of personal resources of pupils, as a means of encouraging recognition of a variety of skills. A section of the directory was to be set up for those who were working at getting better, with their specific goals listed (e.g., "better at doing story problems," rather than just at "arithmetic"; "better at swinging a baseball bat," rather than just "better at playing baseball").

She devised an interesting project to give the group experience in recognizing the various abilities possessed by different members. In it she planned to assign several short, specific tasks to be done within a limited time. Then children were to report upon their reactions, responding to such questions as, "How do you feel when you are done and no one else is?" "How do you feel when you don't finish when time is called?" "How do you feel when you know you are doing a good job? A poor one?" "If everyone seems to be better, would you quit or keep on going?" She planned to select her tasks so that many types of skills would be employed (e.g., copying material from the board, looking up words in the dictionary, writing number facts, running a specified distance, drawing a picture, cleaning out desks, throwing balls into a waste-paper basket, tying a package).

She proposed to use these reports on feelings as a basis for role playing and increasing understanding of the position of the individual in the group.

Altogether the plan was an impressive one. It contained a great variety of alternative ideas and specific plans for working toward her major objective.

Action in the classroom

In the fall of 1960, following the summer workshop, Teacher "A" moved into action with her new class. The first major activity directed toward carrying out the summer's plan was to administer a questionnaire, "Resources in our Classroom," which Teacher "A" designed. Compiling the data thus obtained, she explored ways of using them. She tried various types of sociometric groupings. She devised ways of sharing information with the pupils about the resources that each class member had to offer, such as keeping a card file on her desk listing resource people for various types of tasks, or reviewing with the class as a whole the best available resources for accomplishing a particular assignment or project.

During this period of exploration and trial of different approaches, Teacher "A" conferred with her project consultant, and extended an invitation for him to visit in her classroom. This opportunity for exchange of ideas resulted in the teacher's feeling some support for what she was trying, brought out some possible additional approaches that might be tried, and encouraged continued efforts.

Subsequently, Teacher "A" tried most of the various action ideas originally listed in her plan for change. The more successful are reported in an inventory of innovative efforts gathered from various project teachers (Fox & Schmuck, 1962).

A typical innovation. One of these, by way of illustration, had to do with giving small peer groups increased responsibility for planning and carrying out learning activities in the classroom. The groups were originally set up by the teacher on the basis of congeniality, common interests, and friendship. It was her notion that the elements of an effective working relationship might be more easily understood by pupils working in small groups prior to dealing with total class problems. Individual pupil involvement in planning through such compatible groups might lead to more participation in subsequent classroom activities.

Initially, Teacher "A" introduced the arrangement by conducting some preparatory training for the groups. She assigned discussion topics or specific tasks to each group, helping them to analyze their process. The groups were then ready to check assignments together. Teacher "A" circulated to help groups, reminding pupils to keep their voices down. Later, the pupils themselves arranged groupings and initiated activities.

Among the obstacles or difficulties encountered, according to Teacher "A" 's report, was frustration on the part of some pupils in not having the answer handed down to them. One group decided to vote on the correct answer. In general, Teacher "A" felt it was a good learning experience for the pupils—it "made them do more thinking on their own." She plans to continue use of this procedure, giving further attention to (1) identifying those classroom activities which can be most effectively and profitably dealt with through small group interaction, (2) helping the class clarify the values inherent in the use of peer resources, and (3) structuring more carefully the sequence of training events that would help pupils become more secure in working in small groups.

Clinic sessions

One of the important elements in the year's activities, as far as Teacher "A" was concerned, was the opportunity to participate in monthly clinic sessions with other project teachers and staff members who had been a part of the summer workshop. These meetings were held once each month, with most participants gathering at a local cafeteria for supper and then joining the remainder of the group at the home of one of the staff members for an evening session. A typical agenda included a "round robin" of progress reports on new developments in each classroom, and a general discussion around a problem of major interest to the group. Illustrative of the latter were such questions as:

1. Under what conditions, and how, can negative feedback be given to pupils with constructive results?
2. What is the relationship between teacher standards and peer group standards?
3. How can the teacher influence peer group standards?
4. How can administrators and teacher colleagues be helped to see the significance of human relations in the classroom?

Some attention was given to further practice with skills, such as role playing.

About midway through the first semester, project staff members reviewed the statements of change intentions which had been prepared by participants at the conclusion of the workshop, summarizing each on a one-page sheet. Each teacher then attempted to report what kinds of progress had been made, what modifications had taken place in the original plans, and what prospects the future held. Teacher "A" reported a number of things that seemed to be going well for her:

Group acceptance of individual differences seems to be good.

Spirit of group helpfulness seems to be developing.

Some of the slower learners are showing a greater degree of confidence and are achieving at a higher level.

Individual feelings of responsibility for completing assignments have increased.

In the Library Aide group (with which I have done some role playing) I am told by the librarian that members show a greater degree of responsibility and resourcefulness than is observed in the other schools serviced by this same person.

On the other hand, some things seemed not to be going so well:

Group feeling of responsibility for the conduct of individual members is still weak.

A few members still have not been convinced that they need to change (i.e., that their level of performance is not good enough, that they are satisfied with too little).

She reported that some of the problems she would like to see solved were:

How to channel the energy of the too-competitive member of a group.

How to arouse the self-satisfied (or acquiescent) child.

How to help the child interpret achievement scores and other data to his parent. (Children claim their big concern is that parents don't understand the "facts of life"; that is, parents expect higher grades from them than they think is reasonable.)

Teacher "A" appeared to find in the clinic sessions a pleasant opportunity to continue the friendships established during the summer workshop. In addition, and possibly more importantly, the clinic seemed to provide an opportunity to share ideas about an area of professional concern, as well as to gain some sort of continuing support regarding the importance of personal and group interaction phenomena and her efforts to improve her own classroom situation.

Data collection, fall of 1960

The design for the project called for the collection of some classroom data in the late fall. This would provide teachers with information about their classes early enough in the year so that it might be useful in initiating or modifying plans for change. Therefore, Teacher "A" found herself involved in thinking about the social structure of her classroom, what group standards the pupils had developed, what special resources pupils saw each other as possessing, and what kinds of changes in the teacher's behavior might be desirable. Pupils completed questionnaires on group standards toward the classroom and learning, classroom social structure, importance of classroom life relative to other aspects of their life space, and changes they would like to see in their teacher.

These data were summarized and shared with each project teacher through personal consultation with a staff member. Teacher "A" made frequent comments as she looked at data on class standards or at the ratings individual pupils had been given on the sociometrics: "Well, I'm glad to know that!" or "This is certainly changed from the beginning of the year." She noted particularly and with considerable interest that the pupils thought they should be involved more in decision-making. She had expected they would wish to be involved less. She also tied this up with their concern about her getting angry. She had thought they were looking for more structure, whereas it appeared they may have been interested in more opportunity to participate. She noted that all but two children in her class of thirty felt they were doing at least as well as the others in the class! This she attributed to the fact that the class as a whole had above average achievement and intelligence; they may have been comparing themselves with children in general rather than with their own classmates.

Evaluation of change

In the summer of 1961, project staff members began to evaluate the efforts of participating teachers and to analyze changes in the teachers' perceptions, attitudes, and classroom activities. Evidence of these changes was obtained from a number of sources:

—Pupil and teacher interviews, 1960 and 1961.
—Teacher listings of mental health and learning factors, 1960 and 1961.
—Sociometric choices of pupils, fall of 1960, spring of 1961.
—Pupil requests for changes in the way teacher teaches the class, fall of 1960, spring of 1961.

Teacher "A" showed considerable change in the kinds of character-istics she valued most in the pupils:

1960	1961
1. Sharp	1. Interested
2. Responsive	2. Modest
3. Respond to challenge	3. Helpful to other pupils
4. Highly stimulated	4. Flexible
	5. Cooperative with teacher

She showed shifts toward a more positive view of self. On the instru-ment measuring self perception, items such as *happy, sympathetic,* and *democratic* appear in 1961; not in 1960. Added comparisons appear below.

Learning Conditions Valued by Teacher "A"

1960	1961
1. Emphasis on materials and phys-ical environment.	1. Emphasis on participation, mo-tivation, involvement, oppor-tunity for initiation.
2. Priority items rather general, such as "mental and physical health."	2. Priority items much more "child dynamic" centered (e.g., "high participation," "under-standing of goals," "encourage-ment of all members").
	3. More emphasis placed on teacher attitudes and on demo-cratic orientation.

Mental Health Conditions Valued by Teacher "A"

1960	1961
1. General statements of conditions or relationships: "good rela-tions," "healthy class climate."	1. Much more child-centered items: "acceptance by peers," "helping less expert child," "freedom to express feelings."
2. Listed static categories and no sub-categories: "physical en-vironment," "curriculum," "at-titudes."	2. Differentiated more among cat-egories and listed sub-categories based on interaction concepts: "sharing goals and leadership," "mutual trust," "absence of fear."
3. Emphasized traits: "trust," "tol-erance," "friendliness."	3. Emphasized relationships: "mu-tual self-respect," "doesn't rid-icule others."

In both 1960 and 1961, Teacher "A" evidenced quite a high level of sophistication regarding connections between mental health and learning factors. She showed an increase in mental health insights in 1961, and in use of elements of child motivation and learning theory as a basis of connections between the two.

Such information, together with additional data about the classroom and possible implications for change, was periodically "fed back" to Teacher "A" through a number of techniques and devices, such as personal conferences, group conferences, charts and graphs, and tape-recorded discussion between two staff members.

Planning for the spread of innovation

Choosing sites. As the project moved into a final phase, focused on examining factors involved in the spread of innovation, decisions needed to be made regarding which school sites and which teachers should be involved. The following criteria were utilized:

1. The participant's innovation should be worthwhile (from evidence gained through interviews with pupils, teacher's perceptions of success of innovation, changes effected in the innovator, and changes in pupils).
2. The participant should be remaining in the same building, so that his relationships with the faculty would be relatively well established.
3. There should be evidence of the teacher's potential as a change agent (i.e., he is a person whose ideas might be accepted by his colleagues).
4. Balance between elementary, junior high, and senior high sites is needed.
5. Not more than seven or eight sites can be handled.
6. Areas should be geographically close enough to permit cross-building sessions.
7. Variations in size of system are desirable.

Teacher "A" rated high on both the quality of her innovations, as judged by the project staff, and her attitudes toward change. Her building met the other criteria and was eventually selected as one of the spread sites.

Spreading innovations. A project staff member contacted Teacher "A", described the plan to enter several sites to study the process of spread of innovations, and inquired about her interest in becoming involved with her principal and one of the staff consultants as a member of a change-agent team. She expressed interest, saying she felt quite indebted to the project staff for helping her solve some "real problems." She made arrangements for a meeting with her principal and ascertained his interest in becoming involved.

Subsequently, the three-person change-agent team for the building (Teacher "A", the principal, and the project consultant) developed a strategy for sharing with the faculty some of the ideas about classroom mental health stemming from the project. They described some of the resources that might be made available to teachers wishing to embark on personal attempts to modify their classroom situations. Opportunities were provided for interested faculty members to gain continuing support and assistance with the adaptation of promising practices to their own classroom needs, and with the creation of innovative procedures of their own.

Helpful resources. While there has not yet been opportunity to study fully the kinds of assistance that teachers find to be of most value, it is apparent that some of the resources proving to be of particular help include:

1. The enthusiasm and assurance of practicality provided by the teacher member of the change-agent team (Teacher "A").

2. The booklet describing some of the innovative practices developed by teachers in the project the preceding year (Fox & Schmuck, 1962).

3. The booklet illustrating some of the devices and instruments developed by teachers for getting information about their classrooms (Lippitt & Van Egmond, 1962).

4. A tape recording simulating responses of pupils in Teacher "A" 's classrooms of 1960 and 1961, giving evidence of the kinds of changes brought about in attitudes and behavior among the pupils.

5. The calling in of the other teachers from the project (in other buildings and school systems) to serve as special resource people relative to specific techniques or problems.

Conclusions

This project, directed toward the introduction and spread of teaching innovations relative to classroom learning atmospheres, is not yet at the stage where final conclusions may be drawn. Study of the process of spread is just getting under way at this writing, and extensive analysis of data gathered from earlier stages has yet to be accomplished.[3] However, several tentative conclusions seem to be emerging:

1. Those teachers participating in the intensive summer workshop experience became the most highly involved, attempted the greatest number of new ideas in their classrooms, and were most successful in bringing about some changes.

2. Teachers experiencing summer workshop plus consultation plus monthly clinic sessions produced a higher rate of innovation than those who were involved less extensively.

3. Clinic sessions (periodic meetings of project participants from different school buildings or school systems) provided opportunities for support and sharing of ideas not existent within the normal school faculty communication system.

4. A good place to start toward classroom improvement is at the point of getting facts about the interpersonal situation in the classroom. A teacher's generalized concern for improvement can move toward a more precise attack on a specific problem as information about the real state of affairs becomes available.

5. The innovative efforts of teachers can be highly useful to their professional colleagues who find themselves facing similar problems in their own classrooms. However, the channels of communication whereby successful innovations can be shared are so poorly developed in most school situations that little such sharing takes place.

6. To help make educational innovations visible and available to potential adopters usually requires descriptive effort and conceptual help by a trained outsider.

7. To stimulate active adoption efforts by appropriate colleagues of innovators often requires value re-education to overcome the attitude that using someone else's discovery is a lesser value than "creating your own." The creativity of the adoption process needs to be clarified and promoted as creative activity.

---

[3] Reports dealing with two aspects of the interpersonal situation in the classroom, utilizing data from the 30 classrooms in this project, are available in thesis form (Schmuck, 1962; Epperson, 1962).

Implications of some of the problems encountered in the process of introducing and supporting change in the classroom are presented in journal articles by Fox (1962) and Fox & Van Egmond (1962).

8. In promoting instructional improvement, the collaborative effort of school administrators, teachers, and outside resource people (as represented by the teacher-principal-consultant change-agent team) provides a more vigorous and productive leadership arrangement than does reliance on any one of these roles alone. Innovative efforts by the classroom teacher, with informed and sympathetic support from school administration and professional colleagues, are much more likely to succeed than attempts without such support.

References

Epperson, D. C. The dynamics of two variants of classroom alienation. Unpublished doctoral dissertation, University of Michigan, 1962.

Fox, R. S. Innovation in the classroom. *NEA Journal*, 1962, 51 (4), 41–42.

Fox, R. S., & Schmuck, R. A. (Eds.) *Inventory of teaching innovations directed toward improving classroom learning atmosphere.* Ann Arbor, Michigan: Inter-Center Program of Research on Children, Youth and Family Life, Institute for Social Research, University of Michigan, 1962.

Fox, R. S., & Van Egmond, E. Trying out new ideas. *NEA Journal*, 1962, 51 (7), 25–27.

Lippitt, R., & Van Egmond, E. *Inventory of classroom study tools for understanding and improving classroom learning processes.* Ann Arbor, Michigan: Inter-Center Program of Research on Children, Youth and Family Life, Institute for Social Research, University of Michigan, 1962.

Schmuck, R. A. Social-emotional characteristics of classroom peer groups. Unpublished doctoral dissertation, University of Michigan, 1962.

CHAPTER 12

Resistance to the adoption of audio-visual aids by elementary school teachers: contrasts and similarities to agricultural innovation

GERHARD EICHHOLZ
EVERETT M. ROGERS

IN 1955, one of the authors chanced upon an issue of the *Journal of Educational Research* devoted to reviewing research studies on the diffusion of new educational ideas. This was the first convergence between two research traditions, education and rural sociology, that had both been investigating the spread of new ideas for over seventeen years!

The purpose of the present chapter is to illustrate the convergence between these two major intellectual traditions focusing on the diffusion of innovations, using data from an investigation of the rejection of audio-visual aids by elementary school teachers.

Traditions of Diffusion Research

Diffusion is the process by which an innovation spreads. The diffusion process is the spread of a new idea from its source of invention or creation to its ultimate users or adopters. Thus diffusion entails the communication or dissemination of an idea, and culminates in its adoption by individuals.

THE AUTHORS are, respectively: Director, Division of Educational Resources, The University of South Florida, Tampa, Florida; and Associate Professor of Rural Sociology, The Ohio State University, Columbus, Ohio.

One might expect that various scientists studying the spread of new ideas would be in adequate communication with each other regarding their findings and research methods. Nevertheless, any review of the available literature on the diffusion of innovations must arrive at one conclusion: there has been a very inadequate diffusion of diffusion research findings among those researching the topic.

A *research tradition* is a series of research studies on a similar topic in which successive studies are influenced by preceding investigations. Six major diffusion research traditions will be briefly described: anthropology, early sociology, rural sociology, education, industrial, medical sociology. Each of these intellectual traditions is shown in Table 1. There are important differences among the traditions in terms of the disciplines represented, methods of data-gathering and analysis, units of analysis, and types of findings.

The research tradition that has produced the greatest number of publications and studies on the diffusion of new ideas is rural sociology. Most of these studies deal with the transmission of farm innovations from agricultural scientists to farmers. Rural sociology is probably "the only research tradition within the social sciences that can boast so long and so continuing a concern with the social aspects of diffusion" (Katz, 1961). Most rural sociologists are employed in state universities and conduct their research with funds provided by state agricultural experiment stations. The rural sociology diffusion tradition really got under way with the Ryan and Gross (1943) analysis of the spread of hybrid seed corn in Iowa. Since then, about 300 different publications have appeared to report research findings in this tradition (Rogers, 1962).

The educational research tradition is second largest in number of studies (over 150 are listed in a recent bibliography by Ross, 1958). The educational diffusion studies illustrate strong intercommunication within the tradition, but no close attention to other diffusion traditions. Ross (1958, p. 553), after his review of educational diffusion studies, concluded, "Seldom has dispersed research in some phase of education [educational diffusion] been so well articulated and formed such an integrated pattern as a whole."

The majority of educational diffusion studies have been done at one institution, Columbia University's Teachers College, under the sponsorship of one researcher, Paul Mort. The data were most often

Table 1. A Comparison of the Diffusion Research Traditions *

Tradition	Main Disciplines Represented	Main Method of Data-Gathering & Analysis	Main Unit of Analysis	Major Types of Findings
Anthropology	Anthropology	Participant observation combined with descriptive analysis	Societies or tribes	How idea diffuses from one society to another; consequences of innovation
Early sociology	Sociology	Data from secondary sources & a type of statistical analysis	Mainly communities, but also individuals	S-shaped adopter distribution; correlates of innovativeness
Rural sociology	Sociology	Personal interviews & statistical analysis	Individual farmers	Correlates of innovativeness; characteristics of ideas related to rate of adoption; source of information at adoption process stages; S-shaped adopter distribution
Education	Education	Mailed questionnaire & statistical analysis	School systems	Correlates of innovativeness; S-shaped adopter distribution
Industrial	Ind. economics Ind. history Ind. engineering	Case studies & statistical analysis	Industrial firms	Correlates of innovativeness
Medical sociology	Sociology Public health	Personal interviews & statistical analysis	Individuals	Opinion leadership in diffusion; correlates of innovativeness

* Source: Rogers (1962).

301

gathered by mailed questionnaire from school superintendents or principals. The unit of analysis was the school system in almost all of these investigations.

Diffusion in Education

The problem of "lag" in diffusion

Technology has given education and the educative process a tremendous and sometimes bewildering array of innovations. Yet there is criticism of schools for what is commonly called a "lag" in the acceptance of these new ideas. All bowling alleys built within the last few years have an overhead projector installed in every lane for scorekeeping, yet it is the exceptional school that has even one overhead projector.[1] Does this constitute a "lag" and is such a "lag" measurable? Mort (1953) defined the lag, and measured it.

> A period of about 50 years may elapse between insight into a need and the invention of a solution which will be accepted. Fifteen years typically elapse before it is found in three per cent of the school systems . . . additional twenty years usually suffices for an almost complete diffusion in an area the size of an average state.

Eighty-five years may elapse from insight of a need to complete diffusion. Certainly this may be considered a "lag" when we recall that it was only 58 years after the first successful flight of the Wright brothers that a manned rocket sped into outer space.

Rejection and adoption

Most of the 500-odd diffusion studies in all traditions mentioned have primarily been concerned with those individuals *adopting* innovations. Resistance or rejection of a given innovation has been mentioned only indirectly. Rejection is treated as a "barrier" to be overcome in most diffusion studies. Rejection of an innovation is considered almost abnormal behavior, to be overcome at any expense by those involved in promoting the new idea. Theoretically, rejection might be considered the opposite of adoption. If adoption is the full-scale use of an

---

[1] An informal survey (by the authors) of audio-visual equipment available in 25 schools located in a metropolitan school system disclosed that no overhead projectors were used.

innovation, rejection is the non-use of an innovation. If acceptance is worthy of study, rejection should be also. (One example of the importance of rejection is community decisions regarding the fluoridation of water supplies, an idea recommended by the U. S. Public Health Service in the early 1950's. U. S. communities rejected fluoridation in about 80 per cent of the referenda held in 1961.)

The rejection of an innovation is the antithesis of acceptance. When a given innovation is introduced, the entire population that might use such an innovation are potential adopters or rejecters. The process whereby adopters ultimately use an innovation has five distinct and separate stages (North Central Regional Rural Sociology Subcommittee, 1955). These stages are:

1. *Awareness:* The individual learns of the existence of the innovation.
2. *Interest:* The individual seeks more information and considers the merits of the innovation.
3. *Evaluation:* The individual makes a mental application of the innovation and weighs its merits for his particular situation.
4. *Trial:* The individual applies the innovation on a small scale.
5. *Adoption:* The individual accepts the innovation for continued use on the basis of a previous trial.

Thus the potential accepter moves through five stages to become an actual adopter and full-scale user of an innovation. It can be hypothesized that an individual might follow a similar five-stage process as a potential rejecter, leading to actual rejection based on a trial of a given innovation.

Thus the problem of "lag" in the acceptance of educational innovations is not only one of overcoming barriers, but also that of decreasing the time required in the five-stage process leading to actual acceptance. Furthermore, a study of rejecters might determine if a similar five-stage process leads to rejection, as well as indicate why innovations of proven worth are not immediately acceptable to the very teachers for whom they were designed.

A Study in Rejection

An investigation has been conducted to test a theory of rejection compatible with research findings from adoption studies, and also to explain the "lag" in the adoption of educational innovations. The study attempted to develop a rejection classification for newer educational media (Eichholz, 1961). The newer media were defined as electromechanical innovations such as film projectors, tape recorders, television receivers, etc., and static innovations such as the flannel-board, mock-ups, models, programed instructional materials, etc. The classification system was part of a postulated rejection theory. The theory of rejection attempted to incorporate what is presently known of the adoption process, and to explain some seemingly incongruent behavior on the part of adopters. For example, Johnson and van den Ban (1959) found that some adopters of farm innovations did not continue using them. This phenomenon was labeled a "discontinuance" and seemed to remain an isolated phenomenon, outside of the normal adoption process. Allen (1956) found discontinuances of certain educational practices (including remedial reading) in 12 of 54 schools that he studied.

Figure 1 shows a postulated theory of rejection combining much of the basic research in adoption. This theory is an attempt to formulate a rejection–adoption theory based primarily on rejection, and incorporates "discontinuances" as a logical result of either the rejection or the adoption process.

Procedure

In an effort to test this theory of rejection and validate the classifications postulated, forty-five teachers in a metropolitan school system were selected for interviews in 1960 on the basis of three criteria:

1. *Grade taught*: 15 teachers were selected from each of the following grade levels: 1–2, 3–4, and 5–6.
2. *Teaching experience*: 15 teachers were selected from each of the following ranges of experience: 1–3 years, 7–10 years, and over 15 years.
3. *Known rejecter*: A short six-question test was given to determine the non-users or rejecters of electromechanical innovations.

The criteria of grade taught and years of teaching experience were used because Kelly (1960) found them to be significant factors in the adoption of educational innovations. The sample of forty-five teachers made possible a comparison in terms of grade level and teaching experience, with five teachers at each grade level and five at each

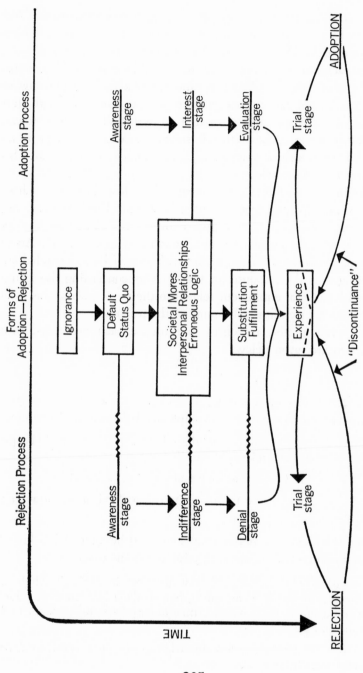

Figure 1. Diagram of a proposed rejection theory

305

experience level. A six-item pre-test was given to all teachers; only those teachers found by this test to be rejecters of electromechanical innovations were included in the sample.

Each teacher included in the sample was interviewed with an open-ended questionnaire designed to uncover teachers' feelings toward the newer media. All interviews were over an hour in length, tape recorded, transcribed, and evaluated in terms of attitudes toward specific innovations. These attitude statements were tabulated on the basis of a previously developed rejection classification system. (See *Rejection Responses* below.)

The sample of forty-five teachers came from five elementary schools in a large metropolitan school system. Each school principal was also interviewed concerning his attitudes toward the newer media, and was asked to evaluate each teacher interviewed in his school. An inventory of the newer media available at each school was compiled and checked against the responses of the teachers concerning this equipment. The fact that equipment related to the newer media was available gave added significance to some of the responses.

Some representative responses to illustrate each postulated form of rejection are given below.

Rejection responses

1. *Rejection through ignorance* was assumed to exist when a given innovation was unknown, or its complexity led to misunderstanding.

> We have an opaque projector in the school. I never use it. [The projector available was a micro-projector.]

> I don't always know what audio-visual materials are available.

> I don't know how to use the movie projector; kind of embarrassed to admit it.

2. *Rejection through default* was expressed by admitting a knowledge of the innovation without any interest in its usage.

> I never use a tape recorder . . . just don't use it, that's all. Might be very helpful in speech. I can run it, but we don't have time . . . Let's be honest about it, we don't have time to do everything we want to do with the children.

> By the time we get through teaching what we have to teach, there is not too much time left for extras.

3. *Rejection by maintaining the status quo* was expressed when the teacher did not accept an innovation because it had not been used in the past.

I tend to do the teaching process [arithmetic] mechanically, because the book does it that way.

I refuse to tell you that I use these aids all the time. I don't. I am an old-fashioned teacher and feel that we should use the text once in a while.

4. *Rejection through societal mores* was expressed when the teacher thought her society did not find an innovation acceptable, and therefore did not use it herself.

I find that children are watching lots of TV programs they should not be watching, and at hours they should be in bed.

Use the record player once a week. I use it more when the children bring in records. . . . they were rock-and-roll, and I discouraged it because they were not worth listening to.

I don't use the museum. There are only certain classrooms that visit the museum.

5. *Rejection through interpersonal relationships* was expressed by indicating that friends did not use an innovation, or that a particular school environment made using an innovation unacceptable. When some teachers or a principal were enthusiastic over the newer media, these attitudes were similarly reflected by rejecters.

The equipment we have at school is excellent . . . we have enough of everything.

We have three television sets. Don't you think that is very good? But then the principal is very audio-visual minded, and sees that we get things.

On the other hand, indifference toward the newer media in other schools was expressed by rejecters.

The principal doesn't think less of a teacher for not using audio-visual materials. She would probably like to see them used. We never talk about this sort of stuff at teacher's meetings . . . they are all business.

Other personal relationships influence the use of the newer media.

We sort of cooperate . . . we tell each other what we have available and how good we think it is.

I don't use the art program. One of the teachers in the second grade used it and said it was too complicated . . . so she gave it up.

6. *Rejection through erroneous logic* was expressed by giving "rational" but unfounded reasons for the rejection of a worthy innovation.

The upper grades use the A-V materials more than the lower grades do.

I suspect the lower grades use them [newer media] more than we do in the upper grades.

I haven't used quite as many audio-visual materials this year because I have a slower group.

Quite often my students think that when they go to see a movie it is fun . . . so I don't use them. I don't use filmstrips either.

7. *Rejection through substitution* was expressed when a teacher spoke of using one practice over another that would have required the use of a particular innovation.

I use two pieces of tag board instead of a screen . . . there is a screen available but this is easier.

If you are going to have a radio program . . . something else will have to be dropped.

I do more work on charts and things like that than on A-V materials.

8. *Rejection through fulfillment* was expressed when a teacher was certain she knew the "best" or "only" way to teach, making any innovation completely unnecessary.

I would not take additional instruction in A-V materials because I think you take those things you are interested in, and I am interested in music and art.

I have a cadet teacher that uses a flannelboard, and the children enjoy it; but I find I can use the blackboard just as well.

I use one film a morning for six weeks. . . . Some have asked why I don't use the radio; but why should I, if I study the material and know what I can present to the children?

9. *Rejection through experience* was expressed by telling of some incident when an innovation was tried and failed.

I signed up one summer to take an audio-visual course, but it was filled.

There are some teachers that order films and ask other teachers to show them.

Now this year I don't use one program that is very good. Sort of ashamed of myself, but I get tired of hearing the same thing year after year.

The children like filmstrips at the beginning because they are a novelty but after a while they get bored.

Results

The findings of this study were not completely conclusive. For example:

1. Attitudes of rejecters were not related to the grade level at which a teacher taught, or to the number of years of teaching experience. This finding is not consistent with the prior findings of Kelly (1960).

2. No teacher, even though classified as a rejecter on the basis of the six-item scale, was a rejecter of *all* the newer media. Every teacher, while rejecting many of the electromechanical innovations, used many of the static innovations.

3. Each form of rejection postulated was expressed by at least 50 per cent of the sample. About 50 per cent of the sample expressed rejection through default, while 93 per cent of the sample expressed rejection through experience.

4. It became obvious that, for the teachers interviewed, the real reasons for rejection and the stated reasons for rejection were not always the same. The postulated forms of rejection could be considered neither complete nor mutually exclusive. Therefore, it became necessary to establish a revised framework for the identification of rejection forms, reducing the nine original postulated forms to five basic forms.

Table 2 illustrates the revised framework for the identification of rejection responses. This framework gives typical responses for various forms of rejection, and differentiates between "real" and "stated" reasons for rejection. These forms of rejection appear to be more inclusive and parsimonious. Each form now stands in a direct one-to-one relationship with stages in both adoption and rejection processes. It is further possible to conceptualize a total process that might be known as an adoption–rejection (or "decision") process that incorporates the five forms and five stages of adoption–rejection. Figure 2, incorporating the revisions made as a result of this study, shows such a process.

Table 2. A Framework for the Identification of Forms of Rejection

Form of Rejection	Cause of Rejection	State of Subject	Anticipated Rejection Responses
1. Ignorance	Lack of dissemination	Uninformed	"The information is not easily available."
2. Suspended judgment	Data not *logically* compelling	Doubtful	"I want to wait and see how good it is, before I try."
3. Situational	Data not *materially* compelling	1. Comparing	"Other things are equally good."
		2. Defensive	"The school regulations will not permit it."
		3. Deprived	"It costs too much to use in time and/or money."
4. Personal	Data not *psychologically* compelling	1. Anxious	"I don't know if I can operate equipment."
		2. Guilty	"I know I should use them, but I don't have time."
		3. Alienated (or estranged)	"These gadgets will never replace a teacher." ("If we use these gadgets, they might replace us.")
5. Experimental	Present or past trials	Convinced	"I tried them once and they aren't any good."

Further Research Needs

This study attempted to define the area of rejection in a limited field. The revised theory and classification of rejection noted here is neither complete nor final. While the classification seems substantiated in the light of the limited sample used, another study is contemplated to further substantiate these findings and to investigate the question of potential adopters–rejecters. There is some reason to believe that a person may be either a potential adopter or a potential rejecter, ap-

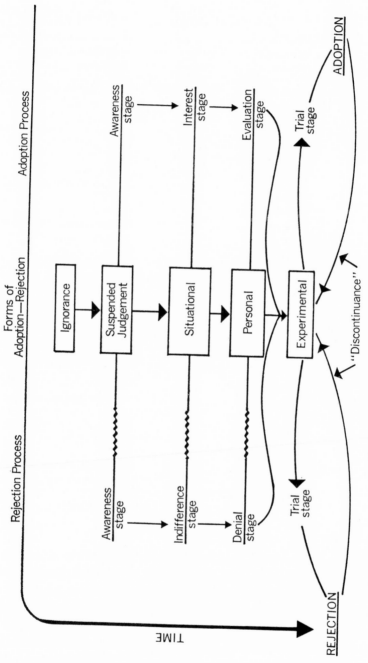

Figure 2. Diagram of revised rejection theory

311

proaching an innovation with adopter or rejecter "sets." Other questions still unanswered are:

1. What factors differentiate the rejecters and accepters of the newer media?

2. Does a given innovation cause a certain form of rejection, or are all forms of rejection common to all innovation?

3. What happens when a series of many innovations related to teaching methodology is available in a short period of time? Are they adopted as a "cluster"? Is such a cluster or complex of innovations adopted more quickly or slowly than single innovations?

4. Are the means for shortening rejection time common to all forms of rejection, or must each form be treated differently?

5. Can tests be devised to isolate attitudes of rejection on the part of teachers, thereby giving administrators some indication of the potential "lag" they can expect in the acceptance of innovations?

6. Should school administrators be responsible for pressing adoption of the newer media to secure an improved quality of education?

7. Are teachers morally obligated to reject the newer media until such time as they are personally certain of its worth and willing to alter their method of teaching to include the innovation?

Although these and other questions are yet to be answered, technology continues to force upon education a vast and complex number and variety of innovations. Devices from teaching machines to airborne television will meet with resistance. Rejection is the only defense left to a teacher who feels threatened by these innovations. Yet it is on the teachers' acceptance of these innovations that their success ultimately depends.

Similarities to Rural Sociological Research

Common elements

There are five crucial elements in the analysis of the diffusion of any type of innovation. These elements have been shown to be the same in studies in rural sociology and education.

1. The *innovation,* defined as an idea perceived as new by the individual.

2. The *communication* of the innovation from one individual to another. Diffusion is defined as the process by which an idea spreads.

3. The innovation diffuses through a *social system,* defined as a

population of individuals who are functionally differentiated and engaged in collective problem-solving. The social system under analysis in a research study may be all the farmers in a county, all the teachers in a school system, or the members of an aborigine tribe. The farmer, teacher, or aborigine is the unit of analysis in each case. The norms of the system, whether traditional or innovative, affect the diffusion of innovations in that system.

4. Diffusion occurs over *time*. Not all individuals adopt an innovation at the same time. Innovativeness is defined as the degree to which an individual adopts new ideas relatively earlier than other members of his social system. Adopter categories involve the classification of individuals on the basis of their innovativeness: (1) innovators, the first to adopt, (2) early adopters, (3) early majority, (4) late majority, (5) laggards, and (6) non-users. Adopter categories have been studied both by educational researchers (Ross, 1958) and by rural sociologists (Rogers, 1962).

5. The time differential in adoption or rejection can be explained in part by the forms and *stages* of adoption–rejection. These forms (ignorance, suspended judgment, situational, personal, and experimental) are directly related to the stages found in both the adoption and the rejection process. Thus the time at which any given individual becomes an actual adopter or rejecter will depend on two factors: (1) how quickly he passes through the forms of adoption or rejection, and (2) the predisposition of the individual to either the adoption or the rejection process. It may also be that certain forms of adoption–rejection lead to a greater or lesser time differential. For instance, rejection for situational reasons will probably remain rejection until the situation is altered, in spite of a personal willingness to adopt.

Common generalizations

Some generalizations found in educational studies seem to be applicable to rural sociological studies (Rogers, 1962). For example, educational researchers have found that schools which are more innovative are characterized by teachers who attend out-of-town educational meetings and who read widely to find new ideas. Similarly, Ryan and Gross (1943) found that farmer-innovators were more likely to travel to metropolitan cities than were laggards. These findings suggest the generalization that *innovativeness varies directly with cosmopoliteness* (defined as the degree to which an individual's orientation is external to a particular social system). This generalization is also supported by evidence from industrial and medical sociology studies (Rogers, 1962).

Another generalization supported by evidence from several research traditions is that *innovativeness varies directly with financial resources.* Rogers (1962) found that innovative farmers operated larger farms, earned higher gross farm incomes, and had a higher net worth than less innovative farmers. Ross (1958) summarizes research evidence to the effect that the more innovative school systems are located in communities with higher average personal incomes and greater school tax support. Similarly, innovativeness has been found to characterize medical doctors with richer patients and industrial firms with larger operations.

Contrasts to Rural Sociological Research

The unit of analysis

One of the important differences between the "typical" research study in rural sociology and the "typical" investigation in education of adoption–rejection lies in the unit of analysis. In rural sociology, the unit of analysis is usually the individual farmer.[2] In some 150 educational studies completed to date on the diffusion of innovations, the unit of analysis has been the school or the school system. It should be noted, however, that the study described in this chapter utilizes the individual teacher as the unit of analysis, although school norms relevant to innovativeness were considered. When the school or school system is used as a unit of analysis, much of the individual variation in innovativeness and other variables is cancelled. The authors, therefore, feel there is a need for further investigation of adoption–rejection using the individual teacher as the unit of analysis, while taking account of school or group norms concerning innovativeness.

Differences in diffusion-adoption rates

Mort (1946, pp. 199–200) found the average school ". . . lags 25 years behind the best practice." Why is the diffusion and adoption of

[2] It is interesting to note that a recent rural sociology study (Armstrong, 1959) used Kentucky counties as the unit of analysis in investigating farmer innovativeness.

educational ideas so much slower than that of farm innovations or medical drugs? The following reasons are offered.

The absence of scientific sources of innovation in education. This is the constant problem of physical versus social research. The drug laboratories and the vast network of agricultural experimental stations make possible accurate and precise measurements under controlled conditions for a given innovation. Education, on the other hand, has only the "campus" or "university" schools and those classes in the nation's schools that are willing to cooperate in experimentation. In either case, the first responsibility is to the student, not to research. Thus, results of innovation trials are often ambiguous, incomplete, and confusing.

The lack of change agents to promote new educational ideas. In agriculture, the Extension Service, through a system of county agents, forms a communication link between scientists and farmers. In education, the school principal is probably in a position similar to the county agent; but, as shown in the Eichholz study, only one of the five principals acted in a "change agent" role with his teachers. It should be noted here that the major role of a principal is probably not to promote change but to administer the *status quo.*

The lack of economic incentive to adopt. The lack of economic incentive to adopt an innovation is two-fold in nature: (1) The results of adopting an educational innovation are not so easily measured as those following the adoption of innovations in agriculture. The innovation in agriculture will result in direct economic profit through increased yield. On the other hand, the only measurable result of an educational innovation may be the dollar cost of the innovation itself, since the amount of increased learning through the use of the innovation cannot be easily measured. (2) Teachers are generally paid on the basis of longevity and personal educational attainment. Thus, what is accomplished in the classroom seldom influences the economic level of the teacher. Teachers adopting innovations are paid the same as those rejecting innovations, and the teacher adopting an innovation faces the added risk of possible failure. As Pelley (1948, pp. 170–171) stated, "Unfortunately, there seems to be no possible profit motive in being an educational innovator."

Concluding Comment

The present study illustrates a type of convergence between two of the intellectual traditions dealing with the diffusion of innovations, education and rural sociology. There is need for greater diffusion of diffusion research findings and methods from one tradition to another. The result will be a greater standardization of terminology, a freshness of approach, and a greater sophistication of research methodology.

References

Allen, H. E. The diffusion of educational practices in the school systems of the Metropolitan School Study Council. Unpublished doctoral dissertation, Teachers College, Columbia University, 1956.

Armstrong, J. B. County agent activities and the adoption of soil-building practices. Unpublished master's thesis, University of Kentucky, 1959.

Eichholz, G. Development of a rejection classification for newer educational media. Unpublished doctoral dissertation, The Ohio State University, 1961.

Johnson, D., & van den Ban, A. The dynamics of farm practice change. Paper read at Midwest Sociol. Soc., Lincoln, Nebraska, 1959.

Katz, E. The social itinerary of technical change: two studies on the diffusion of innovation. *Human Organization*, 1961, 20, 70–82.

Kelly, G. B. A study of teachers' attitudes toward audiovisual materials. *Educ. Screen & Audiovisual Guide*, 1960, 39, 119–121.

Mort, P. R. *Principles of school administration*. New York: McGraw-Hill, 1946.

Mort, P. R. *Educational adaptability*. New York: Metropolitan School Study Council, 1953.

North Central Rural Sociology Subcommittee on the Diffusion of Farm Practices. *How farm people accept new ideas*. Iowa Agricultural Extension Service Special Report 15. Ames: The Service, 1955.

Pelley, J. H. Invention in education. Unpublished doctoral dissertation, Teachers College, Columbia University, 1948.

Rogers, E. M. Categorizing the adopters of agricultural practices. *Rural Sociol.*, 1958, 23, 345–354.

Rogers, E. M. *Diffusion of innovations*. New York: Free Press, 1962.

Ross, D. H. *Administration for adaptability: a source book drawing together the results of more than 150 individual studies related to the question of why and how schools improve*. New York: Metropolitan School Study Council, 1958.

Ryan, B., & Gross, N. C. The diffusion of hybrid seed corn in two Iowa communities. *Rural Sociol.*, 1943, 8, 15–24.

CHAPTER 13

Studies in educational innovation from the Institute of Administrative Research: an overview

PAUL R. MORT

OVER the past two decades, approximately 200 studies have been carried on in the Institute of Administrative Research dealing with the adaptability [1] of public school systems, and with the adaptation process. Forerunners of the work of the Institute were a series of studies of the pattern of diffusion, and a rather intensive survey to identify agents of innovation and factors of community, legal structure, and administrative organization affecting the adaptability of school systems. These studies were carried on in the late 1930's. The studies through 1957 (150 in all) were analyzed by Ross (1958), and were organized under three headings: "What happens in the adaptation process"; "Influences on the adaptability of school systems"; and "Who are the adapters?" The fifty studies completed (to June, 1961) since the Ross book went to press deal almost exclusively with

---

[1] Adaptability is defined as "capacity of an institution to respond to its role in society and to new insights concerning its techniques of operation." (Vincent, 1961, p. 1) It can be seen in a sense as a measure of the relative "modernity" of a school system's practices.

THE AUTHOR was Professor Emeritus of Education, Teachers College, Columbia University, and former executive officer of the Institute of Administrative Research. The manuscript for this chapter was edited posthumously with the aid of William S. Vincent, present executive officer.

influences on the adaptability of school systems, though three deal with the adaptation process itself.

The Early Studies

The early studies indicated that change in the American school system comes about through a surprisingly slow process and follows a predictable pattern. Between insight into a need (for example, identification of school children's health problems) and the introduction of a way of meeting the need that is destined for general acceptance (for example, health inspection by a school doctor) there is typically a lapse of a half-century. Another half-century is required for the diffusion of the adaptation. During that half-century of diffusion, the practice is not recognized until it has appeared in 3% of the systems of the country. By that time, fifteen years of diffusion—or independent innovation—have elapsed. Thereafter, there is a rapid twenty years of diffusion, accompanied by much fanfare, and then a long period of slow diffusion through the last small percentage of school systems.

These studies also indicated that, except for amount of schooling, the factors given emphasis (in the late 1930's) in the selection of teachers did not appear to have very much bearing on adaptability, and that there was a relationship of surprising magnitude between the community and adaptability of school systems. The measured relationship of school support (defined *financially*, and to a lesser degree in terms of public interest) to adaptability confirmed earlier hypotheses.

The early studies also gave considerable information on the place of teachers, administrators, and the public in bringing about innovation. For example, school systems with high adaptability were those where teachers were more highly trained and more accepting of modern educational practices (though community size and wealth appear to be the basic factors underlying these); where administrations provided active support for adaptations rather than remaining neutral; and where the public's attitudes favored modern practices (especially in the case of "visible" adaptations such as kindergarten and adult classes—in the case of "professional" adaptations, such as use of supplementary reading, public attitudes made little difference) (Mort & Cornell, 1941, pp. 199–224, 244–312).

Applications of Early Findings

During the early 1940's, findings of the previous studies influenced analyses of state school finance programs in New York, Rhode Island and West Virginia. They, and the later studies, have continued to influence—and be influenced by—the theoretical evolution of public school finance. They also played some part in the designing of various programs for the introduction of innovations in the American school system.

Experience with one of these innovations gives an idea of how under certain circumstances the tempo of diffusion can be speeded up. The innovation was the program of high school pre-flight training developed by the government to give potential fliers in the Armed Services a better start. The specifications influenced by the adaptability studies were these: (1) a public demand must be built up; (2) the professional leadership of the schools must be made receptive to the demand; (3) instructional materials must be inexpensive; (4) instructional materials must be all but self-teaching. This program, involving radio, press, theatre, conferences and intensive experimental development of instructional materials, was carried through from its initiation to the introduction of the materials in the schools in less than a year. From publishers' reports, there are indications that approximately half of the high schools in the nation were reached within the year. Here the half-century gap between insight and innovation was reduced from decades to months, and a quarter-century of diffusion was achieved in less than a year. It would appear to be very improbable that such a rapid change could be obtained except under emergency conditions, such as those existing in the early 40's. But it also appears likely that even with all the urgency the rapid results could not have been achieved without taking account of insights gained from the adaptability studies.

A similarly rapid diffusion of a program of practices (in this instance centering on the use of the community as a laboratory for purposes of citizenship education) may be observed in the numbers of school districts cooperating with the Citizenship Education Project at Teachers College within a period of six years. The number increased from 5 to more than 1200, a diffusion stimulated principally by foundation support. (Vincent et al., 1958)

Another line of development was the establishment of three "laboratories" for the study of adaptability of public school systems and the adaptation process: the Metropolitan School Study Council, the Associated Public School Systems, and the Central School Boards Committee for Educational Research. They represent a marshalling of the resources of some 700 school systems, selected for their potential contribution toward inquiry into what were judged to be critical areas in the study of adaptability and the adaptation process.

Tempo and Diffusion Patterns

During the past two decades, the work carried on by the Institute of Administrative Research has dealt chiefly with the analysis of the setting for educational innovation—legal structure, community characteristics, administrative organization, and patterns of administration. However, various aspects of the tempo theory (the time lag in diffusion described above) have been examined.

For example, Bigelow (1947) found more rapid diffusion in those communities of the Metropolitan School Study Council which had higher financial support in schools and higher levels of parental education and occupation. Pelley (1948) put the spotlight on the invention period and made some evaluation of the attempts of the Metropolitan School Study Council to spur invention through the organization of long-term committees. Cocking (1951) showed that adaptations appear in every region of the United States during that early period when there is no recognition of the innovation in the professional journals or press. Rothemich (1953) showed that except for the short period of years following the announcement of an insight, there is usually no publicity of consequence for approximately sixty-five years, when the innovation that grows from the insight emerges from the "3% period" of early, slow diffusion. Barrington (1953) showed that the tempo and pattern of change in teachers' colleges and their laboratory schools are essentially the same as those found in the public school systems. Bushnell (1957), by comparing the patterns of diffusion of adaptations introduced in this century with those introduced in the latter part of the nineteenth century, showed that there has been some increase in tempo (perhaps 20%) in recent decades.

Considerable has been done to follow up observations of the patterns of change, on the hypothesis that invention is hindered by the short-term character of study projects organized in institutions and school systems. Long-term committees were established in the Metropolitan School Study Council, designed to come to grips with what were thought to be areas of need. One of these committees, dealing with changes in the teaching of English, has been in operation for eighteen years.

On the hypothesis that a reason for the early slow diffusion period is in part the lack of communication, extensive, systematic and continued studies were made of variations in practice in the schools.[2] Reference to this is made in the discussion of the search for the "emerging design" later in this chapter.

Legal, Organizational, and Administrative Policy

Following the Pennsylvania study (Mort & Cornell, 1941), there was extensive exploration of factors in the community, in financial and administrative policy, and in school personnel to obtain clues to the "handles" for administrative action to improve the adaptability of school systems.[3] The studies of Pierce (1947), Newell (1943), and Eastmond (1950) are examples. Out of this work, two conclusions appear to be justified:

1. There is no single factor, in and of itself, which is highly related to adaptability.

2. Differences in the complexes of factors making for adaptability

[2] Active dissemination of information about educational innovations was also carried out through publications such as *What Schools Can Do: 101 Patterns of Educational Practice* (MSSC, 1947), various versions of which sold over 100,000 copies; and specially-designed periodicals such as *Exchange, Central Ideas* and *Know-How,* which went to school systems associated in such groupings as the MSSC, New York Central School Study, and Associated Public School Systems.

[3] Typical factors studied under the *community* heading were percentage of college graduates in the community, and attitudes toward modern educational practices; under *financial and administrative policy,* net current expenditure per pupil, professional staff per 1,000 pupils, and expenditures for small items (materials, etc.); under *personnel,* age, amount of training, and origin within or outside the local system. For a description of these measurements, and their correlations with school adaptability measures, see Vincent (1961).

among communities are so great as to obscure the relative influence of a particular condition or policy; these differences cannot be ironed out sufficiently by traditional methods of matching by community size, wealth, and expenditure level.

The challenge of these findings is to identify the factors of greatest yield among those available, to measure their usefulness to the local administrator, and to shape them into a control instrument capable of ironing out the differences among communities enough to make effects of particular policies or practices sensitive to measurement. This challenge provided an important guideline for the work of the Institute during these two decades. The results have been what appear to be useful "quality control" guides for local administrators (Vincent, 1961) and a model for equalizing community differences for research purposes, the "sequential simplex" (Mort & Furno, 1960).[4]

Approximately 140 of the 150 studies analyzed by Ross (1958) were carried on in the Institute. One third of the studies dealt with the community (e.g., public attitudes and their relation to the school), and one third with administrative mechanisms and arrangements (of which eleven had to do with class size). The other third were about equally divided among staff characteristics, expenditure analysis, and administrative setting (including ten studies of the special problems of large-city school district organization).

Studies carried on since 1957 have emphasized staff characteristics and patterns of staffing, a new approach to the study of public attitudes by the use of the critical-incident technique, advances in the field of measurement of adaptability, taxation, and extensive work in the development of control models (the sequential simplex variety) for the Associated Public School Systems group and the Central School group (Swanson, 1961).

---

[4] The quality control guides present data collected from approximately 240 school districts in 14 indices of community, financial, and school staff variables, arranged in standard score form (thus, profiles can be drawn and examined). Standard scores on a measure of school system adaptability are also presented. The sequential simplex displays the intercorrelations among these same variables for a sample of school systems, and specifies steps which a researcher can follow to draw inferences about the relative effects of various administrative policies on school adaptability.

Search for the Fruits of Fifty Years of Turmoil

In the wake of the early findings on the tempo of change and the patterns of adaptation in the American school system, one idea emerged as the stimulus for a line of inquiry that has been present in the work of the Institute for the past two decades. This was the idea that discoveries such as those made by Thorndike and Woodworth at the turn of the century with respect to the ineffectiveness of faculty psychology and "formal discipline" approaches to teaching would trigger off approximately fifty years of fits and starts of invention. The expectation that adjustments to such a major disturbance would require a long period of time could explain the abortive character of major reorganization plans that appeared early in this period, such as the platoon school movement, homogeneous grouping, and various multiple-track plans. According to the theory, any movement coming early in the period of turbulence is destined to be abortive, because the critical facts cannot all be in. As one theorist has put it, "the perimeters of the problem could not have been defined and all the parameters could not have been identified."

The theory suggested that the new design coming from this turbulence would appear somewhere around the middle of the century, but would not be identified until the middle of the seventh decade.

There was thus hope in the early 1940's that diligent searching would lead to earlier identification of the fruits of the turbulence. Accordingly, extensive efforts were made in the work of the Metropolitan School Study Council to identify the new practices which were appearing in the schools. They were harvested by systematic visitations of large numbers of people and by continuous reporting associated with the three "pooling and sharing" magazines (*Exchange, Know-How* and *Central Ideas*) that had developed to serve the three major organizations affiliated with the Institute. In this pooling, every effort was made to keep any preconceived notion about school program operational design out of the picture. The instrument for measuring adaptability, *The Growing Edge* (Mort, Vincent, & Newell, 1945), while it drew upon these pools of practice, attempted to define the "character" of teaching in terms of sound psychological insight, rather than by means of set descriptions (e.g., the presence or absence of the platoon system).

In the late 1950's, it was apparent that ten years of the postulated fifteen years of early diffusion were nearing their close. If the design of the school destined to spread rapidly after the middle 1960's was in fact in being, it was following the normal pattern of going unnoticed, in spite of the efforts to stir up an awareness of change in the school systems affiliated with the Institute. In 1960, it was deemed propitious to launch a more vigorous search for the school that is emerging. Carefully selected groups of teachers and supervisors in five groups of states are now working on this, under the auspices of the Institute.

One point of some interest is this: not all important innovations spring fully armed from the brow of some Jove. Some of them are old strands in new patterns. The question, then, as to when an innovation had its beginning is a difficult one. From an analysis of *Growing Edge* scores of Metropolitan School Study Council communities for 1945 and 1954, it appears fairly clear that an important metamorphosis was going on in both elementary and secondary schools in the decade spanned by the data. One could make something of a case for the conclusion that the now emerging school was already in being in 1945, although it was enmeshed in a complex of strands of the old school. This holds for both elementary and secondary levels.

In summarizing the findings of the studies in adaptability and the adaptation process in a series of articles (Mort, 1953–54) the present writer gave this as the first of a series of implications:

> Within the next few years we may expect important new designs in education to emerge. These designs will spring from the combination of hundreds of inventions which have been stimulated during the past half-century by new insights into educational psychology and social change. Following an important discovery such as the one made at the turn of the century—that the theory of formal discipline is untenable—we may expect a long adjustment period characterized by thousands of inventions of know-how designed to put the insights into operation. The latter part of this period will be more prolific than the early part. It is out of the accumulation of inventions that new composite inventions or designs emerge.

In the light of recent experience with the working committees associated with the Institute, there now, eight years later, seems to be little occasion to change this estimate of the situation. It is apparent that the situation has developed to the point at which in no school system of any size will there be failure to find examples, now in being, of practices characteristic of the 1980 school. In some instances such practices may have been created by sheer administrative accident; in others for specialized reasons—for example, the flexible use of subgrouping in instruction to meet individual learning needs. In theory, the school of 1980 is here in bits today. The task that these committees have undertaken is to find the framework which these manifestations illumine.

Some Overarching Findings

The following are findings which seem to be of considerable consequence, and which have reasonably firm support in these studies:

1. Typically, an extravagantly long time elapses before an insight into a need (or a discovery that past practice is indefensible) is responded to by innovations destined for general acceptance in the schools. This period is measured in terms of decades. The same phenomenon can be observed in other fields. Witness the long period of lapse between Pasteur's discoveries and the Flexner report; or the long period of lapse between the establishment of the colleges of agriculture and the marked changes in agricultural practices that followed the first decade of this century.

2. The spread of an innovation through the American school system proceeds at a slow pace. This likewise must be measured in decades. It is very slow for a decade or so, very rapid for a couple of decades, and then very slow during the mopping-up period. Under extraordinary conditions, and with extraordinary expenditure of effort, the decades of invention and the decades of diffusion may be telescoped into months, as with the pre-flight aviation project.

3. The rate of diffusion of complex innovations appears to be the same as that for simple innovations; innovations that increase cost move more slowly than those that do not.

4. During the slow early period of spread of an innovation, the innovation receives no recognition. Recent studies indicate that during this early period the innovation is seen piecemeal; no one sees the forest which comprises the trees. Its rapid spread follows recognition of the inclusive design. For example, according to the theory, some

of the bits of adjustment we find in our schools today are limited but authentic adjustments to fundamental needs. They are now lost in the maze of ephemeral innovations and are seen, along with a myriad of other innovations, as ways of patching, splicing, adding accessories to or otherwise tinkering with the old mechanism to make it more tolerable.

5. Communities vary in the degree to which they take on new practices. Indications are that this is a community characteristic. A community that is slow to adopt one innovation tends to be slow to adopt others. A pioneer in one area tends to be a pioneer in other areas.

6. Explanation of the differences in educational adaptability of communities can be found in no small degree in the character of the population, particularly in the level of the public's understanding of what schools can do, and citizens' feeling of need for education for their children. This appears to set the posture of the community toward financial support, and toward what teachers are permitted to do—and tends to shape the staff by influencing personnel selected and kept in the community.

7. The strength of these population factors appears to be in understandings and expectations. While understandings and expectations are somewhat associated with factors like occupation and education of parents (and of those in political power in the community), they can be altered. Thus they would appear to offer one of the most responsive areas for administrative action, both to capitalize on good understandings and expectations present, and to build up better understandings and expectations where they are not present.

8. It may be hypothesized that a far stronger school is now in the making, and that its threads are present in every community of any size. As the image becomes clearer, the threads that fit the pattern will prosper. Those that represent a multitude of other changes will prove to be ephemeral. With clarification of the image, diffusion through most of the country's school systems will occur rapidly, regardless of what the cost implications may prove to be.

9. The golden strand among the bundles of haywire about us would appear to be *adoption of responsibility by the school that all children shall learn,* and the giving up of the guiding principle of *offering opportunity* that was adequate for the 19th century. A corollary to this would appear to be that the schools must provide sufficient teachers capable of exercising such responsibility.

10. As a guide to innovators, these studies seem to show that a valid assessment of an innovation requires examination of the effect of the innovation on the entire system. For example, there are indications that a centering of overt concern on secondary schools to the exclusion of concern for the elementary schools may result in failure to recruit and keep high-quality people at the elementary level, and vice versa. Or, broad involvement of the public in matters of curriculum may be considered so much an invasion of the rights of the professional staff that not only staff operation but staff recruitment and retention may be negatively affected. The control models developed in the Institute (the sequential simplex) show promise of providing a basis for making broad-gauge evaluations of policies, practices, and structural organization.

11. As another suggestion to innovators, it would appear that knowledge of the slowness of spread of an innovation—among the teachers in a school, among the schools in a school system, and from school system to school system—is essential. Lack of such knowledge has resulted in the abandonment of many good innovations before they had a chance to put down their roots.

12. As a third suggestion to innovators, it is proposed that any innovation which is spreading even more slowly than the slow pace that seems normal may well be questioned with respect to authenticity. There must be a goodly number of practices supported for diffusion today which, in spite of Herculean efforts, do not maintain even the normal slow tempo of diffusion.

References

Barrington, T. M. *The introduction of selected educational practices into teachers' colleges and their laboratory schools.* New York: Bureau of Publications, Teachers College, Columbia University, 1953.

Bigelow, M. A. Discovery and diffusion in pioneer schools. Unpublished doctoral study, Teachers College, Columbia University, 1947.

Bushnell, M. Now we're lagging only twenty years. *School Executive,* 1957, 77, 61–63.

Cocking, W. *The regional introduction of educational practices in urban school systems of the United States.* New York: Bureau of Publications, Teachers College, Columbia University, 1951.

Eastmond, J. N. An analysis of elementary-school staff characteristics related to the quality of education. Unpublished doctoral study, Teachers College, Columbia University, 1950.

Mort, P. R. Educational adaptability. *School Executive,* 1953–54, *71,* (1), (3), (6), (7), (9), & (10).

Mort, P. R., & Cornell, F. G. *American schools in transition.* New York: Bureau of Publications, Teachers College, Columbia University, 1941.

Mort, P. R., & Furno, O. F. *Theory and synthesis of a sequential simplex.* New York: Institute of Administrative Research, Teachers College, Columbia University, 1960.

Mort, P. R., Vincent, W. S., & Newell, C. A. *The growing edge.* New York: Metropolitan School Study Council, 1945. (Revised and reissued, 1953.)

Newell, C. A. *Class size and educational adaptability.* New York: Bureau of Publications, Teachers College, Columbia University, 1943.

Pelley, J. H. Invention in education. Unpublished doctoral study, Teachers College, Columbia University, 1948.

Pierce, T. M. *Controllable community characteristics related to the quality of education.* New York: Bureau of Publications, Teachers College, Columbia University, 1947.

Ross, D. H. (Ed.) *Administration for adaptability.* New York: Metropolitan School Study Council, 1958.

Ross, D. H., & McKenna, B. *Class size: the multi-million dollar question.* New York: Metropolitan School Study Council, 1955.

Rothemich, V. J. Communication in educational change. Unpublished doctoral study, Teachers College, Columbia University, 1953.

Swanson, A. D. *Effective administrative strategy.* New York: Institute of Administrative Research, Teachers College, Columbia University, 1961.

Vincent, W. S. Quality control: a rationale for an analysis of a school system. *IAR Research Bulletin,* 1961, *1* (2), 1–7.

Vincent, W. S. et al. *Building better programs in citizenship.* New York: Citizenship Education Project, Teachers College, Columbia University, 1958.

CHAPTER 14

School superintendents and adoption of modern math: a social structure profile

RICHARD O. CARLSON

RESEARCH on the spread of educational innovations has several characteristics which set it apart from many other streams of diffusion research. One distinctive feature is that a vast amount of work has been done. It seems fair to say that the diffusion literature is as sophisticated and as well developed as any other area of scientific study to which educators have given their attention. Further, the study of the spread of educational practices bears the mark of one man. The late Paul Mort and his students seemed almost to have cornered the market on educational diffusion studies. This last feature has, however, apparently permitted a third and very important characteristic of such studies: an implicit assumption that characteristics of chief school officials are unimportant in explaining rates of adoption of innovations.

Mort and his students have displayed considerable ingenuity in the isolation of variables—usually relating to the economic base, ranging from expenditure per pupil to teachers' salaries—and in fitting the variables into accounting schemes. But they have seemed steadfast in their refusal to deviate from the implicit assumption that the chief

---

THE AUTHOR is Research Associate, Institute for Community Studies, and Associate Professor of Education, University of Oregon.

school official is simply a victim of the local school budget and is therefore not relevant as an explanatory element in the adoption process. The lack of attention given to the chief school official is even more noticeable when coupled with the awareness that the common procedure for the adoption of a new practice involves his approval.

The research reported here, which is part of a larger study, is based on the assumption that the position a superintendent holds in the social structure of school superintendents is directly related to his rate of adoption of educational innovations. In this respect it parallels more closely the research on diffusion of agricultural innovations and the spread of new drugs among physicians than it does the traditional research on the diffusion of new educational practices.[1]

The process of adoption of innovations has been defined as the "(1) acceptance, (2) over time, (3) of some specific item—an idea or practice, (4) by individuals, groups or other adopting units, linked to (5) specific channels of communication, (6) to a social structure, and (7) to a given system of values or culture" (Katz, Levin, & Hamilton, 1963, p. 240). This definition forms the general framework underlying this chapter.

The use of "modern" mathematical concepts (so-called modern math) in teaching mathematics in public schools is the specific practice which will occupy our attention. And we will be solely interested in its rate of acceptance over time by school systems in one county. Variables measuring the superintendent's position in the social structure of chief school officials will be used as explanations of the rate of adoption. Variables dealing with communication channels and the surrounding culture will not be treated here.

Because of our limited purpose here, it does not seem necessary to indicate the nature of modern math in any detail.[2] As an innovation, it does not call upon the school system to provide a completely new service or teach a completely new subject. Modern math is simply a new way of ordering and teaching a firmly established part of the school program. Acceptance of modern math involves the use of new

---

[1] For reviews of this research see Rogers (1962); Lionberger (1960); Katz, Levin, & Hamilton (1963); and Ross (1958).

[2] For a discussion of modern math, see National Council of Teachers of Mathematics (1961).

textbooks and instructional material, and some retraining of teachers.

Modern math was first accepted in a school district in Allegheny County, Pennsylvania, in 1958; by 1963 it had been adopted by about 80 per cent of the districts in the county. There were 68 school districts in the county with chief school officials. Of this number, 46 superintendents held the same position from at least one year prior to the introduction of modern math until 1963; that is, from at least 1957 on. The remaining 22 superintendents were appointed to their superintendency after 1957, and therefore did not have an equal opportunity (with respect to time) to adopt modern math, and are eliminated from consideration here.[3] Data were obtained by interview from 43 of the 46 superintendents who were in their positions at least one year prior to the introduction of the innovation into the county.[4] (Two superintendents would not grant interviews, and one was on extended sick leave.)

Rate of acceptance (or time at which a program of modern math was adopted) is the dependent variable. Acceptance was determined by asking each superintendent if there was a modern math program in his school system and, if so, when it was first adopted. This measurement of rate of adoption was dependent on the superintendent's recall ability, since the superintendent's word was taken as the only evidence of adoption or non-adoption. Thus the dependent variable is subject to error corresponding to the superintendent's inability to recall accurately an event which took place in the past. It seems important to note that the recall period was not excessively long, and that all of the superintendents responded unhesitatingly and categorically regarding the presence or absence of a modern math program. No superintendent needed a definition of modern math before he could decide whether or not his school system had such a program. This simply is evidence that the characteristics of a modern math program were well known among the sample.

[3] In a number of studies of diffusion, it is not clear whether the factor of equal opportunity in respect to time has been controlled. This is an obvious concern in studies involving school superintendents, because of their short tenure.

[4] These school districts ranged in size from 325 to 10,342 students, with a mean size of 3,095 students. The mean annual expenditure per child was $416, with a range from $322 to $713.

Rate of Adoption

When the cumulative percentage of Allegheny County adopters of a modern math program is graphed from the time of its introduction into the county until 1963 (when the program was 88 per cent diffused), the curve produced has the S-shape which has been commonly associated with the phenomena of diffusion of new practices. This curve, shown in Figure 1, indicates that the adoption rate was

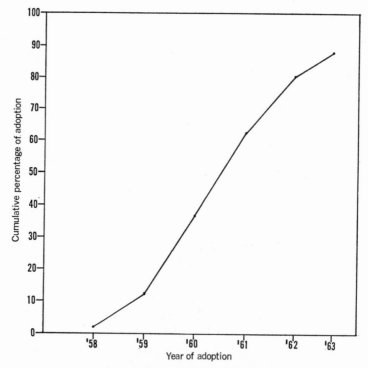

Figure 1. Cumulative percentage of superintendents adopting modern math in Allegheny County, Pennsylvania (N=43)

slow in the early period, when only a few superintendents accepted the innovation, was much faster in the middle period, and then slowed down again as the late adopters gradually accepted the new practice. The curve shows that 10 per cent of the superintendents accepted the program during the first year after its introduction, 28 per cent accepted it in the third year, and 9 per cent in the fifth year.

The curve produced from graphing the rate of adoption of modern math does not show the prolonged initial lag which marks the curve depicting the rate of adoption of hybrid corn, nor does it rise as fast as the curve showing the rate of use of "gammanym" (a new drug) by physicians. (See Katz, 1961.) The slope of the modern math adoption curve would seem to be influenced by the characteristics of the innovation [5] and the accepting population, but the nature and extent of the relationships cannot be stated at this time.

Similar S-shaped curves were plotted by Mort (see Ross, 1958; and Mort's chapter in the present book). According to his research, fifty years is required for the complete diffusion of an educational practice. Note that this generalization grossly exaggerates the time currently needed to achieve almost complete diffusion of modern math programs within one county.

One more important implication can be drawn from the shape of the curve, which commonly represents the acceptance process over time. The implication is this: the act of adoption on the part of some acceptors is itself a means of influencing others to adopt the practice. In other words, there is intercommunication among adopters; they do not accept the practice completely independently of each other. It is precisely this implication that gives meaning to variables relating to position in the social structure.

Social Structure and Adoption

Social structure involves the relations that exist among people. It is defined in terms of the distribution and differentiation of statuses, roles, and patterns of interaction or communication among members of a social system. Because the spread of new ideas takes place in a social network in which the act of acceptance by an individual seems to influence others, knowledge of a superintendent's position in the social structure of superintendents can be used to explain varying rates of adoption of new ideas.

A superintendent's position in the social structure can be measured in many ways. We will now look at some of the factors bearing on

[5] See Katz, Levin, & Hamilton (1963) for a discussion of characteristics of innovations and their rate of adoption.

a superintendent's position in the social structure, and see how various social structure positions are related to the rate of adoption of a program of modern math in one county.

Social network involvement. One aspect of a superintendent's position in the social structure is the extent to which he is immersed in the social system or moves around its fringes. Does he interact with other superintendents or stay aloof from them, either from personal preference or for other reasons? This type of question focuses on his *involvement.*

We raised three questions which have a bearing on the superintendent's position in the social structure with respect to involvement. One question—a straightforward sociometric question—asked the respondent to name his three best friends from among the population of school superintendents within the county. Of course the numbers of friendship choices received by the superintendents varied greatly; seven men received no choices, and one man received fourteen.

The number of friendship choices received by a superintendent is directly related to his rate of acceptance of modern math. The rate of acceptance is accelerated among those superintendents who received a high number of choices, and it is decelerated among those who received a low number of friendship choices. Also, superintendents who are close to their colleagues, in the sense that they received a large number of friendship choices, are quicker in accepting modern math. Those who are less integrated or involved are slower to adopt the new practice.

An alternate way to measure a superintendent's involvement in the social structure is to ask him for his perception of the amount of his interaction with other superintendents, as compared with that of his colleagues. We did this by presenting the respondent with a continuum representing amount of interaction ranging from less than average to more than average, and asking him to indicate his own perceived standing. Those who perceived their amount of interaction to be above average accepted modern math more readily than those who perceived their interaction to be less than average in amount.

At best, perception of interaction is only a fair indicator of actual interaction. Measurement of actual interaction seemed out of the question, so we reasoned that a superintendent who had high interaction with his colleagues would be able to make an accurate judgment of the general rate of adoption of new practices in his own school district as compared with the rate of adoption of new practices in other districts in the county. By the same reasoning, we assumed that the superintendent who had limited interaction with his colleagues would be unable to make an accurate judgment in this respect. We obtained this measure by asking each superintendent if his system had adopted each of seven new educational practices. From the responses we determined the mean number of adoptions for the population. Coupling this mean number with each superintendent's judgment as to whether the adoption rate in his own system on these innovations was above or below average gave us a criterion for evaluating the accuracy of his judgment, and, as we reasoned, an indirect measure of the amount of his interaction or involvement.

Now let us combine these three measures of social network involvement and see their relation to rate of adoption of modern math. Superintendents who scored above the median on all three measures of involvement are designated as "3 highs," those who scored below the medians are "3 lows," and the middle group which had a combination of high and low scores are "highs and lows." The results are shown in Figure 2. It seems sufficient to say that these three measures of social network involvement, when combined, are directly related to rate of adoption of modern math, and achieve a fair separation of early and late adopters.

Status. Another indicator of a superintendent's position in the social structure is his status. Status makes reference to a person's rank or position along some continuum. We obtained status scores for the sample of superintendents along three continua: education, professionalism, and prestige. Amount of education was scored directly, a B.A. degree being scored 1, an M.A. scored 2, graduate work beyond the M.A. scored 3, and a Ph.D. or equivalent scored 4.

Professionalism was measured by means of the superintendents' judgments of each other. Each superintendent was asked to "indicate the characteristics of the truly professional school superintendent." Then, after some discussion and examination of the suggested characteristics, each superintendent was given a deck of cards containing the names of all of the superintendents in the county, one name per

card. He was asked to sort the cards on the basis of his own definition of the professional superintendent and his judgment of the individual superintendents. Six piles, numbered one through six, were
used. Number one was a "no opinion" pile, and from there on the

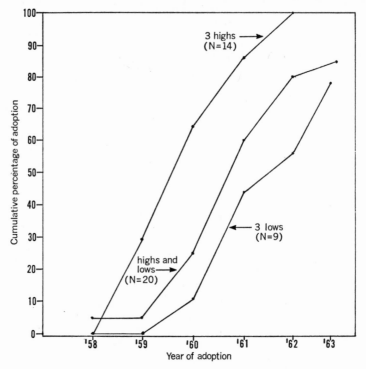

Figure 2. Cumulative percentage of adoption of modern math by
superintendents over time, by composite of high and low
scores on three measures of social network involvement

higher the number the more the superintendent being judged con-
formed to the judge's definition of being professional. The respondents were instructed to place no more than twelve cards in any one
pile. This necessitated an almost complete use of each category if the
respondent made a judgment about each of his colleagues. (Ideally,
we should have asked for a complete ranking of the cards, that is,
asked the respondents to sort out the top professional, the second
ranked and so on. The above procedure was used in order to reserve
time for other questions.) The scoring was achieved by recording
for each superintendent the number of times his name was placed

in the various piles, multiplied by the number of the pile, and dividing this total by the number of times he had been placed in any one of the piles numbered from two through six.[6] The "no opinion" pile was omitted in the above scoring procedure.

Prestige was measured indirectly. Mason & Gross (1955) have reported that salary alone accounted for 79 per cent of the variance in prestige among school superintendencies in a large sample they studied. We used the superintendent's salary as an indicator of the prestige of his office in the status system.

The combined relationship of the status variables (amount of education, professionalism, and prestige) to rate of adoption of modern math can be seen in Figure 3. As in the preceding figure, there are

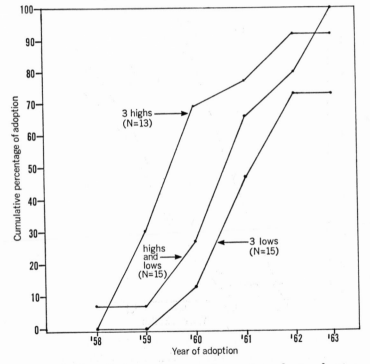

Figure 3. Cumulative percentage of superintendents adopting modern math over time, by composite of high and low scores on three status variables

[6] An examination of distributions of received category assignments found that from 30 to 93 per cent of raters agreed on a modal category for a particular superintendent. The mean rater agreement was 45 per cent.

three curves: one for those men who scored above the median on all three status measures, another for those who scored below the median on all three measures, and another curve for those who had high and low scores. The figure demonstrates that a direct relationship exists between a superintendent's position in the status structure and his rate of adoption of modern math.

When the six social structure variables, three concerning involvement and three related to status, are combined, their total relationship to rate of adoption of modern math can be seen in Figure 4. The figure shows a curve representing rate of adoption among superin-

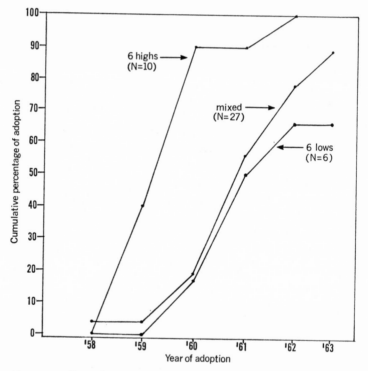

Figure 4. Cumulative percentage of superintendents adopting modern math over time, by composite of high and low scores on six social structure variables

tendents who were above the median on all six social structure variables, a curve showing the rate for those superintendents with mixed high and low scores in respect to the median, and a curve for those superintendents scoring below the median on all six variables.

The figure clearly suggests the utility of variables dealing with the superintendent's position in the social structure for explaining the rate of diffusion of modern math among the school districts in Allegheny County. It is evident from the figure that those high on measures of social network involvement and positions in the status structure tend to adopt modern math earlier than those scoring low on social structure variables. The explanatory power of the variables can be seen in part from the fact that of the fifteen superintendents who adopted the new practice early (in 1958, 1959, or 1960), nine superintendents, or 60 per cent, had scores above the median on all six social structure measures. Of the twenty-eight superintendents who adopted the practice late (in 1961, 1962, or 1963) or had not yet accepted it, one superintendent, or 4 per cent, scored above the median on all six social structure measures.

The Superintendency and the Adoption Process

As the first chapter of this book indicates, there are many important questions to be asked in the study of educational innovations. Here we have focused on a narrow segment of the total complex of problems, that of accounting for or explaining the rate of diffusion. Further, the data have been provided for only a small segment of the general accounting scheme, that of position in the social structure. But it seems that the data presented here contain an important argument with respect to the traditions of research on the diffusion of educational innovations. The argument has to do with conceptions of the school superintendency.

The vast amount of research on diffusion of educational innovations has virtually ignored characteristics of the school superintendent in the "accounting schemes" used. The question is: What conception of the superintendency is implicit in the research? How is the office of the formal educational leader of the school district conceived so that the officeholder is deemed unworthy of attention in attempting to explain the rate of diffusion of educational innovations?

Questionable assumptions

Two assumptions about the nature of the superintendency, if held, would seem to permit research on the spread of educational practices to ignore this officeholder.

The superintendent as budget victim.   One assumption would be that the superintendent is trapped by the local school budget. This seems to have been a guiding assumption in most of the previous research. On this point Ross has said, "If but one question can be asked, on the basis of the response to which a prediction of adaptability is to be made, the question is: 'How much is spent per child?' " (Ross, 1958, p. 15)

In this respect, it is instructive to note a finding from the larger study from which this report is drawn: annual expenditure per child had a Spearman rank correlation of $-.02$ with the rate of adoption of modern math in Allegheny County, Pennsylvania. Further, expenditure per child had a small negative correlation with the adoption of *all* the innovations we studied. The data presented here—indicating the predictive power of two sets of social structure variables in respect to superintendents and the spread of an educational practice, and the relationship of expenditure level with the rate of adoption—make an important argument against the assumption that the school superintendent is a victim of his budget and is therefore of no consequence in the adoption process. The data argue very much to the contrary. They argue that the characteristics of the superintendent are indeed important variables in accounting for the diffusion of educational practices.

The superintendent as powerless officeholder.   A second assumption may have been present though implicit in prior studies of diffusion in school districts which have ignored the superintendent. It is that his position in the organizational structure, specifically his subordination to the school board, renders him powerless and thus not consequential in the matter of acceptance of new practices. The data presented here argue against the validity of this assumption also, though the line of argument is less direct. These data show that the value of social structure variables relative to school superintendents in explaining rate of adoption of modern math is roughly similar to their value in explaining the rate of diffusion of innovations among farmers and physicians. Neither farmers nor physicians are subordinate in their "organization" structures. But variables that go some distance in explaining diffusion of innovations among these populations have comparable ability to explain rate of acceptance of new practices among school districts.

Conclusions

The data, then, do two things. First, they demonstrate the utility and power of certain social structure variables as related to the school superintendent in the explanation of rate of adoption of a specific new educational practice. Second, by doing this, the data argue against the traditions of educational research on adoption rates, by indicating that the school superintendent is neither a helpless victim of his local budget nor a powerless officeholder dominated by a super-ordinate school board. The data suggest that characteristics of the holder of the superintendency which have been ignored in past diffusion research in education must be taken into account in efforts aimed at a complete explanation of school systems' rate of adoption of new educational practices.

References

Katz, E. The social itinerary of technical change: two studies on the diffusion of innovation. *Human Organization*, 1961, *20*, 70–82.

Katz, E., Levin, M. L., & Hamilton, H. Traditions of research on the diffusion of innovations. *Amer. Sociol. Rev.*, 1963, 28 (2), 237–252.

Lionberger, H. F. *Adoption of new ideas and practices.* Ames, Iowa: Iowa State University Press, 1960.

Mason, W. S., & Gross, N. Intra-occupational prestige differentiation: the school superintendency. *Amer. Sociol. Rev.*, 1955, 20, 326–331.

National Council of Teachers of Mathematics. *The revolution in school mathematics.* Washington, D.C.: NCTM, 1961.

Rogers, E. M. *Diffusion of innovations.* New York: Free Press of Glencoe, 1962.

Ross, D. H. (Ed.) *Administration for adaptability.* New York: Metropolitan School Study Council, 1958.

CHAPTER 15

Evaluating an experimental program in medical education

Patricia Kendall

Since the end of World War II, there is probably no medical school in the United States which has entirely escaped experimentation in its educational methods and program. In some instances, such experimentation has been fairly limited in its objectives; for example, new teaching approaches have been tried in particular courses. In other cases, the modifications have been more extensive and the goals more all-embracing. The best example is provided by the School of Medicine of Western Reserve University, which undertook a complete revision of its curriculum in 1956, along somewhat radical and still controversial lines.[1]

The existence—and, indeed, proliferation—of such experimental programs implies the parallel need for evaluation studies aimed at determining the extent to which the modified courses have produced desired changes in attitudes or increases in knowledge. Perhaps the most ambitious and systematic evaluation study was that carried out by Hammond and Kern (1960) at the University of Colorado. More

[1] For a description of the thinking behind this revision, see Wearn, Ham, Patterson & Caughey (1956).

THE AUTHOR is Research Associate, Bureau of Applied Social Research, Columbia University.

usually, however, evaluations (when they are made at all) tend to remain on a rather impressionistic level. The educators in charge of the experimental programs talk in terms of how well the courses were "liked" by the students taking them, or whether they "seemed" to have the desired effects.

There are probably several ways of accounting for the fact that such experimental programs in medical education have not regularly been submitted to systematic evaluation. First of all, an evaluation study worthy of the name requires time and money. It is not always easy to convince the executive faculty of a medical school that available funds or student time should be devoted to rigorous study of a new course. Secondly, the creators of experimental programs often impress one as being men of conviction who have little question about the efficacy of the changes they have introduced. They *know* that the courses they have developed are the best possible under existing conditions; and in the light of this assumed fact, systematic evaluation seems superfluous.

But there is an additional explanation for the fact that such a relatively small number of evaluation studies has been undertaken. Even when there is no reluctance regarding them, actually carrying them out presents certain problems. The present chapter, by means of a case study of an evaluation program carried out over several years, indicates what some of these problems are and clarifies how they were handled in one instance. We shall start with the difficulties one encounters at the beginning of an evaluation study, and then proceed to those which develop later.

The Evaluation Study

The specification of objectives

Obviously, the evaluation of an experimental program presupposes fairly precise knowledge of the objectives of the program. Without such knowledge, it is manifestly impossible to say whether or not the program has been successful. Often the objectives of an experimental course in medical education are stated in rather general terms—"to overcome resistance to psychiatry," "to improve the quality of teaching in a department of anatomy," and so on.

A first step in any evaluation study is therefore a specification of the objectives of the program being investigated. This case was no exception. The program was a newly designed course in medicine, pediatrics, and psychiatry offered fourth-year students in an Eastern medical school. At first the aims of the program were stated in fairly broad terms. It was hoped that through this course in comprehensive medicine, as it was called, students would learn the relevance of social and psychological factors in the diagnosis and treatment of disease, would develop more humanistic attitudes toward patients, and would gain experience in operating as members of a medical team. When we were asked to assist in the evaluation of the program, our first concern was to help the directors of the course define their purposes more concretely, so that these could be translated into testable dimensions, for which suitable indicators could in turn be found.[2]

After interviewing the medical educators who developed the course, and carefully studying all written documents pertaining to it, it was possible to spell out some of the main changes which were hoped for. We were then able to develop attitude questions through which the existence or nonexistence of such changes could be assessed. Space limitations make it impossible to indicate all of these, but a few representative examples can be given.

Attention to social and psychological problems. One of the general objectives of the program was to teach students the importance of taking into account the social and psychological problems of their patients. But, upon further clarification, it turned out that the program's directors did not mean this to be taken literally or applied universally. They recognized that there are some patients who can be treated more routinely than others. Accordingly, they desired more specifically that their students develop an appropriate degree of clinical judgment—the ability to know when attention to social and psychological problems is called for, and when it is not. To measure the degree to which students possessed such judgment before and after their course in comprehensive medicine, we devised the following question:

[2] It is interesting to note that, partly as a result of the evaluation study, the directors did clarify their objectives. Today, some ten years after the research was begun, they talk in precise terms.

Assume that you, as a doctor in a hospital ward or clinic, are caring for the patients described below. In each of the cases, how important—for the kind of care you might give—would extensive knowledge of the patient's *family and social surroundings* be to you?

—20-year old man with pneumonia
—12-year old boy with broken leg
—17-year old girl with menstrual cramps
—60-year old man with heart attack
—30-year old woman with headache
— 5-year old girl with measles
—10-year old boy with bedwetting
—40-year old woman with acute appendicitis
—35-year old man with rheumatic heart disease
—75-year old man with cancer of the large bowel

For some of the cases described, it clearly would be imperative to have extensive knowledge of the patient's family and social surroundings; in other cases, such knowledge, while perhaps useful, would be less urgent. In the evaluation study, we investigated whether students were better able to make this distinction after participation in the program.

Attitudes toward patients. The directors of the program also hoped for changes in attitudes toward patients. They felt that, all too often, advanced medical students viewed the patients whom they saw solely as specimen cases from whom to learn medicine, and were only secondarily concerned with what they were able to accomplish for the patients. Those in charge of the course considered this attitude incompatible with the kind of medicine they were trying to teach their students; they therefore hoped to engender student interest in the welfare of patients. Again, the specification of this desired effect of the program led to the development of several questions. One of them read:

Do you look upon your contact with patients while in medical school primarily as an opportunity to learn medicine? primarily as an opportunity to help patients? as presenting equal opportunities to learn medicine and to help patients?

In the evaluation study, we examined changes in responses to this question to determine whether students had become more interested in patients as a result of the course.

Professional relationship. At the same time, however, the directors of the program believed that the students should not become overly involved with their patients. They contended that a physician who becomes too friendly with patients may endanger his ability to provide optimal medical care: his sympathy for the patient may prevent him from ordering painful or dangerous procedures when these are indicated. Accordingly, it was hoped that the students would learn that a strictly professional relationship with patients is most appropriate. To ascertain whether or not this was the case, the following question was devised:

> Would you prefer a patient who wants to know you only on a doctor-patient basis? wants to know you also on a friend-to-friend basis? it makes no difference?

Quality of medical care. Finally, those responsible for the program wanted students to learn how to provide medical care of high quality. Once again, however, this objective needed specification. Indicators were found for many of the dimensions which were ultimately spelled out, and these were included in the questionnaire administered periodically to the students. One obvious dimension, for example, is the amount of time allocated to each patient. If a patient is to receive optimal medical care, his physician must be prepared to devote a lot of time to him, if this is called for on a particular occasion. This means in turn that the physician should not regularly schedule a large number of patients each day. To see whether this aspect of comprehensive care had been learned through the program, the following question was developed:

> Dr. W is a general practitioner who, at the age of 50, is financially well off, respected and admired in the middle-class suburban community in which he lives. Each day Dr. W sees thirty to forty patients whose illnesses range from measles to cancer of the cervix. To you, does the fact that Dr. W sees thirty to forty patients a day suggest
> —that he is a very competent doctor to be able to care for so many people
> —that he can hardly provide competent care if he treats so many people
> —neither

The specification of the objectives of any experimental program is a preparatory phase. Once it is accomplished, the investigator is ready to undertake the evaluation proper.

Evaluation

Ideally, an evaluation study is modeled after a classical controlled experiment. As in any experiment, one wants to eliminate the possibility that observed changes in attitude and behavior are caused by extraneous factors, and not by the program being evaluated.[3]

The classical design. To eliminate this possibility, one introduces controls. Parallel to the group being exposed to the experimental program, one sets up a control group exactly similar in all essential respects; the only difference is that the experimental program is withheld from this control group.

In the case of the educational program which we studied, this would have meant dividing the fourth-year class into two more or less equal groups, matched according to such characteristics as class standing and initial attitudes toward patients, and then exposing one of the groups to the new course in comprehensive medicine while the other group studied the traditional course in fourth-year medicine. Schematically, this would have looked as follows:

Experimental group	*Control group*
Pretest	Pretest
Exposure to course in comprehensive medicine	Exposure to traditional course in fourth-year medicine
Posttest	Posttest

If the experimental group experienced more change than the controls in the directions hoped for by the directors of the program, then these shifts could be attributed to the program.

This arrangement would have been the simplest and safest for evaluation of the new course in comprehensive medicine. However, the executive faculty of the medical school refused to sanction it. Their

[3] This danger is always particularly prominent in the evaluation of educational programs; as students grow older and gain experience, their attitudes are likely to be modified by the very fact of maturation.

argument was that if the new course were really superior to the old one, it would be unfair to students in the control group to deprive them of participation in it; they therefore decided that all fourth-year students should pursue the new course.

A revised design. This decision by the executive faculty forced a modification in the design of the evaluation study. Each fourth-year class was still split into two groups. The A groups, as we designated them, took the course in comprehensive medicine in the first semester of their final year, and then studied surgery, obstetrics–gynecology and an elective subject in the second semester. The so-called B groups reversed this process: they studied surgery (etc.) in the first semester and comprehensive medicine in the second.

Even though each class was thus composed of two groups, there was no assurance that they would be matched to each other. Indeed, there was good reason to fear that they would not be. For example, once the course in comprehensive medicine got under way, students were allowed to indicate whether they would prefer to take it in the first or second semester of their final year. Over 80 per cent of the students queried on this score told us they had received the semester assignments they had asked for. And there was always the strong possibility that their decision had been motivated by their internship plans. Fourth-year medical students have to apply for the internships of their choice at about the first of the year; to be favorably considered their applications should be accompanied by a letter of recommendation from a faculty member in the medical school. Thus, it could have developed that all of the prospective interns in internal medicine, hoping to obtain strong letters of recommendation from the Department of Medicine, would elect to take the course in comprehensive medicine in the first semester, in order to become known to members of the Department before the application deadline. In contrast, all of the prospective surgical interns, similarly motivated, might have elected to take surgery in the first semester.

In actual fact, it turned out that there were no such systematic differences between those taking the course in comprehensive medicine in the first semester and those taking it in the second. But because we had had no hand in the groups' composition, and because we could not be absolutely certain that there were no initial differences between them (even though none were apparent), we decided to adopt a design in which each student would serve as his own control.

This was made possible by the use of a so-called "panel design." Repeated observations were made of the same individual, on the same criteria: (1) At the end of the third year, just before starting their final year, the students were given a self-administered questionnaire; it asked about their attitudes toward patients, their standards of medical care, experiences they had had in medical school, their career plans, and so on. The responses they gave at this time formed the baseline for studying subsequent changes in attitude. (2) Six months later, just as the first term was drawing to a close, the students answered the same questions a second time. In addition, those who had spent the first term in the course in comprehensive medicine were asked a supplementary set of questions about their experiences during the term. (3) Then, at the end of the fourth year, shortly before their graduation from medical school, the students answered our questions for a third time. And now it was the students who had participated in the experimental program during the second semester who were asked about their experiences.

Again, let us represent this design schematically so that it can be contrasted with a classical experimental design.

	End of third year	Middle of fourth year	End of fourth year
A groups	Course in comprehensive medicine	Courses in surgery, ob–gyn and elective	
B groups	Courses in surgery, ob–gyn and elective	Course in comprehensive medicine	
	Test 1	Test 2	Test 3

Assessing program effects

Let us present an actual finding to show how this design permitted evaluation of the effects of the course in comprehensive medicine. The example is based on a question considered earlier, that dealing with the value of patient contacts. It will be recalled that the students were asked whether they viewed such contacts primarily as an opportunity to learn medicine, primarily as an opportunity to help patients, or as an opportunity to do both. Virtually none of the students said they looked on contacts with patients mainly as an occasion to help them. Instead, they said either that they looked upon patient contacts as an opportunity to learn medicine, or as an occasion both to help patients and to learn medicine. From the point of view of the directors of the program, who wanted to see students develop more concern with the welfare of their patients, the latter response is the "correct" one. The question, then, is whether students were more likely to give this response after participation in the program. The results are shown in Table 1.

Table 1. Effect of Program on Attitude Toward Patient Contacts

| Time points | Per cent saying they view patient contacts as opportunity BOTH TO LEARN AND TO HELP PATIENTS | |
	A groups	B groups
End of third year (T_1)	59	52
Middle of fourth year (T_2)	79	53
End of fourth year (T_3)	64	72

N = approx. 165 for all percentages

Before reviewing the substantive conclusions to be drawn from Table 1, let us consider the reasoning by which we shall arrive at these conclusions. A table like this one contains three comparisons of immediate relevance to evaluation of the course in comprehensive medicine. Quite obviously, we should compare the behavior and attitudes of the A and B groups before and after their participation in the program; if the program was effective, both groups should shift in the desired direction during their term in the course. At the same time, however, in order to attribute such shifts to the program and not to some other factors, we must be able to show that the B groups, which only entered the program at the beginning of the second semester, had not experienced a comparable change during the first semester. We can express these conditions in the following way:

$(T_2 - T_1)$A groups and $(T_3 - T_2)$B groups should show shift in desired direction; but

$(T_2 - T_1)$B groups should be zero, or in opposite direction from that desired.

An examination of the figures in Table 1 shows that these conditions are exactly met.[4] Between the end of the third year and the middle of the fourth, while they were participating in the course in comprehensive care, students in the A groups developed a greater orientation to the welfare of their patients. A similar change occurred with the B groups between the middle and end of the fourth year, the period they spent in the program; during this time they too came to be more concerned with the welfare of their patients. But previously, during the first semester, these same students in the B groups had been completely unaffected in their attitudes. On the basis of these three comparisons, made singly and in combination, we can conclude that the course in comprehensive medicine was quite effective in enlarging students' views regarding the value of patient contacts.

Distinguishing short- and long-term effects

But there is still more to a table like this one. In evaluating an educational program, it is often desirable to differentiate between its short- and long-term effects. A classical controlled experiment does not usually provide data relevant to this question. However, a fourth comparison in tables of this kind yields a first approximation to the differentiation of short- and long-term effects, an unexpected bonus of the design used here. This is the comparison of responses given by the A groups at the middle and end of the fourth year—the period when they had already completed their term in comprehensive medicine and had gone on to study other fourth-year courses. If the effects of the program are long-term,[5] then any shift observed at the end of the first semester should be maintained at the end of the second. If,

---

[4] A comparison of the responses given by the A and B groups at the end of the third year (T_1) shows how closely the two groups resembled each other initially, even though they were largely in the program on a self-selected rather than randomly assigned basis. This comparability was generally found in other aspects of the study. But even when groups were noncomparable on some aspect, it made little difference, since each student was serving as his own control.

[5] Of course, "long-term" is used here in a relative sense. In the evaluation study, we were only able to follow the students for six months after their completion of the course in comprehensive care. In a subsequent study of the same students during their internships and residencies, many of the same questions were repeated. It will therefore be possible to investigate which of the shifts found in the present study were maintained for longer periods of time.

on the other hand, the program has only a short-term effect with respect to a particular attitude or mode of behavior, then we shall observe a reversal during the course of the second semester.

Referring again to Table 1, we see that, although the program seemed to have a fairly marked effect on judgments of the value of patient contacts, this effect was short-lived. At the end of the fourth year, the number of students in A groups saying that they looked on such contacts primarily as an opportunity to learn medicine was very nearly as high as it had been at the end of the third year.

In broad outline, then, this is the mode of analysis employed in evaluating a course in comprehensive medicine. Basing conclusions on the four comparisons just specified, we were able to identify the main effects of the program, and to distinguish which of these seemed to be long-lasting and which more ephemeral.

Additional Features of the Study

We have completed our essential task of indicating how, in one case, a program in medical education was evaluated, and so might conclude here. But it may be of some interest to review certain additional features of this evaluation study.

A first addition was suggested by the fact that the program under

Study of trends

consideration was a *fourth*-year course; it is a program to which students are exposed quite late in their medical school careers. Some students, as a matter of fact, participate in the program almost up to the day of graduation. In view of this, it might be misleading to study the effects of the course without at the same time examining the processes of change taking place in the first three years of medical school. For example, one effect of the program was to increase interest in the social and emotional problems which patients present. Quite different meanings should be attached to this finding, according to the nature of the changes taking place in earlier years. Suppose that in the first three years, before coming into personal contact with the experimental program, students had become progressively less interested in these social and emotional problems. Then the effect of the program would have been a reversal of a previously existing trend, and we would feel that the course had accomplished more than if there had been no trend at all over the first three years, or if the previously existing trend had been toward increasing interest.

Let us provide two examples of differing contexts for the effects of the program. Earlier, we quoted a question having to do with the competence of a general practioner who sees from thirty to forty patients a day; one of the program's objectives was to impress upon students that a habitually heavy patient load is incompatible with the provision of comprehensive care. The trend of responses over the first three years of medical school suggests that recognition of this fact developed even before the students came in contact with the course in comprehensive medicine. This is shown in Table 2.

Table 2. Class Judgments on Dr. W's Competence

Class	Per cent saying that DR. W CANNOT PROVIDE COMPETENT CARE	Number of students
First year	52	(309)
Second year	62	(310)
Third year	66	(325)

There is thus a clear-cut trend over the course of medical school, one with which the directors of the experimental program in comprehensive care would be sympathetic. Does the course add anything to this trend? Again we resort to the kind of format used in Table 1. The relevant data are shown in Table 3.

Table 3. Effect of Program on Judgments of Dr. W's Competence

Time points	Per cent saying that DR. W CANNOT PROVIDE COMPETENT CARE	
	A groups	B groups
End of third year	67	72
Middle of fourth year	75	60
End of fourth year	63	66

The two most obvious comparisons—those involving the behavior of the A and B groups before and after their participation in the program—lead to the conclusion that the program did have an effect on the students' standards of medical care. But in this instance the really crucial piece of evidence is provided by the behavior of the B groups during the first semester, before they entered the program. During that time, under the influence of the courses in surgery, obstetrics–gynecology, and an elective subject, the students' appreciation of the need to spend time with patients—fairly high at the start—suffered considerably. Aside from its substantive interest, this reversal is convincing evidence that the effects attributed to the program were real, and not just the continuation of a previously existing trend.

But there is a second set of findings which provides quite a different context, and suggests correspondingly different conclusions about the effectiveness of the program. To show this we turn to a new question. It is a well-known fact that many medical students prefer to work with patients who have well-defined physical illnesses. There are several reasons for this: it is easier to learn medicine from patients in whom it is possible to find an organic disturbance; patients with no apparent positive findings present a particular challenge, and are sometimes considered threatening; finally, patients who do not have easily identified illnesses offer little opportunity to apply therapeutic measures and to study their effects on disease processes.

To find out the extent to which students did in fact have these preferences, they were asked the following question:

Would you prefer a patient whose illness is entirely physical? whose illness is chiefly emotional in origin? it makes no difference?

Since almost no students expressed a preference for patients with illnesses which were chiefly emotional in origin, we are dealing once again with a dichotomy.

Table 4 indicates that from the end of the first year to the end of the third year there is a fairly marked trend in answers to this question.

Table 4. Class Preferences for Patients with Physical Illness

Class	Per cent preferring patients with PHYSICAL ILLNESS	Per cent saying IT MAKES NO DIFFERENCE	Number of students
First year	27	66	(245)
Second year	39	58	(241)
Third year	45	52	(253)

Two-thirds of the freshman students, but only about half of the third-year students, said that it made no difference to them whether they saw a patient with a physical or an emotional illness. On the other hand, only about a quarter of the first-year students, but nearly half of those in their third year, expressed a definite preference for a patient with a physical illness.

From the point of view of those directing the experimental program being evaluated, the trend recorded in Table 4 was an undesirable one. It is the objective of the program to teach students how to provide adequate care for all patients, not just those who present "interesting" problems. What effect did the program have on this trend? The relevant data are shown in Table 5.

Table 5. Effect of Program on Preferences for Patients with Physical Illness

Time points	Per cent saying they prefer patients with PHYSICAL ILLNESS	
	A groups	B groups
End of third year	47	46
Middle of fourth year	46	57
End of fourth year	54	58

The effects of the program are quite different here than in the previous instance. During their term in the program, both the A and the B groups remained stationary in their attitudes toward patients with physical illness. But both prior to and following participation in the experimental course, the trend which had been noted in earlier phases of medical school continued. To put it somewhat differently, the course succeeded in checking a trend considered undesirable, although it was not able to counteract the trend. This, too, of course, was a positive accomplishment of the program, even though it may not seem so striking at first glance.

To sum up, if one views the effects of the program in the context of what has happened prior to the fourth year, one is better able to assess their meaning.

Specification of effective factors

Even though one may feel some satisfaction in identifying the effects of an experimental program, thus being able to judge the extent of its success or failure, an evaluation study is more complete if one can at the same time specify what accounts for program effectiveness. One may be interested in this from a theoretical point of view, perhaps in order to classify the kinds of factors associated with attitude change. But the specification of effective factors also has practical implications. To strengthen an experimental educational program, or to duplicate it in another setting, it is essential to know just which features of the program account for its effectiveness, and with what type of student it is most likely to succeed. This is a problem more easily posed than solved, for in order to test these helpful dispositions and effective features, they must be introduced into the questionnaire. And it requires a certain amount of systematic analysis to think of them at the time the questionnaire is being prepared. It is one thing to ask students to introspect about what they considered particularly effective in the program; it is quite another to test the effectiveness of such factors by the statistical method to be exemplified presently. We do not want to deprecate the value of retrospective studies, but wish rather to show the special aspects of a panel analysis.

To think of relevant factors, one must consider the dimensions along which the experimental program can vary. In this case, for example, some students may have had the good fortune of being exposed to unusually attractive patients, while less lucky colleagues saw a disproportionately high number of unpleasant patients. In some instances, students may have encountered medical problems of special interest, while other students may have seen only routine problems. And the instructors who helped the students interpret their experiences may have had different degrees of skill.

In addition to these intrinsic variations, external factors may affect the success of the program. The students may be overworked; the routine of the appointment system in the clinic may break down; and so on.

Finally, students can differ considerably in their attitudes. As we have already seen, some approach a patient wanting only to learn from him; others want also to help the patient. Students may also differ in the degree to which they feel involved with the patient. This latter item is used here to exemplify our analysis.

Shortly after entering the program, each student was assigned to a family, for whose medical welfare he was to be responsible for the following six months. Whenever a member of the family needed medical care, he was seen by "his" student-physician; if the patient needed hospitalization, this was arranged by the student, who then followed the course of the patient's illness in the hospital. After the patient's discharge from the hospital, his recuperation and rehabilitation were supervised by the student responsible for his care. As one can imagine, some students became very involved with their Family Care families. To find out the extent to which this happened—and to which students it happened—we asked the following question:

> Compared with most of the patients you've seen this term, do you think you were emotionally involved with your Family Care family to a greater extent? to about the same extent? to a lesser extent? [6]

Our central concern at the moment is not with the phenomenon of involvement itself, but rather with its contribution to the observed effects of the program. One of these effects, it will be recalled, was that students were more likely to view their contacts with patients as an opportunity to learn medicine *and* to help the patients, rather than simply as an occasion to learn medicine. To what extent did this effect come about because of the students' involvement with their Family Care patients? The relevant data are provided in Table 6.

Table 6. Change in Attitude Toward Value of Patient Contacts, as Result of Emotional Involvement with Family

| | Per cent saying AFTER program they view patient contacts as opportunity BOTH TO LEARN AND TO HELP PATIENTS | |
| | *Attitude* BEFORE *program:* | |
Emotional involvement with family:	LEARN MEDICINE	BOTH LEARN AND HELP
Greater extent	62 (21)[a]	94 (33)
Same extent	60 (67)	93 (96)
Lesser extent	48 (31)	90 (38)

[a] The figures in parentheses refer to the number of cases in each group.

It is important to understand the format of this table. As in Table 1, the numerical entries are once more the percentages of students saying

[6] The relative nature of this question should be noted. It would have been quite meaningless to ask the students how involved they had been with their families; what seemed like a high degree of involvement to one student might have been considered moderate by another. Asking the question in relative terms circumvented this difficulty.

that they looked on their contacts with patients as an opoprtunity to learn medicine and help the patients as well. But in Table 1, the responses were given at different points in time. The figures in Table 6 refer to responses made immediately after the students had completed their term in the program: at the middle of the fourth year for the A groups, and at the end of that year for the B groups.

As was suggested earlier, experiences in the course in comprehensive medicine might have had differential effects on students, depending on the attitudes with which they entered the program. If students were patient-oriented to begin with, those who had experiences compatible with these attitudes would presumably be more likely to have the attitudes reinforced. If students were originally learning-oriented, then exposure to such experiences would presumably lead to more frequent conversions. Therefore, in Table 6 it was necessary to separate students according to the attitudes they had expressed immediately prior to participation in the program.

Table 6 shows that students' emotional involvement with families did indeed have differential effects, according to their initial attitudes. Among those who entered the program already expressing the attitude considered desirable, the experience of involvement had little effect: in the main, their already patient-oriented attitudes were merely reinforced. But among those who felt initially that patient contacts primarily enabled them to learn medicine, the experience of involvement did have an effect: the greater the degree of involvement, the more likely their conversion toward a patient-oriented attitude.

Through a series of analyses such as this one, we were able to arrive at some tentative conclusions about the factors contributing most to observed program effects.

The need for replication

Our final point can be stated briefly. When one evaluates an educational program—whether in a medical school, a high school, or a kindergarten—the number of cases available for study is obviously limited by the sizes of the classes. The investigator may have the feeling that these are not large enough for sound statistical analysis. This was true in the present case. Each fourth-year class in the medical school numbered about 80 students. But since these were divided into two groups, the conclusions would have been based on only 40 students, had the analysis been confined to only one fourth-year class. One might have felt uneasy about results deriving from such a small number; in addition, more complicated analyses of the kind reported in Table 6 would have been precluded. The solution, then, was to cumulate fourth-year classes until we had a large enough number of cases. Instead of basing the evaluation on only one fourth-year class, we assembled data from four. This gave us a total of about 330 students, half of them in A groups and the other half in B groups.

Such replication has an additional advantage. There is always a possibility that particular findings, even when statistically significant, have come about by chance. But this possibility is reduced if one can show—as we actually did in our preliminary analyses—that the same phenomenon has occurred independently in four instances. Replication can therefore increase our confidence in our results.

References

Hammond, K., & Kern, F. *Teaching comprehensive medical care.* Cambridge, Mass.: Harvard University Press, 1960.

Wearn, J. T., Ham, T. H., Patterson, J. W., & Caughey, J. L., Jr. Report on an experiment in medical education. *Jour. Medical Educ.,* 1956, *31,* 516–529, 530 ff.

CHAPTER 16

Research and practice
in the teaching of reading:
a progress report

ALLEN H. BARTON
DAVID E. WILDER

THE American educational system originally had three main parts: the community, the school children, and the teacher who was hired to educate them. As education expanded in the nineteenth century, especially with the adoption of long periods of compulsory education, other roles and institutions were added to the system—teacher-training institutions, educational administrators to supervise the larger schools and school systems, and authors and publishers to produce the textbooks for millions of students. These new specialists greatly intensified the age-old quest for theories and ideologies of education. Toward the turn of the century, they began to turn to the new social sciences for help, and a new role was added to the social system of education, that of the research scientist. Education became to some extent a system of applied science—a set of interacting roles and institutions within which scientific research is sponsored, carried out, interpreted, communicated, and applied. The activities of the research scientists affect and are affected by the teacher-training institutions, the school ad-

THE AUTHORS are respectively, Director and Project Director, Bureau of Applied Social Research, Columbia University. This study may be identified as No. A-388 of the Bureau of Applied Social Research. It was made possible by a grant from the Carnegie Corporation of New York.

ministrators, the teachers, the textbook writers and publishers, and the community.

Thus any serious treatment of educational innovation must include a close examination of relationships between research and practice. This chapter describes some aspects of these relationships in the special case of the teaching of reading.

Social Problems and Applied Science

The application of science to any field of social activity involves important social problems. Medicine provides a well-known example. Many nineteenth century physicians bitterly resisted such scientific innovations as Semmelweiss' statistically supported plea to surgeons to wash their hands and save child-bearing women from death (Beveridge, 1957). Other innovations, based on inadequate research, created medical "fads" and contentious schools which resisted rational correction. As medical science developed more adequate research methods and knowledge, it required an heroic effort to reform the institutions of medical training and the standards of admission to practice, calling upon strong professional organization, strict government controls on admission, outside support from enormously wealthy foundations, and a public willingness to pay for competent medical care. Despite this progress, there remain to this day serious problems in the organization of medical research and the transmission of scientific knowledge to medical students and practicing physicians, to say nothing of medical economics. Such problems have recently been made the object of the new field of medical sociology. (Coleman, Katz, & Menzel, 1961; Merton, Reader, & Kendall, 1957)

The application of scientific research to education presents similar problems, aggravated by several special factors. First of all, the sciences involved, those of human behavior, have methods that are less well developed than those of the natural sciences, and labor under certain inherent restrictions. Second, the problems of values and goals present in any application of science are more complex and controversial in education than in medicine. The restoration of health is easier to define than the creation of an educated person. The period during which scientific research was introduced into education was also a time of crusades to change—broadening in some ways, narrowing in others—the goals of education (Cremin, 1961). Scientific theories of the ways children develop and learn became deeply entangled with ideological conflicts. And third, the public has not yet been willing to pay for the recruitment and training of professionals comparable to those in medicine to staff their schools.

Some of the social problems of applied science are exemplified in the domain of elementary reading instruction. There has been a great effort to develop scientific research and theory in this field, leading to drastic changes in teaching methods over the last sixty years. At the same time, there have been attempts to formulate new goals and to de-emphasize some old ones.

Research and the field of reading

These developments have not gone smoothly. Educational literature is full of references to the tendency of schools, teacher training, and teaching materials to lag behind in accepting the practical implications of scientific research and theory. On the other hand, many writers note a tendency to run to extremes, to change doctrines and practices without adequate evidence, thus creating new problems which lead to a swinging back of the pendulum and, possibly, new cycles of extremism.[1] The study of "cultural lag" is an old field of interest for sociologists, and focuses on such factors as inadequate communication of the new, vested interests in the old, and lack of rationality among those who might benefit from change. The study of cycles is also a long-standing interest of social scientists, previously monopolized by economists but now being approached by sociologists with new techniques for the study of mass diffusion and influence processes. These deviations from an optimum development, both chronic lags and excessive fluctuations, can be studied by sociological methods.

The current situation in the reading field suggested some merit in studying the social organization of research on reading and the channels by which research findings influence educational practice. Such an enterprise dovetails with new and important developments in the sociology of the professions, the study of communication and social influence, and the analysis of research methodology. It also involves two frontier areas of considerable interest to sociologists: the sociology of science, and the empirical analysis of social systems. Such a study would examine the social organization of reading research, the methods

[1] See Axline (1957). For discussion of the cycles in reading instruction, see Gray (1948) and Russell (1949).

used in this research, the channels by which it is interpreted and communicated, and the response of educational administrators and teachers to it. Thus, the problems can be considered in terms of their interrelationships in a social system of applied science.

The social system of the reading field

To say that something is a social system means, minimally, that it consists of a number of parts which are interrelated. The main components of the social system of applied science in elementary reading instruction, and some of the main lines of influence among them, are shown in Chart 1.

The boxes in the chart indicate statuses within the system; these statuses are usually (but not always) part of the institution indicated on the right. Complex as the chart is, some status groups and institutions have been omitted, notably state departments of education and their specialists, and the local, state, and national professional associations of school administrators and teachers. Anyone familiar with the system can undoubtedly add additional relationships which he feels are important.

The relationships among statuses are actually of several quite different kinds. One of the most important facts about the system is that some people occupy several strategic statuses at the same time, or in succession. Some reading researchers become general "experts" (as indicated, for example, by their authorship of textbooks on reading instruction), are also professors in university schools of education, and are also writers or editors.

Another important fact is that some of these status groups have the job of formally training others. For example, the general reading expert trains both future researchers and future teachers college professors, as well as school administrators and teachers. Similarly, local teachers college professors, school reading specialists, and publishers' representatives give vast numbers of institutes, workshops, and demonstrations to teachers on how to improve their reading instruction.

A third type of relationship among certain statuses is legal authority. Publishers decide what kinds of textbooks they will print; school administrators generally tell the teachers what textbooks to use, and the community, through its board of education, is empowered to tell the school administrator what kind of reading instruction it requires.

A somewhat different form of authority is the professional prestige of the expert. Top experts give scientific authority to certain methods and the text materials embodying them, as well as to research workers and their findings—though to some extent, the basic scientists in re-

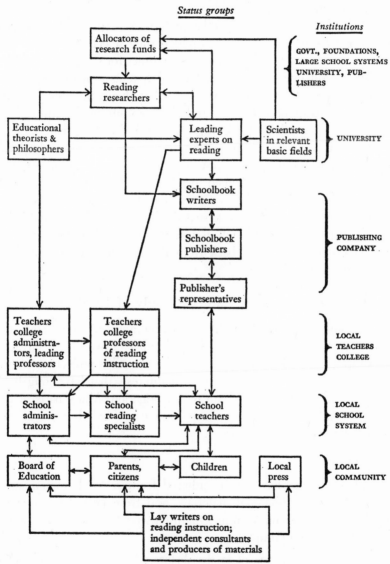

Chart 1. Status groups and institutions involved in the application of scientific research to elementary reading instruction

lated fields (e.g., psychology, linguistics, statistics) must legitimize the scientific status of the reading expert within the university. The local teachers college professors, school reading specialists, and the professionally trained type of publishers' representatives may also claim expert authority for their advice to the teachers.

Finally, there are economic relationships. Various institutions provide support for research projects which they select. Publishers hire reading experts and textbook writers, sometimes for sums much greater than their academic salaries. Local school systems provide the market for the publishers' wares, determining what they can profitably produce. And boards of education and the community determine how much money is available for hiring teachers and buying materials.

The interaction among these many status groups ultimately determines what research is done, how it is interpreted to administrators and teachers, how it is embodied in school textbooks, and how much is actually applied by the classroom teachers. Consequently, it is necessary to examine the component parts of this system, using qualitative and quantitative methods such as interviewing and content analysis, and extending the inquiry back from the present situation into the accessible past.[2]

The Columbia–Carnegie Study of Reading

Under a grant from the Carnegie Corporation of New York, the Bureau of Applied Social Research, Columbia University, is engaged in a study of the sociology of reading research. This project represents an extension of a variety of theoretical interests that have long been pursued in the Bureau's program of investigation. Many parts of the social system described above have been examined, but we cannot claim to know this system fully.

Data collection

Qualitative data have been gathered from research monographs, textbooks, and instructional materials, and from personal interviews with leading experts on reading. Quantitative data have been obtained from the following groups:

[2] The material to this point in the chapter originally appeared in A. H. Barton, The sociology of reading research, *Teachers College Record*, 1961, 63, pp. 94–97. Minor changes and additions have been made.

Reading researchers (647) [3]
Teachers college professors giving courses on reading (727) [3]
Writers of school books and other instructional material (390) [3]
Clinical and remedial reading specialists (704) [3]
Elementary school principals (141)
Elementary school teachers (1580)
A national sample of the public (1500)

Experts.   During 1961–62, 75 leading experts in the field of reading were interviewed at major schools of education in the United States. The interviews averaged over two hours in length, and dealt with the following questions: career history (recruitment into the field, training and financial support received, positions held before and after doctorate); research activities; available facilities for research; present allocation of time and energy; and opinions on reading research and on some controversial issues in the field. The interviews were exploratory and varied a good deal from person to person; material from them will be used extensively in a later report.

As we became more knowledgeable about the field, it became obvious that there were far more experts than we were interviewing. Normally such a problem would be handled by sampling according to some predetermined principle which would allow accurate generalizations about the larger population and express the full range of differences between various kinds of experts. However, the reading field presented special problems (and some advantages) which militated against any systematic sampling. Briefly, the problems were (*a*) that research on reading constitutes a large part of the total of educational research, and is by far the largest body of research on any single topic; and (*b*) that in spite of the constant and increasing output of research articles on reading during the past forty years, the same basic issues are still being debated. To help us understand these problems, we needed data that could be subjected to multivariate analysis so that we could go beyond description to explanation, and to systematic analysis of rather complex social phenomena.

Fortunately, the field of reading is of recent origin. Most of the people who have published research on reading are alive today, and the estimated total universe is not so large as to preclude examining all its members. These were the advantages; thus after the study was under

[3] These are mostly the same persons, since one "reading specialist" in his time plays many parts; 964 different people are represented.

way, the decision was made to survey the whole universe of experts.

Based on the original interviews with reading experts, a sixteen-page questionnaire covering the same topics was prepared and sent during the fall of 1962 to all individuals who could be identified as holding doctorates and as having worked in the field of reading in the United States. (The experts originally interviewed were included.) Usable replies were received from 964 people. This set of people is a large part of all those who can be defined as reading researchers, teachers of courses on reading, and writers of instructional materials for use in teaching reading. They include people who now perform these roles, and those who have done so at some time in their careers.

Teachers and principals. The questionnaire for school principals and teachers was developed in collaboration with a doctoral candidate at Teachers College (see Leahy, 1962), and pretested in the Yonkers school system. In May, 1961, it was sent to a national sample of elementary schools, and a supplementary sample of schools chosen as representing high-quality educational practice from the membership of the Associated Public School Systems, a national group of systems cooperating on research with Teachers College. The 221 schools (182 from the national sample, and 39 from the APSS sample), and the 1,580 teachers cooperating were probably somewhat more concerned with reading instruction, and more professionally oriented, than average. However, a sufficient number of schools from all regions and socioeconomic levels was obtained to permit the analysis of relationships between reading beliefs and practices and a wide range of institutional and personal background factors.

General public. The final phase of data collection in the project has involved preparation of selected questions to be asked of a national sample of the public—questions about the subjects' awareness of current controversies about reading instruction, their own and their children's experience in school, and their relevant beliefs and attitudes. The questions were included in a national survey of 1,500 respondents carried out by the National Opinion Research Center in May and June, 1963.

Analysis

Analysis of data is incomplete at the present time, but the study design will allow some modes of analysis which are usually not possible.

For example, the inclusion of certain attitude and belief items on questionnaires going to all groups will permit comparisons to be made across groups. In addition, information obtained from each group on its frequency of contact with the other groups, and its sources of information, enables measurement of the intercommunication of groups.

Teacher and principal questionnaires were grouped in a limited number of schools, so that the effects of school policies, climates of opinion, and amount of communication can be analyzed as they affect teaching practices and beliefs.

The data on the various types of reading specialists also emphasize problems of communication and influence. The very high response rate to the questionnaire (70 per cent) permits us to study social processes among members of a professional specialty. We know who studied with whom; who they feel influenced them; and who they feel has done the best research. Preliminary analysis reveals a remarkable amount of clustering of "opinion leadership" around a few very famous experts. We hope to apply sociometric analysis to this material.

Illustrative findings from the data analysis so far are presented below. They deal with (1) the characteristics and activities of reading experts; (2) the flow of information in the social system and its effects on beliefs, opinions, and practices; and (3) a significant problem illuminated by the data—the failure of both researchers and practitioners to cope with the teaching of reading to lower-class children.

The Survey of Experts

Characteristics

The reading experts are similar to the population of an earlier study (American Association of Colleges for Teacher Education, 1960) involving recipients of the doctorate in education for the years 1956–58. They too are largely upwardly mobile in terms of their fathers' occupations, education, and income. They are 70 per cent Protestant, and over 70 per cent have parents who were both born in the United States. They are, of course, older than the 1956–58 recipients, since the reading experts' doctorates date back to 1904. They belong to large national organizations, with 65 per cent members of the NEA, and 68 per cent in either Pi Lambda Theta or Phi Delta Kappa. But they also reflect specialization, with 60 per cent in the International

Reading Association, 36 per cent in the National Council of Teachers of English, and 29 per cent in the American Psychological Association.

A larger proportion of the reading experts have Ph.D.'s, rather than Ed.D's (54 per cent of the reading experts and 34 per cent of the 1956–58 recipients), and proportionately more reading experts are women (37 per cent compared with 20 per cent). One can only speculate at this point as to what effects these differences have had on the reading field. But from the standpoint of data analysis, it is fortunate that these variables are distributed evenly enough to allow comparisons between Ph.D.'s and Ed.D.'s, and between men and women. There may be no other field in America where there are enough women with doctorates to make comparisons between the sexes while controlling the effects of other variables.

The experts as graduate students

It is no secret that summer vacations, and the promotion and salary policies of local school systems, have gotten many teachers to attend graduate schools for reasons that have little or nothing to do with the pursuit of knowledge. Apparently, many enter graduate schools seeking promotions or pay increases; receiving the doctorate may even represent a serendipitous event for many educators. Reading experts are no exception. Many entered graduate school as experienced teachers; only 16 per cent have *never* taught in elementary or high school. Perhaps a better indication of original intention can be gotten from the fact that 79 per cent of them did not decide to go ahead for the doctorate until *after* they had already started graduate work.

A common complaint about graduate training in education is that, compared with other fields, it is not research oriented: graduate students are not given training or financial support conducive to research activity. Berelson's (1960) study documented these complaints to some extent, and our data tend to add to this image.

Probably the most encouraging statistic we can present about the reading experts' graduate training is that 30 per cent of them report having worked as research assistants to faculty members. However, this statistic does not look so good when it is juxtaposed with the following: only 17 per cent report ever having had jobs at the university which contributed directly to the degree, and only 21 per cent had fellowships at any time. But 46 per cent did get work at the university which contributed in *no way* to the degree, and 55 per cent had similar jobs outside the university. In fact, 162 (17 per cent) of the experts report having worked away from the university for seven or more years while pursuing the doctorate. Table 1 compares these findings with Berelson's (1960, p. 149) data for other fields. In contrast with other fields, only a minority of the reading experts have had either a fellowship or a degree-related job, and the vast majority (crosstabulation shows 81 per cent) had to work at jobs which did not contribute directly to their degrees.

Table 1. University Support, by Type and Field

	Support requiring no work from me, e.g., a fellowship	Support requiring work that contributed greatly to my degree, e.g., a research assistantship used for dissertation	Support requiring work that did not contribute directly to the degree, e.g., a teaching assistantship
Physical sciences	51% [a]	53%	75%
Biological sciences	45	47	62
Social sciences	45	28	64
Humanities	53	7	63
Engineering	48	52	62
Education	28	13	48
Reading Experts	21	17	46

[a] Percentages in this table (and all succeeding tables) are rounded.

Such a pattern—receiving predominantly the least facilitating kinds of support—suggests that reading experts might feel bitterness or dissatisfaction regarding their period of graduate training. But just the opposite is true. Over 90 per cent are "satisfied" or "very satisfied" with the amount of supervision they received on their doctorates; over 90 per cent feel they were trained "well" or "very well" for their present work. In addition, 85 per cent feel they were trained "well" or "very well" as professional researchers. Obviously, the reading experts are satisfied with less than what people in other fields are getting.

Sociologists have found high satisfaction combined with comparatively bad conditions in other social contexts; this is usually explained by (1) low visibility, or a lack of awareness that others are so much better off, and (2) low expectations for oneself supported by the similarly low rewards, achievements, and expectations of one's peers and reference groups.[4]

It is doubtful that we could now obtain valid information about expectations the experts held when they entered graduate school. However, we can compare them with those holding doctorates in other fields with regard to the purpose of graduate education, because we repeated a question of Berelson's: "Consider the balance in doctoral study in your field between preparing for teaching and preparing for research. What do you think it is now? What do you think it should be?" (But in our question we also included: "What was it when you received your training?") The results are shown in Table 2, along with Berelson's (1960, p. 47) data, and in Table 3.

Table 2. Comparison of Perceived Balance of Doctoral Training in Five Fields

	More for research	More for teaching	About equivalent	Can't say [a]
		Training Is Now:		
Physical sciences	79%	6%	12%	3%
Biological sciences	74	6	18	2
Social sciences	63	15	18	4
Humanities	53	23	20	4
Reading Experts	16	24	22	37
		Training Should Be:		
Physical sciences	60%	5%	28%	7%
Biological sciences	48	4	45	3
Social sciences	37	16	43	4
Humanities	25	32	39	4
Reading Experts	10	15	48	28

[a] Includes "don't know" and no answer.

It can be seen from Table 2 that the reading experts think the emphasis on research is less, and should be less, than do people in the other fields. In addition, Table 3 shows that the reading experts think the research emphasis they received in the past was more than it is now, and that *even now* it is more than it should be. Curiously, most

[4] For an extensive discussion of reference groups see Merton (1957), especially Chapters 8 and 9.

reading experts take the compromise position or can't make up their minds. (This is particularly interesting, because people in other fields could answer the question.) Apparently, it is not felt necessary to emphasize research more than teaching in order to turn out professional researchers in reading.

Table 3. Balance of Training for Reading Experts Only

	More for research	More for teaching	About equivalent	Can't say [a]
Balance received	23%	32%	26%	18%
Balance now	16	24	22	37
Should be	10	15	48	28

[a] Includes "don't know" and no answer.

Post-doctoral research activity of experts

After completing the doctorate, research continues to come out second best in the careers of the reading experts. Fifty per cent of the experts do report publishing research articles or monographs in some area, and 40 per cent have published research articles or monographs on reading. However, there is overwhelming evidence that this research largely consists of individual, part-time efforts done within the confines of the field of education, and receiving little if any financial support.

Table 4. Activities Engaged in by Reading Experts

	Never	Past only	First time this year	Past and this year
Teach on reading	21%	31%	11%	33%
Conduct empirical research on reading	30	41	7	19
Publish instructional reading materials	56	18	9	14
Clinical or remedial reading	24	37	8	28
Special reading workshops or conferences	17	34	11	35
(No answer to whole question: 3.3%)				

It can be seen in Table 4 that although two-thirds of the experts report having done empirical research on reading at some time, they continue to do research less than they continue the other activities. Fewer entered research for the "first time this year" than entered each of the other activities. In fact, a majority of those who have ever done research have done it *only* in the past. Other data showed that only 26 per cent have ever spent a period of six months during which research was their primary activity; presently, while 44 per cent claim to spend some time doing research, only 12 per cent spend one fifth or more of their working time on it.

The limited scope and relative isolation of the experts' research experience are indicated further: while 53 per cent have at one time or another done work with other researchers, only 22 per cent have ever worked on an interdisciplinary research team, and only 9 per cent are currently members of university-connected research bureaus. Furthermore, only 20 per cent have ever applied for research grants, and only 9 per cent have ever received such a grant. Perhaps the most significant statistics are that only 6 per cent (61) of the experts currently receive any income from research bureaus or projects; and only 1.6 per cent (16) of the experts receive half or more of their income from such sources.

Many of the beliefs and attitudes expressed by the reading experts are equally discouraging for research. For instance, 76 per cent agree with the statement that "People in the reading field get more prestige and recognition for editing basal readers than for doing basic research." Only 23 per cent disagreed with the statement that "Teaching is intrinsically more satisfying than research," and only 27 per cent prefer doing research on teams in conjunction with other researchers to doing it alone.

In sum, the reading experts can be characterized as "marginal" researchers. Compared with their colleagues in other fields, they decided to undertake the doctorate late and had to make do with a minimum of degree-facilitating support from their universities. Their research experiences have been largely brief encounters in the past, and were seldom primary occupations. They publish a good many articles *about* research, and 81 per cent plan to do research in the future. However, they would rather work alone than on teams, and financial support for research is rarely sought or obtained. Nevertheless, the experts feel they were trained well for research, and they would, if anything, reduce the amount of emphasis on research at the doctoral training level. In short, the experts feel that research is a good and desirable thing to do, but they are not willing to go at it very seriously, and it is not as interesting to them as teaching.

The Flow of Information

As part of the over-all project, we have also been looking at the content of communications about reading instruction, to get an idea of the problems of communicating scientifically based advice to the practicing profession. Our efforts along these lines are very incomplete, but it does appear from partial analyses of manuals, texts on reading instruction, introductions to readers, and similar advice to teachers over the last 150 years, that almost all of the issues raised in the last ten years were being raised long before there was any such thing as educational research. And some of the stereotyped versions of the history of reading instruction in America (e.g., from the Alphabet method to elaborate Phonics methods, to pure Whole-word methods and back to Mixed methods) are grossly oversimplified.

The impact of reading research

An extensive study of the materials and methods used in beginning reading is now being conducted under the direction of Jeanne Chall of the City University of New York, with support from the Carnegie Corporation. Our own brief examination of the basal reading materials suggests that they have remained substantially unchanged since the 1930's. In other words, with the possible exception of technical laboratory studies of contrast between print and background and illumination, research on reading has had no new effects on the basal readers during the last 30 years. Vocabulary loading has continued to decrease, word repetitions are frequent, and almost all characters in the stories are children. Indeed, 77 per cent of the experts agree that "for all practical purposes, most basal reading series on the market today are alike."

Thus, to the extent that teachers are dependent on these series for teaching reading, they would be largely *uninfluenced* by any research that has taken place during recent years. And as we point out below, teachers do rely to a large extent on these materials.

The impact of particular articles and research reports may be traced by the analysis of citations. Education lacks the ready-made measurement of the "weight" of a paper which the law has for the weight of an appellate decision in the form of Shepherd's citations. By concentrating on certain major texts and articles, however, one can keep the job manageable. (Computers can make such analyses routine, once all the materials are stored away in their "memories.") [5]

It does seem probable that certain pieces of research, often based on quite limited numbers of individuals and subject to the peculiar conditions of one time and place, have been relied on all out of proportion to their scientific weight. The widely quoted evidence that children could not be successfully taught to read until their mental age was 6.5 was not controverted until Gates' (1937) series of experiments, using different methods and different school environments. Meanwhile, this generalization had established such a place in the literature that it took many years to be removed, and it still enjoys an occasional ghostly reappearance.[6] The failure of the system of scientific evaluation and communication to prevent these excesses, which sprang in part from the fact that certain findings were highly congenial to the prevailing educational philosophies of their day, is a topic worth examining both historically and in the present situation.

Communication and influence

Concerning the communications behavior of the various participants in the system, we are now getting some descriptive data from our surveys of reading researchers, people who teach courses on reading instruction, principals, and teachers. We hope to relate styles of communications to knowledge, beliefs, and practices of these people. Just by way of example, take the data of Tables 5 and 6.

In Table 5, these facts are striking:

—The researchers who teach courses on reading are also communicating
frequently with almost everybody. (This may be one reason why only
12 per cent of them can spend more than ⅕ of their time on research!)

[5] During recent years, a series of studies of "citation indexing" have been undertaken by computer. Most notable are those at the Institute for Scientific Information in Philadelphia, which has been working on citation indexing for the physical sciences under grants from the National Science Foundation.

[6] Hunnicutt & Iverson (1958) reprint some of the relevant articles.

Table 5. "How often do you have the following kinds of contacts, on the average over the year?"

Type of contact	Per cent answering "Monthly" or more often, among:				
	RESEARCHERS WHO TEACH READING COURSES (143)	OTHER READING RESEARCHERS (84)	TEACHERS OF READING COURSES NOT ENGAGED IN RESEARCH (238)	ELEMENTARY SCHOOL PRINCIPALS (105)	TEACHERS: GRADES 1–3 (520)
Talking with *teachers* about problems of teaching reading	86	58	74	68	70
Talking with *principals* or other administration people about problems of teaching reading	64	46	56	30	31
Talking with *reading specialist or remedial reading teacher* about reading problems	67	47	50	23	8
Talking to *people from teachers colleges* about reading problems	67	21	54	22	not asked
Talking to *parents* about children's reading	66	43	44	35	30

—The teachers' main contact concerning teaching reading is with other teachers. And the school reading specialists play little part in talking with teachers on the subject—partly because there are so few full-time reading specialists in the schools. (Yet the teachers feel other teachers have been the least important in influencing them, compared with other factors considered, as Table 6 shows.)

—The elementary school principals do not have very frequent discussions of reading with people other than their own teachers.

Looking at sources of influence on beliefs regarding the teaching of reading (in Table 6), it is notable that the reading series and associated teachers' manual used in the school ranks first with the teachers, and fairly high with the principals. In line with Austin's (1961) findings, practice teaching ranks notably higher as an influence for the teachers than do undergraduate courses. Reading books and articles on reading is high for both teachers and principals; "reading reports of specific research studies," however, is important to less than a third of the teachers, and to just under half of the principals. This suggests that the effect of research on teachers is largely *indirect*, through the people who write teachers' manuals and books and articles, and perhaps through the principal, if he is one of the half who read research articles. The role of these mediators and interpreters of research will be subject to further investigation in our analysis.

Finally, it is worth noting that many principals (57 per cent) rank learning from their teachers as a "very important" source of influence —rather more than the proportion of teachers (36 per cent) who give similar weight to the advice of their principals or supervisors.

Practices and opinions

The immediate output of the communications system in education should be some effect on beliefs and practices. Our analysis of reported practices and opinions found a very great uniformity, throughout the country, among all types of teachers and principals. This is not surprising, considering how important the reading series and their manuals are in forming opinions; the country is blanketed by a relatively few series, which, as we have already suggested, are fundamentally very similar in approach.

Practices. Reading instruction in almost all schools starts from a similar basis: basal readers from a graded series are used by 98 per

Table 6. "How important has each of the following been in influencing
your beliefs regarding the teaching of reading?"

	Per cent answering "Very important"	
	ELEMENTARY SCHOOL PRINCIPALS	TEACHERS: GRADES 1–3
Reading series and teachers' manuals	55	63
Practice teaching connected with the teachers college	30	56
Own reading of books and articles on reading	67	51
Advice or example of teachers in your school	57	30
Workshops, institutes, in-service courses	56	48
Reports of specific research studies	48	31
Summer or graduate courses	42	37
Undergraduate courses	23	39
Advice of principals or supervisors	33	36

cent of first grade teachers in our samples, and by 92 to 94 per cent of
second and third grade teachers, on "all or most days in the year."

In addition to this base, however, somewhat different kinds of supplementary materials are used. About a third of the primary grades
use "children's story books which are not part of a reading series" on
all or most days. About a third use special books for slow readers on
all or most days. A quarter of the first grades use experience charts
based on the children's activities or interests on all or most days. Library work in school or public library is used on "many" days in 40
per cent of the first grades, rising to 65 per cent of sixth grades. Field
trips are used more than "just once or twice a year" in 35 per cent of
first grades, falling to 23 per cent of sixth grades.

Films or filmstrips for reading instruction, television for reading
instruction, reading machines for improving speed or training eye
movements, and kits of graded individual exercises ("reading laboratory") are used on all or most days in less than 4 per cent of the
grades from 1 through 6. These devices are as rare as basal readers
are universal.

Almost all classes have a classroom library, but only 16 per cent
of first grades and 30 per cent of higher grades have 75 or more books
in it.

We are currently trying to see how the more frequently used supplemental materials pattern themselves—whether they represent al-

ternative approaches, or form an "enrichment syndrome." We will also see how use of these materials is related to school and community characteristics.

Opinions. Listed in Table 7 are some items on which we find a very high consensus among our samples of reading experts, the elementary school principals, and elementary school teachers.[7] Almost everyone is agreed that some children should start reading instruction before the age of six, and that others should not start until age seven. (But "most children" should begin at age six—which by a strange coincidence is the "official" first-grade entering age in most schools in the United States, as distinct from Sweden and Russia, where it is seven, and Scotland, where reading instruction generally begins at age five.)

There is also a very large majority favoring the present approach to teaching phonetics in connection with words as they appear in reading, rather than through separate periods and exercises, though there is a minority favoring more systematic phonetic training, and, among the experts, a minority favoring a minimum of phonetic training.

All is not complete harmony, however. Table 8 shows some items on which there is considerable disagreement. Over 60 per cent of the teachers find the basal reading series "absolutely essential" for teaching reading; but only 40 per cent of principals and 28 per cent of the experts consider them essential, even though over three-quarters consider them at least "very important."

The experts, by contrast, are more likely to consider a varied classroom library essential, though here again it is a matter of priority, since about 90 per cent of all groups consider it very important, at the least.

About 60 per cent of the teachers find graded workbooks very important or essential, contrasted with 40 per cent of the principals and 32 per cent of the experts. This suggests not so much a failure of communication from experts to teachers as a difference in objective situation: the teachers must cope with large classes of children every day, and the workbook provides something for them to do, especially

[7] The teachers' responses came from (1) the national random sample, and (2) the sample from the Associated Public School Systems referred to earlier.

Table 7. Opinions Held by Experts, Principals, and Teachers on Certain Reading Issues: Items with High Consensus

	Reading Experts	Elementary Principals	Elementary Teachers [a] RANDOM SCHOOLS	"BETTER SCHOOLS"
Is beginning actual reading instruction before age 6 desirable for:				
All children	1%	1%	1%	–%
Most children	8	10	9	10
Some children	82	77	73	75
No children	5	8	6	7
Don't know	5	6	10	8
Is delaying the start of actual reading instruction until age 7 desirable for:				
All children	1	1	—	—
Most children	5	7	7	8
Some children	83	83	75	79
No children	6	5	8	5
Don't know	6	5	10	7
What kind of phonetic training is desirable for most children in the primary grades?				
A systematic program to teach the rules for sounding letters and letter combinations using special class periods and exercises	11	20	27	22
A program of teaching the sounds of letters and letter-combinations mainly as they appear in words in children's reading, but arranged to cover all major rules of sounding	67	74	63	70
Teaching the sounds of letters and letter combinations to some children who need it, when occasions make it necessary	14	2	3	1
Don't know, undecided	8	0	7	7

[a] See footnote 7.

since most classes have two or three reading groups with which the teacher works in turn. So far, the experts have not come up with a technology for handling this situation, so their disapproval of workbooks is not likely to influence the teachers.

Finally, we have two very suggestive differences in attitude. The teachers believe that the suggestions to teachers found in reading manuals are based on "definite scientific proof": almost no teachers disagree. But the experts (as we have defined them) are much less impressed by the scientific status of reading manuals; almost half disagree with the statement that they are based on "definite scientific proof," and only a third agree "mostly." The experts thus think much less highly of their own product, in a sense; perhaps the teachers have been oversold—and the principals are almost as sold as the teachers.

If the experts are more critical of themselves, they are also much more critical of the teachers. About 80 per cent of the elementary school teachers strongly agree that "elementary school teaching is a profession, like law or engineering," compared with about 60 per cent of the principals and only 37 per cent of the reading experts. To be sure, a large majority of experts agree to some extent—but they have qualifications. Further, only 58 per cent of the experts agree that "each teacher should be free to use the methods he thinks best in his classroom," as against 85 per cent of teachers. Most of the reading experts are themselves involved in training teachers; so this failure to endorse their professionalism fully is in considerable part a criticism of their own educational products.

These data show several interesting contradictions. The teachers think they are professionals—but want to rely on basal readers, graded workbooks, teachers' manuals, and other materials prefabricated by the experts. The experts don't accord full professional status to the teachers—but want them to rely less on basal readers and workbooks, and more on a wide range of children's books and more individualized approaches. The teachers are more committed to the standard teaching materials—but they want to have more freedom regarding the methods they use than the experts and principals are inclined to grant.

Clearly, there is a lack of consensus regarding appropriate role definition and role behavior for teachers.[8] The image of the profes-

---

[8] Gross and his associates at Harvard have conducted a series of studies of role conflict and resolution as applied to school superintendents, principals, and teachers. See Gross, Mason, & McEachern (1958).

Table 8. Opinions Held by Experts, Principals and Teachers on Certain Reading Issues: Items with Disagreement

	Reading Experts	Elementary Principals	Elementary Teachers [a] RANDOM SCHOOLS	"BETTER SCHOOLS"
In your opinion, how important are each of the following kinds of materials for teaching reading?				
A basal reading series:				
Absolutely essential	28%	40%	62%	67%
Very important	45	45	30	29
A classroom library of many varied children's books:				
Absolutely essential	64	48	50	52
Very important	27	43	39	40
Graded workbooks:				
Absolutely essential	8	10	24	22
Very important	24	30	35	41
The suggestions to teachers found in reading manuals are based on definite scientific proof:				
Strongly agree	2	10	16	14
Mostly agree	30	48	50	56
Undecided, Don't know	22	33	27	24
Mostly disagree	36	7	5	5
Strongly disagree	10	2	2	1
Elementary school teaching is a profession, like law or engineering:				
Strongly agree	37	59	78	84
Mostly agree	32	29	13	11
Undecided, Don't know	9	9	7	4
Disagree (mostly or strongly)	22	3	2	1
Each teacher should be free to use the methods he thinks best in his classroom so long as he gets good results.				
Strongly agree	16	29	42	38
Mostly agree	42	55	43	48
Undecided, Don't know	16	10	10	8
Disagree	26	6	5	6

[a] See footnote 7.

sional in the United States is based largely on a model provided by physicians and lawyers as private practitioners. Part of this model includes the idea of autonomy with regard to deciding on specific techniques and materials to be used (see Lieberman, 1956). However, teachers are not private practitioners, but part of a highly bureaucratic system, in which decisions about materials and techniques to be used in their classrooms are made by others, many of whom are not teachers. Apparently, teachers are committed to the notion that they are professionals who should be free to decide how to teach in their own classrooms, but when one considers their heavy dependence on basal readers, this commitment to professionalism and autonomy appears to be an expression more of ideology than of reality.

A Failure of Research and Practice: The Problem of Social Class

The inadequacies in the preparation and productivity of reading researchers, the difficulties in the communications flow between researchers and teachers, the disagreements about what *should* influence practice, and the dominance of existing materials—all these would lead us to expect that practice in the teaching of reading has not only avoided innovativeness, but might be found seriously lacking in important respects. This is in fact the case.

Socioeconomic class and reading

Our data show very clearly that the most important single factor in reading progress in school is socioeconomic class. Our national survey of elementary school teachers asked what the average reading level of their class was. We also asked about the predominant income level of their pupils' parents, and their main occupations. When classrooms are divided according to the socioeconomic status of the pupils' parents (using a combination of income and occupation),[9] we find that reading retardation—as measured by the class average—

[9] The levels were defined as follows: *Upper class*—mainly business and professional; *middle class*—mainly white collar, or mixtures of white collar and skilled, and farm owners; *upper working class*—mainly skilled or better-paid industrial workers; *lower working class*—lower-paid industrial and unskilled workers.

rises steadily through the first six grades for classrooms of mainly working-class children, and especially severely for the lower-skilled, lower-paid part of the working class (see Table 9).[10]

Table 9. Percentages of Teachers Reporting Class Reading Average
One Year or More *Below* Grade Level

| Grade | Predominant Socioeconomic Status of Pupils | | | | Difference, lower minus upper |
	UPPER CLASS	MIDDLE CLASS	UPPER WORKING CLASS	LOWER WORKING CLASS	
1	1 (82)[a]	1 (87)	3 (77)	4 (50)	+ 3
2	1 (73)	5 (85)	6 (54)	16 (57)	+15
3	0 (66)	3 (68)	7 (55)	32 (41)	+32
4	4 (51)	12 (60)	10 (67)	50 (30)	+46
5	5 (57)	6 (63)	14 (50)	60 (40)	+55
6	6 (53)	11 (47)	25 (61)	56 (39)	+50
All Grades	3 (382)	6 (410)	10 (364)	33 (257)	+30

[a] Numbers in parentheses are numbers of teachers reporting.

There are very few classrooms mainly composed of upper-class children where the average is a year or more below grade level. Yet by the fourth grade half or more of the classrooms mainly composed of lower-working-class children have a class average which is a year or more below the nominal grade level.

The other side of the picture is reading advancement. Reading advancement, again measured by the class average, is characteristic of the great majority of upper-class children *from the very first grade on;* it occurs in a fair-sized minority of middle-class classrooms; but it is quite rare for a classroom of lower-working-class children to average

[10] The class averages were reported by the teachers on the basis of whatever tests they used; the data need refining, but the major trend can hardly have been influenced by problems of test comparability.

a year or more above grade level. Here the class difference does not rise as we progress through the grades; it exists from the first, and remains throughout (Table 10).

Table 10. Percentages of Teachers Reporting Class Reading Average
One Year or More *Above* Grade Level

| | Predominant Socioeconomic Status of Pupils | | | | Difference, |
Grade	UPPER CLASS	MIDDLE CLASS	UPPER WORKING CLASS	LOWER WORKING CLASS	lower minus upper
1	65	39	27	8	−57
	(82)[a]	(87)	(77)	(50)	
2	60	44	37	10	−50
	(73)	(85)	(54)	(57)	
3	71	49	36	12	−59
	(66)	(68)	(55)	(41)	
4	63	33	22	10	−53
	(51)	(60)	(67)	(30)	
5	68	41	14	13	−55
	(57)	(63)	(50)	(40)	
6	68	38	23	10	−58
	(53)	(47)	(61)	(39)	
All Grades	66	41	27	10	−56
	(382)	(410)	(364)	(257)	

[a] Numbers in parentheses are numbers of teachers reporting.

We are thus confronted with two phenomena: (1) Most rich children are advanced in reading from the first grade on, while very few classes of poorer children are advanced. (2) The poorer children are about average as they go through first and second grade, but fall further and further behind as they go on.

As indicated earlier, we have considerable evidence that the patterns of reading instruction and the materials available are approximately the same for the children of all classes. There is in our schools an almost universal pattern of basal readers, some supplemental reading books, and a mixture of phonics and whole-word recognition training, as advocated in the teachers' manuals of the basal readers. There are some minor instructional differences in favor of the wealthier children in a few respects, but nothing large enough to account for the enormous differences in reading performance.

It seems clear that the major determinants of the retardation of the poorer children and the advancement of the richer ones are to be found in the home—in the differences between the activities, possessions, and values of families of different socioeconomic classes. This has long been known to reading researchers and educational administrators, but it has seldom been made a central topic for research. We have a great many studies of the influence of classroom practices and materials on reading achievement—the amount of instruction in phonics, the use of workbooks, the size of the print, etc. We have relatively few which try to measure the factors in the home environment which are making this enormous difference in reading performance—and almost none which study the interaction between classroom practices and home environment factors.[11]

The interaction of classroom practices and social factors

We have noted that classroom methods are generally very similar for children of all socioeconomic backgrounds. Perhaps this is precisely the trouble. The kinds of activities which could help children from lower-class homes develop reading readiness—going places, getting to talk about experiences with a responsive adult, getting acquainted with symbols, being read to, developing a love for imaginative stories—are not provided sufficiently in the classroom. Such activities might be quite unnecessary for most upper-class children. Many children from better-educated families may be all ready to read from the very beginning of first grade, if not earlier, so that what they need is reading instruction—instead of more readiness training.

We might also expect children who have a very large listening vocabulary, and are strongly motivated to read, to be discontented with a rigidly controlled vocabulary. If these children are taught to rely on memorization of word configurations of a limited sight vocabulary, their ability to engage in a wide range of outside reading may be impeded—unless they are able to figure out the basic phonetic and structural keys to word attack themselves. The extremely large

[11] See W. S. Gray's annual summary of reading investigations in the *Journal of Educational Research,* or any of A. E. Traxler's four volumes on reading research, the most recent being Traxler & Jungeblut (1959). A recent exception which does relate social class to reading achievement is Wilson (1963).

amount of outside reading done by many children of highly educated parents is possible only because they have, in some way or another, developed independent word attack skills and, later on, skill at figuring out from context the meaning of words not in their listening vocabulary. (The part played by dictionaries in extending the meaning vocabulary should be studied, to see whether it can be of much significance.)

The development of a meaning vocabulary, symbol discrimination, and a desire to read in lower-class children will make them ready to learn the mechanics of reading. However, they will *not* maintain the motivation or develop the fluency of reading characteristic of upper-class children, unless something is done (*a*) to make available a wealth of interesting materials for home reading, and (*b*) to continuously maintain the motivation and opportunity to read. Innovations under the first policy require spending a good deal of money and effort in making books very readily available to children—especially children from working-class homes—on loan, as gifts, or for inexpensive purchase prices. As it stands, beautiful, interesting, authentic children's books are distributed in a decidedly class-biased fashion.[12] Lower-class children's tastes are not necessarily the same as

[12] Of course, changing the content and style of basal readers to make them more appropriate for working-class and minority-group children would also help resolve this problem. Two current attempts to do this have come to our attention: the series developed in Detroit by Follett, and the readers being made by the Bank Street College of Education for Macmillan. The latter series has not been circulated yet, but the Follett series appears to be a curious mixture. Many characters in the stories have dark skins, and their surroundings are less affluent than usual. However, vocabulary seems to be even more restricted than is typical for basal readers, and the text is quite repetitious.

For careful attempts to come to grips with the special problems encountered in teaching working-class and minority-group children, see Riessman (1962) and Passow (1963).

So far as we know, the earliest attempt to deal with special problems of the American Negro was *The Lincoln Primer* (American Tract Society, 1864). Its preface states:

"The series of books, of which this little volume is the first, has been prepared with particular reference to the use of colored people in this country, especially of those who have lately emerged from slavery. [It is] intended to aid in teaching them to read and write . . . [in light of] those various domestic and civil duties to which freedom has introduced them. . . . In these respects, the numerous school books already in use in the North, though excellent for the purpose for which they were made, are found to be deficient. It is in compliance

upper-class children's, of course; little is known about this question.

Innovations needed under the second policy would involve less well-educated parents in developing their child's outside reading as the highly educated parents do—reading to the child, helping him maintain his home library, and encouraging rather than discouraging his reading.

Implications

The research itself

The characteristics of reading research have frequently been commented on: that it is abundant, running to several hundred papers per year, and that it is largely inconclusive, noncumulative, and limited in size and scope. Some of the reasons for this situation have been examined in our survey of the experts. A simple way to state the problem is that research needs to be *broader, longer,* and *deeper.* To indicate one line that might be followed to improve this research we will turn again to our crude data on reading level from 1,500 classrooms.

The sheer fact of having *breadth*—information on 1,500 classrooms —permits certain kinds of analysis which are common in sociological survey research, but relatively rare in reading research. To illustrate: we have already reported some striking findings with regard to the advancement and retardation of reading achievement as a function of socioeconomic class. Let us now look at these findings further, introducing two more sociological variables—the size of community and the size of the school class. The results for grades one through three are shown in Table 11.

The effect of socioeconomic class is still the single most striking feature. It remains even when we control for the fact that working-class children are more often in large cities, and in large classes. (Having large numbers of cases permits us to test possible spurious factors of this kind.)

But we can also see that the working-class children do notably bet-

---

with urgent requests from those who are engaged in teaching among the freed people, that the present series has been undertaken."

This book, like many primers of that period, contains religious overtones. Its most unusual feature is the use of Negroes in illustrations.

ter in communities under 10,000. What is there about small communities which has this effect of moderating the influence of social background on reading?

Table 11. Percentages of Teachers Reporting Class Reading Average
One Year or More *Above* Grade Level (Grades 1–3)

Community size	Class Size		Difference, small minus large classes
	UNDER 30	30+	
In classes of predominantly middle-class children			
Under 10,000	62	43	+19
	(67)[a]	(14)	
10,000–100,000	64	36	+28
	(196)	(91)	
Over 100,000	50	43	+ 7
	(36)	(54)	
Difference, small minus large towns	+12	0	
In classes of predominantly working-class children			
Under 10,000	46	34	+12
	(70)	(38)	
10,000–100,000	20	15	+ 5
	(71)	(33)	
Over 100,000	15	17	− 2
	(28)	(94)	
Difference, small minus large towns	+31	+17	
Difference, middle-class minus working-class			
Under 10,000	+16	+ 9	
10,000–100,000	+44	+21	
Over 100,000	+35	+26	

[a] Numbers in parentheses are numbers of teachers reporting.

Further, we can see that class size appears to make a difference—but that the difference is much greater for middle-class children, and in communities smaller than 100,000. Why is this? [13]

We present these figures not so much for their own sake as to indi-

[13] School facilities are one possible answer: we have other data which show that better facilities usually benefit those who are better off to start with. This suggests the difficulty involved in trying to compensate for poor home background by the usual kinds of school facilities.

cate what can be done with data "in breadth"—covering a wide range of types of communities, children, and classrooms, with such a large number of cases that we can use multivariate analysis to isolate the effects of several variables simultaneously. A fairly simple-minded "National Reading Survey," getting reading scores on a standard battery of tests plus family, school, and community characteristics, from, say, 200 schools and 2,000 classrooms, would be immensely useful at this stage in assessing the influence of social and school characteristics on reading. With data on three levels—individual students, classrooms, and communities—some very revealing analysis could be made of the interaction of individual characteristics with social context, in influencing reading.

Such a survey might also form the base line for making reading research *longer*, if the same classes were followed up over a period of years.

Such a longitudinal study would be most useful if accompanied by efforts to make the research *deeper* as well, by breaking down the variables of "reading ability" on the one hand and "social factors" on the other into a set of variables which could be analyzed as a system over time.

What is it about being upper-middle class which helps so much, and about being lower-working class which hinders so much? Undoubtedly, many variables, interacting in a complex "feedback" relationship, are at work. Solely correlational studies cannot show the routes by which good readers "got there."

A very useful type of study, therefore, would measure many variables on a fairly large sample of children once or twice a year for several years, and apply the public opinion research tool of "panel analysis." The variables measured might include:

—size of listening vocabulary
—symbol-discriminating ability
—size of sight vocabulary
—phonetic and structural word-attack skills
—speed and comprehension in reading
—motivation to read
—amount of reading done in and out of school

We might then have the basis of answering practical policy questions about the optimum methods of instruction and types of school materials to employ with various kinds of children at various stages.

For example, do the timing, amount, and type of phonetic training have to be different for children of different backgrounds? Should formal reading instruction begin at different times? How much and what kind of "readiness training" is needed for children of different class backgrounds?

The development of a multivariate system model over time, analyzing the various paths to development of reading skills taken by different children, and the interaction of family behavior, school practices, reading skills, reading motivation, and amount of reading, would lead us toward a *theory* of learning to read. Such a theory is sorely needed, because of the tendency of past researchers to leap from a single correlation or single experimental finding straight to a policy recommendation, without trying to fit the relationship into any system model. For example:

  —If skilled readers are found to read groups of words at a glance, then beginning readers should be trained to read groups of words at a glance. (But perhaps different methods are needed at different phases?)

  —If skilled readers are found to have a high degree of phonetic word-attack skill, then beginning readers should be trained in phonetics. (But what came first in the skilled readers?)

  —If skilled readers have a large vocabulary, then beginning readers should be given vocabulary training.

  —If children can learn to read several hundred words as whole-word patterns without phonetic analysis, then learning of phonetic word-attack must be a waste of time.

This kind of "two-variable, one-time" analysis is wrong: it does not consider the development of reading ability as a complex, multivariate process over time. People have been saying that "development of reading ability is a complex process" for a long time—but we mean something quite specific and quantifiable by this, and suggest that there are research techniques to analyze this process, if we would only use them.

The researchers

In spite of the rather clear implications of the preliminary analysis of our survey of the experts, there are reasons for some optimism concerning the future.

Research on reading has recently begun to attract large amounts of money from foundations and the federal government. This money is going to projects that require full-time efforts on the part of teams of researchers, who often represent many fields. With money available, research will be done by people who regard it as the important focus of their careers—by full-time professional researchers. If our preliminary findings are correct, the foundation- and government-supported projects of today will recruit and train many of the dedicated full-time reading researchers of the future.

The isolation of the reading field has recently been threatened by invasions from experts in others fields, notably linguistics, experimental psychology, medicine, and even sociology and anthropology. Some of the invaders' notions about reading are undoubtedly ridiculous, but there is some good company for these already in the field. More important are the healthy influence, stimulation, and new perspectives their ideas will offer. It is also threatening to the establishment that many of these invaders already have skills in writing research proposals and receiving grants—skills notably lacking among the reading experts. As a result, much of the future research may be done by these invaders.

Another brief allusion to the history of medicine in the United States may be helpful at this point. During the nineteenth century and the earlier part of this one, medical research showed very similar patterns to those we now find in education and reading research. The same physicians who taught at medical schools also had private practices, did part-time research, ran professional organizations, and sometimes even had their own hospitals. The Renaissance-man physician is now a thing of the past. Knowledge is too vast and specialties are too complex for any single man to play all of these roles adequately. In response to this problem, the leading medical schools have recently made policy statements to the effect that their primary goal is to make contributions to medical knowledge through research.[14] There is clear recognition that this can only be done by providing facilities and rewards for full-time research activities at medical schools; with this goal in mind, new positions have been created and organizational changes made at most major medical schools.

[14] See Research and Medical Education, Part 2 of the *Journal of Medical Education*, December, 1962.

Preliminary investigation of our data on reading experts suggests that the minority of reading experts who have been research assistants to faculty members, who have done six months of full-time research, or who are connected with university research bureaus, do behave differently with regard to research and have more favorable attitudes toward it. As shown in Table 12, they apply for research grants more and receive them more often than do the other experts. They rank doing research higher as an occupational preference, and they feel research is more satisfying than do the other experts. Apparently there are deviant patterns of socialization and experiences which are related to more sustained, productive research effort than is character-

Table 12. Opinions and Activities of Reading Experts, by Varying Research Experiences

	All experts [a]	Experts who once worked as research assistants	Experts who have ever done 6 mos. full-time research	Experts connected with research bureaus
Teaching is intrinsically more satisfying than research:				
Agree (strongly and mostly)	44%	35%	31%	29%
Undecided	32	32	27	29
Disagree	24	33	42	42
Proportion who have ever applied for research grant:	20	29	35	47
Proportion who have ever received research grant:	10	16	22	33
Rank of "Doing research in your field" as personal occupational preference:				
First choice	13	20	31	44
Second choice	15	19	20	9
Third choice	18	21	19	17
Not chosen 1, 2, or 3	54	40	31	29

[a] Percentage differences between "all experts" and the other three groups are minimized here because the category of "all experts" includes those in the other categories.

istic of the reading field as a whole. These experiences and training patterns are not yet institutionalized in graduate schools of education, but there are some indications of change in this direction.

Like medical research, reading research is directly concerned with problems that will affect the future of virtually every child in the United States. These problems are far too vast and important to be left to the individual efforts of part-time researchers, and there are strong indications they will not be.

Research–practice linkage

We have already seen that the system we are studying is not working satisfactorily in teaching reading to lower-class children. A better-known example of the failure of the system involves community and national controversies over reading methods and materials. Reviewing these may help point to implications for the improvement of research–practice linkage in the social system.

During recent years, there has been a great deal of public criticism of the methods and materials used in the teaching of reading throughout the United States. Probably the most widely circulated criticism was Rudolph Flesch's *Why Johnny Can't Read* (1955). In this book Flesch called the entire field of education to task for having produced and adopted materials and methods exclusively based on a "whole word" approach to reading, neglecting phonics. In more recent years, additional books have been written which criticize reading materials and methods for using too limited a vocabulary, neglecting the literary quality of introductory materials, failing to observe linguistic principles, falsely justifying methods and materials with Gestalt pyschology, and generally not doing a good enough job of teaching children to read (Terman & Walcutt, 1958; Diack, 1960; Trace, 1961; Bloomfield & Barnhart, 1961; Walcutt, 1961).

Some critics even try to document their claims with evidence, and this creates something of a dilemma. Most of them claim the reading experts are spreading false doctrines and doing bad research; but in order to present evidence in support of their own claims, they must usually resort to data which are less valid than the research they have criticized. For this, they are legitimately criticized in turn by professors of education and other defenders of the educational establishment.[15] Lines are drawn for conflict, and it becomes terribly difficult to find neutral observers.

Such conflicts are probably healthy in themselves, but some of their consequences may not be. In the midst of claims and counterclaims, school administrators and teachers have to justify their own reading programs to parents who have read criticisms, or have children who are having difficulty learning to read. Since most communities are using basal readers which are essentially similar, justification ultimately entails going back to research evidence which is thirty or more years old—and rather inadequate, at that. Some communities have switched radically from a basal reader approach to a heavy phonics approach, and many have tried various combinations.[16] But the decision to alter methods and materials radically can hardly be made on a rational basis when there exists virtually *no* hard evidence as to the superiority of one system over another. In the absence of such evidence, factors such as educational ideology, persuasive ability of book salesmen, sentiment, or exaggerated claims for specific methods may determine how children are taught to read in a given community. Feelings run high in such controversies; professional careers and reputations and millions of dollars are at stake; and the issues may never be settled to the satisfaction of the parties concerned.

Conclusions

An ideal model of the system we set out to study would include such factors as:

1. Highly trained researchers making sustained efforts to solve basic problems in the field.
2. High interaction between these researchers and those in basic sciences which might aid them.
3. Research findings which are cumulative.

[15] One unfortunate aspect of these rebuttals is that they receive widest circulation when made by men who also happen to be editors of basal reading series. However, since many critics are now publishing their own series, almost everyone can argue from a "vested interest" point of view.

[16] A recent extreme case was that of Twin Lakes, Wisconsin, where the famous 19th-century McGuffey Readers were adopted. These contained much sectarian religious material, which had to be covered with brown paper in order to maintain separation of church and state.

4. Changes in materials and methods based on these findings.
5. Feedback about special problems from teachers to researchers and publishers, leading to further research and changes in materials and methods.

Instead we have found that:

1. Reading researchers are largely untrained, and are doing part-time, one-shot research.
2. Contact with other disciplines is infrequent.
3. Research is voluminous, but of poor quality and noncumulative.
4. Materials are largely uniform, unchanged and uninfluenced by new research since the 1930's.
5. Teachers depend largely on published materials, and though ideologically committed to professional behavior, are unable to practice it as traditionally defined.

There are some obvious ways in which this system might be improved: better financial support for research in reading; better training of researchers; better facilities for full-time long term investigation; diversification of teaching materials for special social and ability groups; better "social bookkeeping" on the part of schools, so that accurate records are kept of how different kinds of students perform with various methods and materials under various social conditions; and better implementation of proven practices through improvement of teacher education and in-service training. Some of these changes are being made, or are being seriously discussed. Others are not.

We have presented some data on participant backgrounds, communication, and opinions to illustrate the kind of analysis we are attempting—an examination of the flow of information and ideas within a complex social system, with comparisons of opinions and beliefs among the various participants in the system. We hope that our study will suggest both ways to improve research on reading itself, and ways to improve practice, via dissemination of research-based knowledge.

References

American Association of Colleges for Teacher Education. *The doctorate in education.* 3 vols. Washington, D.C.: the Association, 1960.
American Tract Society. *The Lincoln primer.* Boston: the Society, 1864.
Austin, M. C., Morrison, C., *et al. The torchlighters: tomorrow's teachers of reading.* Cambridge: Graduate School of Education, Harvard University, 1961.

Axline, V. M. Meeting the crisis in educational leadership today. *Educ. Leadership,* 1957, *14,* 330–336.

Berelson, B. B. *Graduate education in the United States.* New York: McGraw-Hill, 1960.

Beveridge, W. I. B. *The art of scientific investigation.* New York: Random House, 1957.

Bloomfield, L., & Barnhart, C. L. *Let's read: a linguistic approach.* Detroit: Wayne State University Press, 1961.

Coleman, J. S., Katz, E., & Menzel, H. *Drugs and doctors.* Glencoe, Ill.: Free Press, 1961.

Cremin, L. A. *The transformation of the school.* New York: Knopf, 1961.

Diack, H. *Reading and the psychology of perception.* Nottingham: Peter Skinner, 1960.

Flesch, R. *Why Johnny can't read.* New York: Harper, 1955.

Gates, A. I. The necessary mental age for beginning reading. *Elem. School Jour.,* 1937, 37, 497–508.

Gray, W. S. *On their own in reading.* Chicago: Scott, Foresman, 1948.

Gross, N., Mason, W. S., & McEachern, A. W. *Explorations in role analysis.* New York: Wiley, 1958.

Hunnicutt, C. W., & Iverson, W. J. *Research in the three R's.* New York: Harper, 1958.

Leahy, M. K. The stated practices and beliefs concerning the teaching of reading of one hundred elementary school teachers. Unpublished doctoral study, Teachers College, Columbia University, 1962.

Lieberman, M. *Education as a profession.* Englewood Cliffs, N.J.: Prentice-Hall, 1956.

Merton, R. K. *Social theory and social structure.* (Rev. ed.) Glencoe, Ill.: Free Press, 1957.

Merton R. K., Reader, G. G., & Kendall, P. L. *The student physician.* Cambridge: Harvard University Press, 1957.

Passow, A. H. (Ed.) *Education in depressed areas.* New York: Bureau of Publications, Teachers College, Columbia University, 1963.

Riessmann, F. *The culturally deprived child.* New York: Harper, 1962.

Russell, D. *Children learn to read.* New York: Ginn, 1949.

Terman, S., & Walcutt, C. C. *Reading chaos and cure.* New York: McGraw-Hill, 1958.

Trace, A. C. *What Ivan knows that Johnny doesn't.* New York: Random House, 1961.

Traxler, A. E., & Jungeblut, A. *Research in reading during another four years.* New York: Educational Records Bureau, 1959.

Walcutt, C. C. *Tomorrow's illiterates: the state of reading instruction today.* Boston: Little, Brown, 1961.

Wilson, A. B. Social stratification and academic achievement. In A. H. Passow (Ed.), *Education in depressed areas.* New York: Bureau of Publications, Teachers College, Columbia University, 1963. Pp. 217–235.

CHAPTER 17

Curricular change:
participants, power, and processes

GORDON N. MACKENZIE

PUBLIC schools today are in the grasp of dynamic forces for change, forces with a power and an energy geared to the accelerating pace of our industrialization and automation. Substantial modifications in school programs are commonplace occurrences. Thus, institutions long viewed primarily as preservers of the heritage and as protectors of traditional values are being molded to assume new functions. The goal is better harmony between schooling and swiftly moving, uncertain world conditions—an education which will fulfill the hopes and ambitions of a vigorous people.

For two years, seminars, classes, and other informal groups in the Department of Curriculum and Teaching at Teachers College, Columbia University, in association with the writer, have secured and developed descriptions of recent curricular changes in elementary and secondary schools. Over thirty case examples were prepared by students as papers or special reports, based on observation of the changes or on interviews with those who had participated in them.[1]

---

[1] Martin Siegel of Teachers College, Columbia University, has a doctoral project based on one such case near completion (Curriculum change: factors which affected the development of three selected changes in the Hackensack school system).

THE AUTHOR is Professor of Education, Department of Curriculum and Teaching, Teachers College, Columbia University.

No standard form was followed in making these reports. Additional brief descriptions of changes were secured from the literature, and from representatives of school systems who visited college classes. Thus, both the focus and scope of the descriptions of change were extremely varied. They dealt with subject-matter areas such as Communism, conservation, foreign language, health, music, science, and social studies, as well as with methods, materials, and organization changes such as educational television, team teaching, and various plans of grouping.

Questions such as the following were asked about each description: What is the precise nature of the change? Who is responsible for the change? How was the change brought about? Usually descriptions were not sufficiently complete to give assurance that all significant details were known. Nevertheless, a continuing effort was made to understand the change process and to find ways of talking about it. What is presented here is a first effort to systematize many observations resulting from an analysis of these descriptions.

This chapter seeks to conceptualize the curricular change process as a whole in such a way as to take its relevant aspects into account, and to suggest further areas of investigation. First, the curriculum is defined as the planned engagements of learners, and the six determiners of these engagements are illustrated. These are the focus of any change effort. Second, the influence of the cultural context on all aspects of the change process is noted. Third, participants in the change process are listed, and an analysis is made of the sources of power and methods of influence through which they achieve change. Finally, several phases in the process of curricular change are described, along with the ways in which internal and external participants relate to this process.

Chart 1 summarizes the analysis presented in this chapter. At the extreme right are the determiners of the curriculum. These become the targets in the process of curricular change. In the left-hand column, participants in the change process have been listed. These participants have control of certain sources of power and methods of influence listed in the second column. They proceed through various phases in a process initiated by internal or external participants, listed in the third column, to influence the determiners of the curriculum listed in the fourth column. These determiners will be presented first.

Participants in Curricular Change →	Having control of certain sources of power and methods of influence →	Proceed through various phases in a process →	To influence the determiners of the curriculum →
Internal participants: Students Teachers Principals Supervisors Superintendents Boards of education Citizens in local communities State legislatures State departments of education State and federal courts External participants: Non-educationists Foundations Academicians Business and industry Educationists National Government	Advocacy and communication Prestige Competence Money or goods Legal authority Policy, precedent, custom Cooperation and collaboration	Initiated by internal or external participants: Criticism Proposal of changes Development and clarification of proposals for change Evaluation, review and reformulation of proposals Comparison of proposals Initiated by internal participants: Action on proposals Implementation of action decisions	Teachers Students Subject matter Methods Materials and facilities Time

401

Chart 1. Participants in curricular change, sources of their power, and phases in the process of change of the determiners of the curriculum

Determiners of the Curriculum

Efforts to describe precisely what had been changed, as the various illustrations were examined, led to the identification of six focal points for change. These came to be seen as the determiners of the curriculum, and made useful a redefinition of the term *curriculum* itself.

The focal points for change were (1) teachers, (2) students, (3) subject matter, (4) methods, (5) materials and facilities, and (6) time. These six components were so consistently present in the illustrations of change that it is reasonable to conclude that to change the curriculum is to change one or more of these six components.

The term *curriculum* has many definitions, and is used in numerous ways in the educational literature. In recent years there has been a tendency to move toward definitions which center on the experiences of learners, ignoring the intent of the teacher. Experience, when viewed as an interaction of the learner with his environment, is undoubtedly of great significance in the teaching–learning process. However, experiences cannot be observed directly. It appeared to be more fruitful, therefore, to define *curriculum* as the learner's engagements with various aspects of the environment which have been planned under the direction of the school. The assumption here is that engagements can be observed and to some extent controlled. The word *engagement* is used to mean what the learner meets face-to-face, what he attends to, or what he is involved in. It is not meant to imply conflict or opposition. It suggests more than mere activity. Obviously there can be engagements with teachers, classmates, or others; with physical factors such as materials and facilities; and with subject matter, ideas, or symbols. The method or procedure followed may pattern the nature of the engagement. The time allocated may influence the engagement in numerous ways. Specific engagements may appear to be primarily intellectual, emotional, or manipulative. Viewing the curriculum, then, as engagements of learners, what was the nature of the *determiners* of these engagements, the focal points of change?

Teachers

In the case descriptions, most curricular changes appeared to involve teachers. For example, the addition of a subject, such as French, to the elementary school program, to provide engagements with the French language, was accomplished through adding new teachers (in person, or by film or television), retraining those already in the schools, or using teacher abilities not formerly employed in the teaching process. New teachers with special preparation in mathematics, art, or guidance often changed the composition of a staff group. Where new teachers were not introduced, a great variety of procedures was used to modify existing teacher skills. New ideas were disseminated through the use of articles, books, films, outside consultants, and visits to other teachers. Workshops were organized to foster discussion of new proposals and to plan experimental programs. In-service courses were introduced to help teachers with new content, and with new methods, such as oral-aural language teaching, and the use of television, films, and programed materials. Specialists in science, mathematics, and social studies were introduced to teach new skills, and to help teachers in the transition to a newly defined program in their area.

The organization or deployment of the teaching staff was altered through securing assistance for teachers on clerical chores or on the task of correcting papers. Similarly, specialization of function was introduced through various kinds of team arrangements.

Students

Changes in the personnel of student groups were used as a means of changing the interactions in teaching–learning situations and thus of influencing the engagements of learners. By court decision, or otherwise, schools were forced to integrate various racial groups. Drastic modifications in learner engagements were intended—and were evident—in the descriptions. Some of the more common approaches to altering the composition of class groups were modification of school district boundaries, and shifts in the bases of grouping (homogeneous, heterogeneous, or inter-age). Changes in class size, and the removal of problem children of various types to special classes or schools, were used as means of modifying the classroom interactions.

Subject matter, methods, materials and facilities

Three of the determiners were very closely interrelated, and constitute the core of the teaching process. Yet, the language used in the description of change, as well as the specific focus of the changes, merits holding them as separate entities. In the discussion which follows, subject matter, methods, and materials and facilities will be discussed separately, with sample interrelationships being shown.

Changes in the curriculum were probably most frequently referred to as changes in subject matter. These were changes in the content, the ideas, or the symbols with which teachers and pupils were dealing. These modifications ranged from a gross type, as in the addition of a new subject to the educational program, to a more limited form, as in the dropping of a specific literary selection. Often changes in subject matter were carried largely by new materials, such as mathematics texts or foreign language tapes. But in many instances the new subject matter was conveyed largely through method, as in the case of a conversational approach to French in the elementary school, or an emphasis on human relations skills or social learnings.

Many change efforts were focused on method, the manner or means by which something is taught or learned. Illustrations were found in the introduction of large-group and small-group methods, of oral-aural methods, of a method of discovery, and of laboratory experiments. However, methods tend to become almost inextricably related to subject matter and materials in many instances, as in the use of the methods of a discipline (history, science) as the method of teaching. The case descriptions also included many approaches to change in which materials and facilities introduced a new method, or a kind of control over methods. Workbooks, programed materials, and language tapes were common illustrations of this.

As just suggested, materials and facilities may influence methods strongly, but they were frequently recognized as determiners of content as well, as in the case of textbooks, pictures, and recordings. The materials mentioned were of many kinds, including paper, paints, chalk, wood, metal, and clay. Materials were regarded as being a very significant part of the environment; their presence or absence, and the ways in which they were used, appeared to be significant in determining the curriculum. Many of the major changes described in the cases would undoubtedly have been long delayed or impossible of achievement without new textbooks, language laboratories and appropriate tapes, or television equipment and appropriate programs. The sheer presence or absence of specific facilities appeared to be crucial in some cases (e.g., the addition of a swimming pool made swimming instruction possible) though not in others (e.g., the addition of a language laboratory or of new kinds of science equipment was not essential for the teaching of language and science).

In the cases, the teacher was obviously an important consideration in relation to the substance of teaching. The teachers' roles varied from that of carrier to interpreter to user of subject matter. Also, methods of teaching tended to be controlled by the teacher, and methods of learning were strongly influenced by him as well. Instances were found in which rich supplies of materials and exceedingly fine facilities were not used at all, or were not used effectively by teachers. Thus, while subject matter, methods, and materials and facilities were revealed as frequent focal points for change, and as significant determiners of the engagements of students, the teacher was usually a vital and related component.

Time

An increase in the time allotment for a subject (such as spelling or language) or a decrease in the time given (as for handwriting practice) was observed to be a sixth way of modifying the learner's engagements, and thus the curriculum. Several instances were found in which the school day was lengthened, or in which supplementary opportunities for gifted students were scheduled in the evening, on Saturdays, or during the summer.

Implications

If these six determiners of the curriculum are the actual focal points through which curricular changes are made, several possible questions suggest themselves.

Does any one determiner, or any combination of determiners, hold more potential than others as a focal point for attention in curricular change efforts? Many would quickly assume that teachers are the most important determiner. There is certainly much evidence of the teacher's influence on the engagements of learners. Yet, many change efforts in the cases focused solely on teachers did not appear to bring about change; many changes appear to have occurred through a major emphasis on students, materials, methods, facilities, or time allocations. It may be that where the focus was on determiners other than teachers, there were changes and adjustments required of teachers which they were able to handle individually. Undoubtedly, the six determiners vary in their significance from one instance to another. Yet, there may be many situations in which the neglect of one or more of the determiners may lead to failure to bring about desired changes.

What is the optimum or necessary interrelationship among determiners? It appeared from the cases that they were often interrelated, and that changes in one were accompanied by or made necessary changes in another. Would more precise analysis reveal the nature or the extent of change in one determiner which calls for various kinds of changes in other determiners?

What is the importance of organization or patterning within each category of determiners? Many of the illustrations of change appeared to involve this feature. For example, a change to a problem or to a subject organization for teaching was a common type of method/subject-matter consideration. An organization of teachers or of materials which sought to foster content integration (the seeing of relationships between two or more subjects) would be similar in nature. A reorganization of the school day, and of its periods, influenced the amount and kind of study time and supervision which students had within the school day. The deployment of staff in self-contained classrooms, in a departmental organization, or in teams of various kinds was noted. The organization of students by ability, inter-age, or achievement groups was another indication of this concern. While these are all variants of the ways in which the determiners are handled, the very large number of the changes concerned with matters of organization suggest this as a special area of inquiry.

What is the precise nature of changes in determiners? These changes appeared to be of many kinds; they included the introduction of a new determiner, a modification of one formerly used, a new use of an old one, or new interrelationships among the determiners. With some modification of wording, this statement could be applied to each of the six determiners. For example, teachers with new or added competencies were employed, teachers were retrained, teachers were reassigned so as to capitalize on strengths, and teachers were placed in a new relationship to programed materials or televised programs. Similarly, in respect to time, a new or initial allocation was made for a new activity, past time allocations were modified, new uses were made of the original time allocation, and time was varied in terms of the kind of student.

Are these six focal points for bringing about curricular change also the keys to stability? If these focal points are the actual determiners of engagements of learners, as now seems to be the case, is it reasonable to assume that stability in the curriculum can be maintained by preventing change in them?

Who is able to manipulate each of the various determiners—and by what methods and under what conditions can they be manipulated? These aspects of the change process will receive attention in later sections of the chapter.

One further observation concerning determiners may be appropriate. Writings about the curriculum, as well as the case descriptions used here, revealed that many attempts at change have focused directly on one or more of the six determiners identified here, treating them as though they *were* the curricular change. Further, many proposals for change (such as team teaching and educational television) have been advanced on administrative or financial grounds, with no consideration of possible implications for the curriculum. Thus, among educators as well as among laymen, there are different criteria in use for defining curricular change. The approach used here is intended to be useful in the further study of curricular change.

When curricular change is referred to in the remainder of the chapter, it will mean a change in the engagements of learners, and will imply changes in one or more of the six determiners illustrated in this section.

Influence of the Cultural Context

In the curricular change illustrations used for this analysis, the impact of the cultural context was very obvious. The precise form and emphasis of the reported changes in determiners could hardly be understood or accounted for without a knowledge of the current scene which they so markedly reflected. Many of the change descriptions suggested one or more community concerns with education; they frequently repeated words and phrases such as "quality," "standards," "gifted children," "college entrance," "reading ability," "television," "teaching machines," "team teaching," "the need for change," and "updating of educational programs."

Ideas from the mass media, several large foundations, and influential citizens were generally reflected in the descriptions. National committees operating in the various subject areas had stimulated much action, as revealed in reports from many communities. There were numerous similarities from community to community; the pervasive influence of the general context within which the schools were operating was evident. This has been noted by the directional arrows in Chart 1 from the "Cultural Context" to each of the four columns of the chart.

The specific influences mentioned in various change descriptions reflected definite but broad individual and social considerations: feelings of national insecurity and a desire for increased personal security; a recognition of the rapid developments in science, mathematics, and technology; an awareness of changes in the occupational pattern with growing mechanization and automation; and a belief in the importance of education for the reduction of international conflict and for personal well-being. Pressures toward centralization and national control were reflected in many areas.

The cultural context was further revealed in these cases as one in which numerous kinds of expectations and sanctions emanated from diverse sources. There were reports of community expectations that the schools should do something vaguely defined as "better" in reading, mathematics, and science. That schools should make changes in the curriculum—and do so rapidly—was often communicated more clearly than was the precise nature of the change desired. Criticisms of schools were often reported as being harsh; funds were withheld and dismissals of administrators were threatened. Revelations of this kind were sometimes cited as descriptive of the conditions under which changes were made. While these expectations and sanctions are basically similar to those which have long been recognized as operating between students and teachers, teachers and teachers, principals and teachers, and parents and teachers, they now appeared to have a new urgency, and possibly a less personal, broader social orientation.

In the next section, a further analysis will be made of the individuals and groups in the cases who were operating to change the curriculum;

later the means which they used are discussed. However, it appears quite clear that the changes made were based on the expectations and the sanctions of those able to influence the school personnel or other determiners of student engagements.

Participants in Change

In the process of summarizing the studies of change, the individuals or groups who were influential relative to curricular change came to be referred to as participants in change. *Participants* are viewed broadly as any individuals or groups capable of a wide variety of actions serving to influence or control the various components of the curriculum which serve as the determiners of the engagements of students.

Participants in change have been classified as internal or external. *Internal* participants are those who had a direct connection with the legal or social system from which a particular description was taken. Because of this relationship, they had a greater potential than other participants for several kinds of direct action in respect to one or more of the determiners of the curriculum. *External* participants are those outside of the immediate social or legal system under consideration. Both groups of participants have a potential for indirect action (influence on those who have the power to take direct action).

Internal participants

Ten major groups of internal participants were identified: students, teachers, principals, supervisors, superintendents, boards of education, citizens in local communities, state legislatures, state boards or departments of education, and state and federal courts. These ten groups of participants differ widely in their influence as well as in their manner of operation. Each will be discussed briefly.

Students. Lest there be confusion resulting from designating students as both determiners of engagements and participants in change, a clarification of the two roles will be presented. In the discussion of determiners, reference was made to the characteristics of students (such as abilities, backgrounds, and aspirations) and the way in which these would influence the nature of the engagements. It was further indicated that by altering the size and composition of groups the student component could be modified.

In addition, however, an examination of cases indicated that students could influence by direct action not only their own engagements but also the engagements of others. Illustrations were discovered of direct student participation in the planning of processes by which content, methods, materials, and time allotments were determined. Students did this both in cooperation with staff members and with other students. Illustrations were also found of student strikes in favor of certain teachers dismissed by the administration. A further example: most teachers modify their practices (consciously or unconsciously) on the basis of feedback from students in the form of interest and satisfaction, or apathy and lack of interest. Thus students do, on occasion, influence all of the determiners directly.

Students are also capable of indirect action. By making their opinions on teachers, students, time allocations, subject matter, methods, materials and facilities known to parents and principals, they have often influenced them to work for modification in the determiners.

Teachers. As players of a double role, teachers are similar to students. The skills, abilities, and personalities of individual teachers cast them in the role of significant determiners of the engagements taking place in their classrooms. They may, of course, work to improve their own skill and operation.

However, teachers have a potential, as students do, for influencing the other five determiners in their own classrooms, *viz.*, (1) students, (2) subject matter, (3) methods, (4) materials and facilities, and (5) time. They can also influence all six determiners in other classrooms than their own. They may invoke sanctions against the teacher who agrees to take his class to the playground. They may decide in cooperation with others that certain subject matter (such as the process of division in arithmetic) will be taught in grade five rather than grade four. They may decide when cursive writing will be introduced, and how much time will be given to specific handwriting practice. Thus, the teacher is not only the determiner of engagements in his own classroom, but is also a participant in changing the determiners of student engagements in other classrooms.

Principals. In the descriptions analyzed, principals were found to be very influential participants in changing the determiners. For example, some principals had the authority to control the assignment of teachers to grade or ability groupings. Also, some principals controlled, within broad limits, decisions on the student composition of class groups, the human and nonhuman resources to be introduced into classrooms, and the time allotments to be followed. They also had much to do with the extent to which parental pressures were brought to bear directly on teachers, and with the provision of in-service educational opportunities for teachers.

Supervisors. While often having less authority than principals, supervisors had considerable influence on all the determiners. However, their actions in the case studies were often those of consultation, cooperation, and recommendation. On the basis of their visits to individual classrooms, or their encouragement of teacher visits to other teachers, they might recommend new or different approaches. Through workshops, committee activity, and a variety of group endeavors they might help individuals and groups move toward modifications of teaching skills and practices, as well as toward policies influencing the other determiners.

Superintendents. In many instances, the superintendent of schools appeared to be the most powerful single participant in change. Illustrations were found in which he intervened directly relative to all of the determiners. For example, he employed new art teachers who were expected to bring about changes in the art curriculum. He added a course in computer mathematics, and decreed new subject matter on Communism in an existing social studies course. He selected new textbooks in American history. He changed the time allotment for physical education from five to three periods per week. He modified attendance areas so as to alter the composition of the student body drastically.

In actions such as these, there were wide variations in the extent to which the superintendent operated independently, under instructions from the board of education, or in cooperation with teachers and other administrators. There are also many instances in which the superintendent did not operate directly in reference to the determiners of engagements, but sought to build parent support for special teachers of reading, or board of education approval for increased materials of instruction, or stepped-up action by principals for in-service education on the use of television.

Boards of education.   In the descriptions collected, boards of education appeared to be influential participants in change. Many instances were discovered where changes were ordered by boards over objections of the professional staff. Included here were changes involving the use of television in classrooms, the introduction of foreign languages in the elementary schools, and the purchase of language laboratories. Boards were observed to exert, in some cases, a very direct influence on the general climate within which education goes forward. Boards also tended to have a major say in determining the pupils to be served, the facilities to be provided, and the staff provisions to be made. Financial controls by boards of education often drastically influenced the situation in respect to availability of materials. Boards also exhibited strong influence on many details of curricular change through their veto action. While boards usually operated through professional personnel, they were in a position to mandate certain changes directly.

Citizens in local communities.   In some instances citizens were very powerful participants in change, operating through citizens' groups, parent–teacher associations, and regularly scheduled elections. They voted directly and specifically on budgets dealing with facilities, organization, and staffing for school systems. A few instances were found in which specific program provisions, such as foreign languages in the elementary school, were demanded. The community was, of course, in a position of power relative to the board of education, the professional staff, and the students.

Through gifts, individuals and groups influenced certain determiners. However, the gift of a swimming pool, which made instruction in swimming possible, required board of education action and approval. Gifts of radios, television sets, and other materials by individuals or groups of parents appeared to occur only with the acquiescence of staff members or boards of education.

State legislatures.   The primary legal bodies responsible for the curriculum are the state legislatures. In some instances, they have laid down the general pattern in respect to several determiners, but they have tended to delegate much of their authority to state boards of education, state departments of education, and local boards. There were numerous illustrations, however, of legislatures requiring specific content and methods (such as foreign languages in the elementary school, and teaching about Americanism), or specifying the way in which pupils must be classified and grouped (for example, in respect to race).

State departments of education. Whether operating under a state board of education, directly under the state legislature, or as a reasonably autonomous state executive agency, the state department of education is often able to mandate or require certain kinds of curricular changes. In the cases analyzed, they influenced content and method through state testing systems. Through financial support and special grants, they stimulated numerous changes, which varied from the pupils served to the content taught. Depending on the nature and size of their staffs, they exerted influence on in-service and other educative activities. In the administration of state laws and regulations they were able to encourage or prohibit specific curricular changes. While state departments carry on many other instruction-related activities not mentioned here, it is clear that they exert both direct and indirect influence.

State and federal courts. The courts have long been recognized as being able to influence the curriculum through rulings and interpretations of laws and constitutions. Incidents were found where the courts had compelled action in respect to content, methods, and the grouping of pupils on an interracial basis. In one well-known instance, the Army was involved in enforcing a court decision.

External participants

Many kinds of participants in curricular change were found to operate from outside the social or legal system of a specific school situation. In most instances, these participants did not appear to have any legal authority or power of direct action relative to the determiners of curricular change. However, they were able to exert substantial influence of an indirect sort (through such methods as disseminating information, raising expectations, or invoking sanctions) on those participants who could influence the six determiners of curricular change directly. These external participants were grouped into six categories: non-educationists (individuals and groups), foundations, academicians (individuals and groups), business and industry (including materials and facilities producers, and agents of the mass media), educationists (individuals, groups, and organizations such as teacher-educating institutions, accrediting agencies, and professional associations), and the national government (primarily the legislative and executive branches).

Non-educationists.   Many individuals and organizations with non-educational affiliations were observed to have an impact upon the curriculum. Through their attacks, acts of violence (as in Little Rock and New Orleans), or persuasion they brought about or resisted changes in the curriculum. Their influence was often directed toward students, boards of education, and materials. Lucille Cardin Crain through the *Educational Reviewer,* Frank Gannett of the Committee for Constitutional Government, Merwin K. Hart of the National Economic Council, and Allan Zoll of the National Council of American Education are among the better known representatives of this group; they were found to be operating through publications and local community sympathizers to influence other participants in change.

Men of outstanding achievement in their several fields were frequently quoted in the descriptions collected. While Admiral Hyman G. Rickover's proposals did not appear to have been directly implemented, he probably contributed to the creation of an environment conducive to change. James B. Conant and Arthur D. Morse did much to inform the public and to build certain expectations about educational programs.

Foundations.   Many illustrations of curricular change were located in which private foundations provided the stimulus to internal participants for such actions as redeploying the teaching staff, introducing educational television, modifying school buildings and facilities, and encouraging massive reorganizations of subject-area content.

Academicians.   Many academicians were found to have shown rather remarkable interest in elementary and secondary education. Some were critics of the schools. Others moved into membership on school survey teams, became temporary internal participants, and recommended specific curricular modifications to other participants in the change process. Not a few sought to remake the curriculum through the re-education of teachers. They frequently worked through national committees which had substantial public and private funds. Examples are Professor Jerome S. Bruner of Harvard, and Professor Jerrold R. Zacharias of M.I.T. Professor Arthur Bestor, formerly of the University of Illinois, and now of the University of Washington, is an academician who has not only attacked modern education through his writing and speaking, but has also allied himself with the Council for Basic Education, a national group consisting largely of laymen; it has influenced internal participants in curricular change in many communities.

Business and industry. An interest in materials and facilities has long been exhibited by many segments of the business and industrial community. The American textbook industry has been an influence for change in some communities and for stability in others. New developments in technology, especially in electronics, have resulted in business opportunities in television, programed instruction, and computers—with considerable implications for curricular change. There can be little question of the impact of materials and facilities on the curricular change process. All of the mass media were found to be concerned with, and all were mentioned as influences for, curricular change.

Educationists. Individual educationists did not appear to be operating outside of the framework of the specific educational institution from which a description was drawn, except insofar as they worked with foundation support, as staff members of higher institutions, or as representatives of national lay or professional organizations. For example, several projects of the National Education Association and its affiliated groups have focused on defining policy and on guiding change. Some of these were noted in the case illustrations. The influence of the National Association of Secondary School Principals, working on team teaching with funds from the Ford Foundation, was mentioned several times.

The federal government. In addition to its long-standing work in vocational education, which appeared in some case descriptions, the Government has entered the curricular arena with new force and influence through the National Defense Education Act. Guidance, foreign languages, mathematics, science, and educational television have been major areas of activity. The President of the United States has been conducting a personal crusade in the area of physical fitness. The Office of Education, even prior to National Defense Education Act or Smith-Hughes funds, appears to have had considerable influence in specific areas such as foreign languages in the elementary school.[2]

While the executive and legislative branches of the national government have had a very substantial curricular impact, they have operated primarily through internal participants for curricular change. Only the judicial branch (in one instance with Army support) has exhibited the ability to make a direct and controlling assault on one or more of the determiners of curricular change.

Interrelation of participants

Relationships among participants within and between the internal and external categories are indeed complex and varied. Some of these relationships will be explored in subsequent sections as the various kinds of action and sources of power available to participants are described.

However, two conditions which have a bearing on participation will be mentioned here: one is distance from the classroom; the other is competence relative to a specific determiner. Thus the legislator, who operates at a considerable distance from the classroom, is only able to lay down (successfully) the most general specifications relative to the determiners. The local board of education or superintendent can be more specific, and in many instances, at least, the classroom teacher is the final determiner.

The second condition, competence, is seen most clearly in relation to the possible impact of the layman (as contrasted with that of the academician) on subject matter. The impact of competence on decisions relative to teachers and teacher education, students, and time is also evident. This implies that decisions probably are and will be differentially distributed among various participants, in terms of their

---

[2] While it did not appear in the illustrations analyzed, research sponsored by the U.S. Office has undoubtedly had an impact on some of the determiners of the curriculum.

distance from the classroom and their competence in respect to the determiners of engagements. Other aspects of the relationships among participants will be considered in the section which follows.

Sources of Power and Methods Used by Participants

To change the curriculum is to modify one or more of the six determiners of the curriculum. One who would modify the determiners must be able to do so directly, or to influence others who are able to do so. Thus the process of bringing about change is one of getting new teachers into the classroom, or changing those who are there; modifying the composition of the student group; introducing new methods, new subject matter, new materials or facilities; or altering the time allocations.

It appears helpful to hypothesize on the basis for the strengths and weaknesses of various participants in bringing about change, as well as to identify the methods used. This will be attempted by a description of the dynamics apparently underlying the operations of participants in the illustrations examined. These have been listed in the third column of Chart 1.

Advocacy and communication

Probably all participants in curricular change engage at some time in advocacy of a change. Unless a change is conceptualized in some form and advocated, it cannot occur on a planned basis. As superintendents, principals, supervisors, and others interviewed consulted and conferred with associates, they often advocated a change and sought to persuade others to accept their way of thinking. The processes here were those of developing a sense of involvement, securing a feeling of identification with a proposed change, or building certain expectations. Many activities used by internal participants to change the curriculum appeared to rely largely on various kinds of advocacy.

Those individuals and groups classified as external participants tended to make more use of mass communication devices in advocating their beliefs. Often they criticized or attacked existing arrangements as well as proposing changes. If they happened to have skills in using the mass media, as well as access to them, they were, of course, in a greatly strengthened position. The activities of agencies like the National Citizens Commission for the Public Schools and of individuals like Admiral Rickover exemplify the skillful use of mass media.

Beyond the advocacy of a change or the communication of a proposal to others, several reasons can be posited for the success of any given effort. The process of exerting influence in favor of a proposed change is based on power, and is essentially political in nature. What are the bases of the power exerted by those able to influence changes?

Prestige

In the cases studied, the prestige of individuals and groups advocating a change was undoubtedly a factor in their effectiveness. Many of the descriptions imply that individuals as well as state or national groups were accorded special deference in the process of making curricular changes, because of their social class membership, personality, attitudes expressed, or unique skills and achievements. In the cases examined, ideas, proposals, and detailed recommendations were often attributed to prestige-bearing sources. James B. Conant had the support of large foundation grants and ample access to the mass media, and appeared to have been treated with exceptional deference in many of the accounts of change which were examined.

Competence

The personality of an individual was sometimes mentioned as a factor in his influence. This was probably linked with outstanding competence in skills of writing, speaking, or conferring, unusual knowledge of a problem, or an ability to relate to people with unusual effectiveness.

Money or goods

The control of this asset is one of the most significant sources of influence which a participant can have. Money or goods can obviously be used in various ways. The national government may provide matching funds in selected areas, to encourage local action. A state may do the same, or may make outright grants for certain minimum programs. An agency without legal authority, such as the Ford Foundation, is able to make a major impact in selected areas through grants-in-aid, or through outright support of special programs. Even an organization of parents may encourage the use of television or library reading through small grants to a local school.

Legal authority

The state government is regarded as the central legal authority in respect to education. This includes its legislative, executive, and judicial branches. Local boards of education are delegated considerable legislative jurisdiction, and in conjunction with the local government and its administrative agencies they have much power. The authority of the federal government relative to education is very real, but operates on a more restricted basis.

The state legislative and executive branches, as well as the local board of education, have clear prescribing or mandating powers, and can also recommend, evaluate, and set standards. State and federal officials have these same powers, and can force compliance through use of police or the armed forces. However, the local board of education is obviously the most significant authority in respect to the day-to-day manipulation of the determiners of the curriculum. It can foster or veto curricular changes within very broad limits.

Policy, precedent, and custom

Much authority is often delegated to the local superintendent of schools, as well as to other professional staff members. This may be by custom and precedent only, or by carefully defined policy. Similarly, students, lay citizens, and others may be permitted to share in the curricular change process. Where precedent or policy clearly establishes a role for such individuals, they come to the task with a most significant asset. However, the authority of various participants to act varies widely with the specific aspect of the curriculum being changed, with the situation, and with the specific participant.

Cooperation or collaboration

Cooperation among individuals and groups having similar (or different) assets may greatly strengthen their influence. Thus, a firm stand by a faculty group on a proposed curriculum change carries more weight than if the proposal is supported by only one or two teachers. Similarly, an influential professional organization working in cooperation with a wealthy foundation can exert an influence considerably beyond the potential of either party working alone.

Briefly, and in summary, the process of changing the curriculum appears to be one of directly changing the determiners of the curriculum, or modifying the expectations and values of those able to change the determiners. The modification of expectations is achieved largely by control of the ideas and proposals communicated and being supported at a particular time. Once proposals, expectations, and values are established, personal and legal sanctions (both positive and negative) can be applied to those able to modify the determiners. This is mostly a matter of the application of personal or group power based upon prestige, competence, control of money or resources, legal authority, policy, precedent, custom, or cooperation and collaboration.[3]

Phases in the Process of Curricular Change

One further series of insights resulted from an attempt to characterize phases in the process of curricular change within school systems. In some situations, these phases appeared as a sequence of orderly steps. However, in other descriptions some phases were not mentioned, and had probably been entirely omitted. Also, the several categories of participants had varying degrees of involvement with each of the phases. These comments will be illustrated in the analysis which follows.

Phases initiated by internal or external participants

Although these phases of change took widely varying forms, the classification below did not appear to force the data. (However, descriptions were often too limited to assure that all relevant data were at hand.)

Criticism. Judgments and evaluations of the curriculum in general, of any determiners of the curriculum, or of the outcomes of curriculum were included here. Illustrations in the field of reading in-

---

[3] The analysis in this section has been strongly influenced by the writings of Lasswell (1958); Lasswell & Kaplan (1950); Lasswell, Leites, & associates (1949); and Merriam (1934).

cluded: general condemnations of reading achievement; belittling of primers and other first and second grade books because of their limited, unrealistic, and uninteresting vocabulary; blaming of the word method, and decrying the failure to teach phonics; citing of specific achievement test results as being unsatisfactory. While such criticisms often came from external participants (such as writers in the mass media), in many cases they were initiated by internal participants (such as board members, principals, or teachers). The purpose frequently appeared to be one of stimulating other participants to take action to change the curriculum.

Proposal of changes. Any attempt to define a specific curriculum problem, or to suggest a specific course of action (often in relation to one or more of the six determiners of the curriculum) was classified here. Such attempts were often closely related to criticism, but went beyond a value judgment on the existing curriculum, and suggested or implied a focal point for action. Thus, the use of phonics was advocated to improve the teaching of reading, French was proposed as an addition to the elementary school program, or the "new mathematics" was urged at both elementary and secondary school levels. This identification of a focus for change efforts was initiated by a wide range of participants, from individual students to national committees.

Development and clarification of proposals for action. This phase was totally absent in many descriptions, yet received extensive attention in others. Thus, a recommendation that French be added to the elementary school resulted in some instances in the appointment to an elementary school staff of a teacher instructed to "see what could be worked out." In other instances, the same recommendation resulted in a careful study of expert opinion and the experience of other schools in order to identify (1) a possible optimum grade level at which to start the study of French; (2) a suitable time allocation per day or week; (3) a clarification of methods and materials to be used; (4) an examination of possible consequences for the language program at the secondary level. It appeared that the care with which proposals for action were developed and clarified had considerable influence on the speed with which an intended change was accomplished, and on the stability of the change. As has been suggested, the development and clarification phase involved gathering data, exploring possible consequences (both immediate and long-term) and working out detailed plans relative to one or more of the determiners.

Evaluation, review, and reformulation of proposals.   Although this phase was initiated by both internal and external participants, its form tended to vary, depending on the participant. Thus a national committee, as well as a local research director, might try out new subject matter, new methods, or new facilities in an attempt to determine their suitability for students of various maturity levels, and their impact on achievement. The national committees working in the sciences and in mathematics illustrated this very well. At the local level, reviews and appraisals were often less formal and thorough, and were frequently related to unique features of the immediate school system in which they were being tried. Teacher or parent reaction provided the basis of assessment in some instances, though carefully planned testing programs were used in others.

Comparison of proposals.   Closely related to testing, review, and reformulation of proposals is the phase of screening or considering various related but alternative proposals. This phase might well have been revealed as being associated with the activities of external participants (such as national curriculum groups) had their complete efforts been analyzed. In a few illustrations of the curricular change process in local school systems, there was clear evidence of a careful process of proposal-screening. This took various forms, such as study groups charged with examining alternative mathematics programs or team teaching efforts, the use of outside consultants or expert opinion, and the establishment of local reviewing committees to examine local efforts.

Phases initiated by internal participants

The two other phases identified, in the cases studied, were action on proposals, and implementation of an action decision. These by their very nature required decisions from internal participants, although external participants might wield considerable influence as well.

Action on proposals. From what has been said, it is probably clear that only internal participants could make the actual decision to adopt a change in a particular school or school system. Often, the initial action or decision involved only the adoption of a purpose or of a general proposal (such as the introduction of science instruction in the elementary grades). In other instances, it involved rather detailed action on one or more of the determiners (staffing, pupils to be served, subject matter or content, methods, materials, and time allotment).

This phase gave evidence of a great variety of practice, both within and among school systems. Authorizing agents and the approval process varied widely, not only from one school system to another, but within a single school system for different change proposals.

Implementation of an action decision. This phase varied widely with the specific change proposal. However, the extent and nature of the implementation or dissemination process was under the control of internal participants. Some changes, naturally, involved only the employment of new staff (such as a teacher of Spanish). Some could merely be announced to existing staff (such as the decision to refurnish a science laboratory). Some changes involved the use of national agencies for retraining teachers, as in the case of the newer mathematics content. Others involved extensive local staff retraining, as in the case of instituting team teaching. Sometimes this dissemination phase was carefully planned in advance; at other times it was disregarded, or attended to only when some intended change appeared to be in danger of failing.

General Observations

The analysis just presented omits some impressions, gathered in working with the case descriptions, which may be worth reporting.

First, many of the illustrations revealed two consequences other than the intended purpose of the change. One was the development of *concomitant or side effects.* For example, one program developed to raise standards and focus more sharply on rigorously defined content increased the failure and drop-out rate. In another instance, the introduction of a plan for the redeployment of staff served to lower morale greatly. One might guess that planning and preliminary exploratory work had been inadequate in many such instances. In some cases, efforts to make a specific change were reported as having resulted in some other program improvements than the one being sought (heightened morale, for example). Another unintended consequence of change efforts, quite commonly observed, was *failure to establish the intended change*. Sometimes this was immediate; in other instances it was a gradual withering away of a change in some later phase. This usually appeared to be a result of inadequate planning, insufficient staff preparation, lack of commitment by the staff or the community, or other deficiencies in resources or power.

A second general observation relates to the source of curricular change. Both internal and external participants initiated changes, as has already been reported. However, external participants (such as foundations, and influential writers and speakers) appear to have been the dominant initiators in the relatively recent examples studied. This seems to conflict with much of the professional literature, which implies that educators themselves have been the primary source of curricular changes.

Finally, this analysis is only a beginning step toward a valid description of the process of curricular change under current conditions. More complete and adequate descriptions should be gathered and analyzed to check the validity of this presentation. Trained interviewers and observers, working more systematically within selected areas (such as mathematics, team teaching, or reading) and studying changes occurring in communities in various parts of the country, might contribute much. Once the existing system by which curricular changes take place is understood, there are further tasks in discovering how this system can be managed so as to obtain desired results.

References

Lasswell, H. D. *Politics: who gets what, when, how.* New York: Meridian Books, 1958.

Lasswell, H. D., & Kaplan, A. *Power and society: a framework for political inquiry.* New Haven: Yale University Press, 1950.

Lasswell, H. D., Leites, N., & associates. *Language of politics.* New York: George W. Stewart, 1949.

Merriam, C. E. *Political power: its composition and incidence.* New York: Whittlesey House, 1934.

CHAPTER 18

Administrative theory
and change in organizations

DANIEL E. GRIFFITHS

THE OBSERVER of social organizations is forced to the conclusion that organizations are *not* characterized by change. Indeed, when organizations are viewed over a long period of time, their outstanding characteristic appears to be stability, rather than change. A social organization is the structural mechanism employed by a society to achieve one or more of its commonly accepted goals. Since the goals do not change noticeably and each organization's activities are rather clearly demarcated, any particular organization comes into existence with a great deal of built-in stability. This stability is so great as to constitute a powerful resistance to change.[1] On the other hand, it is clear that organizations *do* change. In many the increments of change are small, but in others change is so radical as to cause the disappearance of the original organization and the appearance of a new one.

The Roman Catholic Church is an excellent example of a highly stable organization, existing in the same form over a long period of time. Its organizational goals have varied but little since its inception, yet it has changed. The changes have generally been small and well

---

[1] See Presthus (1962), especially Chapters 1 and 2, for an analysis of the way in which system forces prevent change in organizations.

THE AUTHOR is Associate Dean, School of Education, New York University.

spaced, and have tended to vary internal procedures or policies necessary to defend the Church against an unfriendly environment. Radical
changes, on the other hand, are illustrated by governmental revolu-
tions. The overthrow of the Tsarist regime in Russia and the eventual
rule of the Bolshevists point up the fact that an organization (the
governing body) can change to such a degree that it is completely replaced.

It should be noted in both these cases that the stimulus for change
came from *outside* the organization. It would not be a far-fetched pre-
sumption to state that the hierarchies of the Catholic Church and of
the Tsarist government alike would have much preferred to go on
as they had been going.

There are few empirical measures of the initiation of change in
organizations. However, the one most familiar to the writer substanti-
ates the basic assumption of this paper. A measure called *Organizational Change* was developed as part of the scoring procedure in a
study of the administrative performance of elementary school principals in a simulated school (Hemphill, Griffiths, & Frederiksen,
1962). The average score (highest possible, 70) was 5.88; standard
deviation, 2.92; and odd-even reliability, .61. The observer of change
must reconcile himself to study of the infrequent, not the frequent,
in organizational life.

This paper attempts to state a theory of administrative change
which will, at least in part, account for some of the commonly made
observations concerning change in organizations. Space limitations
prevent a full description of detailed observations of change in organizations. The questions to which the theory is addressed are: (1)
Under what conditions does change occur? (2) Under what conditions is change least apt to occur?

Definitions: Organization, Administration, Change

It is necessary to say what is meant by the terms *organization, administration,* and *change.*

First of all, only *formal* organization is being considered; this term
is construed to mean an ensemble of individuals who perform distinct
but interrelated and coordinated functions, in order that one or more
tasks may be completed. Thus we have the public school, the army,

the governmental bureau, the business company. In each type of organization, the task is more or less clearly understood and approved by the public. It is obvious that organizations are, at least to some extent, a consequence of division of labor in society. It follows that any one organization functions as part of a larger social system (Griffiths, 1959, p. 77).

What Kaufman (1961, p. 39) has to say about organizations is also acceptable as contributing to a definition of the concept:

> The term *organization* will refer to all sets of human beings who exhibit the following five properties . . . :
>
> 1. Some criterion or set of criteria by which *members* may be distinguished from non-members (i.e., demarcation of boundaries, though not necessarily territorial boundaries);
>
> 2. Some method of *replenishment* of materials used up by the members (also, for long-lived organizations, some methods of *replacing personnel* lost by the organization through death, departure, disablement, or other factors);
>
> 3. *Elicitation of effort* of some kind by individual members of the organization;
>
> 4. *Coordination* of individual activities—that is to say, some blending of the methods of eliciting effort and the methods of inhibiting activity such that the timing and character of each member's activities facilitate, or at least do not impede, the activities of other members.
>
> 5. Some pattern of *distribution* of materials and messages among the members, and perhaps of movement of people as well.

In summary, a formal *organization* comprises a number of people who perform a task sanctioned by the society in which it functions. The members of the organization are visible as such to the public, work together, and have methods of replenishing the organization with both materials and members.

The term *administration* is used to designate the process (cycle of events) engaged in by all the members of the formal organization to direct and control the activities of the members of the organization. Though all members participate in "administration," there is of course differential distribution of influence within the organization. Those members who are officially charged with the functions of administration are called *administrators* (Griffiths, 1959).

It is assumed that educational organizations do not differ in essential characteristics from any other type of formal organization. When one uses definitions such as those employed above, it is difficult to imagine what the differences could be.

The word *change* is used to mean an alteration in the structure of the organization, in any of its processes, or in its goals or purposes. The revision of a rule, the introduction of a new procedure, or the revision of the purposes or direction of the organization are all subsumed under the concept of change. There are different degrees of change; a variation in a teacher's lunchroom assignment might be considered a minor change, and the reconstituting of a public school system to include a junior college might be considered a major change.

The Model: System Theory

The model employed in building this theory of administrative change is system theory as discussed by Hearn (1958). Although Hearn's ideas are based upon those of Miller (1955) and other system theorists, his careful work is a definite improvement over that of his predecessors.

Systems

A *system* may be simply defined as a complex of elements in mutual interaction. This construct has been used in almost every area of science for a long period of time. Allport (1955, p. 469) offered a more comprehensive definition:

> . . . any recognizably delimited aggregate of dynamic elements that are in some way interconnected and interdependent and that continue to operate together according to certain laws and in such a way as to produce some characteristic total effect. A system, in other words, is something that is concerned with some kind of activity and preserves a kind of integration and unity; and a particular system can be recognized as distinct from other systems to which, however, it may be dynamically related. Systems may be complex; they may be made up of interdependent sub-systems, each of which, though less autonomous than the entire aggregate, is nevertheless fairly distinguishable in operation.

A more succinct definition is that of Hall and Fagen (1956, p. 18): "A system is a set of objects together with relationships between the objects and between their attributes."

All systems except the smallest have *sub-systems,* and all but the largest have *supra-systems* which are their environments.

Systems may be *open* or *closed*. An open system is related to and makes exchanges with its environment, while a closed system is not related to and does not make exchanges with its environment. Further, a closed system is characterized by an increase in entropy, while open systems tend toward a steady state.

Open systems

Open systems, of course, have the properties of systems in general, but also have certain characteristics which distinguish them from closed systems (Hearn, 1958).

1. Open systems exchange matter, energy, and information with their environment; that is, they have *inputs* and *outputs*.

2. Open systems tend to maintain themselves in *steady states*. A steady state occurs when a constant ratio is maintained among the components of the system, given a continuous input to the system. A burning candle is often used as an example of a steady state. Upon being lighted the flame is small, but it rapidly grows to its normal size and maintains the size as long as the candle and its environment exist.

3. Open systems are *self-regulating*. In the illustration above, a sudden draft will cause the flame to flicker, but with the cessation of the draft the flame regains its normal characteristics.

4. Open systems display *equifinality;* that is, identical results can be obtained from different initial conditions. Hearn points out that equifinality in the human being (an open system) is illustrated by the case of two babies, one born prematurely, the other at full term. The babies may look very different at birth, and may be in different stages of development, but within a few months the differences will have disappeared. Even though the initial states may differ, human beings generally achieve the same stages of development.

5. Open systems maintain their steady states, in part, through the *dynamic interplay of sub-systems operating as functional processes.* This means that the various parts of the system function without persistent conflicts that can be neither resolved nor regulated.

6. Open systems maintain their steady states through *feedback* processes. The concept of feedback as used in system theory is more elaborate than its normal usage implies. The reader is referred to Hearn (1958) for a full discussion. In general, feedback refers to that portion of the output of a system which is fed back to the input

and affects succeeding outputs, and to the property of being able to adjust future conduct by reference to past performance.

7. Open systems display *progressive segregation* (von Bertalanffy, 1950). This process occurs when the system divides into a hierarchical order of subordinate systems, which gain a certain independence of each other.

Hearn (1958, pp. 48–49) summarizes the properties of *open* or *organismic systems* in this manner:

> There is a dynamic interplay among the essential functional sub-processes or sub-systems in the organismic system which enables it to maintain itself in a homeostatic steady state. Assuming a sufficient input of material from its environment, the organism develops toward a characteristic state despite initial conditions (equifinality). All of this is accomplished through an automatic self-regulatory process.

A Theory of Administrative Change

It is proposed that system theory serve as a model for a theory of administrative change. As indicated above, any open system has supra-systems and sub-systems. Let an organization be considered as an open system, comprised of human interactions, that maintains a definite boundary. Further, consider administration as an open sub-system, and the environment as a supra-system. The administration sub-system is located at the point of tangency of the three systems, as in Figure 1.

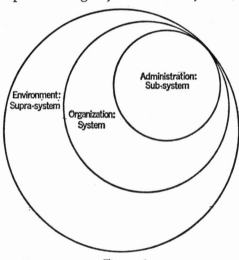

Figure 1

Infrequency of change

The above model for a theory of administrative change would lead one to hypothesize that change would be relatively infrequent. Open systems maintain themselves in steady states (a constant ratio is maintained among the components of the system), whereas change calls for the establishment of new ratios among the components of the system. One could also argue on purely logical grounds that society establishes organizations, or sanctions their establishment, to accomplish rather specific purposes. It is, in part, this original sanction that gives organizations their characteristic steady state.

Conditions aiding change

Although it is infrequent, change does occur in organizations; at times the change is radical. Under what conditions might change be expected to occur?

Several characteristics of open systems were discussed in the presentation of the model. Some of these have relevance here: input–output, steady state, self-regulation, interplay of sub-systems, feedback, and progressive segregation. An examination of these characteristics leads to several ideas about organizational change.

Since the tendency of organizations is to maintain a steady state, the major impetus for change comes from outside rather than inside an organization. Since organizations are open systems, they have a self-regulating characteristic which causes them to revert to the original state following a minor change made to meet demands of the supra-system.

Many organizations bring in outsiders as administrators, believing that change for the better will result. This apparently works in many cases, and the proposed theory can accommodate this observation. All organizations exhibit some form of progressive segregation or hierarchical order. The order makes it possible for change to occur from the top down but practically impossible for it to occur from the bottom up.

These ideas and others are now formulated as a series of propositions.

Proposition 1. The major impetus for change in organizations is from the outside.

Discussion.   It is speculated that when change in an organization does occur, the initiative for the change is from outside the system—that is, from the supra-system. In the study of elementary school principals mentioned above, it was found that those who scored relatively higher on *Organizational Change* were not aggressive leaders as such, but administrators with a tendency to make changes in the organization to please outsiders and superiors, or to comply with suggestions of subordinates (Hemphill et al., 1962). The correlation between the *Organizational Change* score and response to outsiders was somewhat higher than the correlation between the *Organizational Change* score and response to subordinates. The nature of changes made in response to outsiders and insiders was not determined in this study, but it could be hypothesized that changes made in response to insiders will be concerned with clarification of rules and internal procedures, while those made in response to outsiders will be concerned with *new* rules and procedures, and possibly with changes in purpose and direction of the organization. It appears that administrators who initiate change are influenced more by those outside the system than by those inside.

Practical administrators are well aware of this proposition. The use of consultants, evaluation teams, citizens' committees, and professional organizations to bring change to an organization suggests a clear recognition on the part of administrators that an organization is more apt to change in response to an external force than to an internal force.

Proposition 2.   The degree and duration of change is directly proportional to the intensity of the stimulus from the supra-system.

Discussion.   As an illustration of the proposition (but not, of course, as proof of it), it has been noted that the rate of instructional innovation in New York State public schools more than doubled within fifteen months of the launching of the Soviet Sputnik I; this increase was maintained through 1961 (Brickell, 1961, p. 27).

In order that this proposition be tested, it will be necessary to establish ways of measuring degree of change and intensity of stimulus. Duration is simply a matter of time. If the suggested measurements could be made, the proposition could be tested in all of its ramifications.

Proposition 3.   Change in an organization is more probable if the successor to the chief administrator is from outside the organization, than if he is from inside the organization.

Discussion.   The model specifies feedback as a characteristic of open systems. Feedback tends to maintain the system in a steady state. The administrator who comes from outside does not receive feedback from his actions, since well-established channels for feedback to him do not exist. When an insider is appointed to the top post in an organization, the feedback channels which have been established over the years function to keep him operating in the steady state.

An outsider may bring change into an organization out of sheer ignorance. Not knowing the system, he will function in terms of a system which he *does* know. Being without ties in the system, he will not receive the feedback that would keep an insider from initiating procedures and policies differing from those in use.

The insider will also keep the sub-systems functioning without conflicts, since he knows how these sub-systems function to maintain the steady state. The outsider may upset the functioning of the sub-systems, through either ignorance or design. Not knowing how sub-systems function, he can inadvertently throw them into conflict through orders or expectations not customarily held for these systems. On the other hand, he may introduce conflict among the sub-systems, by purposefully changing their functions. This will, of course, upset the steady state and may in time create a state more to the liking of the chief administrator. The notion of controlled conflict as a method of change in an organization may have a sound theoretical base.

In a study of school superintendents, Carlson (1961) found that those appointed from inside the system tend to act in such a way as to maintain the system, while those appointed from outside tend to be innovators.

Proposition 4.   "Living systems respond to continuously increasing stress first by a lag in response, then by an over-compensatory response, and finally by catastrophic collapse of the system." (Miller, 1955, p. 525)

Discussion.   What happens to a system subjected to constantly increasing stress? Miller has formulated the above proposition, which appears to have much relevance to education. As public education is attacked (for example, on the teaching of reading), it responds by proclaiming a strong defense. The schools claim that they have been teaching reading well. In those districts where the defense was not strong enough and the attack grew even stronger, the schools responded by changing their methods of teaching reading. The proposition has not been tested fully, because at this point the stress has always been lifted.

Revolutionary changes occur when the prediction of this proposition is carried through to completion. The collapse of the old system is followed by the establishment of a new system.

Conditions inhibiting change

Many of the characteristics of organizations are such that they make the initiation of change difficult. When organizations are viewed in terms of the system-theory model these characteristics appear very clearly.

Proposition 5. The number of innovations is inversely proportional to the tenure of the chief administrator.

Discussion. The longer an administrator stays in a position, the less likely he is to introduce change. The model indicates some reasons for this. All of the processes which bring about the steady state have been given time to operate. Feedback channels have become fully established. Progressive segregation has set in; the sub-systems have become structured and have gained relative independence. Change is thus more difficult, because the frequency of interaction between sub-systems is decreased, and the chances for effective communication are diminished.

Proposition 6. The more hierarchical the structure of an organization, the less the possibility of change.

Discussion. The system-theory model points out that a characteristic of open systems is progressive segregation, and this occurs as the system divides into a hierarchical order of subordinate systems which gain a degree of independence of each other. The more hierarchical the sub-systems become, the more independent the sub-systems, and the more difficult it is to introduce change.

Proposition 7. When change in an organization does occur, it will tend to occur from the top down, not from the bottom up.

Discussion. Using the same reasoning as in Proposition 6, a hierarchical order would enable change to occur from the top down, but the relative independence of the sub-systems would tend to slow down the rate of change. The structure makes change from the bottom up very difficult; one would expect little if any change to be introduced in this way.

Proposition 8. The more functional the dynamic interplay of sub-systems, the less the change in an organization.

Discussion. As a system operates, the sub-systems develop methods of interacting in which conflict is at a minimum. Each of the sub-systems has a function to perform, and each does so in such a manner as to allow it to maintain a high degree of harmony with the others. Each says to the others, in effect, "If you don't rock the boat, I won't." Change is practically synonymous with conflict, since it means that the arrangements the sub-systems have worked out no longer hold. Sub-systems resist conflict, and in the same manner resist change.

Summary

Using system theory as a model, this paper develops a set of propositions concerning change in organizations. The propositions are restated briefly in the following paragraphs.

Change in organizations will be expedited by the appointment of outsiders rather than insiders as chief administrators. Such administrators will introduce change either because they do not know the system, or because they have a different concept of how the system should function. Most changes result as responses to the demands of the supra-system. The magnitude and duration of change is directly proportional to the intensity of the stimulus from outside. Revolutionary change occurs when a system is placed under continuous, unrelenting stress which is maintained in spite of overcompensating responses, and which results in the collapse of the system and its replacement by a new system.

Change is impeded by the hierarchical nature of organizations. The hierarchical structure makes innovation from the bottom virtually impossible, and the independence of the sub-systems isolates them from innovative activity. The functional nature of the activities of each sub-system generates conflict-reducing behavior which, again, is counter to change-inducing behavior. Further, the longer the tenure of the chief administrator, the fewer the changes.

References

Allport, F. H. *Theories of perception and the concept of structure.* New York: Wiley, 1955.

Brickell, H. M. *Commissioner's 1961 catalog of educational change.* Albany, New York: State Education Department, 1961.

Carlson, R. O. Succession and performance among school superintendents. *Admin. Sci. Quart.* 1961, 6, 210–227.

Griffiths, D. E. *Administrative theory.* New York: Appleton-Century-Crofts, 1959.

Hall, A. D., & Fagen, R. E. General systems. In L. von Bertalanffy & A. Rapoport (Eds.), *Yearbook of the Society for the Advancement of General Systems Theory.* Ann Arbor: Braun-Brumfield, 1956.

Hearn, G. *Theory building in social work.* Toronto: University of Toronto Press, 1958.

Hemphill, J., Griffiths, D. E., & Frederiksen, N. *Administrative performance and personality.* New York: Bureau of Publications, Teachers College, Columbia University, 1962. Esp. Chap. 8.

Kaufman, H. Why organizations behave as they do: an outline of a theory. In *Papers presented at an interdisciplinary seminar on administrative theory.* Austin: University of Texas, 1961.

Miller, J. G. Toward a general theory for the behavioral sciences. *Amer. Psychol.,* 1955, 10, 513–531.

Presthus, R. *The organizational society.* New York: Knopf, 1962.

von Bertalanffy, L. An outline of general systems theory. *Brit. Jour. Philos. Sci.,* 1950, 1, 148.

CHAPTER 19

On temporary systems

MATTHEW B. MILES

WHEN we are asked to examine the social life around us, most of us tend to think of durable, permanent structures. The school, the college, the government agency, the industrial corporation, a particular family, the church, the community agency, the army—all are structures destined for extended life. The participants in such structures ordinarily expect them to exist for an indefinitely long period; they promise to love, honor, and obey until death do us part, and assume that the school, the corporation, and the welfare agency will all outlast the tenure of any particular member. This implied permanency is of course crucial for the continuous existence of a stable social structure incorporating many such substructures. Thus it is natural that almost all sociological inquiry has focused its attention on the properties of enduring social systems. And administrators ordinarily consider the continued survival of their organizations as a primary good.

Yet, reflection shows us this: within the connected framework of organizations and groups constituting any particular society, there is a very large number of interstitial, temporary structures. These structures operate both within permanent organizations and between them;

THE AUTHOR is Research Associate, Horace Mann–Lincoln Institute of School Experimentation, and Associate Professor of Psychology and Education, Teachers College, Columbia University.

their members hold from the start the basic assumption that—at some more or less clearly defined point in time—they will cease to be. The range and scope of such temporary structures is almost bewilderingly wide. For example:

1. *Conferences,* conventions, religious retreats, training institutes, and revival meetings appear everywhere, with objectives as diverse as that of increasing sales of TV sets, developing skills of teaching a foreign language, increasing religious commitment, and creating employment opportunities for promising young Ph.D.'s in history; such systems are designed to alter or benefit their participants in some way.

2. *Games* of all sorts attract vigorous emotional investment from participants and onlookers; they seem to have a renewing, recreating function of a very deep sort, and may indeed be seen as manifesting the major underlying concerns of any given culture, while ministering to them in clever ways (see Huizinga, 1938; Caillois, 1961).

3. *Juries* have a sharply limited lifetime, yet (or perhaps *thus* are enabled to?) exert the power of life and death over others.

4. The very impermanence of *love affairs*—often tacitly agreed to by both participants at the outset—appears to exert special effects (for example, zest and spontaneity) which are difficult to sustain in more durable relationships.

5. *Ad hoc "task forces"* or project teams, focused around the short-term accomplishment of specific goals (e.g., adding a second deck to the George Washington Bridge; developing a miniaturized satellite TV transmitter; investigating philanthropic foundations) are a pervasive feature of most modern organizations, particularly those operating in the midst of steadily changing conditions (cf. Burns & Stalker, 1961, pp. 120–121).

6. Intensive *personnel assessment programs,* such as those carried out by the military services during World War II (OSS Assessment Staff, 1945) and by researchers (Hemphill, Griffiths & Frederiksen, 1962) involve the participants in a residential social system for a clearly marked-off period of time.

7. Some form of *carnival,* as a decidedly temporary, institutionalized release system, appears in many societies. The office Christmas party seems to perform broadly similar functions on a miniature scale.

8. For centuries men have proposed—and in some cases carried out—social systems designed to demonstrate a vision of the world in purified form; these *Utopias* (see Ozmon, 1962; Infield, 1955) are ordinarily not entered into as permanent arrangements, but as fictional or actual demonstrations which may serve as a force toward altering the surrounding society. Most actual Utopias have indeterminate durations, usually terminated by dissolution or incorporation into the surrounding system, but are not ordinarily considered permanent.

9. The basic or applied *research project* is also an undertaking sharply limited at the outset in terms of its effective life. Like the task force, it is a system set up to discover or apply a certain brand of knowledge, and will die, like all temporary systems, at some more or less clearly defined date. The scientific expedition also falls in this general category.

10. Government is rich in temporary systems; the organizations which develop around an *office holder* (executive, legislative, or judicial) are strongly influenced by the defined time at which tenure in the position ends. A particular *session of a lawmaking body,* such as Congress, also contains many temporary system features, although the institution itself can be thought of as permanent. And all sorts of *inter-governmental structures*—disarmament talks, test-ban discussions, and summit meetings —are decisively temporary.

11. The political or social *demonstration* aimed at protesting a policy or correcting injustice also occurs in a limited chronological period. Token strikes, sit-ins, a March on Washington—all require close planning and organization of resources in a system which may only live for a few hours.

12. We may think of a *military battle* as a temporary social system of meaningful sort on a large scale, although termination dates are not fixed ahead of time, as they are in most of the other examples cited.[1]

13. The *psychotherapeutic system* formed by therapist and client is clearly defined as temporary at the outset, although the termination date may be imprecise. The client is entering a two-person (or, in the case of group treatment, multi-person) system which is defined as existing only long enough for certain objectives (self-insight, comfort, increased ego strength, etc.) to be reached.

14. The *consulting system* formed by a consultant and a client group or organization can be thought of as a temporary arrangement as well; a permanent organization has a newcomer attached to it for a (usually specified) period of time, thus forming, in effect, a new system. "Team training" (Blake, Blansfield, & Mouton, 1962), in which a superior, his subordinates and a consultant leave the organization for a few days to analyze their operations and plan improvements, has the same character.

Most of the systems mentioned above are "temporary" for all their members. A special, "impure" type of temporary system involves a permanent cadre, but an ever-changing series of cohorts of "clients"

---

[1] This example leads to the question of whether *unplanned* events which mobilize high effort in a small period of time (such as political crises, mobs, panics, and physical disasters) can be classified as temporary systems. In general, it seems best to exclude them, since the onset of such systems is usually adventitious, and terminal times usually remain vague. This implies that the notion of *willedness* is important in considering temporary systems.

of the system, whose sojourn is defined as temporary. Though these are permanent systems, they are temporary *for the client* (if we except lifers in prisons), and certain temporary system phenomena (such as alteration of time perspective as a function of expected discharge date) are very pronounced. Cumming & Cumming (1962, p. 94) have dramatized perceived temporariness in the mental hospital:

> The individual stands at a nodal point between his past and a future that he expects to be recognizably similar to the present or, more precisely, reconcilable with his projected identity—it should never be forgotten that any therapeutic milieu is a *temporary* arrangement, and the patient must always be helped to project a post-clinic or post-hospital self concept and ego identity.

Some examples of this type of temporary system:

15. The *"total institution"* (Goffman, 1961; Cumming & Cumming, 1962), which has complete or near-complete control over its clients, has many variants: the mental hospital, the prison, the welfare home, the orphanage.

16. So-called *"pathway organizations"* (Landy & Wechsler, 1960), serve to aid an institutional client as he passes from a total institution (for example, a mental hospital) to the surrounding community.

17. And, of course, we have nontotal organizations called *schools* and *colleges*, with a steady turnover of clients who perceive their sojourn in the immediately permanent system to be clearly temporary.[2]

Types and Functions of Temporary Systems

The variety and range of these illustrations indicate the pervasiveness of the temporary system. Two rough typologies (Charts 1 and 2) may be of aid in identifying the foci for this chapter more clearly.

The duration of temporary systems

The defining concept in a temporary system is, of course, anticipated duration. The termination point of a system may be (1) identified chronologically and explicitly (the workshop is over at noon on June 28), (2) linked to the occurrence of a specified event (the research project is over when the manuscript is sent to the printer), or (3) made contingent on the achievement of a general state of affairs

[2] It is illuminating to note, in Watson's chapter of the present book, that students in an experimental college without a defined "graduation" date experienced discomfort about the indeterminacy of their tenure.

(the psychoanalysis is over when patient and analyst agree that the patient can function adequately).

In addition, the distinction between systems which are temporary for all members and those which are temporary for clients only is important.

TERMINATION OF SYSTEM MEMBERSHIP	TEMPORARY MEMBERSHIP HELD BY:	
	All persons	Clients only
Chronological, time–linked	Workshop, conference, etc. Carnival Presidential staff	Prison Personnel assessment program School, college
Event–linked	Game such as tennis Research project "Task force" group	Orphanage
State (condition)–linked	Psychotherapy Game such as poker Love affair Utopia Consultant-client relationship	Welfare home Mental hospital

Chart 1. Temporary systems classified by time use

It seems likely that temporary system phenomena will be strongest in the "pure case"—the cell in the upper left corner where all members enter and leave the system at the same, prespecified, time—and correspondingly more attention will be given here to this type.[3]

The functions of temporary systems

Any temporary system can be examined in terms of its focus of attention (individuals, or larger systems), and in terms of its major function. Presumably temporary systems would not be as pervasive as they are if they did not perform certain necessary functions. Some reflection on the examples listed above suggests that these may be of three general sorts.

Compensation, maintenance. Temporary systems like carnivals, love affairs, Christmas parties, games of all sorts, theatrical entertainments, parades, spectator sports events, political rallies, and conven-

---

[3] Such systems may, of course, have differentiated roles within them, such as those of conference staff member and participant. The point is that such systems are set up from scratch, and do not have durable inhabitants who process a steady flow of clients.

tions of school administrators (Holman, 1961) appear to serve the function of maintaining a person (or group or organization) in the surrounding social system. They supply various sorts of compensation for the slings and arrows of normal social life, and provide expressive outlets not directly related to the accomplishment of any task, or to the alteration of persons, groups, or organizations. That is, such systems serve the function usually assigned to informal organization: that of absorbing, counteracting, and making up for the malformations caused by formal organization, as well as enabling spontaneous, rich participation of the person in areas of his life seen as largely irrelevant to "work."

FUNCTION OF SYSTEM	FOCUS OF ATTENTION	
	Person	Group or organization
Compensation, maintenance	Game Party Vacation, travel	Carnival, office party Recognition banquet
Short-term task accomplishment	Research project Artists' colony	Task force Scientific expedition
Change: treatment	Psychodrama Psychotherapy Social casework	Consultant-organization relationship ("sociotherapy")
Change: re-educative	Sociodrama Human relations training laboratory Teacher training institute Brainwashing	Simulation exercise Survey feedback method Team training
Change: educative	School or college class Golf lesson	Ad hoc committee Educational experiment Utopia

Chart 2. Temporary systems classified by function

Short-term task accomplishment. A second general function of temporary systems is that of providing an arena for the accomplishment of particular tasks—more expeditiously or productively than in a permanent system. The research project, the industrial "task force," the *ad hoc* committee, the scientific expedition, the jury, the political campaign committee—all are assembled to focus on particular tasks, and they dissolve when their mission is completed. They need not carry all the historical freight of the permanent systems from which their members are drawn; in them, all energies can be directed single-mindedly toward the defined task.

The induction of change. Finally—and perhaps most centrally—temporary systems are set up to bring about changes in persons, groups, and organizations. The conference, the psychotherapeutic relationship, the religious retreat, team training, the "pilot project," the Utopia, and the consultant–client relationship are all aimed in this direction.

For many reasons, permanent systems—whether persons, groups, or organizations—find it difficult to change themselves. The major portion of available energy goes to (1) carrying out routine goal-directed operations and (2) maintenance of existing relationships within the system. Thus the fraction of energy left over for matters of diagnosis, planning, innovation, deliberate change, and growth is ordinarily very small. (For example: a professor steadily complains of his work load, but never takes time out to understand reasons for it and plan corrective action; a company finds its share of market steadily declining, but only tries to work harder at what it is already doing ineffectively.)

Other antichange forces—besides sheer unavailability of energy—exist within permanent systems. Feedback loops keep the system in a steady state (see Griffiths' chapter in the present book). Restriction of communication occurs (partly in order to maintain existing status relationships); different parts of the system have incomplete, distorted ideas of what is occurring in other parts. Blame assignment develops; particular persons or groups are seen as "causing" difficulties, which can supposedly be corrected by attacking or eliminating the offending part of the system. Yet status maintenance needs mean that such attacks are very unlikely to result in any lasting improvement.[4]

Thus innovation in permanent systems is very difficult.[5] But by re-

---

[4] Note that these stability-giving forces in permanent systems apply just as centrally to *individuals,* seen as systems, as they do to groups and organizations. Individuals are committed to "business as usual"; they employ durable feedback loops which only confirm their own pictures of themselves; they do not fully understand all that is going on within their skins; they pick out and blame parts of themselves ("I'm lazy," "I'm too impulsive") in a way that dooms any real effort to change.

[5] Huizinga (1938, p. 12) illustrates this charmingly: the innovator in a game is frequently seen as a "spoilsport," one who questions the very structure of the game itself; he thus (in the interests of maintenance of the game as a

sorting to temporary systems, many of these characteristic antichange forces can be avoided or bypassed. It is no coincidence (see Chapter 1 of the present book) that a large proportion of current efforts at educational innovation involve the creation of temporary (or quasi-temporary) systems.

The major focus of this chapter will be on the change-inducing properties of temporary systems. It may therefore be useful to differentiate that function somewhat.

Treatment systems consider their mission to be that of correcting deviancy, or restoring a pathologically functioning person, group, or organization to a state of health (see Vinter, 1962). Examples at the personal level are easy to locate (psychotherapy, etc.); at the level of the larger system, one thinks of Pages' (1959) "sociotherapy of the enterprise," where a consultant helps an organization correct its pathological aspects.

Re-educative systems tend to begin with an unlearning or corrective phase in the change effort, followed by a relearning phase in which new material replaces that which has been discarded. Much adult learning is re-educative, as in the case of human relations training laboratories, National Science Foundation teacher training institutes, and brainwashing attempts; the person must give up or "unfreeze" old, durable habits and attitudes before the new can be assimilated. At the organization level, the survey feedback method seems re-educative; attitude data collected from all organization members are summarized and fed back to help unfreeze existing stereotypes and assumptions, before planning and new learning take place. "Team training," and various simulation exercises, such as business games, also seem to involve an unlearning–relearning sequence.

Finally, though all education has been asserted to be re-education in some fundamental sense, it does seem true that some temporary systems are basically *educative*—designed to add *new* knowledge, skills, practices, or attitudes to a person or group, with little attention to prior unlearning of established (and presumably interfering) material. The usual school or college class is an example, as are the

---

steady state) encounters more resistance (and perhaps more punishment) than does the cheat, who does not publicly question the rules, but only seeks to exploit them for his own ends.

Utopia, the *ad hoc* committee charged with improving some aspect of organizational functioning, and the educational experiment.[6]

The focus of this chapter

This introductory discussion of the duration-types and the functions of temporary systems has indicated their pervasiveness and importance. The emphasis in the remainder of the chapter will be on temporary systems of the "pure" sort—those in which all participants enter and leave at the same time—and on the *change-inducing* aspects of those systems. The general thesis being advanced is that temporary systems are not only powerfully educative in themselves, but can be a prime mechanism for bringing about innovation in "permanent" educational systems.

The chapter will continue with several case studies of temporary systems designed to cause changes in persons and organizations, then focus on recurrent features which seem common to most temporary systems: "input" characteristics involved when the system is designed or set up, "process" characteristics occurring during the life of the system, and "output" characteristics—the resultant changes in persons, groups, and organizations. Following this, some problematic or dysfunctional aspects of temporary systems are reviewed, and concluding implications for educational innovation are drawn. The cases and examples used are not intended, of course, to "prove" the assertions made, but serve to illustrate and clarify them.

Illustrative Cases

To give concreteness to the idea of "temporary system," three cases are described briefly below, with a minimum of analysis. In them, the reader can note the phenomena which flow from the fact that all participants know from the outset that the system is not permanent, but will terminate at a specified time. The three systems described

---

[6] This typology does not include the aspect of time utilization within the life of the system. Some temporary systems operate serially (classes, psychotherapy); others occupy a single, intensive block of time (conferences, institutes, research projects, etc.). The latter (time-concentrated) type tends to produce more pronounced temporary-system phenomena, and thus will receive more emphasis in this chapter.

were respectively aimed at changing the program of an organization, changing persons, and changing the structure of an organization.

Case A: a program-changing system

During the summer of 1962, an educational "experiment" was carried out in the New York City public schools, to test the effects of certain program innovations on the performance of children with academic deficiencies.[7]

The work took place at a junior high school, and involved two principals, forty teachers, and about 1,500 pupils in grades seven to nine. "They taught each other that most of New York's education problems could be remedied with enough good teachers, able leadership, and devotion to effort."

"Most [of the children] arrived with severe academic deficiencies, but more than eighty per cent passed their math work, and seventy-six [per cent] passed English." The undertaking was blessed by an associate superintendent of schools, and used ninety-minute classroom sessions, with classes ranging in size from five to thirty students, depending on the children's needs.

"The general atmosphere and reaction of students and teachers appeared to be more important than the academic arrangements and the test results . . . although the program was devoid of extracurricular activities and recreational periods, the supervisors said there had not been one disciplinary problem. A number of students insisted on attending voluntarily after being refused course credit either because of late registration or illness. . . ." A mathematics teacher said of the children that "they suddenly appeared to enjoy their work as they grasped the meaning of their lessons."

"Observers stressed that the special faculty became a team. An unusual *esprit de corps* seemed to be the secret ingredient of the successful operation." One of the principals who participated said, "For the first time in I don't know how long, I felt like an educator." He and his associate principal were freed of usual administrative details and paper work. Whenever his associate observed a teacher using effective techniques in the classroom, she simply asked one of the other teachers to sit in and watch the lesson.

[7] This account is drawn from a report by F. M. Hechinger (*New York Times*, Sept. 8, 1962). Quoted material is verbatim.

"Many of the youngsters presented the teachers with mementos on the last day of the session. In a surprise ceremony, the faculty presented a plaque to [the associate superintendent] for making the experiment possible and to [the associate and the principal] for supervising it."

"The supervisors said that even incomplete evaluation indicated the program should become a regular summer procedure."

Case B: a person-changing system

In the summer of 1958, a human relations training conference was attended by 38 persons, most of them elementary school principals, and six staff members.[8] Held in an isolated country setting, the conference was scheduled to last two weeks; it was aimed at improving its members' competence in working with others in interpersonal, group, and organizational settings. The school principals who came were self-selected, having seen a brochure describing the conference activities and goals. They stated on a questionnaire that they wished to learn more about "conditions favorable to cooperativeness," and how to work with groups; they wanted to learn skills of leadership and group decision-making; they wished for attitude changes, such as "becoming more patient with other people"; and they contemplated planning changes in their own work situations, such as "having a voice in selection of my teachers," "improved classroom teaching."

The conference methods were primarily inductive in nature. The staff did little didactic teaching, but designed various "laboratory" group situations in which participants could directly discuss and analyze the effects of their own behavior on others and on group progress. For example, in one type of initially unstructured, leaderless group (the so-called "T-group"), participants were responsible for planning and carrying out their own agenda, and intermittently analyzed the group behavior which occurred during this process. Much emphasis was placed on giving and receiving "feedback," or reports of how the behavior of a person struck others in his group, and on increasing the communication between group members as an aid to learning.

The conference had little or no connection with the rural town in

[8] This account is drawn from Miles *et al.* (forthcoming).

which it was held, but became a miniature, self-contained community, with its own duplicated "newspaper," plus a periodic summary of events in the "world outside"; sports and recreation activities; and an evening "community room," open for refreshments, music, and occasional satirical entertainment.

The general climate of the conference itself grew to be friendly, supportive, and very active. Tension was never low, but the tensions of most persons tended to go into active work on the problems with which they were concerned.

The official work schedule was full; all mornings and early afternoons, and most evenings, were occupied. As the conference developed, participants got more and more deeply involved, discussing their experiences vigorously at meals, during free time, and late into the night. They felt a great deal of commitment and urgency, and sometimes spoke of the conference as being one of the most important learning experiences they had ever encountered. So much seemed to be happening that many members commented on their sense of elapsed time—weeks rather than days appeared to have gone by.

Participants seemed to welcome the conference as an opportunity to stand back from the usual pressures of their work, to re-examine their own working behavior in a setting with others whom they would never see again, with the aid of detached, yet helpful, professional staff. The relationships between staff and participants grew increasingly warm and equalitarian.

Most of the first week of the conference seemed to involve "unlearning" and coming to terms with the situation; following initial uncertainty and bewilderment with the "unstructured," inductive approach, participants increasingly defined their own limits and took responsibility for their own learning. Common norms of conduct developed: these included using the language of the social sciences; being objective, yet involved in trying to understand group events; being open about one's feelings and reactions; being experimental rather than rigid.

During the second week, members seemed to take hold of the situation and exploit it actively for their own learning (see Miles, 1960, for data bearing on this). As the second week developed, learning motivation increased even further; participants made remarks like, "We only have three more days, and I'm anxious to get as much as possible before we break up." In the last days of the conference, members planned actions they might take after returning to their home job situations, counseled with each other and the staff on how these changes might be carried out most productively, and tried to specify some of the learnings which they felt they had developed. In general (see Miles *et al.*, forthcoming) these perceived outcomes appeared to parallel conference aims fairly closely; they dealt with group skills, communication, use of feedback, decision-making, and sensitivity to others.

The conference broke up and participants returned to their own home organizations. A follow-up eight months later disclosed that about 75 per cent of the participants (as measured by self-report and accounts of associates on the job) had improved their behavior in working with others. Most of these changes turned out to focus on group and organizational behavior, and included responses like "gives group more responsibility," "more aware of others' feelings," "receptive to suggestions." Some personal changes were also noted: "relaxed," "more direct and frank." Data from two control groups who did not attend the training indicated that changes of this general sort did occur, but in only 10 to 30 per cent of those surveyed. Thus the training experience had clearly affected the job behavior of participants.

An analysis of the reasons for such changes disclosed that those participants who, during the conference, had (*a*) relaxed their defenses; (*b*) become actively involved in the give-and-take of group discussion; and (*c*) received much feedback on their behavior from other members were those who learned the most and who carried through most effectively on the job.

Case C: a structure-changing system

A large British manufacturing company with more than a dozen scattered plants decided to stage a one-week work conference to deal with an increasingly vexing (and threatening) problem: there existed no systematic, coordinated program for the education and development of the firm's managers.[9] Each of the plants carried out sporadic in-service training activities of various sorts, with relatively unmeas-

[9] The author served as consultant in the design and operation of the conference.

ured and uncertain results. Yet the needs for management education were glaringly apparent, and quite crucial for continued productivity of the firm.

The decision was made to hold a work conference composed of managers from the highest level of the organization (those reporting directly to the Board), supported by middle managers and qualified personnel technicians, to hammer out the details of a company-wide policy on management education and development. A planning committee of middle managers and technicians worked for several months in assessing the current state of affairs in the organization, setting up preliminary study groups, collecting data, preparing sessions and procedures for the work conference itself, and deciding on the content to be covered. The assumption behind the conference was this: if high-level managers could work through their vested interests, their struggles for power and their conflicts with other departments, and agree on an over-all management development program based on adequate technical data, the probability of Board acceptance of the recommendations, and subsequent implementation of them, would be very high. The large amount of advance planning, involving twenty to thirty people for about 200 man-days, appeared to deepen commitment and involvement, and helped to insure that the conference itself would be very carefully staged and operated.

The early part of the conference was mainly devoted to presentations on the current state of management education efforts in the company, the numbers of managers who were likely to be involved, and the problems which they felt to be crucial. Small subgroups of the conference worked meanwhile on such topics as the need for a residential training center; on-the-job training methods which might be used to aid managers; and the organization and structure of an over-all management development program.

Much of the early part of the conference tended to be stiff and defensive. Involvement gradually increased as the managers and staff people present became more concerned with the pressing need to produce final decisions by the end of the week. Members of the Board of the organization appeared at luncheon sessions to talk with the total group; this underlined the importance of the enterprise. There was a good deal of intercommunication among the working subgroups of the conference, by means of general session reports.

The final decisions were scheduled to be made at the end of the week by a "policy-forming group," drawn from the senior members of management present at the conference. At a critical turning point, halfway through the conference, this group took control of the procedures decisively, and specified the classes of decision output which were required from the subgroups (of which they too were members). Involvement and work output increased drastically. In several instances groups worked voluntarily until well after midnight. The emotional tone of the conference became one of eager involvement, extremely hard work, and a kind of equalitarian camaraderie which appeared to transcend pre-existing relationships.[10]

The satisfaction with the final product of the conference—a report detailing the new policy, and the structural organizational changes required for an effective management development program—was high. In addition, there were some unanticipated outcomes of the week: a sharp increase in communication between managers from different levels, plants, and departments; improvements in personal relations with specific others; and more understanding of the nature of effective group problem-solving.

The conference report was forwarded immediately to the Board for decision; some senior conference members accompanied it for interpretation and discussion. The nature and scope of the recommendations, the size and complexity of the company, the existence of other pressing demands, and the past history of indecision and in-fighting were all formidable barriers to rapid action. Yet in less than six weeks the Board decided to accept the report, and appointed a top-level, company-wide coordinator of management development activities. (He turned out, interestingly enough, to be the manager who had chaired the work conference.)

In the eighteen months following the conference, program development proceeded vigorously. A company-wide manager appraisal scheme (resisted for years previously) was installed; seminars dealing with on-the-job training methods were held; consultation on problems at the local plant level was supplied; local committees were developed and their chairmen given training in group problem-solving methods.

Thus a one-week conference seems to have succeeded in changing

[10] One manager, after seven years of work with an associate, learned the associate's first name—and used it.

quite drastically both the structure and functioning of a large organization, in an area replete with a history of misunderstandings, conflict, and inaction.

Recurrent Features of Temporary Systems

These three cases show how temporary systems can be used to alter persons, organizational activities, and organizational structure. Certain regularities are apparent across all three, and seem present in more or less visible form in any temporary system set up for change-inducing purposes. In analyzing these recurrent features, the characteristics of social systems referred to in Chapter 1 of the present book are used. They are organized into "input" characteristics appearing at the time of designing or setting up the temporary system; "process" characteristics occurring during the life of the system; and "output" characteristics—the resultant changes in persons, groups, and organizations.

Input characteristics

Time limits. As has been suggested, the defining characteristic of "pure" temporary systems is that they are expected by participants to terminate at a specified point in time, or when some event or end state (such as finishing the project report, "cure," "solving the problem," etc.) has occurred. The possibility of the temporary system's becoming permanent is never in the foreground, often remains indeterminate, and is frequently out of the question completely.

Kimball & McClellan (1962, pp. 273–275) have suggested that the routinized acceptance of impermanence in all forms of association is an integral feature of contemporary life:

> . . . every group is *ad hoc* in the sense that one's association with it is tempered by the deep, implicit awareness that one must be prepared to leave whenever the proper moment arrives.
>
> The ability to relate oneself effectively to other people . . . and yet be prepared to move at any time is without doubt the most difficult demand placed upon personality by the conditions of life in contemporary society. The fact that we can do it, and often in the absence of any clear rationale for our actions, means that we have been consciously or unconsciously trained in a very effective manner. . . . Thus, in contemporary industrial culture one learns to leave the group.

While the difficulties of *ad hoc* relationships are real and should not be underestimated, there are some other features of time-limited systems which make work in them actually easier and more productive than is possible in permanent systems.

Initial goal definition. One such feature is that temporary systems ordinarily deal with a sharply focused range of content. For example, the principals in Case B above were not attempting to work on all of their job problems as principals, but primarily on human relations aspects of them. The efforts of the teachers and supervisors in Case A were aimed at providing a remedial program in certain subject fields —not at revamping the entire New York City curriculum. The managers and personnel technicians in Case C were devoting primary effort to the problem of management development, leaving aside for the moment the pressing problems of production, materials procurement, marketing (etc.) encountered in the operation of a large industrial enterprise.

Such goal limitation reduces the anxieties associated with choice in a complex organizational setting and encourages what might be called hopefulness. Lewin (1948, pp. 103–104) has defined hope as a "coordination of present reality . . . with the individual's wishes for the future." In a time-limited setting it is perhaps easier to identify future wishes which are not only important, but *achievable.* Under these circumstances, we would expect a high degree of persistency in goal-directed efforts, and a higher expectancy of success. In addition, goal focus tends to produce a "clean slate" effect. The temporary system frees members' energies to concentrate on a particular aspect of a keenly felt problem.

Boundary maintenance operations. In most temporary systems, there is close specification of the classes of personnel who may enter the system for its limited life. And the system's boundaries are usually fairly clear and nonpermeable. Membership in *ad hoc* committees, conferences, and the like is ordinarily explicitly defined; additions during the life of the system are discouraged unless they involve an important contribution to the task, and every effort is made to "keep people aboard." This care in maintaining boundaries is ordinarily taken whether the participants in the temporary system are strangers (as in Case B above), quasi-strangers (that is, members of the same organization whose work does not ordinarily bring them into close contact, as in Case C above), or an intact group of a larger organization, as in the case of Argyris' (1962) account of a temporary system set up with the top executive group of a large company.

Sometimes a very high degree of self-selection (because of the sharpened goal focus suggested above) takes place; this was remarked on in Case B above, and Riecken (1952) has pointed out this process in the volunteer work camp which he studied.

This careful specification of personnel encourages further goal focus, minimizes the socialization problems which will be required in order to ensure productive work within the confines of the temporary system, and may also serve the purpose of reducing internal conflict. A further consequence is that those designing the system can get the most competent participants (in terms of the task) and, in the case of a contemplated innovation, those most favorable to its installation.[11] Thus the usual vested-interest and status-maintenance problems existing in permanent organizations can be bypassed.

Physical and social isolation. Games, as Huizinga (1938) has pointed out, occur in a delimited area (the "ground") within which the participants, using the rules of the game, pursue their goals. There is, he suggests (p. 8), a "stepping out of 'real' life into a temporary sphere of activity with a disposition all of its own." Thus participants in most temporary systems are socially—and often physically—separated from their ordinary pursuits. This isolation has its consequences.

First, it removes barriers to change. Lewin (1951, pp. 232 ff.), who coined the phrase "cultural island," suggested that the creation of changes in persons involves, essentially, a changing of the cultures in which the person finds himself. Isolation from the ordinary environment tends to shear away the person's (or group's) preoccupation with, and allegiance to, "things as they are." Thus there is a reduction of resistance to change based on the group norms of permanent sys-

---

[11] I am indebted for some of these observations to Jerald Hage; see also Hage (1963).

tems, and a gradual substitution of new norms aiding change (of which more below).[12]

Secondly, isolation reduces the role conflicts to which members are ordinarily a prey in their permanent organizations; in Case C above, without in-baskets, telephones, secretaries, families, and regular golf partners, the managers and technicians found they could work single-mindedly on the task at hand.

Thirdly, and perhaps most centrally, isolation supplies a very strong *protective* function. The penalties for making mistakes are reduced. Since life in the temporary system is "not for keeps," the participant ordinarily feels freer to experiment, in the knowledge that other members of the system will not be around later to punish his acts, should his experimentation threaten them in some way. One thinks of Pascal's observation:

> We do not worry about being respected in the towns through which we pass. But if we are going to remain in one for a certain time, we do worry. How long does this have to be?

As well as protecting the individual, any temporary structure (such as a game) also serves to protect the *larger environment* from the consequences of behavior within the structure. (Tennis tournaments do not become international incidents, exactly because they are games, defined as temporary, "as if" systems.) [13]

Change in persons or systems always involves risk; one can never be sure at the outset that the costs will not outweigh the rewards of a contemplated action. Thus the importance of protection. It seems al-

---

[12] For an excellent illustration, see Shaw's *Two Weeks in Another Town* (1960); the hero leaves his home to join a film production unit, where he reevaluates and changes many of his existing relationships.

Schein *et al.* (1961, p. 270 ff.) have pointed out that "brainwashing" systems, like other total institutions, "separate the target individual from his normal social context and daily living routines, thus reducing sharply the amount of interpersonal confirmation he can obtain." Though the authors treat this mainly as an "unfreezing" method to make the person more malleable to influence attempts, it has the other consequences discussed here as well.

[13] P. F. Lazarsfeld has pointed out (in the seminar on innovation which preceded the present book) that research centers and institutes are a favorite form of innovation in universities. As quasi-temporary systems, they can fail without damage to the environment; if they are successful, they can be incorporated into the permanent system.

most impossible for a permanent system to commit itself to an innovation until rewards and costs can be assessed in a low-risk setting.[14]

Finally, the physical–social isolation of temporary systems causes participants to have a sense of "being apart together"; this emphasizes the "as if" aspect, while increasing mutual support, cohesiveness, and the feeling of being engaged in a shared enterprise. This "we happy few" sensation is probably quite important for the success of change efforts during the life of the system.

Size and territoriality.   Since temporary systems may include two persons (as in psychotherapy) or thousands (as in a convention or sports event), it is hard to be definitive about numbers and use of space. However, the considerations above suggest that serious change efforts require keeping system size small (perhaps a hundred or fewer persons, probably subdivided into smaller systems) and defining the physical "territory" in a limited way (one hotel, a suite of offices, a

---

[14] Rogers (1962), commenting on the importance of the "trial" stage as a low-risk test before adoption of agricultural innovations, quotes Ryan and Gross (1943):

Most farmers insisted on personal experimentation before they would adopt the innovation completely. Even the last Iowa farmers to adopt the innovation, although often surrounded by neighbors successfully using hybrid seed, planted only a portion of their acreage in hybrid seed during their first year.

The widespread use of simulated activities such as role-playing, business games, and even "war games" also illustrates the importance of *safety* in temporary systems.

The reduction of consequences seems especially important in temporary systems designed for compensatory purposes. Note Caillois (1961, p. 131) on the carnival's

. . . indecencies, jostlings, provocative laughter, exposed breasts, mimicking buffoonery, a permanent incitement to riot, feasting, and excessive talk, noise and movement. Masks are a brief compensation for the decency and prudence that must be observed the rest of the year. . . . In a delimited time and space the carnival results in disorder, violence, cynicism, and unbridled instinct. However, it leads at the same time to disinterested, idle and joyous activity.

And on the "dodgem" cars in amusement parks (p. 136):

. . . in which to the pleasure of being at the wheel (the serious, almost solemn faces of some drivers should be observed) is added the elemental joy . . . of quarrelling, pursuing other vehicles, outflanking them, barring the passage, endlessly causing pseudo-accidents with no damage or victims, doing exactly and until sated what . . . is most strictly forbidden.

meeting room). Larger systems probably require the use of focal events (such as inspiring speakers, contests, etc.) and are more likely to be compensatory/maintaining rather than problem-solving or change-inducing in nature.

Generally speaking, the input specifications described above seem to enable persons "to escape the restraints of historical time and place" (Negley & Patrick, 1952, p. 4), and to create a quasi-hypothetical mode of attack on crucial problems. Yet the people in temporary systems are far from uncommitted. Apparently, the restrictions in time, goal, personnel, and space, and the protection from external stress, help to create conditions for vigorous, productive work; a kind of "committed hypotheticality" ensues. Just how this happens is of some interest; the next section will review some aspects of process during the life of the system itself.

Process characteristics

As any temporary social system develops, certain characteristics predictably occur. They will be discussed here under the headings of time use, goal redefinition, the use of procedures, role definition and socialization, the development of communication and power structures, sentiments, and normative beliefs.

Time use. In permanent organizations, the possibility of postponement of activity always exists, in spite of DO IT NOW signs and deadlines. Thus the future-oriented time perspective of the person tends to become vaguer, and less salient; it exerts less effect on current striving.[15]

This observation should be placed beside one made by Lewin (1951, p. 76): the existence of stress tends to narrow time perspective, so that the person lives more in the psychological present, coping with immediate demands and simultaneously forgetting the past and

[15] This process reaches an extreme in the "Magic Mountain" effect described by Talbot, Miller, & White (1962) as an unintended side effect of hospitalization; because there is indeterminacy as to the length of the mental patient's stay, he does little or no planning and has little achievement drive. But life in *any* permanent organization produces Hans Castorp-like feelings: "I can always do that tomorrow, or sometime."

neglecting plans for the future. This leads to an interesting derivation. If the time perspective of a person were artificially narrowed in some way, so that he was invited to focus on the immediate situation, with less attention backwards and forwards, we might expect greater energy output devoted to the immediate activity.

This narrowing might also reduce anxiety: cf. Barnett's (1953) comments on the management of time as a major means for increasing the sense of *coherence* in the immediate environment. The net effect would also be to make more energy available for work.

A temporary system, designed to achieve certain specified goals within a defined period of time, does, of course, provide this coherent, narrowed time perspective. Several examples suggest that increases in the use of directed energy do, in fact, seem to result. Shlien, Mosak, & Dreikurs (1962) compared psychotherapeutic relationships pre-limited to 15 sessions with relationships of unlimited duration (which averaged about 37 sessions). A measure of therapeutic gain (self-ideal congruency) increased much more rapidly in the time-limited relationships, and ended at a higher level than in the unlimited relationships. The client seemed to be mobilizing energy for vigorous achievement in a system which he knew to be definedly temporary.

Benne (1964), ·Bennis & Shepard (1956), and others have remarked on the striking effect which the approaching end of a human relations training group seems to exert on member participation and learning. As in Case B above, group members who know that the group will cease to exist within the next few days appear to be strongly motivated to seek and receive feedback from other members to aid their own learning. Benne (1964) comments:

> The certainty that the association will not be prolonged lends a freedom of expression and sharing to members that is harder to achieve in a group drawn from an organization where the tenure of continued association is indefinite . . . [There is] a motivation to live the association intensively and to the hilt, with some relaxation of anxieties for the consequences which stretch beyond its closing.

The film (and drama) *Twelve Angry Men* also illustrates the focusing, energizing effects of time limitation. Though the jury's termination time is not fixed in advance, the fact that the group will dissolve upon reaching its decision is an inescapable feature of its life. The film portrays a good deal of early concern about "time-wasting," along with growing involvement and concern for the production of a final decision. The twelve strangers on the jury become much more fully engaged with each other and with the task than they might if they were to meet in a non-time-limited setting (though the importance of the immediate goal cannot, of course, be gainsaid).[16]

Two other related effects seem to occur in time-limited systems. First, *distorted perceptions of elapsed time* take place. Persons at human relations training conferences like that described in Case B, for example, often say they feel several weeks have elapsed, when only a few days have gone by. This effect may stem from removal of the usual time markers from the external world of permanent organizations, and from the intensive work level and high stimulus input; elapsed time may well be measured by the relative number of novel stimulus inputs we perceive.

Secondly, *pacing effects* take place. Initial work level and output are usually low, partly because energy is going into the development of a viable system, but also because the perceived pressure of termination has not yet been strongly felt. When it is, work output goes up sharply. Veterans of *ad hoc* committees know that most of the productive work is often done in the minutes just before closing. And despite the fact that human relations training groups have been staged for periods varying from 8 to 70 hours, broadly similar phases of group development (see Bennis & Shepard, 1956) seem to take place, compressed and miniaturized in shorter groups and deepened and extended in longer ones.

Goal redefinition. Though the goal of a temporary system is ordinarily defined and focused in advance, as suggested above, there nevertheless remains the task of developing redefinitions of the goal which command the commitment and energy of all participants. How does this process occur over time?

First of all, any new situation with structure unknown on *a priori* grounds evokes a good deal of uncertainty. If one is entering a social

[16] Poulet (1956, p. 333) has commented on Poe's use of "closed" time to bound the action of his characters (as in *The Pit and the Pendulum, The Fall of the House of Usher,* and *The Masque of the Red Death*): "a sort of temporal circle surrounds Poe's characters . . . an internal fatality conceived . . . and accomplished in isolation." The poignancy, focus and intensity of these time-limited associations is striking.

situation in which the goals and intentions of others are imprecisely known, where it is impossible to predict what behavior others will produce, and where the precise paths toward goal accomplishment are not clearly perceived, we can expect a good deal of personal anxiety. Such anxiety is ordinarily masked by durable arrangements in permanent settings, but any new setting re-evokes it. Thus at the onset of committees, conferences, or new projects, there is a good deal of defensive maneuvering, formality, attempts to force the new situation to become like old situations, and so on.[17]

This initial uncertainty is heightened if participants have special reason to anticipate conflict. A series of conferences between professional educators and liberal arts faculty devoted to the improvement of teacher education produced these summary reflections:

> As one looks back on that conference, several factors stand out. The first is the dramatic air of tension which existed as the 1,000 participants arrived for the conference. The air was electric—something like the tension that prevails in a college football stadium on the day of the big game. . . . This tension was of course heightened by gratuitous publicity screaming for conflict. . . . It was obvious to the thoughtful onlooker that one incendiary statement or one violently partisan headline could have blown the frail and untried craft of the conference completely out of the water before it got under way. (Hodenfield & Stinnett, 1961, p. 20)

The initial problem, then, is that of creating a relationship in which goal redefinition can begin (which did occur in this example):

> The ground had been laid for fruitful discussion: a rapport had been established by which the most controversial, difficult problems could be laid upon the top of the table and discussed openly and freely. (Ibid.)

As communication increases within the temporary system, participants become more aware of the degree to which their goals are in fact shared, and gradually through joint work one or more superordinate goals (Sherif, 1962) gradually emerge. At this particular conference, a superordinate goal (one which involves meeting the goals of the various parties to a conflict at a higher order of abstraction, and which cannot be achieved by either party alone) did in fact develop:

---

[17] For a very thorough discussion of these phenomena, see Bradford, Gibb, & Benne (1964).

Overall, both sides at the Bowling Green Conference confessed a sense of guilt for the neglect that has divided and hurt the education world. Both demonstrated a lively conviction that the education of teachers is too important to the nation to be left to the sole jurisdiction of either the liberal arts or the teachers education group by itself. There was a sense of need for the strength of union—to achieve the teacher education goals which the liberal arts group has not been able to force by itself, and to win the public support for education which the organized school teachers have not been able to do even in these times. (*Ibid.*, p. 175)

Once shared goals have been defined, one of the most powerful forces for goal achievement in a temporary system is the knowledge that a product must appear within an allotted time. After the Bowling Green Conference, a participant described his experience with this approach in a local university setting:

We told these committees to do the same thing we had done—go off somewhere and reach an agreement and not come back until they had. (*Ibid.*, p. 30)

This force also operated in Case C: the groups of the conference were charged with producing a set of policy decisions by a particular time, but left completely free as to methods employed; within one week problems which had lain unsolved in the organization for nearly a decade were worked through to the satisfaction of all parties involved.

The existence of superordinate goals, which one has personally helped to formulate, combined with the knowledge that the goals must be reached here and now, during the life of the temporary system, appears to cause an associated phenomenon—heightened *significance and meaningfulness* in the activity. In Case A above, one participant said, "For the first time in I don't know how many years, I felt like an educator." Part of the "Hawthorne effect" seems to consist of this heightened sense of significance; since the system is temporary, its members regard the situation as special, as "marked off" in some way from the ordinary run of activities in permanent systems. Watson's chapter in the present book documents this well in the case of an educational experiment.

Heightened significance may explain the fact that almost any educational experiment will show slight increments in learning over that appearing in associated control groups; such gain often recedes as the experiment becomes less temporary and more durably a part of an on-going permanent system.

Placebo effects are undoubtedly related to this phenomenon. Shapiro (1960, p. 114) remarking that "the normative history of medical treatment, until relatively recently, has been the history of the placebo effect," suggests that the effect is essentially a function of the doctor–patient relationship, the placebo itself serving as a symbol of maintenance of faith in the general efficacy of *whatever* treatment is taking place (in the temporary system formed by doctor and patient). The heightened significance of the immediate goal (i.e., cure) undoubtedly serves to make the patient more open to interpersonal influence, as well as distorting his perceptions in the direction of goal achievement.[18]

Associated with this heightened goal significance, there often appears a sense of heightened self-awareness and self-examination. Some systems, such as the human relations training conference described in Case B above, and systems devoted to indoctrination (Schein *et al.*, 1961) encourage this deliberately, of course, but it seems likely that expanded consciousness of self will occur in *any* short-run system with a potent goal, where the person is cut off from his usual supports of habit and institutional routine.

The net effect of these processes of goal redefinition is that the person becomes fully engaged, or "engrossed," as Goffman (1961, pp. 37–40) puts it,[19] in the world of the temporary system. Other con-

[18] Educational researchers examining the effects of innovations would be well advised to post this excerpt from Shapiro's article (p. 112) over their desks:

In 1794, Dr. Ranieri Gerbi, a professor at Pisa, published a manuscript describing a miraculous cure for toothache due to any cause which lasted for a whole year. A worm, species *Curculio* . . . was crushed between the thumb and forefingers of the right hand. The fingers then touched the affected part. An investigatory commission found that 431 of 629 toothaches were stopped immediately. Later, Dr. Carradori, court physician in Weimar, advanced the discovery by substituting a more pleasant ladybird, and an official commission confirmed the immediate relief of toothache in 65–70% of cases.

For a review of the remarkable range and power of placebo effects, see Roueché (1961).

[19] The concept "temporary system" can be seen as a particular case of the useful concept "focused gathering" or "encounter," a here-and-now assemblage of persons who may or may not be members of some durable group. See Goffman (1961, pp. 7–14).

cerns fade; the participant often reports that he is working at the height of his powers on the immediate, focused, short-run goals which he has helped redefine.[20] Thus the over-all work output of the system is often much greater than that sustainable in permanent systems—so much so that it may occur at cost to the individual. Conference participants often report accumulating fatigue and feel they are "living on capital," in energy terms. Riecken's (1952) study of a volunteer work camp found increased passivity (via TAT measures) toward the end of the system's life.

Procedures. Temporary systems, like permanent systems, require timed specification of activities of persons, aimed at accomplishing system goals. Procedures in temporary systems have high importance, for a number of reasons. Huizinga (1938, p. 10), speaking of games, rituals, trials, and dramas as "temporary worlds," points out that:

> . . . inside the play-ground an absolute and peculiar order reigns. Here we come across another, very positive feature of play: it creates order, *is* order. Into an imperfect world and into the confusion of life it brings a temporary, a limited perfection.

In this sense, precise specification of the "rules of the game" provides a temporarily certain way of treating the gigantic uncertainties with which persons, groups, and organizations are faced in ordinary life. Thus, procedures aid predictability and reduce anxiety, while specifying efficacious means for achieving time-limited goals.

Procedures in temporary systems also add to the *controllability* of the immediate system; it is as if the participants in a conference, *ad hoc* committee, or game have succeeded in creating a "mini-world" which is responsive to their needs, desires, and wishes. In this sense

---

[20] The "as if" character of the goal also feeds this work intensity. Cf. Riecken (1952, p. 147) on the volunteer work camp:

. . . [the participant] voluntarily and temporarily subjects himself to hardship, almost always quite genuine and sometimes more severe than that of the inhabitants [of the community where he is working], but he knows that he will shortly return to the relative calm and comfort and security of the middle-class environment he left. He undertakes a task that is ordinarily very trying and exhausting—often a task that is shirked by the very people he is helping—a task that offers comparatively little intrinsic reward as a life work. But the work camper will not become in most cases a bricklayer, ditch-digger, . . . [etc.].

the temporary social system ministers deeply to the person's need for autonomy, as well as his need for certainty and order in his surroundings.[21]

Perhaps for these reasons, the rules of games and the procedures of conferences are intensely compelling. In a social–psychological experiment, subjects will perform all sorts of unusual, difficult, or even degrading tasks (Mills, 1962; Orne, 1962), since they are seen as part of the given procedures of the temporary situation. Or, though the conference planners in Case C above nervously anticipated full-blown conflict, or departures from the conference, neither materialized, of course; the procedures of the "mini-world" were powerful enough to contain the participants and their differences.

These three features of predictability, controllability, and compellingness contribute strongly to the usefulness of temporary systems in bringing about innovation. An excellent analysis of the innovative personality in developing countries (Hagen, 1962) describes the high innovator as someone who sees a *coherent* world about him which he feels will respond dependably to his efforts to change it; he trusts his own evaluation of his experience; he sees the surrounding world as valuing him if he achieves his goals; he has high needs for autonomy, achievement, order, succorance to others, and nurturance from others. It is the understatement of the year to suggest that these conditions are rarely met in mass society today. Feelings of powerlessness, failure, meaninglessness, alienation, and interpersonal distance are extremely common. The temporary social system provides an environment which meets personal needs, reduces defensiveness, and releases potential for creativity and innovation;[22] it can be precisely fashioned by its

[21] Cf. Poulet (1956, p. 333):
. . . the final knowledge, therefore, is a knowledge of the linkage of the causes which constitute duration and destiny. . . . There can be certain knowledge of our temporal destiny only if that particular time is situated off by itself from the ordinary duration, so that it realizes itself independently of chance. For change is incalculable.

[22] deGrazia (1961) has also examined the situational sources of inventiveness: high drive for achievement; marginalism to the surrounding society; operationalism (idea expression through activity); and relationalism (seeing connections among disparate elements). The first three of these are usually accentuated in temporary systems, which have the extra advantage of supporting the person against the usual penalties of marginalism.

designers as a temporary Utopia, flexibly capable of evoking the best possible contribution from its participants.

Many observers have noted the contemporary decay in production of thoroughgoing literary Utopias (in sharp contrast with the ferment of the 18th and 19th centuries), and their replacement by satirical or polemical versions of life in the mass society of the future (e.g., Orwell's *1984*); what has gone unremarked is the enormous proliferation of short-term quasi-Utopias of all sorts—conferences, meetings, "task forces," research projects, experiments, training exercises. It is as if we have traded the grand visions of social life as it might be lived for miniature societies, to which one can become committed intensively, meaningfully, satisfyingly—and impermanently.

Role definition, and socialization. The participant in a temporary system is freed from his usual role conflicts, and need only be a "good conference-goer" if he wishes. Yet the system also offers him striking opportunities for—and exerts certain pressures toward—role redefinition, and the refashioning of his identity.

For one thing, he has a good deal of freedom to experiment in risk-free, controllable circumstances with new roles, unhampered by the role expectations others usually hold for him.

But beyond this, temporary system experience usually actively encourages "unfreezing" of old role definitions. This occurs for two reasons. First, the participant must be "socialized"—taught to participate effectively in the immediate system. Second, if the system is a person-changing one, role changes are an expected long-term output.

Cumming & Cumming (1962), for example, describe how the hospital experience is a challenge to the patient's "assumptive state"; he must learn new roles rather than coping with others in his usual aggressive or withdrawing manner. Heightened self-awareness also serves to keep the person at his task of exploring new behavior patterns. These forces are mainly directed at long-term changes in patients, though there are implications for immediate socialization as well— i.e., aggression is frowned on. (Note, incidentally, that socialization processes in temporary systems are not always helpful to the person. Talbot, Miller, & White (1962), for example, have commented on the dysfunctional role behaviors learned by mental hospital patients, such as complacent acceptance of illness in self and others, and a tendency to regard deviancy as an acceptable mode of life.)

Sometimes this "unfreezing" of old role behaviors is direct and coercive; in "brainwashing" systems (Schein *et al.*, 1961) friends are separated, and physical stress, indeterminate threats, and stimulation of role-attached guilt are employed. Even in permissive environments, such as human relations training conferences, old roles are placed in question: the corporation executive is called by his first name by a foreman, and finds that his usual role of controlling the meeting does not work. Hagen (1962) has commented on the withdrawal of status respect as a profoundly innovative force in traditional societies. When old role definitions are made meaningless or unacceptable, then the way is open for change. Temporary systems offer a protected setting for the "retreat" which Hagen found typically to follow status respect withdrawal, and enable the creative refashioning of roles.

It does seem clear that persons can develop new role definitions as a result of their tenure in temporary systems. For example, Hagen (1962) has quoted Erikson on the importance of the "social moratorium" as a mechanism for defining identity; the classical *Wanderjahr* of European students (emulated by Americans in "junior year abroad" programs) is one example. Schein *et al.* (1961) describe role changes in "brainwashing" systems, and their stabilization via "confirmation" received from others in the prison environment. Most psychotherapeutic systems, of course, are asserted to cause the client to be clearer about who he is. And over half of Riecken's (1952) college-age volunteer work campers, after only eight weeks in a system with strongly altruistic and service-oriented norms, redefined their roles: 29 per cent made immediate or delayed vocational choices in service-oriented professions; 27 per cent shifted toward a more service-oriented emphasis within already chosen vocations.

We may ask why the temporary system seems particularly effective in socializing its members for immediate performance—and in causing durable role changes which persist after the system's death. There are several possibilities.

First, focused goals and clear procedures help to make appropriate role behavior highly visible.

Secondly, most temporary systems involve vigorous participation by one's peers, persons "in the same boat." See, for example, Newcomb's

(1962) comments on the importance of peer culture as a source of influence in college environments. With the climate of heightened awareness often found in temporary systems, the way is open for more vigorous identification with peers as role models. Such identification appears to be more potent than that with authority figures, such as teachers or bosses (Schein *et al.*, 1961).

And, in the protected mini-world of the temporary system, the participant has more opportunity than usual to try out new role behaviors experimentally, and see what their real reward value is. Genuine internalization in this sense (see Kelman, 1961) is even more durable than identification, which may involve dependency on those identified with, and thus result in less carry-through subsequently.

A final comment can be made about two broad types of socialization process. Some temporary systems take a primarily restrictive or convergent approach; others have a freeing, divergent effect (see Schein, 1961). Convergent approaches aim at the development of prespecified outcomes, whether they are deliberate, as in the case of meetings designed to "increase loyalty to the company," or incidental, as in the case of residential child-care institutions; Schuman (1961), for example, found that longer-institutionalized children had less autonomy, less warmth, and less impulse control. Divergent approaches, such as those found in psychotherapy and human relations training, encourage the participant to become more spontaneous, creative, and inquiring (and thus less predictable, in a sense), even though they may have convergent effects at a deeper level (e.g., producing more commitment to the importance of creativity in human relationships).

Communication and power structures.   It is of some interest to examine how the various parts of a temporary system exchange information and influence each other.

Generally speaking, most features of temporary systems appear to encourage communication among participants.[23] For one thing, since communication to groups outside is far less than that within the system, a common language with special meanings for the participants tends to grow up. Secondly, new channels of information transmission tend to develop between persons whose roles in former permanent sys-

[23] Systems with deliberate control of communication (e.g., via interception of letters to prisoners, use of informers, etc.) would be an exception.

tems have kept them apart. Thirdly, since increased interaction leads to increased liking, other things being equal, there is a strong tendency for participants to share more information with each other, become more open and trustful. Finally, under these conditions, equal status relationships develop among participants, so that persons are not seen as having the *right* to withhold or distort information, as is ordinarily the case (for good reasons) in permanent structures.

Such processes occur in any social system, of course, but in a sloweddown, masked form. Temporary systems seem to encourage them; the net effect is that more and better data are available for system problem-solving.

These assertions can be illustrated briefly. The increased openness across hierarchical levels evident at the office Christmas party is one example. At a deeper level, many studies (Star, Williams, & Stouffer, 1958; Thelen, 1954; Cook, 1957) have shown that when members of initially hostile groups come together in the service of a temporary common task (such as sailing a ship, opposing community deterioration, or fighting a common enemy), equal-status contact (and subsequent attitude change) tends to develop.

Another case: during World War II, the Germans imprisoned many high-status personnel from Dutch trade unions, business, and government in the same camp. They found themselves in closer communication than ever before; the trust, the fuller sharing of data, and the action plans which resulted seem to have speeded postwar reconstruction in the Netherlands considerably. (Some permanent crossgroup organizations, such as the union-employer-government Social and Economic Council, seem to have been formed consequentially.) [24]

The importance of this increased communication for *change* in persons and groups is substantial. Existing behaviors seem to be maintained primarily through feedback loops, as Griffiths' chapter on organization change in the present book points out. At the interpersonal level, Lippitt (1962) and Nokes (1961) have shown the crucial importance of feedback in maintaining the person's picture of himself. It follows that the introduction of *new* feedback loops, which appears to be much easier in the new world of the temporary system, can affect behavior considerably.

[24] I am indebted to Marjan Schröder for this example.

For example, a participant in a human relations training conference, after hearing a tape recording of a group in which he participated, may realize that his manner is far more passive and mild than he had thought; changes in a more vigorous direction become likely. Or, in one "organization improvement" meeting which the author helped design, the new feedback loops involved small group discussions containing both top managers and foremen. The managers learned (for example) that many foremen, rather than being apathetic and rebellious by turns, as they had previously seemed to the managers, did in fact have creative, sophisticated, vigorous ideas on how to improve productivity. In the permanent system, these ideas had been ignored by the managers and withheld by the foremen.

New feedback loops can aid change even when this is not planned for. In the intensive assessment programs of World War II (OSS Assessment Staff, 1945) where candidates spent several days in a variety of stressful test situations, many participants reported that they learned a very great deal about themselves, apparently through latent feedback and comparison with others, even though the programs were designed solely for selection purposes.

Some remarks on the power structures of temporary systems are also in order. In permanent systems, there is usually a clearly defined hierarchy of power (with the usual informal bypassings evident). Many temporary systems begin with the question "Who will influence whom?" somewhat in doubt. The conference participants are often not sure how much weight their wishes will carry with the staff; the research assistants do not know whether the project director will give them as much autonomy as they would like; the *ad hoc* committee members need to maneuver for a while to understand who will have his say most consistently.

Three connected points can be made here. First, it seems clear that productive work does not usually ensue until the power structure is *clear* to all; secondly, as implied earlier, there is a tendency for equalitarian notions of power distribution to grow up; thirdly, because of equalitarianism and the limited size of most systems, the net influence of the person on the system's fate can sometimes be very substantial. Some illustrative examples:

Bennis & Shepard (1956) point out that little learning seems to occur in initially unstructured training groups until the group members symbolically demonstrate their joint power to defeat the strongest member (usually the staff trainer). And in Case C above, vigorous work only appeared after the steering group clearly asserted its authority and required subgroups to produce specified results by a certain time.

In another management conference, work seemed very limited until the point when the staff abdicated their role of giving lectures and designing exercises, and gave responsibility for planning to an elected steering committee. Even where authority shifts are not this dramatic, there often seems to be a kind of "tipping point" in many conferences, when roles have been defined to everyone's satisfaction, rather than being accepted passively. If the balance of power which emerges stresses participant autonomy and equalitarianism, high productivity is very typical. (See also the chapter by Clee & Reswick in the present book.)

An example of the high "influenceability" of a temporary system appears in Horton's (1962, pp. 27–28) account of the merger of two large Protestant denominations:

> More than once, when the union was being negotiated the hope for its success hung on a thread of gossamer. There came the time, for instance, when the Congregational Christians were convinced that the Evangelical and Reformed Church was ready to withdraw and [vice versa] . . . After several hours of discussion at a joint meeting at which many were heard who took counsel of their fears, a short devotional address was given by the Reverend Ben M. Herbster . . . in a simple and moving way he stressed one point, one single point—but the cardinal point: What, he asked, is the mind of Christ about this union? . . . This was the turning point: a sub-committee found the courage to report out the recommendation to proceed, for none doubted that union rather than division represented the mind of Him who had had his own *Via Dolorosa*. The whole joint committee, now looking at the matter from a viewpoint higher than that of expediency, accepted the recommendation—and began again its long, slow, unspectacular work . . . The remembrance of this rescue from a defeat considered almost certain by most of those concerned . . . put iron in the arteries of committees facing similar crises subsequently. (It is a pleasure to record that years later Dr. Herbster became the first President of the United Church of Christ.)

The general point here, of course, is that comments like those made by Dr. Herbster had undoubtedly been made at many points in the permanent systems which were considering merger; but in the temporary, if precarious, system formed by the negotiating committee, his reminder of the superordinate goal had unusually potent influence —both on the immediate system and its consequential permanent system.

Sentiments. Certain fairly salient states of feeling, or group "climate," seem to appear regularly in time-limited systems.

Early *defensiveness* and formality is one such shared sentiment. Since the members usually do not have prespecified relationships with others, there is much uncertainty with respect to the goals of others, and the perceived costs of attaining one's own goals tend to be high. Each person withdraws somewhat, and is reluctant to enter the system as a full participant, until he can be assured of its safety for him. The "time-wasting" in early phases of *ad hoc* committee meetings, the "warm-up" phase of role-playing, and the stiff and formal self-introductions usual in most new groups are all exhibits of this tendency. Gibb (1964) has commented on trust formation as one of the central variables in group development; until personal vulnerability is no longer regarded with terror, defensiveness will remain high.

Secondly, an atmosphere of *play* frequently appears in temporary systems, usually further along in their lives. The "as if," risk-reductive character of the undertaking seems to produce more fluid, spontaneous, game-like behavior. As the person comes to trust others and anticipates rejection from them less, he is less self-critical in turn, and "enters the spirit" of the undertaking. Yet the self in the undertaking (whether a conference or a role-playing scene) is somehow "not me," "not my usual self." The maintenance of this fiction, paradoxically enough, seems to enable the person to behave in a way that is more central, more typical of himself—as when the "mild" person shows his deep resentment of others during a hard-fought ping-pong game.

This greater fluidity of behavior also tends to evoke far more inventive, constructive action than in permanent systems (see Caillois, 1961, p. 58), especially since the various constraints of permanent systems are missing.

Thirdly, as suggested earlier, climates in temporary systems tend to move in the direction of more *interpersonal liking*, acceptance, and intimacy. The classical shipboard romance is one such example; the feelings of warmth which develop among some of the jury members in the film *Twelve Angry Men* illustrate this as well. The stresses faced when participants are "apart together" tend to create a kind of mutual identification.

This shades into a fourth kind of shared sentiment—*esprit de corps* and a sense of group identity—perhaps paralleling the clarifications and restatements of personal identity which have been commented on earlier. For example, the summer training institutes sponsored by the National Science Foundation for teachers in various subject matter fields (physics, mathematics, etc.) appear to generate an extraordinary sense of identification with an enterprise thought to be significant and meaningful. And sometimes at meetings of the wholesale distributors, salesmen, and supervisory staff of a large corporation, this song is sung:

(Chorus)
Here's to leadership by Zenith.
It's the leader all the way.
And the heritage at Zenith
Makes it what it is today.
We're a family here at Zenith
Free from jealousies and strife.
Yes Sir! Zenith's more than just a name.
It's a whole way of life.[25]

This seems, perhaps, an artificial attempt to induce *esprit*. Yet a visitor to a Zenith meeting testified that the song seemed to have deep meaning to many participants, and the corporation president reports that the song "has become a very important part of the 'spirit' of Zenith." [26]

Finally, as indicated earlier, a typical sentiment in temporary systems is that of *involvement*, engagement, "engrossment" in the system's goals. This often shows itself as tension early in the system's life (as in Case C above, and in the teacher education conferences described by Hodenfield and Stinnett, 1961), particularly when there is an element of "chanciness," uncertainty as to whether it will "come off" (Huizinga, 1938, pp. 47–48). Later, strong work-orientation often becomes evident. The notion of intensity, of seriousness, as both

[25] From the Zenith "Song of the Leader" (N. Zeno—P. Williams). © 1959 Zenith Radio Corporation. Used by permission.
[26] Personal letter from L. C. Truesdell, President, Zenith Sales Corporation, June 24, 1963.

Huizinga and Caillois point out, is not incompatible with the spirit of play alluded to above:

> . . . This supposed relaxation, at the moment that the adult submits to it, does not absorb him any less than his [usual] professional activity. It sometimes makes him exert even greater energy, skill, intelligence, or attention. (Caillois, 1961, p. 66)

Norms.   Any going social system develops regulatory norms which define and govern behavior. Since temporary systems are new, miniature, temporary, and protected, it seems much easier to develop new norms in them. If the norms are strong, they tend to become internalized as attitudes in the person, or carried over as practices into permanent organizations.

Some temporary system norms are rather specific (such as believing in the importance of Zenith's heritage); others, more general, appear to arise in many different types of temporary system. Six such norms are discussed here. Most of them will sound familiar; they are outgrowths of phenomena reviewed earlier. In a real sense, participants in temporary systems—especially those devoted to producing change—come to value what happens in them.

The first of these norms is *equalitarianism:* an increased belief in the appropriateness of equal-status relationships during the life of the system. The (admittedly useful) distance maintained by hierarchical relationships in permanent systems, cannot, somehow, be generated and sustained in a temporary system. In Case C, for example, the conference was differentiated into groups of two authority levels, a "policy-making" group and a group which came to be called "the rest of us." Though the members of the policy-making group were all high-ranking managers in the permanent organization, they steadily received a good deal of status-equilibrating joking,[27] and could not maintain distance.

A second norm is *authenticity;* a good deal of emphasis is placed on the importance of openness and trust among participants. Genuine

[27] For example, a mock time schedule posted by the lower-status group (mainly middle managers and personnel technicians) identified the senior group as "gentlemen" and themselves as "players," a distinction from the game of cricket. Gentlemen are (usually upper-class) amateurs; players are compensated professionals.

expression of feelings and ideas is valued, and the typically heightened awareness and sense of significance means that interpersonal data
are very closely attended to in the course of the group's work together.[28] Permanent system norms usually (and often functionally)
encourage the reduction of openness as a defense against potentially
disruptive pains and stresses of organized life. But in short-run, equalitarian, highly goal-focused, "marked-off" settings, punishing someone
for being frank not only interferes with goal achievement, but creates resentments which are difficult to manage in such an intimate
milieu.

A third major norm focuses on *inquiry,* problem-solving with use of
all available data. Increased intrasystem communication aids this emphasis, as do equalitarianism and high goal focus. At any rate, temporary systems seem to encourage curiosity and members' attempts to
discover and invent solutions, and to come to grips with the truth as
members see it—rather than relying on *ex cathedra* pronouncements,
avoidance of problems, or use of stock solutions. This general notion is,
of course, related to broad cultural changes stemming from the rapid
historical development of science as a mode of knowing. Dubos (1961,
p. 50) quotes H. G. Wells in this respect:

> The Utopia of a modern dreamer must needs differ in one funda-
> mental aspect from the Nowheres and Utopias man planned before
> Darwin quickened the thought of the world. Those were all perfect
> and static States, a balance of happiness won forever against the forces
> of unrest and disorder that inhere in things. One beheld a healthy and
> simple generation enjoying the fruits of the earth in an atmosphere of
> virtue and happiness, to be followed by other virtuous, happy, and en-
> tirely similar generations until the Gods grew weary. Change and de-
> velopment were dammed by invincible dams forever. But the Modern
> Utopia must not be static but kinetic, must shape not as a permanent
> state but as a hopeful stage leading to a long ascent of stages. Nowadays
> we do not resist and overcome the great stream of things, but rather
> float upon it. We build now not citadels, but ships of state.

Dubos continues: "Thus, it would seem that Utopias can exist as
realities only if they die shortly after being born, to be reborn with
new shapes." This self-corrective and reflexive character of science has

---

[28] See Argyris (1962) for an account of a training conference with a firm's
top executives which emphasized "authenticity" as a major theme.

often been alluded to; temporary systems appear to exemplify it well.[29]

A fourth norm, also science-based, might be called *hypotheticality,* the valuing of experimental, provisional, tentative-until-the-facts-are-in approaches to the solution of problems. Willingness to experiment is in part, of course, a function of commitment to an inquiry model of problem-solving. But hypotheticality seems to flower most vigorously in a new system which is protected from the usual consequences of failure, and does not have an indeterminate future stretching in front of it.

A fifth norm has been discussed by Eaton (1962) under the heading of *"newism."* Most temporary systems set up to cause change in persons or organizations must face the fact that their hoped-for outcomes are uncertain, and—at best—very difficult indeed to measure. In the absence of "hard data," the particular change being contemplated must therefore be validated by means of social support. Thus, norms favoring novelty and innovation—*change for its own sake*—are quite likely to appear in temporary systems. This type of norm can insulate and support the members of the temporary system against the anti-innovative norms of the permanent system or systems from which they come. ("We are deviants together.")

Rogers' (1962) analysis of the diffusion of innovations shows clearly that traditional vs. modern (i.e., newistic) orientations in a particular community or subculture affect adoption rates markedly. In addition, it has been found repeatedly that greater personal innovativeness is associated with "cosmopoliteness," roughly defined as the result of experience in more than one social system (e.g., the pedagogically innovative teacher turns out to have worked in several different school systems). Rogers quotes Tarde (1903, pp. 87–88):

> To innovate, to discover, to awake for an instant, the individual must escape, for the time being, from his social surroundings. Such unusual audacity makes him super-social rather than social.

In a real sense, temporary systems can accelerate cosmopoliteness, through the confrontation of persons with radically differing orienta-

---

[29] Bennis (1962 *b*) has, in fact, suggested that the ethic of science may well generate the most useful criteria for judging the health of permanent organizations; a healthy organization *inquires,* is flexible, has optimal internal communication, and is in accurate touch with external reality.

tions from many different permanent systems; thus "super-social"— and newistic—views are more likely.

A final norm might be labeled *effortfulness.* The expenditure of hard work, energy, and effort are highly valued in temporary systems. This is a function not only of the intense goal focus and heightened significance alluded to earlier, but of the steady awareness that desired learnings or changes must be brought about within a sharply limited period of time. Thus to approach this task casually, lightly, or lazily is reprehensible. Participants are expected to work *seriously;* the effects of this in energy expenditure have already been illustrated in Case B, and in Riecken's (1952) work camp account. In human relations training conferences, at points where progress is felt to be slow, it is not unusual for a participant to estimate average salaries of the persons sitting around the table and announce triumphantly the sum of money which is presumably being "wasted." Yet such calculations are rarely made in permanent organizations—even at coffee breaks.

These norms—and the other process characteristics described above —seem very typical in temporary, change-inducing systems.[30] What sorts of changes can be expected?

Output characteristics

Temporary systems do have consequences; they maintain and support the person, they solve problems, and they bring about change. The main types of change they produce have been illustrated repeatedly in the preceding pages. These are divided for convenience here

---

[30] Examining the special case of the human relations training conference, Bennis (1962 *a*) has identified four underlying norms or "meta-goals," three of which correspond to the norms labeled inquiry, authenticity, and equalitarianism in the analysis above. The other is "expanded consciousness and recognition of choice," which resembles somewhat the "heightened awareness" sentiment reviewed earlier. The position taken here is that these norms are likely phenomena in *any* short-term change-inducing system, and are not limited to the human relations training conference as such.

It is interesting to note that many of the "stock ideas" of literary Utopias reviewed by Negley & Patrick (1952, p. 257) also appear in actual temporary systems, including equality of the sexes, the brotherhood of man, hatred of tyranny, toleration, and a kind of primitivism that may be related to the climate of "play" alluded to earlier. Most Utopias (see Ozmon, 1962) also place a good deal of stress on education (i.e., they are viewed as person-changing systems).

into three: changes in the durable aspects of *persons,* changes in *relationships,* and changes in *action* as a result of decisions made during the life of the temporary system.

Person changes. Some system outputs involve alterations in the durable, continuing aspects of individuals' attitudes, knowledge, or behavior.

For example, a review of those National Science Foundation summer institutes which focused on Physical Science Study Committee material indicates quite clearly that participants received a re-education in modern physics, and in some cases were adequately prepared for teaching the new PSSC course (Marsh & Gortner, 1963, pp. 50–51).

Riecken (1952) found that volunteer work campers became more alienated from the larger society, more pacifistic, less egocentric, and higher in ego strength at the end of a summer program—and that these changes were still apparent ten months later. Hyman, Wright, & Hopkins (1962) found that participation in a workshop for teen-agers caused (for example) increased optimism about the solution of social problems such as race prejudice, more tolerance toward nonconformist views, and more positive attitudes toward the importance of civil liberties; these changes, too, persisted in follow-up measures.[31]

Shlien, Mosak, & Dreikurs (1962) found increased congruence between the client's self-picture and his ideal for himself during and following a temporary psychotherapeutic system prelimited to fifteen counseling interviews.

Analyses of a two-week human relations training conference for elementary school principals (Case B above) found that increased equalitarian behavior, and added skill in aiding group decision-making were detectable eight months afterward (Miles *et al.,* forthcoming; Miles, 1960). Harrison (1962) found that the members of an executive team who participated in a one-week "team training" conference retained a tendency to describe other team members in more person-centered, feelingful terms (as vs. rational, intellective terms).

These examples exhibit a range of possibilities, and help to remind

[31] Perhaps the most basic contribution of this study is its sophisticated use—and analysis—of the procedures necessary to obtain unequivocal evaluation of the person-changing effects of temporary systems. See also Campbell (1957) for an illuminating discussion of these matters.

us that durable changes in persons are not only associated with membership in long-term educational or psychotherapeutic systems. Some of the temporary-system changes reviewed here, in fact, might *only* be achievable by short-term, intensive work.

Relationship changes.   Beyond person changes, it seems likely that membership in a temporary system can durably alter the quality of pre-existing relationships among members of the system. This is well documented in Argyris's (1962) account of work with a group of executives (the same studied by Harrison); he found that their relationships in the home organization had changed toward increased trust and openness in the conduct of their day-to-day work. This type of output also emerged from the teacher education conferences described by Hodenfield & Stinnett (1961):

> The one really important thing to them is the fact that both sides (liberal arts professors and professional educators) have found they want to, and can, work together. This apparent willingness and ability of the two long-divided parts of the education world to collaborate, the conference participants said, is a development of central importance to the American school system. (Hodenfield & Stinnett, 1961, p. 174.)

And note this statement, produced jointly after one such conference by a liberal arts English professor and a professional educator:

> All who attended the Kansas conference (and we hope all who read this report) know now that they cannot afford to neglect the opinions or scant the talents of any of the groups at the conference. Having together defined our ends, we can no longer honestly carry on apart. . . . We came together for the sake of the student whom we would teach to teach. If, in our selfishness, egocentrism, and over-confidence we pull apart, it is he whom we will inevitably hurt. We have talked a good deal about our cooperative enterprise; this report in great part derives from that talk. All of us must put up or shut up. Now we must act, and act together. (National Commission for Teacher Education and Professional Standards, 1959)

There is a (perhaps peculiarly American) tendency to regard only persons as real, and relationships as ephemeral. Yet, with Buber, "all life is meeting," and relationships do constitute the durable stuff of life. Systems—temporary or not—which can alter relationships are thus of considerable importance.

Action decisions. Finally, many outputs of temporary systems do not involve change in persons, or in their relationships—but are simply agreements to *do* some specific thing. The housewives studied by Lewin (1951) experienced no striking personality changes following the group discussions which led to their decision to serve sweetbreads to their families. Yet they did serve sweetbreads for the first time—and continued to serve them. This sort of finding has been replicated many times, perhaps most carefully by Pelz (1958), who found that the act of arriving at a personal decision in a temporary setting where most others were perceived as making a similar decision had great compellingness; such decisions were frequently carried out.

Temporary systems may have other forms of decision output beyond those governing the future actions of individuals as such. Most typically, these involve changes in the structure or operations of one or more permanent organizations. In Case C above, the participants designed a new organizational structure for management education in their firm. The teachers attending NSF summer institutes often plan broad changes in teaching materials and classroom organization, as well as deciding to behave differently themselves. The members of one management team designed a steering committee, both to guide the implementation of action decisions they had reached during their three-day "retreat," and to deal with new problems as they appeared.

Even where temporary-system decisions are rather general and diffuse, they may have important consequences for a wide number of permanent systems. For example, educational commissions and committees (such as the Committee of Ten on Secondary School Studies of the National Education Association, which in 1893 recommended the secondary school curriculum in force until about 1920) seem to have influenced educational practice considerably, since the powerful, prestigious members of such systems are seen by other educators as being in agreement on desirable policies and procedures.

Finally, it seems clear that temporary-system decisions are often carried out more expeditiously than "routine" decisions, because of added support and sanction for the decision. In one three-day management conference with an executive team, certain decisions were made about future recruitment actions. The manager responsible for recruiting methods had, up to this point, not been able to act effectively, because of other job pressures and uncertainty about the priority of his recruiting role. After the temporary-system decision was made, he said, "It's a real zinger. I can't *not* follow through on it now." His subsequent behavior fulfilled his prediction.

The support in this case was provided by other members of the team, back in the permanent organization. One of the most clear-cut findings in all research on temporary systems is that support developed during the system, and provided postsystem, is very crucial for follow-through on action decisions. Lippitt, for example (1949), found that teams of two or three persons carried out more changes after an intergroup relations workshop than did even the strongest individual participant. Riecken (1952) found that those work campers who had continuing contact with others from the temporary system were most likely to retain (or continue) attitude changes. Marsh & Gortner (1962) noted that the growth of Physical Science Study Committee physics courses, following summer institutes, proceeded in regional clusters of "likeminded teachers"; isolated attenders were far less likely to be innovative. Hagen (1962) has commented on the importance of "group protection" supplied to the innovator during the difficult process of installing the innovation in a permanent system. In all these cases, since the temporary system has developed a shared frame of reference, and a shared commitment to action, the innovator is no longer an isolated deviant. He has the double support of change-relevant norms internalized during the temporary system, and the advice and help of other "converts."

Problems and Dysfunctions of Temporary Systems

The discussion so far has indicated that temporary systems of various sorts seem eminently suited to the production of change in individuals and organizations. Yet a number of difficulties or problems with such systems flow from their very nature, and need some discussion here.

Input overload

First, partly because of the typically high involvement in temporary systems, participants may invite or accept an unrealistic amount of stimulus input. Sometimes this is deliberate: Schein *et al.* (1961) have commented on the importance of sensory overstimulation in "brainwashing" systems: the individual is prevented from having privacy, and is constantly engaged in social activity. But input over-load, paradoxically enough, seems even more likely when the tempo-rary system is designed to stimulate or evoke operant responses (i.e., when the person is in control of his own work load). In Cases B and C above, and in many other conferences, it seems clear that given a clear valued goal, a group left to itself will ordinarily work far harder (i.e., provide its members with more stimuli) than would be the case in a more controlled situation. Participants often remark at the end of short-term conferences that they have "a great deal to sort out," and that their learnings are incomplete. Reported feelings of fatigue are frequent; the need for "decompression" is mentioned. Sometimes the individual may not realize how tired and overextended he has be-come until he leaves the hothouse life of the temporary system and returns to his permanent organization.

Unrealistic goal-setting

A closely connected tendency involves aspiration toward grandiose, unattainable goals. The "as if" character of temporary systems invites a feeling of infinite possibility, the sense that "the sky's the limit." Liberation from permanent-system bonds generates a wild surmise; if the temporal bounds of the system are somewhat vague, so that realis-tic, focused goal-setting is less likely, then goals, too, may be general, excessively noble in statement, and impossibly difficult. Most experi-mental Utopias, as Infield (1955) has pointed out, have been aimed at the achievement of extremely ambitious goals. Under these circum-stances, failure and disenchantment are practically guaranteed.

Lack of process skills

The task-relevant and interpersonal skills required in the intensive climate of the temporary system may be substantial. Infield (1955) has noted, for example, that most utopian experiments were dissolved, not because independent economic survival was impossible, but be-cause task skills (such as those involved in farming) and interpersonal skills required to solve problems and accommodate conflict among system members were lacking. He points out that only those experi-ments with a strong religious base (e.g., Hutterite and Doukhobor communities) have survived for more than a few decades; the presence of an overarching religious framework may help absorb interpersonal problems and conflicts. It is possible—though the data are not in yet—that experimental Utopias with well-developed task skills (and methods for teaching them to new members), such as the Israeli *kibbutzim* and the French "communities of work" may also survive for long periods.

The cruciality of process skills in short-term systems is clearly illustrated in Davis's (1960) account of the teacher education conference discussed earlier:

> My group confined itself to meaningless generalities, refused to meet any issues directly, and there was evident feeling that everything would be fine if people like me did not keep asking for some particular recommendation about the reforms needed in teacher certification. . . . [A keynote speech] was supposed to give point to the group discussions, but our group immediately ignored the speech and started talking other issues. . . .

In this, as in any newly met temporary system, the negative effects of missing process skills may well have been accentuated by the initial defensiveness discussed earlier. Even skilled persons have difficulty in functioning well in a stiff, anxious, threatening climate.

Alienation

Because the members of the temporary system are usually isolated from the surrounding environment, and communicate more with each other than with members of permanent systems, they tend to become alienated, detached, uninvolved. Some systems, of course, tend to select already-alienated types of persons (e.g., utopian experiments). But even where this is not the case, alienation seems to develop easily. The controllable mini-world of the temporary system, if things have gone well, has usually proved an excellent device for meeting members' needs—needs which may have existed for months or years in permanent systems. *Esprit* has developed; the sense of "we happy few" is strong.

For example, after Argyris' (1962) one-week conference with a management team, the members did internalize new ways of working with each other on the job. They were more equalitarian, more open and trustful. Yet they experienced much more difficulty than before in communicating with managers who had not been to the conference. And Riecken's (1952) work campers became more alienated and detached from American society, which they perceived as having values contrary to those reinforced by the work camp experience.

Severe alienation, of course, can result in disillusion, cynicism, and despair when the participant returns to his permanent systems. More than this, it can doom his plans for change and innovation—a problem so central that it requires further discussion.

Linkage failure

The siren voices of a smoothly functioning temporary system can deafen the person to the half-forgotten demands of his permanent systems. He may be seduced into the assumption that ideas or innovations developed in the temporary system can be carried over bodily to the permanent system, forgetting the fact that the temporary system may have been created precisely because of the permanent system's inability to tolerate such ideas.

Thus there is a failure of linkage between systems; the very detachment and euphoria which make time-limited systems so fascinating and productive help to blind the participants to what they will be up against when they return to "ordinary" life with its role conflicts, work pressures, and vested interests. If the temporary system exists illegitimately or without the "permission" of permanent systems, linkage problems are even more acute. At best, the decisions reached on the cultural island may be unworkable, inappropriate, or very difficult to communicate to those on the mainland.

These problems are most critical when the temporary system is essentially innovative in intent. The forces making for maintenance of the status quo are poised ready for action. And even where the permanent system is reasonably open to change, many innovations do require a period of protected trial before their effects can be assessed. For example, Brim (1954), in a study of mothers entering a temporary relationship with a doctor, found that about half could be induced (via the doctor's prestige) to make an initial trial of self-demand feeding with their children who had feeding problems. Yet this innovation takes time—usually two to three weeks—to show good results. Only one third of the mothers who did try the innovation were able to continue it; the support of their husbands proved crucial for this.

Generally speaking, the success of action decisions made in the temporary system will depend not only on the quality of these decisions as such, but on the sophistication with which the members have been able to anticipate (and to plan for coping with) the strategic problems they will encounter upon their return. Thus, a good deal of energy should be invested during the closing days or hours of the system in planning strategy—and in inventing institutionalized ways to support the work so nobly begun in the time-limited setting. Yet time and time again the writer has seen this work scanted; the problems of implementation seem in some way to be defended against, almost wilfully ignored.

For example, in one three-day management team conference devoted to the improvement of operations in a chemical plant, the members agreed (during the last three hours of the conference) on a list of forty-seven action decisions, and specified deadlines for them over the next six months, identifying the persons responsible. Yet only at a consultant's suggestion was attention given to the need for a continuing steering committee to guide the implementation of the decisions (and to coping with new problems as they arose). The top manager felt all this could easily be accomplished "through the regular line organization." Yet "the regular line organization," for many reasons, had not been able to cope with the problems which necessitated the conference in the first place.

Thus we have a crucial problem: how to link temporary and permanent systems effectively, without vitiating the advantages of temporal–spatial isolation from the recurring demands of durable organizational life. It is possible that optimal results would be obtained from a series of intensive, but spaced, sessions of a temporary system, with intermittent opportunity to make linkage with permanent systems, and to analyze and plan for the problems of strategy and change process which ensued.[32] We need to know more.

Temporary Systems and Educational Innovation

The discussion so far has been intended to make it abundantly clear that temporary systems are themselves educative in a number of ways;

[32] This model was tried by Edgar H. Schein and Richard Beckhard in an experimental organizational change program sponsored by National Training Laboratories of the National Education Association during 1961–62, with apparently good results.

they accomplish deep changes of many sorts in persons and their relationships with others. But what other freight does the temporary system concept bear specifically for innovation in education?

Some characteristics of educational systems were referred to briefly in the introductory chapter of the present book, including vulnerability to public influence, difficulty in outcome measurement, the tendency toward ritualization of means, and the fact that educational operations are carried out by *persons* as instruments of change, with little use of physical technology.

It seems possible that more widespread use of temporary systems would aid innovation in systems possessing these characteristics. For example, temporary systems provide the opportunity for increased social validation of the desirability of particular innovations, given uncertainty of outcome measurement and public vulnerability. The risk reduction in temporary systems is thus a very attractive feature for most educational systems. Furthermore, the increased innovativeness and creativity which seems evident in many temporary systems can be rather helpful in reducing ritualization of means and the tendency to perseverate with educational procedures of doubtful validity. And the person-changing potential of temporary systems can be very useful, so long as technology is minimal and persons are central as guiding agents of the educational process.

Secondly, it is probable that as broad social changes continue in America (in amounts spent for education, the rate of production of new knowledge, the proportion of persons engaged in formal education, etc.), all existing educational structures will need very substantial revision. The large and growing number of temporary (or quasi-temporary) structures noted in Chapter 1 is perhaps a symptom of this need. Temporary structures can help innovators avoid the temptation to be palliative about the inadequacies of fundamentally bad permanent structures; they can enable vigorous, thoroughgoing development of innovations which might otherwise never make it through the protective fog of the status quo.

Finally, the deliberate use of temporary systems opens the possibility of a more manageable process of educational change. Innovators, either internal or external to a particular educational system, are more likely to be able to control miniature, time-limited systems than those inherently permanent in nature. Systems like committees, in-service institutes and workshops, interinstitutional visiting teams, accreditation groups, and conferences of all sorts are already in wide use. The analysis in this chapter suggests that creative attention given to the invention and use of new types of temporary systems could show very high payoff in the current educational scene. Brickell's proposal (in the present book) of temporary groups for the designing and testing of innovations is one such example. But other inventions are needed, including more imaginative ways of using external and internal consultants to aid with educational system change problems, the use of residential work sessions for portions of educational staffs, and more sophisticated approaches to "pilot" and experimental groups.

Given success experiences with temporary systems which exploit their unique characteristics productively, a given educational system might come to make far more habitual use of temporary systems as an innovative aid. This implies, not the hoary prescription "We need a vice-president in charge of heresy," but the matter-of-fact acceptance of innovative, time-limited subsystems as a natural part of any organization's life.[33]

Under these circumstances, educational administrators may see how thoroughgoing adaptation of their institutions to the stresses of external demands and internal disequilibria need not involve violent revolution, major surgery, or collapse. Without increased sophistication in the management of change, those responsible for the leadership of educational institutions are almost certainly headed for a very difficult time in the next few decades.

As are we all. Perhaps it is not too much to say that until we *genuinely* understand that "the only constant is change," it will be hard for us to realize that our engagement with the stress, adventure, and creative struggle of one temporary system after another is indeed "the way we live now."

Bibliography

Argyris, C. *Interpersonal competence and organizational effectiveness.* Homewood, Illinois: Dorsey Press, 1962.

[33] For examples of this stance toward organizational change, see Foundation for Research on Human Behavior (1960), and Guest (1962); in both cases the regular, judicious use of interstitial temporary systems (meetings, training and diagnostic conferences) brought about striking improvements in organizational effectiveness.

Barnett, H. G. *Innovation: the basis of cultural change.* New York: McGraw-Hill, 1953.

Benne, K. D. From polarization to paradox. In L. P. Bradford, J. R. Gibb, & K. D. Benne (Eds.), *T-group theory and laboratory method.* New York: Wiley, 1964.

Bennis, W. G. Goals and meta-goals of laboratory training. NTL *Hum. Relat. Training News,* 1962, 6 (3), 1–4 (a).

Bennis, W. G. Towards a "truly" scientific management: the concept of organization health. In A. Rapoport (Ed.), *General Systems* (Yearbook of the Society for the Advancement of General Systems Theory). Ann Arbor, Michigan, 1962 (b).

Bennis, W. G., & Shepard, H. A. A theory of group development. *Hum. Relat.,* 1956, 9 (4), 415–457.

Blake, R. R., Blansfield, M. G., & Mouton, J. S. How executive team training can help you. *Jour. Amer. Soc. Training Directors,* 1962, 16 (1), 3–11.

Bradford, L. P., Gibb, J. R., & Benne, K. D. (Eds.) *T-group theory and laboratory method.* New York: Wiley, 1964.

Brim, O. G., Jr. The acceptance of new behavior in child-rearing. *Hum. Relat.,* 1954, 7 (4) 473–491.

Burns, T., & Stalker, G. M. *The management of innovation.* London: Tavistock, 1961.

Caillois, R. *Man, play and games.* New York: Free Press of Glencoe, 1961.

Campbell, D. T. Factors relevant to the validity of experiments in social settings. *Psychol. Bull.,* 1957, 54, 297–312.

Cook, S. W. Desegregation: a psychological analysis. *Amer. Psychol.,* 1957, 12, 1–13.

Cumming, J., & Cumming, E. *Ego and milieu: theory and practice of environmental therapy.* New York: Atherton Press, 1962.

Davis, E. Fiasco at San Diego. *Council for Basic Educ. Bull.,* 1960, 5, 1–2.

deGrazia, A. Elements of social invention. *Amer. Behav. Sci.,* 1961, 5 (4), 6–9.

Dubos, R. *The dreams of reason: science and Utopias.* New York: Columbia University Press, 1961.

Eaton, J. W. *Stone walls not a prison make: the anatomy of planned administrative change.* Springfield, Ill.: Charles C. Thomas, 1962.

Foundation for Research on Human Behavior. *An action research program for organization improvement.* Ann Arbor, Michigan: The Foundation, 1960.

Gibb, J. R. The T-group as a climate for trust formation. In L. P. Bradford, J. R. Gibb, & K. D. Benne (Eds.), *T-group theory and laboratory method.* New York: Wiley, 1964.

Goffman, E. *Asylums: essays on social situations of mental patients and other inmates.* Garden City, New York: Anchor Books, 1961.

Goffman, E. *Encounters: two studies in the sociology of interaction.* Indianapolis: Bobbs-Merrill, 1961.

Guest, R. H. *Organizational change: the effect of successful leadership.* Homewood, Ill.: Dorsey Press, 1962.

Hage, J. T. Organizational response to innovation: a case study of a community hospital. Unpublished doctoral dissertation, Columbia University, 1963.

Hagen, E. C. *On the theory of social change: how economic growth begins.* Homewood, Ill.: Dorsey Press, 1962.

Harrison, R. Impact of the laboratory on perceptions of others by the experimental group. In C. Argyris, *Interpersonal competence and organizational effectiveness.* Homewood, Ill.: Dorsey Press, 1962. Pp. 261–271.

Hemphill, J. K., Griffiths, D. E., & Frederiksen, N. *Administrative performance and personality: a study of the principal in a simulated elementary school.* New York: Bureau of Publications, Teachers College, Columbia University, 1962.

Hodenfield, G. K., & Stinnett, T. M. *The education of teachers.* Englewood Cliffs, N. J.: Prentice-Hall, 1961.

Holman, D. A. An evaluation of the effectiveness of educational conferences as in-service education for school administrators in New York State. Unpublished doctoral project, Teachers College, Columbia University, 1962.

Horton, D. *The United Church of Christ: its origins, organization and role in the world today.* New York: Thomas Nelson & Sons, 1962.

Huizinga, J. *Homo ludens: a study of the play element in culture.* Boston: Beacon Press, 1955. (First published, 1938.)

Hyman, H. H., Wright, C. R., & Hopkins, T. K. *Applications of methods of evaluation.* University of California Publications in Culture and Society, Vol. 7. Berkeley & Los Angeles: University of California Press, 1962.

Infield, H. F. *Utopia and experiment.* New York: Praeger, 1955.

Kelman, H. C. Processes of opinion change. In W. G. Bennis, K. D. Benne, & R. Chin (Eds.), *The planning of change: readings in the applied behavioral sciences.* New York: Holt, Rinehart & Winston, 1961. Pp. 509–17.

Kimball, S. T., & McClellan, J. E., Jr. *Education and the New America.* New York: Random House, 1962.

Landy, D., & Wechsler, H. Common assumptions, dimensions, and problems of pathway organizations. *J. Soc. Issues,* 1960, *16* (2), 70–78.

Lewin, K. *Field theory in social science.* (D. Cartwright, Ed.) New York: Harper, 1951.

Lewin, K. *Resolving social conflicts.* (G. W. Lewin, Ed.) New York: Harper, 1948.

Lippitt, R. *Training in community relations.* New York: Harper, 1949.

Lippitt, R. Unplanned maintenance and planned change in the group work process. In National Conference on Social Welfare, *Social work practice.* New York: Columbia University Press, 1962. Pp. 75–95.

Marsh, P. E., & Gortner, R. A. *Federal aid to science education: two programs.* Economics and Politics of Public Education Series, No. 6. Syracuse: Syracuse University Press, 1963.

Miles, M. B. Human relations training: processes and outcomes. *J. Couns. Psychol.,* 1960, 7 (4), 301–306.

Miles, M. B., Michael, S. C., Whitman, F. L., & Harris, T. M. *To Bethel and back: the processes and results of a human relations training laboratory for educators.* New York: Bureau of Publications, Teachers College, Columbia University (forthcoming).

Mills, T. M. A sleeper variable in small groups research: the experimenter. *Pacific Sociol. Rev.,* 1962, 5 (1), 21–28.

National Commission on Teacher Education and Professional Standards. *The education of teachers: curriculum programs.* Official report of the Kansas Conference, University of Kansas, Lawrence, Kansas. June 23–26, 1959. Washington: The Commission, National Education Association, 1959.

Negley, G., & Patrick, J. M. *The quest for Utopia.* New York: Henry Schuman, 1952.

Newcomb, T. M. Student peer-group influence. In N. Sanford (Ed.), *The American college: a psychological and sociological interpretation of the higher learning.* New York: Wiley, 1962. Pp. 469–488.

Nokes, P. Feedback as an explanatory device in the study of certain interpersonal and institutional processes. *Hum. Relat.,* 1961, 14 (4), 381–387.

OSS Assessment Staff. *Assessment of men.* New York: Rinehart, 1945.

Orne, M. T. On the social psychology of the psychological experiment: with particular reference to demand characteristics and their implications. *Amer. Psychol.,* 1962, 17 (11), 776–783.

Ozmon, H. A., Jr. Educational Utopias. Unpublished doctoral project, Teachers College, Columbia University, 1962.

Pagès, M. The sociotherapy of the enterprise. *Hum. Relat.,* 1959, 12 (4), 317–334. Also excerpted in W. G. Bennis, K. D. Benne, & R. Chin (Eds.), *The planning of change: readings in the applied behavioral sciences.* New York: Holt, Rinehart & Winston, 1961. Pp. 168–185.

Pelz, E. B. Some factors in "group decision." In E. E. Maccoby, T. M. Newcomb, & E. E. Hartley (Eds.), *Readings in social psychology.* (3d ed.) New York: Holt, 1958. Pp. 212–219.

Poulet, G. *Studies in human time.* New York: Harper, 1959. (First published, 1956.)

Riecken, H. C. *The volunteer work camp: a psychological evaluation.* Cambridge: Addison-Wesley, 1952.

Rogers, E. M. *Diffusion of innovations.* New York: Free Press of Glencoe, 1962.

Roueché, B. Peculiar powers of placebos. *Sci. Digest,* 1961, 49, 70–81.

Ryan, B., & Gross, N. C. The diffusion of hybrid seed corn in two Iowa communities. *Rural Sociol.,* 1943, 8, 15–24.

Schein, E. H. Management development as a process of influence. *Indust. Mgt. Rev.*, 1961, 2 (2).

Schein, E. H., Schneier, I., & Barker, C. H. *Coercive persuasion: a socio-psychological analysis of the "brainwashing" of American civilian prisoners by the Chinese Communists.* New York: Norton, 1961.

Schuman, H. Social structure and personality constriction in a total institution. Unpublished doctoral dissertation, Harvard University, 1961.

Shapiro, A. K. A contribution to a history of the placebo effect. *Behav. Sci.*, 1960, 5 (2), 109–135.

Shaw, I. *Two weeks in another town.* New York: Random House, 1960.

Sherif, M. (Ed.) *Intergroup relations and leadership.* New York: Wiley, 1962.

Shlien, J. M., Mosak, H. H., & Dreikurs, R. Effect of time limits: a comparison of two psychotherapies. *J. Couns. Psychol.*, 1962, 9 (1), 31–34.

Star, S. A., Williams, R. M., Jr., & Stouffer, S. A. Negro infantry platoons in white companies. In E. E. Maccoby, T. M. Newcomb, & E. E. Hartley (Eds.), *Readings in social psychology.* (3d ed.) New York: Holt, 1958. Pp. 596–601.

Talbot, E., Miller, S. C., & White, R. B. Some antitherapeutic side effects of hospitalization and psychotherapy. Unpublished paper, Austen Riggs Center, Inc., Stockbridge, Mass., 1962.

Tarde, G. *The laws of imitation.* (Trans. E. C. Parsons.) New York: Holt, Rinehart & Winston, 1903. (First published, 1889.)

Thelen, H. A. *The dynamics of groups at work.* Chicago: University of Chicago Press, 1954.

Vinter, R. D. Analysis of treatment organizations. *Social Work*, 1963, 8 (3), 3–15.

Part III: The American educational system as a setting for innovation

IT MUST be remembered that the case studies, and the research and theory, presented in the first two sections of this book all imply or assume the existence of a larger national context. Some generalizations made so far would hold up in most other industrialized—and perhaps in some developing—countries. Many would not. The American educational system has special properties which are of considerable importance in provoking, discouraging, and maintaining innovative efforts. The five chapters in this section are intended to illuminate these characteristics.

First, Brickell graphically describes the main elements affecting educational innovation in New York State, from local schools to foundations to campus laboratory schools to state education department supervisors. He identifies aspects of the system which presently serve to block innovation, and outlines structural changes needed for sustained innovative effort.

The next two chapters focus on selected aspects of American society which bear on educational innovation. Kiger discusses the financial support which foundations have given to learned societies, councils and institutes, and stresses the importance of the resulting production of knowledge in educational innovation. Jennings' discussion of

491

the mass media illuminates them as centrally educative—and as relatively peripheral in some respects to the education which occurs in schools.

Wayland's chapter undertakes the challenging task of specifying the mechanisms—often not official, usually taken for granted—which make a coherently functioning national system of education out of what most observers treat as a chaotic maze of "local autonomy."

The final chapter of the section offers a set of five independently made predictions—by Cass, Willis, Fischer, Mayer, and Brameld—as to the changes which are probable in American education within the next ten years.

CHAPTER 20

State organization for educational change: a case study and a proposal

HENRY M. BRICKELL

"WE NEED to consider how best to bring the total educational resources of the state in a massive attack on resistance, lethargy, and
blocks to constructive change." Thus New York State Commissioner
of Education James E. Allen, Jr., in 1961, described the need for a
study of instructional innovation in the schools.

In speed and quality of educational change, New York is unquestionably a leader among the states. It may well be first. In 1960, for
example, New York contributed a full 25 per cent of all pupils in the
nation taking the Advanced Placement Program examinations. There
is other evidence of the state's superiority. When Commissioner Allen
described the pace of change as sluggish, he was not measuring New
York against other states, but against his idea of what the state could
and should become.

The Background

The Commissioner called for two studies: (1) an inventory of new
instructional programs being used in elementary and secondary schools,

THE AUTHOR is assistant superintendent of the Manhasset, New York, Public
Schools. He served from February through August of 1961 as consultant on
educational experimentation to the Commissioner of Education, State of New
York.

and (2) an analysis of the dynamics of instructional innovation.[1] The studies were to result in recommendations for state-wide action to accelerate the pace of change, and to improve its direction—without making change an end in itself, and without diminishing local control of education.

Both studies focused *exclusively* on innovations which require significant shifts in the normal arrangement of the six major structural elements of a school: teachers, students, subjects, methods, times, places. Examples of such innovations are television, team teaching, ungraded classes, and large- and small-group instruction. The findings of both studies apply to instructional programs of that type rather than to classroom practice—the behavior the teacher is usually free to exhibit in his own classroom with his own pupils. *Classroom practice as such was not studied.* The findings must be interpreted accordingly.

Taken by questionnaire in the spring of 1961 with the help of the state's college-affiliated school study councils, the inventory of innovations was published in the fall as the *Commissioner's 1961 Catalog of Educational Change* (Brickell, 1961a).

The questionnaire was headlined "What are you doing that is *new for you,* new in your schools, even if someone else has done it before?" It asked schools to list all new instructional programs introduced since 1953 and still in operation. It asked them to omit programs dropped, innovations being planned, and modifications not directly related to instruction—such as the acquisition of data-processing equipment for financial accounting. Because one man's "team teaching" is another man's "large-group instruction," the reporting form was designed so that the actual characteristics of the new programs could be tabulated without regard to their labels.

Of those polled in the state-wide mailing, 564 public school systems (64 per cent of the state total) and 134 nonpublic schools and school systems (39 per cent of the state total) responded. Follow-up inquiries to nonrespondents usually indicated that they had nothing to report. In terms of over-all quality, level of financial support, and responsiveness to public demand, the 698 participating schools probably cannot be matched by any other state-wide group of equal size in the nation. For this reason, the pace and direction of educational change, as re-

[1] The Fund for the Advancement of Education financed the studies.

vealed by the 2,906 innovations they reported, are of great significance.

The analysis showed that the rate of innovation in the public schools (but not in the nonpublic schools) had *more than doubled in the fifteen months following the launching of the Soviet Sputnik I in October of 1957.* (See Figure 1.) Changes had swept not only foreign

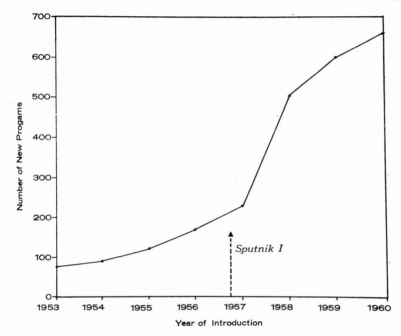

Figure 1. Rate of instructional innovation in New York State public school systems

languages, mathematics, and science—which had led the field by tripling their rate of change—but all other subjects, nonacademic as well as academic, without a single exception. Most of the attention had gone to above-average students in junior and senior high schools.

However, the inventory revealed that despite their increased rate of instructional innovation, *the great bulk of schools as structured institutions had remained stable.* Most changes involved an alteration in subject content (ordinarily different information and more of it), in instructional material (usually a new textbook), or in the grouping of pupils (most commonly class size reduced or varied). Few programs embodied changes in the kind of people employed, in the way they were organized to work with students, in the nature of instructional materials they used, or in the times and places at which they taught. The programs which did embody such changes often touched the work of only two or three teachers.

The second study set out to discover the reasons for structural stability in schools, to identify any forces powerful enough to loosen that stability, and to suggest a new pattern of state organization which would make the modification of instructional arrangements rational, rapid, and continuous. It was published as *Organizing New York State for Educational Change* (Brickell, 1961b). The remainder of this chapter is based upon that study.

The Case Study: Dynamics of Educational Change in New York State (1961)

Like any other state, New York is a massive, complex entity. At the elementary and secondary levels, 2,780,000 pupils are taught by 127,000 teachers in 880 operating public school systems (including that of New York City, which enrolls about 35 per cent of all public school pupils in the state). In addition, there are about 350 nonpublic secondary schools (including all private and parochial institutions) as well as a large number of nonpublic elementary schools. Moreover, there are 189 institutions of higher learning.

New York has a large, influential State Education Department, nine active regional college-affiliated school study councils and one state-wide council, an energetic State Teachers Association, a strong State School Boards Association, a well-supported Parent-Teachers Association, and a vigorous Citizens Committee for the Public Schools. Furthermore, the schools are affected by private philanthropic foundations, commercial organizations, taxpayers' groups, newspapers, and local citizens' committees.

Any study which attempts to describe the dynamic relationships of all the forces which shape elementary and secondary school programs in the state is doomed to oversimplification and threatened with error. The statements made in the original report and in this abbreviated version consist largely of sweeping generalizations. The reader can point to major exceptions. So can the writer. Both must exercise the discipline of omitting those exceptions, in order to illuminate the major vectors in the process of instructional change as it occurs most of the time in most schools. It is always tempting to write about exceptions; they fascinate precisely because of their rarity. But they provide a poor rationale for a pattern of state-wide organization. For that reason they have been avoided.

The tone used here is akin to that used in the original report—straightforward, assertive, often unqualified. The reader of this brief summary is invited to join the writer in a compact: if the writer may be spared the accusation of believing that life is so simple that it can be sketched in bold black lines on a pure white ground, the reader will be spared the labor of reading an endless string of qualifiers which could muddy the text and blur the main points. The length of this chapter prevents adequate illustration of the general statements. For that the reader is referred to the full report.

The writer studied the dynamics of innovation through unstructured interviews in 31 public school systems of all types and sizes in New York, and 5 selected districts located in other states. In the process he visited approximately 100 schools and 1500 classrooms. He also visited 13 college and university schools of education, 9 regional college-affiliated school study councils, the New York State Education Department, schools of medicine and agriculture, and a wide variety of professional, commercial, and school-related citizens' organizations.

The findings and recommendations reported here depend entirely on these interviews for their support. No other data underlie them. Earlier professional literature on the subject played no part in shaping the conclusions, except insofar as that literature had been absorbed into the thinking of those interviewed, or had conditioned the writer's powers of observation.

The three phases of instructional innovation

The key conclusion of the study—drawn only after months of observing puzzling and apparently contradictory phenomena—is that it is one thing to design or invent a new way of teaching, it is another to find out whether the invention is any good, and it is still another to demonstrate it for the purpose of persuading others to adopt it. That is to say, the *design, evaluation,* and *dissemination* of innovations are three distinctly different, irreconcilable processes. The circumstances which are right for one are essentially wrong for the others. Furthermore, most people prefer to work in one phase, and find working in the others uncomfortable if not distasteful. People preferring different phases often have an abrasive effect on each other when brought into close contact.

Phase 1: Design.   Program design is the translation of what is known about learning into programs for teaching. *The ideal circumstances for the design of an improved instructional approach are artificial, enriched, and free.* At their best, they provide a group of highly intelligent people, a somewhat limited problem, time to concentrate on a solution, ample money and resources, freedom to try almost anything, the likelihood that the solution will be used somewhere, and the prospect of personal recognition if the problem is solved. The more artificial, enriched, and free the setting, the more distinctive the innovation it is likely to produce.

Virtually perfect illustrations, characterized by each element listed here, are the settings for the national curriculum studies sponsored by the National Science Foundation. PSSC physics, SMSG mathematics, BSCS biology, and CHEM and CBA chemistry all sprang without exception from artificially created, enriched, free settings. They did not arise naturally from the workaday world. None of them would exist today if a group of talented men had not been paid and freed to concentrate specifically on designing them.

Phase 2: Evaluation.   Program evaluation is the systematic testing of a new instructional approach to find what it will accomplish under what conditions. *The ideal circumstances for the evaluation of a new instructional approach are controlled, closely observed, and unfree.* At their best, they provide conditions in which the forces which might influence the success of the new approach can be controlled when possible, and kept under close surveillance when actual control is impossible. The freedom which is essential in searching for a good *design* is destructive in the making of a good *evaluation*.

Almost every research specialist the writer met in a local school system seemed somehow misplaced. His desire to hold a new program steady in order to evaluate it ran headlong into the teachers' urge to change it as soon as they sensed something wrong. One psychologist in a foundation-sponsored project lamented, "The teachers here don't care anything about objective evaluation—my work is tolerated only because I go with the grant."

Phase 3: Dissemination.   Program dissemination is the process of spreading innovations into schools. *The ideal circumstances for the dissemination of a new approach through demonstration are those which are ordinary, unenriched, and normal.* At their best, they are exactly like the everyday situations in the observer's own school and community. Anything which the observer could label "abnormal" or "unrealistic"—such as the enriched conditions necessary for good *design* or the controlled conditions necessary for proper *evaluation—* is sufficient to rob the observed program of persuasive effect.

A few months before the interviews, Commissioner Allen had announced the possibility of creating a state-sponsored, centrally located experimental education center for the demonstration of novel programs. During the interviews, people all across the state flatly rejected the idea. "Too artificial," they said. "What can we learn from a 'show-off' school where specially selected teachers and specially selected kids, using the best equipment and materials, perform in a sort of convention atmosphere?"

Evidence and comparisons.   Soon after the survey interviews were begun, it began to appear that friction was common between people concerned with innovation. The reasons for the trouble did not become clear for some time. Then gradually, as interview followed interview, a pattern began to emerge.

Probably the most consistently abrasive relationship was that between the State men managing the Education Department's $300,000 fund for local experimentation and the local men spending it. The State view was best summarized in these words: "It's like pulling teeth to get decent experimental designs from the schools." The local view was best summarized in these words: "The Department wants your grandmother's pedigree included in the research proposal." The writer found himself agreeing heartily with the State that the localities should not expect support for slipshod research, and agreeing heartily with the localities that the State should not try to jam their creative impulses into a rigid research framework—then realized that the State men were trying to evaluate programs the local men had not invented yet.

A superintendent, when asked why he had sought a research grant for a program he had already decided would work, answered, "That's just to convince the neighbors." He was using money given for an evaluation to finance a demonstration.

A man who had been freed half time to develop a new program in his school said with pride that fifty visitors had come to see it—but then admitted that demonstrating the program was keeping him from inventing it.

A research specialist was surprised when a philanthropic foundation granted money for his proposal, but suggested that his careful research design be eliminated lest he trip over it in future impulses to improve the program once it began operating. He had asked for money to evaluate a program he proposed to invent; the foundation gave him money to invent it, recognizing that evaluative controls would be a nuisance at that early stage.

People complained repeatedly that outside organizations often promoted the use of unproven innovations. They cited as typical examples the promotion of television by the State Education Department, the promotion of curricular reforms in mathematics and science by the National Science Foundation, the promotion of team teaching by the Ford Foundation, and the promotion of flexible scheduling in high schools by the National Association of Secondary School Principals. Each of these programs had moved directly from the drawing boards to demonstration, with the evaluation stage omitted.

All of this and much more like it convinced the writer that our failure to distinguish—indeed, our dogged refusal to recognize—the three phases of change is the most formidable block to instructional improvement today.

The distinctions between design, evaluation, and dissemination are better recognized, and the circumstances for each better separated, in medicine, agriculture, and industry than in education. In fact, the most striking feature of the innovative systems in these fields is the existence of separate agencies for the different functions.

The distinctions are perhaps clearest in agriculture, where it took fifty years of trial and error to recognize the differences and get organized to deal with them. Beginning with the creation of colleges of agriculture as part of the Morrill Act in 1862, the Federal government started financing agricultural experiment stations in 1887 and established the agricultural extension service with the Smith-Lever Act in 1914. Since that time, the machinery of agricultural research and development has aided innovation vigorously. For example, the staff of an experiment station draws on basic research [2] in agriculture and related fields to develop (invent) a new strain of seed. After evaluating the seed through field testing on controlled plots, the station makes it available for general use. At this point, an extension specialist translates the research findings into a practical plan for farmers. Then the county agent, relying on face-to-face contact and demonstrations on ordinary farms, promotes the use of the new seed.

Medicine and industrial research and development offer generally parallel examples.

But the field of education is organized on the assumption that all phases can occur simultaneously in a single setting. The campus laboratory schools stand as the most spectacular example of trying to put everything into one shell. Their plight will be discussed later.

The process of change within local schools

A possible explanation of the roles played by the public, the board

[2] The reader will note the omission of basic research from the three phases as they operate in education. Basic research in education is the study of the circumstances, processes, and effects of human learning. In a logical sequence of events, basic research would *precede* the *design* phase in the innovative process. Basic research would be Phase 1 and design would be Phase 2. However, the logic of the sequence is seldom followed. Most educational innovation does not flow methodically from basic research findings, but is undertaken quite independently. Consequently, the writer resisted his inclination to discuss basic research at the beginning, and set it aside for treatment in this note.

Our failure to recognize the value of such research, and our refusal to finance adequately the special circumstances needed for it—along with our premature eagerness to have the researcher translate his results into educational programs—have prevented or damaged many basic research efforts. They have led some of our finest minds to try to convert their findings to practical use, to seek recognition through advertising them, and to seek money for further research through selling their findings to schools. Such use of research talent, although understandable, is wasteful. The men talented enough to carry out basic studies should be supported to do what only they can do.

Although the writer believes that the best designs for teaching will come from the conscious, deliberate, planned translation of fundamental studies of learning, he does not propose at the close of this chapter that basic research be supported under a *state* plan. He believes that such research should be supported through *national* funds, because it produces the most universally useful information and should have the broadest financial base.

of education, administrators, and teachers in the dynamics of instructional innovation can be found in the following general formulation.

A school, like any other institution, tends to continue doing what it was established to do, holding itself relatively stable and resisting attempts at restructuring. There is a sound reason for this: Stability in the institutional structure makes for maximum output of the results that structure was designed to produce. Any change in the arrangement of elements tends to cut down production, at least until new habit patterns are formed.

There are two distinct groups of people who might be expected to influence structural change in the local public schools: the public, which is *external* to the institution, and the profession, which is *internal* to it. The process of local educational change is determined by the relationships between and within these two groups: the public and the board of education as external, the administrators and the teachers as internal.

Calls for distinctly different educational results tend to come from outside the school itself, that is, from the public and the board which represents that public. (There is no better example than the doubling of New York State innovation in 1958 following the launching of Sputnik I. It is almost impossible to imagine such an upward thrust coming from within the profession.) However, such external demands seldom specify how better results are to be produced. The choice of methods is left to the staff.

The public and the board.   Public schools are structured in such a way that the chief administrator can be kept responsive to external demands: the superintendent serves in a contractual relationship to a lay board of education.

Parents' and other citizens' groups in most communities do not exert a direct influence on the adoption of new types of instructional programs, probably because they do not know enough about educational methodology to favor or to oppose specific innovations. Their influence is ordinarily limited to creating a climate of interest—or the lack of it— in better results. However, if for some reason the public develops a lively interest in a new type of program—foreign languages in the elementary school, for example—that program is likely to appear in the local classrooms.

The public is not an anchor holding back an eager profession. Community expectations and professional ambitions are usually in reasonable harmony with each other.

Like the public, the board of education in most communities is not a strong agent in determining the path of educational innovation, but its influence is decisive when exerted. Most board members know too little about teaching to suggest that any given new technique be adopted or rejected. Many are only vaguely aware of instructional developments because they devote their time to other matters. Naturally, if the board decides to oppose or to urge a particular innovation, it will have its way. But it is rare to find a board directing the instructional program to that degree. Few boards would do more than demand a generally better outcome. While they may ask that the mathematics program be updated for the space age, they are unlikely to select new content or new methods for the mathematics curriculum.

The administrator and the teacher.   New types of instructional programs are introduced by administrators. Rearrangements of the structural elements of the institution depend *almost exclusively* upon administrative initiative. Teachers are not change–agents for innovations of major scope. Even when free to guide their own activities, teachers seldom suggest distinctly new types of working patterns for themselves.

The administrator may promote—or prevent—innovation. He cannot stand aside, or be ignored. He is powerful not because he has a monopoly on imagination, creativity, or interest in change—the opposite is common—but simply because he has the authority to precipitate a decision. Authority is a critical element in innovation, because proposed changes generate mixed reactions which can prevent consensus among peers and result in stagnation.

The language used almost universally in discussing administration—"shared decision-making," "the team approach," "full staff involvement"—is not descriptive of the actual process. More often than not these euphemisms are intentional disguises. The participation patterns in widespread use are frequently little more than enabling arrangements, employed to persuade the faculty to embark on a course which has been at least partly preselected by the administrator.

The classroom teacher is not an independent professional, much inspirational literature to the contrary notwithstanding. He is instead one member of the staff of a stable institution. His behavior reflects his position.

Classroom teachers can make only three types of instructional change in the absence of administrative intervention:

1. Change in classroom practice—that is, any alteration in instructional procedure which a teacher can accomplish in his own classroom without disturbing the work of other teachers.
2. Relocation of existing curriculum content—an activity which a group of teachers commonly initiates, and can carry forward with little assistance, so long as there is no administrative opposition. A typical example would be the relocating of arithmetic topics between the fourth and fifth grades to assure proper dovetailing.
3. Introduction of single special courses at the high school level—commonly terminal courses in a sequence. They are often begun at the initiative of a teacher who has just returned from an intensive learning experience, such as an NSF summer institute.

Deciding on a change.   Few new instructional programs are invented in any school system. Most local changes involve adopting or adapting something the neighbors are doing.

Suspicion about the worth of innovations in other schools, and even about the sincerity of other innovators, is a widespread and severe inhibitor of change. Most administrators and teachers believe that the bulk of innovations which come to their attention are froth without substance, quite possibly concocted by the sponsoring school in an effort to gain outside recognition.

Many visits are actually undertaken for the purpose of discovering that the new program in a neighboring school is no better—and perchance a trifle worse—than what the home school is already doing.

Among all the ways of learning about an innovation, the most persuasive is that of visiting a successful program and observing it in action. Speeches, literature, research reports, and conversations with participants outside the actual instructional setting are interesting—but relatively unconvincing. Nothing persuades like a visit. However, anything "abnormal," "unreal," or "artificial" in the circumstances surrounding an observed program—that is, anything seen as appreciably different from conditions in the visitor's own school system—can rob a visit of persuasive effect. For this reason, people from an industrial town, for instance, feel they can learn little by traveling to a wealthy suburb.

Introducing the change.   The most successful innovations are those which are accompanied by the most elaborate help to teachers as they begin to provide the new instruction. Whereas initial faculty reaction to the proposed change is not critical in determining its success, the amount of help provided *is* critical. New instructional programs can be successfully introduced despite initial apathy—or even opposition—on the part of a number of teachers. Within four months to a year after a new program gets under way, teachers ordinarily begin to believe that the new program is better than the one which preceded it.

Proposed innovations often arouse feelings of inadequacy and uncertainty. The early questions, doubts, and hesitancies expressed *should be distinguished from outright resistance to the change.* Uncertainties diminish with experience, which is probably why teachers begin to prefer new programs within several months after their introduction.

An innovation which falters is more likely to be suffering from simple staff inability than from conscious or unconscious sabotage.

Evaluating the change.   Almost everything new seems to "work better." One reason is that when a school program is changed, people outside the classrooms give teachers an unaccustomed amount of attention, encouragement, and recognition. That sudden recognition can scarcely fail to have an exhilarating effect. A related reason is that taking part in an innovation often means being surrounded by other adults, who share the risks and are eager for group success. The other adults may be the principal, another teacher on the same team or in the television project, a research worker, a teacher's aide, or perhaps a student teacher or a group of parents.

During the survey interviews, administrators frequently shrugged off any unique value in the *specific form* of an innovation—team teaching, for example—and said, "It succeeded because it brought our teachers into real contact with each other for the first time." Evidently the "Hawthorne effect"—higher production stimulated by a change which does not alter the original resources but which offers recognition and wins group approval of higher goals—goes hand in hand with educational innovation.

Instructional innovations are almost always evaluated by observing the reactions of the students while they are receiving the new instruction. More complex evaluative techniques are seldom used, and never outweigh student reaction as a measure of success. Unimproved achievement test scores, for example, mean little if student enthusiasm for the new program runs high.

The role of outside institutions and organizations

Arranged around the local school system are a number of agencies which attempt to influence instructional innovation. Some are positive; some are negative; some are powerless.

The New York State Education Department. Because of its size and status, the state education agency in New York is powerful and presumably more influential than that in most other states. Its influence is both positive and negative.

In spite of its recent interest in educational innovation, particularly among personnel at the top level, the Department as a whole is still characterized by a prudential outlook. Much of its effort is devoted to regulatory activities. The Department is somewhat encouraging when a school adopts programs it officially endorses, and somewhat discouraging when a school adopts programs not officially endorsed. Departmental discouragement inhibits all but two types of schools: the slow-moving, low socioeconomic districts which never even reach the boundaries of State approval, and the fast-moving, high socioeconomic districts which commonly report that they have learned how to deal with the Department in making instructional innovations ("Don't ask.").

New York State Regents Examinations, beyond any question whatsoever, inhibit educational change. Long and intensive study of old Regents Examinations is a successful pattern of preparing students for the upcoming examinations in a typical high school. Schools are lukewarm about innovations which are distinctive enough in approach or content to disrupt this successful pattern.

The Department's field supervisors—except in selected vocational and technical fields such as agriculture—are so few in number and have such diffuse responsibilities that they have little influence on the schools. There are, for example, *three* field supervisors in English serving approximately seven hundred high schools.

Altogether, the Department employs over 1,900 people. Yet despite its great size and the problems which size inevitably brings, the Department is still too small for the job it is attempting—direct service to nine hundred local school systems—and it can never be made large enough. Even if doubled in size, the Department could not provide direct service to local school systems—on either a supervisory or consulting basis, using either central or regional offices.

Whatever the strengths and weaknesses of the State Education Department, past or present, an urgent cry for State leadership is being uttered by administrators in all types of school districts—large and small, urban and rural, wealthy and poor, active and inactive—across the entire state.

Colleges and universities. Except for their role in training teachers, which is universally regarded as being of critical importance, the colleges and universities have little influence on instructional innovation in elementary and secondary schools. Very few of the local programs studied during the survey had been suggested, planned, or evaluated— or even observed—by college personnel, on either a paid or voluntary basis.

Institutions of higher learning are organized primarily to teach courses of predetermined content and predetermined length to individuals who elect to come to the campuses. For local innovations of major scope, as indicated earlier, the *individual* teacher is not a strong agent of change. To introduce such shifts successfully, it is necessary to deal with the entire staff, rather than with individual teachers. College courses designed for an assortment of individual teachers must offer information and skills which will be useful in a variety of school settings. They cannot be directed narrowly toward the needs of one particular school system. From the viewpoint of a local school system interested in a major innovation, this is a fundamental defect in the structure of the college, rendering it an unsuitable instrument for bringing about local change.

According to the professors interviewed, teacher education programs do not attempt to equip the prospective teacher with specific instructional techniques, but concentrate on developing a general professional wisdom, out of which he can develop the specific techniques he needs for any given task. Actual instruction in specific techniques is said to be the responsibility of the schools which employ the college graduates.

However, few local school systems do have a program of in-service education which could even begin to fill the gap pointed to so insistently by college personnel. Evidently, no one in the profession understands the necessity for continuous in-service education so well as the people providing pre-service education. They understand as no one else does how much more is needed to develop professional competence.

Despite college disclaimers of any serious effort to teach specific techniques, it became evident that teachers *are* taught such things as how to use a textbook, how to make lesson plans, and how to assign homework. These are more accurately described as "techniques currently in vogue" rather than as "basic professional wisdom." Thus the writer concluded that teacher education programs do not train teachers in how to carry out new instructional processes, until those processes are in general use in the elementary and secondary schools.

Campus schools. The campus schools at the eleven state university colleges—schools for elementary or secondary students, located on the campuses—stand as monuments to our inability to distinguish between the design, evaluation, and dissemination functions.

The entire history of campus schools in the United States, up to and including the present day, is replete with conflicting expectations as to what they should accomplish. New York State is no exception. Taking the profession as a whole, it expects the campus schools, all at once and in a single setting, to design new instructional approaches, to evaluate their effectiveness, and to demonstrate them in such a manner as to impress visitors from the public schools—while at the same time showing pre-service teachers the best known ways to teach. All this is to be accomplished while providing sound, dependable instruction for the children of a watchful college staff and the more articulate local parents.

No single institution can perform all these functions simultaneously. The irreconcilability of the functions has meant that the campus schools have found it almost impossible to perform any single one well. Although they enjoy an independence which should enable them to be experimental, they are not; although they presumably should subject their programs to extraordinarily intensive evaluation, they do not; although they demonstrate sound, conventional programs of established quality which should enable them to serve as models for the public schools around them, they are not so used. And although the state spends millions of dollars annually to operate and to maintain them as part of teacher education, observing or teaching in them is not required for teacher certification.

Professional associations. The professional associations are the supreme communicators in the professions, although the communication which they provide is random, disjointed, overlapping, and unfocused. Their effectiveness can be traced not to their periodicals and to speeches at conventions, but rather to informal contact among individuals at meetings. Most administrators and teachers believe that the full truth about programs in other schools is unavailable through professional articles, formal speeches at conventions, research reports, and other information sources which are far removed from the classroom. Informal conversations, particularly with friends who can be trusted, are another matter.

College-affiliated school study councils. These regional associations of school systems seldom participate directly in changing the instructional approaches used in their member schools. With a few notable exceptions, the councils are poorly financed and weak in influence, serving primarily to increase communication among their members.

The core of the problem seems to be that the study councils are sponsored by college professors chiefly interested in discovering new information, but paid for by local systems chiefly interested in learning to do the best of what is already known. This schism in purpose dooms the councils to a finance level so low that they cannot perform either function effectively.

Private philanthropic foundations. The private foundations have sponsored two kinds of activities related to educational innovation:

(1) basic research, most of it in related fields from which education draws its fundamental information, such as psychology, sociology, political science, and other social sciences; (2) the development of specific instructional programs, such as television, team teaching, "dual progress" plans, Saturday science seminars, and the use of teacher aides. Foundation financing has freed able people to concentrate at least temporarily on limited functions. Some important research and some promising new programs have been generated.

One curious paradox is that when foundations which sponsor specific innovations publicize these programs, the publicity (in addition to drawing public attention) arouses suspicion, and tends to inhibit the spread of the programs.

The National Science Foundation.   The high school mathematics and science programs designed under the sponsorship of the National Science Foundation (PSSC physics, SMSG mathematics, BSCS biology, and CHEM and CBA chemistry) are significant innovations in high school course content and methodology. Disseminating these courses is simplified because: (1) they are designed as complete units; (2) the instructional materials are available; (3) in-service training is available at no cost to teachers; (4) like any classroom practice, they can be used by one teacher without disturbing the work of others.[3] However, the current dissemination of these courses *prior* to their evaluation is a prime example of omitting the evaluation phase in educational innovation.[4]

Commercial organizations.   The commercial organizations, such as textbook publishers, are extremely powerful. When they promote an instructional change, a great wave of influence sweeps over the schools. On the other hand, once they begin to market a given product, they

---

[3] The SMSG courses are an exception, since they are sequential.

[4] At the end of the study, the writer hypothesized that *if* his other findings were accurate, then New York State should have less than its share of NSF courses, thanks to Regents Examinations and the "mildly negative" stance of the State Education Department. This hypothesis was quite daring in light of the general alertness of New York schools, and yet the other findings led inexorably to it. Some months later, the Educational Testing Service supplied unpublished data showing that New York, with about 10% of the nation's pupils, had 5% or fewer of the nation's PSSC, BSCS, and CBA courses. In the CHEM group, the state had eleven courses—about 10% of the national total.

serve as powerful inhibitors of further change, because they seek volume distribution and repeated sales of the same product.

One reason for their power is that they innovate early, before the majority of schools have begun to change, and move rapidly and aggressively, by way of advertising and numerous sales representatives, to spread their new products.

The schools depend heavily on instructional materials and can scarcely operate without them. The single fact that commercial companies develop materials to command the widest possible market is a great decisive factor in shaping instructional innovations. Because they draw instructional materials from a common commercial pool, the slower-moving schools are probably pulled forward, while the faster-moving schools are probably held back. One result is a nation-wide tendency toward unification of curriculum content and instructional methods.

The Proposal: Organizing the State to Improve the Process of Change

The report on the dynamics of instructional innovation (Brickell, 1961, *b*) concluded with a new plan for state organization. It had become evident during the study that a little more of anything—even a little more of everything—would not be enough. What appeared to be necessary was a major new solution in which the elements would correspond to each element of the problem. Accordingly the proposed cure was shaped segment by segment to match the diagnosis. The plan was based squarely on the findings presented earlier, and depended entirely upon them for its justification.

The recommendation assumed that the solution would have to be accomplished largely with the people and the funds already available. It expected each level of government and each type of organization to perform, and to finance, the functions most natural to that structure. It avoided the creation of new structures where adequate ones existed, but it recommended the abandonment of some which were inherently defective. Perhaps most significantly, it assumed that the factors influencing instructional change could not be altered appreciably, and that they would have to be guided—not opposed.

A characteristic feature of the plan, proliferated into several structural variants, was the use of generalists to fill long-range permanent

positions, and the use of specialists to fill short-term temporary positions. This feature was used repeatedly for several reasons: (1) it is
exceedingly difficult to attract highly competent specialists into permanent government positions, partly because of salary and partly because
of restrictions on their work; (2) even if attracted, extraordinary
talent does not seem to flourish in bureaucratic organizations; (3) government bureaus have an understandable preoccupation with prudential functions which makes them an unlikely source of innovation; (4)
permanent professional positions in government tend to become managerial, wasting any highly specialized talents of the persons who fill
them; (5) it is shortsighted to limit the sources of talent to persons on
the regular payroll; and (6) it is pointless to hire permanently a
specialist whose talents are needed only on occasion.

Finally, the heart of the proposal was that separate circumstances
be deliberately created for the *design, evaluation,* and *dissemination* of
new instructional programs. (The plan's general structure and the distinction between the three phases of innovation are shown in Figure 2.)

THE UNIVERSITY OF THE STATE OF NEW YORK

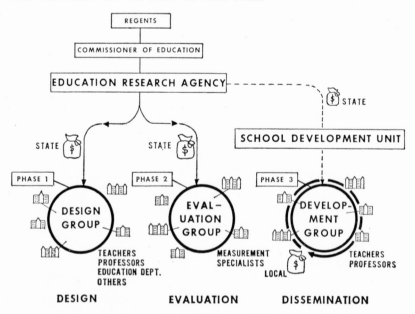

Figure 2. A plan for improving the process of educational change in
the elementary and secondary schools of New York State

The state was urged to create a semiautonomous Education Research Agency with two specific functions: (1) to stimulate and to finance the *design* of new instructional programs for elementary and secondary schools; and (2) to arrange and finance the rigorous *evaluation* of new programs through field testing. At the same time, the state was urged to stimulate (but not to finance) the formation of regional school development units, which would perform a third function: (3) to *disseminate* the programs proven and endorsed by the Education Research Agency.

State financing of design and evaluation was seen as desirable for these reasons: (1) enriched design settings are expensive; (2) state sponsorship gives localities a powerful partner to share the risks of failure; (3) evaluation through field testing must of necessity involve many school districts; and (4) both the design and evaluation efforts produce information which is of very general use. In point of fact, state financing of *design* is not only desirable but necessary, because local schools—if left to their own devices—will neither finance highly artificial design settings, nor expose themselves to the risks of bold invention in teaching children. Moreover, state financing of *evaluation* is also necessary, because local schools will seldom finance rigorous evaluation to ascertain the possible value of an innovation to schools in general. Local schools introduce only those innovations they already believe are better. Any associated evaluation effort is designed to answer the question: "Has our own program improved?" And nearly always the answer is sought merely by observing the reactions of students while they are being taught.

Local financing of dissemination was recommended for two reasons: (1) this is the one phase of innovation which local schools are willing to pay for; and (2) the Commissioner had called for a plan which would in no way diminish local control of education. Local financing of dissemination is more likely to mean local control of dissemination.

The Education Research Agency

The Agency was conceived as an adjunct of the State Education Department, related to but operationally independent of other divisions, with its chief administrator directly responsible to the Commissioner of Education.

During the design and evaluation of new approaches, the Agency would be empowered to suspend (subject to veto only by the Commissioner himself), for schools undertaking sponsored programs, any regulations, rules, and directives of the Department which might hamper such experimentation. Lavish testimony had been gathered on the prudential concerns of the Department. It seemed fruitless to hope that a new "Bureau of Experimentation," buried somewhere in the hierarchy, could succeed in *persuading* its fellow bureaus to move their regulations aside in a wide variety of field locations to allow for experimentation with deviant or even heretical approaches. Therefore the power to suspend regulations was placed in the hands of a man second only to the Commissioner.

The report recommended that the Agency staff be kept small, and that its work be *exclusively administrative*. In no case, said the report, should the Agency staff attempt to design or to evaluate innovations itself. In fact, the staff should not even select the problems to be solved through new designs, or the people who would act as inventors, or the inventions to be field-tested. Recognizing the great difficulty of institutionalizing any innovative process without stultifying it, the report recommended that nothing be institutionalized except a money-management function, staffed by a few generalists. They would be proscribed from doing anything but administering a process which would be (1) located outside their agency, (2) conducted by ever changing clusters of temporary personnel, and (3) guided by a rotating group of school and college leaders.

Probably the best existing illustration of this approach in education is the Cooperative Research Program of the Office of Education. Although it restricts its activities primarily to the support of basic research, and is less complex in structure than what was recommended for New York State, the Cooperative Research Program demonstrates the feasibility of the method. The research programs of the National Institutes of Health offer similar examples in related fields.

Program design: the temporary Design Groups

The report suggested that problems to be solved through new designs should be chosen by a highly capable Professional Advisory Committee, with a rotating membership of school and college personnel. Screening problems directed to it from anywhere in the state, the Committee would select the most significant ones and refer each to a temporary Exploratory Design Panel composed of authorities from inside and outside the state. The Panel would be asked to suggest promising design possibilities, and to help identify people in the state or elsewhere for Design Groups.

At that point, the Agency would solicit applications from clusters of schools, colleges, and other organizations which wished to sponsor Design Groups. Those proposals endorsed by the Exploratory Design Panel would be financed throughout the design phase, which might extend from one to five years. Free communication between Design Groups working on the same problem would be advisable, not only to avoid duplication, but also to generate new ideas.

It was envisioned that several problems would be under attack simultaneously by the Agency. Because the design of an innovation involves the translation of what is known about learning into a program for teaching, the work settings for Design Groups would always include the opportunity to work directly and at length with school children.

To bring together the best of substantive content, learning theory, and practical experience, the typical Design Group would consist of capable teachers, professors in education and in other disciplines, and selected members of the State Education Department. The inclusion of highly capable Department personnel was recommended for these reasons: (1) no source of talent should be neglected; (2) Department officials could be personally associated with promising new developments *without committing their bureaus to the endorsement of unproven approaches;* and (3) since these were the men who would have to shift their positions and their regulations if the innovation were to succeed, early identification with it could ease the way.

The teams which invented new high school science and mathematics courses for the National Science Foundation were outstanding design groups. Those recommended for New York State would differ in the presence of more classroom teachers, some professors of education, and a few qualified members of the state regulatory agency. One may well wonder whether the gain in breadth would be offset by the loss in mutual understanding, shared values, and level of talent; but, on balance, the proposed Design Group composition seems sound.

Because they could have an abrasive or even destructive effect in the early stages of an invention, people interested chiefly in the *evaluation* of instructional approaches would not be placed in a Design Group.

When a Design Group had developed a new instructional approach, it would describe what it believed the innovation would accomplish, for which students, under what conditions, so that a careful field test could be planned. (If this were not done meticulously, what was evaluated might be something other than what had been invented.) Then the Design Group would be dissolved, and its members returned to their regular full-time positions, so that the state's money would be available to set new inventors to work on new problems.

Program evaluation: the temporary Evaluation Groups

The report recommended that innovations be evaluated by field testing in circumstances so diverse that all the forces which play upon learning, even though unknown, would be present to influence the results. A program might prove satisfactory in most schools, while giving spectacular results in one particular setting and abysmal outcomes in another. Only by extensive field testing could the evaluators avoid the error of labeling a program a success or a failure because it happened to be tried *in a single circumstance* where *unknown* factors dictated the results. Moreover, only a field test would indicate which types of schools would find the innovation valuable—and for which teachers, which students, and which learnings.

As each new program was brought in by the inventors, according to the report, the Education Research Agency would employ from schools, colleges, and the Department a temporary Evaluation Group to lay out and to supervise an extensive state-wide field test. The Evaluation Group would be asked to use any existing evaluation instruments suited to the program being tested, but also to be as imaginative in inventing evaluative techniques as the designers were in inventing the program. (A major weakness of current evaluation efforts is the use of old yardsticks to measure new programs which have novel purposes.)

To discover to whom an innovation should eventually be disseminated—if it should be disseminated at all—twenty to thirty school systems of all types would use it over the full range of conditions thought to influence human learning, with all types of students for whom it might conceivably be appropriate. The process might occasionally be concluded within one or two years, but would take longer where longitudinal studies were required.

The state was urged not to ignore innovations incubated under other auspices. Promising new programs not developed under Agency sponsorship, such as PSSC physics, SMSG mathematics, and Advanced Placement courses, would also be field tested.

If comparison studies were made, using experimental and control settings, it would be absolutely essential that equal money, attention, and encouragement be supplied to both control and experimental locations. It would be vital that each group of teachers and students be inspired to compete and to "win," using of course only those techniques assigned to them. Evidence gathered by the Consultant had pointed clearly to the powerful stimulation which groups of teachers experienced when taking part in a distinctive new effort. New group goals, shared problems, and external encouragement tended to infuse the effort with enthusiasm and drive the innovation toward success, giving it an automatic advantage over any stagnant "control group" process used for comparative purposes. Since it is extremely difficult to innovate without stimulating the participants, comparison control groups should be similarly stimulated, so that any differences in the final outcome could be attributed to the treatment used—not simply to the fact that something was changed.

At the conclusion of the field test, the Evaluation Group would describe, for the benefit of prospective users, precisely what the new program had accomplished, for which students, and under exactly what conditions. The Group would then be disbanded and its members released to take up their normal responsibilities. If the innovation had been proved superior in any respect, the Education Research Agency would endorse its use in schools for that purpose under similar conditions.

Program dissemination: the regional School Development Units

The report called upon the state legislature to stimulate, and subsidize with modest initial grants, the formation of regional School Development Units to disseminate the programs proven and endorsed by the Education Research Agency. Structurally independent of the state Agency, the regional Units would be financed and totally controlled by member school systems.

It was recommended that each School Development Unit consist of a limited number of member school systems—probably ten to twenty, depending upon their size—except that each of the largest cities should incorporate one or more Development Units *within its own boundaries*. (New York City, which contains 35 per cent of all public school children in the state, would encompass approximately twenty-five such Units.) Strict size limitation was advised, so that all classroom teachers in each Unit could be reached in the continuous process of retraining in service which the study assumed would be required for an accelerated pace of innovation. A common failing of innovative efforts, according to the report, was that teachers were not given enough help in changing. The regional Units were to be small enough to give all teachers in member schools the kind of direct assistance they needed.

The state was advised to make membership in a Development Unit (or internal subdivision of the largest cities into several Units) mandatory for every school district in the state. While the state would not force the adoption of any innovation, however thoroughly proven, it would require each local district to move into a posture which would make the process of innovation convenient.

Each Unit would be supported by approximately 1 per cent of the current operating budget of each component school district. While such a rate of spending for in-service development would be many times higher than the current rate, the proposed figure would have amounted to only about $100 per year per teacher in 1961–62 in New York State, with teachers' salaries averaging about $6,500. The Consultant believes that spending $100 a year to teach a $6,500 teacher how to use methods definitely proven to be superior is a clear economy. And to spend any less would be to starve the dissemination process, making the state's earlier expenditures on design and evaluation senseless and wasteful.

The report recommended that the chief administrative officer of each regional Unit be appointed by, and be responsible to, a lay board composed of representatives from the boards of education of the component school districts. He would serve in a contractual relationship to his board, and would not have tenure rights. The chief administrative officer in a city Unit would be responsible to the city superintendent. The use of a representative lay board to guide the activities of regional intermediate school districts has been a successful pattern in New York State. So long as lay boards control member school districts, it would seem highly desirable to have representatives of those lay boards managing the dissemination of innovations in those districts. Having the chief administrator of the regional Unit serve on a contractual rather than a tenure basis would enable superintendents in member districts to feel that they had little to fear from the regional Unit, since they could arrange to terminate the employment of the regional administrator by acting through their local lay boards to influence the representative regional board.

Like the Education Research Agency, the report advised, each regional School Development Unit should have a small permanent staff engaging exclusively in administrative work. The Units, like the Agency, would be staffed by long-term generalists contracting with short-term specialists to disseminate innovations.

Three functions were envisioned for the School Development Units: (1) to demonstrate programs proven and endorsed by the central Education Research Agency; (2) to develop in teachers in the component districts the professional skills needed to carry out these programs; and (3) to transfer this professional development function to nearby colleges and universities as rapidly as possible.

Demonstrating new programs. The School Development Units would arrange for the demonstration of each new program throughout their regions with all the types of students and in all the types of school settings for which the program had proven effective. Selected local member school systems would be asked to provide locations for the demonstrations.

All demonstrations would consist of the continuing use of the new approach as a basic part of regular instruction in a normal school setting. That is, the demonstration would not be a special performance by extraordinary teachers working under artificial conditions for a limited time, but would instead be a part of the daily instruction given by regular teachers working under normal conditions for an extended period of time.

The survey had gathered overwhelmingly conclusive evidence that administrators and teachers are primarily persuaded to adopt innovations through seeing them succeed in run-of-the-mill situations in schools very similar to their own; they tend to reject any demonstration which is at all artificial. Inasmuch as normality is the hallmark of a persuasive demonstration, the report exhorted the Units to avoid anything of the hothouse atmosphere in arranging demonstrations.[5]

Teaching teachers to carry out new programs. Each individual member school system in the Development Unit would decide for itself whether it wished to take on a recommended new program.

For those which decided favorably, the Development Unit would employ a temporary Development Group (drawn from nearby colleges and local schools) to teach the new approach to all teachers for whom it would be appropriate. For example, a Group might be hired to teach a superior new approach in the use of electronic language laboratories to *all* teachers of modern foreign languages in those schools choosing to adopt it. The dissemination of a new professional skill throughout a region should be largely completed within three years.

Observations made during the study had indicated that in the best circumstances for re-education, the teacher of teachers knew more about the innovation than those he was re-educating, and had himself succeeded in using the program with children. Successful instruction reached simultaneously all teachers who would use the innovation, extended over a long period of time, involved the use of the

---

[5] In this sense, as in some others, the proposal shows parallels with the structures used to aid the invention, testing, and diffusion of new agricultural practices. Demonstrating in ordinary schools is analogous to demonstrating on neighboring farms, except that the agricultural production unit is an individual farmer, where the production unit in education—the local school system—is an institution. The regional School Development Units, with their associated Development Groups, perform the "county agent" role, and the Education Research Agency is roughly analogous to the agricultural experiment station, including as it does both enriched "laboratory" settings for design of innovations and controlled field settings for their systematic evaluation outside the "hothouse."

One clear difference lies in the temporary nature of design, evaluation, and dissemination teams in the present proposal. The reasons for this have already been discussed. The continuity of staffing which characterizes agricultural innovative structures would be missing, as noted earlier. However, it seems possible that the nonsystematic, noncumulative nature of education as an applied field rather than a scientific discipline makes invention less bound to continued inquiry and more a matter of inspired creation and empirical exploration (as in much medical research). However, this is far from clear.

equipment and materials needed to instruct students, and was interspersed with actual classroom practice. It was that kind of re-education which the Development Groups were expected to supply.

Transferring development activities to the colleges. As soon as a Development Unit had accomplished the general dissemination of a given new program to interested schools throughout its geographic area, the Development Group for that particular program would be disbanded to return to campus and classroom. Money thus freed would be used to hire new Groups to disseminate newly proven innovations.

Before dissolving the Group, however, the Development Unit would arrange for colleges and universities in the region to absorb continuing development activities into their in-service and/or graduate offerings. From that point forward, college courses and college services would provide for: (1) individual teachers who had missed the development in its first general diffusion; (2) newcomers to the area; (3) school staffs which decided late to take on the development; and (4) schools which wanted outside personnel to supply continuing attention to a program already initiated.

The Development Groups were envisioned as the first strong wave in dissemination. Trained in, experienced with, and enthusiastic about a proven program, they would work closely and in depth with the faculties of the alert schools in each region to get the program well under way. But the Groups would not be kept intact indefinitely, if only because their members would not be willing to serve for long periods.

However, some schools would be slow to adopt the innovation, delaying their decision until after the Development Group had been dissolved. Moreover, turnover in local faculties is so high that re-education for an innovation would have to be available continuously to new teachers, even in those schools which had adopted the program early. The colleges, which are not structured to exert rapid, massive influence on elementary and secondary schools, have demonstrated their willingness and their capacity to provide continuous training opportunities for individual teachers. They are the logical institutions to take over the "mopping up" operation after the Development Groups have had their first wide impact.

Related roles of existing organizations

One conclusion of the study was that a number of existing organizations were performing operations which would be of far more significance to the schools if they were part of an over-all plan for accelerating the pace and improving the direction of educational change. Another conclusion was that some organizations were trying to do things which could be better done under an entirely new arrangement. A variety of role shifts was urged.

The State Education Department. After suspending Department regulations temporarily in selected field locations during the *design* and *evaluation* phases, the Education Research Agency would reinstate them at the conclusion of a state-wide field test. At that point, the various divisions of the Department would have to amend their regulations as necessary to allow the immediate *dissemination* of a proven innovation.

The Department was advised in the report to continue its on-going research to ascertain the characteristics of the student, the teacher, the school, the home, and the community which affect learning in school. Out of that effort would come instruments for constructing a School–Community Characteristics Profile on any given school system in the state, to aid in selecting schools for design, evaluation, or demonstration settings.

Saying that the functions of the Department's Field Supervisors could be performed better by temporary Professional Visiting Committees composed of school and college personnel in each region, the report recommended that all Field Supervisors be transferred to regional School Development Units. They would be relieved of the obligation to specialize, and elevated to general administrative positions as Coordinators of Professional Visiting. The effect of such a move would be to place the Department's inspectorial functions in the hands of leading practitioners, who would be chosen and trained by their own professional associations. It should follow that the mildly inhibiting role now played by most supervisors would diminish.

The colleges and universities. Under the plan outlined in the report, college faculty members in all schools and departments, not in schools and departments of education alone, would participate as appropriate in Design Groups, in Evaluation Groups, and in Development Groups.

The participation of professors at the *design* stage would mean (1) that men conversant with basic research could bring its findings to bear on innovations, and (2) that experts in the content of education and experts in the process of education could join with experienced teachers of children to devise improved educational programs.

The participation of professors at the *evaluation* stage would mean that the men inside and outside the specialty of education who had the deepest interest in measurement would be paid and freed to sharpen the evaluative instruments used by schools.

The participation of professors at the *dissemination* stage would mean that they could learn—by teaching—the best new content and the best new instructional procedures used in elementary and secondary schools.

Finally, once a regional Development Unit had concluded an effort and disbanded a Development Group, the colleges would have the conditions they need to teach a new approach in *pre-service* courses. Those conditions are: (1) the knowledge that the approach has been proven through extensive field testing; (2) the presence on campus of professors who know how to teach it, having learned how as members of a regional Development Group; and (3) the general use of the innovation in the schools which surround their campuses. Under those conditions, the colleges would almost inevitably incorporate the approach into their pre-service teacher education courses.

Campus schools.   The report recommended that the eleven campus schools at the State University Colleges be closed, and their elementary and secondary school students returned to the local school systems. It had become apparent during the study that the conflicting roles expected of the campus schools by various segments of the profession were irreconcilable. Because of the artificiality of their location on a college campus—and such other extraordinary features as highly selected students, hand-picked teachers, and crowds of observers—the campus schools were unsuitable for either the evaluation or the demonstration of innovations. And whereas their artificiality would make them likely places for enriched design settings, their location in New

York State on the campuses of teacher preparation institutions meant that the faculties which guided them were understandably interested in using them as demonstration centers for sound approaches—not as experimental laboratories. Stable conditions and strong forces worked against each other so effectively, in short, that the campus schools could perform no job well, and were not worth what it cost the State to finance them. Hence the recommendation that they be closed.

The report went on to say that if candidates for the profession of teaching were to observe conventional programs of established quality, they should see them in ordinary public schools. If they were to observe proven innovations, they should see them in the demonstration settings sponsored by the regional School Development Units in ordinary public schools. And of course the candidates would receive their practice teaching experience (as virtually all of them do today) in ordinary public schools.

The professional associations.   Taking into account the effectiveness of the professional associations as communicators, the report called upon them to exercise their skill at every step in the innovative process. The New York State Teachers Association, as well as the state chapters of national professional associations, would be urged by the Education Research Agency and by the School Development Units to parallel all design, evaluation, and dissemination efforts with energetic communication about those efforts.

The key role suggested for the associations in selecting and training the members of the Professional Visiting Committees was mentioned earlier.

The State School Boards Association.   Although the local school board had shown up in the study as a weak influence on innovation, it had become quite obvious that the board had great potential strength. This meant that new programs would have to be disseminated in a manner which would not arouse the opposition of local boards.

Accordingly, the report concluded that the State School Boards Association should be encouraged and helped to inform its member school boards extensively and in depth about the proposed purposes,

structure, and operation of the state school improvement system. Once
the system went into operation, the Association would be encouraged
to interpret its design, evaluation, and dissemination efforts to school
board members at state-wide and regional meetings. It seemed probable that the best persuaders of board members would be other board
members.

The State Congress of Parents and Teachers. The local Parent-
Teacher Association is the prime organization in most schools for
creating parent understanding and readiness to support the introduction of new instructional programs. Its cooperation should be avidly
sought, said the report, in creating the local climates essential to (1)
imaginative design efforts in community pilot settings, (2) field testing under closely controlled conditions in local schools, and (3) the
rapid spread of distinctive instructional approaches which might break
sharply with community traditions. Toward this end, the Education
Research Agency would work with state PTA leaders, the School
Development Unit would work with regional leaders, and the local
school staff would work with local leaders to provide direction and aid
to the PTA.

The State Citizens Committee for the Public Schools. Though its
role in the state has not been described earlier, the New York State
Citizens Committee for the Public Schools was also considered in the
report's recommendations. The Education Research Agency would
encourage the Committee to determine the patterns of community participation most conducive to building public understanding and acceptance of new programs, in various types of communities. These
successful patterns would be described, and recommended to local
citizens' groups across the state; the Committee would (as it now does)
provide relevant help to community groups on request.

The college-affiliated school study councils. Although it observed
that the state's nine regional school study councils could teach much
about what local schools need from outside agencies, the report went
on to say that the councils were only a fragment of the answer to those
needs. It concluded by suggesting that the councils be allowed to

atrophy in favor of the regional School Development Units—and urged that no attempt be made to convert the councils into such Units.

Despite an aura of good feeling between the professors directing the councils and the superintendents of the member schools, it seemed clear that the interest of the former in studying educational phenomena and the concern of the latter for having their staffs taught the best of conventional wisdom could never be reconciled. At least, they provided a poor basis for establishing a regional dissemination unit. There were better ways for the professors and the superintendents to pursue their bents.

The private philanthropic foundations.   The philanthropic foundations which have supported basic research in the social sciences underlying education—psychology, sociology, political science, and others—could continue to do so under the plan proposed, with the expectation that the state would draw more effectively upon the results of that research in designing new instructional approaches.

As for the foundations which have supported the actual design of new programs, the report strongly recommended that they be encouraged to invest their money exclusively in financing design efforts, and leave dissemination to the schools and colleges of the state after the designs had been evaluated.

The funds of philanthropic foundations are the supreme form of risk capital available to schools. Because of the short supply of this kind of money, the foundations interested in innovation should reserve their funds for design purposes. And there is another point. The study had gathered elaborate testimony as to professional suspicion about the motives of private foundations in promoting specific programs which they had sponsored. This suspicion could be allayed once a program had been evaluated by an independent, state-wide group and was being disseminated by locally controlled School Development Units.

The commercial organizations.   The organizations which manufacture and distribute instructional supplies and equipment are extremely powerful. As the technological side of teaching expands, these organizations will unquestionably become even more influential. In a free-enterprise economy such as ours, there is no hope of insulating schools from the impact of their activities.[6] What can be done, however, is to connect their power in a systematic way to the three phases of instructional innovations. The plan proposed for New York State envisioned the following roles for the commercial organizations at each phase:

1. Design: When the Education Research Agency announced plans to select Design Groups, the schools and colleges submitting proposals would include plans to use commercial organizations when appropriate to help the Design Groups develop new materials and equipment. The commercial organizations would bid for the privilege of assisting, with their bids expressed in terms of the technical personnel, materials, and equipment they could supply. The report assumed it would not be necessary to pay them to take part.
2. Evaluation: When a new instructional program was ready for state-wide field testing, the cooperating commercial organization would supply—at no charge—sufficient quantities of necessary equipment or materials for state-wide use during the field test period.
3. Dissemination: When a program had proven successful through field testing, there would be at least two possibilities for the participation of commercial organizations: (1) specifications for the new material could be made available to anyone interested in producing it; (2) bids could be taken on the exclusive right to produce the material.

Using this plan would have these advantages: (1) the commercial organizations, which at present support innovation in instructional materials only to the extent of having a few authors invest a little time on the promise of future royalties, could instead publish the work of a team of highly skilled, lavishly supported inventors; (2) field testing of commercially produced equipment and materials, managed in such a way that the manufacturers would be aided rather than damaged by the results, would fill one of the most unfortunate gaps in the process of instructional innovation as it operates today; (3) when the time for

[6] This problem is complex in the extreme. It has not been solved in medicine, or in industrial research and development. In agriculture, it is handled reasonably well in the development of seed strains and farming practices, less well in the case of fertilizers and medication, and hardly at all in the case of agricultural equipment.

demonstration arrived, the commercial organizations would already be tooled up to produce the equipment and materials in quantity.

The Aftermath

Within one year after its publication, *Organizing New York State for Educational Change* had clearly discernible effects upon professional thinking about instructional innovation in New York State.

It soon became evident that dissatisfaction with the recommendations was evenly distributed among all types of organizations. Privately expressed reaction within a number of organizations revealed a belief that a better plan than the one recommended would be to supply more money for that organization—the one speaking—to expand its own services as a means of accelerating innovation in the schools. Publicly expressed reactions of the same organizations tended to endorse, albeit mildly, the idea of giving some of the recommendations a trial.

The response of the agents and agencies singled out for extinction—campus schools, school study councils, Department field supervisors—ranged from indifference through distress to antagonism.

On the other hand, the general reaction of people who were not strongly identified with specific existing structures was that although the report was not correct in all its conclusions and recommendations, it merited very serious study. Discussed at first not only in the State Education Department but by professional educators in colleges and local school systems as well, the study began to draw attention at the meetings of various professional associations across the state.

Contributing factors

It was widely agreed that the straightforward manner of presenting the findings had resulted in a highly readable—and provocative—document. But readability was only one explanation of the wide influence of the study. In retrospect, several factors seem to have contributed to its impact:

The time was right. People had sensed in advance of the undertaking what the Commissioner voiced succinctly after reading the *1961 Catalog*: "In short, the backward-forward, restricted, sporadic and unrelated kind of innovation shown in the Brickell inventory is not likely to change the mainstream of education."

The sponsorship was right. The Commissioner of Education in New York State is a towering figure, clothed in prestige and power. His prior expression of interest in planned innovation, and his personal initiative in broadcasting the final results of the study, guaranteed professional attention to it. Under different sponsorship, the report might have been greeted with mild interest as one more ripple in the wave of words about change. But written and circulated under the aegis of the Commissioner, the recommendations could precipitate decisive action if they met with his favor. Thus the report could not be ignored by the profession.

The Consultant was virtually free from restrictions in conducting the study and drawing up recommendations. The most significant dimension of that freedom was the privilege of proposing a solution which did not have to be confined within a single agency, such as the State Education Department. As President of the University of the State of New York, the man who serves as Commissioner of Education is in charge of all schools—elementary, secondary, and collegiate; public, parochial, private, and commercial—in the state. In that capacity he authorized the study. In that framework the recommendations were erected.

Freedom for the Consultant took other forms, too. On temporary leave from one organization to which he was sure to return, the Consultant worked for a second and was supported by funds from a third. At no time did he feel in jeopardy or under pressure. The absence of pressure is perhaps best illustrated by the fact that the report was published before the Commissioner had read it.

The report was quickly and widely distributed. Copies were made freely available on request.

The choice of one man as investigator and author, rather than a commission, weakened the report by narrowing it to the insight and vision one man could supply—and strengthened it by making cavil, caution, and compromise largely absent during the writing of the final document. The net result was a clear, consistent, and dramatic set of recommendations.

The simple, direct writing style made the book highly readable. In a flood of educational writing which is otherwise, that fact alone drew attention and a certain amount of commendation for the work.

The report was largely journalistic—as it had to be, inasmuch as the

Consultant learned almost everything in it during six months of interviews. Although the Consultant exercised a modicum of insight in analyzing the problem, and supplied substantial synthesis in proposing a solution, the great bulk of the commentary was purely reportorial. Many men found the Consultant's observations familiar and sensible. That was not surprising. He had simply said to them in public what they had said to him in private.

Subsequent events

A number of important events took place within the first year after the release of the study. Some of the most significant are summarized below.

Copies of the report were distributed to legislators, school board presidents, selected college personnel, chief local school administrators, Department of Education personnel, and the press.

Newspapers gave extensive coverage to the controversial segments of the report—such as the charge that Regents Examinations inhibited innovation—which resulted in wider currency for the entire document.

When the first printing of 15,000 copies was exhausted during the first year, another 10,000 were printed. (About 200 copies went outside the state in the initial mailing; hundreds more were mailed on request subsequently.)

The Consultant accepted some sixty invitations to explain the recommendations before a variety of state-wide, regional, and local groups.

The Commissioner and other Department leaders accepted a number of invitations to express their own assessment of the report before professional and public audiences.

The Department began extending its sponsorship of field tests in clusters of local schools, hiring college research men as evaluators.

A county association of superintendents planned and moved rapidly toward creating a regional school development organization patterned after the one described in the report.

A professor at a major university sought an extension of an existing foundation grant to test the elements of the proposal in several field locations, with State Department approval.

Seven neighboring school districts joined together with an initial budget of $21,000 to field-test and disseminate innovations. Their first project involved six school systems, forty teachers, and 1800 students.

The Commissioner called a meeting of thirty school and college leaders, and had them spend a day reacting aloud to the report while Department leaders listened. At the end of the day, the thirty men recommended that the plan for a state Education Research Agency and regional School Development Units be given a full-scale pilot run to test its feasibility.

Several professional organizations communicated with the Commissioner (who had appealed for public and professional reaction) and recorded their qualified, favorable support for the proposals.

A Department committee, whose consideration of state-wide research and development possibilities preceded and followed the appointment of the Consultant, scrutinized the final report and endorsed its chief recommendations.

The PTA at its state convention resolved to support enabling legislation.

A private philanthropic foundation signified an interest in subsidizing the agencies envisioned in the plan.

After all of this, the Commissioner made the following announcement at several state-wide meetings: "Plans are under way in the Department, following the recommendations of the Brickell report, to establish a semiautonomous research unit, reporting directly to the Commissioner, to stimulate and finance the design and evaluation of new instructional programs and new methodologies in the schools. The unit will seek the cooperation of the universities, colleges and schools, and will plan its projects on a scale that will produce valid results."

Ten months had elapsed since the publication of the report.

References

Brickell, H. M. *Commissioner's 1961 catalog of educational change.* Albany, New York: State Education Department, 1961 (*a*). Available free from the Commissioner of Education.

Brickell, H. M. *Organizing New York State for educational change.* Albany, New York: State Education Department, 1961 (*b*). Available free from the Commissioner of Education.

CHAPTER 21

Foundation support of educational innovation by learned societies, councils, and institutes

Joseph C. Kiger

DEFINITIONS of what constitutes a foundation vary historically and are subject to exception. The same is, of course, true in defining similar organizations: learned societies, councils, institutes, universities, etc. In order to study foundation support of our national learned societies, councils, and institutes, therefore, some definitions and distinctions must be made in advance; those which follow are the basis upon which this study has been conducted.

In twentieth-century United States a foundation may be broadly defined as a privately-endowed, tax-exempt, eleemosynary organization which has been established to provide wealth for projects useful to society. Estimates of the total number presently in existence in the United States range from 6,000 to 13,000.[1]

Some foundations, because of their similar interests and a common devotion to the advancement of knowledge, bear a similarity to our learned societies, councils and institutes. The category into which these organizations fall is, therefore, a somewhat arbitrary one in some instances. Some authorities, for example, have classified the American Philosophical Society as a foundation because of its sizeable

---

[1] For two works dealing with the development and operation of U.S. foundations, see Andrews (1956) and Kiger (1954).

THE AUTHOR is Professor of History, University of Mississippi.

endowment and its grants program (Walton & Andrews, 1960, p. 554). Also, the fact that all of these organizations can change—and some have changed—their methods of operation makes it difficult to place them in definite categories. Nevertheless, it appears that the main features differentiating the foundations from learned societies, councils and institutes is that they (*a*) are not membership organizations, restricted or open, and (*b*) are not set up or created by other organizations to perform a considerable number of functions for them.

A *learned society* may be generally defined as an organization composed of individuals devoted to a particular learned discipline (or branch or group of disciplines) in the humanities, social sciences, or natural sciences, and primarily committed to the study and advancement of knowledge in that discipline. Such a definition excludes professional societies in medicine, law, engineering, etc., where the *raison d'etre* and primary emphasis is upon the application of knowledge for professional and/or monetary purposes.

Several other characteristics of an American learned society can be noted. It usually carries on no teaching function, except incidentally through studies, publications, etc. Its membership may be open or closed, but normally includes a significant portion of the outstanding persons engaged or interested in the particular discipline or disciplines. Its main source of revenue is usually from membership fees, rather than from endowments, bequests, or grants. Finally, although it performs other functions, the learned society's foremost ones are the holding of periodic meetings where papers are presented and members become personally acquainted and mutually stimulated in their scholarly endeavors, and the provision of a medium or media for publication, usually described as learned journals.

Such societies may be national, regional, or local in scope. The category into which they fall turns on several factors: the stated purpose of the society, the size and composition of its membership, and its activities. In this last connection, national learned societies are usually co-members with other societies in groupings called *councils* or *institutes,* and their major activities, in addition to those enumerated above, are with these groupings, the philanthropic foundations, and the universities. In the last few decades a considerable number of the societies, and most of the councils and institutes, have also worked with the federal government and industrial concerns.

The learned societies

Although many regional and local learned societies have performed and are performing a valuable service to the nation, only the sixty learned societies which are national in scope are included in this study. Their number includes thirty societies which are members of the American Council of Learned Societies; seven associated members of the Social Science Research Council; thirty-two cooperating member societies of the National Academy of Sciences–National Research Council; and five societies which are associate members of the American Council on Education. The total number of societies studied, sixty, is different from the total provided in the figures above because several societies are members of two or more councils.[2]

These sixty learned societies fall into three broad categories: twenty-nine humanistic–social science societies, twenty-nine natural science societies, and two societies which span all areas of knowledge. The study which follows is based on these three divisions.

Also included in the study are the four councils and five institutes.

The councils

The American Council on Education, National Academy of Sciences–National Research Council, American Council of Learned Societies, and Social Science Research Council are the four national associations of organizations concerned respectively with education, natural sciences, humanities, and social sciences. There is, of course, some degree of overlapping in their respective areas of interest.

American Council on Education. This council was organized in 1918 by eleven national educational associations to coordinate the work of educational institutions and allied organizations during World War I. The membership of the Council today consists of approxi-

[2] See Appendix, "Learned Societies Which are Members of Councils and Societal Institutes." This list includes the sixty societies meeting this definition and included in this study.

For a history of each of these organizations, as well as of our national councils and institutes, and a general history of the development of their relationships to each other and to other domestic and international organizations concerned with scientific and cultural advancement, see Kiger (1963). See also Kiger (1958).

mately 150 national and regional educational associations and about 1100 educational institutions. Although it strives to improve education at all levels, the Council has placed particular emphasis on higher education. The ACE operates through its staff and some thirty commissions and committees. For instance, the Committee on Government Relations, through its membership and consultants, has provided congressional committees and government agencies with advice in such areas as veterans' educational benefits, fellowships, and student aid programs. Similarly, the Council's Commission on Education and International Affairs performs analogous functions in its area of interest.

National Academy of Sciences–National Research Council. This council grew out of World War I, but its parent organization, the National Academy of Sciences, extends back to the Civil War period. The National Academy was chartered in 1863 to meet the need of the federal government for competent, objective advice on scientific matters connected with the war. In addition, the Academy was honorific, in that election to membership in it was, and has continued to be, one of the highest scientific honors.

With the advent of World War I, it was decided that an operating arm or agency of the National Academy was needed in order to make best possible utilization of scientists in the war effort. In 1916, therefore, President Wilson created the National Research Council; in 1918 this Council was set up on a permanent basis. The major portion of the membership of the National Research Council is made up of representatives of the natural-science learned and technical societies of the country, and these representatives serve on the working committees, commissions, and panels by which the scientific work of the Academy–Council is accomplished.

In the decade since World War I, the Academy and the Research Council have increasingly meshed and they have come to be designated as the Academy–Council. In effect, the Academy members have come to act as trustees, or as a large board of directors, for the Research Council. The executive body of the two groups is a Governing Board composed of the eleven-member Council of the Academy and the Chairmen of the eight major Divisions of the National Research Council. A staff of approximately 150 executive and professional employees is maintained by the Academy–Research Council.

American Council of Learned Societies. This council was also organized during the World War I period. An initial purpose of the new organization was to provide representation in the newly-organized Union Acadèmique Internationale, in the absence of an official organization to represent the United States abroad. The initiative in calling the organizational meeting for the American Council of Learned Societies rested with officers of the American Academy of Arts and Sciences and the American Historical Association. Ten other humanistic learned societies constituted the original roster of the American Council of Learned Societies, which by 1960 had expanded to include a total of thirty societies. The activities of the American Council of Learned Societies, both here and abroad, are carried on by an extensive system of committees and a modest executive staff.

Social Science Research Council. This council was organized in 1924–25 by seven social-science learned societies. Since its inception the SSRC has operated through various committees, which presently number about twenty-five, with the aid of an executive staff. A third of the committees are primarily concerned with the administration of fellowships or grants for research in social science fields; most of the remainder deal with research planning and appraisal in specific areas.

The institutes

The five institutes—the American Association for the Advancement of Science, Federation of American Societies for Experimental Biology, American Institute of Physics, American Institute of Biological Sciences, and American Geological Institute—are the national associations of organizations (some also including individuals as members) concerned with particular disciplines within the natural sciences.

The first of these, the American Association for the Advancement of Science, is a variant in this group in that its interests also include, to a limited degree, the social sciences and education. It originated in 1848, and it has offered membership to all persons interested in any aspect of science. As a result, it is presently organized into eighteen different sections with a membership of approximately 60,000. There are also some 300 affiliated societies and academies associated with it.

The remaining four institutes, Federation of American Societies for Experimental Biology, American Institute of Physics, American Institute of Biological Sciences, and American Geological Institute, were organized by particular natural science learned and technical societies to accomplish what the individual societies could not do. For example, the Federation of American Societies for Experimental Biology has held annual meetings which facilitate personal contact by investigators in the biological and medical sciences; it has held symposia in which the individual societies could operate more effectively as a group rather than as individual units; and it has engaged in a publication program which spans the fields of interest of the individual societies. Such activities have been characteristic of each of these four institutes.

Each of the five institutes operates through various committees, formed for particular purposes, and with the aid of executive staffs of varying sizes.

Contributions to Educational Innovation

It would be futile to attempt to list all of the innovative educational contributions of the learned societies, councils and institutes. In general, however, the individual learned societies have made their primary contributions in their respective disciplines through various projects, studies, and publications.

The four councils have similarly made contributions in their general areas of interest. The major innovative educational role played by the American Council on Education has involved its consideration of problems connected with the administration and organization of higher education. For example, it has examined the problems associated with the financial structure of colleges and universities; many of the resultant recommendations have been followed by business officers of these institutions all over the country. Since World War II, the ACE has engaged in an almost continuous study of sponsored research conducted by colleges and universities, and the recommendations resulting from such studies have been adopted in many colleges and universities.

From its beginnings and through the years, the American Council of Learned Societies has continued to represent the humanities internationally by providing delegates to the annual meetings of the International Academic Union. In addition, however, the American Council of Learned Societies has engaged in many innovative activities which have broadened the scope of humanistic knowledge. For instance, it laid the groundwork for the study of the Middle East, Far East and Russia that proved so valuable to the nation in World War II. In addition, the ACLS aided in devising ways and means to train linguistic and other specialists in these areas, which were totally unfamiliar to all but a handful of Americans. Many of the innovative educational methods developed in this connection were adopted and have continued to be used in the language and area study programs of many colleges and universities.

Similarly, the Social Science Research Council, through the work of its committees and staff, has engaged in many trail-blazing studies and projects. Various reports of its Committee on Historiography, for instance, have had a considerable influence on historical scholarship.

The five institutes have also sponsored essentially innovative educational programs such as visiting-scientist programs for high schools, colleges and universities; studies designed to provide the best type of buildings for a particular scientific activity; and programs in the construction of new scientific teaching apparatus.

In analyzing foundation support of these educationally innovative activities of the learned societies, councils, and institutes, it is apparent that the point of departure must be the gifts or grants from one to the other. In other words, money flowing from the foundations to the other organizations forms the basis for this study. All of the financial figures given represent the awards made by the donor to the recipient organization, and no account is taken of the relatively small amounts which occasionally reverted to the donor if the funds were not expended for the specified project. Also, it should be noted that payments on many of the larger grants were spread out over a number of years. Data were derived from the annual and special reports of all of these organizations and the replies to questionnaires and letters submitted to them. It should be pointed out that (unless otherwise noted) the study was based on a terminal date of 1960.

Grants to Learned Societies

The Carnegie Corporation of New York; various Rockefeller philanthropies, including the Rockefeller Foundation, the General Education Board, and the Laura Spelman Rockefeller Memorial; and the Ford philanthropies, including the Ford Foundation and the Fund for the Advancement of Education, have rendered by far the major portion (approximately 88%) of foundation aid to fifty-eight learned societies.[3]

Specific analysis of the Carnegie Corporation's operations from its beginning to the year 1960 shows that it aided some twenty-three learned societies, eighteen of them active in the humanities and social sciences and five in the natural sciences. Total aid granted during the period to all twenty-three amounted to approximately $1,257,075, less than one-half of one per cent of the total amount of about $300,000,000 appropriated by the Corporation. One of the largest grants was $67,500 in 1931 to the American Political Science Association for its general support; the smallest, $1,000, in 1940, to the Econometric Society for research and publication purposes. There were a total of approximately 100 grants made to societies during the five decades.

From its inauguration in 1913 until 1929, the Rockefeller Foundation restricted its activities primarily to work in medicine and public health on an international scale. In 1929, a reorganization took place which broadened the area of interest of the Foundation to include all of the natural sciences as well as the humanities and social sciences. Programs in the latter area were taken over from the Laura Spelman Rockefeller Memorial, which was consolidated with the Foundation. At the same time, it was decided that the General Education Board would concentrate its activities in *education*, while the Foundation would engage in *research*, including educational research.

The Rockefeller Foundation has, since 1929, aided some thirteen learned societies, eight active in the humanities and social sciences and five in the natural sciences. Aid granted to these societies during the period amounted to a total of approximately $900,000, 0.13 per cent of the grand total of approximately $711,550,000 awarded by the Rockefeller Foundation during the period. One of the largest grants was $140,000 in 1957 to the American Historical Association for its South Asia program; the smallest, $1,000, in 1929, to the Bibliographical Society of America for support of its publications. The Foundation made a total of thirty-six grants to the thirteen societies during the years 1929–1960.

[3] These figures do not include the American Philosophical Society and the American Academy of Arts and Sciences, since they are concerned with all fields of knowledge—natural sciences, social sciences, and humanities. The former has received about $137,000 in financial aid from the foundations; the latter has received approximately $200,000.

The General Education Board, from its establishment by John D. Rockefeller in 1902 until the termination of its active program in 1956, appropriated in excess of $322,000,000 to aid education in the United States. Over 50% of this total was appropriated for the Southern States, to uplift the educational facilities of that section, the remainder being used for educational ventures all over the country.

A total of four national learned societies received aid from the Board during its period of activity. The American Association of Pathologists and Bacteriologists, in the 1920's, received $45,000 toward the support of its *Journal;* the Mathematical Association of America, during the period 1918–1938, received $61,300 for various studies of the mathematics curriculum in the secondary school; in 1937 and 1938 $7,500 was appropriated to the Botanical Society of America for a study of the first-year college course in botany; and in 1940–41 $2,625 was provided the American Political Science Association for several projects in civic education and the social studies. The total amount of money involved in aid to these four societies was $116,425.

The Laura Spelman Rockefeller Memorial disbursed approximately 74 million dollars from 1918 to 1929.

During this period two learned societies, the American Historical Association and the American Psychological Association, received grants totalling $55,000 and $76,500 respectively. Those to the former were primarily for conference and publication purposes. Those to the latter were made towards the support of the Association's *Psychological Abstracts* and were payable over an 11-year period beginning in 1926.

The Ford Foundation, although it was organized in 1936, did not engage in the large-scale activities characteristic of the Carnegie Corporation and the Rockefeller Foundation until a reorganization which took place in 1950. At that time, as the result of a tremendous increase in funds, which placed it first in size among all foundations, it completely reorganized its program. Previously confined to the local and palliative giving typical of smaller foundations, the new program (arrived at by a special study group named by Henry Ford II and directed by H. Rowan Gaither, Jr.) called for activities on a global scale and in the best "venture capital" tradition (Ford Foundation, 1949; 1952). As a consequence, it was at this time that Ford Foundation grants to learned societies began.

During the ten-year period from 1951 to 1960, the Ford Foundation made grants to twelve learned societies, only two of which operated primarily in the natural sciences. The total amount of aid granted by it to these learned societies amounted to approximately $2,800,000,[4] less than $3/10$ of 1% of the total of approximately $1,300,000,000 appropriated during the period. Thirty-six individual grants ranged in size from $717,000 to the American Political Science Association for its program of Congressional Fellowships for selected individuals who are temporarily attached to the offices of U. S. Congressmen and Senators and Congressional Committees, to a $3,896 grant to the American Historical Association for the expenses of foreign historians attending meetings in this country.

To summarize, the Carnegie Corporation of New York, Rockefeller Foundation, General Education Board, Laura Spelman Rockefeller Memorial, and Ford Foundation provided aid of approximately $4,-615,000 to twenty out of twenty-nine humanistic–social science societies, and approximately $590,000 to nine out of twenty-nine natural science societies. The total amount of aid rendered by them to these twenty-nine learned societies receiving grants was thus approximately $5,205,000.

The same relative pattern of giving shown by the Rockefeller, Carnegie, and Ford philanthropies emerges from an examination of some nineteen other foundations which have provided aid to the learned societies. Only five of the nineteen foundations provided aid totalling $124,000 to five societies operating in the natural science areas, whereas fifteen of the nineteen foundations provided aid totalling $564,010 to fifteen societies operating in the humanistic–social science areas.

Altogether, of the approximate total of $5,894,000 provided some thirty-five learned societies by some thirty foundations, over 88% was provided by Rockefeller, Carnegie, or Ford philanthropies. Of the total, 88% was provided to twenty-three humanistic–social science learned societies, whereas only 12% was provided to twelve natural science societies.[5]

---

[4] This figure includes one grant of $5,000 to the American Philosophical Association from the Foundation's Fund for the Advancement of Education.

[5] These figures on foundation giving do not include the income which the American Chemical Society received from the Petroleum Research Fund.

The Fund was set up in 1944 by a group of oil companies, and it now has assets in excess of $70,000,000. The income from this Fund, which through 1960 amounted to approximately $12,000,000, has been administered by the Society to support research in various fields of chemistry.

Grants to Councils

American Council on Education

For the first few years of its existence, the American Council on Education had very limited relationships with the philanthropic foundations. It had been called into existence and financially sustained by a group of educational organizations for the purpose of aiding the defense effort in World War I; it was not until the late '20's that appreciable sums began to flow from the foundations to the Council. During that period three major projects were sponsored by the foundations: a series of modern language studies, an educational finance inquiry, and a program of international activities.

The first project resulted in various changes in the way the teaching and study of modern languages, both foreign and English, were conducted in educational institutions; the second resulted in considerable clarification of the financial practices employed in educational institutions, and in better accounting procedures; the third involved the maintenance of offices in Western European countries which provided liaison for U. S. nationals with the academic personnel and universities in that area. This project provided useful experience for the Institute of International Education, which began operations in 1927–28.

The period from 1929 to the advent of World War II was characterized by a fluctuating but steadily increasing amount of funds to the ACE, primarily from two foundations: the General Education Board and the Carnegie Corporation of New York. In addition to the general support of approximately $450,000 they rendered the Council, these same two, plus a few others, provided the necessary funds for a score of special projects of the Council. These included studies of college teaching and teachers; surveys of secondary school systems; educational finance inquiries; the use of radio and film as education media; and general education.

Following World War II, there was a substantial increase in the number and size of grants from the foundations to the American Council. By the 1950's, such grants were running in excess of one million dollars annually. They came from some 35 foundations, ranging in size from the very largest to the very small. With the exception of two general support grants of $150,000 each from the Rockefeller Foundation and Carnegie Corporation in 1950, and a number of smaller ones for the same purpose from a few smaller foundations, almost all of these grants were for special educational projects similar to those of the pre-war period.

The total amount of foundation aid made available to the ACE, from its beginning in 1918 to 1960, was approximately 12 million dollars. Of this total, over ninety per cent was for special projects, while the remainder was for general support of the Council.[6]

> Various Rockefeller and Carnegie philanthropies, including the General Education Board, Laura Spelman Rockefeller Memorial, Rockefeller Foundation, Rockefeller Brothers Fund, Carnegie Corporation of New York, Carnegie Foundation for the Advancement of Teaching, and Carnegie Endowment for International Peace, provided the ACE with approximately 70 per cent ($8,400,000) of the total monetary aid it received from foundations. Ten per cent ($1,200,000) was provided by some 25 other foundations, such as the Kellogg Foundation, Lilly Endowment, and Grant Foundation.

> The remaining twenty per cent ($2,400,000) was supplied, entirely in the 1950's, by the Ford Foundation and its Fund for Adult Education and Fund for the Advancement of Education. The bulk of the money appropriated by these Ford philanthropies was for the support of activities in educational television, particularly the Joint Commission on Educational Television, popularly known as the JCET, for which the Council acted as fiscal agent.

National Academy of Sciences–National Research Council

The National Academy of Sciences, from its founding during the Civil War to World War I, had become largely honorific. This fact, plus the pre-World War I lack of concern on the part of the new twentieth century foundations with such organizations as the Academy, militated against the development of relationships between them. It was not, therefore, until the mobilization of scientific effort called

---

[6] In this connection, successive officials of the Council have all expressed the conviction that it would be best if the central office, containing the permanent staff and secretariat of the organization, were supported entirely by dues received from members, thus obviating the need for making requests for general support grants from the foundations. By the 1950's, through a modest increase in dues charged members, plus receipts from administrative fees, this situation was about achieved.

for by the events of 1916–18 that the Academy and foundations were brought together.

The fruit of this juncture was the National Research Council, for the Council was created in 1916 by funds supplied by the Engineering Foundation and the Carnegie Corporation of New York. It was sustained by additional grants from the Corporation and the Rockefeller Foundation, and by small appropriations for work done for the Signal Corps. It was not until 1918 that President Wilson authorized the first of several larger governmental grants to the Council. Immediately following the war, the Council was placed on a permanent basis within the Academy; in 1919, the Carnegie Corporation appropriated $5,000,000 for the erection of a building to house the Academy–Council and an endowment to maintain it.

The post-war role of the Council evolved as the result of discussion and actual operation. Although it was envisioned by some as the scientific coordinator of the government, and had high-level government representatives named to it by the President, the Council was not to play an important role in this way until World War II. In 1919, President George Vincent of the Rockefeller Foundation suggested to the NRC's Robert A. Millikan and a group of fellow scientists the creation of a central institute of science comparable to the Rockefeller Institute for Medical Research. Millikan and a majority of the scientists rejected this idea, maintaining that such centralization would be inimical to the advancement of science. While no definite action concerning the Council's post-war structure was taken as a result of discussions incidental to this plan, it did result in the Council's inaugurating a series of post-doctoral fellowships financed by the Rockefeller Foundation (Millikan, 1950, pp. 180–84. See also Dupree, 1957, pp. 305–313).

The importance of these fellowships, aside from their impact on science and the individuals selected, was that, together with other special projects financed by Rockefeller and Carnegie philanthropies, they became the major operating function of the NAS–NRC between the two World Wars. Begun with an initial grant of $50,000 in 1919 for fellowships in physics and chemistry, they were gradually extended to include medicine, the biological and physical sciences, anthropology and psychology, and agriculture and forestry. By the time the Rockefeller Foundation began to curtail this fellowship program in the 1950's, some 1,500 young scientists had participated in it, at a cost in excess of $5,000,000. The various NRC boards of selection and the Foundation worked in close harmony. For example, European fellows selected for work in this country received advice and aid from the Council and the Foundation, while American fellows working abroad were similarly aided by the various foreign offices of the Foundation.

Other Rockefeller philanthropies providing aid to the Council during the 1920's and '30's were: the Laura Spelman Rockefeller Memorial, General Education Board, and International Education Board. Diverse projects receiving aid included: research in population problems, including migration research; surveys of schools for the deaf; studies of child development; sponsorship of lecture tours by distinguished foreign scientists; and technical studies in various disciplines, such as physics and astronomy.

The Carnegie Corporation also supplied funds for specific projects, including some fellowships; research and study on the preservation of books and records; scientific aids to learning; and problems of human heredity. It tended, however, to concentrate its grants upon general support of the Academy–Council, and the work of its divisions and committees.

Although the Rockefeller and Carnegie philanthropies supplied about ten million dollars (about fifty per cent) of the total funds received by the NAS–NRC during the period 1918–1941, there were a number of other foundations which made important grants to it during that time.

In addition to the Engineering Foundation, these included the Chemical Foundation, John and Mary R. Markle Foundation, Russell Sage Foundation, and Commonwealth Fund. The latter organization made an emergency grant of $12,000 in 1919, which was described in the Council's annual report for that year as preventing a "grave catastrophe."

World War II saw a change in the role played by the foundations vis-à-vis the Academy–Council. The Carnegie Corporation and the Rockefeller Foundation provided hundreds of thousands of dollars for the necessary working capital to initiate preparedness projects during the years 1939–41. This capital was needed because the government during this period was unable, because of statutory restrictions, to supply it. Following United States involvement in the war, this difficulty was surmounted and ever-increasing amounts of money flowed from the government to the Academy–Council.

From 1946 to the present, foundation funds have been an ever-smaller part of the total income of the Academy–Council. Despite this development, these same funds are just as important as they were when they constituted a larger portion of that income. This is because foundation financial support forms one of the major bases upon which the Academy–Council is able to maintain its objective position in regard to the government and government-sponsored projects.

Because of its involvement with government contracts (many of them of a secret nature), the fact that the Academy–Council was until the 1950's a bifurcated organization, and the sheer amount of money involved, it is more difficult to ascertain the nature of the income of the NAS–NRC than is the case with the other three national councils. It appears, however, that the total income of the Academy–Council was about $120,000,000 for the period 1918–1960. The total amount of aid rendered to it by all of the foundations during the same period appears to have been approximately $30,000,000, about twenty-five per cent of the total. In assaying the role of particular foundations, it appears that the various Rockefeller and Carnegie philanthropies have supplied about 80 per cent of such aid, the remainder being scattered among some twenty-five other foundations.

American Council of Learned Societies

The Carnegie and the Rockefeller philanthropies were the first foundations to render support to the American Council of Learned Societies. During the period 1925 through 1960, the Rockefeller Foundation gave about $4,560,000 to the Council, most of it in the 1930's and 1940's.[7]

> Of this total, approximately $1,400,000 was for general support; $1,-100,000 for Council projects, including those of committees on Latin-American and Far Eastern Studies; $1,400,000 for fellowships and grants-in-aid; $500,000 for various publications, such as the *Linguistic*

[7] The General Education Board, a Rockefeller philanthropy, made two grants to the ACLS amounting to $134,000 for general and special purposes: one in 1926, the other in 1945.

The Laura Spelman Rockefeller Memorial made a grant of $15,000 in 1925 and another for the same amount in 1928, for research projects of the ACLS.

Although it lies outside the period covered by this study, it should be mentioned that the Rockefeller Foundation provided $1,000,000 to the ACLS in 1961 for its general support.

Atlas of New England, Dictionary of American Biography, and *Current Digest of the Soviet Press;* and $100,000 for the holding of conferences.

The Carnegie Corporation of New York has given about $1,665,000 to the Council during the same period.[8]

Of this sum, the Corporation appropriated about $700,000 for general support; $500,000 for projects, including the holding of conferences; and approximately $465,000 for fellowships and grants.

The Ford Foundation, during the period January, 1950–November, 1960, provided the ACLS with about $4,337,000.

Of this sum, $2,637,000 was for general support; approximately $700,-000 was for various projects, particularly Near and Far Eastern language studies; $200,000 was for various publications; $300,000 for fellowships, and $500,000 for participation in international conferences.

In December of 1960, the Ford Foundation made two grants, one of $2,500,000 and one of $5,670,000, to the ACLS. These grants are unique, being the largest in the Council's history, and are a tremendous earnest of the interest of the Ford Foundation in the humanities.

In announcing these grants, Frederick Burkhardt, president of the Council, stated that the $5,670,000 grant was for the basic program of the ACLS, including fellowships, grants-in-aid, and travel grants; planning and development; and staff and organizational functions of the central office. He also stated that the grant of $2,500,000 was to be used for a fellowship program in which European scholars would study American subjects in the United States, and for the establishment of professorships in American Studies at European universities.[9]

In addition to the funds from the Rockefeller, Carnegie and Ford philanthropies, the ACLS received subventions amounting to about $550,000 from some seventeen other foundations, for approximately similar purposes.

The total of all foundation aid provided the ACLS from 1925 through 1960 was approximately $20,000,000.

[8] In the 1940's, the Carnegie Endowment for International Peace made grants totalling $11,500 to the Council for publication purposes, and the Carnegie Institution of Washington one of $1,646 for a historical program at St. Augustine, Florida.

Although it lies outside the period covered by this study, it should be mentioned that the Carnegie Corporation of New York appropriated $650,000 to the ACLS in 1961 for its general support, fellowships, and grants-in-aid.

[9] *ACLS Newsletter,* 1960, *11,* 10.

Social Science Research Council

At the time of its founding in 1924–25, the Social Science Research Council had no clear-cut concept of the method by which it should operate. The consensus appears to have been that any projects undertaken by it would be of a coordinating nature and on a volunteer basis. There also seems to have been little anticipation of the substantial research funds which would flow to it from the philanthropic foundations.

The initial grant from a foundation to the Council was one of $18,000 in 1924 from the Laura Spelman Rockefeller Memorial, for a study of the social aspects of human migration. This grant, and a subsequent one of $2,500 from the same source for a study of international news and communication, had an important effect on the Council. The setting up of committees to facilitate the conduct of these studies placed it in the mainstream of social science research activity, and served as a precedent for the future operations of the Council. Thus, for about three decades, it has been Council policy to serve principally in an advisory or facilitating capacity; it does not directly administer research projects except when no other competent sponsor exists.

Throughout the 1920's the Memorial contributed a total sum of about $2,600,000 to the Council.

> Approximately $1,500,000 was for general administration and projects. In addition to giving the Council a considerable degree of flexibility at a time when it was most needed, this money provided the funds for a paid staff, which had become a necessity by 1926 because of the increase in the number of projects undertaken. The Memorial also granted $500,000 for the establishment of a *Journal of Social Science Abstracts*,[10] approximately $490,000 for various fellowships, and about $75,000 for the support of summer research conferences.

When the Memorial terminated its activities in the early '30's, several other Rockefeller philanthropies (the General Education Board, Spelman Fund, and Rockefeller Foundation) began to provide financial aid for numerous purposes. The first two, because of concentration of interest elsewhere, provided sums of only about $300,-

[10] The *Journal* was terminated in 1932 because of its lack of use by social scientists.

000 between the years 1931 and 1935, for graduate fellowships and several study projects.

The Rockefeller Foundation, on the other hand, has been a principal contributor to the Social Science Research Council. During the period 1929–1960, it appropriated approximately $12,000,000 to the Council. Fellowships and grants-in-aid programs conducted by the Council account for approximately $4,800,000 of this sum. The great majority of these awards were granted for work in all of the fields of the social sciences. Some, however, were restricted to specific areas, such as agricultural economics, and recently political theory and legal philosophy.

> Various studies and research projects, conducted primarily by committees of the Council, such as the Committee on Public Administration, received subventions amounting to about $4,500,000. Approximately $2,000,000 was appropriated for the use of the SSRC in defraying its general administrative expenses. The Rockefeller Foundation also made grants of about $300,000 for the preparation and publication of several books and for the purchase and distribution of books and periodicals to foreign libraries following World War II.

Including a $25,000 grant from the Rockefeller Brothers Fund in 1953 for research in psychiatry and the social sciences, and various sums which the Council received from the Rockefeller Foundation as a fiscal agent for other agencies, the total financial aid received by the Social Science Research Council during the period 1929–1960 from all of the Rockefeller philanthropies amounted to approximately $15,-000,000.

The pattern of Council support followed by the Carnegie Corporation of New York was generally that followed also by the Rockefeller Foundation, but it differed in timing and in the relative amounts for specific purposes. Whereas the Rockefeller Foundation began to provide aid for fellowships in the late 1920's, it was not until 1947 that the Carnegie Corporation began such aid. Since that time, however, it has approached Rockefeller munificence with grants of almost $3,-000,000 for fellowships.

> Support for studies and research projects was initiated by the Corporation in 1931, within a year of the date such support was first undertaken by the Foundation, and has continued down to the present. Within the total of almost $1,100,000 for these projects, there appears the same range in size and purpose that prevailed in the Rockefeller grants.

Similarly, sums of approximately $375,000 and $1,000,000 respectively were provided for conferences and general support. Joint grants by both foundations for the same purpose are to be found in only a few instances out of a total of hundreds.

Including $10,000 granted the Council by the Carnegie Foundation for the Advancement of Teaching and various sums from the Carnegie Corporation to be administered by the Council as fiscal agent, these two foundations granted a total of approximately $5,500,000 to the Social Science Research Council during the period 1926–1960.

The new colossus of the philanthropic world, the Ford Foundation, followed the pattern of the Rockefeller and Carnegie philanthropies in grants to the Council for research development and fellowships, appropriating approximately $3,700,000 and $2,000,000, respectively, for those purposes during the period 1950–1960.

In other respects, however, the Ford Foundation departed from the older foundations' practices. It provided only $450,000 for conferences and institutes, and only $250,000 for general Council support, the latter sum in one appropriation in 1955. Two separate funds set up by the Ford Foundation, the East European Fund and Resources for the Future, Inc., have also had dealings with the SSRC. The Fund made $45,000 available to the Council, which acted as fiscal agent jointly with the ACLS, for the publication of the *Current Digest of the Soviet Press*. Resources for the Future, Inc., transferred $5,000 to the Council as its share in the cost of a conference held by a Council committee.

Thus, beginning at the relatively late date of 1950, the Ford philanthropies granted the Council approximately $6,400,000 in the short period of ten years.

Nine other foundations appropriated about $788,250 in grants to the Council. They spanned the period 1925–1960, varied in size from $1,000 to $150,000, and were for general support, studies, and fellowships.

The total financial support provided the Social Science Research Council by all of the foundations from its beginnings in 1924–25 through 1960 amounts to approximately $28,000,000.

Grants to Societal Institutes

Compared to the councils, the five societal institutes (the American Association for the Advancement of Science, Federation of American

Societies for Experimental Biology, American Institute of Physics, American Institute of Biological Sciences, and American Geological Institute) have received little aid from the foundations. The Federation of American Societies for Experimental Biology and the American Geological Institute have not received any foundation grants during their entire period of existence, and the total aid granted the three other institutes by some seven foundations amounts to only about $1,000,000. Furthermore, over 90 per cent of this sum was received in the period from 1950 to 1960.

Several reasons appear to account for this relative lack of financial support. Prior to the 1950's, there was not the near-crisis atmosphere in American science which was produced by the Soviet Union's rise to scientific eminence. At the same time that this occurred, various agencies of the government were prepared to support research and other activities of the institutes with large sums of money. Many foundation executives apparently felt that several of the institutes had long been able to finance their projects from their own resources, and therefore did not need foundation aid. Strengthening this attitude was the view that the members of societies supporting these institutes, particularly the Federation, were composed of relatively well-to-do scientists. Finally, pharmaceutical and medical supply houses as well as industrial concerns had developed an early interest in the institutes, and many of them provided sums of money towards their general and special support.

Nevertheless, as the succeeding analysis shows, foundation grants to institutes, although small in number and size, have often been forthcoming at crucial points. For the private foundation, with its greater freedom and flexibility, can quickly put sums of money into extremely valuable, timely projects, which for one reason or another cannot find support elsewhere.

American Association for the Advancement of Science

The relationship of the AAAS with the philanthropic foundations has been a very recent development and is restricted to nine foundations, some large, some small.

The first grant from a foundation was one of $1,000 from the Commonwealth Fund in 1924 for a study of the place of science in education. During the period 1930–1938, the General Education Board and the Carnegie Corporation of New York supplied the Association with some $17,000 in general support of its educational program. In the 1950's, the Rockefeller Foundation made grants totalling about $48,000 towards the payment of expenses connected with the holding of the Gordon Research Conferences. The Westinghouse Educational Foundation, in the 1940's and 1950's, supplied funds of approximately the same amount for science writing awards. A few other foundations, such as the Wenner-Gren Foundation for Anthropological Research, supplied smaller sums for publication and other purposes.

Since 1954, about sixty per cent of the grants made to the Association have been for the purpose of holding various scientific meetings and conferences. The remainder has been for special projects, such as awards for newspaper and magazine science writing, and provision of scientific books for certain foreign areas. Among the projects, probably the most noteworthy was the Carnegie Corporation's support of approximately $550,000 towards the Association's program for improvement in the teaching of science and mathematics in the secondary schools; this aid formed by far the largest portion of the total sum of approximately $722,000 supplied the Association by all of the foundations.

To summarize, foundation funds have played a relatively minor role in the operation of the Association throughout the period of its existence. Its present-day operating budget of approximately $2,000,-000 is largely derived from membership fees, subscription and advertising revenues, interest on invested funds, and grants from the National Science Foundation.

American Institute of Physics

The American Institute of Physics, although its expenses for the first two or three years of its existence were defrayed by the Chemical Foundation, has received relatively few grants from philanthropic foundations.

The Rockefeller Foundation provided funds in 1945 in the amount of $29,300, to aid the Institute in initiating a program to provide a new kind of income for journal publication by charging authors' institutions a fixed amount per page. This page charge now contributes a large annual sum toward the costs of publication of the physics journals. In 1957, the Ford Foundation provided $15,000 for the AIP's future physicist fund. In 1957 also, the Fund for the Advancement of Education granted $52,750 for studies related to the improvement of physics teaching, such as TV and film evaluation. The Educational Facilities Laboratories, Inc., an organization established in 1958 by the Ford Foundation to conduct research and other activities on educational facilities, including buildings, made in that year a $75,850 grant to the Institute to prepare an informative book for the guidance of institutions planning new physics buildings.

The Rockefeller and Ford Foundations and several other foundations provided smaller sums to the AIP for other purposes, but the total amount of foundation aid rendered the Institute from its inception to 1960 is but a small fraction of its total income during that period.

American Institute of Biological Sciences

The American Institute of Biological Sciences has also received very little aid from the private philanthropic foundations.

The Rockefeller Foundation appropriated $40,000 to it in 1952 for general support over a three-year period. This came at a time when the Institute was still struggling and really needed support. Since that time, this same foundation has made only two small grants to defray the travel expenses of several biologists. The Asia Foundation made two similarly small grants in 1959 and 1960 for the same purposes. The only other foundation making a grant to the AIBS during its entire history was the Ford Foundation. In 1958 it awarded the Institute $172,191 for the development and production of a motion picture film of a basic biology course for high school use.

Thus the total dollar amount of all foundation funds awarded the AIBS through 1960 has been approximately $212,000.

It should be reiterated, however, that although the total of foundation aid to the AIBS and other institutes has been relatively small, it has often come at crucial points in the history of these institutes. In at least two instances, the lack of foundation grants would have seriously impaired the work of several institutes, probably critically so.

Conclusions

Analysis of the foregoing grants of the foundations to the learned societies, councils, and societal institutes shows that a very few, primarily larger, foundations account for most of the support provided these organizations, although there has been a relative increase in the number rendering such support since World War II. This concentration can be explained by the fact that, normally, it is only among these relatively few foundations that the "venture capital" concept of operation prevails. Since one of the purposes of all learned societies, councils, and societal institutes is the advancement of knowledge in their particular disciplines or areas of knowledge, it is readily understandable why the larger foundations have supported their essentially innovative educational activities.

The societal institutes, primarily committed to activities in the natural sciences, have received relatively little foundation support. As has been pointed out earlier, such lack of support apparently stemmed from a belief that these institutes already had sufficient financial support for their activities, and when their activities increased in the 1950's governmental funds were available to them.

Each of the four councils has received large amounts of financial aid from the foundations. Two of them, the American Council of Learned Societies and the Social Science Research Council, have derived the major portions of their annual income from foundation sources. The general reason underlying the consistent and heavy foundation support of these councils is the belief that these organizations have been in a position to undertake projects of a trail-blazing and inter-disciplinary nature that no other organizations—including the individual learned societies—could undertake. In the case of the ACLS and the SSRC, this reasoning has been buttressed by the lack of governmental and industrial support that has, almost up to the present, prevailed in their areas of interest. It may be noted parenthetically that these two councils have been receiving increasing governmental support for their activities in the past several years, and indications are that such support will greatly increase in the next decade.

Most foundation support provided the learned societies has been to those active in the humanities and social science fields. Here again, the foundations have operated on the premise that other means of support are available to organizations active in the natural sciences.

In the case of a goodly number of the learned societies, councils, and societal institutes, foundation aid was rendered at crucial periods in their history, usually when they were first organized and needed outside financial support before they could become self-sustaining.

While most of the money provided the learned societies, councils, and societal institutes can be classified as for educational purposes, the vast portion of it has been for general support, research, or fellowships. Relatively little has been used for actual teaching or demonstration purposes.[11] Nevertheless, the foundation aid rendered these organizations has contributed to educational innovation.

Such innovation, however, is invariably one step removed from these organizations. In other words, these organizations play a tremendous role in educational innovation by providing a fulcrum or base from which scholars operate, and a forum where they can argue the merits of their views with their peers. The actual testing of their work, however, usually takes place in our schools and colleges.

For example, in the 1930's the College Art Association of America, financed by grants amounting to several hundred thousand dollars from the Carnegie Corporation of New York, engaged in a number of art projects that worked what amounted to a revolution in the art offerings, and their methods of presentation, in American colleges and universities.

Or, the Rockefeller Foundation and the Ford Foundation provided funds in the 1950's to the Modern Language Association of America, to enable it to develop methods and prepare material for better, more efficient methods of teaching modern languages. The results of these projects are just now being felt in the remarkable increase in the number of courses in modern foreign languages being taught at all levels of our educational system, and in the new materials and methods of presentation developed (*viz.* the emphasis upon the practical and conversational, and the use of teaching laboratories).

Support by a number of foundations has enabled all of the councils to engage in inter-disciplinary projects which have had wide-ranging innovative effects in the field of education. The application and use of statistics is a case in point. Foundation support of the inter-disciplinary application of statistics has resulted in its being taught and used in areas where economics, mathematics, and other natural and social

[11] The 1958 Ford Foundation grant to the American Institute of Biological Sciences for the development and production of a motion picture film of a basic high school biology course is an exception. It is also an example of how foundation funds have been utilized to get new teaching approaches and course content into the school curriculum with a minimum of lag.

science disciplines converge. Also, wider and wider practical utilization of statistical methods has been made in business forecasting, military programming, etc.

The fellowships provided to individuals (usually connected with education at some level) under foundation-financed societal, council, or institute programs have normally involved research projects on some unexplored subject, or in a new area of knowledge (or both). The effects of the successful completion of such projects upon the individual, upon the area of knowledge, and upon teaching conducted thereafter must be far-reaching, but are of course incalculable.

These examples are a few from hundreds, even thousands, of foundation grants to learned societies, councils and societal institutes. They demonstrate, however, that foundation support of the innovative educational programs and projects of these organizations has been a significant one.

Appendix:
Learned Societies Which Are Members
of Councils and Societal Institutes

American Council on Education [1]
   American Historical Association
   American Political Science Association
   American Psychological Association
   Mathematical Association of America
   Modern Language Association of America

National Academy of Sciences–National Research Council [2]
   American Anthropological Association
   American Association of Anatomists
   American Association of Immunologists
   American Association of Pathologists and Bacteriologists
   American Astronomical Society
   American Chemical Society
   American Geophysical Union
   American Institute of Nutrition
   American Mathematical Society
   American Meteorological Society
   American Physical Society
   American Physiological Society
   American Psychological Association
   American Society for Experimental Pathology
   American Society for Microbiology

American Society for Pharmacology and Experimental Therapeutics, Inc.
American Society of Biological Chemists, Inc.
American Society of Parasitologists
American Society of Zoologists
Association for Symbolic Logic
Association of American Geographers
Botanical Society of America, Inc.
Ecological Society of America
Econometric Society
Electrochemical Society, Inc.
Entomological Society of America
Genetics Society of America
Geochemical Society
Geological Society of America, Inc.
Institute of Mathematical Statistics
Mathematical Association of America
Paleontological Society

American Council of Learned Societies
American Academy of Arts and Sciences
American Antiquarian Society
American Anthropological Association
American Economic Association
American Folklore Society, Inc.
American Historical Association
American Musicological Society
American Numismatic Society
American Oriental Society
American Philological Association
American Philosophical Association
American Philosophical Society
American Political Science Association
American Psychological Association
American Society for Aesthetics
American Sociological Association
American Studies Association
Archaeological Institute of America
Association for Asian Studies, Inc.
Association of American Geographers
Bibliographical Society of America
College Art Association of America
History of Science Society
Linguistic Society of America
Mediaeval Academy of America
Metaphysical Society of America
Modern Language Association of America
Renaissance Society of America
Society of Architectural Historians
Society of Biblical Literature and Exegesis

Social Science Research Council [3]
American Anthropological Association
American Economic Association
American Historical Association
American Political Science Association
American Psychological Association
American Sociological Association
American Statistical Association

American Association for the Advancement of Science [4]
American Anthropological Association
American Association of Anatomists
American Association of Immunologists
American Astronomical Society
American Chemical Society
American Economic Association
American Folklore Society, Inc.
American Geophysical Union
American Institute of Nutrition
American Mathematical Society
American Meteorological Society
American Philosophical Association
American Physical Society
American Physiological Society
American Political Science Association
American Psychological Association
American Society for Aesthetics
American Society for Experimental Pathology
American Society for Microbiology
American Society for Pharmacology and Experimental Therapeutics, Inc.
American Society of Biological Chemists, Inc.
American Society of Parasitologists
American Society of Zoologists
American Sociological Association
American Statistical Association
Archaeological Institute of America
Association for Symbolic Logic
Association of American Geographers
Bibliographical Society of America
Botanical Society of America, Inc.
Ecological Society of America
Econometric Society
Electrochemical Society, Inc.
Entomological Society of America
Genetics Society of America
Geochemical Society
Geological Society of America, Inc.
History of Science Society
Institute of Mathematical Statistics

Linguistic Society of America
Mathematical Association of America
Paleontological Society

American Geological Institute
American Geophysical Union
Geochemical Society
Geological Society of America, Inc.
Paleontological Society

American Institute of Biological Sciences
American Association of Anatomists [5]
American Physiological Society
American Society for Microbiology [5]
American Society of Parasitologists
American Society of Zoologists
Botanical Society of America, Inc.
Ecological Society of America
Entomological Society of America
Genetics Society of America

American Institute of Physics
American Astronomical Society [6]
American Physical Society

Federation of American Societies for Experimental Biology
American Association of Immunologists
American Institute of Nutrition
American Physiological Society
American Society for Experimental Pathology
American Society for Pharmacology and Experimental Therapeutics, Inc.
American Society of Biological Chemists, Inc.

[1] All of the named societies are called associate members.
[2] All of the named societies are called adhering societies.
[3] All of the named societies are called associated societies.
[4] All of the named societies are called affiliated societies.
[5] These societies are called affiliate member societies.
[6] This society is called an associate member society.

References

Andrews, F. E. *Philanthropic foundations.* New York: Russell Sage Foundation, 1956.
Dupree, A. H. *Science in the federal government.* Cambridge: Harvard University Press, 1957.

Ford Foundation. *Report of the study for the Ford Foundation on policy and program.* Detroit: The Foundation, 1949.

Ford Foundation. *Annual reports, 1951–52.* Detroit: The Foundation, 1952.

Kiger, J. C. *Operating principles of the larger foundations.* New York: Russell Sage Foundation, 1954.

Kiger, J. C. The four councils. *Educ. Record,* 1958, 39, 367–373.

Kiger, J. C. *American learned societies.* Washington: Public Affairs Press, 1963.

Millikan, R. A. *Autobiography.* New York: Prentice-Hall, 1950.

Walton, A. D. & Andrews, F. E. (Eds.) *The foundation directory,* Edition 1. Published for the Foundation Library Center. New York: Russell Sage Foundation, 1960.

CHAPTER 22

Mass media, mass mind, and makeshift: comments on educational innovation and the public weal

FRANK G. JENNINGS

Thou shalt not answer questionnaires
Or quizzes upon World Affairs,
    Nor with compliance
Take any test. Thou shalt not sit
With statisticians nor commit
    A social science.

—W. H. AUDEN *

In a forgotten sub-basement in a very old school on Manhattan's fabled Lower East Side, I had my first adventure in educational archaeology. As a student teacher I was a member of a lesser caste, untouchable in two meanings of that unlovely word. I was free to wander about the "plant." I was equally free from any specific assignment other than a minimum attendance in the classes of my cooperating teacher when my university supervisor was expected. So it was possible for me to take two of the less biddable boys on an exploration of the school's lower depths.

At the bottom of a flight of stairs that had not felt the caress of the janitorial mop for a generation, we came upon a pair of handsome oak-panelled doors. On the center panel of each was a thespian mask.

---

* From "Under Which Lyre." Copyright 1946 by W. H. Auden. Reprinted from *Nones*, by W. H. Auden, by permission of Random House, Inc.

THE AUTHOR is Educational Consultant to the New World Foundation and Editor-at-Large, *Saturday Review*.

Above the lintel was a drape of marble laurel leaves and grape clusters. Two handsome doorknobs bore crests that were meaningless to me. All this we could see by the light of an emergency electric lamp. The first violators of the tomb of Tutankhamen could not have been more awestruck, nor more excited. One of the boys found the old tumbler lock hardly any challenge at all and in a moment we were surrounded by a velvet silent darkness. The light beam pointed up eroded sections of auditorium seats. At some past time, this place had been cannibalized to outfit another assembly hall (certainly not in this school, whose top floor was partitioned into classrooms by huge sliding doors). Further down the sloping floor the light touched the apron of a stage, traced a proscenium arch behind which was a half-raised curtain—but on its return sweep, the beam glinted upon something on a man-high mound, a veritable kitchen midden. We picked our way across the rubble-strewn floor and discovered that the mound consisted of stereopticon viewers. The lenses of some reflected the light dully, like uncut gems. Beyond this mound were smaller heaps of dust-silted cards. We collected several handsful of these and three of the viewers and retreated from the site to examine the find under modern light.

Here were remains of an ancient visual-aid program—gelatin slides that required a different kind of instrument were mixed in with the stereo cards on which were printed scenes from village life, from the Scriptures, from the streets of an earlier New York—the pell-mell detritus left over from earlier sorties by other explorers.

The boys were thrilled by the possibilities of other loot. I was romantically urged by the notion that I might be able to rehabilitate a long-forgotten theater. We hurried to report our "discovery" to the principal, who quietly quoted chapter and verse to the effect that that section of the "plant" had long since been condemned as unsafe and that he would immediately instruct the maintenance crew to padlock the doors. The thought of lag screws biting into that old fumed oak made me wince. He said I was to forget what I had seen, and the boys were warned that if anything happened in or to that sub-basement they would be held responsible. No high priest could have been more avid in the keeping of the mysteries.

But an archaeologist on a "dig" who strikes pay-dirt is not so easily dissuaded. I reported to my supervising teacher at the university in such a way that I infected her with my enthusiasm—but she responded differently. She was more interested in the kitchen midden than I was in the reclamation of the theater. We should try to find out what the program must have been that would use so large a number of viewers; more important, we should collect and re-establish the catalogue of the cards . . . there was, apparently, a scholarly debt we should pay. I later realized that this was in part her strategy for opening the padlocks. I also discovered that her interest in educational archaeology was aroused by her curiosity about "early teaching aids."

She was a sharp-tongued lady whose gentle mien belied a tough-mindedness that could often shock an overenthusiastic colleague into silent reconsideration of a half-baked proposal. She was eager for experiment, willing to entertain any new proposal—"providing," she would say, "that what you are trying to do is to help the teacher do better what she is already able to do indifferently well." In a faculty meeting she had once declared that the best audio-visual teaching aid she had ever seen was "a teacher on her own hind legs, her back to the blackboard, a piece of chalk in her hand, talking *with* her class about something that mattered to all." She was for any technological advance, but she thought that all too often, when engineering comes into the classroom, teaching is shoved into a closet. "A smart teacher," she told me, "could do a lot with these viewers. A lazy teacher could squander a dozen useful afternoons . . . What have you said about Professor ——, whose entire course consists of a brief introductory lecture, fifteen films and fifteen student reports on those films?"

She was right, of course: automated learning, the mass media, and teaching aids in general represent resources. Employed purposefully, they can give point and depth to any learning. But the media are also a vital part of the complex of experiences we live through all the days of our lives. Because of them, a six-year-old coming to school today brings along a language experience rich beyond that of his parents and grandparents. Although much of what he knows he has not yet been able to assimilate or to manage, he is conscious that there are wider reaches to his world than he has yet touched.

The pervasiveness of the media, and the impossibility of there being any selectivity in who shall read or see or hear what is broadcasted or printed, forces young and old to participate in unmediated experiences. It is hardly overstating the situation to say that one of the teacher's first tasks is to account for these experiences and help the student—of whatever age—to develop the necessary mediating skills. At the same time, the teacher is confronted with the "engineering" phase of education, in which every new technological advance in communications, in data storage and retrieval, and even in information theory, is forced upon the attention of the school.

The Engineering of Educational Innovation

It is the rare good teacher who is not hospitable to the educational gadget—at first. Anything that will help him help his students will get a hearing or a trial run. It is equally rare for even the least resourceful teacher not to be able to find a way to isolate, hide or ignore whatever is useless or harmful, no matter how official the sanction or instruction for its use. In short, teachers are no less resourceful nor a whit less responsible than members of other professions in their alertness to novelty, in their willingness to experiment, and in their readiness to cast aside what does not work. One of the consequences of this attitude, however, is that the storerooms and basements of schools become cluttered with cast-offs of past programs, with books that didn't quite make it, with monster slide-rules, plaster Parthenons, antique phonographs, and the viscera of AM radios.

This is not to suggest that technology serves the school less fruitfully than it does other institutions in society. Quite the contrary. For example, time and again efforts are made by educators and commercial producers to exploit the fascination the comic book holds for children. Whatever the earnestness that is behind such attempts, the youngsters sense the "hidden commercial." The ploy just does not work. Classroom closets and storerooms pile high with "classic comics," "science made easy via funnies" or the polychrome moralizing messages about good citizenship and proper human relations.

Equipment fares better than the material programed for its use. The optical systems now available for classroom use are merely the most recent generation of designs that go back to the magic lantern of the turn of the century. The tape recorders and playback equipment are descendants of Edison's cylinder record. The teaching machine and the programed lesson have a history even more ancient. Certainly the mnemonic devices of the Sophists are among their antecedents. Surely the good textbook is in fact a good program. We "trade up" the name, change the binding to a container, the pages to a film strip or tape—there it is, the program.

An aside is necessary here: I am not denigrating the performance or the potential of programing as an aid to instruction. There is some evidence, admittedly meager, that both linear and branching programs that are well-designed and well administered can effect some improvement in some relatively simple learning. That the instruments and the materials will improve, there is no gainsaying, but that they will result in some fundamental shift in the formal structure or organization of the school is a notion that is both romantic and nonsensical. The same may be said of television—air-borne, closed-circuit, or clear channel. The same must certainly be said of the film. All have as great a potential as the printed page, and the probability of a similar history. Where there is a skillful combination of excellent material, offered at the right time through dependable equipment, then the work of the classroom teacher is both eased and enhanced. Where there is a failure of the engineering or the content, more than time is lost.

I repeat: the teacher and the administrator are not hostile to innovation. Both are eager to entertain new ideas and to test new equipment. Both are very conscious of the potentially available resources which our technology, and more specifically our mass media, have to offer them in their work. We need only instance the way in which paper-bound books are being ever more widely used in schools at all levels.

Sometimes innovation is planned, the result of carefully designed experiment. Sometimes it is the consequence of a happy hunch or insight by the teacher or administrator who is prepared for surprise. But innovation is more than mere novelty or brute change. It can be distinguished from these by its possession of a history: something has always gone on before. And it results in measurable differences. An innovation may ultimately be rejected—most of them are—but it does leave a mark.[1] Things are never quite the same where it has

---

[1] Sometimes there is a kind of flywheel effect with innovation. A look at the development of American textbooks over the past twenty years shows this: typographical trickery is increasingly used; color photography and magazine layout literally drive the text off the page; overlay transparencies appear in one science book and are soon copied by half a dozen competitors. When the basic value of such innovations is exploited as a sales gimmick, teaching is sidetracked and learning is diffused—where it is not defeated.

been; an emphasis in content is shifted, the tempo of learning is altered.

What Are the Media? Semantic Dust-storms

In thinking about mass media and the classroom, one might be persuaded to believe that the media are ubiquitous; that they in fact alter the very act of teaching; and finally that they are accepted, however reluctantly, as something that the teacher and the child must live with. As evidence of all this, one might offer innumerable studies dealing with the effects on student and teacher of radio, the film, television, magazines, syndicated newspaper materials, comic books, recordings. But immediately one does this, one is overwhelmed with demurrers and disclaimers. There are semantic dust-storms. The big sociological guns are drawn up; we discover that in order for an enterprise to qualify as a "mass medium" certain conditions must be met. There must first of all be an "audience"; this is a multi-bodied creature with certain minimum characteristics and a specific habitat. There are rather ordinary matters that suddenly appear to be arcane —intent, persuasiveness, universality, etc.

For example, Kornhauser (1960, pp. 94–95) makes this distinction:

> Agencies of large-scale communication are not necessarily mass media, however. They become so when they lose their ties to local and personal forms of communication. Mere growth in size of these agencies makes mass relations more probable (but certainly not inevitable), as it encourages national centralization and discourages local relations of those who manage the media. Thus, the genuine community newspaper forms a link in the local chain of gossip and discussion, as its staff members participate in face-to-face relations with their readers. By contrast, the mass media lack such intermediate associations; as a result, instead of sharing a community of value and interest with their audience, they substitute organizational and market relations on a national level.

Notice that the term "mass media" in this context has a clearly pejorative aspect. "Large-scale communications," so long as they do not lose the homey touch, and have a human scale, are respecters of values and tradition. But the mass media are too often believed to be powered by pernicious and often faceless "influences," which generate the "mass mind," create the "consumer personality," and are destructive of "community." Moreover, leaders and directors of mass media often give credence to these interpretations by inadvertence, as did for example Frank Stanton, president of the Columbia Broadcasting System, in a speech to the Institute of Radio Engineers. He is quoted by Siepmann (1950) as saying:

> . . . a true mass medium [has] four basic characteristics which I think apply universally. These are, in order: first, broad appeal; second, speed; third, availability; and fourth, low unit cost.

Siepmann (1950, p. 331) comments on Stanton thusly:

> The mass theory of the public is the illusion which comes over men who become habituated to seeing people in terms of figures, not faces; men too, whose concern with people is as a means to ends, and not as ends in themselves.

Siepmann then makes the point, clearly differing with Kornhauser, that "Mass media differ from other media only with respect to the relative size of the many, differentiated markets available to them." (*Ibid.*, p. 332)

Now, although Siepmann's comments are not concerned with the classroom as such, there are certain instructions to be drawn from them. First, "mass media" is a term without a clear referent, even though we usually use it as if it had one. Secondly, there is an implied opprobrium here. The market place is seen to be in conflict with "true" culture, having bred something almost loathsome—mass culture. Thirdly, there is the further suggestion that there has been a perversion of technology in the employment of mass media materials in the classroom. That which could do so much to extend the range of human dignity diminishes it instead, and is therefore to be deplored.

Mass culture and the mass media. A point must be made about the invidious comparison between mass culture and "true" culture. There is a middle-aged, middle-class, middling intellectual assault upon anything that is offered as evidence that large numbers of our citizens are acquiring something called taste; that they are learning something about art; or that they are becoming increasingly conscious of their intellectual, literary and esthetic heritages. All of this broadening of our cultural base is looked upon as merely the current vector of the Babbitt syndrome.

There is a major cultural innovation that we are benefiting from today, and it is the direct product of the increased efficiency and efficacy of the mass media. Perhaps *Life's* series on the world's religions is only superficial scholarship; perhaps *Time, Look,* and most of the other mass circulation magazines are merely running hard after a quick profit when they offer very competent color reproductions of paintings; perhaps a newspaper's circulation department was only out after more readers when it mounted a campaign to tie classical recordings of symphonic music to a readership drive. Perhaps—but this has been going on for many years now, and with what result?

Museums are crowded the way movie palaces once were. Philharmonic orchestras play to greater audiences than do the big-league ball teams; ballet groups both foreign and home-trained are followed avidly by huge publics; the best-seller list of non-fiction today almost always carries several titles of rather stiff ideational content. We are reading more, and reading more thoughtfully today than we did before World War II. (Of course I know Iceland and Japan read more, proportionally, than we do!) The live theater is more alive than it has ever been in this century, and the "road" is not dead. Architecture is a subject for popular discussion. Even the poets have front-page representation.

This is mass culture. It is not neat. It is not sophisticated in the special sense that the intellectual "in-group" have for that word. It apparently does not, or has not yet, led to any heightening of the critical faculties of the masses. ("Masses" itself is a badly shopworn term used obscurely and romantically by the descendants of the nineteenth-century parlor-quasi-intellectuals.)

Still, the critics of mass culture want it both ways. They want the general population to accept their vision of the world, and at the same time they do not want to be crowded by even our deodorized masses. Their one final telling term of opprobrium is "middle-brow": with this they tag most of our popular magazines which try to offer intelligent comment upon the state of society and the drift of the cosmos. Thus, the *New Yorker,* the *Reporter, Time, Harper's, Atlantic,* the *Nation,* the *New Republic* are rejected out of hand for being pallid imitations of the real thing (which almost always is a periodical printed in another country and sometimes in another language.) And of course, it is added, their writers do not write very well and their editors cannot really edit.

Television, for the critics of mass culture, hardly exists as a target. So far as they are concerned, Newton N. Minow laid its ghost with his "Wasteland" speech. But what will happen when Telstar makes it possible to compare the traffic on our venal channels with the nationalized excellence across the ocean? Most of American television is very bad indeed, as is most of our publishing and most of our filmmaking. But our best (as in France, England and Italy) is very good. The best of our television documentary should make Grierson himself proud. And what of the dance, what of poetry, what of our Shakespeare productions, what of the Picasso programs, what of the Walter Lippmann interviews, what of the science coverage, and those rare and wonderful explorations of great minds at work?

American television is gross, loud, vulgar, and superficial in the main, but through it runs, as with all our mass media, a golden thread of the almost perfect. It does move the people. It does instruct. It sends them to books, to the theater, to the classics in every mode. It sends children to school asking new kinds of questions even as it clutters their minds with silly shadow-violence and a hash of sex and history. It is for the school to do the winnowing and reinforce the good that is learned.

Mass culture, which comes out of our common schools, inches perceptibly upward. Just as we are more sanitary today, more diet-conscious, more aware that graciousness in living is available to almost everybody, so are we becoming sensitive to the farther reaches of the mind and the wider scope of the human condition.

The point that I am making here is that the viewers of these television shows, the readership of these magazines, the audiences at the concerts and theaters, the visitors to the museums, all have come to these modest Rialtos as a direct consequence of their earlier experiences with the mass media, both in school and out. To depreciate this arrival is as easy as it is cheap and nasty.

It makes good newspaper copy, and has stood many an academic speech-maker in good stead, when he has been invited to inveigh against the idols of the market place. He need only set up his mass-culture target and let fly. The practicing educator is less tender-minded (although no less aware of the real dangers). For him the mass media *are* the film, radio, television and mass-distributed magazines, paperbound books and newspapers. He cannot keep them out of his classroom, nor would he want to. He cannot prevent his students or their parents from using them. But he does seek, with some success, to instruct his students in using their experiences with the mass media and so to further the orderly work in the classroom.

The Resources of the Mass Media

The mass media have developed classes of techniques of very high skill. For example, the quality of research and the speed with which facts are assembled in the newsgathering agencies of Time, Inc., or in those of the major television networks, *properly employed,* can put us in touch with events and give us most of the essential meanings of those events with greater fluency and accuracy than we could ever achieve with our own resources.

Consider, too, how much more closely we are able to follow spectator sports on television than by being in attendance at the field. (Or consider the ubiquitous transistor radio at the ball park—we want the announcer to give emphasis to what we see.) There is an obvious danger here. Television, by itself, is only a peephole view of reality. There is lacking most—but not all—of the immediacy of what the French mean by their intransitive verb *assister* (to be actively present). This is at once the danger and the reality. It is dangerous to come to believe that what we see represented on the television screen is the occurrence. The reality, however, is that this is one of the most vital ways by which we come in contact with representations of that reality. And it is for the teacher especially to make that distinction. This means that instruction must be given in the specialized *seeing* one does before big and little screens. (We talk a good game about the need to teach literacy in film and television—but we are laggard in our practice.) To learn how to look at a film is almost as basic a skill as reading itself. It is a skill that is extremely difficult to teach and seductively easy to talk about. And the discussion about the matter all too often degenerates into an exchange of cliches.

The educator's views.   It is easy enough to poke fun at the educator as he struggles to explain, sometimes in graceless phrases, what it is that he is about. He knows that the mass media are among the most potent and pervasive elements in his students' language experience.

This is so even in those media in which there is a strong or even dominant visual element, as in television and the film, for back of every formal act in our society is the printed page or the written word. He knows, too, that all these media are vehicles for potent symbolic elements, some of which can be successfully dealt with in language forms only with great difficulty. And he knows that these media present him and his instruction with competition that is often overwhelming, as he seeks to carry on the often prosaic affairs of teaching. As Witty (1961, p. 138) says, concerning "the influences of standardizing forces and the power of the ubiquitous mass media . . .":

> Certainly it appears that the present pattern of interest is too heavily weighted with activities associated with the mass media. Moreover, the mass media, it seems, may exercise a restricting influence upon the recreation, the vocational ambitions, and the reading of many boys and girls . . .

Here Witty is commenting upon the amount of time spent with television as compared with reading. A similar comment was commonly made about the film during the thirties and forties. And yet the teacher also knows well what few of the marketeers of the mass media seem aware of—the child's capacity for selective and even multiple attention. The adolescent especially demonstrates these "skills"; he can attend to television, do his homework, eat, and carry on a conversation simultaneously and often quite successfully. This should be instructive to investigators of communication phenomena.

LaBrant (1951, p. 190) has dealt with this, and has some valuable suggestions for the classroom teacher. Her point is that there is need to teach listening skills, but she does not proceed in the nitpicking manner of some more recent commentators who fractionate the behavioral gestalt and produce lists of elements and processes to be identified and integrated, in order to teach the student how to listen effectively.

The attitude of the working teacher [2] is stated quite clearly in *The English Language Arts,* produced by the National Council of Teachers of English (Smith, 1952), in a discussion of the relation of the mass media to reading, listening and expression:

[2] What is said here of the English teacher applies with equal force to the teacher of social studies and the sciences or, in fact, to any teacher of any subject and grade level.

It is essential to note that in considering the media of mass communication, teachers are not really divorcing themselves from the four essential skills around which the language arts revolve. Mass communication modes are not radio or newspapers or television or movies. They are seeing and listening, reading, writing and speaking adapted to reach large audiences by means of specially devised techniques and mechanisms.

It would be easy to take this isolated paragraph and have a field day at the teachers' expense. But what is being said here is that the job of the teacher is to meet the student where he is (granted the educational cliche) and help him to develop language skills (and even felicities) of an order high enough so that none of his other talents or capacities will suffer in comparison to the richness of these experiences.

More, there is a note of quiet courage here. The increasing rapidity of our technological development is such that what we now have to confront in our language experiences and our management of information is being multiplied enormously. Some of the consequences will make for difficulties and unpleasantnesses (consider again the omnipresent transistor radio which is now complementing the comic book as part of the youngsters' armamentarium). Some of the consequences will produce a richness of resources that will confound our choosing of what to use and when to use it. The whole area of information storage and retrieval, the new technology of thermoplastic recording, and the new methods of photo-copying open still other flood-gates of printed and illustrative matter. The very young student today now has access to material that once could only be gained through hours of research by someone with considerable scholarly sophistication.

Whether these gains in getting bits of information can be translated into gains in learning will depend upon how the teacher exploits them. What, after all, does it signify if a classroom of bright-eyed moppets can display fat little folders of polychrome illustrations of the cultural wonders of the city of Brasilia; what does it mean to have the wallboards festooned with the handouts of half a dozen of the great corporations' "educational divisions"; what is represented by the fact that the librarian—or some other designate—can produce on short notice a beautiful film or strip or slide-set on the behavior of Alfven waves?

The communications revolution. There is a revolution going on today that is reinforcing and accelerating the cultural revolution we have been living with for more than half a century. There are increasingly more aspects of our world that are susceptible of understanding, even to the very young. I suspect that much of the success in the so-called "new math" programs and other discipline-based curricula is a direct result of the recognition of this fact. Partly, too, the sharply accented concern with science and the products of science filters down very quickly to the borders of the nursery.

What was once a far-out joke of the *New Yorker* cartoonists is now a commonplace reality. Kids *do* talk of the Doppler effect and can pluck it out of their real experience. Many of them have seen man-made satellites course across the sky and understand something about transit. Even before some of them can read with much skill they have succeeded in assembling gasoline-powered model boats and planes, walkie-talkie sets, and simple-minded computers. They will know about the Mohole project and some button-nosed little monster will expect his third-grade teacher to know all about the Mohorovicic Discontinuity.

This communications revolution has been affecting us, in school and out, and with increasing intensity, since World War II. It has wrought changes in the very quality of the teacher's lack.

Fifteen years ago John Grierson wrote of these changes in terms that are ever more pertinent today:

> We ought today to be grateful for one especial gift which the technological revolution has brought us. It may have faced us with difficult issues in education, but it has also blessedly handed us new tools for their solution. We have in radio, in film, in television, in traveling exhibits, and in the infinitely cheap reproduction of newssheets, paintings, posters, pamphlets, books and wall newspapers, vital new media by which the world can be elucidated and brought to our understanding. (Hardy, 1947)

"Stupid Ideas Can . . . Spread Abroad"

There is as much innovation and experimentation with the use of mass media in the schools as there is in business and government. It is true that the best "educational films" can rarely compete with the best industrial or commercial films. Educational radio and television almost never achieve the high competence of the broadcasting industry. Again—these comments are trivially true. The history of the documentary film is a record of high educational achievement. (And teaching and training films have a very different history, a different order of success and a most informative record of failure.)

But it is on this issue of the difference in performance between educational and commercial uses of the mass media that one finds some educators trying to reject the mass media. For example, Wright (1962, p. 519) almost seems to be echoing Stanton's thesis:

> It seems to be that mass communicated materials fail as educational enterprises precisely because they operate in isolation from the larger framework of an educational enterprise.

He goes on to make the not unusual comment that:

> One reason why the mass media fail to have a greater educational effect than they do is that most people consciously use them primarily for entertainment and news rather than for education. (*Ibid.*, p. 522)

This is a distinction without a real difference. To act as if the intent of the producer and the behavior of the user aborts the basic resource, and vitiates the evident function of a medium, is more than failure of nerve. It is a rejection of the humane potential of our technology that is identical with that of the sixteenth-century humanists who lamented the coming of the printed book on the ground that it vulgarized learning. There is a story told that when a certain Bernardo Cennini opened a printing shop in Florence in 1471, Politian, who had a good job collecting manuscripts for Lorenzo the Magnificent, saw his world coming to an end. ". . . now," he said, "the most stupid ideas can in a moment be transferred into a thousand volumes and spread abroad."

When the printing of books became a business of some profit toward the latter half of the eighteenth century, Oliver Goldsmith in "The Distress of the Hired Writer" warned of "that fatal revolution whereby writing is converted into a mechanic trade; and booksellers, instead of the great, become the patrons and paymasters of men of genius."

During the same period, the spread of the circulating libraries caused the contemporary guardians of culture to warn that these "slopshops in literature" (as the libraries were called) would debauch the minds of "school boys, plough boys, servant women of the better sort, and every butcher and baker, cobbler and tinker of the three kingdoms." (Wright, 1962, p. 552)

In Sheridan's "The Rivals," Sir Anthony Absolute says to Mrs. Malaprop: "Had I a thousand daughters, by Heaven! I'd as soon have them taught the black art as their alphabet." For him the source of infection was clear:

> "A circulating library in a town is an evergreen tree of diabolic Knowledge! It blossoms through the year!—and depend upon it, Mrs. Malaprop, that they who are so fond of handling the leaves, will long for the fruit at last."

The very people whose accepted responsibility it is to "bring education to all" reject available instruments on the grounds that they are "vulgar" (and does not this betray a strange semantic ignorance? What, after all, does "vulgar" mean?).

Max Lerner, as active a democratizer as one can find, falls into this position too.

> It is important to understand that the corrupting principle does not lie in the machine principle—itself, only a duplicative force—nor in the popular standards of taste, which are product rather than source. At the core is the apathy of people who have never been exposed to quickening ideas, and the slackness of thought which makes them victims of cynical and greedy men. In this sense there is no great difference between the sleaziness of the "comic books" (a hundred million copies of which flow into the American market every year) and that of the "slick" magazines produced on coated stock and selling for much higher prices. They have in common the assumption of an inert reader who will respond to a formula. In both cases the situation is contrived and the solutions are easy. The difference is largely that the comic books contain stronger ingredients, including violence and sadistic terror, that they take less pains at simulating plausibility, and that they mainly reach young readers. (Lerner, 1957, p. 799)

Now there is no denying the relevance of Lerner's assessment. Much mass media content is unsuccessful by his or any standard, except as the media reach large audiences and make a lot of money. But it requires a peculiar construction of the meaning of "education for all" to give this emphasis. The corrupting principle does not lie in the machine *or* its use.

Yet these assertions are understandable. The press in all of its aspects does have some perverse elements. One can speak of "mass culture" as popular debasement. One can, at a more sophisticated level, deplore the production of the *non-book*.[3] One can, with Gieber (1962), say, "Whatever it is, the press isn't education." He goes on:

> The mass media inherently respond to mass audiences with an icono-clastic [sic] respect for major institutions (is this not part of the liberal tradition?) with terse, simple style, with names instead of issues, with drama instead of abstractions, with denotative rather than connotative discourse. (Gieber, 1962, p. 14)

This is rather like saying that the school is a tight little island in a dangerous cultural sea. It must protect itself and its inhabitants from wind and wave. It must be aware that with richness comes corruption, and it must strive for elegance in simplicity. True, its people must someday become navigators, but it would be far better that they learn by indirection.

This, of course, goes counter to the basic American educational commitment to engagement. But it allows one to talk of "excellence" in a safe way. It allows one to see *a* man as potentially good while seeing mass-man as essentially corrupt. It allows, in fact, a pseudo-scientific distance to develop between the individual and society. Then one can speak of "human engineering," of the "manipulation of consent," and of the creation of the flaccid "consumer personality."

There are Luddite echoes of fear of the machine in such attitudes, and an almost superstitious dread of what may happen if something called "science" is given free rein in the affairs of men. Thus the responses to automation, to programed learning, to television in all of its forms, and to any activity which exploits the potential of the "educational market."

The Media and the School

But more to the point are the communication-facts-of-life in the modern world. Not only are we better informed than our ancestors,

---

[3] Often, a publisher's device for filling out a lagging production schedule. The non-book may be little more than the sweeping together of some articles that are vaguely related to a currently popular theme or taste. It may be the work of an informed literary hack who pieces together the story of a forgotten event and so "recreates" an era. A non-book at its best can be an informative visit to the graves of the Hittites, or a reconstruction of an ancient controversy over the railroad "right-of-way" through our Western mountains. At its worst it might be a committee-book with four score authors and not a scintilla of editorial control.

we are better instructed in the uses of information. We take it as a matter of course that we can know the shape of society, the drift of the cosmos, and the dreams of men everywhere on the planet. There are in effect tremendous and intricate feedback loops, through which it is possible to take readings of the results of our actions as a nation among nations, of the results of our responses as citizens to what our several governments plan and act upon.[4] Today it is almost a childish commonplace to say that we know our brother and, whatever the occasional reluctance of some of us, we tend to accept the Biblical injunction (now properly mis-read) that we are his keeper. None of this would have come about without the primary contribution that the mass media have made to the way we address reality.

These observations make it plain that the mass media not only extend the range of the teacher's responsibility, but provide the student, at a far earlier age than in the recent past, with the possibility of learning experiences and intellectual challenges that once were deferred to the late years of secondary school. The direction that education must take will be profoundly affected in consequence.

Again, we must be wary of the cheap fear that sees in all of this a debasing of our cultural and intellectual currency. Siepmann (1950, p. 267) suggests:

> . . . as a consequence of mass communication, we are witnessing a convulsive upheaval of our culture, marked by a shift in its center of gravity. It is probably safe to say that of all matter printed fifty years ago, the proportion of intelligent matter was higher than it is today. But fifty years ago the literate were comparatively "few and select"— and there was much less printed matter. Today, as the market for mediocrity is greater, the supply is greater. This is the combined consequence of universal and still very elementary education and of the mass marketing of communicable matter that technology has made possible.

Though Siepmann betrays hostility to certain classroom practices, he is not an unfriendly critic. He is responding, as sensitive and responsible people have for generations now, to the great gap between potential and performance in our democratic processes. We should and could be better than we are, and the history of the mass media is rich

---

[4] See Chase (1962) for a discussion of the development of the opinion-gathering and assessing services that have become part of the fabric of our daily lives.

with instances of apparent opportunities of quick good growth. Edison immediately saw the educational possibilities of his phonograph and his film projector. Herbert Hoover, as Secretary of Commerce in 1923, conceived of broadcast radio as too precious an educational instrument ever to be used for commercial purposes.

Using the media.   Yet though children and their parents are living in a world that is larger and more attractive because of our audio-visual technology, Dale (1958) reports that:

> Only 26% of English teachers make adequate use of audio-visual equipment. Results of a study of 189 secondary school teachers in Michigan revealed that the average teacher used the equivalent of a one-reel film every four weeks. The average English teacher used one such film every ten weeks. Whether this indicates good or poor judgment is not indicated.

In all probability, both kinds of judgment were operative here. The quality of educational films is rarely as high as it ought to be. On the other hand, there is available—at what cost in time, effort and money, it is hard to say—a veritable treasure-house of film, television programs, and recordings to support every element of the curriculum at almost every level. The problem is to get it at the right time to the right place with equipment that will work . . . and have permission to use it and the skill to do it right.

Here the *mea culpa* comes quickly to the teacher's lips. "If only we had grasped the opportunity . . .," "When the first commercial message went over the air waves, the school lost its chance . . .," "When teachers were offered a second chance in radio with the invention of the frequency modulation circuit they did not know how to grasp it . . .," "For almost two decades now it seems as if the nation as a whole has been unsuccessful in luring the schools to exploit the educational potential of television." All of these confessions are so patently true that they are trivial. Education is *not* isolated from society's other institutions. Our technology is not selective in what it affects; the automobile, television, frozen foods, the ball-point pen all permanently and drastically change the way we work and live—and even the way we perceive reality.

Hardware is not enough.   Yet Jerome Bruner has a pointed warning here:

The film or television show as gimmick, the television system without substance or style in its programs, the pictographically vivid portrayal of the trivial—these will help neither the teacher nor the student. Problems of quality in the curriculum cannot be dodged by the purchase of sixteen-millimeter projection equipment. (Bruner, 1961, pp. 91–92)

"Hardware" (that bravado-term we so like to use for things we fear we do not understand too well) never built a curriculum. A film cannot respond to a child's wonder. The teacher alone can discriminate and act upon what he believes to be the needs of his students. Feedback is a human enterprise, even if it has excellent electronic analogues.

One educator, in a speech to the NEA's Department of Audio-Visual Instruction, recently dreamed of a fully-automated classroom, wired for sight and sound, complete with tape recorders, access to memory banks, and computers, where whatever a teacher or a child would need to know could be had at the touch of a button or the shuffle of a deck of cards.

Suppose we place the teacher at the center of the process, assume from the beginning that he will serve as the master of ceremonies or the producer rather than the main actor. Now, suppose he can be equipped with the ability to use effectively the techniques and devices that are available and that his function is to focus these along with his own talents on a given learning situation. Graphically, the design would appear something as follows. We would place the teacher in position as a sort of central sun which controls certain satellite processes. (Beggs, 1962)

The speaker then goes on to suggest that these "processes" would include all the mass media, all of the best A-V equipment, programed instructional materials, research and teaching teams, etc.

Beggs has narcotized himself into a wild world of dreams. Gadgets are wonderful. Imagine a cigarette lighter that always works! or a camera that corrects your mistakes even if you did not intend to make them!! or a teaching console that warns you with a buzzer-blinker-alert that you are not responding to the class ambience!!!

What is teaching if it is not the engagement of minds contending over the nature of reality? What is teaching if it is not the attempt to impart to others a "sense of the horizon," the range of possibilities open to man-in-society, or the discovery of what is needed for the mastery of some subject matter? What is teaching if it cannot produce persons who are at once individuals and members of publics, who know what is of value and have the capacity to pay for what they need to make life significant for themselves and their fellows?

The "unknown public." Over a century ago, Wilkie Collins discovered the "unknown public" which bought the cheap fiction sheets of his day in great quantities. He saw this audience as hardly literate but certain to become so quite rapidly, for it "must obey the universal law of progress." It would learn to discriminate. It would grow to the millions and it would become the arbiter of literature. "When that great public shall discover its need of a great writer, the great writer will have such an audience as has never yet been known." (Altick, 1957, p. 6)

Collins was right, if overly sanguine. That public is here—it has been with us for half a century. Most of us are its children. We come to literature, to the professions and to public responsibility, out of this mass. We are the products of public schooling which helped that unknown public grow more quickly than the good ladies of the Society for the Diffusion of Useful Knowledge ever hoped. The schools themselves were supported by those who had tasted the fruits of these new leaves. In turn, the "literate" public coming out of the schools was ready to accept the ever-increasing "product" of the mass media. This does not mean that the schools made them ready for this acceptance. What is available in society is taken and used by its members, if what is offered either provides satisfaction or reduces frustration. Here we apparently come back to the "Stanton" thesis— of broad appeal, speed, availability, and low unit cost.

The functions of the media. That thesis should be given a more generous interpretation than its bald statement allows. Leaving aside for a moment the quality of program, what the mass media provide is the possibility for any area of society to have rapid and continuous contact with all other areas. What the modern media provide to their users is surcease from gross cares—what can simply be called escape. They also provide for the development of elasticity of temperament, for a toleration of the new, the complex and even the alien idea.

And perhaps the media's most important function is as channels for news; we need instance only the coverage of the Glenn orbits and the amount of information (instruction is a better word here) which even quite young children were able to receive. The sandpile set that day was dealing with Newton's laws of motion, trajectories, and orbital velocities.

Network radio and television (and with Telstar, network will very shortly be planetary), mass circulation of national magazines and paperbound books, and the national editions of the *New York Times,* the *National Observer,* and others to follow, presage an era of increasing efficiency in the operations of the mass media. *What* they will disseminate is the question that has haunted these pages. It can be good or bad; it can be quite literally world-saving. It can be propaganda in its virulent forms—and there will never be any guarantee that this will never be its use. But these are such potent possibilities—if the teacher uses them as means toward teaching ends.

The educational impact.   The schools do respond to the uses of technology. The teachers are more experimental than they would be ready to admit. They may scoff at air-borne television (and are they wrong?), they may resist the closed circuit, they may forget the cans of film that lie waiting for them in the A-V office, they may ignore the piled up copies of *Life* (is it as good as it used to be?)—but not always. There are the right times, the happy accidents, the sudden realization that what has been happening on Channel 2 or 7 or 31 is what they should have paid attention to (and making a note to check the program listing so the mistake will not happen again).

The mass media will never be deliberately instructional (except in a propaganda phase). They may take occasional bold flights to culture so long as it is safe enough or sacred; Shakespeare is always a good loss-leader, Bernstein is tax-deductible, Science brings in the advertisers. So, there it is in bits and pieces. It is for the teacher to pick and use.

Would anyone compare the level of cultural literacy abroad in the United States today with that of thirty years ago? Imagine Picasso on Main Street? Imagine Shakespeare in Central Park, in Stratford, Connecticut, or on NBC or CBS or ABC? Imagine a profit in classical recording? And what about issues and ideas?—the Congo, capital punishment, the Common Market, existentialism?

This is not to suggest that we are *as a people* as alert, as responsible and as selflessly sophisticated about these matters as some of us are *as individuals*. Nor does this portend the soon approach of a more humane commonwealth. Disaster is always a possibility, but as C. S. Lewis has remarked, "The task of the modern educator is not to cut down jungles, but to irrigate deserts." The mass media, in all of their present and future forms, will be exploited with increasing efficiency. Used by the teacher with conscience and talent, they will contribute increments of good to classroom practice. They can provide more than a peephole view of reality. Under adult guidance—never a plentiful commodity—the child can learn to come to terms with that reality without succumbing to it. The middle-class virtues against which Bernard Shaw inveighed can be seen in proportion and focus. One can learn without debilitating trauma that even good people can be stupid, that sex is not a misspelling of sin. Perhaps, most important, one can learn—in fact one *must* learn—that change is not necessarily destructive, that conflict is not a disaster, and that, as President Kennedy once observed, "Life is not always fair."

References

Altick, R. D. *The English common reader.* Chicago: University of Chicago Press, 1957.

Beggs, W. K. The teacher of tomorrow. Talk given to Department of Audio-Visual Instruction, National Education Association convention, March 28, 1962. Mimeographed.

Bruner, J. S. *The process of education.* Cambridge: Harvard University Press, 1961.

Chase, S. *American credos.* New York: Harper, 1962.

Dale, E. A. Impact of the new media on the secondary school curriculum. In G. Z. F. Bereday & J. A. Lauwerys (Eds.) *Yearbook of Education.* New York: World Book Co., 1958. Pp. 304–317.

Gieber, W. Whatever it is, the press isn't education. *Teach. Coll. Rec.*, 1962, 63 (7), 510–516.

Hardy, F. (Ed.) *Grierson on documentary.* New York: Harcourt, Brace & Co., 1947.

Kornhauser, W. *The politics of mass society.* London: Routledge & Kegan Paul, 1960.

LaBrant, L. *We teach English.* New York: Harcourt, Brace & Co., 1951.

Lerner, M. *America as a civilization.* New York: Simon & Schuster, 1957.

Sheridan, R. B. *Sheridan's dramatic works & his life.* London: Bohn Standard Library edition, 1852.

Siepmann, C. A. *Radio, television and society*. New York: Oxford University Press, 1950.

Smith, D. V. (Director) *The English language arts*. The National Council of Teachers of English, Curriculum Series, Volume I. New York: Appleton-Century Crofts, 1952.

Witty, P. A. The role of interest. In N. B. Henry (Ed.), *Development in and through reading*. 60th Yearbook, National Society for the Study of Education, Part I. Chicago: University of Chicago Press, 1961. Pp. 127–143.

Wright, C. R. The dilemma of education through mass communication. *Teach. Coll. Rec.*, 1962, 63 (7), 517–526.

CHAPTER 23

Structural features of American education as basic factors in innovation

SLOAN R. WAYLAND

AMERICAN educators like to point with appropriate horror to the statement attributed to a French Minister of Education that he knew at any hour of the day exactly what was being taught in any of the classes anywhere in France. It is understandable that a cabinet member in charge of a highly centralized bureaucratic system could offer this statement as a valid, if oversimplified, description of the situation under his jurisdiction. But to accept the statement literally would be to assume that formal organizational structure is a fully meaningful picture of the way in which a system actually works.

In a similar manner, American educators seem to accept the formal organizational structure of American education as a sufficiently meaningful picture of this system. A survey of textbooks, designed as introductions to American education for teachers, indicates a high degree of consensus in their presentation of a picture which is the reverse of the French statement. The essence of this picture is that each school in the American system is an autonomous unit with local determination of its organization and program, with the result that

---

THE AUTHOR is Professor of Sociology and Education, Teachers College, Columbia University.

each school is unique. This conclusion, again, may be reached only if one assumes that the formal organizational structure is an adequate basis for describing how the system works. The French Minister was presenting a false picture, and the American textbooks are also seriously in error.

A deeper understanding of the structure of American education—both the structure of local units and the relationships between these units—is essential as a background for understanding educational innovations, whether one is an innovator or a student of innovation. If, in fact, one's assumptions about the structure are erroneous, the content of proposed innovations may be open to serious question, and explanations of success or failure will be inadequate.

When proposals for innovations such as team teaching, programed instruction, or ungraded schools are made, the advocates' assumptions about the structure of the schools are not usually made explicit. Attention is usually focused on the attributes of the proposed innovation and the points at which the innovation differs from those aspects of the existing system which are being modified or supplemented. Implicit in this approach is the assumption that parts of an on-going system can be modified without giving attention to the possible impact on the other parts of the system. However, this assumption has proved incorrect in many efforts at innovation, with predictable consequences: the innovation is ultimately rejected, or new problems are created which were not anticipated by those favoring the innovation.

In this chapter, one way of viewing the structure of the educational system in the United States is presented. There is no single, correct description of the sociological structure of any social system. The framework which is used for such a description is a function both of the state of theoretical development, and of the purposes for which the description is made. Although the sociological literature on complex organizations is growing rapidly, comparatively limited attention has been given to the educational system specifically. The analysis presented in this chapter should be critically examined in terms of the extent to which the concepts employed bring the complex characteristics of the American educational system into meaningful order. In addition, the analysis may be considered in reference to its utility as a framework for understanding innovations in education.

The first task undertaken is a presentation of some of the key concepts which are used. Other concepts will be presented later as they become relevant. After the presentation of the concepts, three aspects of the educational system are examined in some detail. In each instance an effort is made to suggest some of the ways in which the analysis may shed light on the problems of innovation. In many instances, empirical data are not available to test fully the validity of the propositions which are advanced.

The Concept of Structure

The word *structure* is used here to refer to those regularities of human behavior within a specified social system which are so fully institutionalized that they persist within a limited range of tolerance, in spite of changes in membership of the system. For purposes of this analysis, however, it is necessary to differentiate between four types of structure which are intricately interrelated in complex systems such as education.

Types of structure

The first of these types is the *formal organization* of education, as it is publicly understood. This includes such features as the U.S. Office of Education, the state departments of education, local school boards, and local school systems as they might appear on a line-and-staff chart. Private and parochial school systems would also be included here.

The second type is *ancillary structures:* deliberately and formally organized systems, not a part of the formal organization, which contribute to the functioning of the educational system in specific ways. Some of these are highly visible and have relatively well-established linkages to the formal structure (Parent-Teacher Associations, for example); others are more remote (school committees of local mental health organizations, companies engaged in the manufacturing of school buses, etc.).

The third type of structure is the *autonomous group* made up of individuals within the educational system. Friendship groups or cliques of this type may be viewed individually, or the linkages between them (within a particular system) may be examined as a network which constitutes an informal organization. This type of structure is less stable than the first two types, since it is partially dependent on the particular persons who are members of a system at any point in time.

The final type, *institutions*, is made up of those relationships within a system which are functions of prescribed norms. Explicit formulations of appropriate behavior of this type are not necessary, since they have come to be accepted as given in the system. For example, much of the interaction between teachers and students follows prescribed norms which have been learned (for example, hand-raising as a way of seeking permission to speak) but which are not explicitly covered in formalized rules of conduct. When norms governing institutions are brought into question, explicit rules may be established, and thus a shift occurs from institutions to formal organizations. Each school system has its own institutions which have developed over a period of time, and, in addition, certain institutions have developed within the larger systems of education—e.g., relative status among universities (Ivy League and others) and among fields of study ("pure" and "applied").

An example

The location of particular structures under one or another of the four types in this classification scheme poses several problems. These may be illustrated by a brief examination of the structures involved in the publication and distribution of instructional materials.

In the United States, most instructional materials are prepared by educators on their own time, outside of the commitments called for by the formal organization. These materials are then published and marketed by private companies. However, in some instances, the preparation of instructional materials is an assignment for a regular staff member, and publication and distribution may be in the hands of an educational organization. In countries with centralized educational systems, the preparation and distribution of such materials are a part of the formal organization.

Several aspects of the structure of education may be seen in this illustration:

1. The use of prepared instructional materials is an institutionalized practice at almost all points in educational systems.

2. Since this cannot be left to chance or *ad hoc* arrangements, some type of structure develops or is established to meet this need.

3. The location of this structure may be in the formal organization, or among the ancillary structures.

4. The character of American education is such that (in this instance as in many others) ancillary structures, such as textbook departments in publishing companies, have developed to meet this need.

5. At some points, the line of demarcation between the ancillary structures and the formal organization is not sharply drawn (e.g., a cooperative bookstore run by students).

6. Over time, the location or type of a structure may change. For example, a school may decide to furnish instructional materials, rather than ask students to buy such materials from a private store. A staff member is then charged with setting up a formal system to implement this decision.

Selected areas of analysis

A full analysis of the structure of American education, using this framework, would involve an identification of all of the various structures, their location in one of the four types, and a specification of their operational interrelationships. Obviously, such an analysis cannot be fully presented here.

The scope of this paper is limited to the discussion of three areas in the field of education to which attention has been given in recent years. In each of these areas, various proposals for modification have been made; in some instances, innovations have been attempted. For each of these areas, an effort will be made here to consider the relevant structural dimensions. Proposals for innovation in these areas have sometimes taken some aspects of the formal organizational structure into account, but the other types of structures involved have received limited attention. In view of the intrinsic interrelationships of the various structures in education, as in other social systems, change in any of the structures will involve changes in other aspects of the system.

The three areas to be considered are: (1) integration of various levels of the educational system; (2) interrelationship between school districts in the American system; and (3) formal organization of local schools.

These three areas are closely related to each other, as indicated in the diagram below. The third represents a focus of attention on a particular educational unit; the unit selected is a school (A). The second deals with horizontal interrelationships, i.e., relationships between school systems $(A-A^n)$. The first examines vertical integration, i.e., integration between the different levels in the educational system $(A-D)$.

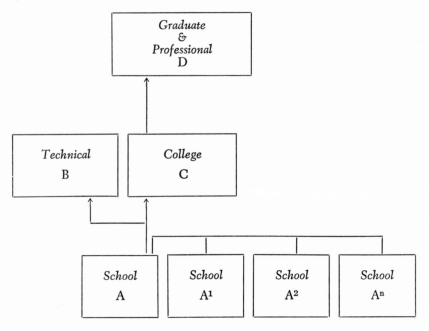

A detailed analysis of areas of such magnitude and complexity cannot be made here. However, an examination of certain aspects of these three areas will serve to illustrate the utility of the approach.

Integration of Various Levels

At the outset, one may raise the question as to why pressure for integration of the various levels in education is apparently present in all societies with developed educational systems. Several quite different but interrelated factors are involved.

1. For any specific group of students who go from one level to another (such a group will be called a "cohort" here), serious discontinuities in content would result in difficulties for the students involved, particularly if members of the cohort vary in their educational background.

2. Each higher level is selective in its recruitment, and wants the best from the lower level. The interests of the higher levels can be better served if the programs at the lower levels have been such as to provide a good basis for selection.

3. Efficiency in the use of resources of the higher levels is most likely if the recruits have attained at least a minimum common level of competence. A law school which has to spend time on the development of English composition skills may well feel that this is not the best use of its resources.

4. The leadership personnel in the lower levels are likely to be products of the higher levels, and will tend to give expression to the orientation or values of the higher system.

5. The presumed unity of knowledge in any area leads to pressure for the removal of basically different orientations at different levels.

Although the four units of the conventional educational system in America—schools, colleges, technical schools, and graduate and professional schools—depend on each other at many points, they have only limited formal organizational structures providing for integration. For example, in most states the legal structures controlling the schools are separate from those regulating higher education. Teachers in schools are licensed, and college teachers are not. Since many colleges are privately controlled, the states have only indirect control over their programs. Attendance in school is compulsory, but is voluntary in the other units.

The fact is, however, that these different levels do have a relatively high degree of integration. College officials sometimes complain about the poor standards of secondary schools in their offerings in such areas as English composition. In such instances, the complaint is directed toward the administration, which permits some students to reach college without adequate competence, and not toward the failure of secondary schools to offer the appropriate curriculum as such. In the same way, preprofessional programs in colleges are specifically geared to professional school admission requirements. Since, however, this integration is not fully provided for in the formal structure, it is necessary to look to other types of structures to explain the integration. Our attention will be focused particularly on ancillary structures and institutions. A number of efforts at innovation have ignored or underplayed the significance of the structures insuring integration. They have assumed that schools were free to make changes, since the formal structural ties with higher levels were limited.

A fundamental assumption of this analysis is that the top level in the educational system is in a determining role for other parts of the system, and that this power is exercised primarily through ancillary structures and institutions. This is not an unusual—or inevitable—role, as will be shown later.

The top level of the American educational system is the graduate and professional school. A major feature of this school is its national character. Staff and students are recruited nationally, and the standards for degree–granting are not primarily local. The graduates find employment in a national market.

The graduate department

The significant unit is not the graduate school as such, but the graduate department; the graduate school is essentially a loose *confederation* of such departments. The graduate department is also a unit of a larger body of scholars in a particular discipline. This discipline group is an ancillary structure in reference to the graduate school, but the status arrangements in this structure are likely to be of great significance for the relationships within a department. A strong department is usually one in which the status of several of its members in the associated discipline body is high. High status in a discipline body involves a cosmopolitan orientation, whereas leadership in a graduate school involves a substantial measure of localism, or (in Riesman's terms) "home-guardism."

In a sense, each graduate department is a professional school for its discipline, allocating its resources in varied ways to train specialists and to advance knowledge in that discipline. The administration and facilities of the graduate school may facilitate the work of the departments, or aid (by recruitment policies) in building strong departments. However, the department is, in fact, the key or basic unit.

The discipline bodies working through the graduate departments are thus the ultimate groups in the educational structure. Since the discipline bodies are ancillary and do not have the continuing character of a structure like a department, their power is muted. Structures outside the graduate schools which bring together *various* discipline bodies are even weaker confederations—e.g., the AAAS and the American Council on Education.

The graduate departments, then, are the capstones of the *formal structure,* and control the levels below them in various ways:

1. Although knowledge production can and does occur at various points, the graduate departments are in a controlling position. A combination of two functions—(*a*) knowledge production and (*b*) control over the admission of candidates to doctoral standing—places the graduate departments in a strong position for any who aspire to be recognized in a particular field.

2. The self-contained and self-perpetuating character of the educational system gives the top position a strong determining role in reference to the lower levels. Most college staff members will have had some graduate work, and college leaders will usually have graduate degrees. School teachers, in turn, will have earned college degrees (and, in increasing numbers, graduate degrees). The interpenetration of personnel in this manner is an important aspect of the structure which insures a measure of integration in the total system.

3. In a related fashion, the admission requirements of higher levels serve as a framework for the program of the lower units. This has become even more important as the number of students moving through several levels of the system has increased. Secondary schools take seriously the need to prepare students for college; the college departments, in turn, want their majors to be able to get into the graduate and professional schools of their choice. For each of the lower levels, the requirements of the upper level are taken as given, and any adjustment must be made by the lower level.

Ancillary structures and vertical integration

Elaborate structures have been developed which establish standards for admission to higher levels; most of these are ancillary structures. As noted above, a latent function of these structures is pressure on lower levels to prepare students to meet such standards. (In various countries with centralized systems of education, examinations at the end of the secondary level, and at other points, are developed and administered as external examinations.)

Mechanisms have developed in the United States which serve as systemic linkages (in this instance, links between different levels) not provided for by the formal organization. They include such practices as the Carnegie unit system, National Merit Examinations, College Board Examinations, advanced placement programs, and the

Graduate Record Examinations. The accreditation associations represent another type of mechanism, with a somewhat more elaborate organizational character. Each of these has its own special function, but all are ancillary structures employed by higher levels in the educational system to implement, on a wide scale, logistical control of movement of students through the system. *Structures which are parts of the formal organization in many countries of the world are defined as ancillary structures in the United States.*

In summary, in any educational structure a measure of integration between the various levels is achieved. In societies with highly organized formal controls over all aspects of the system (e.g., the USSR or France), the structures providing this integration are highly visible, and problems involving relationships between subsystems will require attention to the formal organization. Structures of the other types described above are, of course, present. To the extent that the formal organization does not adapt to changing conditions, institutionalized evasions of the formally established system are likely to develop.

Innovation and nonformal structures

In societies in which the formal organization does not include provision for integration, linkages are maintained through other types of structures (e.g., accreditation associations provide a linkage between schools and colleges). These linkages are not likely to be as visible or as subject to control as formal structures, but may be highly effective in maintaining integration. In such societies, efforts at innovation which take only the formal organization into account are certain to meet resistance from the other types of structures. But the lower visibility of these structures may prevent the innovator from understanding the nature of the resistance.

An unsuccessful innovation attempt. The Eight-Year Study anticipated the resistance to innovations in the secondary school curriculum which might come from the colleges, and gained prior approval for the innovations. However, many other elements in the system which were not taken into account served as barriers to the development and maintenance of innovations. A careful study of these elements would be illuminating. (Some of the elements which were probably operating are also considered in the discussion of interschool and intraschool relationships below.) A background factor was World War II, which was at the least diversionary, and may also have facilitated the reassertion of the established pattern. Turnover of staff was probably an important factor, since the organizations which prepared teachers were not changed. The usual process of institutionalization must have forced the schools involved to regularize features of a program which, essentially, required flexibility. As a corollary of this, the administrative difficulty involved in managing a large number of students as exceptions was probably an unfavorable element. The movement of students in and out of these schools probably increased parental pressure to restore a pattern which would involve fewer difficulties.

In any event, little residue of the innovations of the Eight-Year Study remains in these schools, and the impact on American education was slight, even though the experiment seemed to have met its goals.

A successful innovation attempt.   Education for the mentally retarded was successfully incorporated in school systems throughout the country in a relatively short period of time. The leadership for this innovation came from ancillary structures—parents and lay organizations. After efforts at the local level which were not very successful, action was taken at the state and federal levels; this included pressure for the enactment of legislation which established a pattern and provided funds for local schools, teacher training programs, and research activities. Local, county, state, and national groups were organized to bring pressure to bear on appropriate groups at all levels. In addition, the nature of this innovation was such that it could be added onto the existing program without serious disturbances to other parts of the system.

Implications for innovation

In the analysis above, two central points are being made which have significance for innovation in education. In the first place, the formal system represents only a part of the educational structure, and efforts at innovation must take into account ancillary structures and institutions. In the second place, the educational system has a relatively high degree of integration,[1] and innovations which do not take the integrated character of the system into account will encounter difficulties at many points.

Interrelationship between School Districts

One of the dominant elements in the formal organization of the American school system is the independence and autonomy of the local educational system. Under the Constitution, the provision for education is a state function; the states in turn have delegated the responsibility for the operation of schools to local school districts. The consequence is that education is administered through some 37,025 local districts. These districts hire and fire their administrators and teachers, establish their curricula, and handle the finances for the schools. Lateral relationships between districts are not usually provided for in the organizational structure of a state system, as they are between schools within a single district. Sometimes, collaboration for specialized functions may be officially established between districts on a regional basis. In some instances, local districts collaborate with other districts under state regulations in the provision of secondary or other special schools. In general, however, there is no authority in a line position between the local school district and the state. Local control of schools is a well-established feature of the American ideology.

We are faced at this point with a paradox. The 37,025 school districts are ostensibly locally controlled; this is socially valued as a grassroots system which will permit the local area to have the kind of educational system it wants. Yet the differences among these districts are

[1] This analysis is not designed to convey the impression that the American educational system has *tight* integration. Subsystems deviate in varying degrees from the dominant pattern. For example, the linkages between the Negro school system and the white school system of the South were not strong enough to make the separate systems equal. The Roman Catholic parochial system has few formal organizational ties with the dominant system; but linkages through other types of structures (e.g., teacher training institutions) have been such as to make these two systems essentially similar. Finally, although certain professional schools, such as those in business education and teacher education, have developed their own patterns, the influence of the graduate school has tended to reassert itself as linkages have increased (both through formal organizational and ancillary structures), and closer integration has occurred.

relatively small, as will be seen below. *The formal organization of the schools, and their curricula, do not vary markedly throughout the country.* Since this similarity is not the function of an over-all formal organization, and cannot be assumed to be a matter of chance, other types of structures must exist which have brought it about.

The assumption underlying this section of the paper is that *we have, in fact, developed a national educational system, with the consequence that serious innovation at the local level is extremely difficult to introduce and to maintain.* The fact that this national sysem is not provided for in the formal organization (i.e., that there is no central ministry of education charged with the responsibility for running a national system) does not mean that a national system does not exist. Assuming that such a system does exist, our task becomes that of identifying the types of structures which make it function.

No effort will be made here to demonstrate in detail the common character of the school system throughout the country. Several aspects will be considered, however, and others will be analyzed in the process of looking at the types of existing structures.

Evidence for a national system

In countries with a legally established national educational system, the courses of study which are to be offered at each level are specified, the instructional materials are provided for all, and an evaluation system, including inspectors and external examinations, is provided. As noted above, none of these exist in the United States as publicly controlled activities. State departments of education do issue curriculum guides, and these serve as a framework within which local curriculum decisions are made. *However, no one knows in any detail what is taught in the American schools.* Since we do not have direct data, it is necessary to rely on indirect evidence. The four items listed and discussed below constitute such evidence, and at the same time are factors which partially account for the common curriculum.

1. *National recruitment of teachers.* Although each state has its own system of certification of teachers, the training process for teachers makes it relatively easy for teachers to move from one state to another. Teachers trained in Arkansas are regularly recruited by suburban schools around Chicago. California school systems send repre-

sentatives to the East Coast to recruit teachers. Active negotiations are under way to prevent the loss of pension rights when teachers move from one state to another. If differences exist between these systems as they affect teachers, they are apparently of minor importance. These minor differences are a function both of the similarity in educational systems and the ease with which the college graduate can learn to do what he is assigned to do.

2. *Successful movement of students from school to school.* The extensive mobility of the American population results in frequent tests of the degree to which the instruction in one school system meshes with that of another. Research on the problems associated with such movement has been limited, but the few studies at hand indicate that students do not suffer from such mobility, unless they move many times in a short period.

3. *National market for instructional materials.* Although teachers are urged to prepare their own instructional materials, textbooks and similar instructional materials serve as the central feature of most courses. The textbook industry functions on a national basis. In order to take advantage of large-scale production, extensive adoption of texts is a desirable goal for any one publisher. And in view of the sequential or cumulative character of many segments of the curriculum, series of texts are issued for different levels, with the expectation that a particular school system will buy an entire series. Many publishing companies publish such series, in a variety of different subject areas.

Texts are prepared by educators, and the textbook editors and their consultants are frequently people who have had some association with the school system. Authors of texts frequently test out their materials in their own classrooms, or gain the cooperation of others in trying them out before they are published. However, most of the structures involved in the preparation and distribution of texts are ancillary, and not part of the formal structure. The linkages referred to above, and others such as feedback from teachers to salesmen, serve as mechanisms to insure that the formal and the ancillary structures mesh with each other. (This pattern operates in the Roman Catholic parochial school system as well as in the public educational system. Private publishing companies specializing in production of textbooks for such schools are not part of the formal structure of the church.)

In summary, textbooks are a central feature in setting the framework of what students are taught, and they are distributed on a national basis. Although it is not contended that textbooks by different companies are the same, their differences in most areas of instruction are not marked. Furthermore, school systems do not like to change textbooks as long as the existing inventory is usable. Three- to five-year use of such materials seems to be common, and retention for much longer periods is not unusual.

4. *National examination systems.* Over a period of years, several different testing and examination systems have been developed which operate on a national basis. The factors giving rise to these testing and examination systems vary. The National Merit Scholarship system has the manifest function of providing opportunity for college study for qualified students, regardless of their financial resources. The tests developed and administered through the College Entrance Examination Board have been devised to provide colleges with standardized information about applicants, supplementing data from local school systems, which may be difficult to interpret. The various achievement tests, such as the Iowa or Stanford tests, make it possible for local school systems to measure their achievement against a norm established on a national basis.

The fact that such tests and examinations could have been developed and administered on a national basis—and the fact that the results are taken as a basis for action—indicates the extent to which a basically common system has developed. In a sense, these ancillary structures have an effect which is in the direction planned for (through the use of inspectors and external examinations) in countries with formal national educational systems.

Variations in content and quality of school programs are frequently *not* sources of pride, but of concern. Dr. Conant has followed the logic of many educational leaders in urging the building of large educational systems, to facilitate the introduction of courses which cannot be provided economically in small schools. State and federal aid is urged as a means of insuring that inadequate education is not due to lack of resources. The argument is usually made in terms of the extent to which school systems deviate from a norm; inability of a deprived area to establish its unique program is not usually mentioned.

Structures supporting a national system

To the extent that a relatively common educational program exists, it is necessary to look for explanations outside of the formal structure. The various ancillary structures which exist are numerous and of quite different orders, and only brief and general examination of their operation can be made here.

In the first place, the structures which have been cited as indicators of the common character of the program are also contributory structures. For example, the movement of teachers and administrators from place to place is a mechanism for diffusion of educational practices. Similarly, the parents who move around the country serve as a diffusion mechanism. The textbook industry, through its publications and the actions of its salesmen, makes available to local school systems curriculum patterns which are in existence in other school districts. The results obtained through the administration of national tests and examinations serve as a guide for modifications of the curriculum— modifications designed to insure more favorable results on subsequent administration of the same tests.

Another major set of structures is composed of *national organizations* of persons involved in various ways in the educational system. State and national organizations for teachers (at all levels and for all specialties) and for administrators, school board members, parents, textbook publishers, and teacher training personnel serve as communication devices and also as status-giving and rewarding systems. Through formal papers, informal discussions, publications, and policy-making actions, models for appropriate actions are made available on a national basis. Although most of the personnel involved are parts of the formal structure, these organizations are ancillary structures, and provide systemic linkages which the formal organization does not. A special case in this general category is the Council of Chief State School Officers, an organization which has no legal status but which is a very significant mechanism in a society without any formal structural provisions for handling interstate problems.

Teacher training institutions usually have no direct formal relationships with the schools. A significant proportion of teachers is trained in private institutions which take state requirements into account as they choose. Only about 120 of 1,300 institutions engaged in teacher preparation are teachers colleges. Graduate schools of education, whether public or private, tend to function as nonlocal institutions, as noted earlier. Leadership personnel in teacher training programs are likely to have strong professional ties outside the local area. Too strong a commitment to local ties may hinder advancement within the profession, and the rewards for strong professional ties are high.

Accreditation associations represent another ancillary structure which brings local school systems and teacher training institutions within a common framework. Although these are extralegal associations, they can exercise sanctions which cannot be ignored by educational systems. For example, college admissions officers usually discount units offered by students graduating from nonaccredited high schools. Recently, the threat of loss of accreditation status at the University of Mississippi has apparently been of more serious concern to state and university officials than legal sanctions had been. Although accreditation associations may try to reject the concept of a single pattern for the institutions which they serve, they do have an evaluative function, and also communicate a system of values. Since the members of accreditation teams are also on the staffs of accredited institutions, they serve as additional linkages between formal systems.

In addition to the types of structures which have been identified above, another type exists which is not as closely tied to the educational structure. This is the *ad hoc* group—either an independent group, or an agency of an organization with a program which may involve education. For example, national organizations interested in safety, alcoholism, conservation, patriotism, and mental retardation attempt to focus attention on their areas of concern by gaining inclusion of materials in the curricula of schools throughout the country. Once such programs are adopted, the organizations resist efforts to eliminate or reduce the attention given to their interest.

Groups in special positions in the educational system, or operating as ancillary structures, may serve to reinforce the national character of the system. For example, an influential figure such as Dr. James Conant, with support of a respectable foundation like the Carnegie Foundation and using national media, has been able to set a pattern which mediates between somewhat different emphases. In a similar way, new programs in physics (and other disciplines) have been developed by ancillary structures; through linkages with the formal structures at many points, such programs have been established throughout the country.

Since ancillary structures are not a part of the formal organization of the school, they are not easily subject to public control. However, changes in the formal system will be felt in these ancillary structures, and such changes may or may not be in the self-interest of such structures. To the extent that a proposed change is not in their interest, resistance to it may be anticipated.

Implications for innovation

In this section, attention has been directed to the set of structures which serve to develop and maintain a national educational system. These structures are primarily ancillary, since the formal organizational structures are limited and weak. At a number of points, the functions of ancillary structures in the United States have been shown to be parallel to those of elements in the formal organizational structure of nations with centralized educational systems.

However, the central point of this analysis is not the demonstration of the existence of a national educational system, but the identification of features of the American system which influence innovation. If in fact local school districts functioned as autonomous units with no significant linkages outside the local area, the problems of innovation would be limited to the type discussed under formal organization of local schools, below. But as the Arkansas–Ford Foundation experience shows, even the states, which are legally autonomous educationally, are in fact so linked with other states through ancillary structures that real limits on innovation exist.

It is particularly instructive to compare the relative success of the Ford Foundation, with all its resources, and that of the special education movement, working as an essentially lay movement. Although the content of the interests of these two ancillary structures is of some relevance to the comparison, the special education movement has apparently operated with substantially greater appreciation for the structure of the American educational system. Its leaders have not been deceived by the ideology of local autonomy of schools or by the assumption that well-trained teachers will solve all educational problems. No judgment is being made here as to the merits of the innovations which have been proposed; nor is it assumed that the leadership of the special education movement ever made explicit their understanding of the structure of American education. It *is* assumed that their actions were sufficiently in conformity with the demands of the structure to lead to success.

Formal Organization of Local Schools

The major problem for consideration in this area is quite different in character from those which have been considered in the two previous sections. The structural analysis for the first two areas was focused on the role of the ancillary structures as complements to the formal organizational structure. In this section, the focus is on the nature of the formal organizational structure itself, and in particular on the degree of discrepancy between the demands of the formal organization and the ideal pattern as seen in professional literature. The basic premise of this analysis is that the gap between "is" and "ought" is in part a function of the requirements of the formal organization—and is not solely due to inadequate professional preparation, lack of commitment, or human frailty. Efforts at innovation which assume the latter as the only problems to be overcome will encounter difficulties.

One of the central themes in the literature of professional education is the centrality of the role of the individual teacher. A significant proportion of the educational research of the past fifty years has been focused on methods of instruction. One implicit assumption underlying much of this research is that the teacher is in a position to decide what he will teach, and how he will teach it. The fact that a teacher is a member of a formally organized system is largely taken for granted, and resistance to proposed innovations, whether suggested by a new teacher or by established members of a staff, is frequently interpreted as due to the recalcitrance of other members of the system, rather than seen as stemming from system problems. Similarly, proposals such as teacher aides or team teaching, which are intended to meet educational problems engendered by the operation of the school as a social system, are frequently denounced, since they are perceived as mere rearrangements which do not deal with the "real" problem of teaching and learning. Although there have been literally thousands of studies of teaching methods, with the individual teacher and one or more classes as the unit, there is no study of a school as a social system which gives attention to all of the elements in such a system. Several studies have been made of the student population in particular schools, and a few studies have focused on the staff.

System problems requiring solution

As a social system, a school must solve a number of problems that are qualitatively different from those faced by the individual teacher with his own group of students.

Social control.   In the first place, the school directly serves a given number of students at any one point in time, and has to devise some system by which social control of such a population is insured. For this age group, this means continuous supervision, since the student is away from home, and free use of time by students is not culturally acceptable. Adult supervision, by someone officially delegated for this task, is provided from the time the student comes under the jurisdiction of the school until he leaves.

Sequential organization of program.   In addition to meeting the problem of social organization and control as a day-to-day matter, the school must also organize its resources to serve each cohort of students from its entrance into kindergarten until graduation. Some of the students in any one cohort will withdraw from that cohort, and new members will be added to it. The goals of the system require that a program be developed to insure that any given cohort has an experience which is integrated and cumulative in character, and results in an acceptable degree of attainment at the end of the period of tenure in the school.

Goal attainment.   As noted earlier, any particular school system must meet the problem of matching its goals and its attainment with the expectations of other systems with which it has linkages. These other systems include not only higher educational systems but also the various other systems into which the high school graduate moves. Actions of individual staff members which do not contribute to the system goal cannot be tolerated. This was the underlying issue in a recent controversy in Westchester County, New York, involving an English teacher who refused to submit lesson plans for review by the administration. The New York State Department of Education upheld the dismissal of the teacher, holding in effect that the school administration was responsible for the achievement of system goals, and that the requirement of submitting lesson plans in advance was a legitimate means of insuring that the system goals were honored.

Public accountability.   A school is a public institution, and attendance is compulsory. Even if a particular school is privately supported, it still has a public character. The compulsory and public character of a school involves certain modes of social behavior and organization. In the first place, the individual students have a claim on the system for equality in treatment. The teachers are public employees, and are subject to public scrutiny of their actions. As schools are presently organized, the public holds the chief administrative officer of a school accountable for the operation of the school system. Although a teacher may be sensitive to the support or criticism of parents and others, he knows that positive and negative sanctions are in the hands of the administrator.

Once again: the attainment of system goals, the provision of continuity and integrity of program for each cohort of students as it moves through the system, and the day-to-day need for effective social control are *system* problems, which exist independently of the particular persons who happen to be members of the staff at any point in time. One of the facts of life about school systems is the rapid turnover in their teaching and administrative personnel. On an average, the annual staff turnover rate of 8 to 10 per cent is such that the rate for the period of tenure of one cohort of students in a school system will be more than 100 per cent. Continuity and integrity cannot be left to informal arrangements among individual teachers. The curriculum is established, and new personnel in the system will normally be assigned to fill slots in the organization chart. Curriculum revisions worked out at any point in time (whether initiated by the administrative staff or teachers) are a form of rational allocation of duties;

they are binding on the existing staff—and on subsequent staff—until such time as a new allocation of duties takes place.

Staff allocation. Another problem the system must meet is the allocation of a given number of staff members to meet the problems of social control and continuity of program. The number of students to be served is not subject to control, since all persons within a given age range must be served. The absolute number in any cohort will vary from year to year as noted above, and the numbers in the different cohorts in the same year will vary.

In addition, within any one cohort the number who will take particular courses of study is not subject to rigid control. Some measure of control may be exercised through guidance of students, but (particularly at the secondary level) classes will vary in size at any point in time, and the same classes will vary from year to year. Furthermore, the social control function usually involves assignment of staff to such functions as supervision of study halls, cafeteria, and extracurricular activities.

The matching of a given number of teachers (with a special combination of primary competences) and a given number of students (with varied interests) is a logistical problem, which is usually solved on an administrative level. This almost invariably means that some teachers are assigned to teaching functions other than those in which they have most interest and competence. For example, social studies class time may be required beyond the number of hours which those prepared to teach in that area have available. But this surplus may not be enough to warrant the hiring of a new teacher, and norms of class size may preclude the possibility of absorbing added students in the classes taught by the trained staff. The extra classes will usually then be assigned to someone whose work load is not filled, such as the football coach, or the English teacher who has only three classes in English.

Logistically, problems of this type are inevitable with the present pattern of school organization; this in part accounts for the large number of teachers who are shown in state and national studies to be teaching courses for which they are not certified, or in which they have minor interest and competence.

It may be noted in passing that this logistical problem is a particularly difficult one in smaller secondary schools, and is one of the major factors which has led to pressure for elimination of smaller schools. Under present patterns of school organization and curriculum structure, the alternatives available to the administrator of a small school—limited offerings, or courses given by teachers without adequate training—are unacceptable to many. Certain other factors being equal, the larger the school, the smaller the proportion of students who must be served by teachers assigned to functions other than those they are best qualified for.

One of the factors which may intrude is the tenure status of the existing staff. As noted earlier, rapid turnover of staff is characteristic of many schools; this has the function of permitting annual modification of the pool of competences which are represented in a total staff. But tenure status of a high proportion of a staff introduces a potential difficulty in meeting the logistical problem. The system has a large number of "given" employees, and they must be used. (Tenure status, however, does not include the right to teach a particular level or subject, and the individual teacher with tenure may thus face the necessity of accepting an assignment which he does not like, or of resigning.)

It should be emphasized again that this logistical problem is inherent in the organizational structure. The more rapid the changes in the four key variables involved, the more difficult the logistical problem. These variables are: (1) changes in the absolute numbers within the succeeding cohorts; (2) changes in the interests of students, as reflected in changing enrollment in different courses by succeeding cohorts; (3) changes in the curriculum offerings; and (4) changes in combinations of staff competences (resulting both from changes in competences of continuing staff, and from replacement of staff members).

Teacher competence and system decision-making

A number of the factors discussed above have been shown to be forces reinforcing the maintenance of a curriculum which will be effective *regardless* of the particular persons who happen to be members of the staff at any one point in time. For example, an administrator can handle the logistical problem described above if he knows that the teacher assigned to a course outside his area of major interest and competence will not have to begin *ab initio* in preparing for it—i.e., if the basic content, goals, instructional materials, and evaluation standards for the course have been predetermined. The administrator is well aware of this factor, because he has already faced essentially the same problem at all levels with the majority of his staff, which *is* teaching in its areas of major competence.

The school, as it is presently organized, is based on the assumption that all teachers in the system are equally competent within an acceptable range of tolerance. The parents of a fourth grade student have the right to expect their child's teacher to be as good as that of their neighbors' child, who is in the same grade but has a different teacher. The factors which lead to the assignment of a student to one section of tenth grade geometry rather than another presumably do not include the fact that one teacher is highly competent and the other mediocre.

The fact is that teachers do differ. Efforts are made at many points, of course, to insure that a minimum level is attained. The recruitment, training, certification, and hiring of teachers all represent points at which floors are established. Supervision, in-service training, and probationary periods for new appointments serve as control mechanisms.

Curriculum decisions. However, the variations which exist in spite of these mechanisms need to be faced; it is at this point, again, that an extrapersonal solution seems called for. Since neither individual decisions by the teacher nor informal determinations among various teachers can be trusted as a means of curriculum determination, system decision-making is usually the pattern followed. (Schools do differ somewhat in the extent to which they involve the staff actively at any one point in time, of course.) The consequence of this pattern is that those teachers at the minimum level of competence are not faced with the necessity of making a set of basic decisions. In more concrete terms, these decisions take the form of an established curriculum. Courses at various levels are specified, and the amount of time to be spent in each area is established. In elementary schools, where one teacher may handle a number of different subjects, there is frequently a specific number of minutes designated to be spent each week on science, language arts, arithmetic, etc. In systems where curriculum guides are less detailed, the basic decisions may be made at the point where textbooks are selected.

Once the decisions have been made, all teachers are expected to follow the basic patterns which have been established. (These basic patterns include areas of teacher action such as student management, teacher–parent relations, and use of school resources, as well as curriculum activities.) The sources of the system decisions may not be local in origin, but they are local in application. Such system decisions do not make all teachers equally competent, but they are designed to raise the quality of the performance of the less competent above the level which they might reach if left to their own resources. Even the teacher who is competent in some areas of his role may not be equally competent in other areas. The implementation of system decisions may at times have the effect of serving as a constraint on the creative teacher, but it also serves to reduce the potential range of differences among teachers.[2]

Time utilization. Another factor which sets limits on the individual teacher's range of freedom of action, and in turn reinforces the significance of system decisions, is the time utilization pattern for teachers. As noted earlier, the age of the population served in schools is such that, in our culture, continuous adult supervision is the rule. As our schools are presently organized, teachers are usually involved in a teaching or supervisory role for almost all the time school is in session. (Also, some time during the working day often needs to be spent in giving attention to system problems. This includes meetings of department or grade level teachers, the total faculty, or special committees.) At any minute of the day, just as a parent can find out from the principal's office where her child is, so the principal can also locate any teacher, knowing without asking what kind of activity he is engaged in.

Almost all the preparatory and follow-up work involved in teaching must be handled before or after school is in session. The management problems involved in developing lesson plans, assembling or preparing instructional materials, checking students' work, preparing tests,

[2] One other possible interpretation could be made of the relationship of teachers with different competence to a population which has a claim on equal treatment. If, within any given cohort of students, the assignment of students to teachers occurs on an essentially random basis, it can be assumed that over the period of tenure of the cohort, any given student's combination of teachers will not differ significantly in competence from that of other students in the same cohort.

and grading papers for 150 to 180 student hours daily—all these are "presumably" tasks which can be handled without much expenditure of time after a working day. (The teacher of a freshman in college will normally spend less than half of his working time during the week in teaching or supervisory activities.) Professional advancement activities also usually take place during "free" time.

Such a pattern of time utilization is possible because of the extensive institutionalization and routinization of many aspects of the job of teaching. Basic decisions about the curriculum are anticipated in textbooks or curriculum guides. The use of curriculum resources which are not fully institutionalized has, by and large, not been successful. For example, audio-visual equipment has not been extensively and effectively utilized in most schools, in spite of promotional actions in professional circles for a generation.

Implications for innovation

From the analysis presented above, it is clear that the schools face a number of problems which are similar in character to those in other complex organizations. The attributes which have been described indicate that *schools are essentially bureaucratic structures, and the teacher's role in the system is largely that of a functionary.* The school differs from many bureaucratic structures in the relatively high proportion of its staff members who have received advanced training. Thus the rationalization of functions, an ordinary feature of bureaucracies, is somewhat more difficult than usual. Accordingly, one factor in the introduction of innovations is the problem which Veblen referred to as "trained incapacity." Although the structure of schools would seem to lend itself to innovation through administrative decision, reallocation of duties is actually made difficult by the type of specialized training which the existing staff has received.

Some of the possible implications of this general picture of the local school system for innovation are suggested briefly here:

1. Innovations which are difficult to institutionalize are likely to encounter greater resistance, and to have a short life, if they are introduced.

2. Successful innovations are more likely to be achieved when initiated by administrative officials, not only because of the power of their office, but also because they are in a position to handle the system

problems inevitably associated with innovation in an on-going system.

3. The more extensive the subject–matter training of teachers, the greater the possibility that they will be intolerant of system demands.

4. The greater the division of labor which is worked out in a system, the greater the need for specificity in role definition and the greater the likelihood that system demands will increase. For example, the use of special music or art teachers in elementary schools results in a complex set of problems of scheduling, co-ordination, and follow-up by the classroom teacher—which can be met only through the establishment of a higher level of control and supervision.

In this section, we have pointed to a series of system problems which schools face, and have described the formal organizational structure of local school systems. In the earlier sections, attention was given to the significance of ancillary structures as elements in the structure of American education. Although attention has not been given to the role of ancillary structures at the local level, a more complete analysis would require it. Finally, efforts at innovation must take into account system problems of the type which have been identified here.

Conclusion

Innovation in education, as in any system, involves changes in the social organization of the system. Although much attention has been given to the formal organizational structure of American education, analysis of other dimensions of this structure has not received the same attention. An effort has been made to present a way of looking at the American educational system in structural terms. Particular attention has been given to the dominant role of ancillary structures in the American system, as means for meeting problems handled in other societies by the formal structure. The integration of various levels in the system, and the interrelationships between different school systems, have been shown to be achieved largely through ancillary structures. In an examination of the structural properties of the local school system, particular attention has been given to their significance for understanding the role of the teacher in that system. It is believed that a framework of the type presented above is necessary in order to understand the success or failure of efforts at innovation.

CHAPTER 24

Changes in American education
in the next decade: some predictions

THE TEST of our understanding of a system lies in our ability to predict its future state, to anticipate change accurately. Or so the scientist has it. Mark Twain once commented that predicting the future was actually very easy—being truthful about the past was what made for difficulty.

But predicting the future *responsibly* is not easy at all. Each of the five persons asked to contribute to this section—journalist, school superintendent, graduate school president, writer, and professor—took his assumptions and predilections in hand, and attempted, with more or less confidence, to say what things educational would be like in 1974. The results show a diversity which suggests (with apologies to Wallace Stevens) that the section should be called "Five Ways of Looking at a Blackboard," and invites despair, or at least skepticism, about the possibility of change predictions in education. Yet this very diversity is informing. It tells us that a man's view of what is coming depends on what he chooses to look at here and now, and on his understanding of its present meaning. But we cannot look at and understand everything, of course, and so predictions differ. Fortunately.

615

The reader has an advantage over the five contributors who follow in having sampled a wide range of cases and concepts relevant to educational innovation in the preceding pages. The editor's heuristic suggestion for the reader at this point is: jot down *your* predictions, now, before going on to examine the predictions which follow.

M. B. M.

James M. Cass

THE DIRECTION that educational change will take in the elementary and secondary schools during the coming decade is relatively clear. The major experimental programs of the ten years just past will be expanded and extended as they are adopted by an increasing number of school systems. Four factors make this a reasonably safe prediction.

Numbers—of children and teachers—constitute the fundamental reality with which the schools will have to continue to deal. An increasing number of children will attend each year, and the schools will find it impossible to improve quality and at the same time organize and man the classrooms in traditional fashion. Therefore, a growing number of school districts will explore the possibilities of such innovations as independent study, non-graded schools, and team teaching.

New knowledge—of subject matter areas and of the teaching–learning process—will stimulate innovation. New curricula and fresh approaches to teaching will be developed in the social sciences, language arts, and foreign languages, as they already have been in math, physics, chemistry, and biology. And more advanced subject matter will be taught at lower grade levels all along the line, as more effective teaching and better understanding of children's capacity for learning develop.

Technology will spark the most dramatic changes in elementary and secondary classrooms in the next decade. Educational television, lan-

JAMES M. CASS is Associate Education Editor, *Saturday Review*.

guage laboratories, teaching machines, films, and the whole range of other mechanical and electronic means of communication will become increasingly important. Not long ago the potential of these devices for improving classroom learning was largely theoretical, but today they have proved themselves in many experiments. What remains is to rub the gloss of novelty off these innovations and find how they can best contribute to learning day by day.

Popular attitudes have been changing slowly for a dozen years—and they have been changing rapidly since Sputnik was launched in 1957. Today, popular realization that education at an ever higher level is the *sine qua non* for success in almost every job has stimulated a growing proportion of the school-age population to complete high school and enter college. It has also sparked a higher degree of academic rigor in the classroom, and more emphasis on academic achievement. There is no sign that this trend will be reversed or even slowed in the next decade, and there is considerable evidence that it will be intensified.

Not all schools will adopt all of the changes being tried currently in school systems scattered across the country. In fact, it is likely that fewer than half of them will make major changes in the organization and content of school programs. But those that do will be educating far more than half of the nation's elementary and secondary school students. And it will be the rare school system that is wholly untouched by the winds of change that are blowing through America's classrooms.

The changes that face American higher education in the ten years ahead are less well known and understood, but are no less revolutionary. The same underlying factors will affect the nation's colleges and universities, and to them—for many private institutions—will be added the crucial problem of financial survival. In some cases, these factors will force radical departures from traditional practices; in others they will merely continue and speed trends of long standing.

Public colleges and universities will serve a progressively larger share of the college population. Few private schools have either the desire or the capacity to expand their facilities greatly. They will, therefore, serve a constantly smaller proportion of the nation's college students. Two-year colleges will provide one important means by which the states will provide facilities for more students.

In addition, a growing number of both public and private colleges will seek to serve a larger college public through more efficient utilization of plant and personnel. Year-round operation, independent study, large lecture courses, and television courses offered to off-campus students are among the means that will be used more widely to serve a larger public without major expansion of plant or faculty.

College Board scores will continue to rise, year by year, and admissions officers at the better schools will become progressively more concerned about factors other than academic aptitude and achievement. Some progress will probably be made toward the difficult goal of identifying more accurately, at college entrance age, those personal qualities that make for creative, productive adults.

Higher education in the decade ahead will go through a vast sorting-out process, as the pressures of money, space, and numbers become more acute. Public institutions, and some of the stronger private schools, will continue to offer a wide range of studies for students of diverse talents and interests. The smaller private schools, however, will have to define their objectives and programs more specifically if they are to survive. The best ones will probably become, even more exclusively than at present, feeder institutions for the nation's top graduate schools—though most will continue to deny it. The better ones, just below the top echelon, will narrow their focus to provide higher-quality liberal arts and teacher education to prepare students for graduate or professional–occupational courses. The weaker colleges will continue to serve a local or denominational constituency—or they will merely cease to exist.

A growing number of colleges and universities, both public and private, both the strong and the less strong, will enter into cooperative programs with neighboring institutions. In this way it will be economically possible for them to offer their students a wider range of special studies and facilities than any one institution could provide alone. In an era in which there will be far more than enough students to go around, the traditional competition among institutions of higher learning will give way to cooperation.

American education will, indeed, change profoundly in the course of the next ten years. On the surface, the schools and their activities may not appear very different. But behind the exterior, where the process of education is planned and carried out, the changes will be many and fundamental. And we may hope that change will bring improvement.

BENJAMIN C. WILLIS

THE DIRECTION of change in American education during the next decade will be charted by the challenges we face today—the rising population, the nation-wide mobility of people, the advancement of technology, and the rapid accumulation of new knowledge. All of these telescope into a kind of directional signal toward future courses of action: Better ways must be found for more people to know more in less time through more avenues for reaching the individual, at the point of greatest need.

Time is of the essence. College enrollments will double in the next ten years, and it is estimated that fifty per cent of this increase will occur during 1963–65. Such numbers call for a level of articulation not yet achieved between colleges and secondary schools, and for equally close articulation between scholars in the academic disciplines and those in teacher education.

The need for increased articulation in all subject areas between the elementary and high schools must follow. Already there has been a rapid expansion in the numbers enrolled in advanced placement courses, and in the numbers who write the College Board examinations. Sequentially developed kindergarten-through-grade-twelve educational programs are increasing.

Not only has there been a concern for some time about the quality of what we teach, but there has been an equally important movement to emphasize the process of education. More and more people are engaged in research in cognitive learning, and in the period ahead there will be an equal concern for affective learning.

Pre-service education of teachers will change greatly, and an effective means of continuing, mass in-service education will be developed.

BENJAMIN C. WILLIS is General Superintendent of Schools, City of Chicago.

For many reasons, increasing provision will be made for easy access to life-long learning for adults.

Employment trends indicate a steadily increasing shift in composition of the work force from wage employees to salary employees. Industry and education will join forces in creating opportunities for meeting requirements for supervision, research, engineering, maintenance, and cost analysis.

Training and retraining in job skills to keep pace with technological progress will require a continuing canvass of the labor market and a corresponding reappraisal and revision of vocational curricula.

Civic, industrial, and community agencies will close ranks with the schools in helping youth who are out of school and out of work. Dropouts, culled through a teen-age census in high schools, will respond to invitations to counseling services, to encouragement of full or part-time school attendance, and to work-oriented courses.

The surging mobility of people across the nation will require more literacy classes for both youth and adults who do not have a basic command of the three R's. Broader programs of urbanization for newcomers to the big cities will follow in the wake of this mobility.

Part-time, evening, and TV college courses, which have mushroomed in the past few years, can be expected to expand greatly within the next ten.

Health and medical services in the schools will be expanded; closer coordination will be achieved between the work of the schools and that of health and welfare agencies, both public and private.

Counseling services will be expanded at the elementary, secondary, and college levels. A pattern of continuity in guidance will emerge.

Automated systems will augment the inventory of pupil strengths for more effective guidance and for grouping by ability, interests, and aptitudes; they will also enhance the inventory of teacher strengths for assignments which make more effective use of their talents and training.

More involvement of parents in the school life of their children will follow today's efforts to have parents "team up" with the school and the pupil in the realization of his goals.

How to provide large-group instruction and at the same time obtain an understanding of individual learning problems will be a determining factor in the use of instructional media.

Closed-circuit television will be developed for clusters of schools by means of a coaxial cable which will link schools having similar pupil population characteristics into a network. Thus, the best teaching talent of the connected schools will present television lessons to children of similar needs, possibly through team teaching utilizing the strengths of the combined staffs.

Programed learning, now in its infancy, may be the answer for some kinds of learning, if properly developed and utilized. The automated classroom, hardly more than a dream, could prove the answer to providing for the individual—if the American scientist and business-man give serious attention and adequate sums of money to development in this field.

There will be changes in procedures of recruitment, selection, placement, and orientation of personnel. In the immediate future, these procedures will take into account the need for teachers who are skilled in orienting the in-migrant child and those of limited background to urban ways of life.

We will seek more teachers with backgrounds in the liberal arts and sciences to open doors to cultural opportunities for all children. In this regard, a five-year program of pre-service teacher education including an internship period will become the mode. Fellowship programs for teachers will be strengthened. Study teams, workshops, teacher-exchange programs, and internships will play a more important role in continuing professional growth.

Tomorrow's school buildings will provide for flexibility of scheduling to accommodate team teaching and varying sizes of learning groups. Adaptability to the changing needs of youth and better ways of learning will be the basic factors in architectural design. Facilities which permit extensive use of electronic instructional equipment will be typical rather than atypical.

The tendency to regard education as an investment in America's economic future will take hold. Raising educational levels is fundamental to America's concept of the dignity of the individual and the goal of self-realization; raising educational levels, particularly of the unskilled laborer, is also a dollar-and-cents proposition in the light of relief rolls and unemployment compensation. In this connection, federal aid to vocational education and closely allied programs will be expanded.

Financial aid from the federal government will be allocated to the big cities to offset the effects of urbanization, mobility, and technology for the same basic reason as that underlying federal aid to impacted areas. Migration to urban centers from many states is a national as well as a local problem and will continue to be for some time.

Perhaps the most promising change in the next decade of American education is the current lessening of resistance to change itself. Time lags are shortening. New concepts in teaching and learning are increasingly viewed as areas of adventure into the world of research and development.

John H. Fischer

VIRTUALLY every innovation in American schools during the coming decade will be influenced by two strong currents of change. One of these is the growing effort to improve relations between races. The other is the increasing insistence of teachers on the right to express their views on school policy questions. Rather than predict specific innovations at this point, I would like to discuss these two underlying forces, and their probable impact on education.

As, one by one, the barriers that have prevented the Negro's full participation in American life are being struck down, race relations are changing at an unprecedented rate. Yet the very speed of that progress emphasizes how much remains to be done to correct the errors of the past. The consequences of excluding millions of Negro Americans from the mainstream of the nation's culture present the schools with an urgent agenda of unfinished and new business.

For many Negro children, equal educational opportunity requires more than a seat beside a white classmate. Integrated enrollment is a primary objective, to be sure, and one to be sought as quickly and in as many schools as possible: children of all races need to know and work with each other. But if in every school a wholly satisfactory bal-

JOHN H. FISCHER is President, Teachers College, Columbia University.

ance of the races were achieved at once, serious difficulties would still remain. The handicaps many Negro children suffer as a result of the legal and social treatment they and their families have undergone pose academic and social problems that call for wise and imaginative teaching.

As a group, Negro children present the same range of gifts and handicaps as white children, and require the same variety of school arrangements to cultivate their gifts and talents, to reduce the effects of their disabilities, and to stimulate their interests and ambitions. But having been denied so much for so long, many Negro children need additional teaching and other compensatory services to mitigate the effects of earlier deprivation and discrimination.

All children—of whatever race—who have grown up in disadvantaged conditions are entitled to cultural experiences that will broaden and deepen their knowledge of the world about them and strengthen their confidence in themselves. In many instances, and often for the same reasons, they will need remedial instruction in the traditional academic subjects.

In making the transition from segregated to integrated schools, children of both races (but Negro children perhaps more frequently) may encounter problems of emotional and social adjustment. Schools and other community agencies will therefore be expected to offer counseling, diagnosis, and treatment on a basis commensurate with the needs. To help parents as well as children deal with new situations and requirements, many schools will have to establish more effective relationships with homes.

Emphases and innovations of these kinds may appear to conflict with what some see as the school's overriding obligation to stress its academic responsibilities. Yet, if the school is to encourage the best intellectual development, it cannot properly ignore the major factors that influence formal learning. To be successful, curricula and teaching procedures will have to be designed not to serve theoretical abstractions or merely to conform to currently fashionable "standards," but with deliberate attention to the live boys and girls who are actually present in the classroom.

The second broad current of influence that is likely to affect major innovation in American schools stems from teachers' changing views of their roles and their power in the educational establishment. Recent efforts to establish collective bargaining between teacher organizations and school boards reflect a condition more complex than immediate differences about salary rates. As teachers become aware of their collective power to influence policy decisions, they are forcing a similar awareness upon school boards. But the principal question which the teachers themselves—even more than the boards—must face is: will this new-found power be used only to improve the personal position of the teacher, or will it be employed also to raise the quality of schools? If teacher organizations restrict their activity to pressure tactics of the kind traditionally used by industrial unions to wring concessions from private corporations, the results will almost surely prove disastrous for both schools and teachers. Strikes and similar coercive devices were not designed to strengthen the status of professional workers, nor to apply the talents and wisdom of highly trained men and women to intricate questions of educational policy. They were intended, rather, to arm negotiating agents with the collective strength of a mass organization for use in industrial situations where personal responsibilities and the unique professional contributions of individuals are of small significance. But school boards or administrators who deny teachers a recognized role and a reasonable voice in determining school policies will inevitably encourage the mass approach and the power play.

Because the necessity is so clear, and because no existing alternative is likely to meet the needs of modern education, it is predictable that new patterns of working relations will be developed among school boards, administrators, and professional staffs to take account of the contributions that individual teachers, as well as organized groups, can make in the shaping of school policy. These arrangements will undoubtedly provide for collaboration, not only on salary and personnel matters, but on issues of curriculum, teaching procedures, and general school administration.

Although strong professional organizations will continue to be needed at state, local, and national levels, it will also be necessary to enable the individual teacher to participate directly in policy development. The intermediary and representative function of the independent professional organization will have to be distinguished from the right and responsibility of the teacher, as a member of a faculty, to take part directly in making school-wide and district-wide decisions.

In the next decade, we may expect important changes in the operating procedures, and perhaps even in the composition and structure, of school boards and administrative staffs.

MARTIN MAYER

BECAUSE the crisis in American education over the last decade was caused primarily by failures of intelligence and leadership, it is not possible to predict where we are going to wind up. Too much depends on accident. The quality of reform movements is largely a function of the ability and devotion of the people who lead them, and we have no demonstrated way to attract people of the necessary scholarship, imagination, and wit into work for education.

Many of the factors that now operate as a drag on educational motion will certainly persist. There is at present no American alternative to the superintendency system, which typically places politicians and businessmen of limited speculative intelligence in charge of directing educational enterprise. By and large, with obvious exceptions, educators in positions of power and visibility are not among the most able members of their profession. Organizations like AASA and ASCD, and the Educational Policies Commission of the National Education Association, have an almost unbroken record of fearful objection to the introduction of ideas not yet vetted by the shopkeeper communities which control school board elections.

The acceptance of "progressivism" by the superintendents was misleading in this regard. What they took for "progressivism" was, like the later "life adjustment," a wholly conservative doctrine which assumed that the function of the school was to make children as much as possible like their parents (only happier). What progress has been achieved in education over the last decade was made possible by the action of confused but angry commentators who kept the superintendency terrified about the loss of jobs, and thus willing to look for leadership to the intellectually more competent and daring. The ability of educational reformers to maintain this fear in the breasts of educa-

MARTIN MAYER, a writer, has just completed *Where, When and Why: Social Studies in American Schools,* based on a study sponsored by the Carnegie Corporation for the American Council of Learned Societies.

tional bureaucrats will be one of the major determinants of our future schooling. The history of political reform movements offers little encouragement to the belief that the pressure can be maintained.

What has enabled the relatively small group of intellectuals in education to scare the superintendents is, of course, the national fear of the Russians. Economists are working on the problem of what would happen to the economy if a sudden *détente* relieved us of the need to produce great quantities of armaments; educational theoreticians ought to examine what would happen to our effort in the schools if the beat-the-Russians mentality were to disappear. Generally speaking, the scientific, scholarly, and artistic achievements of this century are discomfiting to the average man—more so, perhaps, than any similar set of achievements since the firm rejection of geocentricism in the seventeenth century. Freud, Weber, Frazer, Einstein, Rutherford, Planck, Poincaré, Picasso, Schönberg, Joyce—these names still symbolize esoteric and avant-garde matters to the great majority of Americans (and especially to educators), even though all of them stand for work accomplished, in the main, half a century ago.

The central effort of the educational reformers is to find a way to bring American schools into the twentieth century. But the community at large still resists the intrusion of the twentieth century, and goes along, grumbling, only because competent authority has asserted that the Communists might gain some advantage by reaching the twentieth century first.

By itself, fear produces only incoherence, frustration, and eventual loss of contact with reality. What passes for educational reform in many places right now is a set of spasm reactions—homework for its own sake, ability grouping down to first grade, ill-conceived flounderings in misunderstood "modern math," technology-worship, etc. Over all lies the blight of an essentially superstitious faith in "research" as something more than a means of acquiring evidence to which judgment must be applied. The great need is not research; it is taste, style, judgment. The worth of any investigation is far more closely related to the hypotheses it explores than to the methodology it employs.

Given almost unimaginable good luck, American education could develop into a predominantly scholarly enterprise, in which the masters of a study would feel an obligation to communicate, and the teachers of children would feel an obligation to discipline their common sense and seek out the uncongenial idea. Streams of teaching ideas could flow from academicians for the purposes of training and retraining teachers, and of preparing valid written materials and "hardware" for teaching use. Teachers could participate in the invention and propagation of teaching ideas, in the elimination of what is inconsequential, stupid, misleading, or unnecessarily difficult, and in the adaptation of pedagogic models for differing groups of students. Every other summer, and for a regular sabbatical year, the teacher would return to the universities for scholarly labor, to keep the central faith that nobody is worth much as teacher unless he is primarily a learner. Examinations would be designed to discover what is going on, not to assess the barren achievement of somebody's "objectives." All new technical devices—teaching machines, television, feelies—would be judged by their contribution to improving the ideational content of education, and by this criterion alone. Superintendents would permit the tone of the schools to be set by the most able teachers, on the understanding that the least able are easy to replace anyway. And so forth.

Betting that such a future will arrive is like buying a policy slip. The probability is not zero, but it's a lot nearer to zero than to one. And we are asking people to bet their life's work on it. Still, they have to put their life's work into something, and the odds against significant accomplishment are always high.

THEODORE BRAMELD

I FIND it impossible to offer any certain educational predictions, except quite obvious ones (e.g., barring a major catastrophe, the amount of money spent annually on schooling will increase substantially). Those who do offer less obvious predictions are the fortunate possessors of extrasensory powers of clairvoyance which I lack. Therefore I do not pretend to know what important changes will occur in the next ten years.

Moreover, I refuse to identify wishes with predictions. There are, to be sure, many changes that I would like to see occur, a remarkably

THEODORE BRAMELD is Professor of Educational Philosophy, School of Education, Boston University.

large proportion of them contrary to trends now under way. But I find no scientifically ascertainable ground for declaring that what one wishes would happen will actually happen. The only ground I am reasonably sure of is this: the course that education pursues depends very largely upon the course that the nations of the world themselves pursue. And, because the ongoing struggle for power is fraught with profound contingencies, with fears precariously counterpoised against hopes, one can only predict with assurance that the status of education in, say, 1974 will be conditioned chiefly by the status of international relations.

Upon this premise, I see at least as much reason for short-range pessimism as for short-range optimism. Surely the course of world events in the past six decades is hardly conducive to rosy expectations that peace, security, and opportunities for human fulfillment on a planetary scale will be assured in the seventh. Given this grim record, I am afraid rather that the scales are more heavily tipped against sure educational advancement in the near future than in its favor.

The rapid spread of programed instruction, to take an important example of which this volume speaks, is by no means to be counted exclusively on the positive side. Whatever its form, programed instruction is, in and of itself, a strictly amoral innovation. Granting that they are able to increase learning at impressive rates, what do we find in teaching machines, in closed-circuit television, or in similar inventions that cannot just as adroitly be utilized for cultural and educational goals destructive of the democratic ethos, as for goals that serve to strengthen that ethos? In contemporary perspective, their dangers, indeed, loom larger than their promises. For by concentrating public as well as professional attention upon dramatic technological devices, they also succeed in diverting attention from the more elusive—but far more fundamental—question of the individual and cultural purposes that every such device ought to advance, and by which alone it can be justified.

This is not to say that programed instruction fails to contribute powerfully to the building of habits saturated with value preferences. Of course it contributes, as every kind of learning does. The relevant question, however, is not whether programed instruction avoids values, but whether it is likely to function much more generously in behalf of values sanctioned by an efficiency-centered, corporately organized and directed culture, rather than values that maximize creative individuality, critical-mindedness, and conscientious involvement in the crucial social, economic, political, and moral conflicts of our time.

Programed instruction is chosen to exemplify the key issue which innovation, the more encompassing concept, generates. That education requires far greater attention to its innovative role than has been typical of an institution freighted with transmissive, reinforcing practices is surely a defensible view. The preceding pages point out how fruitful the study of innovation can become, especially when it draws from the expanding resources of anthropology and other behavioral sciences. I, for one, am particularly encouraged by the recognition of these resources in Professor Miles' introductory discussion.

Yet it must never be forgotten that innovative means without commitment to ends appropriate to our crisis-age are hazardous in the extreme. I would therefore like to suggest as an urgent requirement the creation of innovative experiments in behalf of the examination and delineation of such ends as these. More precisely, I am suggesting that schools and colleges undertake curriculum adventures in the study and testing of value orientations, and that they do so not indirectly or intermittently, but directly and systematically.

May I illustrate? For two years I have been directing a project in the Lexington (Massachusetts) Senior High School, the purpose of which is to seek answers to this question: "How far are we, as young citizens of an American middle-class subculture, similar to and different from people of cultures in other parts of the world—similar to and different from them especially in what we and they aspire to, cherish, struggle against, and struggle for?"

The project draws heavily upon anthropology and philosophy, but history, psychology, and sociology are among the additional resources. Without in any way prejudging outcomes, it carries participating students vicariously to the South Seas, to India and Africa, and directly through field experiences to ethnic communities of New England. The motivation stems from the kind of conviction expressed in my opening paragraphs: problems of international relations are so central today that no education deserves to be called responsible that fails to give searching attention to them. And, while many approaches to the task are open, one of the most neglected yet needed ways is to shift the focus from the usual descriptive study of international events to normative concern with obstacles and opportunities confronting any attempt to move toward world order and human unity.

The optimistic overtones of the Lexington project help to neutralize, perhaps, some of the pessimistic overtones of my earlier comments. Certainly one detects many signs that education in the years ahead will pay attention to desirable goals as well as to effective processes. Please recall my adjective "short-range." While I remain dubious that the period immediately before us will see much, if any, genuine educational progress, the constructive resources waiting to be used are far richer than they have ever been. The concept of innovation itself is one of these resources. Another, still more far-reaching, is the emerging—in fact revolutionary—knowledge of human nature, understood for the first time in cross-cultural range. Predictions as to how this knowledge *will* be used are, to be sure, still unwarranted. But that it *could* be used by education in behalf of potentialities for magnificent new levels of human achievement is not at all unwarranted. On the contrary, the image of man that begins to appear in its light affords the strongest of all supports for long-range confidence in the future of man as the only evolution-shaping animal on earth.

CHAPTER 25

Innovation in education: some generalizations

Matthew B. Miles

Editors have temptations. To aim at The Grand Theory, to pontificate, to have the all-wise last word, to apologize, to withdraw inconspicuously in despair—each of these stances becomes a possibility when it is time for concluding commentary.

The realities at hand are something like this. The studies of innovation offered in these pages are undoubtedly a biased sample from the universe of all possible studies. They occupy a very wide range, in terms of size of system involved, methods used, and position on a theoretical–practical continuum. The 250-odd generalizations produced by the authors come in various sizes, shapes, and degrees of potency. There is no systematically drawn theory of social change within which they can be elegantly (or even compulsively) organized.

In such situations, it is fashionable to quote Einstein: "We know nothing." But this is hyperbole. The contribution of this book is precisely to indicate that we *do* know something about how educational innovation proceeds. Here, it is useful to make a meaningful summary of what we now know and to speculate about it. This chapter will review generalizations made explicitly or implicitly in the preceding chapters, with intermittent commentary.

631

A loose accounting scheme has been used, covering characteristics of educational systems; the innovation itself; innovating persons or groups; states of the relevant systems prior to and during change processes; and the eventual fate of innovations advocated.[1] The reader, according to his profession or discipline, may be able to see ways in which these first-level generalizations can be subsumed within more general theoretical frameworks. If so, one primary purpose of the book will have been achieved: that of causing thought about educational innovation to take place.

Educational Systems: The Context

Does the American educational system have particular characteristics which influence innovation rates—and do educational institutions, as such, show different innovation rates than organizations devoted to producing things, services, or knowledge? Some generalizations are relevant to these questions.

A national educational system

The existence of a *de facto* national system of education in America has been asserted (1,23);[2] it may serve to brake local innovation attempts (and, it might be pointed out, can increase the potential for vigorous, comprehensive innovative attempts as well). The autonomy of local districts is suggested to be a myth (7); the reality of a national system is said to be indicated, supported, and reinforced by such factors as the national recruitment of teachers, successful mobility of students and teachers from school to school, the national market for instructional materials, and national examination systems (23).

The subsystems at work in the American educational scene have been reviewed (1,17,23); it is suggested that any innovation attempt will be conditioned by forces working within or between subsystems

---

[1] Other schemes could have been used, of course: cf. that suggested by Katz, Levin, & Hamilton (1963), who define the process of diffusion of innovations as the (1) *acceptance,* (2) over *time,* (3) of some specific *item*—an idea or practice—by (4) *individuals,* groups, or other *adopting units,* linked to (5) specific channels of *communication,* (6) to a *social structure,* and (7) to a given system of values, or *culture.*

[2] In this chapter, numbers in parentheses indicate the chapters from which the generalizations are drawn.

falling in the general categories of educational agencies, government systems, and commercial and nonprofit organizations. These are interdependently connected; for example, the foundations, rather than being all-powerful, are seen as dependent on the educational and scientific organizations to which they make grants (5). Within the educational establishment, hierarchical ordering is evident, so that higher schools influence lower (1,23), with the apogee of influence turning out to be the graduate department in the university, which not only influences lower programs but also produces new knowledge, controls admission to itself, and trains related practitioners (23).

With this evidence for an interdependent national educational system, it is not surprising that large-scale innovative efforts must of necessity require careful strategy planning, be complex, and—above all—be expensive (1).

For example, an experimental statewide program in teacher education, though it did appear to strengthen the fifteen institutions participating and may have influenced teacher education elsewhere, nevertheless only produced 194 teachers during the experimental period, and cost over $3 million (5). Similarly, the cost of producing a new set of materials for one nationally distributed high school physics course (10) exceeded $4.5 million.

American mobility is high, averaging about 20 per cent annually; the mobility of teachers and students undoubtedly influences innovation rates (24:Willis), since it forces national standardization of practices (23). At the local school level, turnover also makes for stability, since particular innovations are often difficult to initiate and install without what has been called a "product champion" who will work continuously to further them (Schon, 1963).[3]

The nature of educational systems

Even though the innovation rate in New York State schools showed a three-fold increase after the launching of Sputnik (20), a stern reminder of the stability of educational institutions is given by the fact that the schools in Brickell's sample averaged about *one* innovation

[3] Of course, the influx of new personnel helps to start local innovation (see the discussion below of "cosmopoliteness" and initiation of change by outsiders), but local change processes take time, and are likely to falter if stimulating outsiders do not stay long enough to become "insiders."

annually, and the great bulk of schools remained stable as structured institutions. Why should this be so?

The diffusion rates in educational systems may be slower than those found in industrial, agricultural, or medical systems for several reasons: the absence of valid scientific research findings (12,16); the lack of change agents to promote new educational ideas (12); and the lack of economic incentive to adopt innovations (12) (since educational products do not have immediate economic payoff, and educational practitioners are paid on the basis of longevity and personal educational attainment rather than on net output, itself very difficult to measure).[4]

It is also possible that certain ideological beliefs in the educational profession serve to block effective innovation by effectively insulating educational practitioners from reality. For example, beliefs that American schools are locally controlled (1,7,23), that the school teacher is an independent, autonomous professional (16,23), and that teaching can never be effectively measured or specified in other than intuitive terms, all appear to serve the function of protective myths.

To discuss one of these in more detail: the teacher's ideological commitment to professional autonomy appears to be belied by heavy classroom reliance on texts and materials (16). Confused role expectations for the teacher may be at work; for example, reading experts do not accord full professional status to teachers, yet expect them to act autonomously and rely less on texts (16). Thus it seems likely that local innovative efforts are restricted by the fact that the teacher's role is actually that of a bureaucratic functionary (16,20,23) who has little power to *initiate* system-wide change, but—because of the ideology concerning professionalism alluded to above—tends to *resist* innovative demands, like most professionals in bureaucratic organizations.[5]

It has also been asserted that existing educational product specifica-

---

[4] Clark (1963, p. 13) while noting that amount of education is directly related to personal life income, and to output of goods and services in the economy, concludes helplessly:

About all we can say is that the schools produce an output roughly equal to the learning that goes on during twelve, thirteen, fourteen, or fifteen years of schooling. The data from results of standardized tests are not helpful in appraising the quantity of learning.

[5] Cf. Etzioni's (1959) discussion of the ways in which "expert" authority is wielded in professional organizations, and some of the role strains which result.

tions, as manifested in state or national examinations, serve to inhibit change in educational procedures (1,20,23). (The existence of adequate measures tends to aid innovation by improving outcome measurability, of course—see Walsh (1963), for example—but there appears to be a conservative back effect as well: teachers teach "for the exam.")

Other aspects of educational systems have been alluded to; it certainly seems possible that vulnerability to outside influence, the use of persons rather than physical technology as primary instruments of change, and lay control may all serve to lower innovation rates in educational organizations, seen comparatively with other organizations (1). Much more conceptualizing and empirical measurement is needed.

The Innovation Itself

A kind of axiom seems visible in almost any of the studies reported in this book: educational innovations are almost never installed on their merits. Characteristics of the local system, of the innovating person or group, and of other relevant groups often outweigh the impact of what the innovation *is* (see especially 2,4,5,8,12,14,16,20).

Yet it does seem likely that some properties of the innovation itself are likely to affect its adoption and continued use. (The fact that modern math diffused more rapidly in a county-sized area than hybrid corn, but more slowly than a new drug, was suggested (14) to be an indication of this.) What are some of these properties?

Cost

On the face of it, it seems likely that innovations requiring inordinate outlays of money, energy, or time by the adopting person or group are likely to move slowly (13). These costs may be incurred during preliminary procurement operations (if the innovation is a technological device)—thus the importance of simple marketing procedures (8) —as well as at the point of purchase and during use (maintenance costs). In the absence of good measures of output, educational organizations tend to stress cost reduction (Thomas, 1963), since other potential rewards of the innovation remain only vaguely seen.

If the innovation is divisible (i.e., can be adopted on a partial, flexible basis), the obstacle of cost may be less formidable (10). Such flexibility, however, must be *permissible* rather than mandatory, since mandatory flexibility in the use of an innovation tends to conflict with the tendency for organizational practices to move in the direction of routinization, stability, and regularity (23).

Finally, the cost question interacts, of course, with the profit-making possibilities associated with the innovation. In America, if these are minimal, widespread diffusion is unlikely.

Technological factors

It is often pointed out that technological innovations are relatively easy to adopt. It is important to remember, however, that such innovations are equally easy to reject or discontinue (12,22).

Even prior to the point of adoption or rejection, many problems occur during the development of diffusable models of the hardware involved. Relatively small technical decisions may have a strongly blocking effect on the development of a particular device, and the opinions of a relatively small technological elite may exert disproportionate influence (8). In addition, devices which rely on associated materials (such as film projectors) may be hampered by a chicken-or-egg problem, since producers of materials are reluctant to produce them if no device for using them exists, while producers of the device are reluctant to proceed in the absence of available materials (8).

At the user level, it appears that many features of technological innovations influence diffusion, including (as well as cost) feasibility, ease of availability when use is desired, and convenience of use (8, 22). Direct experience with a particular device and any associated materials seems essential for an adoption decision (8,10).

Associated materials

Materials aid the diffusion of educational innovations very considerably (1). The reasons for this are suggested to be the relative degree of ease with which they can be designed and altered to fit the demands of teaching situations, their ease of reproduction and distribution, and their retention of substantial integrity when used by a wide variety of teachers in different situations (10). The existence of a very wide range of competence among teachers makes routinized procedures—including supporting materials—an inevitable part of an educational system (23). If the materials are comprehensive, and designed as complete units, as in the case of those distributed by the Physical Science Study Committee, teacher adoption becomes more likely (20).

It is not surprising, then, that materials have exerted far more influence on practice in the teaching of reading than has the available research; the available reading series and their manuals have induced national uniformity in practice, in spite of the fact that only one third of a sample of reading experts—peers of those who prepared the materials—had confidence that they were based on "definite scientific proof" (16).

Implementation supports

More generally, it seems fairly clear that, the motivational reactions of potential users aside, the difficulty of use or implementation of a particular innovation is a genuine barrier to adoption and continued use. Although complexity or simplicity of innovations has been asserted not to influence innovation rates (13), it does seem very likely that innovations which are difficult to operate (that is, require extra administrative energy, are disruptive to the local system, or are puzzling or threatening *in a technical sense*) will diffuse relatively slowly (23). Thus the potential use of technological innovations in the classroom depends on a number of anticipated implementation factors, such as availability of the device, how easy it is to use (8), the working condition of the equipment, authorization from the local organization, and the skill of the operator (22).

Therefore, innovations with built-in implementation supports should diffuse more rapidly than those not so supported. For example, in the case of certain curricula prepared by national groups, training in use of the innovation *is part of the innovation,* and is available at no dollar cost (10,20). If the support is via materials, the more "self-teaching" they are, the more likely are adoption and continued use (13).

Innovation/system congruence

Some innovations bear characteristics which do not necessarily serve to slow adoption rates in themselves, but do retard diffusibility because of their incongruence with a potentially accepting system. For example, innovations developed in a temporary system outside the potentially adopting system usually face problems of feasibility and practicability, by-passed during the design stages of the innovation, but crucial during implementation stages (3). The fact that false starts often occur in the diffusion process during the period of early invention and trial before a diffusible device gets launched (1) suggests a similar problem.

It is difficult to specify in *a priori* terms what characteristics of an innovation—*vis-à-vis* the adopting system—will block or aid innovativeness. For example, it does not seem automatically clear that substantial structural innovations, such as changes in teacher role definition, diffuse at lower rates than technologically based ones (1).

However, other things being equal, innovations which are perceived as *threats* to existing practice, rather than mere additions to it, are less likely of acceptance (8); more generally, innovations which can be added to an existing program without seriously disturbing other parts of it are likely to be adopted (23).

It also seems clear that an innovation which is relatively easy to *institutionalize* is more likely of acceptance than innovations (such as "meeting the individual needs of children") which require steady creativity and cannot be routinely managed (23).

It has been suggested that the spread of an innovation may be retarded when a potential user regards it as *familiar*—as only a slightly different version of an existing procedure or practice—and thus not worth the extra cost required to shift over to it (8).[6] However, an innovation regarded as a means of reducing a well-known (familiar) gap between ideals and practice may achieve adoption (4), particularly if the gap is a genuine, keenly felt one and not solely an ideological protestation.[7]

[6] For commentary on familiarity/unfamiliarity, and the general notions of congruence and compatibility, see Kushner *et al.* (1962); their inventory of empirical propositions on factors underlying sociocultural change is very useful.

[7] An example of a genuine ideal/practice gap might be the serious lag in the content of high school physics education prior to the launching of the Physical Science Study Committee (10). A pseudo gap is exemplified by the idea that the schools should "meet individual differences," a task which most schools do badly at; many educators choose to ignore the fact that the task is in some respects incompatible with effective functioning of the school as an institution. Thus an innovation aiming at meeting individual differences, like the experimental college described by Watson (4), does not diffuse, partly because of the noncompellingness of the original concern.

Any innovation implying or requiring important *value changes* in accepters (such as those dealing with interpersonal relationships, race relations, religious commitments, etc.) (7,11,24:Fischer), will encounter difficulty, since much more than the nature of the innovation itself is at stake.[8]

The sorts of *interaction* which the particular innovation requires also affect adoption and continued use. Innovations which—in a particular system—will have the consequence of decreasing personal initiation, increasing dependence on others, and violating important values are likely to be resisted by persons in the accepting system (2). Conversely, innovations are more likely to be accepted when they increase and reinforce initiative-taking and autonomy (2). The fairly rapid diffusion of team teaching (apparently a radical role shift) may well be explained by the fact that it increases initiative and autonomy —while reducing isolation, and adding perceived support from peers. It may also reinforce values centering around "professionalism." (Note, however, that a teacher may use autonomy in apparently self-restrictive ways—for example, through adoption of and overreliance on standard texts (16).)

Innovative Persons and Groups

Most innovations appear to be stimulated, triggered, shepherded, and nurtured by some active person or group, either external to or within the "target" (innovation-receiving) system (see particularly 2,3,4,5,8,10,11,14). Some generalizations can be made about their characteristics.

Interdependence of innovators and others

The first is that the concept of the innovator as isolated hero seems inappropriate. The progress of any innovation must be examined in relationship to a complex network of groups, individuals, and organizations having a stake in the innovation (1). Thus the professional, political, and economic context of an organization's operation must

[8] Kushner *et al.* (1962) make the useful distinction between "malleable" cultural traits, such as those dealing with instrumental techniques and esthetic matters, and "persistent" traits, such as those involved with ideological security, status maintenance, communication, and child-rearing.

be considered when innovations are being studied or attempted (5). Interinstitutional power struggles are probably inevitable in the installation of any substantial innovation, and may become more important than the innovation as such, or what "research has said" about its merits (5). The interdependence between innovating groups and others may or may not have "coattail" effects—e.g., 8mm sound film may diffuse more rapidly if connected with the work of a national curriculum group (8)—and may or may not be directly relevant to the content of the innovation as such (e.g., developments in race relations, and changes in teachers' power in local decision-making, were predicted to affect the progress of virtually every innovation during the next few years) (24:Fischer).

Community support.   A special case of the interdependence discussed above is the fact that innovativeness in school systems in the 1930's appears to have borne much more relationship to community (and thus financial) factors than to characteristics of administrators or teachers in local school systems (13). Community size and wealth appeared to exert the most powerful effects, of course, in the case of "visible" innovations (13). Some recent data, however, indicate that rate of innovation adoption within a county was *not* correlated with annual expenditure per school child (14). Thus money as such is not a sufficient predictor. Rather, community influence—as in the case of agricultural innovation (Rogers, 1962)—is exerted through traditional or innovative norms, which set lower and upper bounds for financial support, provide latitude for teacher experimentation, and influence the selection and retention of educational personnel (13).

External initiation of change.   The importance of community factors may also be explained by another near-axiomatic generalization: in most cases the initiation for change in an educational system appears to come from outside (2,5,6,10,17,18,20,24:Mayer). Most local changes appear to involve adoption or adapting, rather than direct invention (24); outside commentators can induce fear and movement toward change on the part of local administrators (24:Mayer); and the school board and public create general pressures toward innovation (20), while local system inhabitants are naturally much more preoccupied with successful operation of the existing educational program (6).

The reasons for this appear to be many: outsiders or newcomers are ignorant of established methods of doing things and are not committed to them; they may, like Atwood's new principal, Mr. Daubner (2), inadvertently or purposefully cause conflict among existing subsystems (18); they do not receive steady-state-maintaining feedback through regular channels (18); they are not wholly bound by the existing norms of the social system (19). If we remember that "cosmopoliteness" is operationally defined as the degree to which an individual's orientation is external to a particular social system, it is not surprising that cosmopolites, rather than "locals," are most often seen as champions of change (12); also, new members in a social system, whose orientation is not yet fully "within," have less to lose and may thus support innovation (2).

Profit. There is a final aspect of innovative interdependence. Educational change rates are undoubtedly influenced by the speed or slowness with which commercial firms are able to produce and distribute relevant materials, and to continue to reap a regular profit from them (1).[9] Producers of commercial materials may overemphasize novelty in the attempt to increase adoption (22); commercial interest usually acts to increase adoption early in the life of the innovation, while materials are new—but to *inhibit* later changes which would render obsolete or noncompetitive materials that have been successfully launched and institutionalized (20). This stabilizing effect of profit motives is well shown in the case of reading materials, which have remained substantially unchanged for thirty years (16).

Innovative persons

Authority figures. Moving now to the local system, it seems very clear that administrators, as authority figures, are crucial in introducing innovations, particularly those which involve structural change (2,4,14,18,20). Administrators have more power, since institutions are hierarchically ordered, and thus can handle the system problems ordinarily associated with the introduction of an innovation more effectively than other system members (18,23). If the local adminis-

[9] Of course, many schools are themselves operated for profit. The effects of this stance on innovation rates have not been analyzed, and should be.

trator is highly legitimated in his reference group of other administrators in a state or region, his innovativeness is even more assured. For example, school superintendents who interacted frequently with other superintendents and were often chosen as friends by them, and who were seen as well-trained, well-paid, highly professional types, tended to be the earlier innovators in a county (14).

Personality characteristics. Official authority aside for the moment, it has been asserted that strong, benevolent persons often find themselves in an important and central role in utopian change efforts (4). In addition, intelligence and verbal ability seem important (4, 24:Mayer); the innovator also appears to be less bound by local group norms, more individualistic and creative (4). Intelligence and creativity have been suggested not to be enough, however. When the innovator must persuade or enlist the support of others, and overcome resistance, authenticity (3) and enthusiasm for the innovative enterprise (3,15) also seem to be important.

Not all of the characteristics of innovative persons are heroic, apparently; they are said to be rebellious, alienated, excessively idealistic (and thus unable to cope with problems of the survival of the innovating unit), emotionally unstable, and prone to resentment and rebellion in the face of adversity or disillusionment (4).

The relative paucity of generalizations on personality traits of innovators is interesting; though it offers a useful counterpoise to the popular tendency to assume that change only occurs through the efforts of isolated heroes, there is also the possibility that the selection of studies in this book is biased in the direction of attention to larger systems. Further attention to the innovative personality is undoubtedly desirable.[10]

Innovative groups

At any rate, group support for individual innovators does seem particularly important (3), whether it is group support for a single innovator, or mutual support among a number of innovators (11).

[10] Such work should take note of the observation that most innovative enterprises seem to require considerable division of labor. Thus we have the agitator, the dreamer, the skillful navigator *vis-à-vis* the environment, and the internal administrator as recurring and presumably crucial roles. Another prominent role (pointed out by L. A. Cremin in the seminar preceding this book) is that of the "committed nut"—the monomaniac, fanatic, or "true believer."

If the innovative group draws high-status members from the target system in which innovation is contemplated, it is more likely to have its recommendations accepted, particularly if the group is strongly legitimated by the system, and maintains clear, open communication with it (7). However, these conditions, if met thoroughly, also mean that the norms and demands of the target system exert a good deal of influence on the innovating group; thus the innovations achieved are likely to be moderate rather than radical in nature (7).

New structures. This difficulty can often be avoided by creating new innovative structures which by-pass vested interests, provide protection for the development and trial of innovations, and aid high focus on the work at hand (19); such isolation also frees the innovative enterprise from the (usually anti-innovative) norms of the target system (4). The essential problem here appears to be that of linking new structures with their associated target systems closely enough to aid the construction of innovations which are feasible, meet the realistic demands of the target system, and are likely candidates for trial (1,19), while avoiding the problems of restraint associated with too-close linkage with the target system (4) and the tendency to become trapped in its assumptions (1).

Temporary systems. Innovative systems set up on a temporary basis have the advantages, mentioned above, of any new structure, plus the extra one of not having permanent status to threaten the existing order (19). In addition, temporary systems appear to aid educational innovation for other reasons. They are asserted to: increase creativity, involvement, and work level because of the time limitation; enable easier recruitment of appropriate persons; have a minimum of bureaucratic restrictions, and minimal managerial requirements; deal with special-purpose, short-run problems expeditiously; cause pronounced attitude, relationship, and action changes on the part of their members; and provide increased social validation for particular innovations (19,20).

Prior States of Relevant Systems

There appear to be certain conditions in the target system—and in its environment—which facilitate or hinder change processes.

Stability-maintaining forces

The conditions which develop "ripeness" for change in a system may be illuminated by clearer understanding of the forces acting to maintain any system in a steady state. It has been suggested that systems tend *not* to change for a variety of reasons. First, maximum energy goes into current operations and maintenance (19); the development and implementation of new programs appear to require the addition of money and staff over and beyond that required for regular operations (6). Second, the hierarchically arranged subsystems in the over-all organization tend, over time, to become progressively segregated and independent from each other (18).[11] Third, durable feedback loops tend to develop between individuals and subsystems (18,19), and operate to restrict communication in self-confirming, stabilizing ways. Thus the longer the tenure of individuals—either administrators (18) or those lower in the structure (2)—the more stable the patterns of interaction which develop, and the more difficult change becomes.

Another set of forces for conservatism arises from the connection of the target system with other relevant systems. For example, the target system's autonomy may be limited by other systems (23). In addition, comparison processes occur; innovations in other systems, when noted at all, are often defined as "no better—and perchance a trifle worse than what . . . [we are] already doing" (20).

The surrounding context

It has been suggested that educational innovation in the next few years will depend very largely on the course of international relations (24:Brameld). More generally, it does seem apparent that the over-all cultural context serves as a backdrop for innovation: the going *Zeitgeist* creates specific pressures toward change and applies sanctions for not changing (4,10,17,20). In the American school system, such general concerns for change are often expressed as specific public demands on the schools, which are by general agreement vulnerable to public opinion.

[11] Cf. the finding by Mott & Neff (1962) that members of organizations with good internal integration (i.e., communication within elites, vertically and horizontally) tended to accept change more readily.

The existence of *Zeitgeist* effects can usually be inferred when multiple innovations occur independently at about the same time (4,10, 13), implying a common underlying concern. It has been suggested that this period of independent invention reflects turbulence and impending change in a social system, with a resulting search for innovations which will re-establish equilibrium (13). In any event, once a "family" of innovations develops (particularly a technological one), its existence tends to stimulate and support further innovative work. For example, the development of 8mm sound film has occurred in a setting of high interest in educational technology—programed learning devices, educational TV, and the like (8).

Some present features of American society are said to be accelerating educational change rates. These include widespread social change; [12] affluence and the resultant need for intellectually sophisticated manpower; the growth of cultural and aesthetic activities; growth in the rate of production of knowledge; and increases in information-handling and information-retrieval capacity (1). In addition, it seems very likely that the mass media influence the processes and rate of educational innovation by stimulating the desire for change, aiding communication between educational decision-makers and the larger society, and serving occasionally as a kind of feedback device on the public's attitudes toward particular innovative efforts.

A special case of pressures for change from the surrounding context involves the exertion of threat, as in the case of competition with the Soviet Union (20,24:Mayer), and the emergency pressures of wartime (13). It is suggested that stress exerted on a system from outside tends to produce first a response lag, then an overcompensatory response, and subsequent change; if overcompensation and the outside stress are maintained past some critical point, then catastrophic collapse of the system is likely (18).

Internal pressures for change

Though, as we have seen, most change initiations come from external sources, there are also sources internal to the target system. Sheer size and growth of a system tend to force adaptive changes and in-

---

[12] Dubos (1963) has pointed out that periods of rapid social change (e.g., the early Renaissance, and the Enlightenment) also appear to have been periods of educational reform.

creased concern for innovation (1). Discrepancies between ideals and existing practice (4,10), and conflict among subsystems (18) over the allocation of scarce personnel, money, or time (2), are also likely precursors of change.[13]

Most organizational analysis has stressed the "return to equilibrium" following a disturbing stimulus. However, it is also entirely possible that there may be organizational analogues of the wish for change, growth, and development in the individual (as discussed in Shachtel, 1959). Organizations, like individuals, may actively seek the excitement and drive of change for its own sake, rather than solely wishing to return to a familiar equilibrium.[14]

Limiting and enabling factors

It seems likely that, in addition to basic motivation for change in the local system, other prior-state factors must be considered which serve to define the limits of change, and/or to permit it to occur.

One of these appears to be financial resources. If we think of innovation as requiring *extra* system effort, it is not surprising to find, across many types of systems, that innovativeness varies directly with available money (12,13), though this is not, as we have seen, an invariant finding (14).

Secondly, underlying norms concerning the appropriateness of change in general (i.e., traditionalism vs. modernism) affect the diffusion rate of potential innovations (12). Such norms can be seen as "meta-norms," since they regulate the speed with which other norms change. It has also been suggested that norms dealing with adoption of another's invention (as against creating one's own) may also affect innovation rates (11).

[13] For an illuminating discussion of change processes in general, and preconditions in particular, see Moore (1963); in addition to the strains suggested here, he proposes competition for *loyalty* (among subsystems); failure in the existing rationale for unequal distribution of rewards; and disputes over goals, means, and the distribution of legitimate power.

[14] Cf. Watson's (4) comments on the adventurous climate in utopian experiments. It was suggested in the seminar preceding this book that boredom in organizations often serves a profoundly innovative purpose; not all change is terrifying, and the excitement usually engendered in innovative projects is highly salutary for both individual and organization. Another possibility is pointed out by Moore (1963, p. 58); organizations often deliberately *create* problems for themselves via departments of research and development, rather than waiting passively for change stimuli to appear.

Other such factors could undoubtedly be listed; the general point is that the properties of the target system in existence prior to the introduction of an innovation operate to reject, modify, accept, and maintain the innovation (1). Informal, less visible, structures are not less important than official ones in this respect (23). The general implication seems to be that successful innovation at the local school level is likely to require work with the entire organization, as such, rather than solely with individual teachers (2). Such an approach appears to have been under-used in education, perhaps because of norms stressing the autonomy and individuality of teachers.

Interestingly enough, the chapters of this book have not been terribly explicit as to whether there is some optimal condition of system prior to the introduction of an innovation. Apparently ripeness is not all, if one is attempting to predict impending change in a school system. Johnson's (6) comment on the importance of *commitment* of the target system (via the provision of matching funds) emphasizes system readiness, but it is important to remember with Brickell (20) that "new instructional programs can be successfully introduced despite initial apathy or even opposition on the part of a number of teachers." Perhaps the infrequency of generalizations about pre-innovative states in target systems is accidental; perhaps it is significant. It does suggest, however, that careful attention to the anticipation and management of change processes as an innovation proceeds is of considerable importance, and to this we now turn.

The Planning and Execution of Change Processes

The installation of an innovation in a system is not a mechanical process, but a developmental one, in which both the innovation and the accepting system are altered (2,3,5). This process obviously requires continuing technical attention. Yet for various reasons—perhaps connected with existing educational ideology—deliberate planning of change is more often than not slighted, rejected as "manipulative," or ignored completely. Often, much more attention is put on constructing the innovation itself than on planning and carrying out the strategy for gaining its adoption (1,4,10).

Yet it seems very clear that for almost all innovations the process of implementation itself needs careful study, planning, and experimental work (1). This is true both in general and for specific situations. For example, working out the changes in teacher role, administrative support, and classroom organization required for effective use of a new type of educational technology, such as programed learning, may require nearly as much attention as did the step from original conception to hardware (9). And when a particular programed learning device is introduced to a particular target system, much energy is required to shepherd its adoption and continued use. The understanding—and management—of change efforts thus becomes important to the success of any innovative effort.

Strategies

The idea of a strategy is essentially that of a general set of policies underlying specific action steps ("tactics") expected to be useful in achieving the durable installation of a particular innovation.

A strategy may also involve deliberate causation of innovation in associated areas, beyond use of the innovation itself (9). This is connected with the idea of "multiplier effects" as a strategic goal. Strategies devoted to encouraging extra communication among system members about the existence and efficacy of innovations (11), to the creation of facilitating, supporting, legitimating groups to aid diffusion of a series of innovations (7), and to teaching system members to use an innovation (such as the PSSC physics course) and help spread it to others (1) all fall in this category.

More generally, it seems likely that the most theoretically powerful strategies are likely to be those designed to produce "meta-changes"—second-order changes which will lead to further changes. Examples of these are the installation and use of new feedback loops, such as citizen surveys; regular use of diagnosis and improvement sessions which aid organizational self-consciousness; and use of consultants on organizational problems.

Certain characteristics of strategies have been asserted to make for effectiveness: comprehensive attention to all stages of the diffusion process (1); creation of new structures, especially by systems outside the target system (1); congruence with prevalent ideology in the target system, such as beliefs about the importance of "local control" (1); reduction of pressures on relevant decision-makers (7); and use of coalitions or linkage between existing structures, or between old and new structures (1).

Certain types of strategy seem less effective: those which attempt to use only existing structures, and are thus hamstrung by the *status quo* (1,18); those self-initiated by the target system (1), since (in addition to suffering from *status quo* problems) they tend to avoid attention to cross-system problems, such as interorganizational power struggles (5) which are likely to affect the progress of the innovation; and those which rely on arousing excessive degrees of conflict (1), though the intriguing idea of "controlled conflict" has been suggested as being promising (18).[15]

Change processes

Seen in the large by Mort and other researchers in the 1930's (13), the complete process of adoption of an innovation appeared to occupy a period of about 100 years, beginning with the existence of an educational need, followed by a period in which sporadic, nondiffusible inventions were made. The first 50 years closed with a period of turbulence and simultaneous invention, culminating in the production of a diffusible educational device of some sort. This diffused through 3 per cent of the school systems in a state (or nationally) in approximately 15 years; diffusion rates then accelerated rapidly for the next 20 years; the remaining 15 years of the century were occupied in diffusing though late adopters of the innovation (13). It should be remembered that adopters influence each other; adoption is *not* an independent, isolated act (14); hence the curve's acceleration after Mort's "3 per cent" point.

It seems clear that present diffusion rates are *much* more rapid than these (1,14), but it is likely that the conception of stages remains plausible; the postinvention stages noted by Mort have also been found in agricultural and medical studies (12).[16]

Seen at the level of the target system, change processes are said to involve the following stages following the design of innovations:

[15] See also Mann & Neff's (1961) comments on the "controlled explosion" as an approach to major organizational change.

[16] For an extremely thorough review of the chronology of diffusion, and conceptualization of the stages which potential adopters go through, see Rogers (1963).

the development of awareness and interest concerning the innovation; evaluation (in the sense of reaching a judgmental decision about the potential rewards and costs of the innovation); actual trial of the innovation in the local system (1; Rogers, 1963). This process results in a decision to adopt, adapt, or reject the innovation.

Another proposed formulation of stages includes: criticism of existing programs, presentation of proposed changes and their clarification; review and reformulation of proposals and comparison of alternate proposals; action decisions; and implementation of action decisions (17). It has also been suggested that durable innovations are most likely to result when an innovation is tried out tentatively, and modified on the basis of feedback from potential users (10).

Stage formulations such as these lead to operational suggestions. It has been proposed, for example, that the stages of design, scientific evaluation, and dissemination of innovations require mutually incompatible skills, personnel, and operations (20), and therefore should be sharply separated and assigned to different decision-making bodies. It also seems likely that structures which separate the investigation and problem-solving phases of decision-making from the action or implementation phase are helpful, since issues can be looked at on their merits, and anxiety about the action to be taken is postponed in time and place to another body (7).

Optimal conditions during each stage of change

Considering stages separately also leads to analysis of optimal conditions in each.

Design. It is suggested that effective design requires protected, enriched, autonomous environments (20). Professional or discipline groups, and interdisciplinary associations, often seem able to encourage major change, since their design work is removed from the immediate necessity of demonstrating or testing innovations, and can focus on adequate conceptualization and invention (10,20,21).

It is quite important to remember, particularly in the case of technological innovations (though the same may be true for procedural or other nontangible educational inventions), that much design-relevant communication must occur among technical experts before the innovation can be said to be adequately diffusible to the environment of "users" (8).[17] Thus devices to develop awareness and interest concerning the innovation, such as journals, papers, and conferences, may be very crucial.

Awareness–interest. Dissemination seems to be aided when the circumstances of the innovation's use by disseminators or early adopters are perceived as congruent with conditions in the target system; perceived artificiality and unrealism are contraindications for adoption (20). This is particularly important because of widespread suspicion about the genuineness of communication concerning innovations (2,20); the discrepancy between public pronouncements and private reactions to the progress of an innovation is often large (5). Thus we have the report of a state commission contrasting with the private view of a prominent editor. The commission:

> There has been a natural tendency for the General Assembly to consider the problems of each institution—and they are usually financial—separately. The institutions, therefore, have had no option but to compete for legislative favors. The result has been a piecemeal approach to legislation . . . (5)

The editor, in an interview:

> . . . the Legislature . . . was damn sick and tried of the squabbling and jockeying for positions and appropriations. They had [had] a bellyful of that sort of thing. (5)

Or compare the same editor's editorial on the acceptance of a new program with what a university official said to an interviewer. The editorial:

> In the next few months, the affected educational agencies and colleges will have to decide whether or not they will go along with the program. The indications so far are that the great majority will and it is difficult to see how any could hold out [of such a promising program]. (5)

The official, in an interview:

[17] This raises the interesting possibility that elite groups of many sorts (technical, administrative, prestige-holding) must in effect proceed through stages of diffusion at least a stage or two ahead of "user" groups.

It wasn't all beer and skittles by any means . . . After I made my rounds of the colleges here and saw how the wind was blowing . . . I told [the foundation] just how the land lay. I wasn't trying to kid them . . . I told them it wasn't going to come off. (5)

Thus credibility often becomes crucial. It can be aided if a genuinely dispassionate group serves as a clearinghouse for information on an incipient innovation (8). In addition, structures which provide for peer communication appear helpful. Potential users of an innovation seem to trust the accounts of peers who have actually tried the innovation, and can testify as to its worth, give aid with skills required, etc. (11). Peer development of awareness–interest may or may not be influential in an adoption decision, however. For example, teachers' main contacts on the subject of teaching reading appear to be with other teachers—yet this contact is seen by them as less influential than the impact of materials, in-service education, and pre-service education (16). The use of early adopters to stimulate awareness–interest is well developed in agriculture; less so in education. It is suggested that support and conceptual help provided by consultants or other outsiders (cf. the role of the county agent) may be essential for adequate development of awareness–interest (11), and later adoption.

Evaluation. Complex processes occur when a potential user makes a subjective evaluation of the potential rewards and costs of an innovation. Inadequate communication of its characteristics, the operation of vested interests, and "lack of rationality" appear to be at work (16). It has been suggested elsewhere (Mann & Neff, 1961) that a potential user's initial reactions to a proposed innovation are a function of matters such as the amount of control he has over his own destiny, how ambiguous he sees the situation ahead to be, and how much trust he places in local authority figures. The user then engages in "search behavior" to assess the likely net consequences of adopting the innovation. A good deal of ambivalence can be expected; this serves as personal (and organizational) defense.

The making of evaluative judgments seems easier when potential adopters can visit and actually observe (not hear reports of) the operation of innovations (10,20). Perhaps for this reason, innovations tend to develop in geographical clusters (10).

Initial trial and posttrial. During the early period of an innovation's use, there seems much importance in supplying support and help to users. (This may be another reason for the geographical clustering noted above.) It has been suggested, for example, that user inability is much more frequent than sabotage as a factor in discontinuation of innovations (20); thus early questions, doubts, and hesitancies on the part of users should be distinguished from resistance to the change as such. Successful innovation appears more likely if users receive careful training, and can use supporting materials (6, 20,11). The training may be carried on in an external system, with users returning to the local system to implement their learnings (6), or also involve close supervision and follow-up support in the local system (11).

There is a connected point: the rationalistic, high-involvement model of curriculum change long advocated by some educators seems seriously inadequate as a model of actual innovative processes. The sequence is *not* that of careful school-wide or system-wide assessment of the pros and cons of an innovation, accompanied by various forms of rational persuasion and missionary fervor, culminating in a general decision to "go ahead." Rather, there is a decision (usually administrative) to add particular equipment or materials on a modest ("pilot study") scale; consultant help and special training are then employed to teach teachers to handle the innovation effectively. This essentially *fait accompli* approach appears in several chapters of this book (2,6, 10,20) and is consistent with a conception of the teacher as a bureaucratic functionary, rather than an autonomous professional (23).

Linkage problems

The question remains: How will innovations established in an innovating, "pilot study" group diffuse outward to the remainder of the target system? Effective innovative enterprises usually require physical and social isolation, but intellectual and professional connectedness (i.e., linkage) to the surrounding context.[18] The isolation frees new projects from conformity restraints, aids focused work on the innovation, and protects both innovating group and target system from

[18] Loomis (1963) has, indeed, suggested that linkage between systems is the *essential* process in any effort at planned social change.

the consequences of failure (19). But adequate linkage is required as well, or the pilot group may not even be able to survive, let alone cause diffusion of its work in the wider system (4).

Linkage difficulties. Certain dysfunctional consequences of isolation tend to recur. Since any innovative enterprise represents a voyage on uncharted waters, away from the reassuring support of the familiar, members of innovating groups tend to turn their concern inward; they become alienated from the surrounding environment, including potential target systems (3,4,10,19,20). This lack of communication reduces support from the environment, makes recruitment difficult, brings about lack of credibility in the evangelistic reports of the innovation (20), and may lead to inadequate coping with the problems of sheer survival (4).

Under these circumstances, intergroup conflict and hostility become likely; innovative attempts receive hostility from the surrounding context (4); coalitions develop, with each group magnifying its own virtues and attributing satanic qualities to the enemy (4). Such intergroup conflict can galvanize the members, and produce high solidarity and needed mutual support *within* the groups (4,19). Yet denial and minimization of threat are occurring; if *severe* threats to the survival of the innovative group are finally made plain, members may become self-preoccupied, rather than working to advance the innovation's development (4), and system collapse is more likely.

Usually the environment of an innovative group can (almost by definition) exert more power than the group itself. Thus the members of utopian or experimental enterprises, lacking the power to cause change directly, develop substitute satisfactions, such as unrealistic enthusiasm, fantasies that the more powerful out-group will be convinced of the worth of the innovation "on its merits," and grandiose, vague images of what "the future" will look like.

Finally, even if an innovative group does manage close linkage with a target system, often by having membership in it, innovators are likely to (*a*) be restricted by existing system norms, (*b*) encounter problems of conflicting loyalties, when the extra energy needed for innovating must be taken from existing commitments to the target system (3).

Conditions aiding linkage. In what ways can adequate linkage between innovating groups and target systems be facilitated? Member selection is one; if the innovators are chosen so as to have a direct, pre-existing relationship with persons responsible for making political or financial decisions relevant to the innovation, linkage failure is less likely (7). Reasonably stable tenure in the innovating group, and operating stability via constructive norms and clear goals also seem helpful (7).

In addition, it seems essential to create explicit communication channels between persons in and out of the innovating group, particularly at a peer level (11). Such channels not only supply feedback on the progress of the innovation's acceptance and development (3), but serve to increase the credibility of innovators and add support from the environment (3).[19] The creation of new structures to aid linkage is often overlooked, particularly when the innovating group has been set up on a temporary basis (19), but seems essential.

Processes in innovating groups

Certain phenomena have been said to characterize groups designed to induce change in their members or the environment; they are thought to be particularly strong in temporary groups with a predefined life span (19).

Functional aspects. Some of these are favorable to group survival and effectiveness. These include increased energy devoted to the accomplishment of novel, significant, focused, internalized, shared goals (3,19,20); effective, controllable procedures for achieving the goals (19); *esprit de corps,* group support, and mutual identification with peers (4,19); high autonomy and spontaneity, with freedom for creative experimentation, along with norms actively supporting change itself (19); higher-quality problem-solving via increased communication among participants and fuller use of member resources (19); active meeting of members' needs for autonomy, achievement, order, succorance, and nurturance (19); high involvement and commitment

[19] The problem of adequate linkage also has importance when more diffuse groups, such as "researchers" and "practitioners," are considered. The fact that most reading researchers seem relatively isolated from researchers in other disciplines, and to some extent from teachers, does a great deal to reduce the quality of their work (unbeknownst to them), and to minimize its impact on practice (16).

to decisions, followed by group support for implementation after the termination of the temporary group's life (19).

Dysfunctional aspects. But other predictable behaviors seem likely as well—ones which cause strain and threaten the accomplishment of group objectives. For one thing, the sheer newness and ambiguity of most innovations tends to induce anxiety in members of an innovating group (3). Under these circumstances there may be regression to traditional behavior patterns (3), along with denial and minimization of threat from the environment (4).

Another source of stress is that early stages in the implementation of an innovation strategy usually involve a good deal of frustration and difficulty (3). Such frustration is likely to be accentuated by tendencies toward unrealistic goal-setting (19) and too-high aspirations (4), which in turn encourage input overload and fatigue, particularly in time-limited innovative systems (19).

The inevitable failures which follow unrealistic goal-setting tend to bring about internal blaming and splintering (4), and the loyalties of more conservative elements in the innovative group may tend to be "recaptured" by the norms of the surrounding community (4). More generally, loyalties to other groups, both in and out of the target system, always make for internal difficulties (3). Yet if efforts are made to avoid external loyalty problems by heightening internal cohesiveness, alienation and linkage failure are likely, as we have seen.

The need for aid in process skills. Some of the natural process difficulties suggested above are accentuated when members are unsophisticated about change processes, or lack needed skills (19). Thus attention to process skills can be extremely helpful (3,11). Methods for help in this area include direct teaching of participants about difficulties of the change process; training in the interpersonal, research, and professional skills required in the process of innovation; and steady collection and feedback of data on the vicissitudes of the innovative enterprise (11). It is suggested that the use of internal or external consultants can be helpful (11), particularly if supplemented by occasional intensive work sessions detached from the job setting for data-collection, diagnosis, goal-setting and plans for further innovation (11,19). The importance of continuing support during innovation attempts is repeatedly stressed (3,10,11,19).

The Fate of Innovations

The ultimate aim of any particular strategy is to gain adoption of an innovation by a target system, though shaping and development of the innovation are of course likely during the adoption process (3). Once adoption is gained, the usual hope is that the system will continue or accelerate its use of the innovation.

Thus the question of the fate of innovations is an extremely crucial one, for which most of the preceding generalizations have been a sort of process prelude. However, the question of adoption and continuation begs the more fundamental question, the one which an innovation's proponents usually answer automatically and positively: *Is it really effective?*

Infrequency of systematic evaluation

Yet, judging from the chapters of this book, a near-axiomatic statement is this: Educational innovations are almost *never* evaluated on a systematic basis. Perhaps every educational researcher ought to spend part of his apprenticeship painstakingly illuminating this text on parchment:

> The creators of experimental programs . . . have little question about the efficacy of the changes they have introduced. They *know* that the courses they have developed are the best possible under existing conditions; and in the light of this assumed fact, systematic evaluation seems superfluous. (15)

To illustrate: it has been pointed out that less than half of 1 per cent of nationally financed experimental programs in a large state were systematically evaluated (6); that it was never really decided whether a multimillion-dollar program of teacher education was worth the money and effort (5); and that reading instruction has not really been influenced by research findings for the past thirty years (16).[20]

---

[20] If we conceive of an educational organization as an open system with inputs and outputs (18), it becomes quite apparent that changes typically occur because of *input* changes (e.g., a sudden influx of students from a different social class, or a shortage of teachers), not because of noted changes in *output*. When there are no output data (or inadequate data, as in the case of the usual local school follow-up study) getting into existing feedback loops, little change is likely to result.

In the absence of evaluatory evidence, substitute bases for judgment are used, such as educational ideology, sentiment, or persuasive claims by advocates or salesmen (16). Most educational decisions appear to be made in an intuitive, prudential manner. Sometimes the merits of an innovation are said to be "self-evident"; for example, the various positions on methods of teaching reading seem to have antedated the advent of research to test them (16). More frequently, the opinions of users and clients are invoked. Informal student reactions and teacher responses are assessed (20); perceived student boredom is taken as an indicator of lack of learning (9), and the extra enthusiasm of teachers and students usually found in a new program (with its additional encouragement, recognition, and shared wishes for goal accomplishment) is mistaken for the success of the innovation (20). *Yet no hard data have been collected,* and decisions to terminate or continue the innovation are founded on sand.

For these reasons, among others, many apparently promising innovations have been abandoned before they have had a chance to "put down their roots" (13); and apparently poor (or at least implausible) educational practices have persisted for decades. Faddism, cycles of educational practice, and capricious shifts based on single research studies of doubtful validity are further consequences (16).

Several reasons for the infrequency of evaluation have been suggested. The primary one is that there are few clear criteria of educational effectiveness (1,5). Since *really* confronting this possibility would be too alarming, it is usually suggested that educational objectives are "difficult to evaluate." They may be, but they are not impossible to assess, as Kendall's chapter in this book (15) well illustrates.[21] Adequate evaluation of an innovation *is* expensive in time and money; for example, serious evaluation and revision of a new physics curriculum cost three times that required for the original production (10). It also requires the use of controlled situations and measurable procedures, maintained for a significant period of time, and careful measurement of effects (20); these conditions are not usually met in educational practice (5).[22]

[21] See also Thomas (1963) for a thoughtful discussion of the criterion problem, and some illuminating data on school output as a function of differential use of internal resources.

[22] They are not usually met, either, in other enterprises aimed at changing attitudes and behavior: psychotherapy, counseling, social work, and human

Two other forces may serve to block adequate educational evaluation. The innovative enthusiasm and messianic zeal often noted in experimental enterprises may come to have a self-justifying strength; systematic evaluation *might* prove risk-takers wrong and dampen the satisfying ardor of the mutually converted (4).[23] And, the imperatives of organizational survival inevitably enter into the evaluation of any particular innovation. Struggles for organizational autonomy and economic security may well be more potent than the question of the actual educational legitimacy of the innovation as such (5). Even when there is direct focus on the innovation itself, members of the organization may be more concerned with its potential effect on relations with the public, with accrediting bodies, and other educational organizations, than with its impact on learners (5).

The failure of innovations

Because of the infrequency of evaluation, what might be called *substantive* failure of an innovation—inability to achieve desired results—often goes unnoticed, or is defended against vigorously when it is pointed out (1).

Adoptive failures occur when an advocated innovation is rejected, or discontinued, by target system members. Generally speaking, it has been suggested that negative or conservative reactions (which are natural given the innovation's usual incongruence with existing target system norms and procedures) serve to give confirmation to teachers whose only first-hand "proof" of efficacy is attached to existing procedures and materials (10). Other general reasons for failure to achieve adoption of an innovation have been suggested to be inadequate planning, insufficient attention to "preparing" teachers for the change, lack of commitment by teachers or community, and other deficiencies in resources or power (17).

Looking at rejection more specifically, at the potential user level, it is suggested that steps in a theoretical process of rejection may paral-

---

relations training. A recent review by J. H. Mann, prepared under the auspices of the Russell Sage Foundation, examined 187 studies (*limited to those with control groups*) in such fields, and found that "few, if any" of them could be said to be scientifically satisfactory.

[23] Eaton (1962) has shown in an ingenious experiment that resistance to evaluative research findings is a durable feature of treatment-oriented organizations.

lel the steps of awareness, interest, evaluation, and trial in the adoption process (12). Thus rejections may occur basically because of sheer ignorance, because of a lack of logical, material, or psychological compellingness, or because of direct experience with the innovation. A more phenotypical listing of modes of rejection may include default, maintenance of the *status quo,* appeal to societal norms, substitution of alternate practices, invocation of others' attitudes, and use of erroneous logic (12).

Innovative success

Adoption and continued institutionalized use of the innovation by the target system, *assuming that efficacy has been demonstrated,* presumably represent basic criteria for judging the adequacy of an innovative effort.

Other frequently used success criteria include: use of the innovation to accomplish broader purposes than originally envisioned (9); subsequent use of portions of the innovation, or its "flavor" (4); the existence of publications designed to draw the attention of a wider audience to the innovation (4); improved attitudes or skills of the innovating group members which may affect their later innovativeness (4). Others can be suggested: spread or diffusion of the innovation to other systems; stimulation of innovation in similar areas of school practice; and upward job mobility on the part of practitioners who use the innovation. The importance of concomitant or side effects on parts of an educational system other than the point of direct concern has also been stressed in general terms (1,2,6,13,17,23).

However, it must be emphasized that all these associated criteria for innovative success, while serving more or less well as proximate criteria, are largely irrelevant to the crucial question of the *actual* efficacy of an innovation in increasing system output—namely, learning of students. If this difficult, much-avoided, and undoubtedly threatening question is not confronted, it does not seem likely that our understanding, or practice, of educational innovation can advance very far.

Concluding Comment

This book was designed to stimulate more inquiry into the nature of educational innovation, and to widen the range of coherent possibilities for innovative practice. The reader should judge his own residues from it accordingly.

Charles Beard was once asked for his version of the lessons of history: he replied with aphorisms such as "When it is dark enough, you can see the stars." A reader wishing to play this game with this book might emerge with items like these: "No evaluation without misrepresentation!" "Act first, teach next. This should be the changer's text." "He who innovates must pay." "Outsiders know best." "The merits of the case be damned!" "When in doubt, make it *ad hoc*." "Innovators love company." "Professionalism is the refuge of scoundrels." Or maybe (the despairing cry from Milt Gross' *Nize Baby*): "Is diss a system?"

The editor's favorite, perhaps, is "THINK." He is not the first to suggest that the domain of education—both its practice and its study—constitutes a kind of anachronistic folk subculture, a pocket of *Gemeinschaftlich* life in the midst of an otherwise rationalized world. Intelligence does have its uses; the theory and practice of educational innovation may well turn out to be one of them. At least, let us hope so.

References

Clark, H. F. *Cost and quality in public education*. Economics and Politics of Public Education Series, No. 5. Syracuse, N. Y.: Syracuse University Press, 1963.

Dubos, R. Growth, learning and purpose. Paper delivered at 75th Anniversary Distinguished Lecture Series, Teachers College, Columbia University. March 14, 1963.

Eaton, J. W. Symbolic and substantive evaluative research. *Admin. Sci. Quart.*, 1962, 6, 421–442.

Etzioni, A. Authority structure and organizational effectiveness. *Admin. Sci. Quart.*, 1959, 4, 43–67.

Katz, E., Levin, M. L., & Hamilton, H. Traditions of research on the diffusion of innovation. *Amer. Sociol. Rev.*, 1963, 28 (2), 237–252.

Kushner, G., Gibson, M., Gulick, J., Honigmann, J. J., & Nonas, R. *What accounts for sociocultural change? a propositional inventory*. Chapel Hill, N. C.: Institute for Research in Social Science, University of North Carolina, 1962.

Loomis, C. P. Social change and social systems. In E. A. Tiryakian (Ed.), *Sociological theory, values, and sociocultural change*. New York: Free Press of Glencoe, 1963. Pp. 185 ff.

Mann, F. C., & Neff, F. W. *Managing major change in organizations.* Ann Arbor, Michigan: Foundation for Research on Human Behavior, 1961.

Moore, W. E. *Social change.* Englewood Cliffs, N. J.: Prentice-Hall, 1963.

Mott, P. E., & Neff, F. W. Some criteria for the effective acceptance of organizational change. Paper read at American Sociological Association meetings, 1962.

Rogers, E. M. *Diffusion of innovations.* New York: Free Press of Glencoe, 1962.

Schon, D. A. Champions for radical new inventions. *Harvard Bus. Rev.,* 1963, *41* (2), 77–86.

Shachtel, E. G. *Metamorphosis.* New York: Basic Books, 1959.

Thomas, J. A. Efficiency in education. Paper read at Amer. Educ. Res. Assoc. meetings, 1963.

Walsh, J. J. Testing: a catalyst for educational innovations. *Theory into practice,* 1963, 2 (4), 218–225.

Wayland, S. R. The teacher as decision-maker. In A. H. Passow (Ed.), *Curriculum crossroads.* New York: Bureau of Publications, Teachers College, Columbia University, 1962. Pp. 41–52.

INDEX

Index

Academicians, influence on curricular change, 414

Accelerated Learning of Logic (ALL) project, 3

Acceleration in change rates, 5–7, 7n, 42–43, 333, 645
  causes for, 8–10, 42

Accreditation agencies, 37, 603

Achievement rates, with programed instruction, 243

Achievement tests, 601

Action decisions, in temporary systems, 479ff., 483

Action research, 20, 272ff.

Ad hoc groups,
  as change participants, 412ff.
  as structures supporting a national system, 603
  as temporary structures, 438

Adams High School, case study, 53–76

Adaptability,
  measurement of, 323ff.
  of public school systems, 317ff.

Adelphi College, 113

Adler, Mortimer, 28

Administration,
  as open sub-system, 430
  case study of small-scale change, 49–76
  definition, 427

Administrative change, theory of, 430–35

Administrators,
  crucial innovative role, 100, 339–40, 503–04, 612, 641
  definition, 427
  external and internal influences on, 432
  influence on adaptability of school systems, 318, 329ff.
  outsiders as change initiators, 433
  tenure of, 434
    see also Principals, school, Superintendents, school

Adoption of innovations,
  and social structure variables, 329–41
  and superintendency, 339–40
  rates, 5–7, 7n, 332–33
  resistance to, 299–316
  reviews of studies, 299–302, 317–28
  theory, 20, 302–03
    see also Diffusion, Change

Adult education, 9

Advanced Placement Program, 37, 493

Advanced School of Education (Teachers College, Columbia University), 49n

Affluent society, demands of, 8

Agency for International Development, educational efforts, 31

Agricultural innovation, 20n, 299ff., 312, 314, 330, 333, 500–01

Alexander, Thomas, 98, 100, 106, 108

665

The text of this book is set in *Fairfield*, the first type face designed by the artist and engraver Rudolph Ruzicka. Born in Bohemia in 1883, Ruzicka came to the United States in 1894; he began his work as apprentice to a wood engraver. Fairfield was cut in 1940. Although it has roots in the "old style" family of type faces, it has a distinctly contemporary feeling.

The main display heads are set in *Deepdene*, an evenly colored face designed by Frederick W. Goudy between 1927 and 1929. It was the fifty-eighth of the one hundred twenty-eight faces which he designed.

The secondary display heads are set in *Electra*, designed by the late W. A. Dwiggins (1880–1956). A refinement of his own hand lettering, it is deliberately not based on any other face.

Composed and printed by the Hamilton Printing Company, Rensselaer, N. Y. Bound by the J. C. Valentine Company, New York. Designed by Laura R. Whitehall.